The **XML** companion

Third Edition

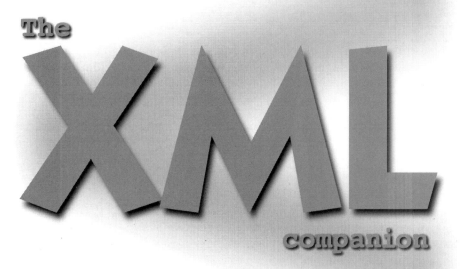

The XML companion

Third Edition

Neil Bradley

ADDISON-WESLEY

An imprint of Pearson Education

Boston · San Francisco · New York · Toronto · Montreal · London · Munich
Paris · Madrid · Cape Town · Sydney · Tokyo · Singapore · Mexico City

PEARSON EDUCATION LIMITED

Head Office:
Edinburgh Gate
Harlow CM20 2JE
Tel: +44 (0)1279 623623
Fax: +44 (0)1279 431059

London Office:
128 Long Acre
London WC2E 9AN
Tel: +44 (0)20 7447 2000
Fax: +44 (0)20 7240 5771
Website: www.it-minds.com
www.aw.com/cseng

_____

First published in Great Britain 2002

© Pearson Education Limited 2002

The right of Neil Bradley to be identified as Author of this Work has been asserted by him in
accordance with the Copyright, Designs and Patents Act 1988.

ISBN 0 201 77059 8

British Library Cataloguing in Publication Data
A CIP catalogue record for this book can be obtained from the British Library.

Library of Congress Cataloguing in Publication Data
Applied for.

10 9 8 7 6 5 4 3 2 1

Typeset by the Author
Printed and bound in Great Britain by Biddles Ltd of Guildford and King's Lynn

The publishers' policy is to use paper manufactured from sustainable forests.

Preface

XML

The *Extensible Markup Language* is a powerful document publishing and data interchange format. It was released in 1998 by the *World Wide Web Consortium*, to immediate and widespread acclaim. *XML* has a superficial resemblance to HTML, the established language of the Web, but information held in this format is self-describing – it can be extracted, manipulated and formatted to the requirements of any target audience, publishing medium or XML-enabled software application. XML should be of interest to HTML designers who need more flexibility to manage and customize their documents, to SGML users seeking advanced yet modestly priced applications, and to software developers requiring a flexible storage or interchange format that benefits from powerful, often freely available supporting tools.

This book

The XML Companion serves the *programmer*, *analyst* or *consultant* involved in the management, processing, transfer or publication of XML data and documents. Detailed study of the standard is supported by the inclusion of cross-referenced 'road maps' of the building blocks that comprise the standard, and an extensive glossary. Related standards for cataloguing, processing, linking and styling XML documents are also covered in detail.

The third edition

This is the third edition of *The XML Companion*. While the standard itself has not changed since its release in 1998, many important supporting standards have emerged, progressed, or been finalized and officially released. New editions are needed to keep up with this progress. But a significant issue that arises when writing a book on XML today is deciding what to leave out. Hundreds of XML-based standards have now been developed. A book several times the size of this one could be written, but it would not be practical to publish it, or indeed to carry it around. Apart from the core chapters on the XML standard itself, this book concentrates on related standards developed by the W3C, and on the two most popular applications of this technology (document publishing and data exchange).

Standards for navigating, describing, processing, transforming, presenting, resolving relative URL links, and linking XML data, previously described in their draft form (or too new to have been mentioned before), have now been completed and released. This includes *XPath* (November 1999), *XML Schema* (May 2001), *SAX 2.0* (June 2000), *DOM 2.0* (November 2000), *XSLT* (November 1999), *XHTML 1.0* (January 2000), *XML Base* (June 2001) and *XLink* (June 2001). Another draft proposal for advanced XML linking has matured significantly: *XPointer* (September 2001). Finally, a proposal for merging XML structures has been announced: *XML Inclusions* (May 2001). Selected loosely-related standards, such as *XHTML* and *CSS*, are included because of their historical significance and widespread use, and because they form the basis of several other standards.

Despite the wealth of new material, very little from the previous edition has been omitted (the HTML 4.0 chapter has been replaced by one on XHTML, and the chapter on XSL has been dropped (see *The XSL Companion* for a full description of this language)), so this book is larger than before. Yet it is hoped by the author that this book can still serve as a 'companion' for those who are constantly on the move.

Acknowledgements

Thanks to Michael Will for proofreading the first draft, to Viki Williams and Katherin Ekstrom at Pearson Education for steering this book to completion, and once again to Adobe for *FrameMaker+SGML* (which was used both in the preparation and publication of this book). Finally, thanks to those readers of the second edition who mailed corrections and suggestions.

Feedback

Comments and suggestions for a possible future edition are welcome. They should be sent to the author, who can be contacted at *neil@bradley.co.uk*. Updates, additions and corrections can be obtained from the author's Web page, located at *www.bradley.co.uk*, which also contains links to various XML- and SGML-related sites, and all the standards covered in this book.

Neil Bradley
October 2001

Contents

Reference

1. Using this book

Book structure

The chapters in the first part of this book, *The XML Standard*, cover all the features of the XML language. They should be read in the order provided, as they each build on concepts described in previous chapters. The second part of this book, *Underlying Standards*, covers other standards that XML relies upon to operate, including standards for representing characters in data files, as well as means to locate data files. *Extension Standards*, by contrast, explores more recent standards that have emerged to enhance the core language, including mixing document fragments from different domains, improved document classification rules, changing the document location context, and querying, inter-linking and merging XML document fragments. In *Processing and Transforming*, tools and techniques for accessing XML documents, and converting them into other formats are covered. This section is mainly aimed at software developers. On the other hand, the *Formatting XML* section is aimed at document publishing professionals who need to prepare XML documents for display or printout. Finally, the *References* section includes condensed information on a number of topics, including a Road Map of the XML standard and a glossary.

Although XML is heavily influenced by SGML and HTML, familiarity with these languages is not assumed. The text describes XML in isolation, starting from first principles. However, it is recognized that readers may be familiar with one or both of these languages, and some of the features and limitations of XML could surprise or confuse readers with prior expectations. Notes targeted at these audiences appear at relevant points in the text (see below). These notes should be ignored by readers unfamiliar with the language concerned.

HTML Note: Although XML is similar in appearance to HTML, there are many fundamental, and some counter-intuitive differences in approach. These notes highlight and explain any differences, as they are encountered.

SGML Note: Although XML is similar in concept to SGML, there are many limitations and a few differences of approach. These notes draw attention to details that may otherwise be missed.

Style conventions

Names or terms that appear in **bold style** have specific meaning within XML or related technologies, and appear in bold typeface on their first significant occurrence, and thereafter whenever their roles are further defined. They are described in the *Glossary* (except for model-specific element and attribute names and default values), and each occurrence is referenced in the *Index*.

Example data appears 'in this style'. Larger examples are separated from the text thus:

```
This is an example
```

For the sake of brevity, examples often include an indication of omitted material using '. . .', which often represents essential material, or appears where text is not allowed by the XML standard, so should never be considered to be a valid part of the example.

XML has a superficial resemblance to SGML and HTML. To avoid confusion, whenever example fragments of these languages appear, they are preceded by one of the following comments:

```
<!-- SGML -->                    <!-- HTML -->
```

In addition, when the discussion includes XML examples in close proximity to HTML or SGML examples, each XML fragment is preceded by the following comment:

```
<!-- XML -->
```

Though bold typeface may be used to emphasize part of an example, such as 'look at **this** word', it does not have the significance described above.

Examples of presented material (printed or displayed output) appear as follows:

This is a presented example

Words displayed in *italic style* are either quotations or simple 'attention grabbers'.

For the sake of clarity, element and attribute names are capitalized in the text, such as 'the Name element contains a name', but are usually lower-case in XML fragment examples, as in '<name>Smith</name>', or follow the requirements of the XML-based standard it illustrates. As XML element and attribute names are case-sensitive, the examples are to be considered authoritative.

Editorial policies

This book rarely mentions specific vendor products, or even free-ware tools. XML-sensitive products develop very rapidly, and whole new classes of product can also quickly emerge. It would be both misleading and dangerously biased to describe or even show individual tools. It is now easy to discover what is available in any category of product from a few key Web sites, such as www.w3.org, www.xml.org, www.xml.com and www.xmlsoftware.com.

Examples from the book are *not* included on a CD-ROM, and are *not* available for downloading from the Web. The vast majority of samples are very small and serve no practical purpose beyond the need to illustrate a concept. In addition, it is the author's firm belief that people learn best by doing; they learn little from simply copying material.

Note that UK spelling conventions are used in the text, but some terms and key-words appear with US spelling when compliance with a standard described in this book is important. For example, 'centre' is used in the text but 'center' is a para-meter value in the HTML table formatting model.

2. Elementary XML

XML elements divide data into meaningful components, and lie at the heart of the standard. The remaining features of the standard take supporting roles, along with some peripheral standards, and focus on the refining, annotating, storing, controlling, mixing, linking, processing and formatting of these components.

Introduction

The name 'XML' is an acronym for '**Extensible Markup Language**' (with 'X' replacing 'E' for aesthetic impact). This language is not owned or dominated by any single commercial interest. It was developed by the **W3C** (the *World Wide Web Consortium*), and has been shaped by experience of previous markup languages.

XML has almost unlimited application. However, the two primary uses are as a data exchange format and as a document publishing format. These two applications are often complementary, as data can be formatted for human consumption.

The XML data format appears at first sight to be very simplistic, and indeed it is possible to learn the basics in a matter of minutes. But there are a number of constraints and hidden complications (covered in later chapters). Nevertheless, it is possible to do a lot with very little XML, and a feel for the language can be gained from a brief look at the background, and detailed study of a few of the core concepts.

Text

The XML data format is always supported by an underlying text format. It therefore exploits the already great advantages this approach gives to information exchange. **ASCII** text is the near-universal format for text-based information storage and transfer. It is possible to copy text between computer applications, and to transfer it over networks, using tools that have been around for a very long time. While ASCII is not the only text format available, most alternatives are minor variants or enhancements of this format (see Chapter 29 for details). The following news item could easily be created in any text editor or word processor, then saved to disk, and opened and amended using any other editor:

```
              XML Standard Released
  The XML standard was released today by the W3C.
  This is an important new standard for data exchange
  and document publishing ...
```

It is the simplicity of text formats that make universal support so easy to achieve. But this very simplicity also reveals a major weakness: a format like ASCII cannot divide data into more meaningful units, or at least cannot do so without ambiguity. For example, a line-end code might signify the end of a paragraph, or perhaps consecutive line-end codes (creating blank lines) would be necessary to indicate this meaning. Maybe a heading is indicated by centring it with leading spaces (as shown above), or by using all capital letters.

Markup

ASCII text can be made smarter, simply by adding on an extra layer of meaning. This is done by assigning significance to certain characters or sequences of characters in the text.

For example, the comma and line-end codes are deemed significant in the CSV format. This standard is used to unambiguously isolate embedded units of information within a line of text, simply by separating each unit from its neighbours using a comma. Between them, the line-end codes and commas create a grid structure. This is therefore an ideal format for representing tabular information that is to be exchanged between database tables or spreadsheets:

```
SGML standard released,1986,ISO
HTML 4.0 standard released,1997,W3C
XML 1.0 standard released,1998,W3C
```

This CSV document could be imported into a spreadsheet to create the following:

SGML standard released	1986	ISO
HTML 4.0 standard released	1997	W3C
XML 1.0 standard released	1998	W3C

The commas and line-end codes in CSV are not part of the data. They are considered to be **markup** constructs that are used to manage the data. Chapter 31 provides background information on the markup formats that influenced the design of XML, and its approach to document formatting.

The weaknesses of CSV and similar alternatives are readily apparent. First, only tabular information can be represented, so every row must hold the same kind of information. Second, each column must have a pre-defined purpose, so if repeatable items are required then the maximum number of occurrences must be defined in advance. Also, as the ordering of the columns is fixed, the order cannot change between entries, and so cannot ever be deemed significant. Finally, the meaning of each column is not identified within the data file, so could be misinterpreted by recipients of the data, or simply forgotten over time.

Some of these issues are addressed in other markup languages, such as **RTF** (*Rich Text Format*), which are focused much more on the presentation of documents rather than the simple transfer of raw data. This kind of markup language uses sequences of characters, called **tags**, to provide more information on the data they affect. In the following RTF example, a paragraph is identified that contains bold words, using the '\par' and '\b' tags:

```
\par This paragraph contains some \b bold text.
```

XML has been described as the ultimate 'smart-ASCII' format, and makes extensive use of markup tags. While it can easily replicate the functionality of CSV (though in a less compact manner) and RTF, it also addresses all of the remaining weaknesses outlined above.

XML documents

The term **document** tends to be employed when discussing XML data objects or files, because XML is based on earlier standards that were primarily used to prepare narrative text for publication. This terminology still tends to be used, even when XML is being employed to exchange data between software applications, is never stored in a data file, and is never published or otherwise presented to a human audience. To simplify the discussion in this book, the term 'document' is therefore used to cover all possible ways of storing or exchanging XML data objects.

Naturally, it is still common for XML to appear in stored data files, and in some cases for these files to contain narrative text intended for dissemination and publication. This 'traditional' use of XML and its forebears is still a significant application, and forms the basis of many of the examples in this book.

Elements

XML allows documents to be decomposed into smaller, meaningful **elements** that can be recognized and, when required, processed as individual units. This concept is at the heart of the XML standard. Every XML document must contain at least one element, and the first element always identifies and encloses the entire document. But most documents contain many elements. Indeed, XML documents often consist of either nothing but elements, or of a mixture of elements and text.

Container elements

The term **container element** is used to describe an element that encloses the data it identifies. Such an element is comprised of three parts: a **start-tag**, an **end-tag** and the data between these tags. This data is known as the **element content**. The element content is both identified and bounded by the two tags.

The start-tag is identified by the surrounding markup characters '<' and '>', and the end-tag is very similar, but begins with the sequence '</'. The content is simply the data between the two tags:

```
... <...> ..... </...> ...
         |    content    |
      start-tag       end-tag
```

Element names

A criticism already levelled at languages like CSV is that they do not contain any information about the meaning of each distinct unit of information. It is necessary to find explanations elsewhere, or rely upon analysis of the data to determine its meaning. Neither approach is very satisfactory when the data is complex, has a long life span or is widely disseminated. In XML documents, the names are embedded in the data itself, so are never lost.

An element name is actually stored in both the start-tag and the end-tag of a container element. As the following example shows, the name of a data format could be identified as such by enclosing it within a Name element. In this example, the content of the Name element is the text 'XML':

```
The <name>XML</name> standard was released today...
```

Probably the most significant freedom that XML permits beyond most traditional markup languages is that there are no pre-defined element names. The XML standard does not define an element called 'Name'. Instead, document authors may invent names to suit their purposes. When people talk about an **XML application**, they are discussing a particular use of XML for which a number of element names have been defined. For example, WML is an XML application; it defines the element name 'card' for a purpose that is specific to this application.

There is no limit to the length of an element name, beyond the obvious fact that it must consist of at least one character (though Chapter 6 discusses some recommendations). However, there are some limitations on the characters allowed in a name. An element name must begin with a letter, an underscore character, '_', or a colon, ':' (though there are restrictions on the usage of the colon), and may additionally contain digits and some other punctuation characters ('.' and '-'). Valid names include 'P', 'X:123' and 'aVeryLongElementName'.

Sequential significance

Instructions may need to be followed in strict order, and narrative text, such as the paragraphs in a book, must retain their original sequence in order to make any sense. Sequential context is therefore very important. Fortunately, the contents of text-based data files have an implied order. The data is processed as a **data stream**, as a sequence of characters, starting at the top of the document. The following examples illustrate this concept. The instructions and the paragraphs both have an implied order that XML can maintain without effort:

```
<instruction>insert key</instruction>
<instruction>turn key</instruction>
<instruction>open door</instruction>
<instruction>enter</instruction>
```

```
<para>The next paragraph will not make sense unless
it is preceded by this one.</para>
<para>The previous paragraph explains the purpose
of this paragraph.</para>
```

This may appear trivial and obvious, but some alternative data storage technologies (such as relational databases) do not maintain the order of individual document components quite so easily.

Empty elements

Elements do not have to be containers, but can act as **placeholders** instead. They can anchor important document features to specific points in the text. They hold their place in the sense that edits to text preceding the element have no effect on the position of the element in respect to the text on either side of it. For example, a page-break may need to be inserted between two specified words when the document is published, and the break-point could be represented by an empty placeholder element:

```
The page ends here <pageBreak></pageBreak> and the next
page starts here...
```

The act of adding or removing text before the break-point does not cause the page-break to appear in another, less appropriate location. The first example below shows how the page-break must occur between the words 'here' and 'and'. The second example shows how this break is not affected by edits to preceding text:

```
The page ends here <pageBreak></pageBreak> and the next
page starts here...

The edited page ends here <pageBreak></pageBreak> and the
next page starts here...
```

While the use of a start-tag and end-tag is permitted for empty placeholder elements, the need for two tags cannot be justified. First, there is no data to be contained, so the end-tag is superfluous. Second, the presence of an end-tag is misleading, as it suggests that text could be meaningfully inserted into this element. A more concise and appropriate alternative is provided by the **empty element** tag. This is a single tag that ends with '/>':

```
The page ends here <pageBreak/> and the next page starts
here...
```

Special characters

It is evident that chevron characters have a significant role in XML markup. If they were also present in the document text, this could confuse software that attempts to read and interpret the document. For example, fragments of some programming languages would often include these characters:

```
<code>if ( x < y ) { ... } </code>
```

In order to avoid such ambiguity, significant characters need to be replaced by safer equivalents when used as data characters. Traditionally, this has been achieved using a special sequence of characters, known as an **escape-code** (though the XML standard does not use this terminology). In XML, the '**<**' (less than) code represents the '<' character, and the '**>**' (greater than) code represents the '>' character.

Consider the problem of creating an XML document that explains XML markup, and therefore needs to include XML tags in the text as examples. To include a representation of an element start-tag, these codes are needed:

```
The &lt;name&gt; tag identifies a name.
```

The codes are converted back to the characters they represent when the text is presented. The user sees an XML tag:

The <name> tag identifies a name.

The software fragment is therefore properly coded as follows:

```
<code>if ( x &lt; y ) { ... }</code>
```

Note that an **XML-sensitive** document editor may perform this substitution on the author's behalf. Such editors are similar to traditional text editors and word processors, but understand the XML data format and constantly maintain the distinction between data and markup. They can hide this issue from the author, who may enter the characters as normal (and is given other ways to conveniently create element tags). Despite the on-screen appearance of these characters, however, these editors must write the equivalent codes out to the file when the document is saved:

Using these codes immediately raises another example of the same problem. The ampersand character, '&', has now also become a significant markup character. The solution is the same. If an ampersand character is required in the text, it must escape *itself*, and is therefore actually represented by the '**&**' (ampersand) code:

```
<code>if (( x &lt; y ) &amp;&amp; ( y &lt; z ))
{...}</code>
```

if ((x < y) & & (y < z)) {...}

Parsing

Software that reads XML data needs to distinguish between the markup and the actual content of the document. It needs to understand the significance of the markup characters and escape codes. The process of interpreting data in this way is called **parsing**.

The act of parsing may reveal errors in the document markup. Validating documents is one of the primary reasons for performing this operation. Sometimes, a **parser** may exist only to perform this validation. But, the parser may also be a module in a larger application, and be used to pass on required information from the document to the rest of the application.

The kind of parser needed to perform basic checks on markup is called a **well-formed** parser. The following XML fragment is not well-formed, because the wrong chevron is used to complete the start-tag, and an un-escaped ampersand character is used in the text. These errors would be detected by a parser:

```
<para< This is not valid XML data & is therefore
illegal.</para>
```

Strictly speaking, a parser is a component of an **XML processor**, which also performs entity management (see Chapter 4), though 'parser' has always been the popular term used to describe the whole package (and is used in place of XML processor throughout this book).

Element types

Elements with the same name may appear many times in a document. The following text fragment contains three occurrences of the Name element:

```
The <name>XML</name> standard was released today.
It is based on the earlier <name>SGML</name> and
<name>HTML</name> standards.
```

All three are said to be of the same **element type**. Quite simply, *all* elements with the same name (within the same document) are deemed to be of the same element type. Each occurrence of an element of a particular type is said to be an **instance** of that element type. In the example above, there are three instances of the Name element type.

Unlike previous markup languages (excepting SGML), XML does not in fact predefine *any* element types. In this sense, the 'eXtensible' part of the XML name is actually a little misleading, as there is no existing list of element types to be extended. Instead, element types are chosen to match the need of a particular XML application.

Element names are case-sensitive, so 'name', 'NAME' and 'Name' would refer to three different element types. Consequently, the name appearing in the end-tag must exactly match the name that appears in the start-tag. Although case-sensitivity allows different element types with the same name to be defined and used, such as 'Name' and 'name', this is not advisable as it only leads to confusion and the significant possibility of error. The following example is another well-formed error:

```
<badtag>THIS IS WRONG</BADtag>
```

Caution: For reasons of legibility, element names always appear mixed-case in the text of this book, and will usually not match the case used in examples. In such cases, the examples are considered to show the correct usage. This distinction becomes important when looking at standards that are based on XML. If the text says 'Xyz' and the example says '<xyz>', then 'xyz' is the correct usage.

Appropriate element types

The primary strength of the XML data format is that it is a **self-describing** format. In practice, this simply means that elements normally have names that describe their contents. The elements explain themselves. An element type called 'Name' should only exist if names need to be identified within the document. Even then, perhaps more specific alternatives such as 'AuthorName' may be more appropriate.

An XML document that contains quotations would have element types such as Citation and the quotation itself:

```
<quoteText>The surest way to make a monkey of a man is
to quote him</quoteText>

<citation>Popular Quotations - Page 123</citation>
```

An XML document that contains news items would have element types such as Dateline and Byline:

```
<byline>J. Smith, Ace reporter</byline>
```

When all information items are unambiguously identified, it is possible to select and extract portions of a document that are relevant to a particular audience.

Consider the following paragraph, taken from an instruction manual, which contains information specifically relevant to North American and to British audiences:

```
<para>The <us>color</us><gb>colour</gb> green is used on
buttons in ACME <us>elevators</us><gb>lifts</gb> to indi-
cate the <us>first</us><gb>ground</gb> floor.</para>
```

> *USA*: The **color** green is used on buttons in ACME **elevators** to indicate the **first** floor.
>
> *GB*: The **colour** green is used on buttons in ACME **lifts** to indicate the **ground** floor.

A practice that is certainly discouraged in XML circles is the use of names that describe the appearance rather than the meaning of the content. Those familiar with HTML, for example, would recognize tag names such as 'B' (bold) and 'I' (italic), which say nothing about the content except how it should look when presented in a Web browser:

```
who knows why <B>this</B> is so important?
```

> who knows why **this** is so important?

Document modelling

When a number of documents have similar or identical structures, they should naturally contain the same element types. Furthermore, they should be considered to be a group of documents that both define and conform to the same document class, or **document model**.

For example, all news items would include a location, a source and the name of the writer, so they all conform to the same model. A document model provides the technical specification of an XML application, such as XMLNews-Story. This particular model defines a number of element types, including the following:

- Nitf (news item)
- Body (body of the news item)
- Title (title of the news item)
- Byline (writer of the news item)
- Dateline (date the item was submitted).

Similarly, a model could be defined for quotations. This model might include element type definitions such as:

- QuotationItem
- QuoteText
- Citation

- AuthorName
- PublicationName.

Modelling rules

Software can be developed to interpret all documents that conform to a particular model, and stylesheets can be created to format all these documents for presentation or printout. But the programs will break, and the stylesheets will fail, if the documents they process do not conform to the model they expect and understand. For this reason, it is very important that all documents that claim to conform to a particular model can be tested to ensure that they really do so.

A document model is nothing more than a number of rules. These rules define the elements that can be used, and may also specify which elements are required and which are optional, where the elements are allowed to be inserted into the document, and what attributes each one may contain. For example, element types called 'Book' and 'Chapter' could be defined, and it might be made clear that while a chapter can be embedded within a book, the reverse should never be true.

Configuration schemes

Rules that build a document model can be encoded electronically, so that they can be read by computer software. When the rules are stored in a data file, software can treat this as a configuration file. The software first reads the rules to 'learn' the document model, so that it can then detect any problems in the documents that claim to follow this model.

Many attempts have been made to decide on a scheme for codifying document model rules, and two main issues have driven these attempts. First, the scope of the rules is of major interest, such as the degree to which attribute values can be constrained by templates, and to which the location of elements can be restricted. Second, the syntax of the rules themselves.

The XML standard contains one such scheme (inherited from SGML), which uses markup tags to define a **DTD** (*Document Type Definition*). However, this is an optional feature of the XML standard (see Chapter 5). When a DTD is not in use, the document may still be deemed valid, providing that it is well-formed.

One reason to avoid using a DTD is to take advantage of a more sophisticated alternative. A few alternatives have arisen since the release of XML, and a new standard called **XML Schema** (Chapter 14 and Chapter 15) has recently been released (note that, for the sake of brevity, the term 'DTD' is used in the following discussion as a shorthand for all of the alternatives; and whenever the term 'permitted to contain' occurs, it can be taken to imply that a DTD or schema is in use).

This concept underpins the idea of the XML application, as each XML application, such as XHTML, WML or XMLNews-Story, is defined using one or more DTDs (with supporting documentation).

Validating parsers

A **validating parser** is a software application that reads a DTD, then also reads a document that claims to conform to the rules in the DTD, reporting any discrepancies it may find. For example, an error will be reported if the document contains a Name element and the DTD does not define this element type.

Validation can also be undertaken during construction of a document. The **XML-sensitive** editor introduced earlier may interrogate the DTD and create a menu of allowed element types, for the author to select from as required. The element names displayed in the menu may change, depending on the current editing context. In the first illustration below, the highlighted text can be enclosed only by the elements in the list. In the second illustration, the location of the cursor is outside the paragraph, so a different list of options is presented:

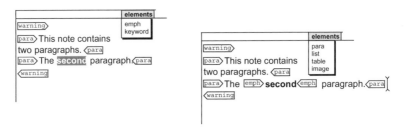

HTML Note: A DTD is not directly relevant to HTML because the tags allowed and rules dictating their use are already hard-wired into **HTML-aware** editors and Web browsers. However, DTDs for each version of HTML *do* exist, primarily to document these standards, but also for the benefit of SGML users (who may employ SGML tools to create, modify, store or validate HTML documents). The new XHMTL variant of HTML is an XML application, so is defined by a DTD (actually several DTDs).

Element hierarchies

A key feature of container elements is that they are often permitted to contain other elements. For example, a Book element should be expected to be able to contain Chapter elements, and Chapter elements should be able to contain Section elements. This is termed an element **hierarchy**.

The document element hierarchy may be visualized as boxes within boxes, or as branches of a **tree**. A tree representation can be drawn in any direction, but left-to-right or top-to-bottom is perhaps the most natural way to view it:

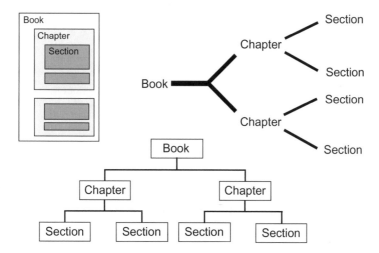

Ultimately, a complete document must be enclosed by a *single* element. This element lies at the root of the tree, and is informally termed a **root element** for this reason, though it is properly called the **document element**. The Book element in the example above is therefore a document element.

Layout of element hierarchies

Embedded elements can be placed on the same line:

```
<book><chapter><section>...</section></chapter></book>
```

For increased clarity, they can be placed on different lines instead:

```
<book>

<chapter>
<section>...</section>
<section>...</section>
</chapter>

<chapter>
<section>...</section>
<section>...</section>
</chapter>

</book>
```

For even greater clarity, it is common practice (at least in example documents) to indent embedded elements. In the following example, the start and end of each chapter is easy to see at a glance:

```
<book>
  <chapter>
    <section>...</section>
    <section>...</section>
  </chapter>
  <chapter>
    <section>...</section>
    <section>...</section>
  </chapter>
</book>
```

The following example shows a fictional XML application for handling quotations. In this example, it is clear to see that the publication and author details are both part of the citation:

```
<quotation>
  <quoteText>The surest way to make a monkey of a man
  is to quote him</quoteText>
  <citation>
    <publication>Quick Quotations</publication>
    <author>
      <name>Robert Benchley</name>
      <born>1889</born>
      <died>1945</died>
    </author>
  </citation>
</quotation>
```

Mixed content

Sometimes, it is permitted for an element to contain both text and other elements. This is called **mixed content**, though in some cases the content will happen to be just element or just text. In the following example, a paragraph contains both text and Name elements:

```
<para>The <name>XML</name> standard was
released today by the <name>W3C</name>.</para>
```

Line-ending codes are significant in text content. The example above shows the ideal, or safe way to format the content of a mixed content element. The line-end code after the word 'was' should be considered equivalent to a space character by an application that is formatting the text for display or print (there is much more information on line-ending and space significance in Chapter 8).

Element content

An element that does not directly contain text, but does contain other elements, is said to have **element content**. For example, it would not usually be reasonable for a Book element to directly contain text. Instead, it may contain Title, Preamble and Chapter elements.

Unless a DTD is in use, it is not possible to know for certain that an element has only element content. A human reader may make reasonable deductions from the name of the element, but software cannot reach such conclusions so easily. Just because there is no actual text between the elements, this does not mean that there cannot ever be. Whether this matters or not depends on a number of factors, mainly concerned with how an application might interpret line-end codes, and also has implications for advanced hypertext linking schemes.

Recursion

Some hierarchical structures may be **recursive**. This means that an element may directly or indirectly contain other instances of the same type. The term **nested element** is also used to describe an element that is embedded within another element of the same type. In a typical example, a list consists of a number of items, and one of the items contains a further complete sub-list. Some of the List and Item elements are therefore nested:

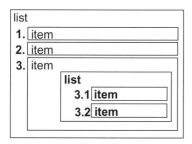

However, this leads to the possibility of infinite recursion, which may cause problems for processing or publishing software. It is not possible to limit the degree of recursion once it has been allowed at all by the DTD:

```
<book>
  <chapter>

    <list>
      <item>...</item>
      <item>

        <list>
          <item>...</item>
          <item>

            <list>
              <item>...</item>
              <item>...</item>
              <item>

                <list>
                  ...
```

Contextual significance

A book such as this one contains many titles. Apart from the title of the book itself, each chapter, section and sub-section also has one. A different element type could be defined for each usage, with names such as BookTitle, ChapterTitle, SectionTitle and SubSectionTitle.

But this approach is both unwieldy and unnecessary. Document authors, in particular, should not need to have to learn so many element types (though readers familiar with stylesheets in DTP software and word-processors will be familiar with this requirement).

The presence of hierarchical and recursive structures allows the meaning of elements to be at least partially defined by their location in the document. For example, the content of a Title element may be processed or formatted differently, depending on whether the element occurs directly within a book, author, chapter, section, table or illustration:

```
<book>
  <author><title>Mr</title>...</author>
  <title>Book Title</title>
  <chapter>
    <title>Chapter Title</title>
    <section>
      <title>Section Title</title>
      ...
      <table><title>Table Title</title>...</table>
      ...
      <figure><title>Figure Title</title>...</figure>
    </section>
    ...
  </chapter>
  ...
</book>
```

For example, it would be possible to target and extract a list of chapter titles to create a table of contents.

Structure constraints

Hierarchical structures are strictly enforced. A document is not well-formed if the structure is broken for any reason. An element must be completely embedded within another element, or must be completely outside of that other element.

For example, a section may not straddle two chapters:

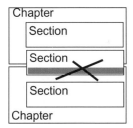

Those familiar with HTML tags may be aware that Web browsers would not object to the following fragment, where the bold and italic text ranges overlap:

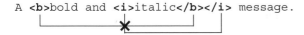

This is illegal in XML documents. A document that contained this structure would not be considered to be well-formed. In this simple case, it is only necessary to re-arrange the end-tags in order to make it valid:

```
A <b>bold and <i>italic</i></b> message.
```

However, the following example could not be rectified so easily:

```
A <b>bold and <i>italic</b> message</i>.
```

Here, it is necessary to split the range of italic text into two separate elements. One of these elements must be inside the bold element, and the other outside of it:

```
A <b>bold and <i>italic</i></b><i> message</i>.
```

These constraints may appear to be inconvenient and unnecessary, but are required to build a strict, hierarchical structure. Hierarchies are very useful structures. They give each element an unambiguous contextual location within the document. This is useful for finding, controlling and manipulating XML document fragments (as later chapters will show).

However, there are tricks that have been developed to overcome this constraint, involving pairs of empty elements (see Chapter 6).

Terminology

It is often necessary to discuss a particular element in an XML document, and relate it to other, nearby elements. When describing the relationship between elements the terminology of the family tree is often adopted (an analogy that clearly fits a tree-like view of structures).

From the perspective of a specific Chapter element, for example, adjacent Chapter elements are **siblings**, like brothers or sisters, the Book element is its **parent**, and any contained sections are its **children**:

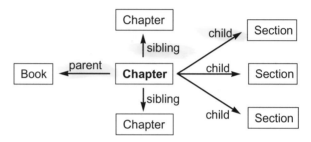

This concept can be further illustrated with an example XML document that happens to contain appropriate element names in respect to the element named 'target':

```
<parent>
  <sibling>...</sibling>
  <target>
    <child>...</child>
    <child>...</child>
    <child>...</child>
  </target>
  <sibling>...</sibling>
</parent>
```

Taking this analogy further, all elements directly or indirectly enclosed by the Chapter element are **descendants** of that element (including its children), and the Book element can be described as its **ancestor** (as well as its parent). If the Book element were part of a collection of books in the same XML document, then the Collection element would also be an ancestor:

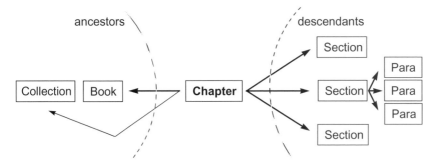

Again, an example with appropriate element names demonstrates this concept:

```
<ancestor>
  <ancestor>
    <target>
      <descendant>...</descendant>
      <descendant>
        <descendant>...</descendant>
        <descendant>...</descendant>
        <descendant>...</descendant>
      </descendant>
      <descendant>...</descendant>
    </target>
  </ancestor>
</ancestor>
```

However, terminology based on the concept of the family tree has its limitations. First, the plural term 'parents' has no meaning, because XML elements can only have one parent. Also, an element that has no child elements is not 'childless', but is termed a '**leaf**' element (just as the only element with no parent is called the 'root' element).

Attributes

It is possible for an element to hold additional information about its content beyond just its name. For example, the target audience for the content of a particular Paragraph element may be governed by a security level value, and each paragraph may be associated with a particular author. This 'information about information' is termed **meta-data**, and is stored in an **attribute**. An attribute has both a name and a value. In the following example, a paragraph is designated as secret using an attribute which is embedded within the start-tag:

```
<para security="secret" >
  ...
</para>
```

Attributes can also be embedded within an empty element tag. For example, a placeholder for an image would need to use an attribute to identify the image to be inserted:

```
The boat looks like this <image file="boat.gif" />.
```

A single element may contain more than one attribute. The following paragraph is both secret and has an identified author:

```
<para security="secret" author="J. Smith" >
   ...
</para>
```

Attribute construction

Each attribute in an element start-tag or empty element tag must include the attribute name, the attribute value, and the additional markup characters shown above. The equals symbol, '=', separates the name from the value, which is held between quotation marks.

HTML Note: Most HTML users will be familiar with the short-hand form '`<hr noshade>`' or '`<ol compact>`'. The attribute name is not present, and the attribute has only one allowed value, such as 'compact'. When the value is not present, the element has an implied value, such as 'shaded' or 'not compact', so its presence acts as a simple switch-on instruction. As XML requires the presence of the attribute name, the equals symbol and the surrounding quotes, this technique is not available.

There must be at least one space between the element name and the first attribute, and between attributes. Spaces may also optionally appear around the equals sign:

```
<topic keywords = "XML SGML" id   =   "x123"   >
```

Attribute names

An attribute name is case-sensitive. Just as with element names, care must be taken to get the name exactly right, as 'Type' is a different attribute to 'type' or 'TYPE'. Attribute names follow the same constraints as element names.

Just as the precise meaning of an element may depend in part on its location in the document structure, the precise meaning of an attribute could depend on the element that contains it. For example, an attribute called Key would have one meaning in an element called Song and another in an element called Password:

```
<Password Key="x123yz" ... />

<Song Key="C" ... />
```

Some attribute names are reserved by the XML standard, or will be reserved by future adjunct standards. In all cases, these attribute names begin 'xml:'. For example, the standard reserves the name xml:lang for an attribute that holds information on the human language used in the content of the element, and is recognized as such by all (interested) XML-aware applications (a user may wish to see only the content of elements conforming to a specific language, or a spell-checking application may switch dictionaries as the language changes).

Attribute values

The attribute value is enclosed within quotes because it may contain spaces and it would otherwise be impossible to detect the end of a value when it is followed by more attributes. Consider the following start-tag:

```
<topic keywords="XML SGML" id="x123">
```

The Keywords attribute currently has a value of 'XML SGML', and the Id attribute currently has a value of 'x123'. If the quotes were not present, it would be assumed that the Keywords attribute had a value of 'XML SGML id=x123', and if the space character was interpreted as a value terminator, the Keywords attribute would be assumed to have a value of just 'XML'.

Although double quotes are usually used, it is possible to use single quotes instead. One reason for using single quotes would be to enclose a value that contained a double quote as part of the text:

```
<bolt diameter='2"'>
```

Similarly, there is no problem with single quotes in attribute values delimited using double quotes:

```
<pillar diameter="2'">
```

If both types of quote are used in the value, it is necessary to use an escape code ('**"**' for the double quote or '**'**' for the single quote (apostrophe)). Which one is needed depends on which character is used for the delimiters:

```
<pillar diameter="2'5&quot;">
<pillar diameter='2&apos;5"'>
```

HTML and SGML Note: It is important to remember that the surrounding quotes are required, and the attribute name must always appear.

Any tab, carriage return or line-feed in an attribute value is considered to be equivalent to a space character, and will be translated into a space (further manipulation of whitespace is performed for some attribute types when a DTD is in use). The combination CR (carriage return) then LF (line-feed) is translated into a single space. The following examples are therefore equivalent:

```
name='John Smith'
```

```
name='John
Smith'
```

Uses of XML

The uses of XML are many and varied. It is not possible here to cover the huge number of XML applications in depth, but here are some examples of common usage to illustrate its breadth of application.

XML emerged from earlier technologies that focused on the publishing industry, and continues to serve in this area. It can be used to mark up semi-structured documents, such as reference works, training guides, technical manuals, catalogues, academic journals and reports. Among many other niche applications, XML can also be used to mark up patents, examination papers, financial statements and research papers.

Despite this background, XML was released as the solution to an entirely different problem. The most exciting new application – the one that has caused the most interest in the press – is as a solution to the problem of transferring complex data between software applications, particularly over the Web. The self-describing nature of XML data is fundamental to this application.

XML is now also seen as an ideal data format for configuration files. The fact that XML-sensitive editing tools can both control and assist people who need to configure software for a particular purpose can be exploited.

XML can be applied even when text plays little or no part in the application. XML is used for representing graphical information. A standard called **SVG** (*Scalable Vector Graphics*) has emerged and gathered widespread support. Like all 'vector' formats, this is only directly suitable for images that can be built from lines, curves and text strings. The following element tells an SVG application to draw a red rectangle, two inches wide by one inch high:

```
<rect style="fill:red" width="2in" height="1in" />
```

XML has even been used as a multimedia data format. XML can be applied to create multimedia presentations, allowing documents to be created that instruct a **SMIL** (*Synchronized Multimedia Integration Language*) player on how to play a presentation.

3. More document markup

XML documents may contain more than just elements and attributes. While these are the most fundamental constructs, and the only essential components of an XML document, other important markup structures are also defined in the standard. They need to be understood, if only to recognize their significance when seen in documents created by others.

Introduction

It is possible to create valid and useful XML documents using nothing but the markup already introduced. The markup described in the previous chapter performs the important task of creating a self-describing document, including useful meta-data. However, elements and attributes are essentially passive explanations of the document contents. Software can choose to ignore some or all of this markup. Almost all of the remaining XML features are much more active, and are mainly instructions to software to perform certain operations.

This includes comments to the document author, links to a DTD or stylesheet, clarifications on the character set and version of XML the document conforms to, and identification of sections of the document that do not contain element markup. New markup constructs are required for most of these purposes, and reserved attribute names are used for others.

Reserved attributes

There are some universal characteristics that elements in many different applications may share. To avoid conflict with user-defined attribute names, the prefix 'xml:' is reserved by the standard for these and other purposes.

There are only two **reserved attributes** in the XML core standard. They are used to identify the human languages used for the text in the document, and to indicate whether whitespace characters are used to format the XML markup, or to format the text of the document itself.

Languages

There are any number of reasons why it may be useful to identify the language used for the text contained in a particular element. The '**xml:lang**' attribute name is reserved for storage of both language and sometimes also country details (as the same language may differ slightly between countries). The value of this attribute is a single token, or code, which conforms to one of three possible schemes, as outlined below and defined in **RFC 1766**.

The content may comprise a simple two-character language code, conforming to **ISO 639** (Codes for the representation of names of languages). For example, 'en' represents English (a list of these codes appears in Chapter 33):

```
<para xml:lang="en">This is English text.</para>
```

Alternatively, the content may be a user-defined code, in which case it must begin with 'x-' (or 'X-'). For example, 'x-cardassian'. Finally, the code may be one that is registered with **IANA** (the *Internet Assigned Numbers Authority*), in which case it begins with 'i' (or 'I-'). For example, 'i-yi' (Yiddish).

It is possible for sub-codes to exist, separated from each other and from the main code by a hyphen, '-'. If the first sub-code is two letters (and is not part of a user-defined code) then the sub-code must be a country code, as defined in **ISO 3166**, such as 'GB' for Great Britain (see Chapter 33 for a list of country codes):

```
<instruction xml:lang="en-GB>Take the lift to
floor 3.</instruction>

<instruction xml:lang="en-US>Take the elevator to
floor 3.</instruction>
```

Note that although attribute values are case-sensitive, interpretation of these codes is not case-sensitive, so any combination of upper- and lower-case letters may be entered, though convention dictates that lower-case be used for language codes and upper-case for country codes, giving 'en-GB'.

Significant spaces

Some space characters, line-end codes and tabs may be inserted into an XML document to make the markup more presentable, but without affecting the actual content of the document. The following two examples should normally be considered equivalent, in the sense that published output should be identical:

```
<book><chapter><section><p>The first paragraph.</p>...
```

```
<book>
  <chapter>
    <section>
      <p>The first paragraph.</p>
```

Some XML-sensitive software is able (in certain circumstances) to distinguish space characters in elements that contain other elements (as in the Book, Chapter and Section elements in the example above) from spaces in elements that contain text (as in the Paragraph element examples), which is termed **significant whitespace**. It is normally assumed that spaces in elements of the first type are not part of the document, so can be considered to be **insignificant whitespace**.

Yet in some circumstances the document author may wish this space to be considered significant, in which case the **xml:space** attribute may be used to override the default handling. The **xml:space** attribute has two possible values, 'default' (the assumed value when this attribute is not present) and 'preserve' (do not discard). All whitespace in an element can be explicitly made significant, even though the element may only contain child elements.

Most publishing applications are liable to reduce multiple spaces back to a single space, and replace line-end codes with spaces. The 'preserve' value may also be interpreted as an override to these actions, but this is not made explicit in the standard (Chapter 8 covers this topic in more detail).

Processing instructions

It is sometimes necessary for an XML document to contain instructions aimed at a particular software application, or at any application that needs to perform a specific process on the document. A **processing instruction** contains document-specific information, and is bounded by the characters '<?' and '?>':

```
<? ..... ?>
```

SGML Note: the '?' at the end is required.

The content begins with a keyword, significant to an application that will understand the instruction. This is followed by a space, then the instruction itself. The instruction may include any valid XML characters:

```
<?keyword instruction?>
```

The syntax used for the instruction is assumed to be significant only to the target application. In the example below, a Paragraph contains two processing instructions, each forcing a new page in the required syntax of differing pagination applications (which happen not to be able to interpret an otherwise more suitable PageBreak element):

```
<p>It would be nice to end the page
<?ACME-WP   (NEW PAGE)?>
<?BigDTPSystem   DO:page-break?>
<pageBreak/>
here.</p>
```

In most circumstances, processing instructions are not generally considered to be desirable. Elements and attributes are the ideal carriers of information about the document. But there are some very high-profile exceptions.

Processing instructions are used to provide information about an XML document (see below), and to identify a stylesheet that is to be used to format the document. The following example identifies an XSLT stylesheet that is to be used to transform the document into an output format (see Chapter 17 for details):

```
<?xml-stylesheet href="mystyles.xsl" type="text/xml"?>
<Book/>
   . . .
</Book>
```

XML declaration

The XML standard employs a processing instruction to impart important information about an XML document to any software application that wishes to access it. Called the **XML Declaration**, this processing instruction has a target name of 'xml' (always lower-case):

```
<?xml ... ?>
<book>
   . . .
</book>
```

Each piece of information in this processing instruction resembles the syntax of an attribute embedded within an element start-tag. But this resemblance is purely superficial, and the more accurate term used here is 'parameter'. There are no standards for parameters, and in other processing instructions they will often bear no similarity to attributes.

The required **Version parameter** tells the XML processor which version of XML the document conforms to. At present there is only one version, identified as '1.0':

```
<?xml version="1.0" ... ?>
```

The optional **Encoding parameter** reveals the character encoding scheme used in the document. If present, it must follow the version parameter. If this information is not present, then 'UTF-8' or 'UTF-16' encoding is assumed (see Chapter 29):

```
<?xml ... encoding="UTF-8" ... ?>
```

The optional **Standalone parameter** indicates whether or not an externally defined set of declarations (in a DTD) contains information that affects interpretation of the content of the document (see Chapter 5). If present, it must follow the other parameters described above:

```
<?xml version="1.0" encoding="UTF-8" standalone="yes" ?>
```

If the XML declaration is present, it must occur before everything else in the document. Even a single preceding space character would render the document invalid. The very first character of the file must be the left chevron, '<', that begins this declaration. The reason why this is so important concerns recognition of character sets (and is fully explained in Chapter 29).

If the XML declaration is not present, the version of XML in use is assumed to be '1.0'. It is probable that the XML declaration will not be optional in later versions of the language, as it would otherwise not be possible to detect which version was in use. Other defaults adopted are the same as listed above for missing parameters (the character set encoding is assumed to be UTF-8 or UTF-16 (see Chapter 29), and the processing of externally defined entity declarations (see Chapter 4) is assumed to be required).

Markup declarations

All remaining XML markup involves a single additional markup construct, called a **markup declaration**. Declarations identify or specify important features of the document. They create comments, re-usable document components, identify the DTD the document conforms to, and construct the DTD itself. The following sections and the next two chapters all involve the extensive use of markup declarations. A markup declaration is delimited by the characters '<!' and '>':

```
<! ... >
```

In a few specific circumstances, markup declarations may be embedded within other markup declarations. The embedded declarations are held in a subset structure, identified using the square bracket characters '[' and ']':

```
<! ... [
   <! ..... >
   <! ..... >
] >
```

A specific type of declaration is indicated using a keyword; which must appear at the start of the declaration, without any intervening spaces. The declaration types described below have the keywords '**DOCTYPE**', '**[CDATA[**' and '**--**':

```
<!DOCTYPE ..... >
<![CDATA[ ..... ]]>
<!-- ..... -->
```

The remainder, which are described in following chapters, have the following keywords:

```
<!ENTITY ..... >
<!NOTATION ..... >
<!ELEMENT ..... >
<!ATTLIST ..... >
<![IGNORE[ ..... ]]>
<![INCLUDE[ ..... ]]>
```

If some of these keywords look odd or obscure, the explanation lies in the historical roots of XML, which is a simplified subset of the SGML standard. XML, like English, is complicated due to its history (and Chapter 32 clarifies some of these apparent oddities). When XML was designed, backward compatibility with those parts of SGML it retained was considered paramount.

It is important to remember that, despite the name 'XML Declaration', the construct described in the previous section is actually a processing instruction, *not* a markup declaration.

Document type declaration

A markup declaration is used to identify the document class that the document belongs to. The **document type declaration** sits at the top of an XML document. The keyword '**DOCTYPE**' is used to indicate a document type declaration:

```
<!DOCTYPE ...>
```

The example below shows a document type declaration in its simplest form. It merely identifies the name of the document element, which it precedes:

```
<!DOCTYPE myBook>
<myBook>
   ...
</myBook>
```

Note that if an XML declaration is present, it still appears first, before the document type declaration:

```
<?xml version="1.0" ... >
<!DOCTYPE myBook>
```

More complex variants are used to hold entity definitions (see Chapter 4) and contain the DTD (see Chapter 5). These variants use the square bracket groups, because this markup declaration contains other declarations (to build entity and DTD definitions):

```
<!DOCTYPE myBook [
......
]>
```

It may also call-in declarations that are held in a separate data file. The keyword 'SYSTEM' precedes a quoted URL that identifies the file containing these declarations (a slightly more sophisticated variant of this feature uses the 'PUBLIC' keyword which creates an indirect reference to the remote resource):

```
<!DOCTYPE myBook SYSTEM "declarations.xml" [
......
]>
```

This declaration may be omitted if the document does not use entities, and is not associated with a DTD. In its simplest form it merely indicates the name of the root element, so adds no value to the document at all. In most real-world cases, the document type declaration only appears when a reference is needed to a DTD file:

```
<!DOCTYPE myBook SYSTEM "book.dtd" >
```

Character data sections

When a document author wishes to use characters that could be confused with markup delimiters, such as '<' and '&', it is normal practice to employ the codes introduced earlier (including '<' and '&'). But, if one portion of a document contains many such characters of this type, the use of these codes could be considered very inconvenient. Consider the following example:

```
Press the &lt;&lt;&lt;ENTER&gt;&gt;&gt; button.
```

Press the <<<ENTER>>> button.

The text is difficult to read and interpret. It may also be inconvenient for an author to generate this text, and for software to interpret it quickly. In more extreme cases, a significant impact on the size of the document can even be expected.

It would be useful to be able to identify a range of text that cannot contain markup constructs, so that these significant characters could be used in the data, as normal, without confusing a parser.

It is therefore possible to identify a block of text as **character data** (data that consists of characters, but not markup). A **Character Data Section** declaration identifies a character data document segment. The keyword '**[CDATA[**' begins the declaration, and ']]>' ends it. As markup characters are not expected in character data, apart from the sequence ']]>', there is no possibility of confusion when using markup-related characters in the text:

```
<![CDATA[Press the <<<ENTER>>> button.]]>
```

Press the **<<<ENTER>>>** button.

If escape-codes are present in a character data section, they are not considered to be significant, so are treated as normal character sequences:

```
<![CDATA[In XML the &lt; reference is built-in.]]>
```

In XML the **<** reference is built-in.

SGML Note: The other marked section types, 'IGNORE', 'INCLUDE', 'TEMP' and 'RCDATA' are not available in an XML document instance, though the first two of these are available in the external subset of a DTD.

Comments

It is possible to add a **comment** to an XML document. A comment is never considered part of the document text, so would not appear in published output. A comment may be inserted by a document author or editor to mark text that needs further treatment.

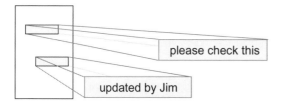

A comment declaration is used to create a comment. The keyword '--' identifies a comment declaration. For backward compatibility with SGML, the declaration must also end with the same two characters, and two adjacent hyphens must not appear within the comment text:

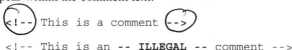

```
<!-- This is an -- ILLEGAL -- comment -->
```

SGML Note: A markup declaration that contains a comment can contain only one comment, and nothing but that comment. It is not possible to embed comments in other declarations.

HTML Note: HTML adopted its comments scheme from SGML, so there should be no surprises here. Other forms of comment that Web browsers support are not legal in XML.

Comments may be inserted by a document author or editor to mark text that needs further treatment. But they should probably not be used if they need to be preserved when the document is processed. Some tools (such as those reading the document using the SAX API, as discussed in Chapter 18) will 'lose' the comments in the process of generating an output file. It is often a better idea to use an element, perhaps called Comment, instead (stylesheet languages are able to prevent such elements from being included in published output):

```
<p>A completed paragraph</p>
<comment>PLEASE REVIEW THE FOLLOWING PARAGRAPH</comment>
<p>This is a suspect paragraph.</p>
```

Comments are more typically employed in DTD files, where they help to organize and document the rules that DTDs contain. However, they can often also be found in applications of XML that are similar to programming or scripting languages, such as XSLT.

Syntax overview

These initial chapters have introduced XML elements and attributes, and a few other constructs, but there is still much more to this standard. The following illustration includes examples of almost all the important features of the XML format. Many of the mechanisms shown are optional, including some that are rarely used (many of these are in the process of being replaced by new, separate standards that are discussed later). Each major feature of XML is labelled in the diagram below to facilitate quick look-up of any unknown concepts:

Note.XML

```
Ⓐ <?XML version="1.0" encoding="UTF-8" standalone="no" ?>
Ⓑ <!DOCTYPE Note SYSTEM "Note.DTD" [
Ⓓ <!ENTITY XML "eXtensible Markup Language">
   <!ENTITY history Ⓔ SYSTEM "History.XML">                    Ⓒ
   <!ENTITY XMLimage  SYSTEM "/ents/XML.TIF" NDATA TIFF> - - - ▶
   <!ENTITY Ⓕ % images "INCLUDE"> ] >
Ⓖ <note>
   <p>The Ⓗ &XML; format is a very important move
   to bringing the benefits of structured markup
   to the masses.</p>
   &history; Ⓘ
   <p>The following image shows a fragment of XML:</p>
Ⓙ <image filename="XMLimage" />
   <p>The tags Ⓚ <![CDATA[<note>, <p> and <image../> are
   used in this document]]>.</p>
   </note>
```

XML.TIF
Ⓦ

Ⓛ History.XML

```
Ⓜ <?XML encoding="UTF-8" ?>
   <p>Its roots can be seen in HTML, in that the tags
   have the same delimiters, Ⓝ &#60; and &#62;, but its
   real Ⓞ cestry is SGML.</p> Ⓟ
   <p xml:space="preserve" xml:lang="en-GB">
   --- XML |-/-|
   |          | / |
   SGML      / HTML</p>
```

Ⓠ Note.DTD

```
Ⓡ <!-- The Note DTD version 1.3 -->
Ⓢ <!NOTATION TIFF SYSTEM "TIFFVIEW.EXE" >
   <!ENTITY % images "IGNORE" >
Ⓣ <![%images[<!ENTITY % noteContent "p | image">]] >
   <!ENTITY % noteContent "p">
Ⓤ <!element note (%noteContent;)*>
   <!element p (#PCDATA)>
   <!element image EMPTY>
Ⓥ <!attlist image filename ENTITY #REQUIRED>
```

Key:

- (A) the XML Declaration – *XML declaration*
- (B) the document type declaration – *Document type declaration*
- (C) the internal subset – *Declaring an entity* (Chapter 4) and *DTD Markup* (Chapter 5)
- (D) an entity declaration – *Declaring an entity* (Chapter 4)
- (E) an external entity declaration – *External text entities* (Chapter 4)
- (F) a parameter entity declaration – *Parameter entities* (Chapter 4)
- (G) the document ('root') element – *Element hierarchies* (Chapter 2)
- (H) an entity reference to an internal text entity – *Entity references* (Chapter 4)
- (I) an entity reference to an external text entity – *Entity references* (Chapter 4)
- (J) an empty element – *Elements* (Chapter 2)
- (K) a character data section – *Character data sections*
- (L) an external XML entity file – *External text entities* (Chapter 4)
- (M) an encoding declaration – *XML declaration*
- (N) a character reference – *Character entity references* (Chapter 4)
- (O) preserved space – *Reserved attributes* (Chapter 3) and *Preserved space* (Chapter 8)
- (P) text language – *Reserved attributes*
- (Q) the external subset file (the DTD) (Chapter 5)
- (R) a comment – *Comments*
- (S) a notation declaration – *Notation declarations* (Chapter 5)
- (T) an ignored or included section declaration – *Conditional sections* (Chapter 5)
- (U) an element declaration – *Element declarations* (Chapter 5)
- (V) an attribute list declaration – *Attribute declarations* (Chapter 5)
- (W) a binary entity file – *Binary entities* (Chapter 4)

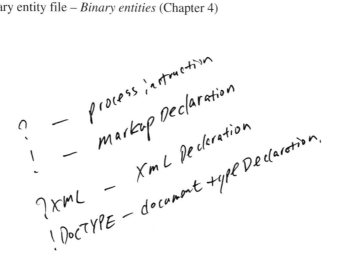

4. Physical structures (entities)

The markup described in previous chapters plays the important role of dividing a document into its logical components. It can also be useful to split documents into physical components. Entities allow components to be shared and more easily managed, for unusual characters to be easily represented, and for non-XML data to be included in the document.

It needs to be acknowledged that the least popular aspects of the XML standard are its entity-based features. Some of the adjunct standards described in later chapters attempt to replicate and improve on these features, using simpler techniques (such as XInclude (see Chapter 12) and XLink (see Chapter 27)). Applications of XML, including XML Schema and XSLT also provide their own features in order to avoid the need for entities. But entities can be very useful, and are well supported by software with an SGML heritage.

Introduction

Some thesauri give **entity** as a synonym for 'element'. But XML entities are very different to XML elements. They are concerned with the physical components of a document, rather than its logical components. The entire XML document is an entity. Entities are not as simple as elements, since they are used for several distinct purposes. In fact, a number of the key features of the standard are supported by entities. They are used to:

- create escape-codes for significant markup characters
- provide a mechanism for representing characters that are not available from the keyboard, or in standard character sets
- divide long documents into smaller, more manageable chunks

- create re-usable components that can be shared by many documents
- include by reference external binary data, such as images
- assist in the construction of DTDs (see the next chapter).

There are therefore several different kinds of entity, which the following sections explore in detail. But one thing that all entities have in common is that they are divided into two conceptual parts. First, there is the entity itself, which is either an implied or explicitly declared object. When an explicit declaration is required, a markup construct is used to create an **entity declaration**. But, for its existence to have any meaning, there must be at least one **entity reference** present to make use of the entity. For most types of entity, there may be any number of references. References generally take the form of names. The **entity name** is part of its declaration, and also appears in each reference to the entity. The entity name is used to find the relevant entity (and the content of the entity then replaces the reference):

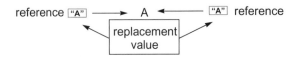

Entity references

Usually, an entity reference is a simple markup construct that begins with an ampersand character, '&', and ends with a semicolon, ';'. The body of the construct is a reference to the name of the entity. The following example is a reference to an entity called 'XML' (which might have a replacement value of 'eXtensible Markup Language'):

    The &XML; format is useful.

SGML Note: The semicolon is always required, even when followed by a space.

The entity reference is detected by an XML parser as it reads the data, and is removed. Its place is taken by the replacement value, which is then also parsed as if it had always been an integral part of the document:

    The eXtensible Markup Language format is useful.

Entities can also be referenced from attributes (with some limitations):

    <dataFormat name="XML (&XML;)">...</dataFormat>

When DTDs are in use, the value of an attribute in an empty element can also be identified as an entity reference. In the following example, the Pic element refers to the entity called 'JSphoto' (Chapter 5 explains how to specify such attributes):

```
Here is a photograph <pic name="JSphoto" /> of J. Smith.
```

In DTDs, the format is slightly different.

Built-in entity references

The first and most widespread use of entity references is to avoid the problem of confusing markup delimiters with data characters. Depending on the context of its usage, document authors may need to use the references listed below instead of the actual characters they represent:

- **<** for '<'
- **>** for '>'
- **&** for '& '
- **'** for ' ′ ' (in attribute values)
- **"** for ' ″ ' (in attribute values).

The true nature of the 'escape-codes' introduced earlier is now evident. Although entities are far more flexible than escape-codes, they do serve this simple purpose very well.

As previously indicated, the angle bracket entity reference must be used in place of the actual character within text, so that the XML processor can safely assume that every occurrence of these characters represents a markup delimiter:

```
<p>The &lt;p&gt; tag is used to represent
a paragraph.</p>
```

> The <p> tag is used to represent a paragraph.

These references must also be used in attribute values:

```
<if test="x &lt; y">...</if>
```

The ampersand entity is used within text to avoid confusing an XML processor, which assumes that the '&' character represents the start delimiter of a general entity reference:

```
<title>&XML; &amp; &CSS;<title>
```

> eXtensible Markup Language **&** Cascading Style Sheets

The quote entity references are only needed within attributes (and within entity declarations). Even then, they are only required when both types of quote appear in that text, and a conflict with the delimiter character would otherwise be unavoidable:

```
<size height="3' 6&quot;">
```

Character entity references

Entity references can be used to represent any character. Though rarely needed for widely used characters such as 'a' and '3', this mechanism is widely used for less familiar characters, and as an alternative means to represent characters that could be confused with markup delimiters. All **character entity** references are built-in entities, so no explicit declarations are necessary. The entity names in this case consist of a leading '#' symbol:

```
&#...;
```

The rest of the name is a number that represents the position of the character in its character set. A decimal value in the range '0' to '127' represents an ASCII character. The reference '&' refers to the ampersand character, '&'. A value in the range '0' to '255' represents a character from the extended ASCII set, ISO 8859/1, as used under Windows and UNIX (see Chapter 33). The reference 'é' represents the character 'é' (French acute e):

```
The caf&#233; is owned by Smith &#38; Son.
```

> The caf**é** is owned by Smith **&** Son.

A decimal value in the range '256' to '65535' represents a character from the larger Unicode/ISO10646 set (see Chapter 29). As keyboards have a very limited number of key-press combinations, this mechanism is very useful for accessing such a huge range of characters.

Immediate replacement

In all circumstances, these references are immediately replaced by the characters they represent, as the parser reads the text from the source file or data stream. Once inserted, the replacement character is not re-parsed. This means that if, for any reason, there is a need to retain the reference in the parsed data, a simple trick can be used to achieve this, involving the replacement of the ampersand markup delimiter with the ampersand reference:

```
The caf&#38;#233; is owned by Smith &#38;#38; Son.
```

Both the references in the example above are converted to ampersand characters as the document is parsed, resulting in the creation of two new references that will only be interpreted when the data is eventually parsed again:

```
The caf&#233; is owned by Smith &#38; Son.
```

Hexadecimal references

Computers perform calculations using **binary** notation, which only uses the digits '0' and '1' to construct all numbers. But even small numbers are difficult to read and write using this notation. For example, '10101' is equivalent to the decimal value 21, but is much harder to remember. Converting numbers between binary and decimal is also non-trivial, because decimal (base 10) is not a multiple of binary (base 2). However, **hexadecimal** notation (base 16) is a multiple of 2, and produces even shorter representations of numbers than decimal does, so has long been used to more conveniently represent values stored on computers. This notation requires symbols for 16 digits. Apart from the usual '0' to '9', the first six letters of the alphabet have been recruited ('A' = 10, 'B' = 11, 'C' = 12, 'D' = 13, 'E' = 14 and 'F' = 15). In a character entity reference, a hexadecimal value is preceded by an additional 'x' character:

```
&#xE9;
```

The reference '&' refers to the '&' character, because the hexadecimal value '26' is equivalent to the decimal value 38 ('26' represents two multiplied by 16, plus 6, giving 38). Similarly, 'é' represents the 'é' character, as 'E9' is equivalent to the decimal value 233. Larger values may be used to refer to any Unicode character, such as '￸' (Chapter 29 discusses character issues in more depth):

```
The caf&#xE9; is open
```

> The café is open

Declaring an entity

For remaining entity types, a declaration is almost always required. The declaration specifies the entity name, and either directly contains the entity itself, or contains a reference to an entity held elsewhere.

Usually, the declaration takes the form of a markup declaration. The '**ENTITY**' keyword identifies an **entity declaration**:

```
<!ENTITY .......>
```

This keyword may be directly followed by the name of the entity being declared. The name can be any length, but the characters allowed in the name are restricted in the same way as element and attribute names. Legal names include '_MyEnt' and 'my.ent'. The name is case-sensitive, so an entity named 'MyEntity' is *not* the same as an entity named 'myentity', or another named 'MYENTITY':

```
<!ENTITY MyEntity .......>
```

SGML Note: a default entity cannot be defined.

It is possible to define the same entity more than once, but only the first declaration is acknowledged:

```
<!ENTITY myentity .......>

<!-- IGNORED -->
<!ENTITY myentity .......>
```

Entity declarations cannot appear within the document content. Instead, they must be inserted at the top of the document, within the **document type declaration**:

```
<!DOCTYPE MyBook [
  <!ENTITY .......>
  <!ENTITY .......>
  <!ENTITY .......>
] >
```

Internal text entities

The simplest kind of declared entity is an **internal text entity**. This type of entity allows a document author to pre-define any phrase or other text fragment that will be used repeatedly in the document. For example, in a book on XML the name 'eXtensible Markup Language' may appear often. To avoid keying the whole name, and also to prevent inconsistencies and misspellings that may result from this tedious task, an internal text entity may be created to hold the text.

But internal text entities are most commonly used to represent unusual characters that cannot be accessed from the keyboard, or are represented by different character values on different computer systems. It may be easier and safer to create and transfer data containing the reference 'é' instead of 'é'. There are standard names for many such characters (see Chapter 29 for more details on character handling, and '*ISO 8859/1 character set*' in Chapter 33 for a list of entity names).

An internal text entity is contained within quote delimiters that follow the entity name:

```
<!ENTITY XML "eXtensible Markup Language">
```

Either single or double quotes may be used to enclose the replacement text. When double quotes are used, it is not possible to also include a double quote in the text, as this would prematurely signify the end of the entity. However, it would be possible to include a single quote without ambiguity:

```
<!ENTITY DemoEntity "The ladder is 6' long.">
```

One reason for choosing single quotes as delimiters would be to allow double quotes to appear in the text (the same as for attribute values):

```
<!ENTITY DemoEntity 'The rule is 6" long.'>
```

When both kinds of quote are used in the value, this technique is inadequate. The '"' and ''' entity references may be used to overcome the problem.

An entity that contains XML data is known as a **parsed entity**, because it can be validated by an XML parser. A parsed entity contains **replacement text**, meaning that the content of the entity replaces the reference to it in the data stream (and is then parsed):

```
┌─────────────────────────────┐
│ eXtensible Markup Language   │
└─────────────────────────────┘
        ↙
The &XML; format includes entities.
```

When a parser is providing this service on behalf of a larger application, the application may not be aware of this activity, and may therefore be ignorant of the existence of the original entity. The application 'sees' only the final result:

```
The eXtensible Markup Language format includes
entities.
```

Entities can also contain elements. These element tags are parsed as normal once the value has been inserted in place of a reference to the entity:

```
<!ENTITY Water 'H<sub>2</sub>O' >
```

```
Water consists of &Water;.
```

Water consists of H_2O.

External text entities

Internal text entities are not appropriate when:

- the entity is large
- the entity needs to be shared with other documents.

An entity may be too large to be conveniently stored in the declaration. It may, for example, consist of several paragraphs of text. XML editing tools are generally ill-equipped for editing the content of internal entities. The entity content may need to be accessed from a number of documents, and it would be both time-consuming and error-prone to redefine it in each one.

An **external text entity** differs from an internal entity in one important respect. Instead of the entity being held in the entity declaration, it is held elsewhere. Usually, this means that it is held in another data file. This file may be stored on the user's own system, and accessed by reference to its location on this system, or may be held on another system, for access over the Web using a URL.

Using an external text entity, the size of the information unit is not limited, the content is easy to edit in isolation, and the entity can be referenced from declarations in each document:

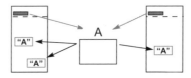

The other major difference is that references to external entities are not valid if they occur within an attribute value. They can only appear in element content. This makes sense, as external entities are generally quite large, and attribute values should not be.

Uses of external entities

Every data file that contains text, XML markup or both, can be considered to be an entity. This includes the file that the user initially tells a processor to process. However, this file is only ever referenced directly by the user or process, so does not need to have an entity name. This is almost the only entity that does not have a name (there is one other exception). This entity is known as the **document entity**, because it represents the entire document, and either directly or indirectly *contains* the entire document. Large fragments of the document could be held in external entities, or, at the furthest extreme, the document entity may be nothing more than a framework, used primarily to position the content of other entities:

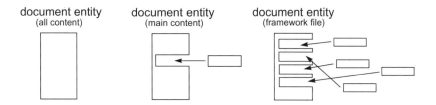

document entity
(all content)

document entity
(main content)

document entity
(framework file)

Another use of external text entities is to hold a convenient group of internal text entities. For example, letters and symbols not covered by ASCII, such as accented European letters, Greek letters and mathematical symbols, have standard ISO entity declarations and are grouped into entity files. The most commonly required groups are the following:

- **ISOnum** (symbols, including '<', '>' and '&')
- **ISOlat1** (accented Western European letters)
- **ISOgrk1** (Greek letters)
- **ISOpub** (publishing characters)
- **ISOtech** (technical symbols).

HTML Note: Some of the entities declared in this list should be familiar to HTML authors, where references such as 'é' are used to incorporate foreign, accented characters.

System identifier

The location of an external text entity is provided by a **system identifier**, which is indicated using the '**SYSTEM**' keyword, followed by a quoted string that locates the file. The system identifier must conform to the URL standard (see Chapter 30 for details):

```
<!ENTITY MyEnt SYSTEM "file:///C:/ENTS/MYENT.XML" >
```

This should be familiar from the discussion on the document type declaration in the previous chapter. The mechanism used there is now revealed to be an entity declaration (and is discussed again below).

Public identifier

An additional mechanism for indirectly locating an external entity can be provided, using a **public identifier**. This method of identifying remote information is more flexible, as it offers more information on the content of the data file and because it does not directly specify the location and name of the file. The keyword '**PUBLIC**' is used to indicate a public identifier:

```
<!ENTITY MyEnt PUBLIC
     "-//MyCorp//ENTITIES Superscript Chars//EN" "...">
```

A standard that describes a recommended format for such identifiers exists, and the example above conforms to this standard. Also, as public identifiers usually do not contain a direct reference to a physical file, some form of look-up is needed to match the identifier with a physical file location (see Chapter 26).

When a public identifier is used, the system identifier must still be present, and it must follow the public identifier. This is the only thing that can follow a public identifier, so there is no requirement to include the 'SYSTEM' keyword, and in fact this keyword must not be entered:

```
<!ENTITY MyEnt PUBLIC "...." "file:///C:/ENTS/MYENT.XML">
```

SGML Note: The system identifier is *always* required.

Using both a public and system identifier has the advantage of allowing local resources to be used when they are available, and is particularly suited to Web usage. The application should first test the public identifier against a **catalog** of locally stored entities (see Chapter 26 for more on catalog management, and details on a standard catalog data format). If the entity already exists on the local system, it does not have to be fetched from a remote Web server. Should the public identifier not resolve to any locally held entities, the system identifier is then used to fetch the entity from the Web server.

Entities within entities

The replacement value of an entity can itself contain entity references. In this way, a hierarchy of entities may be built, beginning with the document entity. However, entity content cannot contain declarations for the entities they reference. The declarations must all be known to the main document. In the following example, the document must declare both A and B entities, even though it directly references only the first of these:

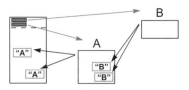

However, it is not permitted for an entity to directly or indirectly contain a reference to itself (a cyclical relationship would confuse XML processing software).

In this example, the TimeCorp entity value contains a reference to the Division entity:

```
<!ENTITY Division "Headquarters">

<!ENTITY TimeCorp "TimeCorp Int. (&Division;)">
```

TimeCorp Int. (**Headquarters**)

However, this example is a little misleading, as it can be taken to imply that the reference in the TimeCorp entity is replaced by the value of the Division entity immediately, before any reference to the TimeCorp entity is found in the document. In reality, though, references in entity content are not parsed immediately. When the parser reads the entity declaration, it does not deal with the embedded reference. In this example, therefore, the replacement value is 'TimeCorp Int. (&Division;)'. Only when this value is inserted in place of a reference to it, and is immediately parsed in this location, does the embedded reference get replaced by *its* content.

This distinction is often unimportant, and would certainly have no effect on the outcome in the example above. But it *is* important when each document has a different definition for the embedded entity. In the following document, the Division entity is given the value 'Watches', and this value becomes part of the TimeCorp entity value on insertion:

```
<!ENTITY Division "Watches">
...
<title>Accounts for &TimeCorp;</title>
```

Accounts for TimeCorp Int. (**Watches**)

In another document, the Division entity is given the value 'Clocks', and this value becomes part of the TimeCorp entity value on insertion:

```
<!ENTITY Division "Clocks">
...
<title>Accounts for &TimeCorp;</title>
```

Accounts for TimeCorp Int. (**Clocks**)

Binary entities

Not all data held on computer systems is text-based information. Documents typically contain images that are usually stored in more compressed data formats such as CGM, JPEG, GIF and TIFF. Sound and video components are no longer unusual, so WAV, MPEG and other data formats need to be handled as well. These are all **binary formats** that cannot be edited or even presented using text-based tools. Many documents have a textual infrastructure, but need to incorporate binary data at appropriate points (such as the illustrations in this book), and this can be done using entities. A **binary entity** is any entity that does not conform to XML syntax, so cannot be parsed using an XML parser.

Separate data

Binary data must be kept separate from XML data, so that XML parsers will not be confused by unintelligible data sequences. Binary entities are therefore always external entities. For this reason, binary entities cannot be merged into the document by the parser. Instead, they must be handled by the application itself.

The parser provides the name and location of the file, along with the data **notation**, such as GIF or WAV. The application is expected to use this information to either process the data directly, or launch another application that can deal with it.

For example, a browser could either integrate a binary entity directly, so that the user is not even aware of this mechanism, or it may insert an icon which prompts the user that an entity is present, and can be viewed by selecting it:

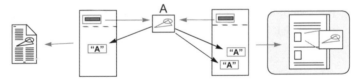

Binary and notation declaration

A binary entity is otherwise very similar to an external text entity. The public and system identifiers are used in the same way to locate the data file that contains the entity:

```
<!ENTITY JSphoto SYSTEM "file:///C:/ENTS/JSphoto.tif" ... >
```

But there is an additional requirement to identify the format of the data, so that it can be associated with an application that understands this format. After the system declaration, there is a name that identifies the data format used, following the '**NDATA**' keyword. This name is actually a reference to another declaration, called a **notation declaration**, which explains the meaning of the notation (and is explained in the next chapter).

In the example below, the file 'JSphoto.tif' is identified as a 'TIFF' file. Although, in this case, it may be thought possible to identify the format from the filename extent of '.tif', that mechanism cannot be relied upon:

```
<!ENTITY JSphoto SYSTEM "/ENTS/JSphoto.tif" NDATA TIFF>
```

References of the kind discussed previously cannot be used to refer to binary entities. Instead, an empty element is used, with an attribute specified to be of type 'ENTITY' (see Chapter 5 for details on attribute types):

```
A photograph of J. Smith :<photo ent="JSphoto"/>.
```

General entities

All entity types previously discussed are referenced from within XML documents, so are used to enhance the content of the document. All such entities are known as **general entities**. They can be used in a 'general' manner within documents.

An attribute value cannot *be* the name of a general entity (except for a binary entity). The following example will *not* identify the entity declared above (even when the DTD is configured to recognize the Owner attribute as identifying an entity). Indeed, this is considered to be a serious error:

```
        <!-- ERROR -->
  <book owner="TimeCorp">...</book>
```

However, an attribute value may *contain* a reference to an internal entity (complete with '&' prefix and ';' suffix), though not to an external entity (so excludes binary entities by default):

```
<!ENTITY TimeCorp "MyCorp International">

<!ENTITY TimeCorpAddress SYSTEM "address.xml">


                        <!-- ERROR -->
  <book owner="&TimeCorp; at &TimeCorpAddress;">
```

Parameter entities

Entities can also be used to assist with the construction of the rules that govern the document. But a different category of entity is required for this purpose. A **parameter entity** cannot be referenced from within a document, but *can* be referenced from within the document type declaration in order to help build the content of this important preamble to the document.

Declaration and reference

Parameter entities are declared in similar fashion to general text entities. The replacement value may be held in the declaration, or in an external file, in exactly the same way. The only difference in the declaration is the presence of a '%' symbol before the entity name:

```
<!ENTITY % aParameterEntity SYSTEM "anEntity.ent" >
```

A reference to a parameter entity is again similar to a reference to a general text entity. However, in place of the '&' symbol, a parameter entity reference is identified using the percent symbol again:

```
%aParameterEntity;
```

Constraints

As indicated above, parameter entities cannot be referenced from the document text. They have no significance and are simply not recognized in document text and attribute values:

```
              <!-- IGNORED -->
<book owner="%AnEntity;">...</book>


              <!-- IGNORED -->
<title>All About %AnotherEntity;</title>
```

    All About %AnotherEntity;

They are only used in the DTD, and specifically between declarations, within element and attribute declarations, and within internal entity values (see Chapter 5 for details).

Reusable entity sets

When a large number of general entity declarations are needed, it can be inconvenient to place them directly within the document type declaration. Also, when a number of documents require the same set of declarations, it can be even more inconvenient to repeat them all in each document. It is therefore possible to place the declarations in a separate data file. This file is an entity in its own right. It can be referenced from every document that requires the entities it defines. In the following example, both documents declare and reference entity A, and therefore acquire all of the declarations it contains, including those for entities B and C, which are referenced in these documents:

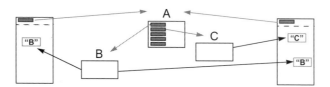

A good example of this idea is the practice of using entities for non-ASCII characters, where each character must be defined by its own entity declaration. For example, an entity named 'eacute' could be declared to represent the 'é' character. Clearly, a large number of these declarations are needed to represent all possible characters, and it would not be convenient to directly insert hundreds, or even thousands of declarations into every document that requires them. The ISO (*International Organization for Standardization*) has specified standard entity names (such as 'eacute'), and has also divided the huge range of characters into convenient groupings (the 'eacute' entity is in a group called 'ISO Latin 1'). All the declarations for a single group are typically stored in a single data file (such as 'ISOLat1.ent'). The declarations in this file can therefore be used in any document, simply by referencing it using a parameter entity declaration, followed by a reference to this declaration:

```
<!ENTITY % ISOnum SYSTEM "/ents/isonum.ent">
%ISOnum;
```

Rational for parameter entities

It may not be immediately obvious why a new type of entity is required to provide this functionality. General text entities would appear to offer the required capabilities. The answer is that this distinction provides a clean separation between entities that can be used in the document, and entities that can be used to help configure the document. Entities with the same names can be used in these two locations, and separately referenced without confusion:

```
<!DOCTYPE myBook [
  <!ENTITY % ents SYSTEM "file:///C:/ENTS/entities.ent">
  %ents;
  <!ENTITY ents "XML entities">
]>
<myBook> ... and &ents; are very powerful ... </myBook>
```

It could be argued that a document author can easily remember what names have been used to identify entities that are used in both locations, and is therefore able to avoid using conflicting entity names. While this is certainly true, potential problems could still arise when a DTD is referenced. Many DTDs include entities to assist with their construction, and are usually not created by the document authors. It should not be necessary for document authors to read the DTD and make note of the entities it uses. Likewise, the DTD author cannot be expected to anticipate and avoid every possible entity name that could later be assigned by document authors. For example, if the DTD author defines an entity called 'Styles' to group the names of elements that affect the style of a range of text, this should not prevent a document author from also defining an entity called 'Styles' to hold a paragraph describing the aesthetic options available on a new vehicle.

Document type declaration

There is another way to create a parameter entity declaration for an external entity. A single, un-named declaration can be embedded within the **document type declaration**, before the start of the optional internal subset. This declaration was introduced in the previous chapter.

A name is not needed for this entity, because there can only be one reference to it, and this reference automatically occurs at the end of the internal subset. The URL for this external entity is preceded by the '**SYSTEM**' keyword:

```
<!DOCTYPE book SYSTEM "declarations.xml" [
  <!-- INTERNAL DECLARATIONS -->
  ...
  <!-- "declarations.xml" INSERTED HERE -->
]>
```

The implied insertion point for the entity content is very significant. It should be recalled that only the first occurrence of an entity is acknowledged. Declarations in the internal subset precede declarations in the inserted file, so take precedence. This mechanism can therefore be used by document authors to override some of the declarations in the entity. Authors can use, but customize a pre-defined package of entities.

Although this feature is widely used, mainly to integrate externally defined DTD constructs, this approach is not strictly necessary. It can be seen as a simplification of the following, where a normal parameter entity declaration and reference are inserted at the end of the internal subset:

```
<!DOCTYPE [
  <!-- INTERNAL DECLARATIONS -->
  ...
  <!-- EXTERNAL DECLARATIONS -->
  <!ENTITY % declarations SYSTEM "...">
  %declarations;
]>
```

Alternatives to entities

XML inherited all of the entity-related features described above from the older SGML standard. In part, the entity concept was retained simply for backward compatibility with this standard, and was already considered by many to be an overly engineered approach to solving some of the problems introduced above. In particular, the separation of the declaration from the reference is often considered to be difficult to manage. Recently, alternative approaches have emerged to solve many of the issues handled by entities and discussed above.

Character referencing

As more operating systems and software applications become Unicode-sensitive, the need for entities to represent unusual characters will finally begin to diminish (see Chapter 29).

XML fragment inclusions

The proposed **XML Include** standard (see Chapter 12) offers a simpler, more direct way to call-in XML document fragments, and if the merging of data is only required to be a transitory visual effect for on-line viewing of narrative text, then the proposed **XLink** 'embed' feature (see Chapter 27) may also be considered.

Binary object inclusions

Again, **XLink** 'embed' feature (see Chapter 27) may be considered as an alternative mechanism for presenting referenced binary data to users, but in this case the embedding is no more transitory than the entity approach.

5. Document type definitions (the DTD)

Much of the XML standard is dedicated to the concept of document modelling. A DTD (*Document Type Definition*) can be used to ensure that documents conform to pre-defined rules. This chapter explains the purpose, scope and syntax of DTDs.

Some readers may have already determined that DTDs will not be relevant to their needs. Some simple applications of XML do not require them. In other cases, DTDs may be considered inadequate, and XML Schemas (see Chapter 14 and Chapter 15) may be a better choice. In either case, this chapter can be safely ignored. Basic principles common to both DTDs and XML Schemas are explained in both chapters. However, the principles outlined in the next chapter are relevant to both, and should be read whichever modelling scheme is preferred.

Introduction

It is possible to define in advance which elements can be used within a document, and where in the document these elements may be employed. This concept is similar to, but more powerful than, the stylesheet mechanisms that all modern word processors and desktop publishing packages provide.

HTML Note: There are SGML DTDs that describe HTML 2.0, HTML 3.2 and now HTML 4.0. These DTDs are not compatible with XML, primarily because they use some of the additional features of SGML. There is now also an XML DTD for the new XHTML standard.

SGML Note: XML DTDs use the same syntax as SGML DTDs, but have a more limited scope (Chapter 32 covers the differences in detail). Also note that the XML Schema standard re-introduces many of the features omitted from XML DTDs.

Models

A **document model** specifies the names of the elements that may be used in a document. It also dictates which elements have element content, mixed content and text content, and which elements are empty. When elements can contain other elements, restrictions on the content may include the names of the elements allowed, and even the order in which they may occur. The names of attributes each element may hold are given, and constraints may be placed on the possible value of an attribute.

The document modelling scheme provided by the standard is used to create a **DTD** (*Document Type Definition*). But a DTD is not a single object; this is the collective name for a model built from definitions in a number of markup declarations.

DTDs are typically used to describe such document types as journals, training guides, technical manuals and reference books, as well as to help define other standards that utilize XML syntax (including XHTML, NewsML and VML).

Model tree

The DTD creates a document tree model. This model is related to the tree structure of all the documents that conform to the DTD, but is rarely identical. Unlike a document tree, the model tree contains a branch for all the options, and does not include repeating elements.

In the example below, the model tree specifies that a book contains a number of Chapter elements, with each chapter containing either a number of Paragraph elements, or a single Sections element. A particular document tree, on the other hand, will have a branch for each chapter in the book, and any one of these chapters would typically contain a number of paragraph elements:

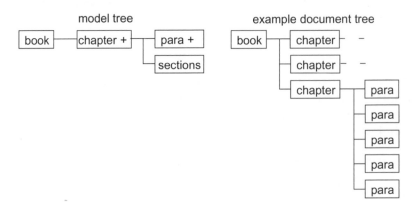

When to use a DTD

Creation of a DTD is rarely a trivial exercise, but there are several important benefits to having one:

- Characteristics of a set of documents can be codified in a formal, unambiguous manner, for later reference.
- Programmers can write extraction and manipulation filters without fear of their software ever having to process unexpected input.
- Stylesheets can be written with the same degree of confidence (a style rule can be defined for each element, and each context of significance, defined in the DTD).
- Using an XML-sensitive word processor, authors and editors can be guided and constrained to produce conforming documents.

Avoiding a DTD

However, some applications of XML will not require the creation of a DTD. Where raw information is automatically tagged by software for reading by a specific client program, the tagging may be relied upon to be accurately generated. Although strict rules will apply, these will probably be defined in a written specification. In fact, much more specific checks may be made by the receiving software than could be implemented in a DTD.

For example, the content of a Date attribute may be checked for valid values in the format 'ddmmyyyy'. Also, where documents are created on an *ad hoc* basis for one-off projects, the effort of producing a DTD may be too great for the limited rewards.

Attributes

The DTD also specifies the names of **attributes**, and assigns them to specific elements. It specifies whether an attribute is optional or required, and what kind of value it may hold. An attribute can hold a simple text phrase, a token, list of tokens, hypertext link anchor, or a reference to an entity or notation.

An attribute may also have a default value, to be applied only if no value is supplied by the document author. For example, a DTD may define Version and Date attributes for the Book element, and a Section Number attribute for the Section element. The Version attribute value may default to '1.0'.

Validating parsers

Some parsers are able to read the DTD, and use it to build the document model in memory. The template is then compared with the content of a document instance to search for errors. Such parsers are said to include a **validation** feature (it is a **validating parser**).

Batch validation

A **batch validation** process involves comparing the DTD against a complete document instance, and producing a report containing any errors or warnings. For example, if the DTD states that a title must appear in every chapter, but the Title element is missing from one chapter, this is flagged as an error.

The recipient of a document instance from another source may perform batch validation to ensure the document is correct, before loading it into a database or attempting to edit it. Software developers should consider batch validation to be analogous to program compilation, with similar types of errors detected.

Interactive validation

Interactive validation involves constant comparison of the DTD against a document as it is being created. The application simply prevents an illegal operation from happening. For example, if the DTD states that a Paragraph element can contain only Emphasis and Keyword elements, an XML-sensitive editor may only make these elements available for insertion when the cursor is located within a Paragraph element:

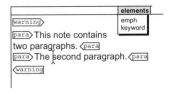

Parsing limitations

When a DTD is used, it should be understood that parsing a document does not replace careful visual checking of the document content. For example, a parser cannot detect a missing chapter. Likewise, if the title of a book appears in the Author element, and vice versa, this cannot be detected. Some of the limitations of DTD validation are addressed by the newer XML Schema adjunct standard (discussed in Chapters 14 and 15).

DTD location

The declarations that comprise the DTD may be stored at the top of each document that must conform to the model it creates. Alternatively, and more usually, they may be stored in a separate data file, referred to by a special instruction at the top of each document. Finally, there may be good reason to split the declarations between these two locations. Some declarations are then stored within the document, where they are described as the **internal subset** of the DTD. The remaining declarations, stored in a separate data file, are described as the **external subset** of the DTD.

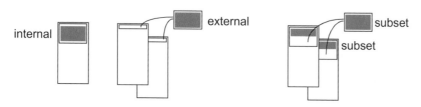

When an external subset applies to many documents, each document is known as a **document instance**, as it is just one instance of a document that is in the set of related documents. The external subset is considered to be the second part of the DTD. Though this often does not matter, there are cases where it is important because it gives the document author some control over how the external subset is used in a particular document:

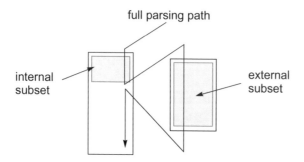

One way in which the document author can be given access to optional configurations is by allowing the author to include instructions that enable or disable declarations in pre-defined segments of the external subset. A **conditional section** encloses a number of other declarations, and contains a keyword that renders the content 'visible' or 'invisible' to XML processing software:

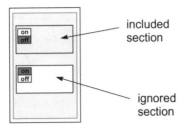

included
section

ignored
section

DTD markup

A DTD is composed of a number of declarations. Each declaration conforms to the markup declaration format, and is classified using one of the following keywords:

- ELEMENT (tag definition)
- ATTLIST (attribute definitions)
- ENTITY (entity definition)
- NOTATION (data type notation definition).

Declarations are grouped together, and may (like entity declarations) be held within the **internal subset** of the **document type declaration**:

```
<!DOCTYPE MYBOOK [
<!-- The MYBOOK DTD appears here -->
<!....>
<!.......>
]>
```

This approach makes the DTD part of the document it describes. This can be convenient. If the document is moved, the DTD automatically moves with it, as only a single data file or stream is involved.

External subsets

But the problem with this approach is that a DTD is only worth defining if it is going to apply to a group of documents, and this technique would require the same set of declarations to be repeated in every document. This is inefficient, and also difficult to manage, as any modifications to the model must be repeated in each document. To resolve this problem, some or all of the declarations can be stored in an **external subset** file. This file can then be referenced from all relevant documents, by placing a URL that locates the file after the '**SYSTEM**' keyword:

```
<!DOCTYPE MYBOOK SYSTEM "../DTDS/MYBOOK.DTD" [
  <!-- Rest of MYBOOK DTD appears here -->
  <!....>
] >
```

Of course, this is the technique previously described for handling large sets of entities. Indeed, the file referenced may contain both DTD-building declarations *and* entity declarations.

Internal subsets

Typically, only a few document-specific declarations are left in the **internal subset**, and only entity declarations at that. They may define special characters, commonly used phrases or embedded images that are not used elsewhere. In such cases, all the important document structure describing declarations are contained in the external subset file, which is why many people describe this file as *the* DTD file, despite the technical inaccuracy of this statement. Although it is possible to put element declarations in the internal subset, and thereby create document-specific structure models, caution is advised. DTD-specific processing software and stylesheets cannot be developed with confidence when some documents arbitrarily re-define or extend the rules.

Overriding declarations

An entity declaration in the internal subset can be used to override the value of an entity in the external subset. To understand how this is done, two important points must be recalled. The first point is that when an entity is defined more than once, only the first declaration is used. The second point is that the internal subset is processed before the external subset. Therefore, if an entity is declared in the internal subset that has the same name as one in the external subset, it will be processed first and take precedence.

In the example below, a local entity declaration is used to define the content of an element that is defined in the external subset:

```
<!DOCTYPE MYBOOK SYSTEM "C:\DTDS\MYBOOK.DTD" [
<!ENTITY % paraModel "#PCDATA | SUB | SUP">
] >
```

Note that this is a parameter entity, so all references to it must be in the DTD.

This technique can also be used to exert some control over the use of optional or alternative segments of the DTD, but involves the use of conditional sections, which are described later.

Attribute list declarations work in a similar way. An attribute specified in a declaration within the internal subset overrides a definition in a declaration in the external subset.

SGML Note: The SGML specification has been updated so that it also allows attribute declarations to override external declarations.

Element declarations

An **element declaration** is used to define a new element and specify its allowed content. The keyword '**ELEMENT**' introduces an element declaration. The name of the element being declared follows (recall the constraint to an initial letter, underscore character, '_', or colon, ':', and thereafter also digits, '.' and '-'), separated by at least one space character:

```
<!ELEMENT title ..... >
```

A statement of the legal content of the element is the final required part of the declaration. An element may have no content at all, may have content of only child elements, of only text, or of a mixture of elements and text. If the element can hold no child elements, and also no text, then it is known as an **empty element**. The keyword 'EMPTY' is used to denote this. In the example below, the Image element is declared to be an empty element, as it is used only to indicate the position of the image. When child elements are allowed, the declaration may contain either the keyword 'ANY', or a **model group**. An element declared to have a content of 'ANY' may contain all of the other elements declared in the DTD (in practice, however, this approach is rarely used because it allows too much freedom, and therefore undermines the benefits that derive from defining document structures):

```
<!ELEMENT p ANY>
<!ELEMENT image EMPTY>
```

```
<book><p>An image <image.../> in the text.</p></book>
```

Note that an element that is allowed to hold child elements, text or both, may just happen to have no content at all. In this case it is legal to employ both a start-tag and end-tag, or to use an empty element tag:

```
<title></title>                          <title/>
```

Likewise, an element declared to be empty may be represented by a start-tag, immediately followed by an end-tag, though there must be no elements or text between these tags.

A model group is used to describe enclosed elements and text. The structure of a model group can be complex, and is explained fully in the next section.

```
<!ELEMENT book (para*, chapter+)>
```

SGML Notes: The optional minimization codes, '- -' and their variants, never appear in an XML DTD because minimization is not supported (though a DTD can be compliant with both SGML and XML by replacing these characters with a parameter entity, which in the XML version must have an empty replacement value). It is not possible to embed comments within other declarations. Also, an element cannot be declared to have CDATA or RCDATA content.

Model groups

A **model group** is used to define an element that has mixed content or element content. An element defined to have **element content** may contain only **child** elements. An element defined to have **mixed content** may contain a mixture of child elements and free text. When applied in a document, however, this element may equally contain only text, only child elements or a mixture of the two, and it is not possible to specify the order in which text and elements may intermix.

A model group is bounded by brackets, and contains at least one **token**. The token may be the name of an included element. In this way document hierarchies are built. For example, a model group used in the declaration for a Book element may refer to embedded Front Matter and Body elements. The declarations for these elements may in turn specify the inclusion of further elements, such as Title and Chapter.

When a model group contains more than one content token, the child elements can be organized in different ways. The organization of elements is controlled using two logical connector operators: ',' (**sequence connector**) and '|' (**choice connector**):

```
(token, token, token)
```

```
(token | token | token)
```

SGML Note: The 'and' connector, '&', is not available. The reason for not including this connector type is related to the added complexity it introduces to document structure models, which complicates development of parser software. At the loss of some flexibility for document authors, it can simply be replaced by the sequence connector.

Sequence control

The **sequence** rule '(a, b, c)' indicates that element A is followed by element B, which in turn is followed by element C:

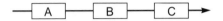

Note that other markup, such as comments and processing instructions, may be inserted between these elements. Such markup is not part of the document structure. In an article, for example, it may be important for the title to appear first, followed by the author's name, then a summary:

```
... (title, author, summary)...
```

```
<article>
  <!-- this is an article -->
  <title>Article Title</title>
  <?PAGE-BREAK?>
  <author>J. Smith</author>
  <summary>This is an article about XML.</summary>
  ...
</article>
```

Choice control

The **choice** rule '(a | b | c)' indicates a choice between the elements A, B and C (only one can be selected):

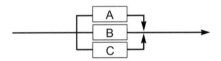

For example, an article in a magazine may be factual or fictional:

```
... (fact | fiction)...
```

```
<article>
  <fact>...</fact>
</article>
```

```
<article>
  <fiction>...</fiction>
</article>
```

Embedded model groups

It is not legal to mix these operators because this would introduce ambiguity in the model. The rule '`(a, b, c | d)`' is invalid, for example, because it may indicate that 'D' is an alternative to *all* the other elements, or that 'D' is an alternative only to element C (A and B still being required). To take a more realistic example, consider the need to place a title before a factual or fictional article, but the following model would not make it clear that the title is required regardless of whether the article is factual or fictional:

```
... (title, fact | fiction) ...
```

The solution to this problem is to use enclosed model groups. Further brackets are placed according to the meaning required – '`((a, b, c) | d)`' indicates the first meaning, whereas '`(a, b, (c | d))`' indicates the latter. In this way, operators are not actually mixed in the same group. In the last example, the outer model group makes use of the choice connector and the inner model group makes use of the sequence connector. The article example is also clarified:

```
... (title, (fact | fiction)) ...
```

Quantity control

The DTD author can also dictate how often an element can appear at each location. If the element is required and may not repeat, no further information is required. All of the previous examples indicated a required presence (except where the 'I' connector specified a choice of elements). It is also a simple matter to specify a fixed number of reoccurrences of an element. For example, if every article in a magazine had three authors, the following model would ensure that three names are present:

```
... author, author, author, ...
```

But is also possible to make an element optional, to allow it to repeat any number of times, and even to make it both optional and repeatable. These occurrence rules are governed using **quantity indicators** (the symbols '?', '*' and '+').

Optional element

If an element is optional, and cannot repeat, it is followed by a question mark, '?'. For example, '`(a, b?)`' indicates that element B is optional:

In an article, the Title element may be required, but the Author element may be absent.

Required and repeatable element

If an element is required and may repeat, the element name is followed by a plus, '+'. For example, '(a, b+)' indicates that element B must appear, but may also repeat:

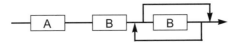

For example, a Book element may require the presence of at least one embedded Chapter element.

To take another example, a list has a number of items so a List element would have repeatable Item child elements. At least one must occur, but it may then be repeated:

```
<list>                          <list>
   <item>...</item>                <item>...</item>
   <item>...</item>             </list>
   <item>...</item>
</list>
```

Minimum occurrences

The DTD author can ensure that an element appears at least twice. For example, a list that contains a single item should not be a list at all. A List element may therefore be obliged to hold more than one Item element. This can be achieved using the model '(item, item+)', though care must be taken to place the '+' occurrence symbol after the second Item, as the alternative would be ambiguous, for reasons described below.

Optional and repeatable element

If an element is optional, and also repeatable, the element name is followed by an asterisk, '*'. The '*' may be seen as equivalent to the (illegal) combination '?+'. For example, '(a, b*)' indicates that element B may occur any number of times, and may also be absent:

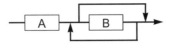

An Article element may contain any number of Author elements, including none.

To take another example, a chapter may have preliminary paragraphs, but (as in this book) may not always do so:

```
<chapter>                        <chapter>
  <para>...</para>                 <section>...</section>
  <para>...</para>              </chapter>
  <para>...</para>
  <section>...</section>
</list>
```

Model group occurrences

A model group may itself have an occurrence indicator. The entire group may be optional, required or repeatable. The example '(a, b)?' indicates that the elements A and B must either occur in sequence, or both be absent. Similarly, the example '(a, b)*' indicates that the sequence A then B may be absent, but if present may also repeat any number of times. The example '(a, b)+' indicates that elements A and B must exist, but may also then repeat.

Note: When creating a DTD, there may be several ways to achieve a required effect. The shortest representation possible should always be used for the sake of clarity. For example, the rule '(a+)?' is more simply defined as '(a*)', though '(a+, b+)' should not be confused with '(a, b)+', which is a very different model.

Text

The locations where document text is allowed are indicated by the keyword **'PCDATA'** (*Parsable Character Data*), which must be preceded by a **reserved name indicator**, '#', to avoid confusion with an element that has the same name (as unlikely as this seems). This keyword represents zero or more characters. An element that may contain only text would be defined as follows:

```
<!ELEMENT emph (#PCDATA)>

<emph>This element contains text.</emph>
```

There are strict rules which must be applied when an element is allowed to contain both text and child elements. The PCDATA keyword must be the first token in the group, and the group must be a choice group. Finally, the group must be optional and repeatable. This is known as a **mixed content** model:

```
<!ELEMENT emph  (#PCDATA | sub | super)*>
<!ELEMENT sub   (#PCDATA)>
<!ELEMENT super (#PCDATA)>

<emph>H<sub>2</sub>O is water.</emph>
```

SGML Note: These strict rules are to avoid the ambiguities that alternative arrangements have caused in SGML DTDs. Most SGML DTD authors have adopted these restrictions as an informal rule.

Model group ambiguities

Some care should be taken when creating model groups as it is possible to confuse the parser. There are several ways to inadvertently create an **ambiguous content model**.

Ambiguities arise when the element encountered in the data stream matches more than one token in the model. The example below illustrates such a case. On encountering an Item element, the parser cannot tell whether it corresponds to the first token in the group (the optional item) or to the second (the required item). If the parser assumes the first case then discovers no more Item elements in the data, an error will result (because the second item is required). If the parser assumes the second case, then encounters another item, an error will also result (because no more Item elements are allowed). The parser is not expected to look ahead to see which situation is relevant, because some examples of this problem would require the parser to search a long way (possibly to the end of the document), complicating the process and hindering efficiency. The example below could be made valid simply by switching the '?' to the second token:

```
(item?, item)
```

If alternative model groups contain the same initial element, the parser cannot determine which model group is being followed:

```
((surname, employee) | (surname, customer ))
```

On encountering a Surname element, the parser is unsure which model group is active and, as before, will not look ahead to determine which is in use. Such problems can be resolved by redefining the model groups as follows:

```
(surname, (employee | customer ))
```

One severe cause of ambiguity in mixed content models has been avoided by only allowing the choice connector in such models. This decision was made in response to the problems that using other connector types in SGML has raised in the past.

Attribute declarations

Attributes are declared separately from the element, in an **attribute list declaration**. All the attributes associated with a particular element are usually declared together, in a single attribute list declaration. An attribute declaration is identified by the keyword '**ATTLIST**'. The name of the element that will contain the declared attributes appears first:

```
<!ATTLIST  chapter ... .....
                   ... .....>
```

When there is more than one declaration for a particular element, the individual attribute definitions are combined. However, the first declaration takes precedence when the same attribute is redefined in declarations that are encountered later. Note that this allows an attribute declaration in the internal subset to override external definitions, though this is not usually advisable as it alters the document model for individual documents.

The rest of the declaration consists of at least one **attribute definition**. An attribute definition specifies the name of an attribute, dictates an attribute type, and sometimes provides a default value.

Name

The first parameter in the declaration is the attribute name, which is of type **Name**, and therefore follows the same restrictions on character usage as element names. In the example below, three attributes are defined for use in the Sequence List element:

```
<!ATTLIST  seqlist first .....
                   offset .....
                   type ..... >
```

Type

The second parameter describes the type of the attribute, which can restrict the range of possible values it may hold, or identify special attributes of significance to a parser:

- CDATA
- NMTOKEN
- NMTOKENS
- ENTITY
- ENTITIES
- ID
- IDREF
- IDREFS
- notation
- name group.

For example:

```
<!ATTLIST  seqList first  CDATA
                   offset NMTOKEN
                   type   ( alpha | number )>
```

SGML Note: This is a subset of the types allowed in SGML. The missing types are 'NUMBER', 'NUMBERS', 'NAME', 'NAMES', 'NUTOKEN' and 'NUTOKENS'.

Three of these types are divided into singular and plural forms, for example 'NMTOKEN' and 'NMTOKENS'. The plural form simply indicates a series of values that conforms to the same restrictions as the singular form. As a NMTOKEN attribute may contain '123abc', a NMTOKENS attribute may therefore contain '123abc 987xyz thirdToken'.

All attribute types are considered case-sensitive. This means that any difference in letter case is important. For example, 'MyToken' is not considered the same as 'mytoken' or 'MYTOKEN'.

Character data

The **CDATA** type indicates a simple string of characters, providing exactly the same flexibility as would be allowed if a DTD was not in use.

```
<book author="J. Smith">
```

Name tokens

The **NMTOKEN** type indicates a word, or token, with the same limits on character usage as previously described for the attribute name, except that there are no special restrictions on the first character (so a token can begin with a digit):

```
<doc size="A4">
```

Whitespace is used to separate tokens when a value is allowed to contain multiple token values:

```
<picture boundary="5 12 35 55">
```

Entities

The **ENTITY** type is a special case, indicating that the attribute value is actually an entity reference. The entity must be unparsed (binary data). For example, an element may be used as a placeholder for images:

```
<!ENTITY ACMElogo ..... >
<!ELEMENT picture   EMPTY>
<!ATTLIST picture   file ENTITY ...>

<picture file="ACMElogo" />
```

Identifiers

The **ID** and **IDREF** types are also special cases, used to provide a platform for hypertext linking (they are covered in detail in Chapter 7).

Notations

It is possible to embed non-XML data within an element. However, the embedded data must conform to an identified format. The name is used to link various references to the data type, found in notation declarations (see below), entity declarations and attribute declarations.

In an attribute declaration, the **NOTATION** option specifies which data types may be embedded within the element. The **notation type** declaration begins with the keyword 'NOTATION', and concludes with a list of previously defined notation names, such as 'T$_E$X'. In the example below, the Format attribute to the Image element has been defined to be a notation attribute:

```
<!ATTLIST image format    NOTATION (TeX | TIFF) >

<image format="TeX">
-$${ \Gamma (J^psi ......
</image>
```

Because the embedded data does not conform to XML syntax, the XML processor must assume that the element has ended when it encounters the end-tag start delimiters, '</', so this combination must not appear in the embedded data.

Name token groups

The **name token group** option restricts values to one of a finite set. For example, the definition '(left | right | centre)' specifies that the value must be one of these tokens:

```
<title align="centre">
```

SGML Note: Attribute token names do not have to be unique across all attributes assigned to a given element. For example, more than one attribute could have a 'yes' or 'no' value. The lack of minimization techniques makes this restriction redundant in SGML.

In some cases, it is practical for a group to contain a single option:

```
<!ATTLIST list  type  (indented)  .....>
```

In this example, the List element has an attribute called Type, which can take only one value, 'indented'. An application should assume that a missing value indicates the alternative form:

```
<list> <!-- normal list -->

<list type="indented"> <!-- indented list -->
```

HTML & SGML Note: Recall that the attribute name, equals sign and quotes are all required in XML, so '`<list indented>`' is not allowed.

Normalization

Attribute values are 'normalized' before they are passed to an application. In all cases, any line-end codes are replaced by spaces to create a simple string of text. Then all entity references are replaced by the entity content. Finally, for attribute types other than CDATA, multiple spaces are reduced to a single space and surrounding spaces are removed. The attribute values below are normalized to 'X123', 'John Peter Smith' and '15mm 35mm':

```
<!ENTITY MiddleName "Peter">
<!ATTLIST pic    id    ID            #REQUIRED
                 owner CDATA         #REQUIRED
                 size  NMTOKENS      #REQUIRED >

<book id=" X123" owner="John    &MiddleName;
        Smith " size="15mm    35mm " >
```

Note that CDATA attributes are allowed to contain general entity references.

Required and default values

The final parameter is the **default value**, which specifies a default value to be applied when the document author does not enter a value. Alternatively, this parameter can be used simply to state that the document author must enter a value, or that the value is optional. It is even possible for a default value to be made compulsory (the only value allowed for this attribute).

The DTD can specify that a particular attribute must be present each time the element it belongs to is used. This is termed a **required attribute**. If a value is not given, an error is reported. The '**#REQUIRED**' keyword is used for this purpose. In the example below, the DTD dictates that the Separator Character attribute to the Sequence List element is a required token. This token must be provided every time a Sequence List element is used:

```
<!ATTLIST seqlist sepchar   NMTOKEN  #REQUIRED>
```
optional

Alternatively, the DTD may specify that the attribute can be absent. This is an **implied attribute**. When a value is not explicitly provided, the application just assumes some default behaviour. The '**#IMPLIED**' keyword is used for this purpose. In the example below, the DTD dictates that the Offset attribute to the Sequence List element is an implied token (which, if used, specifies an indentation width for the list items):

```
<!ATTLIST seqlist sepchar   NMTOKEN  #REQUIRED
                  offset    NMTOKEN  #IMPLIED >

<seqlist sepchar="*">...</seqlist>

<seqlist sepchar="*" offset="5mm">...</seqlist>
```

An attribute may be required, yet also given a **default value**. When an explicit value is not provided in the document, this default value is used. The benefits of this approach are that each time the default value is applicable, the size of the data file or stream is reduced, and a document author has less work to do. In the example below, the Type attribute is a choice group, with possible values of 'alpha' and 'num' (indicating an alphabetical list or a numeric list). When a value is not specified, the default is 'num' (numerical list), perhaps because this is deemed to be the most frequent requirement:

```
<!ATTLIST seqlist sepchar   NMTOKEN     #REQUIRED
                  offset    NMTOKEN     #IMPLIED
                  type      (alpha|num) "num" >

<seqlist sepchar="*">                <!-- number -->

<seqlist sepchar="*" type="num">     <!-- number -->

<seqlist sepchar="*" type="alpha"> <!-- alphabet -->
```

Note that a default value *cannot* be added to required or implied attributes. It is an alternative to these types of attribute. It can, however, be considered as a special kind of required attribute, as the XML processor is guaranteed to be given a value, by the DTD author if not by the document author.

Fixed values

If a default value is preceded by the keyword '**#FIXED**', then the value provided is the only value the attribute can take. This may seem odd, but using this feature the DTD author can place permanent markers that attach application-specific roles to DTD-specific elements or attributes. Xlink and HyTime utilize this concept to identify elements and attributes with linking roles, and it also has a possible role in the Namespaces standard to identify the namespaces allowed.

Reserved attributes

Attribute names beginning 'xml:' are reserved for use in the standard, and the attributes **xml:lang** and **xml:space** are already assigned meanings. Previous examples have shown these attributes embedded in element start-tags. But when a particular element always has the same value for one of these attributes, it is more economical to store this information in the attribute declaration. For example, when elements called English and German are defined to hold text in each of these languages, it would be sensible to define suitable values in the DTD. The document author then only has to insert the relevant element:

```
<!ATTLIST english  xml:lang NMTOKEN "en">
<!ATTLIST german   xml:lang NMTOKEN "de">
```

Note that this example illustrates another possible use for the #FIXED feature. It would not be wise to allow a document author the option to override the values attached to each of these elements.

Multiple declarations

More than one attribute list declaration can be assigned to the same element. The attribute definitions they contain are combined. When the same attribute name appears, the first declaration has precedence:

```
<!ATTLIST book   id  ID #REQUIRED
                 type (novel | fact) #REQUIRED>
<!ATTLIST book   type (thick | thin) "thin"
                 author CDATA #IMPLIED>

<book id="X123" type="fact" author="J. Smith">
```

For reasons of backward compatibility with SGML, which does not allow this, using multiple declarations is not advised. In any case, there seems to be little advantage in doing this. For reasons already stated, it is certainly not a good idea to include overriding declarations in a document's internal subset.

Parameter entities

Just as a document author may use a general entity to avoid unnecessary repetition, so a DTD author may use a **parameter entity** in a similar fashion to aid construction of the DTD. The use of entities can reduce the workload, make authoring errors less likely and clarify the DTD structure (although they can also, if used too frequently, render the DTD unintelligible).

For example, a model group that is in common use may be stored in an entity:

```
<!ENTITY % common   "(para | list | table)">
```

Within element declarations a reference is made to the parameter entity:

```
<!ELEMENT chapter  ((%common;)*, section*) >
<!ELEMENT section  (%common;)*>
```

Note that an entity reference must not be qualified by an occurrence indicator. In the example above, a model group is used to hold the '%common;' reference. It would not be legal to use '%common;*' instead. The double pair of brackets this introduces into the model has no effect, though to avoid such redundancy, models defined in entity declarations tend not to include the brackets. But omitting brackets in the entity declaration can also cause problems if the DTD author forgets, and also omits them in the element declaration. In the end, this is just a matter of personal preference.

Automatically inserted spaces

A space character is added to the start and end of the content as it replaces the reference. This is to ensure that the entity contains complete tokens.

The following example would break the Superscript element into two tokens, 'supersc' and 'ript', and this would be illegal anyway because there would be no vertical bar between them:

```
<!ENTITY % PartModel "emph | supersc" >

<!ELEMENT para  (%PartModel;ript)* > <!-- ERROR -->
```

Using this feature, portions of a DTD may be stored in separate files, for reuse in other DTDs. Parameter entities are also useful when used in conjunction with conditional sections, as described in the next section.

Illegal general entities

General entities may not appear in the DTD, in either the internal or external sub-sets. The following example contains two general entities that are incorrectly used:

```
                                    <!-- ERROR -->
<!ELEMENT para (#PCDATA | emph | &MoreTokens;)>
<!-- ERROR -->
&MoreDeclarations;
<!ELEMENT emph (#PCDATA)>
```

Conditional sections

Portions of a DTD may be identified as optional segments, which can be easily included or excluded from processing to build alternative document models. This facility is provided using **conditional sections**. Once a segment of the DTD is marked as a conditional section, the content is made visible or invisible to XML processing by changing a single keyword.

It should be noted that conditional sections can only be used in the external subset of the DTD. It is not possible to use them in a document's internal subset, or in any external entity referred to from this place. It is also not possible to use them in document content.

SGML Note: The included and ignored section markup cannot be used in a document instance. In XML, this is purely a DTD feature.

Included sections

Marking the DTD segment for possible exclusion is achieved by surrounding the appropriate declarations with an **included section** declaration. An included section declaration is an example of a markup declaration that includes a subset. It is therefore indicated by the declaration start characters, '<!', and an open square bracket, '['. This is followed by the keyword '**INCLUDE**'. However, unlike the CDATA construct described previously, spaces *are* allowed around the keyword. The contents are enclosed by embedded square brackets, and the declaration is closed with the combination ']]>':

```
<![INCLUDE[
     ......
]]>

<![  INCLUDE  [
     ......
]]>
```

Ignored sections

Simply surrounding some declarations with an included section has no effect on the processing of the DTD. The included section declaration is effectively invisible. The only reason for its presence is that it allows the segment to be 'switched out' easily. Simply changing the word 'INCLUDE' to '**IGNORE**' converts the included section declaration into an **ignored section** declaration. The content of an ignored section is not processed by an XML processor. The embedded declarations are effectively omitted from the DTD:

```
<![IGNORE[
    <!-- THIS COMMENT IS NOT PROCESSED -->
]]>
```

Entity-controlled switching

Entities may be used to facilitate the use of conditional sections. If marked sections are used to define optional parts of the DTD, or to create two variants of the same DTD within one file, then the active group of marked sections at any one time can be identified using an entity. In the example below, all the conditional sections containing parameter entity reference 'MyStandard' are to be included (along with all their embedded element and attribute list declarations), and the other marked sections are to be ignored. The effect is to include the first Text entity declaration, which includes the Temp element:

```
<!ENTITY % MyStandard "INCLUDE">

<!ENTITY % MyVariant  "IGNORE">

<![%MyStandard;[
    <!ENTITY % Text "#PCDATA | sup | sup | temp">
]]>

<![%MyVariant;[
    <!ENTITY % Text "#PCDATA | sup | sup">
]]>
```

By redefining such entities in the internal subset, a document author can choose to omit or include pre-defined (tightly controlled) segments of the DTD.

When two conditional sections are used to select alternative entity definitions, as in the example above, there is a simple technique that can be employed to dispense with one of the entities. This technique depends on the fact that duplicate entity definitions are ignored. There is therefore no need to surround the second entity declaration, or declarations, with included section markup.

In the following example, the second Text entity declaration is ignored if the first is included by setting the MyStandard entity value to 'INCLUDE':

```
<!ENTITY % MyStandard "INCLUDE">

<![ %MyStandard; [
      <!ENTITY % Text "#PCDATA | sup | sup | temp">
]]>

<!ENTITY % Text "#PCDATA | sup | sup">
```

Notation declarations

An element or entity may contain non-XML format data. An element declaration must specify which formats may be embedded, and an entity declaration must specify which format *is* embedded. In both cases, this is done by referring to a notation name, which is defined in a **notation declaration**.

It should be noted that this feature was included in XML as part of its SGML inheritance, and that new applications of XML tend not to make use of it. Instead, non-XML data is usually included by reference from an attribute value, and the data format is identified using a MIME type, or even just the filename extent, as in '.gif'.

As with other declaration types, a notation declaration begins with the '<!' delimiter and ends with '>'. The keyword '**NOTATION**' identifies a notation declaration, and is followed by the notation name, which is at the discretion of the DTD author but should be an obvious name for the format:

```
<!NOTATION TeX ..... >
```

Note: T_EX is a typesetting language.

The notation name is followed by an external notation identifier, possibly involving both a public and a system identifier. If no information on the format is available, and no application is identifiable that can process the data, the declaration must be present in its minimum form, which includes a system identifier with no value (the keyword 'SYSTEM' followed by two quotes):

```
<!NOTATION PIXI SYSTEM "">
```

When an application is available that can process the data, the system identifier should specify the location and name of that application (though this approach may not work well across the Internet, where the location and name of the user's application will not be known in advance):

```
<!NOTATION TIFF SYSTEM "C:\APPS\SHOW_TIF.EXE">
```

Information about the data format should be provided, if present, in the public identifier:

```
<!NOTATION TeX PUBLIC "-//MyCorp//NOTATION TeX
                 Help File//EN" "C:\APPS\SHOW_TEX.EXE">
```

The declared notation may be referred to in entity declarations, following the '**NDATA**' (notational data) keyword. Note that the parser can make no use of this information, but passes it to the application (which, it is hoped, can):

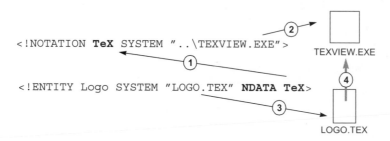

The declared notation may also be referred to in attribute declarations, for elements that contain formats other than XML (but conforming to legal XML character usage):

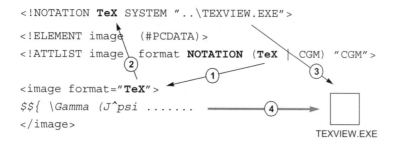

DTD processing issues

When a document contains neither an internal nor external DTD subset (and does not belong to an alternative schema model), there are some restrictions on the use of markup:

- Attributes cannot have a default value, so must always be specified in full.
- Attributes cannot be entity references, identifiers or identifier references, nor

a token or series of tokens. All attributes are assumed to be simple strings (CDATA).

- Attributes cannot be made compulsory. All attributes are optional, and implied if not present.
- Entities cannot be defined, and the only entity references that can (and should) be used are the hard-wired references: '<', '>', '&', ''' and '"'.

Also, because no document structure rules are available, it is not possible to determine which elements have element content, as opposed to mixed content. Therefore, all spaces and line-end codes may be considered part of the document:

```
<p>Here is a list:</p>
<list>
<item>
<p>First item</p></item>
<item><p>Second item</p></item>
<item>
<p>Third item</p></item></list>
```

Here is a list:

First item
Second item

Third item

These restrictions are relatively trivial in the cases where software is both generating and processing the document. The document rules need not be passed from application to application if they are already built in to both applications. The writer program can easily ensure that required attributes are always produced, and repeated generation of 'default' values takes no effort. Unnecessary spaces and line-end codes can also be consistently avoided. It is assumed that the client application can perform its own check for required attributes, and determine for itself which of the attributes hold either references to entities or hypertext link codes.

Internal DTD processing

When present, an internal DTD subset *must* be processed. Typically, this subset contains document-specific declarations, such as local entity definitions.

Though much less common, the internal subset may also contain document structure building declarations. Even a non-validating parser needs to read these declarations, as they may contain default or fixed attribute values, or attributes that provide the name of a binary entity (indicating that the element should be replaced by the content of that entity). For example, the DTD may state that a Security attribute is required in every paragraph, and that it has a default value of 'secret'.

Without reading the attribute list declaration, it would not otherwise be possible to tell that the second paragraph in the example below should not be presented to all readers:

```
<!ATTLIST para    security   (secret|normal)  "secret">
...
<para security="normal">A normal paragraph.</para>
<para>A secret paragraph.</para>
```

For this reason, an XML processor that is not capable of reading and interpreting element and attribute declarations should abort processing the document if they are encountered.

External DTD processing

Typically, an external subset contains document structure rules. Although some applications may not be very interested in the external subset, especially when they have no intention of validating the content for correct structure, they still need to know if entities or attribute values of the kinds described above are stored there. The **Standalone parameter** of the **XML Declaration** includes the keyword 'yes' or 'no', to inform a non-validating XML processor whether or not the external subset of the DTD must be read for the document to be processed accurately:

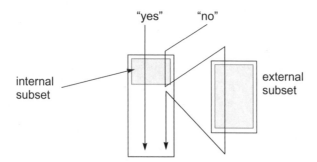

When no information is provided, the value 'no' is considered to be the default, so external processing is assumed to be necessary (unless, of course, there *is* no external subset). It follows that the parameter need only be included when an external subset exists, but is not needed to interpret the document content:

```
<?XML ..... standalone="yes"  >
```

6. Document modelling techniques

This chapter explores issues relating to the development of a model or template for XML documents, including document analysis, future-use analysis and general model design.

Most of the concepts covered are applicable to both DTD and XML Schema modelling (though Chapter 14 and Chapter 15 should be read first by those only interested in schemas). When the term 'DTD' is used in place of 'model', this indicates that the concept is not applicable to XML Schema.

Stages of development

Development of a DTD should ideally involve the following steps:

- analysis (including document and database schema analysis)
- model definition (including use of existing standards)
- writing the DTD (or schema)
- testing and debugging.

Analysis

DTD and XML Schema document models are very important. They are used to guide authors and ensure that relevant documents conform to agreed standards. If a model is in some way inadequate, or simply defines inappropriate rules, the implications can be very significant. Later corrections may involve modifications to many documents (perhaps thousands) that were built to conform to the incorrect model, as well as to software filters and stylesheets. Great care should therefore be taken to ensure that the model is correct first time.

The creation of a document model requires a number of skills that in most cases cannot be found in any single person. Specifically, it is necessary to consider the features and limitations of the modelling language (as well as significant adjunct standards, such as XPath), the level of complexity and its impact on any custom software development, the existing document model (which may not be fully apparent from simply studying previously published material and style guides) and likely future electronic publishing or information dissemination needs.

The following roles are likely to be spread across a small number of individuals:

- document author or editor
- editorial system administrator
- software developer or integrator
- XML consultant
- database designer.

Model definition

Ultimately, the results of analysis are used to create a concrete model. But there may be many ways to implement a valid model. There are choices to make, such as whether or not to adapt an existing model, whether to describe a feature of the document with an element or an attribute, and what names to assign to each element and attribute. The following sections discuss appropriate element and attribute names, how to choose whether to use an element or attribute in a given circumstance, when to consider using or adapting an industry standard model, how to model lists and tabular matter, and whether to consider a concept called 'architectural forms'.

Writing the DTD

The layout of the model deserves consideration, such as the arrangement of declarations, the use of comments, and the division of the DTD into re-usable entities. XML allows a lot of freedom in the construction of the DTD. A recommended approach to formatting a DTD is outlined below, followed by a look at DTD writing tools.

Debugging

Testing a model is an important exercise that requires a number of considerations. These are also discussed below.

Document analysis

Document analysis is often only applicable to publishing applications of XML, and not to the development of data exchange applications.

Existing rules

It is typically the case that a new XML-based publishing system replaces a system that adopted procedural markup principles, whether an old-fashioned typesetting system or a more modern DTP package. Existing books or documents to some degree conform to in-house style guides (whether formally defined, loosely described in notes, or existing simply in the heads of senior editorial staff), and naturally form the foundation of document analysis. The better the style guide, and the more rigorously it was previously applied, the easier it is to define a suitable model (and to convert these legacy documents to XML format too).

Human expertise

Studying existing documents reveals much about the required structure. However, an author or editor with widespread experience of the content of these documents should still be involved in the process. When the document collection is vast, only a small proportion of the material can realistically be assessed, and it is very important that the selected material be representative of the whole collection.

Another important principle to adopt is to be realistic about the technology and its capabilities. DTP operators have become accustomed to a degree of artistic freedom that cannot be sustained in a controlled XML environment.

Formatting constraints

XML is usually implemented in order to improve the efficiency of publishing and republishing to different target audiences on a variety of media. Software is used to provide the necessary automation, but programs require predictable input. Utilities that locate, extract, manipulate and present information from XML documents must be given manageable tasks to perform. In particular, regard must be given to the limitations of stylesheets and structure-oriented publishing products.

Creating complex coding structures to deal with document structures that appear infrequently may not be practical. One common example of such a problem is a small, vertically aligned fragment, as shown below. Compromise may be necessary. Perhaps these structures can be formatted slightly differently, more simply, without any loss of legibility:

> 300
>   25.6
> and   1.3

Relevant features

For every feature identified in existing documents, the following set of questions may be asked:

- can it be given a name?
- does it always appear?
- may there be more than one?
- must it always appear before (or after) some other feature?
- does it deconstruct into smaller objects (to which these same questions apply)?
- is some of the textual content always the same (if so, it could be generated automatically)?

The answers to these questions form the basis of a document specification. Every object in the document is given a descriptive name, and is assigned rules governing where and how often it may appear, and what it may contain.

Database schema analysis

All or part of an XML document may consist of data extracted from a relational database. If the database schema has been created professionally, there should be documentation that describes the design. Database analysis frequently involves the production of entity relationship diagrams (E-R diagrams), which may be of use in helping to determine the XML data model. The reverse is also true; an existing XML document model may be used to help design the database schema, including the E-R diagrams describing it. In either case, it is interesting to compare DTD definitions with entity relationship diagrams. Note that an 'entity' in this case may actually be equivalent to an XML element.

In a **one-to-one** relationship, one entity is related to one other entity. For example, a chapter may contain one title, and that title belongs only to that chapter (note that the Chapter element is not mandatory to the Title element if the Title element may also be used elsewhere):

chapter (title, ...)

If the Title element is not mandatory, the black circle is replaced with an empty circle:

                                        chapter (title?, ...)

In a **one-to-many** relationship, a single entity is related to many instances of another entity. For example, a Chapter element may (or perhaps must) contain at least one Paragraph element:

                                        chapter (para+)

                                        chapter (para*)

Alternative relationships can also be described in XML, and in the **SSADM** (*Structured Systems Analysis and Design Method*) version of an E-R diagram. For example, a Chapter element may contain either a set of Paragraph elements or a single Sections element (note that the Title element may be part of a chapter or a section):

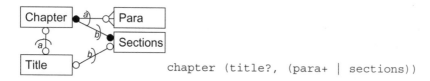

                    chapter (title?, (para+ | sections))

However, these diagrams say nothing about the order of appearance because relational databases have no concept of internal order (though output may be sorted alphabetically).

Future-use analysis

A major reason for adopting XML is the possibilities it offers for information reuse. Analysis should therefore not end at describing current practice, unless it is certain that the data will never be put to any new purposes.

The advent of electronic publishing has been a major factor in popularizing the generalized markup approach. Analysis must therefore include looking ahead to the features offered by these new publishing media, and to possibilities for niche publications derived from subsets of the data.

Hypertext linking

One benefit of electronic publishing over traditional paper publishing is the capability of software to support hypertext links. The original document may contain obvious linking text, such as 'see section 9 for details', but there may also be other, more subtle links 'hidden' in the document structure. In both cases, it is necessary to determine a linking strategy, including a scheme for producing unique link values for each target object. The XLink (Chapter 27) and XPointer (Chapter 28) standards may be considered.

Granularity

The degree to which an element's content is organized into sub-elements is often termed its **granularity**. Grains can be coarse (like sugar) or fine (like flour). The issue of granularity is often raised at this point, because future-use analysis tends to identify structures that need to be identified, but which have no distinctive visual appearance in existing paper products.

For example, while a person's name may be highlighted in the document, it is unlikely that the last name will be styled differently to the first name, yet an on-line publication or associated database may be envisaged that includes a list of names, sorted by last name. To achieve this automatically, each part of the name should be tagged:

> The name *John Smith* is very popular in England.

```
The name <name><f>John</f><s>Smith</s></name> is
very popular in England.
```

Legally overlapping structures

There are occasions when it is absolutely essential that ranges of data that span structures must be identified and isolated, despite the strict rules concerning proper element nesting defined in the XML standard. For example, it is common practice in technical documentation for text that has changed since a previous release of the document to be marked as 'revised text', perhaps using a vertical bar in the margin. Yet such text may begin part of the way through one paragraph, and end in the middle of the next. Breaking the range into smaller pieces is always possible, but this would add a number of tags to the document, and would also destroy the significance of the complete unit (if there *was* any significance to the grouping).

Instead, pairs of empty elements can be employed to describe a block of text that spans element structures. In the example below, the empty Revision element is used to indicate the start of a block of revised text, and the empty RevisionEnd element to indicate the end of the block. The parser is unaware of the particular significance of the two empty elements, so cannot object to their usage to define the boundaries of a range of text that does not fit into the formal document structure:

```
<para>In this paragraph there is
some <revision/>revised text.</para>
<para>This text is also changed,
but<revisionEnd/> this text is not.</para>
```

In this paragraph there is
some **revised text.**

This text is also changed,
but this text is not

This mechanism can be used to extract arbitrary ranges of material, but only for non-XML processing, as the embedded structures will be invalid when taken out of context. This example fragment is not well-formed, because the fragment begins with an empty element, followed by text, then an end-tag, and only the first half of the following paragraph:

```
<revision/>revised text.</para>
<para>This text is also changed, but <revisionEnd/>
```

Appropriate names

There are few restrictions on the naming of elements, but some guidelines are worth considering. A number of software and markup language conventions are available to choose from.

Letter-case

A coherent and easily remembered policy on the use of upper-case and lower-case letters is essential, as element names are case-sensitive. The most obvious options are all lower-case ('myelement') and all upper-case ('MYELEMENT'). Lower-case letters are, for two reasons, generally considered to be better. First, they are easier on the eye, whether viewing elements in XML documents, or options from an XML editor menu (and tests have shown that upper-case words take 30% longer to read). But they also make documents compressed for transfer smaller, because the same words, consisting of identical characters, are more likely to appear in the document text.

However, mixed-case ('MyElement') has the benefit of clearly distinguishing each part of a name that is derived from multiple words:

```
<CompanyPresident>J. Smith</CompanyPresident>
```

Software conventions

When developing software to process XML data, one common approach is to use the same name for an element or attribute as the variable that holds its value while in memory.

For example, Java conventions include the use of lower-case for the first letter, and capitals for the start of each embedded word, such as 'theTag' (this convention is generally used throughout this book):

```
String companyPresident = "J. Smith";
```

```
<companyPresident>J. Smith</companyPresident>
```

HTML and XHTML conventions

Another common approach now is to adopt HTML tag naming conventions. A number of recent standards have taken HTML as a starting-point, simply removing unwanted elements and adding new required ones. For example, both WML (*Wireless Markup Language*) and OEB (*Open Electronic Book*) standards adopt this practice. Familiarity with HTML makes learning the new standards relatively simple, as people already know what element names such as 'P' (paragraph), 'UL' (unordered list) and 'TR' (table row) mean. The second benefit is that HTML is currently used as the core storage format for a huge range of information. The ability to extract and copy HTML-based text into documents that conform to other standards, with a minimum of fuss, is of clear benefit.

The HTML standards are based on SGML, rather than XML, which is not (by default) case-sensitive. This means that 'p' and 'P' are both valid ways of identifying the HTML Paragraph element. To distinguish the original HTML-originating elements from the domain-specific new ones, the HTML elements could be made upper-case, and the others mixed- or lower-case:

```
<P>Company president:
<companyPresident>J.Smith</companyPresident>.</P>
```

As XHTML is an XML application, names *are* case-sensitive, and all names are lower-case.

Length of names

The other factor to consider is the length of the name. Unfortunately, there are two conflicting aims to keep in mind. The desire to create unambiguous, self-describing structures would tend to suggest the need for longer names. Clearly, the name 'PriceCode' is more meaningful than 'PC', or even 'PriCd'. But in contradiction to this is the need to minimize document size, so as to increase the speed of transfer over networks.

One practical solution is to use short names for commonly used elements, and long names for infrequently used elements. This approach addresses both problems, as document authors will use the shorter named elements so frequently that memorizing their meaning is not an issue, and, at the same time, document size is not greatly affected by the increased length of a few, rarely used elements.

Naming of attributes should follow the same considerations, with a reasonable balance between clarity and brevity, perhaps also taking into account the likely number of occurrences of both the element and of the attribute itself.

Note that HTML tends to follow these rules, with 'P' standing for 'paragraph', a commonly used element, and the longer but less common 'FRAMESET' representing an entire document containing frames.

Consistency

Consistency is particularly important, regardless of which convention is chosen. If an underscore character is used to separate words within one element name, this character should be used for the same purpose in all compound element names. Confidence in a model is easily undermined if there is little or no consistency.

Element or attribute

In a few cases, there is no choice of whether to use an element or an attribute for a given piece of information. For example, if it is a reference to a binary entity, then it must be an attribute value, as the XML standard does not allow such references in element content.

More usually, information could be represented either by a child element or by an attribute. In some cases, either an element or an attribute would be equally well suited to the task, and even professional model designers would argue over some decisions. But in other cases, one or the other would be more suitable, and there are some guidelines that may assist in making this decision.

An element should be chosen if the information:

- is a sub-division of the element content, rather than information about the content
- contains sub-structures
- is a long text string
- is to be presented to the audience when used in a publishable document
- is *not* constrained to be a single word, or to be one possibility from a list of options.

Candidate reasons for choosing an attribute include the following factors (largely simply the inverse of the factors listed above). The information:

- describes the content of the element, rather than being a sub-division of the element content
- has *no* sub-structures
- is a short text string
- is *not* to be presented to the audience when used in a publishable document
- must be a single word, or one option from a list of possible values.

Data and meta-data

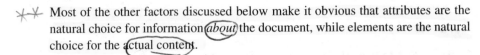 Most of the other factors discussed below make it obvious that attributes are the natural choice for information about the document, while elements are the natural choice for the actual content.

The very name 'attribute' makes the point most clearly. In English, this word is synonymous with 'characteristic'. An attribute is not the thing itself, but a quality of that thing.

Sub-structures

If the embedded information may itself contain sub-structures, then an element should be used, because attributes are not capable of holding structured markup.

For example, if the title of a book may contain subscript characters, or emphasized words, it should be held in a Title element:

```
<book>
  <title>Qualities of H<sub>2</sub>O</title>
  . . .
</book>
```

The subscript start-tag and end-tag will not be recognized if inserted into an attribute value. Indeed, an error should be reported if any '<' symbols are found within an attribute value:

```
                <!-- WILL NOT WORK  -->
<book title="Qualities of H<sub>2</sub>O">
   ...
</book>
```

If the information is a small unit of text that cannot itself contain markup, it can reasonably be represented by an attribute. Otherwise, it should be element content.

Text length

Although, strictly speaking, there is no limit to the number of characters allowed in an attribute value, most software developed to parse, edit or display the content of attributes expects to find short values. Long values may be difficult to work with at best, and may crash the software at worst. Most XML-sensitive editors have more primitive interfaces for attribute editing, and may truncate the data or at least make scrolling necessary to see the whole string.

Published output

In a document that is to be published, meta-data is information about the content of the document, and is not itself part of the content. It is for this reason that stylesheet languages have tended to focus on the ability to format element content, rather than attribute values. Instead, attribute values have often been used to help decide *how* to format the content. Some products and stylesheet languages have limited or non-existent capabilities for presenting attribute values.

Restricted values

If the information needs to be constrained to one of a small set of possible values, then an attribute should almost certainly be used, as it is possible to enforce the restrictions, and the full set of options can (with a typical XML-sensitive editor) be presented for document authors to choose from (though the XML Schema standard allows element content to be restricted in this way too):

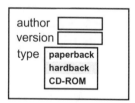

Conformity issues

Using the recommendations discussed above, a first draft of the model could be produced that consists almost entirely of elements, or almost entirely of attributes (with most elements being used only to hold these attributes). At this point, it would be worth taking another look at the few remaining elements or attributes, to see if the benefits of conformity with the rest of the model could outweigh the factors that originally determined the current choice. In an XML-sensitive editor, it is often inconvenient to switch between element inserting mode and attribute editing mode.

Software that needs to process XML input (perhaps using the SAX or DOM interfaces discussed in later chapters) would be less complex if it only had to deal with elements or attributes, instead of both.

Summary

To summarize, an attribute is usually easier to manage. It can be constrained and validated by a parser, whereas text in an element cannot. However, stylesheets tend to have limited capabilities for extracting, styling and positioning an attribute on-screen or on the page. When in doubt, and a small number of attributes are involved, an element should probably be used instead.

Other modelling tips

Using the context

It is generally good practice to define as few elements as possible, and use context to help refine the meaning of elements with similar purposes. A good example of this is titles. When a book, chapter, section and table can all have a title, it is not necessary to define elements such as 'bookTitle', 'chapterTitle', 'sectionTitle' and 'tableTitle'. The context is sufficient to identify each usage, and the name 'title' can be used for all these purposes:

```
<book>
  <title>The Book Title</title>
  <chapter>
    <title>The First Chapter</title>
    <section>
      <title>The First Section</title>
      <table>
        <title>A Table</title>
        ...
      </table>
      ...
    </section>
    ...
  </chapter>
  ...
</book>
```

Headings or wrappings

It would be very natural to consider headings that appear in the text of a document to be isolated elements, and to encode them as such. This approach is seen in HTML, where H1, H2, H3, H4 and H5 elements are used to hold headings of various weight. In the following example, headings appear amongst some normal paragraphs:

```
<chapter>
  <para>...</para>

  <heading>...</heading>
  <para>...</para>
  <para>...</para>

  <heading>...</heading>
  <para>...</para>
  <para>...</para>
</chapter>
```

But the fact that a heading identifies the purpose of the following paragraphs may be considered a significant clue that this is a meaningful unit of information. The heading can be considered to be the title of this unit, and all the components can be wrapped in a single element to make their relationships explicit:

```
<chapter>
  <para>...</para>

  <section>
    <title>...</title>
    <para>...</para>
    <para>...</para>
  </section>

  <section>
    <title>...</title>
    <para>...</para>
    <para>...</para>
  </section>
</chapter>
```

However, this approach uses more tags, and can slow down document authoring (especially when adding XML tags to existing text, when the editor must scroll down to encapsulate the material in a section).

Dangerous attribute assumptions

The order in which attributes appear within the start-tag is not significant, and software should never imply any significance from the actual ordering. Processing software that reads and outputs modified XML documents may inadvertently switch the order of the attributes, and this is considered to be both legal and acceptable practice.

Likewise, there should never be any implied difference between the default value of an attribute as assigned by a DTD, and the physical presence of this attribute with the same value in the document. Again, processing software often tends to add default attributes to the document before outputting it (software that uses the SAX API, discussed in Chapter 18, is particularly likely to do this).

Appropriate granularity

When a document uses elements to isolate and identify every possible unit of information, it is said that the document has a **fine granularity**. In the following example, the name of the author is divided into the maximum number of useful sub-components:

```
<name>
  <salutation>Dr.</salutation>
  <initial>J</initial>
  <last-name>Smith<last-name>
</name>
```

When less than the optimum number of elements are used, the document is said to have a **coarse granularity**. The following example illustrates a person's name that could potentially be divided into smaller meaningful components (as shown above):

```
<name>Dr. J. Smith</name>
```

The finer the granularity, the larger the document. When created manually, such documents are also more expensive to produce. On the other hand, the document is 'richer'; it is potentially more amenable to analysis and processing.

Industry standard models

Some government organizations and industry-wide standardization committees have produced standard DTDs and XML Schemas. The case for adopting a standard for exchange of information with other organizations is incontrovertible.

But when exchange is not a core issue, or when data could be stored locally in a more appropriate format, the picture then becomes more complex.

Advantages

There are powerful reasons for considering the adoption of a standard model:

- The costly and time-consuming task of developing a custom model is avoided.
- The model usually benefits from the wisdom of many expert contributors.
- The model usually benefits from the contribution of at least one XML expert.

In addition, consider the case of two organizations who wish to both produce and exchange documentation:

- There are no arguments regarding who is going to build the model.
- The organizations have equal rights to the model.
- The recipient is at a particular advantage, as this organization will have a data repository that understands the document structures (and stylesheets already configured to present it), or software that can already interpret their contents.
- The model itself is already available, so does not have to be exchanged along with the data.

Issues

Unfortunately, matters are rarely as simple as the arguments above imply. The exact needs of one organization will rarely match the exact needs of another. Each party will tend to make different decisions concerning the content of their data or documentation, even in tightly regulated industries, perhaps for reasons of commercial advantage, or because their products differ in some detail. These factors tend to introduce three major drawbacks to using an industry standard model:

- lack of required features
- surplus of undesirable elements and attributes
- too much freedom.

The model may not identify every feature of the documents produced by the implementor, in which case important information will either not be tagged at all, or be tagged inappropriately, and such information will then be difficult to identify when it is required for indexing, styling or extraction.

Conversely (or simultaneously), the model may contain elements that will never be used by the implementor, and the presence of these elements on selection menus will both confuse authors and add unnecessary work for software developers (who may be unaware that they are not used).

Note that a subtle variant or combination of these two factors may be encountered. For example, if a standard model contains several elements to describe paragraph levels, such as 'P0', 'P1' and 'P2', but the implementor only requires a single level of paragraph, then there are both unnecessary elements which are to be ignored ('P1' and 'P2'), and an inappropriately named element for a simple paragraph, 'P0', which would be better named 'Para' (or just 'P').

In order to attempt to satisfy the varying needs of many organizations in the industry, the model rules may be too flexible, and so fail to enforce an appropriate template. As an example of this issue, the model may allow an author name to appear before or after a publication title, and also allow it to be absent (if there is no author), despite there being an in-house style rule that states an author's name must always appear, and that it must always precede the title. Every unnecessary degree of freedom will also add to the work of software filter developers and stylesheet designers. Worse still, there may be more than one mechanism included to model a particular data structure, due to compromises made by various contributors to the design during development of the model, and it would be unfortunate if document authors were able to choose a model at random.

Adapting standards

The issues described above are not insurmountable, and rarely constitute a reason for dismissing the standard model from consideration. A pragmatic approach can be adopted, taking account of the standard model, but modifying it to fulfil the actual need.

Although this approach undoubtedly hinders the transfer of documents between organizations that have modified the model in subtly different ways, there will be at least some community remaining to help reduce confusion. For example, if the model contains an element called 'PriceCode', all modified versions of the model are likely to have retained this name (not changed it to 'PC', for example).

The model designer should therefore compare the results of analysis against a suitable standard. Redundant elements should be removed, additional ones added, and loose occurrence rules tightened as appropriate.

This process is not as destructive as it first looks when considering how to transfer data to an organization using the standard (or their own variant of it). Tightening of context and occurrence rules has no effect on the validity of the documents when parsed against the original DTD or XML Schema (the recipient's parser does not know or care that the documents were created using a stricter data model). Also, removal of redundant elements usually has no implication beyond making them unavailable to document authors, providing that they were originally optional elements. Only the addition of new elements guarantees problems, which can simply be resolved by either removing or renaming these elements before the data is transferred.

Lists

Lists are just complex enough to raise a few specific issues regarding their design.

List structure

It is almost always a good idea to surround a set of elements that define list items with another element that defines the scope of the entire list:

```
<!ELEMENT list   (item+) >
<!ELEMENT item   (#PCDATA) >


    <list>
      <item>Item One</item>
      <item>Item Two</item>
      <item>Item Three</item>
    </list>
```

This approach is particularly important when using the same item elements in both numbered and non-numbered (also known as 'random', 'bulleted' or 'unnumbered') lists, as the enclosing element then specifies how the items are to be formatted:

```
<!ELEMENT numList      (item+) >
<!ELEMENT nonNumList   (item+) >
<!ELEMENT item         (#PCDATA) >
```

At least two items

Some 'purists' will state that a list should only be created if there are going to be at least two items in the list, and that a list with only one item should not be a list at all. This constraint can be specified in the model:

```
<!ELEMENT list (item, item+) >
```

Simple or complex content

The first decision to make about list items is whether they can hold more than a single paragraph of text. If they are constrained to a single paragraph, then the content model for the item element can be #PCDATA, along with any elements that are allowed to appear in the text:

```
<!ELEMENT item (#PCDATA | sub | super)* >
```

But if there is ever a possibility that an item needs to contain more than a single paragraph, or contain other structures such as notes and warnings, tables or even embedded sub-lists, then the content model should not allow direct entry of text. Although it is possible to avoid creating an ambiguous content model, as in the example below, this kind of model can still cause problems for applications, particularly when trying to decide whether whitespace is significant or not (see Chapter 8):

```
<!ELEMENT item  (#PCDATA | para)* >
```

It is far safer to disallow direct entry of text, even though this causes more work for document authors when they are creating lists that only ever contain a single paragraph:

```
<!ELEMENT item  (para)+ >
```

```
<item><para>content of item</para></item>
<item><para>content of another item</para></item>
```

Embedded sub-lists

A relatively minor modelling issue arises when allowing a list item to contain a complete further list, and this is a common requirement in document models.

It is usual to indent embedded lists, to show that the items are all part of a single item in the outer list, but a simple model cannot constrain document authors to a maximum number of list levels, so there is a danger that an author will use more levels than allowed for by a given stylesheet.

The only way to overcome this problem is to pre-define list elements with a level indicator as part of the name. In the following example, authors are constrained to use no more than three levels of list:

```
<!ELEMENT list1  (item1)+ >
<!ELEMENT item1  (para | list2)* >

<!ELEMENT list2  (item2)+ >
<!ELEMENT item2  (para | list3)* >

<!ELEMENT list3  (item3)+ >
<!ELEMENT item3  (para )* >
```

Custom lists

If edits to lists after initial publication of a document are not allowed to affect the number of existing items in the list, then automatically numbered lists are not the solution. For example, when inserting a new item between item '5' and item '6', it may be that the new item has to be numbered '5a', in order to avoid renumbering the later items. This is common practice where there may be references in the text to a specific item, such as 'see item 6 for details'. In such a case, the model needs to include a list type that does not pre-define the numbers of each item.

Definition lists

Using the same technique required to provide custom lists, many document models can also include a 'definition list' type. This is also known as a 'glossary list' type, as they are often used for glossaries. These lists are actually more akin to two-column tables, with fixed column widths and the first column much narrower than the second. In the first column, a term that required clarification appears. In the second column, the clarification (or 'definition') itself appears. Typically, the term is constrained to simple text, but the definition can be large, and possibly include multiple paragraphs:

```
<!ELEMENT defList (term, def)+ >
<!ELEMENT term    (#PCDATA) >
<!ELEMENT def     (para)+ >
```

```
<defList>
  <term>XML</term>
  <def><para>eXtensible Markup Language</para></def>
  <term>HTML</term>
  <def><para>HyerText Markup Language</para></def>
</defList>
```

HTML lists

It is common practice to use element names defined for HTML in other DTDs. The names OL (Ordered List), UL (Unordered List) and LI (List Item) are therefore often seen. For definition lists, HTML defines the DL (Definition List), DT (Definition Term) and DD (Definition Description) elements.

However, the HTML model allows both direct entry of text and block-level sub-elements, which is not wise to adopt (see above).

Table standards

Industry standards play an important role in defining models for constructs that are difficult to render on screen or paper, and the most common example of this is tabular matter. Structures like paragraphs, lists and warnings form a simple linear sequence, but table cells are arranged into a two-dimensional grid. An application must recognize the elements that represent column or row boundaries. Other complications include border lines, cells that straddle over adjoining rows and columns, and the various ways in which text can be aligned within each cell.

These typical table features may be described using additional elements or attributes, but if every document model designer adopted a different approach, an application that is required to present the information in a tabular format would have little chance of being able to interpret the markup.

CALS and HTML tables

In the SGML community, recognition of this problem led to the establishment of a *de facto* standard. From a few competing models, widespread use of applications that supported DTDs developed for the US Department of Defense meant that the **CALS table** model was the inevitable winner (and was used in the DTD for this book). This table model requires the use of specific elements, including Table, Thead, Tbody, Tfoot, Row and Entry.

This model also influenced the approach taken to add table support to HTML. Introduced in HTML 2.0, this scheme has been extended in later versions, and is now quite similar to the CALS model (see Chapter 23 for details). The HTML model is rapidly becoming the *de facto* standard. Certainly, this model is retained in XHTML (an XML compatible version of HTML 4.0), and other HTML-derived standards.

Meaningful element names

Although there is nothing to prevent the creation of XML elements that reflect the names of HTML elements, such as Table, Tr (table row), Th (table header) and Td (table data), the freedom to use names that are more meaningful to the content of the cells remains an important XML principle.

For example, when the table contains a list of product codes and prices, the following structure may be deemed more appropriate:

```
<prices>
  <prod><code>XYZ-15</code><price>987</price></prod>
  <prod><code>XYZ-22</code><price>765</price></prod>
</prices>
```

In this example, the information is sufficiently well identified for product details to be automatically located and extracted, and it is possible to locate the price of a specific product. The content can also be presented in a number of different ways. Nevertheless, the most obvious presentation format is a tabular structure. Close study of the elements reveals that the Prices element is analogous to the HTML Table element, the Prod element encloses a single row of data, and the Code and Price elements both represent individual cells.

CSS mappings

An application must be informed of the specific significance of each of these elements. This can be achieved using a stylesheet. Fortunately, the CSS specification now includes property values that map an element name to a table part role (see Chapter 25 for full details). The values 'table', 'table-row' and 'table-cell' may be used in the display property:

```
prices { display:table }
prod   { display:table-row }
code   { display:table-cell }
price  { display:table-cell }
```

XYZ-15	987
XYZ-22	765

Care should be taken to adopt a row-oriented approach, as shown in the example above, so that the elements can be easily mapped to the HTML model. It is not possible to map elements in a structure that takes a column-oriented approach, as in the example below:

```
<table>
  <products>
    <code>XYZ-15</code>
    <code>XYZ-22</code>
  </products>
  <prices>
    <price>987</price>
    <price>765</price>
  </prices>
</table>
```

Note that another reason for avoiding this approach is that it is more likely to separate related items (such as a product code and the price for that product), which complicates analysis and extraction of these items.

Architectural forms

When an application is tuned to a specific DTD or XML Schema, it directly understands the significance of each element and attribute. For example, an HTML-sensitive Web browser recognizes and responds appropriately to each occurrence of the Image, Table and Form elements it encounters in a document. But when an application must perform specific tasks on data that conform to a variety of different models, the names of the significant elements and attributes are unlikely to be the same across all the models involved.

Harmonizing different models

Software that requires specific information from documents that conform to various models should expect to find the information in elements or attributes with different names.

For example, an indexing application may need to identify the author and title of each document in a collection that is composed of documents from many different sources (placing them in a database table). The title may be tagged with an element called 'Title', and the author name with an element called 'Author', but in another model these elements may be named 'Tel' and 'Auto'. Foreign language models may further increase the range of possibilities, including 'Titel' and 'Verfasser' (the German equivalents of 'title' and 'author'):

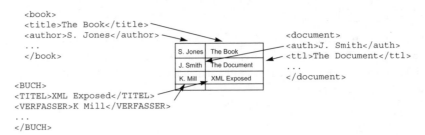

```
<book>
<title>The Book</title>
<author>S. Jones</author>
...
</book>

                              <document>
                                <auth>J. Smith</auth>
                                <ttl>The Document</ttl>
                                ...
                              </document>

<BUCH>
<TITEL>XML Exposed</TITEL>
<VERFASSER>K Mill</VERFASSER>
...
</BUCH>
```

S. Jones	The Book
J. Smith	The Document
K. Mill	XML Exposed

Avoiding the problem

Naturally, the ideal solution would be to avoid this problem entirely, and harmonize the models (the Namespaces standard, discussed in Chapter 10, provides a suitable approach to the problem). But this can be impractical to enforce when the models were produced by different authorities, or were developed primarily for other purposes.

Assuming that the problem cannot be avoided, the issue of how to tell the software what the significant element names are in each document type must be addressed. The solution is an **architectural form**. An architectural form is a mechanism that enables standard templates to be added, as an extra layer of meaning, to documents that conform to diverse models.

Standardized forms

It would be useful if all applications that perform identical functions could understand documents conforming to various models, without any further preparation by the user of a particular application. If all applications adopt the architectural form mechanism, and an independent group devises an appropriate architectural form model, this laudable goal can be achieved.

One obvious example is hypertext linking, where each browser must be made aware of the linking elements and attributes in order to provide active linking. The **HyTime** standard (ISO/IEC 10744) takes this approach, though XLink and XPointer (Chapter 27 and Chapter 28) now offer a better way forward.

Reserved attributes

Architectural forms work by storing the roles that each significant element or attribute plays in the DTD or XML Schema itself, so that no additional data files need to be maintained, and document authors are not affected.

Typically, an architectural form involves the use of significant, or 'reserved' attribute names. When a model is analysed, and some elements are found to contain these attributes, the application can match its capabilities to documents conforming to this model. For example, the application may have the capability to create a simple database table of names and works, as shown above, and assign significance to elements that contain attributes named 'IndexTitle' and 'IndexName'.

To keep the number of reserved attributes to a minimum, the **fixed attribute** type may be used to distinguish roles. For example, a single attribute called 'WorkIndex' could be defined, with possible values of 'TITLE' and 'NAME', but having a different fixed value in each element:

```
<!ATTLIST title      workIndex CDATA #FIXED "TITLE">
<!ATTLIST author     workIndex CDATA #FIXED "NAME">
```

The reason for using fixed attributes is to prevent document authors from changing the values. In fact, document authors can completely ignore these attributes.

Unfortunately, it is possible for a reserved attribute, such as 'WorkIndex', to conflict accidentally with an attribute of the same name already residing in the DTD. In some cases, it is hoped, this can be avoided by assigning very specific names, such as 'HyTime' and 'SDARULE' (see below). A more secure workaround is to define a single required reserved attribute, which is used to override the default names for other reserved attributes.

ISO standard

A standard for the use of architectural forms, released by the ISO under the designation ISO 10744, is aimed at their use in SGML documents. Applications that are expected to process documents containing unknown architectural form markup need some indication that one or more forms are present, and which ones they are. A processing instruction of the following form is specified:

```
<?IS10744:arch name=MyForm ?>

<!ATTLIST book myForm NMTOKEN #FIXED "MyForm-Document">
```

Case study (the ICADD initiative)

Some practical issues regarding the use of architectural forms can be covered through analysis of a real application: an attempt to help print-impaired readers by making documents accessible in large print, Braille or voice synthesis forms.

The **ICADD** (*International Committee for Accessible Document Design*) organization produced a suitable SGML DTD for use with software that can re-publish information in these forms.

Developed for use with SGML, and having played a fleeting role in some earlier versions of HTML, the ICADD DTD should now be viewed as an example, rather than a recommendation.

The software developed by ICADD to process documents relies upon a custom DTD, so that both generic and formatting tags can be unambiguously translated (in the same way that Web browsers have relied upon conformance to the HTML element set in order to present material). The ICADD DTD is relatively simple, and contains the following basic elements:

Anchor	(mark spot on page)	Lhead	(list heading)
Au	(author)	List	
B	(bold)	Litem	(list item)
Book	(document element)	Note	
Box	(sidebar information)	Other	(emphasize)
Fig	(figure title)	Para	
Fn	(footnote)	Pp	(print page number)
H1–H6	(header levels)	Term	(or keyword)
Ipp	(Ink print page)	Ti	(title of book)
It	(italic)	Xref	(cross reference)
Lang	(language)		

In order to make a wide variety of information available via this means, it would normally be necessary to either impose the ICADD DTD on all contributors, or translate information between DTDs. But both options have drawbacks. The first is impossible to enforce, so is clearly impractical. The second is very costly because such translations can rarely be performed without human guidance.

For these reasons, the **SDA** (*SGML Document Access*) architectural form was developed. When SDA rules are embedded in a DTD, a special converter application learns how to map document instances into the ICADD DTD format, without manual intervention:

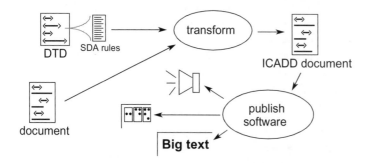

A number of special attributes are defined. They are SdaRule, SdaForm, SdaBdy, SdaPart, SdaPref and SdaSuff. Each dictates a different action to be taken by the transformation software. For example, the SdaForm attribute is used to map an element to an ICADD DTD element. In the following example, the Title element is mapped to the Ti element:

```
<title>The Title</title>
```

```
<!ATTLIST title SDAFORM CDATA #FIXED "ti">
```

```
<ti>The Title</ti>
```

The SdaPref attribute is used to specify a prefix to be generated. In the following example, the original meaning of the Abstract element is kept intact by specifying that the paragraph is to be preceded by an appropriate header:

```
<abstract>The Abstract</abstract>
```

```
<!ATTLIST abstract
            SDAFORM CDATA #FIXED "para"
            SDAPREF CDATA #FIXED "<h1>Abstract</h1>">
```

```
<h1>Abstract</h1>
<para>The Abstract</para>
```

DTD writing tools

The XML tags used to construct a DTD have a complex syntax that hinders DTD authoring. It is far too easy to make a mistake when generating the necessary markup, or to create an incorrect document model that allows elements to appear where they should not (or not appear where they should).

There are products that can overcome these problems. They hide the markup behind a visual interface that reveals the hierarchical structures in the model. The author receives visual feedback on the document model as it is built, is prevented from making many mistakes, and the software generates the necessary markup when the model is complete. Such tools are also useful for interpreting DTDs developed elsewhere, and for training editorial staff:

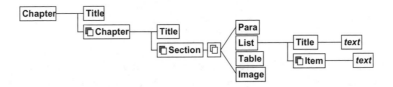

A relatively new additional strength of these tools is their ability to output the model in the different modelling languages now emerging, and to convert models between them. The most obvious use of this feature in the short term is to convert the vast legacy of DTD models into XML Schema models.

The one disadvantage of such tools is their tendency to output markup that is not elegantly formatted, creating even greater problems for those who may later need to work with the model, without access to such tools. However, the decreasing cost and increasing power of these tools means that few people likely to edit a DTD will soon have any excuse to not have them.

DTD formatting

An illegible DTD is difficult to analyse and maintain, whether created by hand or using a design tool. A DTD can be written using a standard text editor, providing that the DTD author understands the declarations that comprise it, as described in the previous chapter. However, some thought should be given to the location and layout of the declarations.

Header and footer details

The DTD should contain a header that describes its purpose and scope, and identifies the current version and the author (including contact details).

At the end of the DTD there should be a comment that makes it clear that the DTD is complete. When the comment is missing, the DTD may have been truncated or corrupted:

```
<!-- COMPANION BOOKS DTD
         AUTHOR: N.Bradley (neil@bradley.co.uk)
         VERSION: 1.4 (7/5/2001) -->
...
...
...
<!-- END END END -->
```

Declaration groups

In some respects, the rules of the XML language dictate the general layout of declarations in the DTD. Notation declarations should appear first, and entity declarations should follow. Most DTD authors then place element declarations in order of
their approximate location in the structure hierarchy, starting with the document
element and ending with in-line elements:

```
<!-- NOTATIONS -->
...

<!-- ENTITIES -->
...

<!-- MAJOR SECTIONS -->
...

<!-- SUB-GROUPS -->
...

<!-- IN-LINE ELEMENTS -->
...
```

Element declarations

Element declarations should be separated from other element declarations by at
least one blank line:

```
<!ELEMENT quotation .....>

<!ELEMENT citation .....>

<!ELEMENT quoteText .....>
```

Short element names should be preceded by a comment that includes the full name:

```
<!-- Quotation Text -->
<!ELEMENT quoteText .....>
```

Legibility is increased if the model groups are aligned vertically throughout the
DTD, or the local section of the DTD, as shown in the first case study below.

Within model groups, it is good practice to insert a single space after each comma,
and around each vertical bar, as in the following examples:

```
(a, b, c, d, e)

(a | b | c | d | e)
```

Attribute declarations

Attribute declarations tend to be placed immediately after the elements to which they apply:

```
<!-- Company President -->
<!ELEMENT comPres .....>
<!ATTLIST comPres ........>
```

When more than one attribute is being defined, each attribute should be specified on a separate line:

```
<!ATTLIST book    version   CDATA           #REQUIRED
                  date      CDATA           #REQUIRED
                  author    CDATA           #IMPLIED
                  type      (fiction|none)  "none"
                  pages     NUMBER          #IMPLIED>
```

Although aligning parts of the definition in columns, as shown above, is the most common approach used, there is no universal consensus that this is the best technique. Some people consider the following to be more legible than the example above:

```
<!ATTLIST book    version CDATA #REQUIRED
                  date CDATA #REQUIRED
                  author CDATA #IMPLIED
                  type (fiction|none) "none"
                  pages NUMBER #IMPLIED >
```

Debugging the DTD

Model editing

There is often a number of different ways that the legal content of an element can be specified. But in all cases, the most terse and efficient alternative should be chosen, as this approach reduces ambiguity. The following is a list of some of the most common mistakes:

```
good practice               bad practice

(a+)             instead of  (a, a*)
(a*)             instead of  (a?, a*)
(a | b)?         instead of  (a? | b?)
(a, b, c, d)     instead of  (a, (b, c), d)
(a, b?, c?, d)   instead of  (a, (b?, c?)?, d)
((a | b), c)     instead of  ((a, c) | (b, c))
```

Badly designed models have been seen in many publicly released DTDs. They cause confusion because they tend to imply that some other model was intended, and cast doubt on the quality of the model itself.

Syntax testing

When a DTD has been developed using a standard text editor, it may contain errors. The first and most obvious kinds of error are syntax errors in the markup tags. Missing chevrons or keywords are detected and reported by XML parsers. Validating parsers will also detect such errors as content models that refer to elements which do not exist.

Model testing

The time needed for testing the document model defined by the DTD is often underestimated. Even relatively simple DTDs usually contain a surprising number of possible document structures. Even if a DTD design tool is not used to construct the DTD, these tools can be useful for revealing content models in a tree form that is easy to analyse.

Testing should also involve the production of conforming documents that contain all possible combinations of elements. This process should reveal any gaps or redundancies in the structure, and the resulting documents become a useful product for the purposes of training future authors and editors. If realistic data is placed in this document, it may also be used to test translation software and stylesheets.

Case study (quotations)

Consider a simple use of XML to hold famous quotations. From studying a number of entries in an existing book of quotations, some basic conclusions can be drawn:

- details of the author must be handled, if known
- details of the publication it first appeared in must be handled, if known
- the quotation itself must be included
- the birth date of the author should be given, but may not be known
- similarly, there may be a date when the author died, but it may not be known or the author may still be alive.

The following example is copied from Chapter 2 (and models the quotes that appear at the top of each chapter of this book):

```
<quotation>
  <quoteText>The surest way to make a monkey of a man
  is to quote him</quoteText>
  <citation>
    <publication>Quick Quotations</publication>
    <author>
      <name>Robert Benchley</name>
      <born>1889</born>
      <died>1945</died>
    </author>
  </citation>
</quotation>
```

It is possible to reverse-engineer the DTD from the sample, and this is not uncommon practice when developing DTDs. A possible DTD for this example follows:

```
<!-- XML Quotations DTD
          AUTHOR: N.Bradley (neil@bradley.co.uk)
          VERSION: 1.0 (15/2/2001) -->

<!ELEMENT quotation    (quoteText, citation?)>

<!ELEMENT quoteText    (#PCDATA)>

<!ELEMENT citation     (publication?, author?)>

<!ELEMENT publication (#PCDATA)>

<!ELEMENT author       (name, born?, died?)>

<!ELEMENT name         (#PCDATA)>

<!ELEMENT born         (#PCDATA)>

<!ELEMENT died         (#PCDATA)>

<!-- END END END -->
```

Case study (this book)

It can be imagined that this book is part of a collection of 'companion' books, which conform to a standard style and layout. The editors of existing books and authors of new books are to use XML-sensitive word processors in order to ensure consistency of structure and style. All new issues will then be paginated automatically. Initial analysis will focus on one book in the range: *The XML Companion*.

Note: This book was actually produced using *FrameMaker+SGML*, which (as the name implies) is compatible with SGML (the older brother of XML), and includes a semi-controlled authoring environment based on an SGML DTD. The following example is based on this DTD, but is simplified for XML compatibility.

Book structure

This book obviously follows general structure conventions, including division into three main segments: front-matter, body and back-matter:

```
<!ELEMENT book  (front, body, back)>
```

Front-matter

The front-matter segment contains, amongst other items, the title and edition, author name and contact details, publisher name and address, and the date of publication:

```
<!ELEMENT front     (title, edition, author,
                     publisher)>

<!ELEMENT title     (#PCDATA)>

<!ELEMENT edition   (#PCDATA)>

<!ELEMENT author    (first, second, e-mail?)>

<!ELEMENT first     (#PCDATA)>

<!ELEMENT second    (#PCDATA)>

<!ELEMENT e-mail    (#PCDATA)>

<!ELEMENT publisher (pubName, address)

<!ELEMENT pubName   (#PCDATA)>

<!ELEMENT address   (#PCDATA)>
```

```
<front>
  <title>The XML Companion</title>
  <edition>Third Edition</edition>
  <author>
    <first>Neil</first>
    <second>Bradley</second>
    <e-mail>neil@bradley.co.uk</e-mail>
  </author>
  <publisher>
    <pub-name>Pearson Education Limited</pub-name>
    <address>Edinburgh Gate, Harlow, CM20 2JE,
    United Kingdom</address>
  </publisher>
</front>
```

Body

At first sight, the body of the book appears to be a simple sequence of chapters. However, close study of the contents list reveals a higher level of structure. Although not named, this can be thought of as major book divisions. It may be decided that this layer is not mandatory in the series of books:

```
<!ELEMENT body     ((chapter*, division+) | chapter+)>
<!ELEMENT division (title, chapter+)>


<body>
  <division>
    <title>The XML standard</title>
    ...
  </division>
  <division>
    <title>Extension standards</title>
    ...
  </division>
  ...
  ...
</body>
```

Note that the Division element contains a Title element, which has already been defined and used to title the book. The purpose of a particular Title instance is dependent on its context, so it is easy to distinguish a book title, which appears in one style in the first pages, from a division title that appears in the contents. The Title element is also used in other contexts:

```
<!ELEMENT chapter  (title, (...))>
```

Sections

Most chapters contain headings, some larger than others. In fact, there are two levels of heading, and it may be tempting to define elements called Header-one and Header-two, which surround only the heading text. However, another way to look at this is to recognize that the headings are identifying a block of text. In this case, the whole block of text should be isolated, perhaps by an element named Section, and the heading text itself is then identified by an embedded Title element. The smaller headings identify sub-sections. The advantage of this approach is that it becomes possible to extract the sections and sub-sections for possible reuse in other publications. In addition, a hypertext link to a section may return the entire section to the browser:

```
<!ELEMENT chapter    (title, quote, ..., section*)>

<!ELEMENT section    (title, (..., subSection*))>

<!ELEMENT subSection (title, (...))>
```

Blocks

At the next level down in the book structure, there are miscellaneous 'block'-level structures. They are called blocks because they do not share horizontal space on the page with other elements. The most obvious block-level element is the Paragraph element. In addition, there are List, Table, Graphic and Markup Paragraph elements (and a PageBreak element for forcing page-breaks where appropriate). As all these block structures may be used in various places, it is appropriate to create an entity to hold the content model that groups them:

```
<!ENTITY % Blocks     "(para | list | markupPara |
                       graphic | table | pageBreak)*" >
```

Blocks can be used as introductory material in a chapter and section, and form the content of sub-sections:

```
<!ELEMENT chapter     (title, quote, %Blocks;, section*)>

<!ELEMENT section     (title, %Blocks;, subSection*)>

<!ELEMENT subSection (title, %Blocks;)>
```

The Markup Paragraph is used to hold multi-line fragments of XML example data. The content appears in a monospaced font, and is indented (as in the fragment above this paragraph). So that the author can control line-break positioning in the example data, each line is enclosed by a Markup Line element:

```
<!ELEMENT markupPara   (markupLine*)>

<!ELEMENT markupLine   (#PCDATA | ... )*>


<markupPara>
  <markupLine>Line one of markup</markupLine>
  <markupLine>Line two of markup</markupLine>
</markupPara>
```

The List element contains further block-type elements, called Item, which contain the text of each item in the list:

```
<!ELEMENT list   (item+)>

<!ELEMENT item   (...)>


<list>
  <item>Item One</item>
  <item>Item Two</item>
  <item>Item Three</item>
</list>
```

The List element contains a Type attribute to specify whether it is a numbered or random (bulleted) list. It defaults to random, as this is the most common type used:

```
<!ATTLIST item        type    (number|random)    "random">
```

For tables, the popular CALS model is used. This is to take advantage of the capabilities of some SGML-sensitive typesetting and DTP software. In future, this model may be replaced by the HTML table model.

The Graphic element is empty because it is a placeholder for an image. It contains an Identifier attribute, which holds an entity name. An entity declaration is required for each picture in the book:

```
<!ELEMENT graphic     EMPTY>
<!ATTLIST graphic     id      ID       #IMPLIED
                      ident   ENTITY   #REQUIRED>
```

In-line elements

There are various classes of in-line element, which may be used in varying combinations within the block-level elements. To help describe these classifications, three entities are defined:

```
<!ENTITY % SuperSub "sup | sub" >

<!ENTITY % Hilite   "markup | emphStrong | emphWeak" >

<!ENTITY % Inline   "(#PCDATA | %Hilite; |
                     %SuperSub; | x-ref)*" >
```

The Superscript/Subscript entity refers to superscript and subscript text, such as 'H_2O'. The Hilite entity refers to the Markup, Emphasis Strong and Emphasis Weak elements, which are used to enclose example fragments within a paragraph. Typically, different fonts would be used to identify them in the text. In this book, the Markup element content is presented in a monospaced font, as in 'this is markup', the Emphasis Weak element content is presented in italic typeface, for '*important terms*', and the Emphasis Strong element content is presented in bold typeface, for '**key terms**'. The Inline entity includes the previous entities and adds the #PCDATA token and Cross Reference element (X-ref). Each element definition is carefully designed to avoid including itself:

```
<!ELEMENT markup      (#PCDATA | %SuperSub; |
                      emphStrong | emphWeak)*>

<!ELEMENT emphStrong  (#PCDATA | markup | emphWeak |
                      %SuperSub; | xRef)*>

<!ELEMENT emphWeak    (#PCDATA | markup |
                      emphStrong | %SuperSub; | xRef)*>

<!ELEMENT sup         (#PCDATA) >

<!ELEMENT sub         (#PCDATA) >

<!ELEMENT xRef        (#PCDATA) >
```

Examples

The MarkupLine element can, in addition, contain a Presented element. This is used to show the published output, using a sans-serif font:

```
<!ELEMENT markupPara    (markupLine*)>

<!ELEMENT markupLine    (#PCDATA | ... | presented)*>


   <markupPara>
     <markupLine>XML fragment</markupLine>
     <markupLine>
       <presented>XML fragment</presented>
     </markupLine>
   </markupPara>


   XML fragment

   XML fragment
```

Some markup fragments may be quite large, in which case it is likely that a page-break would naturally appear somewhere within it. The Splitable attribute is used to specify whether or not the block can be split across pages. The default value of 'loose' means that a page-break may appear within the block. The alternative value of 'together' means that the lines must be kept together (even at the expense of leaving whitespace at the bottom of the page):

```
<!ATTLIST markupPara   splitable
                        (loose | together) "loose">
```

Back-matter

The back-matter consists of only the Glossary element. The Glossary element is a simplified version of a Chapter. There is no Title element, because the title 'Glossary' can be assumed, and can therefore be generated automatically:

```
<!ELEMENT back          (glossary)>

<!ELEMENT glossary      (para*, section*)>
```

The index is generated automatically, so no data or tags are required.

7. Hypertext links

The ability to link one part of a document to another part is a fundamental feature of electronic document publishing, and is also an important information modelling technique. This chapter covers the linking features provided by the XML standard. Advanced requirements will require the more extensive capabilities provided by the XLink adjunct standard (Chapter 27), and perhaps also the XPointer standard (Chapter 28).

Background

Publishers of printed material typically provide a number of features to assist with the locating of required information. This may include a table of contents, numbered pages and an index. But some of these navigation techniques may become irrelevant when the document is published electronically. Document browsers have a number of new features for locating required material, including full-text and keyword searching. Most also include a **hypertext linking** capability. In the simplest case, when the reader encounters such text as 'see *More Information* for details', a software link provides instant access to the specified section.

Basic links

The simplest kind of link imaginable can be visualized as a length of string, attached to different parts of the document at both ends with a pin.

One pin represents the '**source**' (or start-point) of the link. This would typically be a phrase that directs the reader's attention to other information. From here, the string leads to the '**target**' (end-point) pin, which is located around or at the start of the required text. This is termed a '**basic link**':

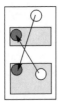

A document browser emphasizes source text, providing a visual clue to the user that it is possible to instantly access the material referenced:

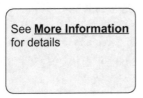

Formally, the target object is called a **resource**, and the source is a **linking element**. The act of moving from the linking element to the resource is termed a **transversal**:

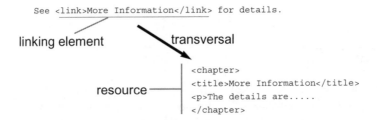

Attribute types

The XML specification includes reserved attribute types, **ID** and **IDREF**, which enable a simple linking scheme to operate. In this scheme, source and target attributes hold a matching **locator** value. This facility is backward compatible with SGML, so will work with SGML-sensitive browsers:

```
                                    locator
See <xref link="X123">More Information</xref> for details.

      <section target="X123">
      <title>More Information</title>
      <p>The details are.....
      </section>
```

Basic Link

There are no special restrictions on the names of elements and attributes that have significance in this linking scheme. For example, a linking element could be called 'A' (Anchor), 'Xref' or 'Link', and the attribute that contains the locator of the resource may be called 'Name', 'Id' or 'Target'. The attribute that holds the locator value in the linking element is identified in the DTD, using a special attribute type.

However, the link code is limited to alphabetic or numeric characters, and the symbols '-' and '.', but must start with an alphabetical character. Valid examples include 'X-123', 'peter' and 'ABC.DEF'. Names are case-sensitive, so a target value of 'mytag' will not be matched with a source value of 'MyTag'.

Limitations

From this description of how XML links work and are validated, a fundamental weakness becomes apparent. The source and destination points must reside in the same document. Links *between* documents are not supported.

While limiting, this restriction can be surmounted. A collection of XML documents may be merged together for publication. This technique is quite common when preparing material for publication on CD-ROM or large printed books (and is discussed in more detail later).

Another major constraint is the reliance on special attribute types (ID and IDREF), as a DTD is required to identify these attributes. Well-formed documents cannot contain such links.

Advanced linking concepts, such as bi-directional, multi-destination, out-of-line and inter-document links are not supported. Adjunct standards such as XLink and XPointer are required to supply these features.

ID/IDREF

The XML standard relies upon the two special attribute types, 'ID' and 'IDREF', to identify attributes that serve as the target and source of a link. Using this technique, the target object must be enclosed by an element that has an attribute defined to be of type **ID**. A unique value must be placed in this attribute:

```
<!ELEMENT section (...) >
<!ATTLIST section target ID #REQUIRED>
```

```
<section target="S6">
  <title>This is Section 6</title>
  ...
  ...
  ...
</section>
```

Every reference must be contained within an element that has an attribute defined to be of type **IDREF**. For example, a referencing element called 'XRef' may use an attribute called 'Link' to point to the required element:

```
<!ELEMENT xref (...) >
<!ATTLIST xref link IDREF #REQUIRED>


<para>Please refer to
<xref link="S6">Section 6</xref>
for more details</para>
```

An XML parser uses the ID and IDREF attribute type designators to identify and validate these values. Every ID value must be unique, to avoid ambiguity, and every IDREF value must match the value of an attribute of type ID in order to avoid 'hanging' pointers:

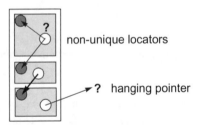

The following fragment is invalid because two sections have the same identifier value. They both have a locator value of 'S6':

```
<section target="S6">
  <title>This is Section 6</title>
  ...
  ...
</section>
<section target="S6"> <! -- ERROR -->
  <title>This is Section 7</title>
  ...
  ...
```

The following fragment is invalid because no element with an identifier matches the reference value:

```
<section target="S1">
  <title>This is Section 1</title>
  <para>Refer to <xref link="S0"> <!-- ERROR -->
  Section 7</xref> for more details.</para>
</section>
<section target="S2">
  <title>This is Section 2</title>
  . . .
```

Link value strategies

For many purposes, unique identifiers can be generated automatically by software, and references can also be inserted automatically. But issues arise when unique identifiers, or just the references to them, must be created by hand. In such cases, the scheme chosen for assigning identifiers must be convenient for authors to use.

Sequential assignment

One approach is to use simple code numbers. If the last element likely to be the target of a reference was assigned an identifier of 'X-77776' (recall that identifiers cannot start with a digit), then the next element is assigned an identifier of 'X-77777'.

These identifiers may be inserted automatically by editorial or database software. But, because the identifiers are not intuitive, and hard to memorize even when frequently referring to the same target element, it is necessary for authors to look up the identifier (in the most extreme case by scrolling to the target element itself and looking at its attribute value). This can be a time-consuming, and therefore costly, process.

Meaningful names

A simpler and more intuitive technique that many HTML users will be familiar with involves identifiers that describe the content of the target element. When the target element is a title, or has a title, this could even be a copy of the title:

```
See <xref idref="Summary">Summary</xref>
. . .
<title id="Summary">Summary</title>
```

This approach is suitable for small documents (such as Web pages), especially when distinctive titles are used throughout the document.

Standards for abbreviating longer titles must obviously be established, or there will still be a need to check each reference against the target locator. For example, the identifier could be built from the first five (legal) characters of the first word, a dash, then the first letter of each subsequent word, with all letters folded to lower-case, so 'Contents List' becomes 'conte-l'. But duplicate names are still a danger using such a scheme. For example, 'Contemporary Life' would be coded in the same way as 'Contents List'.

Reference numbering

For long, numbered documents, an abbreviated reference scheme may be considered appropriate. This scheme makes use of the navigation methods devised for printed output, such as 'see Chapter 7, Paragraph 12', but codifies this information, for example, 'ch7pa12'. This approach allows for automatic generation of resource identifier values. Second, and more importantly, document authors can deduce the target value from the reference text itself, so do not have to look up the value anywhere else:

```
see <xref idref="#ch7pa12">Chapter 7, Paragraph 12</xref>
```

But the problem with this approach is that when new material is inserted into the document, the numbering of material beyond this point will change. However, the reference text will also be affected, and it is assumed that procedures for correcting such problems are already well established. With clever software, it is even possible to automate the updating of both target and source locators.

Merging to publish

It was suggested earlier that the inability of this scheme to work across documents is not an issue when the documents are destined to be merged into a single large document prior to delivering or publishing the contents. When this is the case, linking can still be supported, though there is one complication involving the DTD.

There is a need for two versions of the DTD. The first is used for the separate documents. The second is used only with the final merged document.

The first DTD needs to assign the attribute type CDATA to the attributes in the source linking elements. This prevents a parser from trying to find the target elements (which will often be in a different document). The second DTD assigns the IDREF type instead, but may otherwise be identical. Checking and activation of links then only take place during validation, and broken links can be identified.

Note that there is no problem with using ID attribute types in both of the DTDs, as this type simply ensures that the values are unique. However, duplicate locator values may not be detected until after document merging.

8. Whitespace issues

Spaces and line-end codes are sometimes important characters in the document, and at other times are used simply to lay out XML tags. Within the document, a consecutive series of whitespace characters may be significant, or unimportant and expected to be reduced to a single space. This chapter describes an XML mechanism for preserving all space, explains how related standards cope with identifying significant document spaces, and concludes with suggestions for default handling of ambiguous spaces in XML documents.

Whitespace

The term '**whitespace**' is used to describe a small number of miscellaneous characters that have no visual appearance, but in some way affect the formatting of a document.

The **space** character is usually used to separate words, and the **tab** character is usually used to help align columns of text. Depending on the computer platform concerned, the **carriage return** and **line-feed** characters are used, either alone or in combination, to indicate the end of a line in the text (so can be collectively termed 'line-end' codes). All of these characters may be used in the text of a document, to separate words, lines and columns:

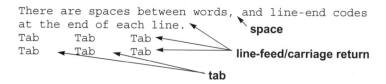

But in addition, they may be used in an XML file simply to assist with the tagging of the document:

```
<tag>
    <embeddedTag>      </embeddedTag>
   /</tag>
```
space   **line-feed/carriage return**

Whitespace becomes an issue for XML processing when it is not certain that it is intended to be present in the published document. Ambiguities may arise when a document author introduces line-end codes simply in order to make it easier to read the text when using a standard text viewing utility, or to edit the text in a standard text editor.

At certain locations in the body of the document, the significance of whitespace characters can be set by the document author. In other circumstances, their significance is determined by the processing application.

Line-end normalization

The ASCII standard includes two special characters that may be interpreted as a signal to end a line of text. These are the **CR (Carriage Return)** and **LF (Line-Feed)** characters. The names of these characters are taken from the actions of a typewriter. When starting a new line, the lever on the typewriter carriage forces the roller to move the paper up by one line (the line-feed), then the typist pushes the carriage to the right so that the next letter will appear at the left edge of the paper (the carriage return). The line-feed character has an ASCII value of 10, and the carriage return character has an ASCII value of 13. On IBM mainframe systems, these characters are used to surround one record of text, so are given the names 'record start' and 'record end', but MS-DOS/Windows systems use the pair together as a line-end code sequence. The Macintosh and UNIX platforms use just one of these characters (but different ones) to signify a line-end:

```
A Macintosh[CR]
data file.[CR]


A Unix[LF]
data file.[LF]


An MS-DOS[CR][LF]
data file.[CR][LF]
```

An XML processor uses the line-feed character to terminate lines. This is compliant with UNIX. When a carriage return is encountered in the data stream, the XML processor converts this to a line-feed (so dealing with Macintosh input). When both characters are found together, in the sequence CR followed by LF, the carriage return is removed (so dealing with MS-DOS/Windows input). But a sequence of identical line-end codes, such as three carriage returns in a row, is treated separately.

Whitespace in markup

Within markup, all whitespace is equivalent to a single space character, and may be used to separate attributes and other parameters. The two examples below are deemed to be equivalent:

```
<book issue="3" date="15/3/97" >


<book
issue    = "3"
date     = "15/3/97"    >
```

Element content space

Document authors may choose to insert whitespace, particularly line-end codes, around elements that contain other elements, in order to improve the presentation. For example, the second document fragment below is easier to read than the first:

```
<sec><auth><first>Neil</first><second>Bradley</second></
auth><e-mail>neil@bradley.co.uk</e-mail>...


<sec>
<auth>
  <first>Neil</first><second>Bradley</second>
</auth>
<e-mail>neil@bradley.co.uk</e-mail>...
```

In the second example above, the Section element directly contains a line-feed character, and the Author element immediately contains two line-feeds and two spaces. It is clear that these whitespace characters are not part of the document text. The fact that they occur in elements that are only allowed to contain other elements is a clue to this fact, as shown in the following DTD fragment (they do not contain the #PCDATA keyword, indicating the possible presence of document text):

```
<!-- element content -->
<!ELEMENT sec    (auth,e-mail,...)>
<!ELEMENT auth   (first, second)>

<!-- mixed content -->
<!ELEMENT first  (#PCDATA)>
<!ELEMENT second (#PCDATA)>
<!ELEMENT e-mail (#PCDATA)>
```

A validating parser has access to the DTD, so is able to determine which elements can only contain other elements. Such parsers are obliged to inform the application of whitespace characters in element content (termed **ignorable whitespace**), and a publishing application may choose to omit these characters from the presented document.

But a non-validating parser (which does not interpret the DTD) cannot tell which elements have element content by design (as opposed to by accident in a specific instance), so cannot discriminate between significant and insignificant whitespace so easily. In fact, one reason for including a **standalone parameter** value of 'no' in the XML declaration at the top of a document is to warn such parsers that they cannot process the document without misinterpreting some of the whitespace.

Some may consider this technique to be inadequate even when a validating parser is in use. For example, the Paragraph and Emphasis elements below both have mixed content, so are not distinguished by this mechanism, yet many would argue that the leading and trailing spaces in the Paragraph element should be removed, while spaces in the same positions in the Emphasis element should not:

```
<para> A paragraph with<emph> space </emph>. </para>
```

Ambiguous space issues are discussed later, and the suggested solution completely ignores this feature of the XML standard.

Preserved space

A distinction is made between the act of leaving all whitespace characters intact, and **normalizing** whitespace down to a single character. When left intact, the whitespace is said to be **preserved**. When normalized, it is said to have **collapsed**, and this is usually what is desired.

XML:space attribute

The document author has some control over normalization of whitespace in the text, using a reserved attribute named '**xml:space**'.

If this attribute is applied to a specific element, and given a value of '**preserve**', then all whitespace in that element is deemed to be significant:

```
<para xml:space="preserve">ISO Central Secretariat
1, Rue de Varembe
CH-1211 Geneva 20
Switzerland</para>
```

```
ISO Central Secretariat
1, Rue de Varembe
CH-1211 Geneva 20
Switzerland
```

Fonts

More advanced formatting is possible using multiple spaces to align text. However, care must be taken over which font is used to present the content. Each character has a different width in most fonts. Unless the same font is used to present the material as was used to create it, the output will be distorted. The safest approach is to use a **monospaced** (fixed-pitch) font:

```
<preform xml:space="preserve">
     O
  --I--
     I
   / \
</preform>
```

A fixed pitch font must also be used to display the content (though it does not have to be the same font):

```
     O
  --I--
     I
   / \
```

If a variable-pitch font is used to present the material, the content is distorted because the space character is no longer the same width as other characters:

```
  O
--I--
  I
 /\
```

Embedded instructions

If an element embedded within a preserved element has content which must not be preserved, the same attribute may be used to explicitly '**collapse**' its content:

```
<preform xml:space="preserve">
   . . .
   <p xml:space="collapse">Collapse the white
   space in this paragraph.</p>
   . . .
</preform>
```

DTD control

When an element is created specifically to hold pre-formatted text, its content status can be set in the DTD:

```
<!ELEMENT preform (#PCDATA)>
<!ATTLIST preform xml:space #FIXED "preserve">
```

```
<preform>
     O
  --I--
    I
   / \
</preform>
```

Note that this is a good example of the use of the FIXED attribute type.

Line ending interpretation

Separate lines of text are often found in XML documents, and indeed in other text-based document formats. Text may be broken into lines for various reasons; either for convenience, or to signify and isolate important sub-units of information. Either way, the presence of multiple text lines can also cause complications.

Line-end codes

The points at which line-end codes appear may have been carefully chosen to avoid corrupting the text. It is possible to interpret line-end codes in three ways. The line-end code can:

- be retained, and used to force a line-break when presented
- be removed
- be replaced by a space.

These interpretations can be illustrated with three examples:

```
<software>10 PRINT "Hello World" [CR]
20 GOTO 10.</software>
```

```
<geneSequence>TCTCGATTACACCGC[CR]
TAATCGCGATTACAC</geneSequence>
```

```
<para>This is a normal[CR]
paragraph.</para>
```

These examples each require a different interpretation, giving the following output:

```
10 PRINT "Hello World"
20 GOTO 10.
```

```
TCTCGATTACACCGCTAATCGCGATTACAC.
```

This is a normal paragraph.

Each application of XML requires a clear policy on this issue. In most cases, line-end codes are deemed to stand in for spaces, as this is standard practice in the publishing application that underlies the historical roots of XML.

A further issue to consider concerns identification of line-end codes that do not belong to the document text at all (discussed below).

Hyphenation

To complicate matters further, many documents are converted into SGML or XML format directly from previously typed or published material (possibly using OCR or ICR technology). This material often contains hyphens at the end of lines, where the author or publishing software has chosen to split a word so as to better balance the text over lines:

```
This paragraph is too long to comfor-[CR]
tably fit on one line of text.
```

In this case, an application may be intelligent enough to simply remove the line-end code (not replace it with a space), and also remove the hyphen:

This paragraph is too long to **comfortably** fit on one line of text.

But it must be careful not to remove the hyphen from a double-barrelled word:

```
The hyphen must not be removed from 'line-[CR]
end' when re-formatting.
```

The hyphen must not be removed from '**lineend**' when re-formatting.

Because software is not usually sufficiently intelligent to make this distinction, an alternative strategy is to manually separate the two kinds of hyphen. Extended character sets include a special 'soft hyphen' character (character 176, '°'), which looks the same as a normal hyphen, but is interpreted as one that *can* be safely removed. The normal hyphen is assumed to be a 'hard' hyphen, which must be retained. When the hyphen is soft, it is manually identified as such and changed to the soft hyphen character.

Ambiguous space

Earlier, it was suggested that the XML mechanism for distinguishing significant space from insignificant space (which relies totally upon the distinction between element with element content, and elements with mixed or text-only content) is not sophisticated enough for many real-world situations. Spaces and line-end codes that are considered by this mechanism to be significant, may not really be so.

The following example could be treated in two different ways. The problem is deciding whether or not the line-end code after the Paragraph start-tag is part of the text of the document:

```
<para>[CR]
This paragraph is bounded by element tags.[CR]
</para>
```

Perhaps the line-end code should be interpreted as a space. Similarly, the line-end code at the end of the paragraph could also be treated as a space. Although retaining them would usually have no visual impact, there is no guarantee of this (the '^' symbol is used below to represent spaces that are otherwise impossible to see):

^This paragraph is bounded by element tags.^

Most would argue that they should not be seen:

This paragraph is bounded by element tags.

This issue does not just affect publishing. Applications of XML that rely upon exact text string comparisons need to address this issue too.

Note that these issues are quite separate from stylesheet considerations. For example, though there is no space in '<name><f>Dick</f><s>Whittington</s></name>', this is a reasonable construct because a stylesheet would be used to add a space between the first and second names. In these cases, additional formatting rules are applied to specific elements.

According to the standard, there are no issues relating to ambiguities in the use of whitespace, as it appears to be assumed that different rules or conventions may be applied in different applications. Some consider this decision 'to ignore the issue' to be naive, if only because the same XML processors, document handling software libraries, editors and browsers should be universally applicable.

However, it is true to say that some applications of XML could vary from the most typical scenario. The following text therefore concentrates on information that is to be published. In this arena, it is possible to look to SGML and HTML solutions for some guidance. HTML-based editors and browsers, and SGML-based document management systems and pagination engines, have been adapted for use with XML. Unfortunately, there is no agreement between SGML and HTML regarding whitespace handling. It is therefore necessary to look at both in isolation, before attempting to define a suitable position for XML.

Note that in the following discussion, the term 'ignored' will be used to describe a whitespace character that appears in the data file, but is not considered to be part of the document it contains, so will not appear when the document is presented. An XML-sensitive application should remove these characters if it is preparing the content for display.

HTML

Rules for whitespace handling in HTML have arisen in a haphazard fashion, though the two most popular browsers are now almost compatible. It is useful to first define two classes of element. An **in-line element** does not generate a break in the flow of the text, whereas a **block element** contains text that is separated from preceding and following text. The Emphasis element is an in-line element, whereas the Paragraph element is a block element:

```
<p>This block element contains an <em>in-line</em>
element, which does not break the flow of the
text.</p>
<p>This paragraph block is separated from the
previous block.</p>
```

This block element contains an **in-line** element which does not break the flow of the text.

This paragraph block is separated from the previous block.

Note that the CSS stylesheet language (see Chapter 24 and Chapter 25) allows the default settings for each element in the HTML format to be changed. For example, the Paragraph element could be changed into an in-line element.

Except for text contained in the Preformatted element, a Web browser removes any whitespace not considered to be part of the actual document. All whitespace between block elements is ignored. All whitespace preceding the first 'genuine' character in a block element, and all but one trailing whitespace character, is also ignored. A fixed amount of vertical space is re-inserted between block elements as they are presented:

```
<p>The first paragraph.</p>[CR]
[CR]
[CR]
<p>^^^The second paragraph.^^^</p><p>[CR]
^^^[CR]
^^^The third paragraph.[CR]
^^^</p>
```

The first paragraph.

The second paragraph.^

The third paragraph.^

Within a block element, all line-end codes are replaced by a space (as discussed in the previous section), and multiple spaces are reduced to a single space. The browser re-inserts its own line-end codes when presenting the material, at points dependent on the width of the screen or frame:

```
<p>This paragraph is split over[CR]
lines.^^^The browser may re-insert some^^^[CR]
line-end codes as it 'composes' the[CR]
paragraph.
```

This paragraph is split over lines. The browser may reinsert some line-end codes as it 'composes' the paragraph.

The only disagreement between Netscape Navigator and Microsoft Internet Explorer is in regard to comments. Explorer simply ignores them, but Navigator also ignores any immediately following line-end code. This may be considered dangerous, as demonstrated in the following example, where two words are inadvertently joined together. Comments should therefore not be placed on the same line as any text:

```
<p>The following words are joined<!-- COMMENT -->[CR]
together in Netscape.</p>
```

The following words are **joinedtogether** in Netscape.

SGML

The advantage that HTML-sensitive applications have over SGML-sensitive applications is that they already 'know' the meaning and purpose of each element in the language they are processing. On the surface, an SGML application can only deduce a few characteristics of the document structure from its DTD construction.

A distinction is made between an element that has **element content**, as opposed to one that has **mixed content**. A typical Chapter element has element content, such as lists, paragraphs and tables, and an element called Emphasis may have mixed (or text only) content.

This concept seems to be analogous to the block and in-line distinction made in HTML. But both the Emphasis element and the Paragraph element have mixed content, despite one of these elements being a block element, and the other an in-line element.

In SGML, the focus is on the line-end codes rather than on whitespace in general. Specifically, two characters are defined in the SGML standard that take the roles of record delimiters. The **RS** (**Record Start**) character identifies the start of a record (or line) and the **RE** (**Record End**) character identifies the end of a record (or line). By default they are mapped to the ASCII characters LF and CR respectively. It is, therefore, strictly speaking incorrect to think of the CR plus LF combination as indicating the end of a line on MS-DOS/Windows systems, when the second character is really indicating the start of the next line.

In element content, both these characters are simply ignored (element content is always identifiable because DTD processing is not optional as it is with XML).

The record start character is ignored everywhere (except in markup), but the record end character may be interpreted as a space (or retained as a line-end code) within text:

```
[RS] <chapter>[RE]
[RS] ^^^ [RE]
[RS] <p>A normal[RE]
[RS] paragraph.</p>[RE]
```

A normal paragraph.

If a line of text contains only markup declarations (including comments) and/or processing instructions, the record end code is also ignored. Note the similarity of this behaviour to comment handling in Netscape Navigator.

Finally, the record end character is also ignored if it immediately follows a start-tag, or immediately precedes an end-tag. Again, this is similar behaviour to the HTML browsers, except that only the one character is affected:

```
<para>[RE]
This paragraph is bounded by element tags.[RE]
</para>
```

This paragraph is bounded by element tags.

Note that multiple whitespace characters within a line are not normalized down to a single space in SGML:

```
<para>This is a ^^^ paragraph.</para>
```

This is a ^^^ paragraph.

Recommendations

It seems desirable to provide rules that allow some latitude to the author, while producing common sense 'standardized' output. If the standardization authorities are unwilling to tackle this subject, the best that can be hoped for is consensus amongst application developers.

There has been much discussion on this topic in the XML newsgroups, and many people have contributed thoughts based on experience with SGML and HTML. The following is the author's own stab at a set of rules, but readers should be prepared to discover the 'real' rules as they emerge.

If Web browsers become the first major applications that process XML for presentation (as, at the time of writing, seems to be happening), then HTML conventions should be of most relevance to XML. A stylesheet is needed to identify block elements and in-line elements, but CSS and XSL both have this capability. This would probably be appropriate, because the block/in-line definitions are more informative in this regard than the element/mixed model details that a DTD can supply (and a DTD may not even be available).

When a space mode is not made explicit for a particular element, the application should imply a default setting, which it should additionally interpret as implying 'collapsed' mode. If the DTD or document author requires preserved content for a specific element, the XML-Space attribute should be used.

A string of whitespace characters should be reduced to a single character, except when 'preserve' mode is in operation:

```
<para>A ^^^ normal
^^^paragraph.</para>
```

    A normal paragraph.

When a line of text consists of nothing but comments and/or processing instructions, the entire line should be removed, including the line-end code.

```
<para>A normal
<!--Comment-->
paragraph.</para>
```

    A normal paragraph.

The line-end code after 'normal' becomes the space between this word and 'paragraph'. The middle line is effectively non-existent. Actually, this rule is implied from previous rules. The comment is removed anyway, leaving two consecutive line-end codes. The normalization process then converts the first one to a space and removes the second.

To summarize the rules in the order they should be applied:

- Block and in-line elements must be identified (using a configuration file or stylesheet).
- Whitespace surrounding a block element should be removed.
- A line containing nothing but declarations and/or comments should be entirely removed.
- Leading and trailing whitespace inside a block element should be removed (except when content is explicitly preserved).
- A line-end code within a block element should be converted into a space (recall that alternative line-end codes are already normalized to a line-end code).
- A sequence of whitespace characters (including converted line-end codes) should be reduced to a single space character.

9. XML extensions

XML can stand alone, but benefits from the assistance of adjunct standards. This chapter introduces the most significant general-purpose standards. These standards significantly enhance the functionality of XML, and the interoperability of compliant XML-based tools. This chapter also introduces the two main applications of XML that are covered in later parts of the book, and explains the purpose of further adjunct standards applicable to each of these areas.

Extension standards

One key design decision that was made during the development of XML was to keep the language small. This was done in order to encourage application developers to support the standard, and to help ensure that the cost of development would be minimized: a strategy that has worked extremely well, as the subsequent widespread availability of low-cost (sometimes free) XML tools has demonstrated.

Another key decision made was that XML should be backward compatible with SGML, so that existing SGML tools could be utilized in XML projects, and protecting the investment of organizations that had already adopted SGML.

These two decisions were certainly valid, but as a result there has been pressure to:

- replace some of the more archaic SGML-compatible features with simpler yet more powerful, alternatives
- improve upon or simplify some existing SGML-based adjunct standards
- enhance XML to better support data exchange applications
- generally extend XML in new and interesting ways.

It was understood that the only way to do these things, without complicating XML itself, was to introduce a number of adjunct standards. Individual applications could then choose whether or not to support a particular extension standard as appropriate to their purpose.

One by one, functional areas not tackled by the XML standard have been addressed by new, adjunct standards. Some of the old SGML-related standards have been dusted down and re-worked (often simplified in the process), and most of the more significant ones have been developed by the W3C (see www.w3.org).

General extensions

There are a number of standards that do not apply to a specific usage of XML, but are applicable to most or all possible applications of this standard (they are introduced here, then discussed in detail in the following chapters).

Namespaces

When an XML document conforms to a specific DTD, all the elements in this document can be said to be in a single 'namespace'. The element and attribute names are assigned by the same authority, and are either unique, or contextually unique, so there is no ambiguity about their purpose.

But it is often desirable for an XML document to contain elements from multiple DTDs, or 'namespaces'. This could confuse software (and people too), especially when two DTDs define an element or attribute with the same name. The **Namespaces** standard (see Chapter 10) provides a mechanism to avoid such confusion:

compound document

Relative URLs

When an XML document contains a relative URL reference, there may be some debate about what the reference is actually relative *to*. It may be to the location of the document that contains it, or to the application that is processing the document, or to the root directory of an area controlled by the Web server that delivered the document to the application:

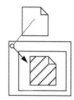

It can be useful to set the base address to an explicit location instead, and the **XML Base** standard (see Chapter 11) was devised for this purpose.

Composite documents

It is sometimes convenient for an XML document to be able to 'include' another document by reference. For example, the 'skeleton' of a book could include references to other XML documents representing each chapter, and the whole book could then be assembled for publication using these references.

In a limited way it is possible to do this already, using external entities, but with this method the files to be included cannot be complete XML documents (see Chapter 4), and the need for entity declarations only complicates the procedure. The new **XInclude** standard (see Chapter 12) promotes a simple yet powerful way to achieve this.

'skeleton' document

Navigation

The ability to identify a specific instance of an element within a document, without necessarily having to assign an identifier to that object, can be important for a number of applications of XML.

The **XPath** standard defines a flexible scheme, and a simple syntax that can be used in URL references. Other standards (such as XSLT and XPointer) utilize this standard.

Alternative modelling techniques

The DTD feature of XML is directly inherited from SGML, and long before XML was invented this approach to modelling SGML documents was considered inadequate for some applications.

Many people wondered why the syntax used to create DTD instructions should be different to the syntax of SGML documents, thus creating difficulties for both DTD authors and parser developers. Others argued that this modelling language was inadequate in various ways (for example, it is not possible to constrain an attribute value to a maximum or exact number of characters). For still others, the whole modelling approach was simply wrong.

The popularity of the newer XML standard, especially in its application as a data exchange language (as well as a document modelling language), further fuelled the demand for alternative modelling techniques.

The **XML Schema** standard is one well-backed alternative to DTDs. It uses XML document syntax, so can exploit existing XML authoring, management and rendering techniques and tools, and can replicate all DTD features (see Chapter 14 for an introduction).

Advanced schemas

Although an **XML Schema** can exactly replicate the modelling functionality of an equivalent DTD, the reason for the development of this standard was primarily to improve on the modelling features that DTDs can offer (for example, it does permit the model to constrain attribute values to a given length). In particular, the need to model highly structured data is met by this new standard (see Chapter 15).

Significant XML domains

Some significant applications of XML require additional, but very different adjunct standards to support them. This book explores the standards developed to support the two most prominent of these applications.

Data exchange applications

Wherever complex data must be exchanged between two programs, XML has the potential to play a significant role. Its self-describing nature, and its simple text-based data format, together ensure its utility in maintaining complex structures and relationships:

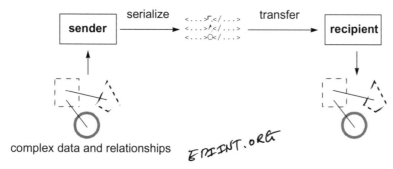

complex data and relationships

The electronic exchange of commercial information between software applications, usually in different organizations, is very important for efficient business transactions. Although **EDI** (*Electronic Data Interchange*) has been a reality for some years, this technology has been based on proprietary (and often expensive) solutions. There is now a lot of activity in this field based around the use of XML and other Internet standards, aiming not only to reduce the price of electronic commerce solutions through the use of freely available tools (such as Web browsers), but also to bring much needed standardization to this domain.

Another prime area of interest is the passing of information about information, commonly known as 'meta-data', between systems. Standards for the exchange of meta-data have been suggested by various parties, including most recently the **RDF** (*Resource Description Framework*) proposal from the W3C.

XML may also be used as an exchange format for **relational database** systems. The XML tags are used as a convenient data wrapper during the transfer of records, fields and relationships between systems:

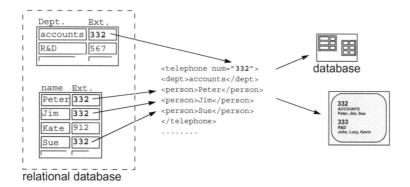

relational database

The most significant aspect of all of these applications is the need for software to read and write XML data files. Writing XML files is relatively simple, but reading them requires a suitable interface to an XML parser, and some standard interfaces exist.

But when an application is required only to manipulate an XML file (simply to read it, modify it, then write it out to a new file), then it may be more appropriate to use a transformation tool instead.

These issues are covered in the next part of this book: *Processing and transforming XML.*

Publishing applications

Although XML has many uses, the application that drove the development of its ancestors remains relevant. At its heart, XML is still a document markup language, and inherits from SGML its particular ability to separate formatting from content.

XML can be used to hold semi-structured documents, including textbooks (including those covering XML), training guides, technical manuals, catalogues, academic journals and reports. Among many other niche applications, XML can also be used to create and describe patent applications, examination papers, financial statements and research papers.

There are two significant components to this usage of XML. The most fundamental is the formatting of XML documents for presentation or publication. But the creation and management of documents prior to formatting is also very important.

A number of standards assist with the formatting of XML. Typically, a **stylesheet** is used to map XML elements to output styles:

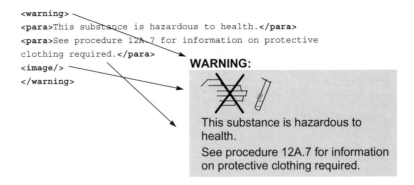

Advanced formatting tools must deal with more than simple text. XML documents may include mathematical and chemical formulae, and both vector and raster image formats. XML can be used to describe page layouts, and even multimedia presentations.

It should be noted that XML documents created primarily for data exchange may also benefit from the rendering capabilities developed to support XML-based document publishing. Also, sophisticated stylesheet technologies may act as general XML transformation tools.

Formatting issues are covered in the fourth part of this book: *Formatting.*

XML document management may be achieved using a number of technologies and techniques, including simple storage of XML files on a disk, the use of catalog files to simplify the management of these files, and search engines to enable flexible identification of required documents. The adoption of sophisticated databases and document management systems are essential for large-scale document management problems.

The standard XML method for creating hypertext links is extremely limited. These links are one-directional, have a single end-point, and work only within the same document. All of these limitations are overcome using the **XLink** standard (see Chapter 27). But even XLink links are limited to targeting complete elements that have a unique identifier. But it can be inconvenient or even impossible to add such identifiers, especially when the target object is read-only, or is a range of text instead of a complete element. The **XPointer** standard (see Chapter 28) overcomes this issue using contextual location identifiers:

The management of documents, and links between documents to be published, is discussed in the fifth part: *Document management.*

10. Namespaces

This chapter describes a standard for building documents that include components from different domains, defined within disparate DTDs or XML Schemas. It is used to support XSLT, XLink and other important standards.

Compound documents

It is possible for a single XML document to contain fragments that are defined in a number of different DTDs or schemas. The ability to do this resolves a number of issues.

To facilitate rendering of complex structures in a browser, it may be necessary to embed HTML elements within a document that does not otherwise conform to this standard. For example, HTML tables (see Chapter 23) are powerful, and well supported by the popular Web browsers, so it would be useful to be able to use HTML elements whenever a table is needed:

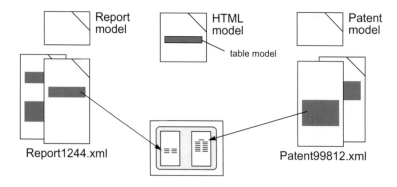

This is actually just one case of a general need to match data to the expectations of widely used tools that have a specific purpose, beyond the individual domains that DTDs are associated with. Another example would be a Web crawler searching documents for specific forms of meta-data to improve the classification of sites for a search engine (but see Architectural forms in Chapter 6 for another approach). The XSLT standard also requires this concept to allow the mixing of formatting instructions with target document element tags, and the XLink standard (Chapter 27) uses namespaces to add linking roles to elements from any DTD or XML Schema model.

Mixed model problems

The well-formed nature of all XML structures makes it relatively easy to embed 'foreign' structures in documents. However, doing so raises two issues that must be addressed. Element and attribute names must be unique, and easily associated with the model they are defined in.

Context identification

The first problem is to identify which DTD or XML Schema each element belongs to. Normally, of course, the element names might be considered sufficient to identify which models they belong to, but in practice it would be necessary for an application to hold a list of elements from each domain, in order to distinguish between them. This would be inconvenient, certainly, but not as serious as a side effect of the second problem, which is discussed below.

Duplication conflicts

The second problem is how to avoid duplication of element and attribute names, as there is nothing to prevent different models defining objects with the same names. XML does not allow two elements or attributes to have the same name, as it would then be impossible to identify which is indicated when one of them is used in a document.

Consider the possibility of a DTD that describes musical compositions, and includes elements that identify the composer, the title of the composition, and the name of the person who provided a particular score (arrangement). Another DTD describes the performance of a musician at a competition, and include the score that the individual obtained for the performance:

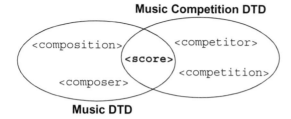

Music Competition DTD

<composition> <competitor>
<score>
<composer> <competition>

Music DTD

In this scenario, both DTDs have an element named Score. If a single document were to contain both sets of elements, there would be two Score elements in the document:

```
<competitionEntry>
  <competition>Piano</competition>
  <competitor>J Smith</competitor>
  <score>57<score>
  <composer>George Gershwin</composer>
  <composition>Rhapsody in Blue</composition>
  <score>Ferde Grofé</score>
</competitionEntry>
```

This example illustrates a side effect of the problem that compounds the first problem (identification of the context), because it is not possible to identify which model an element or attribute belongs to if more than one model contains an element or attribute with its name. While in this case it is easy for people to distinguish between the two Score elements, by reading their contents, it would be far less easy for software to make such a distinction.

The standard

The Namespaces standard, or '**Namespaces in XML**' to give it its full title, is a scheme for building documents from fragments defined in different domains, by addressing the problems outlined above. It was produced by the W3C, and gained recommended status in January 1999. The standard can be found at http://www.w3.org/TR/1998/REC-xml-names.

This standard focuses on solving the two issues raised above. First, it provides a mechanism for identifying the namespaces used in the document. Second, it identifies which namespace a particular element or attribute belongs to.

A single XML Schema (or DTD) is considered to own a '**namespace**', an environment in which all element names are unique, and all attribute names (within the context of a particular element) are also unique. Any reference to an element name is therefore unambiguous. Any reference to an attribute within a particular element is also unambiguous. The term **multiple namespaces** is used to describe the concept of a single document that contains information defined in a number of namespace domains.

Namespaces are now supported by the two most popular parser interfaces for XML processing. SAX 2.0 (see Chapter 19) and DOM 2.0 (see Chapter 21) both support this standard, and are both now well supported by parser developers. Indeed, the main reason for the development of these updates is to support namespaces.

Namespace identification

Most standards can now be identified with a specific location on the Web. For example, HTML 4 is defined at http://www.w3.org/TR/REC-html40. As these Web addresses must be unique, this string of characters can be deemed to be a suitable namespace identifier. In addition, it is already known to anyone interested in the DTD or standard in question, and it is genuinely informative to any readers of the document who were not aware of its existence, as they can use the identifier to find and read the standard itself.

The Namespaces standard uses URLs (see Chapter 30) to identify each namespace, but it must be understood that Namespace-sensitive applications do not have to be connected to the Internet. In this context, a URL is only a useful and well-known text string. An application is expected to compare the URL against a list of standards it can meaningfully process: not try to open a link.

Elements and attributes from different namespaces are distinguished from each other by adding a prefix to the name. The prefix is separated from the name using a colon. The resulting object is known as a **qualified name**:

```
prefix:name
```

Having noted that URLs are a good way to uniquely identify a namespace, it also has to be said that they are not suitable for use as element and attribute prefixes. First, they tend to be quite long, as in the HTML example above, but, more importantly, they often contain characters that are not allowed in element and attribute names. To solve this problem, the standard includes a mechanism for defining short, legal prefixes, and for mapping them to the full URL identifier.

For example, HTML paragraph elements and XSLT template elements may be given appropriate prefixes:

```
html:p

xslt:template
```

It cannot be left to the standard's bodies to define the prefix, because the collision problem could easily re-emerge. The DTD, XML Schema or document author has full control over prefix names, and can avoid conflicts simply by ensuring that each prefix is unique within the confines of that document, or class of documents.

Using namespaces

Namespace declaration

Namespaces are defined using attributes. The attribute name 'xmlns' is used to declare a namespace. The value of this attribute is a (complete, not relative) reference to the namespace concerned. For example:

```
<html xmlns="http://www.w3.org/TR/REC-html40">
 ...<p>An HTML paragraph.</p>...
</html>
```

However, this attribute is also used to supply the replacement prefix to be used in element and attribute names. This is done by extending the name to include the prefix. The prefix is separated from the 'xmlns' part of the name using a colon. This can be confusing at first, because the namespace *prefix* is defined by the attribute name *suffix*. In the following example, the HTML 4.0 namespace is referenced, and given the local prefix 'X':

```
<X:html xmlns:X="http://www.w3.org/TR/REC-html40">
 ...<X:p>An HTML paragraph.</X:p>...
</X:html>
```

In the following example, the music DTD or schema is referenced:

```
<competitionEntry xmlns:M="...">
  <competition>Piano</competition>
  <competitor>J Smith</competitor>
  <score>57</score>
  <M:composer>George Gershwin</M:composer>
  <M:composition>Rhapsody in Blue</M:composition>
  <M:score>Ferde Grofé</M:score>
</competitionEntry>
```

Declaration locations

Although namespaces may be defined within the root element, as in the examples above, they can actually be specified in any element. In the following example, an HTML table has been included in an XML document:

```
<document>
  <description>...</description>
  <X:table xmlns:X="http://www.w3.org/TR/REC-html40">
    ...<X:td>An HTML table cell.</X:td>...
  </X:table>
  <summary>...</summary>
</document>
```

Multiple declarations

An element may declare more than one namespace:

```
<D:document xmlns:D="file:///DTDs/document.dtd"
            xmlns:X="http://www.w3.org/TR/REC-html40">
  ...<D:description>...</Q:description>...
  ...<X:td>An HTML table cell.</X:td>...
  ...<D:summary>...</Q:summary>...
</D:document>
```

This example does not contain duplicate attribute names. It is legal XML because the suffixes serve the purpose of making each attribute name unique:

```
xmlns:D
```

```
xmlns:X
```

Indeed, the ability to place multiple declarations in the root element can be very convenient. As the music example demonstrates, it would be a good idea to keep the declarations in the root element, as otherwise they would be needed on every element. The example below is clearly over-burdened by namespace declarations:

```
<competitionEntry>
  <C:competition xmlns:C="...">Piano</C:competition>
  <C:competitor xmlns:C="...">J Smith</C:competitor>
  <C:score xmlns:C="...">57</C:score>
  <M:composer xmlns:M="...">
    George Gershwin
  </M:composer>
  <M:composition xmlns:M="...">
    Rhapsody in Blue
  </M:composition>
  <M:score xmlns:M="...">Ferde Grofé</M:score>
</competitionEntry>
```

Mixed attributes

Attributes from one namespace can be used in elements from another. The attribute names contain the same prefixes as the elements. The following example of a House element contains two Style attributes. The first one is from the house namespace, and explains what kind of property the House element describes. The second one is an HTML attribute that is used to format the content of the element (in this case colouring the text red):

```
<property:house property:style="Georgian"
                html:style="color:red">
   ...
</property:house>
```

Defaults

When every element has a prefix, the document can become difficult to read, and the extra characters certainly add to its size. Fortunately, the standard includes the concept of a **default namespace**.

Element defaults

Elements can belong to a default namespace, but this is done by declaring the namespace using an attribute named 'xmlns', with no suffix (as suggested earlier):

```
<document xmlns="file:///DTDs/document.dtd"
          xmlns:X="http://www.w3.org/TR/REC-html40">
  ...<description>...</description>...
  ...<X:td>An HTML table cell.</X:td>...
</document>
```

Overriding defaults

The default namespace can be changed at any point in the document hierarchy. This is an ideal technique when a sufficiently large XML fragment is embedded:

```
<document xmlns="file:///DTDs/document.dtd"
          xmlns:X="http://www.w3.org/TR/REC-html40">
   ...
  ...<para>A normal paragraph.</para>...
  ...<X:td>An HTML table cell.</X:td>...
  ...<description>...</description>...

  ...<html xmlns="http://www.w3.org/TR/REC-html40">
     ...<td>An HTML table cell.</td>...
  ...</html>
   ...
  <summary>...</summary>
</document>
```

Attributes

When an attribute belongs to the same namespace as the element containing it, there is no need to include the prefix on the attribute. Attributes with no prefix are *not* considered to belong to the default namespace, as elements with no prefix would be. In truth, an attribute with no prefix is deemed to belong to no namespace at all, and it is the job of the application processing the XML data to assume that it therefore belongs to the same namespace as the element containing it.

Note that the standard is a little confused on this point, since an appendix to the standard includes an example showing that an attribute would conform to the same namespace as the element it belongs to, rather than to no namespace at all. But there is little practical difference, as both interpretations are unambiguous and consistent about which namespace an unqualified attribute belongs to.

DTD handling

When a document requires elements or attributes from multiple DTDs, it is not possible for it to simply refer to each DTD, as the following diagram would imply to be required:

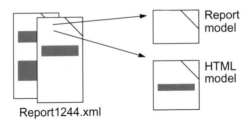

Report1244.xml

The XML standard does not allow multiple DTD references. Instead, it is necessary to create a new, single DTD, that incorporates all the required elements and attributes:

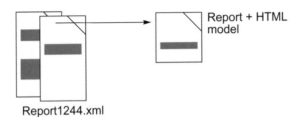

Report1244.xml

Note that XML Schemas *are* namespace-sensitive (see Chapter 14), and merging of models is therefore not necessary when using that modelling language.

Namespace modelling

In order to parse documents against a DTD, it is necessary to include the prefixes in the element definitions:

```
<!ELEMENT competitionEntry
                (competition, competitor, score,
                 M:composer, M:composition, M:score)>
```

In addition, the namespace definition can be included in the DTD, and shows one good use of the FIXED attribute type:

```
<!ATTLIST competitionEntry xmlns:M
                         #FIXED "file:///c:/Music.DTD">
```

This all means that namespace and prefix selection is performed by the DTD author instead of the document author. But this is not a problem, because the DTD author should be aware of which namespaces are allowed in all documents that conform to the DTD, and consider this to be an important part of the modelling process. It also simplifies the authoring of documents considerably. Document authors should not need to concern themselves with discovering which namespaces are needed, finding the namespace URLs, inventing suitable prefixes, and creating the declarations.

Prefix flexibility

It is possible that the DTD will need to cater for documents that use different prefixes for the same namespace. Parameter entities and the document's internal subset can be used to provide this flexibility. In the following example, the default prefix defined in the DTD is 'acme', but a document that references this DTD overrides this prefix with the prefix 'A':

```
<!ENTITY % prefix "acme:">
<!ENTITY % book "%prefix;book">
<!ELEMENT %book; ... >

<!DOCTYPE A:book [
  <!ENTITY % prefix "A">
]>
<A:book>...</A:book>
```

Constraints

Despite the benefits that DTDs can bring to simplifying use of namespaces outlined above, it has to be recognized that the DTD feature of XML was designed long before namespaces were invented, so DTDs are not namespace-aware. This causes some difficulties when both namespaces and DTDs are required for a particular application of XML.

As usual the DTD must include references to all allowed children in an element's content model, regardless of the disparate namespaces they may belong to. In one sense this is a good thing, because it continues to give the DTD author total control over where elements and attributes can appear in relation to each other.

But the inventors of the namespaces concept were seeking the flexibility to include XML fragments from any model at any location within another. One could envisage this working by switching between DTDs as elements from different models are encountered. With each switch, parsing against the current model ceases, and re-starts with the new model. The element where the switch occurs does not cause an error in the original model. But, at the time of writing, no tools take this approach. Some alternative modelling schemes such as XML Schemas address this issue. Even when possible, however, this approach is not always advisable, as it can lead to very unpredictable document structures.

Examples of usage

Some of the other important XML-related standards described later utilize the Namespaces standard.

XLink

The latest draft of the XLink standard (see Chapter 27) uses namespaces to embed linking attributes in arbitrary elements. This standard relies upon the use of namespaces:

```
<document xmlns:xlink="http://www.w3.org/1999/xlink">
   ...
   ... <reference xlink:href="otherDoc.xml" />Other
   Document</reference> ...
   ...
</document>
```

XSLT

The XSLT standard (see Chapter 17) allows the use of namespaces to embed output elements in an XSLT stylesheet document. Most stylesheet developers tend to use the default namespace either for XSLT element or for output elements:

```
<xslt:stylesheet
        xmlns:xslt="http://www.w3.org/1999/XSL/Transform">
    ...
  <H1>Normal HTML Header One</H1>
  <xslt:if test="...">
    <P>Normal HTML paragraph.</P>
  </xslt:if>
    ...
</xslt:stylesheet>
```

11. Relative URLs (XML Base)

The XML Base standard provides the flexibility to reset the base location of relative URL references within a document, a feature that is important to both XLink (see Chapter 27) and XInclude (see the next chapter). This standard also generally promotes the increased use of relative references, and the shortening of such references, by allowing the base location to be re-set numerous times within a single document.

Background

The URL standard includes the concept of 'relative' URL references (see Chapter 30 for details). With such references, it is necessary to determine a starting point, or '**base**' location, from which to follow the URL path to the required resource. By default, the starting point is the directory containing the document that includes the URL reference. While useful, this assumption can be too limiting. If the document is moved to a new location, but the related resources are not, the URL reference becomes broken. When many references are involved, it can be a considerable editing task to fix them all.

A better solution would be to enable the base location to be changed, within the document, in order to fix all of the broken references. This is one of the purposes of the **XML Base** standard. Its other purposes are to allow relative URLs to be used more frequently, by re-setting the base location, perhaps several times within the same document, and to drill down further into an existing location, so that the relative paths in the URL references can be made shorter.

The XLink standard (see Chapter 27) relies upon the XML Base standard. Indeed, the idea for the XML Base standard emerged from a need for this feature within the XLink standard.

However, other standards, such as the XInclude standard (see the next chapter), are beginning to refer to XML Base too, thus justifying the decision to make it a separate standard.

Relative URLs

Normally, all relative URL references in a document assume that the location of the document is the starting point for calculating the target resource location. For example, consider a document called 'maindoc.xml' that is currently situated in the 'books' directory on the 'D:' drive:

```
d:/books/maindoc.xml
```

If there is a relative URL reference in this document that only contains the name of another file, this file will be assumed to be in the same directory. A slightly more complex relative URL, such as 'fiction/1984.xml', would be resolved as follows:

```
d:/books/maindoc.xml
        fiction/1984.xml
```

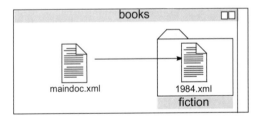

New base location

XML Base is used to set the base address to a new location, such as 'file:///d:/new-books', and the relative URLs are then updated to start from this location.

The example above would be re-located as follows:

```
d:/books/maindoc.xml
```

```
d:/newbooks/fiction/1984.xml
```

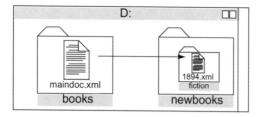

It is even possible for the base address to be re-set a number of times within the same document, and the document hierarchy is exploited to give each definition a specific scope.

Also note that the characters allowed in this value must conform to the constraints of the URL standard (see Chapter 30).

XML Base markup

The **xml:base** attribute is reserved for the purpose of re-setting the base location for relative URLs (the 'xml' prefix is reserved in the Namespaces scheme for significant XML-enhancing schemes, such as this one). The value of this attribute is a URL that points to the new base location. When attached to the root element of an XML document, it takes effect throughout the entire document, applying to all relative URLs that the document contains.

xml:base attribute

In the following example, the Link attribute contains a relative URL reference to the document '1984.xml', which would normally be expected to be present in the same directory as the source document, but is now expected to be found in the 'Orwell' directory instead:

```
<collection author="G. Orwell"
            xml:base="file:///d:/colls/Orwell/">
  ...
  <bookLink title="1984" link="1984.xml" />
  ...
</collection>


    d:/colls/Orwell/1984.xml
```

Overriding declarations

The scope of a base declaration is the element it is declared in, and all descendants of that element, except for any descendant elements that contain overriding definitions.

An overriding definition may be used to re-set the base to a totally different location, or, as in the following example, simply to drill down into the existing base location in order make the embedded relative URL references shorter. In the following example, the declarations on the Fact and Fiction elements both override the one on the Collection element. This allows the individual book references to avoid including the parent directory, for example giving '1984.xml' instead of 'fiction/1984.xml':

```
d:/colls/Orwell/fact/DownOut.xml
                 WPier.xml
         fiction/BDays.xml
                 1984.xml
                 AFarm.xml
```

```
<collection author="G. Orwell"
            xml:base="file:///d:/colls/Orwell/">
  <fact xml:base="file:///d:/colls/Orwell/fact/">
    <bookLink title="Down and Out in Paris and London"
              link="DownOut.xml" />
    <bookLink title="Road to Wigan Pier" link="WPier.xml" />
  </fact>
  <fiction xml:base="file:///d:/colls/Orwell/fiction/">
    <bookLink title="Burmese Days" link="BDays.xml" />
    <bookLink title="1984" link="1984.xml" />
    <bookLink title="Animal Farm" link="AFarm.xml" />
  </fiction>
</collection>
```

More specifically, a relative URL reference in an attribute value is within the scope of the element it is attached to, a relative URL reference within the text content of an element is within the scope of that element, and a relative URL reference within a processing instruction is within the scope of the element containing that instruction:

```
<outer xml:base="file:///d:/outerBase/"
       url="outerBase/...">
  <?url outerBase/... ?>
  <url>outerBase/...</url>
  <inner xml:base="file:///d/innerBase/"
         url="innerBase/...">
    <?url innerBase/... ?>
    <url>innerBase/...</url>
  </inner>
</outer>
```

Relative bases

An xml:base attribute may itself contain a relative URL reference. In this case, the complete URL must be calculated by searching up the document hierarchy for another xml:base attribute (if an absolute ancestor definition is not found, the location of the document is taken to be the base location).

This technique avoids unnecessary repetition, and the example above can be simplified as follows:

```
<collection author="G. Orwell"
            xml:base="file:///d:/colls/Orwell/">

  <fact xml:base="fact/">
    ...
  </fact>

  <fiction xml:base="fiction/">
    ...
  </fiction>

</collection>
```

External entity declarations

A base definition has no effect on external entity references that use a relative reference. This is due to the fact that these declarations occur outside of the root element, so are not in the scope of that element (or of any other element).

In the following example, the DTD file 'coll.dtd' will not be sought in the 'Orwell' directory, and neither will the document '1984.xml':

```
                    <!-- NOT AFFECTED -->
<!DOCTYPE collection SYSTEM "coll.dtd"
[ ...
    ...             <!-- NOT AFFECTED -->
  <!ENTITY book1984 SYSTEM "1984.xml">
  ...
]>
<collection xml:base="file:///d:/colls/Orwell/">
  ...
  &book1984;
  ...
</collection>
```

External entity content

External entity content may include relative URL references. These references are almost inevitably created without knowledge of the (possibly disparate) locations of the documents that will eventually include this entity content. Clearly, these references will break once the content of the entity is placed in such a document.

However, an entity containing XML markup may include an xml:base attribute (or attributes). The presence of such attributes would neatly overcome this problem.

In the following example, an image is assumed to be located in an 'images' directory that is a sibling of the directory containing the entity text. The path to the image is maintained after entity merging, as it is a combination of the specified base location, 'file:///d:/books/', and the relative location of the image, '../images/boat/gif', giving the complete path 'file:///d:/books/../images/boat.gif' (which is a slightly roundabout way of saying 'd:/books/images/boat.gif'):

```
<!DOCTYPE collection ...
[
  ...
  <!ENTITY book9 SYSTEM "file:///d:/books/book9.xml">
  ...
]>
<collection>
  ...
  &book9;
  ...
</collection>


    <book xml:base="file:///d:/books/">
      ...
      <image href="../images/boat.gif" />
      ...
    </book>
```

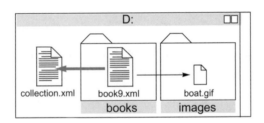

The XInclude standard (see the next chapter) utilizes this concept, but automatically adds an xml:base attribute to the root element (or elements) of each included fragment or document. Consider the following example (explained in the next chapter):

```
<collection xmlns:xi="...">
   ...
  <xi:include href="file:///d:/books/book9.xml" />
   ...
</collection>


    <book>
      ...
      <images xml:base="../images/">
        ...
        <image href="boat.gif" />
        ...
      </images>
      ...
    </book>
```

After inclusion of the book file, the added xml:base attribute on the Book element provides the information needed to find the image file:

```
<collection>
   ...
  <book xml:base="books/">
    ...
    <images xml:base="../images/">
      ...
      <image href="boat.gif"/>
      ...
    </images>
    ...
  </book>
   ...
</collection>
```

But note that the standard does not make clear what would happen if the xml:base attribute in the included file had appeared on the Book element instead of the Images element. It is not permitted for a single element to contain two attributes with the same name, yet both 'books/' and '../images/' are required. Perhaps these two relative URL references would be combined into the single attribute value 'books/../images'.

DTD declarations

When a DTD is in use, the xml:base attribute needs to be defined explicitly for each element it may be allowed to appear in:

```
<!ELEMENT collection  xml:base  CDATA  #IMPLIED>
```

When the element name is significant enough to imply a specific base location, this location can be inserted into the DTD as a default value:

```
<!ELEMENT image  xml:base CDATA "file:///d:/images/">
```

It is even possible that the value should never be changed, in which case it could be made into a fixed attribute value:

```
<!ELEMENT image  xml:base CDATA
                          #FIXED "file:///d:/images/">
```

Warning: These techniques should not be used if there is any possibility that the XML documents will be processed using parsers that do not validate them against a DTD or schema, or when the paths are likely to vary because document instances will be placed in different locations.

12. Composite documents (XInclude)

The proposed XInclude standard permits composite documents to be created from disparate XML fragments (or complete documents) in a simple but powerful manner. This chapter discusses the draft proposal of 16 May 2001. It relies upon the Namespaces standard (see Chapter 10) and XML Base (see the previous chapter).

Overview

It is the very nature of XML document structures that encourages information re-use, and the building of documents from many components. Indeed, the XML standard includes support for this concept, employing internal and external general entities to achieve this effect. But XInclude takes a fresh approach, addressing some of the perceived weaknesses in the entities feature built in to the XML standard.

The XInclude standard defines a single 'inclusion' element that can be used to reference another document, or just a fragment of another document, or even a fragment of the current document, with the intention that the referenced content should replace this inclusion instruction:

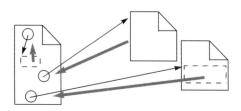

In general, this standard is one of several attempts to move away from the 'old SGML' way of doing things, towards the 'new Web-based' world. It is intended that current XML-based markup languages that currently define their own standards for including remote material will gradually adopt this standard instead, and then benefit from authoring and processing tools that understand it.

Note that an application can only support this standard if it also supports the Namespaces standard (see Chapter 10) and, in addition, it should also support the XML Base standard (see the previous chapter). Like many other peripheral standards discussed in this book, this standard uses URLs (see Chapter 30) to work with remote resources. In fact, both URL references and XPointer expressions (see Chapter 28) are exploited (examples of both appear below, but explanations of the syntax are not repeated here).

Identifying objects to include

Any inclusion mechanism can only work if it is possible to 'point to' the resource that needs to be included. Existing standards (described elsewhere in this book) are utilized for this purpose.

URLs

Other documents are identified for insertion into the current document using URL references. For example, a document representing an entire book may need to include other documents that represent individual chapters:

```
file:///c:/book/chapters/chapter1.xml
```

XPointer expressions

URL references may conclude with the '#' symbol, which is used to identify specific resources within the document referenced (or within the current document, when not preceded by a URL reference). This symbol is followed by an XPointer expression (see Chapter 28).

An XPointer expression can be used in this context to emulate the internal entity mechanism of the XML standard. Instead of having an entity declaration that either directly contains the entity value, or contains a reference to an external value, in this case it would be the first occurrence (probably) of the text within the document that is referenced.

For example, if the name of a company occurs many times in a document, and its first occurrence is in a document header, then this header could be given an identifier, such as 'CompanyName', that can be referenced from all other occurrences:

```
#companyName
```

```
<company>
  <name id="companyName">Acme Corp.</name>
  ...
</company>
```

The same approach may be taken to identify specific objects within other documents (the following example is more clearly shown to include an XPointer expression):

```
chapters/chapter1.xml#xpointer(id("chapterTitle"))
```

Ranges

When an XPointer expression is used to identify a range of items, rather than a single element, there are some possible complications to consider.

In the simplest case, the range neatly surrounds a set of elements, as in the example below. In this scenario, the complete list simply replaces the include instruction in the output. Note that the start-point and end-point of the range are both within the same enclosing element:

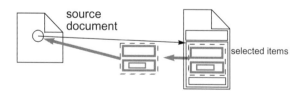

However, it is also possible for the start-point to occur in a different element to the end-point, as in the example below, where the range starts in the middle of one element, and ends in the middle of the next. Under these conditions, the elements containing each end of the range are included, but only the children of these two elements that occur within the range are also included (child elements outside of the range are ignored):

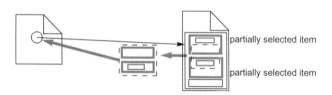

Recursive processing

Inclusions are processed recursively. When included text contains further inclusion instructions, these instructions are in turn detected and processed:

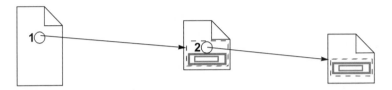

As mentioned above, a document may contain an include instruction that selects material from elsewhere in the same document (rather than from another document). This possibility raises a potential complication, because the material to be selected could itself contain an include instruction, and this instruction may or may not have already been processed:

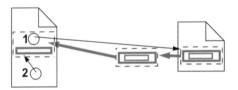

Various XInclude processors could be inconsistent with regard to the order in which they process these instructions, and different results might therefore be expected. In some cases, the original text (including the include instruction) would be inserted, but in other cases it would be the updated version that gets included. The following two examples show how the inclusion indicated above could be interpreted:

To avoid such problems, the standard makes it very clear that it is the *original* text that is copied, as in the first option shown above. However, this only means that the included material will definitely contain an include instruction, and this embedded instruction will subsequently be processed too, so finally still creating a document like the second option above (in this case creating the same final result, but in other, more complex scenarios, creating different results).

Inclusion markup

The Namespaces standard (see Chapter 10) is used to identify the element that takes the role of an inclusion instruction. The namespace for XInclude is 'http://www.w3.org/2001/xinclude'. In the following example, this namespace is mapped to the local prefix 'xi', though any convenient name may be chosen:

```
<book xmlns="my_book_namespace"
      xmlns:xi="http://www.w3.org/2001/xinclude">
  ...
</book>
```

Include element

The XInclude namespace defines a single **Include** element. The Include element is meant to be replaced by the material it refers to:

```
<book xmlns="my_book_namespace"
      xmlns:xi="http://www.w3.org/2001/xinclude">
  ...
  <xi:include ... />
  ...
</book>
```

Three attributes are defined for use within this element. The first, and most important, is the **Href** attribute. The name of this attribute will be familiar to many, though it is perhaps a little misleading in this context, as it actually stands for 'Hypertext REFerence'. As in other standards (such as XHTML), this attribute holds a URL reference, but in this case the URL is not used to create a hypertext link: it is used to locate material that needs to be copied to the current location:

```
<xi:include href="file:///c:/book/chapter1.xml"/>
```

Note that there is no implication here that merging will be prevented if the remote material does not conform to the constraints of a local DTD, or causes the enclosing element to be invalid according to this DTD. In practice, however, a validating parser may perhaps include such a constraint.

Include element content

The Include element is always completely removed during the inclusion process, even if it has content. Therefore, such content cannot ever be treated as anything more than a comment on the intended replacement text:

```
<xi:include href="file:///c:/book/chapter1.xml">
  INSERT CHAPTER ONE HERE
</xi:include>
```

Text inclusions

The assumption made so far is that XML material is to be inserted. But material to be included can also be treated as simple 'text' data. The **Parse** attribute is used to indicate how the material is to be treated:

```
<xi:include href="quote.txt" parse="text" />
```

Although unnecessary, this attribute can also take the value 'xml', to make the default action explicit. In 'xml' mode, the included fragment must conform to XML well-formed rules, and will be parsed for further Include elements (it is therefore assumed that an XML parser will be used to read this resource, and may reject it if it does not conform to XML rules).

In 'text' mode, XML parsing is not desired, regardless of whether or not the fragment happens to consist of XML data. Any special characters, such as '<', are escaped as they are merged in (so '<' becomes '<'). Note that processing is therefore *not* recursive, because the text is not parsed to try to find embedded Include elements.

When inserting plain text, the character set used may not be known to the application. It is possible to specify what character set has been used in the **Encoding** attribute. This attribute holds a character set code, such as 'UTF-8' or 'ISO-8859-1' (see Chapter 29):

```
<xi:include href="quote.txt"  parse="text"
                              encoding="ISO-8859-1" />
```

Duplicate entity and notation declarations

There may be entity references present in material collected from another document. While an XInclude processor may be blind to parsable entities processed by an underlying parser, it will always have to cope with binary entities. The relevant entity and notation declarations must be copied with the references into the document that contains the Include element, in order to ensure that the references can continue to be resolved within their new environment.

However, it is possible that a copied entity or notation declaration will have the same name as an entity or notation declaration that already exists in the source document. The XInclude application then needs to rename one of the declarations (and all of the references to it). But it is also possible that the two declarations have the same name because they are identical definitions. In this case, the second declaration is redundant and should simply be ignored.

Including complete documents

It is possible for one document to contain inclusion instructions that refer to other complete documents. This feature is ideal for building large, compound documents from a number of smaller documents.

For example, a book could be divided into chapter-sized documents that can be worked on separately, while a book 'skeleton' file could also be maintained that contains the preliminary text and back-matter material, surrounding a number of Include elements that are used to build the whole book:

```
<book ...>
  <xi:include href="chap1.xml"/>
  <xi:include href="chap2.xml"/>
  <xi:include href="chap3.xml"/>
</book>
```

Using entities, this concept was always hindered by the fact that each document to be included may have a document type declaration, or an XML declaration, and it would not be legal for these items to be merged in to another document. External entities cannot be complete documents (although an external entity may have no XML declaration and no document type declaration, these files would not refer to a DTD, so hindering independent validation and possible editing of the content).

Fortunately, this problem is addressed and overcome in the XInclude standard. The root element and any surrounding comments and processing instructions are merged in, but the XML declaration and document type declaration are not copied:

```
<?xml version="1.0"?>
<!DOCTYPE book SYSTEM "book.dtd">
<book xmlns:xinclude="...">
<xi:include href="chap1.xml"/>
...
</book>



              <?xml version="1.0"?>
              <!DOCTYPE chapter SYSTEM "book.dtd">
              <!-- INITIAL COMMENT -->
              <chapter>
                <title>Chapter One</title>
                ...
              </chapter>
              <!-- FINAL COMMENT -->
```

Contextual base URLs

An issue arises when included material contains relative URL references, and originates from a different location to the document it is being copied into. It would appear that these references would adopt the base location of the destination document, and therefore become invalid. In order to avoid this problem, the XInclude application is expected to retain information on the original location of each merged fragment. This can be done by including XML Base attributes in the merged output file (see the previous chapter).

The XML Base standard can also be used to resolve relative URLs in the Href attribute of the Include element:

```
<book xml:base="file:///d:/book/" ... >
  ...
  <xi:include href="chapters/chapter1.xml" />
  ...
</book>
```

Namespace complications

Included elements could conform to any namespace. Unfortunately, namespaces are often declared at a higher level in the document hierarchy than the elements to be extracted, but are still needed to make sense of the element name prefix (or to identify the default namespace, if no prefix is present). Consider the following example, and the effect of copying just the embedded chapter title, which includes a bold word enclosed in the XHTML B (bold) element:

```
<book xmlns:XHTML="http://www.w3.org/1999/xhtml">
  <chapter>
    <title>A <XHTML:B>BOLD</XHTML:B> Title</title>
  </chapter>
</book>
```

This title is to be copied into the following document, which does not define the same namespace:

```
<chapterTitles xmlns:xi="...">
  <xi:include
      href=".../#xpointer(book/chapter[1]/title[1])"/>
  ...
</chapterTitles>
```

For this inclusion to work properly, the Title element needs to be given a name-space declaration. The XInclude application should do this automatically, during the process of inserting the element (or elements) to be included:

```
<chapterTitles ...>
  <title xmlns:XHTML="http://www.w3.org/1999/xhtml">A
  <XHTML:B>BOLD</XHTML:B> Title</title>
  ...
</chapterTitles>
```

Essentially, the namespace declaration is copied down into the element that is being included during the process.

Illegal inclusions

Software that supports this standard must make additional checks that the incoming data can sensibly be inserted into the document.

Inappropriate inclusions

One problem that could arise is that an XPointer expression identifies an object that cannot sensibly be included (such as an attribute). Only information that could be directly embedded within an element can be inserted, including an element or elements, a comment or processing instruction, or even just a text string.

If the root element of a document is an Include element, it can only be replaced by a single element, not a range of elements. If allowed, this would create a new document that had multiple root elements (which is not well-formed XML).

Recursive inclusions

The danger that must be avoided with recursive inclusions is the possibility of creating an infinite loop. This can occur if the included material directly contains an Include element that refers back to the original document, or to any ancestor of the original Include element in that document:

A more subtle variant of this problem occurs if there is a chain of inclusions that eventually lead back to the starting point:

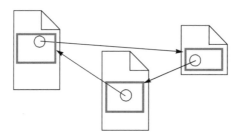

Neither of these conditions is legal, and both should generate an error.

Document modelling

As with many other adjunct standards, inclusion markup may need to be added to an existing DTD or XML Schema model.

The appropriate markup for inclusion of the Include to a DTD is as follows:

```
<!ELEMENT xi:include EMPTY>
<!ATTLIST xi:include
        xmlns:xi          CDATA          #FIXED
                          "http://www.w3.org/2001/XInclude"
        href              CDATA          #REQUIRED
        parse             (xml|text)     "xml"
        encoding          CDATA          #IMPLIED>
```

Note that the default value for the Parse attribute is 'xml', though this is not strictly necessary because a missing Parse attribute is assumed to indicate this mode in any case. This attribute need not be defined at all, if the 'text' mode is not applicable to the application of XML concerned. At the other extreme, however, this attribute could also be defaulted to 'text', if this mode is expected to be more popular than 'xml' mode, or even fixed at this value.

A roughly equivalent XML Schema instance follows (see Chapters 14 and 15):

```
<x:schema
    xmlns:x="http://www.w3.org/2001/XMLSchema"
    xmlns="http://www.w3.org/2001/XInclude"
    targetNamespace="http://www.w3.org/2001/XInclude">
  <x:element name="include">
    <x:complexType mixed="true">
      <x:attribute name="href"
                   type="x:anyURI"
                   use="required"/>
      <x:attribute name="encoding"
                   type="x:string"/>
      <x:attribute name="parse" default="xml">
```

```
      <x:simpleType>
        <x:restriction base="x:string">
          <x:enumeration value="xml"/>
          <x:enumeration value="text"/>
        </x:restriction>
      </x:simpleType>
    </x:attribute>
  </x:complexType>
</x:element>
</x:schema>
```

Note that in this case the content of the Include element is not empty (as it is in the DTD variant above). The decision on whether or not to allow the Include element to contain commentary text is left to the author of the schema or DTD model.

Alternatives to XInclude

It can be quite difficult to distinguish between the concepts of including, linking, and generally associating resources. Both the XML standard itself, and other adjunct standards, offer similar features to XInclude.

It could be observed that the XLink 'embed' feature (see Chapter 27) performs a similar role to XInclude. Indeed, this XLink feature has the additional strength that it also supports binary formats. However, XInclude is a lot simpler than XLink and actually creates a new merged document, while XLink only creates a temporary merged view (usually in a browser window).

A more realistic overlap in functionality is seen when comparing this feature with external XML entity referencing (see Chapter 4), and it could be argued that the XInclude standard is being developed as part of a wider strategy to avoid the use of entities entirely (considered by many to be an ungainly solution to this task, and to many of the other problems that they attempt to solve). XInclude takes an approach that offers a number of advantages over entities. First, it does not require separate declarations to be made; the inclusion is defined and used in a single step. This is not only easier to learn, to create and to understand, but has particular advantages when creating a document incrementally, as it is not necessary to move back to the top of the document in order to insert a declaration. Second, this is not necessarily a parsing feature, but can be used at any time.

XSLT implementation

It is possible to create an application that merges XML documents that conform to the XInclude standard using only an XSLT stylesheet (see Chapter 17). The following stylesheet would suffice, but only when complete documents are to be included, as it does not look for or even cope with a possible '#xpointer(...)' on the end of the URL:

```xml
<?xml version="1.0" encoding="ISO-8859-1"?>
<!-- XINCLUDE Merger Application -->
<!-- Main file that includes <xi:include.../> elements
     is processed -->

<stylesheet version="1.0"
            xmlns="http://www.w3.org/1999/XSL/Transform"
            xmlns:xi="http://www.w3.org/2001/xinclude" >

  <output method="xml" encoding="ISO-8859-1" />

  <template match="xi:include">
    <comment>
      MERGED "<xsl:value-of select='@href'/>" START
    </comment>
    <copy-of select="document(@href)" />
    <comment>
      MERGED "<xsl:value-of select='@href'/>" END
    </comment>
  </template>

  <template match="node() | @*">
    <copy><apply-templates select="@* | node()" /></copy>
  </template>

</stylesheet>
```

13. Navigation (XPath)

The ability to navigate through XML documents is vital to many applications of XML, including the querying of XML documents to find and retrieve required material, the creation of hypertext links to objects that do not have unique identifiers, the merging of documents and document fragments, and the formatting of document components for presentation. The XPath standard has been incorporated into several XML-related standards, including XPointer, XSLT, XML Schema, and indirectly by the XInclude standard. Readers intending to cover one or more of these topics are advised to read this chapter first. Standard-specific extensions are explained in the relevant chapters. Chapter 35 provides a series of maps that explore the XPath standard in fine detail, but these maps are best explored after reading this chapter.

Background

The meaning of an element can depend on its contextual location. For example, a Title element that is embedded within a Book element has a different meaning to one that is embedded within a Name element. The format will certainly differ, and a query that is used to extract a list of book titles should not include entries such as 'Mr', 'Dr' and 'Miss'.

Unique context

Every element in an XML document has a specific and unique contextual location. The hierarchical and sequential structures in an XML document can be used as stepping-stones, and any element in the document can be identified by the steps it would take to reach it, either from the root element, or from some other fixed starting location.

For example, the last name of the author of a book may be held in a specific instance of a Name element. It could be obtained by stepping through the 'book', 'front', 'author', 'name' and 'last' elements. This would select the name 'Smith', but not the name 'Jones':

```
<book>
  <front>
    <author>
      <name>
        <first>John</first>
        <last>Smith</last>
  </name></author></front>
  ...                             <!-- NOT SELECTED -->
  <chapter><name><init>F</init><last>Jones</last></name>
```

Common requirements

A number of XML-related standards discussed in later chapters need to 'tunnel in' to XML documents in order to target specific elements, attributes, other markup constructs, or even text fragments. The proposed XQuery standard (see http://www.w3.org/TR/xquery/) may be used to locate and extract information of interest, and needs a mechanism for specifying the queries to do this. The proposed XPointer standard (see Chapter 28) will be used to create hypertext links to objects that do not have unique identifiers, and requires a mechanism for identifying each target object by its location. Similarly, the XSLT standard (see Chapter 17) needs to match formatting templates to appropriate elements in the source document in order to transform or style the content:

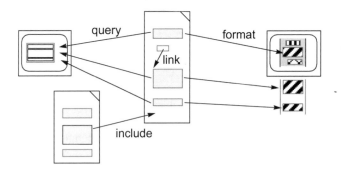

XPath

XPath has been developed to support all of the needs described above, and more (it also plays a role in XML Schema). One advantage of such a common approach is that skills learned from adoption of one of these standards remain relevant when working with another. The XPath standard can be obtained from www.w3.org/TR/XPath, was released in November 1999, and is illustrated in Chapter 35.

Using XPath expressions, it is possible to select the first paragraph in each chapter of a book, in order to give it a different style to all other paragraphs (using XSLT), to create a hypertext link to the paragraph that is separated from the current paragraph by five intermediate objects (using XPointer), and to retrieve a list of all author names that appear in the bibliography section of a textbook (using XQuery).

XPath can also be used as a validation language, taking a very different and potentially far more powerful approach to validating document structures than DTDs and XML Schemas do. The Schematron proposal adopts this approach (and is briefly discussed in Chapter 14).

Limitation of IDs

It could be argued that navigation techniques are not needed when elements contain unique identifiers. Indeed, when a specific element needs to be extracted using a query, or made the target of a link, or styled in a specific way, then the presence of a unique identifier is invaluable. Referring to a unique identifier is the most direct, efficient, and sometimes only way to locate such an element. However, limitations of this technique include the effort required to create identifiers, the restricted places where they can be used, and the need to discover and remember the identifier (these issues are explored further in the final section of this chapter).

Expressions

The XPath standard defines the syntax of a text string, called an '**expression**', that consists of instructions for selecting objects, such as elements, within an XML document. The following simple expression selects a Title element that is the child of a Book element:

```
book/title
```

```
<book>
  <title>...</title>
  ...
</book>
```

Expressions may also be used to select attributes, comments, processing instructions and the text content of an element. The term **node** is used to represent every item of significance in an XML document, including elements. The reserved function '**node()**' represents any such item. The reserved node-test functions '**text()**', '**processing-instruction()**' and '**comment()**' represent any object of these specific types. Note that it is not possible to select a range of text within a text node, but that the XPointer standard (see Chapter 28) has extensions that permit this.

Environments and syntax

How expressions are used depends on the technology in question, and on the application of that technology. Typically, however, an expression may appear in an attribute value, or be appended to a URL reference:

```
http://MyCorp.org/getQuery#xpointer(/book/front/title)
```

```
<xsl:template match="chapter/title">
   . . .
</xsl:template>
```

The characters allowed in an expression are constrained by the various environments in which they may be used (of which the most limiting of these is the constraints of the URL standard). Perhaps the most significant restriction is that line-feed characters are not allowed; the expression must be a single line string.

This standard also takes account of widespread knowledge of techniques used in command-line operating systems (such as UNIX and MS-DOS) for navigating through file-system directories (the 'folders' in a graphical user interface). Symbols such as '/' ('\' on MS-DOS systems and ':' on the Macintosh), '..', '.' and '*' have significant and relevant meanings to users of these systems. For identical historical reasons, '/' and '..' conveniently have the same purpose in XPath as they have in URLs (see Chapter 30 for more on URL syntax).

Types of expression

Expressions are used in different ways for different purposes. Some expressions are **location paths**, used to identify and extract, link to or re-use targeted information in the document. Some location paths can take the role of a **pattern**, and be used simply to confirm or deny that an element of interest is in a specified location in the document (the XSLT standard (see Chapter 17) makes use of this concept). The following sections discuss these concepts in more detail.

Single and multiple selections

Most XPath expressions select multiple elements in a document. Depending on the characteristics of the application the expression is being used within, the expression 'para' may select every paragraph in the document, or every paragraph that is the child of a currently selected element. However, it is possible to create expressions that are guaranteed to only select a specific element instance, or simply to establish whether this instance actually exists in the document or not.

Simple location paths

Expressions often identify items by their location in the document structure. A 'path' is a series of steps to a target location. A **location path** may burrow down into the structure, skip over siblings, or work back up the structure.

Relative paths

A **relative path** is one that starts from an existing location in the document structure. The element that is ultimately targeted depends entirely upon where the starting point is. The same relative expression selects different elements when applied from different context locations:

The simplest form of relative path is a reference to an element name. In the following case, the reference is to any Paragraph element that happens to be a child element of the currently selected element:

```
para
```

This is in fact the simplest possible form of a 'node test'. In this case, a test for the presence of an element node with the name 'para' is made. This is also an abbreviation of the expression 'child::para', which makes the meaning more explicit.

To re-emphasize the point, this expression does not select children of a paragraph, but children of the *current* element that have the name 'para'. The current element may, perhaps, be a Chapter element:

```
<chapter>
  <title>A TITLE</title>
  <para>First paragraph.</para>
  <para>Second paragraph.</para>
  ...
</chapter>
```

Some applications that could use XPath may have no concept of a current element. For example, an expression may be a query that searches the entire document. On these occasions, a relative path will never be appropriate.

Some other applications may process a document from start to finish, selecting each element in turn, so that all elements eventually take their turn to become the current element. In this scenario, the expression shown above would apply to all paragraphs in the document, as they would all be children of elements selected during the process.

An objection may be raised to the suggestion made above that all elements are the children of other elements. The root element has no parent, so a Book element should not be selected by the expression 'book'. But even the root element has a parent *node*. This node represents the entire document, including any markup, such as comments and processing instructions, that may surround the root element.

Multiple steps

When an expression includes a number of steps, these steps are separated from each other using the '/' symbol. The steps in the expression are read from left to right, and each step in the path creates a new context for remaining parts of the path. The following example includes two steps. First, the Book element is selected and made the current context, then each Title element directly within the Book element is selected:

```
book/title
```

Both steps in this expression refer to child elements. However, it is important to emphasize that the '/' symbol itself does not denote a parent/child relationship. It merely serves to separate the steps, and is also used in many other circumstances. This distinction is much more obvious when the more verbose form of expression is used:

```
child::book/child::title
```

Wildcard steps

Sometimes, the names of elements between the context element and the required descendant may not be known, but this does not need to be an obstacle. The '*' symbol can be used as a 'wildcard', standing in for any element name (like the joker in some card games).

This technique can be used to select elements in a number of different contexts simultaneously. For example, it may be necessary to select all chapter titles, and also the title of an introduction. The first example below is equivalent to both of the following, more explicit expressions:

```
book/*/title
```

```
book/intro/title
book/chapter/title
```

But this approach can be dangerous. The example above may inadvertently also select titles in other structures, such as an Appendix element that follows the Chapter elements. Used with care, though, it is a powerful technique. The unabbreviated version simply adds the asterisk symbol to 'child::':

```
child::*
```

Although multiple asterisks can be used to indicate unknown elements at several levels in the expression, it is necessary to know in advance exactly how many levels deep the required elements will be. This approach clearly does not work when the elements to be selected lie at different levels within the document structure. Instead, a more powerful feature allows selection of all descendants. In the abbreviated syntax, two slashes are used to indicate this intent, '//' In the following example, paragraphs that occur anywhere within a chapter are selected:

```
chapter//para
```

```
<chapter>
  <para>...</para>
  <note><para>...</para></note>
  <para>...</para>
</chapter>
```

It is also possible to use this technique at the beginning of an expression. However, for reasons that will become clear later, using '//' at the beginning would not produce the desired effect. Instead, it is first necessary to explicitly declare that the starting point is the current element. This is done using a full-point '.' The following example selects all paragraphs within the current element:

```
.//para
```

Parents and grandparents

The parent of the context element is represented by two full-point symbols '..'. This mechanism is typically used to help select siblings of the current element. The following example selects a Title element that shares the same parent as the context element (the Para element):

```
../title
```

```
    <ch>
      <title>...</title>
".."   ...
      </para>...</para>
    </ch>
```

To move up to the grandparent element, the '..' notation is simply repeated as a further step. The following expressions select the title of a chapter, when the current element is embedded within a section of the chapter:

```
../../title
```

```
        <ch>
          <title>...</title>
 "..."
          ...

          <section>
 "..."
            <para>...</para>

          </section>
        </ch>
```

This technique for accessing ancestors of the context element can be clumsy when many intermediate levels exist, and does not work at all when the number of levels to be traversed varies. A more advanced technique for accessing ancestors is described later.

Absolute paths

In some circumstances a relative path is not suitable. For example, it may be necessary to select the title of the book, irrespective of the current context. The location relative to the document as a whole may be known, whereas the offset from the current location (if there *is* a current location) may not. In this case, an **absolute path** is more appropriate. This is a path that begins at a fixed 'landmark'. Essentially, an absolute path is the same as a relative path, except for the first step, which identifies such a landmark.

One kind of absolute path begins with a '/' symbol, indicating that the landmark is the root of the document:

```
/book/title
```

Note that by placing '//' at the beginning of an expression, it is possible to select all occurrences of a specific element type within the document (and is necessary if the expression is not being employed by an application that traverses the document structure, applying the expression to each element it finds):

```
//para
```

The other kind of absolute path is one that begins from a specific 'anchor point' in the document. An element that has a unique identifier can be targeted using the '**id()**' function:

```
id("para33")/...
```

Note that, for this to work, the identifier attribute must be declared in a DTD (or other modelling language) to be an identifier attribute.

Complex location paths

Apart from the selection of children, it has already been shown that parents and further ancestors of the current element can also be selected. But there are many other options available, and each can be thought of as a direction, or an '**axis**'. A particular axis is indicated using an '**axis specifier**'. One axis specifier has already been seen; the 'child::' axis specifier selects the child axis.

Close family

Parents, children and siblings can be selected using the '**parent::**', '**child::**', '**preceding-sibling::**' and '**following-sibling::**' axis specifiers:

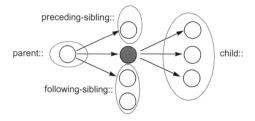

The '**parent::**' prefix, along with the 'node()' function, is equivalent to '..':

```
../title
```
```
parent::node()/child::title
```

The reason for needing 'node()' here, instead of just '*', is to cater for the parent of the root element, which is not an element, but a node that represents the entire document.

Note that sibling elements are divided into those that appear before the context element, and those that appear after:

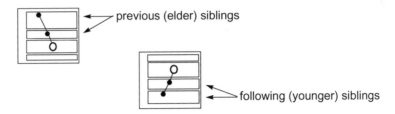

previous (elder) siblings

following (younger) siblings

The counting order is important. Previous siblings are counted backwards from the context element. In the following example, the paragraph closest to the current paragraph is selected:

```
preceding-sibling::para[1]
```

```
<para>Target paragraph.</para>
<note>A note</note>
<para>Source paragraph.</para>
```
> 1

Note: The meaning of the square brackets is explained later.

Following siblings are counted up from the context element. In the following example, the next Para element is selected:

```
following-sibling::para[1]
```

```
<para>Source paragraph.</para>
<note>A note</note>
<para>Target paragraph.</para>
```
> 1

Ancestors and descendants

Ancestors and descendants can be searched for matching criteria using the **'ancestor::'** and **'descendant::'** axis keywords:

more than one
parents

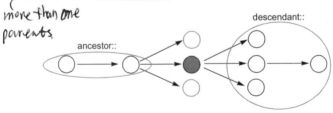

ancestor::

descendant::

Note that descendants include children, not just lower levels in the hierarchy. Elements are also counted in 'breadth' order, meaning that, at each level, all sub-elements of one element are counted before going on to the next sibling of that element:

This can be seen as stepping through the elements in document order, as they would be encountered by a parser.

Ancestors are counted backwards up the hierarchy. Siblings of each ancestor element are ignored:

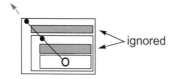

There is no abbreviated format for descendant and ancestor axis navigation. To select the title of the chapter containing the current element, the following verbose expression is required:

```
ancestor::chapter/title
```

Ancestors and descendants including current object

The current context node can be included in ancestor and descendant searching. The search works as described above, except that in both of these cases the context element itself is the first node in each list:

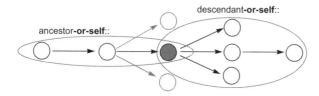

The **ancestor-or-self::** axis is the same as the ancestor:: axis, except that the first ancestor is the current object.

The '**descendant-or-self::**' axis is used to select all descendant nodes, including the original context node itself. It is therefore equivalent to '//', as the following examples demonstrate:

```
chapter//para
```

```
child::chapter/descendant-or-self::node()/child::para
```

Note the presence of the 'node()' function in the second step above. It is necessary to specify any constraints on what class of node is acceptable, and here there is no desire to rule out anything. As already stated, the 'node()' function is even less discriminatory than '*', particularly because it includes the document root node (which is not an element node).

Remaining axis specifiers

Finally, there are some axis specifiers that select the current object, its attributes, all preceding and all following objects:

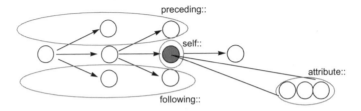

Self axis

The current context node itself can be selected using '**self::**'. As the current object may be an element, or the node representing the entire document, the node test should again be 'node()'. This is equivalent to the '.' operator. It can now be seen that the verbose equivalent of the following expression is in fact *very* verbose:

```
.//para
```

```
self::node()/descendant-or-self::node()/child::para
```

First, the 'self::node()' step is used to identify the current element (or root node) as the starting point. Second, the 'descendant-or-self::' step is used to indicate that all descendants, and the current node itself, are to be selected (and again, the node() function is used just in case the current node at any point is not an element). Third, the 'child::' step is used to indicate which children of these objects are to be selected:

Attribute axis

The attributes of the context node can be selected using '**attribute::**'. This is equivalent to '@'.

Preceding and following axis

The **preceding::** axis takes a flattened view of the document, and provides access to all elements that occur, and are completed, before the context element begins (thus eliminating ancestors of the context element):

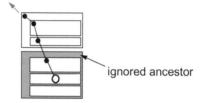

ignored ancestor

The **following::** axis provides the same service for the remainder of the document, only counting elements that begin after the current element ends, so ignoring all ancestors and descendants of that element:

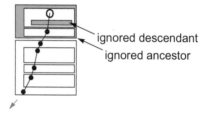

ignored descendant
ignored ancestor

Patterns

A **pattern** is a form of expression that is used to establish if an object of interest matches some given criteria (rather than to locate and select the object). Location paths, of a certain limited kind, are used in patterns to decide if the currently selected element occurs in a specific context. Instead of the expression 'chapter/ para' being interpreted as a request to find paragraphs in chapters, it is interpreted as a question about the identity and location of a particular element instance. Is the current element a Paragraph element, and is it also the child of a Chapter element? The answer can only be yes or no ('true' or 'false').

XSLT makes significant use of XPath patterns (indeed, the formal definition of a pattern can be found in the XSLT standard, not the XPath standard). For example, paragraphs tend to be styled in different ways in a book, depending on where they appear. A paragraph in the introduction may be styled differently to one in a chapter, and a paragraph anywhere within a warning section may need to be highlighted. These circumstances can be expressed as 'book/intro/para', 'chapter/para' and 'warning//para'.

Because there is no concept of a source location in patterns, the symbols '.' and '..' are meaningless, as are many of the axis types, such as 'ancestor-or-self::'.

The '/' and '//' instructions are permitted, including an initial '/' or 'id(x)'. But when used in patterns they simply add a final constraint on the contextual location of the subject element. If the Book element can only occur at the root of the document, there is no practical difference between 'book/intro' and '/book/intro'. The concept of relative and absolute paths simply does not arise.

The 'I' symbol may be used to specify multiple patterns. For example, 'note|warning|caution|/book/intro' matches all Note, Warning and Caution elements, as well as an Intro element that is a child of the Book element.

Predicate filters

Location paths are quite indiscriminate. For example, the path 'book/chapter/para' selects all of the paragraphs in all of the chapters. But there is often a need to target a more selective set of elements, and possibly a single element instance.

A **predicate filter** is used to qualify any step in the path. The list of matches at each step is reduced by asking questions about the nodes in this list. Square brackets, '[' and ']', are used to hold the predicate:

```
para[....]
```

The predicate filter holds one or more test expressions. The results of the test (or tests) is a single boolean value, and the selection only succeeds when the value is true.

Position tests

The '**position()**' function returns the sequential location of the element being tested. This value can be compared to a desired location. The following example selects only the first paragraph:

```
para[position() = 1]
```

This form of query can be abbreviated to just a number. The following test is equivalent to the one above:

```
para[1]
```

This number does not refer to the position of the element among all sibling elements, but only among those elements already selected by the pattern (the current 'context list'). In this case, as only Paragraph elements are selected, the position refers to the first Para element in the list. To select a Paragraph element when it is the first *child* of its parent, a more complex expression is required. The following example illustrates this, and shows that it is necessary to first select all the sibling elements, using '*', then check both the position and the name of each element. In this case, the element is only selected if it is the first in the list, and is also a Paragraph element (see below for the purpose of the 'and' expression):

```
*[position() = 1 and self::para]
```

Locating the last sibling, when the number of elements in the list is unknown, can be achieved using the '**last()**' function. The following pattern applies to the last paragraph (not to the last sibling, if it just happens to be a paragraph):

```
para[last()]
```

The '**count()**' function has the same purpose, but requires a parameter to specify the node list to count. Using this function, it is possible to discover how many occurrences of a particular element there are in a document. The following example selects notes that contain a single paragraph:

```
child::note[count(child::para) = 1]
```

An element may have an identifier, and this unique value can be used to select the element. The '**id()**' function is used for this purpose:

```
chapter[id("summary")]
```

The '**name()**' function returns the name, as a string, of the node specified as a parameter. When the parameter is '.', it returns the name of the current node.

Contained element tests

The name of an element can appear in a predicate filter, and as normal represents an element that must be present as a child. In the following example, a Note element is only selected if it directly contains a Title element, and makes no distinction between one and many titles present:

```
note[title]
```

The content of an element can also be compared to a fixed string value:

```
note[title="first note"]
```

```
<note>
  <title>first note</title>
  ...
</note>
```

Attribute tests

Attributes can be tested. An attribute name is distinguished from an element name using a prefix '@' symbol. The following example selects every paragraph with a Type attribute value of 'secret':

```
para[@type='secret']
```

The verbose equivalent of '@' uses the '**attribute::**' axis:

```
para[attribute::type='secret']
```

Boolean tests

Many expressions, including those described above, are either valid or invalid in a given circumstance. A boolean test is performed, with a result of 'true' or 'false'. The tests shown above are only successful if the expression returns a 'true' value. The '**not()**' function can be used to reverse the result, and so greatly extends the number of tests that can be made. For example, all notes except for the third one, a note that does not contain a Title element, and all chapters except for one with a specified identifier, can be selected in this way:

```
note[not(position() = 3)]

note[not(title)]

chapter[not(id("summary"))]
```

The '**boolean()**' function evaluates an embedded expression and returns a boolean value. All valid numbers except zero are considered to be true, and a node list that contains at least one entry is also true. A text string is true if it contains at least one character. All the following tests return 'true' (assuming, in the last case, that there is at least one Title element):

```
boolean(3)

boolean("some text")

boolean(title)
```

It follows that the following expression returns false:

```
not(boolean(3))
```

Comparisons also return a boolean result. The most obvious comparison is for equality, using the equals symbol, '='. Examples of such comparisons appeared above. In the following example, when the position of the current Note element matches the value '3', then a 'true' value is returned:

```
note[position() = 3]
```

The example above compares two numbers for equality, but it is also possible to compare boolean expressions and strings:

```
note[title = "first note"]
```

Testing for non-equality is possible using '!='. For example, to select all but the last note:

```
note[position() != last()]
```

Other comparisons can be made that require the expressions to be interpreted as numbers. These are tests for the first expression being greater than the second, using '>', and the other way around, using '<'. By combining symbols, it is also possible to test whether the first expression is greater than or equal to the second one ('>='), or less than or equal to it ('<='). The two examples below are equivalent, as they both filter out the first two Note elements:

```
note[position() > 2]
```

```
note[position() >= 3]
```

Note that the '<' and '>' symbols are significant in XML. When inserting expressions into an attribute, it is necessary to remember to use '<' and '>' to represent these characters (except when using an XML-sensitive editor, which performs this translation on behalf of the author):

```
note[position() &gt; 2]
```

An expression can be divided into separate sub-expressions, and the whole expression can be considered to be true only if all the sub-expressions individually evaluate to true, using an 'and' expression. In the following example, a Note element is selected only if it is preceded by at least two others, and followed by at least one more:

```
note[position() > 2 and position() < last()]
```

Alternatively, the whole expression may succeed when at least one of the sub-expressions is true, using an 'or' expression. In the following example, both the second and fourth Note elements are selected:

```
note[position() = 2 or position() = 4]
```

Finally, the '**true()**' and '**false()**' functions simply return a value of true or false respectively.

Strings

String objects can be analysed to discover if they contain specific characters or sub-strings. The '**contains()**' function returns 'true' if the string contains the given text. The first parameter is the string to test. The second parameter is the string to find in the first string. In the following example, each Note element is tested to see if it contains the word 'note':

```
note[contains(text(), "note")]
```

```
<note>This is a note.</note>
```

Note that, in this example, the string to test is the child node of the Note element, which of course needs to be a text node, as represented by 'text()' in the first parameter. But only the first node is tested. The test will fail if the word is actually in a sub-element, or in another text node that follows a sub-element. The safer way to use this function is to refer to the Note element itself, using '.' (the current node). Although the Note element node does not contain the string, its children may do, and these are analysed too:

```
note[contains(., "note")]
```

```
<note>This is a <emph>note</emph>.</note>
```

If the specified text needs to appear at the start of the string, the function '**starts-with()**' should be used instead:

```
note[starts-with(., "Note")]
```

```
<note>Note to myself</note>
```

The '**string()**' function converts an embedded expression into a string. For example, the following test selects Note elements that contain the character '2':

```
note[starts-with(., string(2))]
```

```
<note>This is note number 2</note>
```

When converting a number into a string, an invalid number is converted to the string 'NaN' (Not-a-Number), and an infinite value is converted to the string 'Infinity' (negative infinity becomes '-Infinity' and negative zero just becomes '0').

The '**translate()**' function converts characters according to a mapping scheme. The first parameter is the string to convert. The second parameter lists the characters to modify in the source text. The third parameter lists the replacement values. One use for this function is to allow case-insensitive text comparisons, as in the following example, which matches both of the Note elements below:

```
note[starts-with(
        translate(.,
          "abcdefghijklmnopqrstuvwxyz",
          "ABCDEFGHIJKLMNOPQRSTUVWXYZ"),
            "HELLO THERE")]
```

```
<note>Note to myself</note>

<note>NOTE:  ...</note>
```

Additional characters in the second parameter represent characters that are to be removed from the source string. To convert semicolons to commas, while also removing all existing plus symbols from a string, the following would be used:

```
translate(., ";+", ",")
```

A leading or trailing fragment of a string can be extracted, providing that the fragment ends or begins with a given character or sequence of characters. The '**substring-before()**' function takes two parameters: the string to extract text from, then the character or characters that terminate the prefix to be extracted. The '**substring-after()**' function works in the same way, but extracts text from the end of the string. The following example retrieves just the year from a date:

```
substring-after( ., "/" )
```

```
<date>12/08/1999</date>
```

To extract any fragment of a string, the '**substring()**' function takes three parameters: the source string, the character offset position and the number of characters to extract:

```
note[substring(., 9, 5) = "XPath"]
```

```
<note>This is XPath</note>

<note>This XPath is not a match</note>
```

When using namespaces (see Chapter 10), element names are separated into two parts: a local part, such as 'h1', and a namespace prefix part, such as 'html', giving a complete name of 'html:h1'. The prefix is mapped to a URL, such as 'http://www.w3.org/Profiles/xhtml1-strict'. The '**namespace-uri()**' function returns the URL of the first node in the list that forms its parameter. The '**local-name()**' function returns the local part of the name:

```
*[namespace-uri(.) =
            "http://www.w3.org/Profiles/xhtml1-strict"]
```

```
<html:h1>An HTML Header One</html:h1>
<html:p>An HTML paragraph.</html:p>
```

```
*[local-name(.) = "score"]
```

```
<music:score>Ferde Grofé</music:score>
<competition:score>57</competition:score>
```

The '**normalize()**' function removes leading and trailing spaces, and reduces a sequence of whitespace characters down to a single space character: The following Note element matches, despite the leading and additional embedded spaces:

```
note[starts-with(normalize(.), "Hello there")]
```

```
<note>   Hello    there</note>
```

A number of strings can be concatenated into a single string, using the '**concat()**' function, which takes one or more string parameters:

```
concat("Original string.", " Append this", " and this.")
```

This can be used with substrings to create fixed-length strings. For example, to ensure that a string is exactly ten characters in length, by padding with spaces if necessary:

```
substring(concat(node(), "                "), 1, 10)
```

Finally, the number of characters in a string can be determined using the '**string-length()**' function:

```
note[string-length(.) = 15]
```

```
<note>fifteen letters</note>
<note>123456789012345</note>
```

Numbers

Objects can be converted to numbers, using the '**number()**' function. Boolean expressions are interpreted as '1' for 'true' and '0' for 'false'. Strings that cannot be interpreted as a valid number are translated to a special default value called 'Not-a-Number' (or 'NaN' for short).

Real numbers can be converted to integers. Using the '**round()**' function, the real number is rounded up or down to the nearest integer equivalent. Using the '**floor()**' function, the number is rounded down to the nearest integer, so '3.9' becomes '3', and using the '**ceiling()**' function, the number is rounded up, so '3.1' becomes '4'.

The '+' and '-' operators may be used, as well as '*' for multiplication, and the following four examples are all equivalent:

```
note[ 4 ]
note[ 2 + 2 ]
note[ 4 - 2 ]
note[ 2 * 2 ]
```

The '**mod**' operator supplies the remainder of a truncated division. For example, '9 mod 4' returns '1' (there is a remainder of one after dividing nine by four). This feature is useful for selecting alternate items, such as even numbered paragraphs:

```
para[ position() mod 2 = 0 ]
```

The '**div**' operator returns the divisor. For example, '9 div 4' returns '2', because four goes into nine twice.

Precedence

The operators introduced above ('*', 'mod', 'div', '+', '-', '=', '!=', '<', '>', '<=', '>=', 'and' and 'or') are *not* processed in a simple left-to-right manner. Some have higher precendence than others.

Starting with the highest, the precedence levels are:

- '*' and 'div' and 'mod'
- '+' and '-'
- '<', '>', '<=' and '>='
- '=' and '!='
- 'and'
- 'or'

The lower the precedence, the more significant an operator is. Because 'or' is processed last, it is very significant: everything to the left of the 'or' operator is calculated, then everything to the right of it, and finally the two halves are both checked, and the whole expression succeeds if either sub-expression is true.

Similarly, the '+' and '-' operators are always dealt with before '='. For example, the expression '4-1 = 5-2' returns true, because '3 = 3'.

Multiple filters

Multiple predicate filters are used when both an abbreviated position and another type of test need to be combined, because they must not appear together. The following example first selects company names, then extracts the third name in this list:

```
child::name[company][3]
```

```
<names>
  <name><person>...</person></name>
  <name><person>...</person></name>

  <name><company>...</company></name>
  <name><company>...</company></name>

  <name><person>...</person></name>

  <name><company>...</company></name>

  <name><person>...</person></name>
</names>
```

The order in which these two tests are carried out is very important. Only elements that successfully pass the first test are subjected to the second. Reversing the order of the tests in the example above therefore produces a very different result. This time, the third name is selected, providing that it is also a company name:

```
child::name[3][company]
```

```
<names>
  <name><person>...</person></name>
  <name><company>...</company></name>
  <name><company>...</company></name>
  <name><person>...</person></name>
</names>

<names>
  <name><person>...</person></name>
  <name><company>...</company></name>
  <name><person>...</person></name> <!-- NOT SELECTED -->
</names>
```

Multiple predicate filters are also useful in other circumstances, although in many cases a single filter can be used that includes the 'and' token instead. The second example above can be reformulated as follows:

```
child::*[position() = 3 and self::company]
```

ID limitations

Earlier, it was suggested that the justification for a standard like XPath is to avoid the need to create unique identifiers for all elements and other markup constructs that might be the target of a link. Of course, if such identifiers already exist, and are known, they should be used. Identifiers are the safest and most direct way to locate an object. In addition, they can be relied upon if new material is added to change the context location. But there are limitations to this technique. First, assigning unique identifiers to every element in a document can be an arduous task. Second, identifiers cannot be used to isolate individual comments, processing instructions or ranges of text. Third, the identifier of a required element may not be easily made known to those who wish to refer to that element. Finally, it would not be convenient to identify many similar objects by listing all of their identifiers. These objections are discussed in more detail below.

Required effort

A large XML document may contain thousands of elements. It would be very difficult to invent meaningful identifiers for them all. This can be illustrated by considering the paragraphs in this section. It is not obvious what meaningful identifiers they could be given. The obvious solution would be to give them simple identifiers, such as 'P1', 'P2' and 'P3'. There may be good reasons to do this, but not just, for example, to return a list representing the first paragraph within each chapter.

Of course, such identifiers are very useful when a specific paragraph is the target of a hypertext link, and the link must be retained even if the paragraph is moved (this topic is covered further in Chapter 7).

Limited scope

A hypertext link may need to refer to only a short range of text in a large paragraph. The XML standard includes no mechanism for assigning an identifier to such a range. It would always be necessary to enclose the text in an element.

Knowledge of identifier

There is little point in an identifier if it is not known by those wishing to refer to it. If a list of all the document authors needed to be retrieved from a document just received from elsewhere, it would be necessary to open the document and note the identifiers in order to reference them.

Necessity for identifiers

All the paragraphs in this section are styled in the same way. It should not be necessary to list their identifiers in order to apply the same style to them all (using XSLT):

```
para[@id='P1']  |  para[@id='P2']  |  para[@id='P3']  |  ...
```

14. Schemas

A number of new, more powerful alternatives to the XML DTD have recently emerged. Most notably, this includes the XML Schema standard, which is introduced and compared with DTDs in this chapter, and further explored in the next. The XML Schema standard relies heavily upon namespaces (see Chapter 10), and one feature also relies upon the XPath standard (see Chapter 13).

DTD limitations

XML inherited its modelling capabilities (its DTD-building instructions) directly from SGML, its older, bigger brother (see Chapter 32). This was done in order to ensure that both relevant expertise, and existing SGML-based tools, could be utilized to give the new standard an initial impetus. But even before XML was completed and released, considerable opposition to the decision to adopt SGML DTDs was raised. There were several reasons for this resistance, but criticism tended to focus on the general lack of modelling functionality in the DTD language, as well as its specific lack of support for data exchange applications, its lack of namespace sensitivity (though this is understandable, given that the Namespaces standard was finalized and released later), and its unique and complex language syntax.

Limited functionality

XML DTDs are quite modest in their capabilities. Indeed, XML DTDs are simpler than the SGML DTDs they are derived from. This decision was made to encourage the development of simple-to-build supporting tools, and the development of many such tools across a wide spread of computer platforms (a strategy that clearly worked).

However, although there is now increasing demand for more flexible document and data modelling capabilities, there has been pressure to reintroduce only a few of the SGML features that were omitted. Many other features are now redundant, or were never widely used in the first place (though most long-serving document architects regret losing at least one favoured feature or other).

Namespace insensitivity

Although XML documents that use namespaces can be validated with a DTD, there are some severe limitations. The DTD must be aware of all possible combinations of elements and attributes from all the namespaces concerned, and must pre-define the prefixes to be used.

Data exchange applications

The SGML standard was developed to support the creation and publication of documents, rather than the interchange of rich data structures. Even the more sophisticated SGML DTD modelling language has almost non-existent support for data-typing. It cannot, for example, specify that an attribute value must be a date, or even dictate that the value must consist of a specific number of characters.

DTD syntax

Another weakness of DTDs is that they have their own syntax. This is unnecessary, because the models that DTDs create could just as easily be built using normal XML document markup. There would be at least three benefits to using XML document syntax for document modelling. First, a DTD could be parsed using a normal XML parser. Second, a DTD in this form could be edited using an XML document editor (with authoring assistance driven by a DTD-for-DTDs); or, when using a standard text editor instead, it would at least not be necessary to learn a different language syntax. Third, a DTD could be easily formatted for viewing with an XML browser.

While it would be very easy to re-formulate XML (or SGML) DTD models using XML document syntax, this has not been done, primarily because all efforts in this area have focused on also improving modelling functionality. A DTD that has a different syntax, and different capabilities, is no longer a DTD; it is an entirely new modelling language (and the following section discusses some of these new languages).

Alternative modelling languages

A number of alternatives to the DTD have arisen since the release of the XML standard. They differ in capability and scope, but on two things they all agree: name and syntax.

'Schema' languages

The term **schema** is used to describe all of the alternative modelling languages. In the IT field, this name has its roots in database technologies. It is used to describe the tables and fields in a database, including constraints on the values of particular fields, and the relationships between tables (to those familiar with these concepts, the similarity to document modelling should be obvious). More generally, the term simply means a representation of something using a diagram, a plan or an outline.

Note that the plural of the word 'schema' is often given as 'schemas', but 'schemata' can be used as well.

XML syntax

In every case, these languages adopt standard XML document syntax. This approach has a number of benefits, as outlined above. The only disadvantages of this approach are that the syntax is quite verbose (hindering legibility, and slowing down data transfer), and that, due to the rather obvious choice of element and attribute names, explanatory texts (including this chapter) cannot easily avoid such clumsy phrases as 'the Element element defines an element'.

Multiple languages

A single, universally supported standard is generally considered to be desirable. Yet, in recent times, the following proposals have all been in contention:

- RELAX
- TREX
- RELAX NG
- Schematron
- XML Schema.

For the moment, the DTD modelling language remains dominant, simply because it has a significant head-start on the competition. At the time of writing, it is the only universally supported language. But almost all of the alternatives are superior, and it is widely expected that DTDs will eventually fade into obscurity. There will no doubt be a shake-out of these proposals (and this is already happening, as the third language listed above is a consolidation of the previous two); though whether there will be a single survivor, rather than a small number with different strengths, is too early to say. While it is possible that more than one will succeed, the only one that is almost guaranteed to do so is XML Schema, if only because it is backed both by the W3C and the major software vendors. But, while the XML Schema standard deserves particular attention, the others cannot be ignored.

RELAX

RELAX was initially developed by INSTAC (*Information Technology Research and Standardization Center*), and a small number of volunteers contributed to its design. The Core standard has been approved as an ISO Technical Report (ISO TR 22250-1). RELAX has been described by its originators as 'a specification for describing XML-based languages'. RELAX grammars use XML document syntax, and have adopted the data types developed for XML Schema (see Chapter 15). This proposed standard aimed to provide eighty percent of the functionality of the XML Schema standard, for only twenty percent of the complexity, and many have agreed that early drafts of this language met this objective.

Based on the theory of tree automata, RELAX has a modular design, is namespace-aware, and has a number of powerful features. For example, grammars can be compared for upward compatibility, by computing the difference between versions, and the functionality of SGML exclusions and inclusions can be supported (see Chapter 32), without the processing complexity.

However, work on RELAX has now ceased (for the reasons given below).

TREX

The **TREX** (*Tree Regular Expressions for XML*) proposal was developed by James Clark (see jclark.com). The following example shows how this standard uses XML document syntax, and an intuitive structure for modelling XML document structures:

```
<element name="book">
  <optional>
    <element name="intro">
      <element name="title"><anyString/></element>
      <element name="author"><anyString/></element>
    </element>
  </optional>
  <zeroOrMore>
    <element name="chapter">
      <element name="title"><anyString/></element>
    </element>
  </zeroOrMore>
</element>
```

```
<!-- DTD EQUIVALENT:
<!ELEMENT book      (intro?, chapter*)>
<!ELEMENT intro     (title, author)>
<!ELEMENT title     (#PCDATA)>
<!ELEMENT autor     (#PCDATA)>
<!ELEMENT chapter   (title, ...)>
```

However, work on TREX has now ceased (for the reasons given next).

RELAX and TREX combined

Because RELAX Core and TREX are very similar, they are going to be unified by OASIS (see www.oasis-open.org/committees/relax-ng). The unified language is to be called **RELAX NG** (*Relax Next Generation*), which is pronounced 'relaxing', and there are plans to submit the same proposal to the ISO. See relaxng.org for details.

Schematron

Schematron (now at version 1.5) is described as a 'simple XML-based assertion language using patterns in trees'. It can be used for validation, for automated link generation, and for triggering actions based on very complex criteria.

The Schematron language is not grammar-based, like the other languages covered here. Instead, it is 'rule-based', allowing validation to include the kind of checks that grammars cannot achieve, such as ensuring that a particular element is present when another element has a particular attribute value. This language uses the XPath expression language (see Chapter 13) to interrogate a document. It uses expressions to discover whether or not a pattern can be matched in the document. Any 'false' return values means that the document is invalid.

Recent changes have added a way of grouping patterns together to allow dynamic validation (different rules and assertions are tested according to the phase), and 'abstract rules', which permit more convenient declarations and type extensions. See www.ascc.net/xml/resource/schematron for the latest details.

This language is recognized by the namespace 'http://www.ascc.net/xml/schematron'. It is envisaged that Schematron validation instructions could be embedded within other documents, and would typically form an extension to another, grammar-based document validation scheme (one suggestion makes use of the XML Schema AppInfo element for this purpose (see below)).

XML Schemas

In May 2001 the W3C released the **XML Schema** standard. This standard had a very long gestation and this is not surprising, as the aim was to create a single modelling language that would please all interested parties. It had to be very flexible and powerful, yet remain elegant and relatively simple to implement.

In terms of features (though not syntax), XML Schema models are backward-compatible with DTDs. This is very important, for the practical reason that it eases the transition from DTD modelling to XML Schema modelling. It is always possible to convert a DTD into an XML Schema model automatically. (The remainder of this chapter focuses on the features of the XML Schema standard that replicate the functionality of DTD models, but also hints at some extensions to these 'core' features. Readers unfamiliar with DTDs should also read this material, as the concepts covered here are not re-visited in the next chapter.)

Schema document structure

Because an XML Schema model is an XML document (unlike a DTD), it must be enclosed by a root element, in this case, the **Schema** element:

```
<schema ...>
   ...
</schema>
```

The Schema element has a **Version** attribute, but this attribute is not used to identify the version of XML Schema in use; it is instead used by schema authors to identify the version of the schema, assuming that the schema undergoes periodic updates.

All schema elements have an **Id** (Identifier) attribute. These attributes have no purpose within the schema language, and are included for convenience only. For example, it could be anticipated that hypertext links may be created from an XML document that documents the schema, with each link targeting the element in the schema that is currently under discussion.

Within the root element, there can first be any number and combination of inclusions, imports, re-definitions and annotations, followed by any number of combinations of simple and complex data type definitions, element and attribute definitions, model group definitions and annotations. Some of these top-level elements are described in the next chapter:

```
<schema>
  <!-- ANY NUMBER OF FOLLOWING -->

  <include.../>
  <import>...</import>          <!-- see Chapter 15 -->
  <redefine>...</redefine>      <!-- see Chapter 15 -->
  <annotation>...</annotation>

  <!-- ANY NUMBER OF FOLLOWING DEFINITIONS -->

  <simpleType>...</simpleType>
  <complexType>...</complexType>
  <element>...</element>
  <attribute />
  <attributeGroup>...</attributeGroup>
  <group>...</group>
  <annotation>...</annotation>
</schema>
```

Schema namespace

The XML Schema standard is namespace-sensitive. It can be used to intelligently process documents that include elements and attributes from numerous namespaces. In addition, namespaces are used within the schema document itself to distinguish between references to built-in data types, and other types that can be defined by the schema author. The XML Schema standard belongs to the http://www.w3.org/2001/XMLSchema namespace:

```
<schema xmlns="http://www.w3.org/2001/XMLSchema">
  ...
</schema>
```

Note that in the standard, the namespace prefix 'xsd' is used in the majority of the examples. Most of the following examples avoid prefixes, because they hinder legibility, though they become essential later (ironically, when dealing with the validation of XML documents that do *not* use namespaces).

Comments

While it is possible to include normal XML comments in an XML Schema document, there is also an **Annotation** element that serves this purpose, and can distinguish between comments aimed at humans and comments aimed at software processing (supplanting processing instructions). For human consumption, the **Documentation** element contains the actual comment text, and may also carry a **Source** attribute, containing a URL reference that may, for example, point to a document or document fragment that explains further:

```
<annotation>
  <documentation source="...">
    This is documentation
  </documentation>
</annotation>
```

However, note that the examples below use normal comments, both for brevity and because comments can include un-escaped chevrons. This is important because comments are used here to show equivalent instructions in the DTD modelling syntax:

```
<!-- <!ELEMENT ... > -->
```

The **AppInfo** (Application Information) element may be used in place of the Documentation element, when the information contained is to be digested by software, as a form of 'processing instruction'. Again, it may carry the **Source** attribute. One possible use of this element is to carry Schematron extensions (see above), in order to perform validation checks that XML Schema itself is unable to perform.

A single Annotation element may contain any number of Documentation and AppInfo elements, in any combination.

Element definitions

The **Element** element is used to define an element. (As mentioned previously, awkward sentences like this are hard to avoid with this standard). The **Name** attribute specifies the name of the element to be defined:

```
<element name="book" ... />
<!-- DTD EQUIVALENT: <!ELEMENT book ...> -->
```

This definition permits the 'book' element to occur within a conforming document instance:

```
<book>...</book>
```

Note that the Element element may be empty, as in the example above, but complex element definitions require this element to be a container for other instruction elements.

Any content

In the simplest possible form of declaration, the Element element is not only empty, but also has no attributes. This indicates that the element may contain anything, including text and other elements:

```
<element name="anything" />
<!-- DTD EQUIVALENT: <!ELEMENT anything ANY> -->
```

```
<anything>text and <emph>other</emph> elements
in this element</anything>
```

Simple content

When an element to be defined can have no attributes, and no sub-elements, it is termed a 'simple element'. Generally, this means that the element is just a container for a simple value, such as a number, word or text string. The **Type** attribute is used to specify what kind of text the element can hold. The type 'string' is the most straightforward, as it represents any string of text:

```
<element name="para" type="string" />
<!-- DTD EQUIVALENT: <!ELEMENT para (#PCDATA)> -->
```

```
<para> This is a text
string.    </para>
```

Complex content

Anything more sophisticated than simple value content (and *any* content) is defined using a **ComplexType** element:

```
<element name="book">
  <complexType>...</complexType>
</element>
```

Complex types are needed to specify the complex content model of the element being defined, and also any attributes that can be attached to this element.

Empty elements

Some elements can act as 'placeholders', with no content and no attributes (in the DTD for this book there is a 'pageBreak' placeholder element, which forces page-breaks to occur at earlier and more convenient points than they otherwise would). This involves a relatively simple form of element declaration, because the ComplexType element has no content:

```
<element name="pageBreak">
  <complexType></complexType>
</element>
<!-- DTD EQUIVALENT: <!ELEMENT pageBreak EMPTY>
                     <!ATTLIST pageBreak > -->
```

```
<para>...</para>
<pageBreak/>
<para>...</para>
```

This example is a little misleading, however, because there is quite a lot of implied content within the ComplexType element. The following example is equivalent, but more explicit. Additional elements specify that the content is a modified version of an existing data type, then that it is a restriction of 'any' content, then finally that there are no restricted options to choose from (the elements used are explained in the next chapter):

```
<element name="pageBreak">
  <complexType>
    <complexContent>
      <restriction base="anyType">
        <!-- NO ELEMENTS REFERENCED OR DEFINED -->
      </restriction>
    </complexContent>
  </complexType>
</element>
```

Note that this model does not distinguish between '`<pageBreak/>`' and '`<pageBreak></pageBreak>`', any more than a DTD model does. Both forms are legal representations of an empty element in the XML standard.

Child element content

Elements that need to contain other elements as children can do so by referring to elements that have already been defined elsewhere. Each reference requires another Element element, but this time holding a **Ref** attribute (instead of a Name attribute) to refer to the declaration concerned. However, these references cannot be placed directly within the ComplexType element; they must be wrapped in another element that indicates how they are to be combined with each other. If the embedded elements must occur in a pre-defined order, then the **Sequence** element is used to enclose these references:

```
<element name="last">...</element>

<element name="first">...</element>

<element name="name">
  <complexType>
    <sequence>
      <element ref="DOC:first"/>
      <element ref="DOC:last"/>
    </sequence>
  </complexType>
</element>
```

```
<!-- DTD EQUIVALENT:
     <!ELEMENT first ... >
     <!ELEMENT last ...>
     <!ELEMENT name (first, last)> -->
```

```
<name><first>...</first><last>...</last></name>
```

Namespace issues

Note the 'DOC:' prefixes on the reference values of the example above. These look suspiciously like namespace prefixes, and this is indeed what they are. Namespace issues are discussed in detail later; but for now, it is only necessary to understand that all definitions belong to a 'target' document-type namespace, which is distinct from the XML Schema namespace, and that references can be made to objects in either namespace. In this case, it is assumed that the target document-type namespace is defined with a prefix of 'DOC:'.

Note that if the default namespace is *not* used for the schema elements (unlike all previous examples), the prefix adopted must also be added to data type values (in order to distinguish them from any data types with the same names that the schema author may create). For example, if the prefix 'xsd' is used for XML Schema elements, then the data type 'string' becomes 'xsd:string':

```
<xsd:schema xmlns:xsd="http://www.w3.org/2001/XMLSchema">
  ...
  <xsd:element name="para" type="xsd:string" />
  ...
</xsd:schema>
```

Occurrence options

By default, referenced sub-elements must be present, and cannot be repeated. But it is often desirable to make a sub-element optional, or to allow it to repeat, or to allow it to be both repeatable and absent. Two attributes can be added to the reference to specify these options. The **MinOccurs** and **MaxOccurs** attributes by default have the value '1'. This means that the element must occur at least once, and also at most once, and this is just a complicated way of saying that it is required and not repeatable. The following two examples are therefore equivalent:

```
<element name="last">...</element>
```

```
<element name="last" minOccurs="1" maxOccurs="1">
  ...
</element>
```

An element is made optional by giving it a minimum value of zero. When no maximum value is appropriate, the value 'unbounded' can be used instead, representing infinity. Negative values are not allowed (and would be meaningless). The following table shows the equivalent values for the options that a DTD allows:

Common occurrence requirement	minOccurs	maxOccurs	DTD equivalent
required (the default)	1	1	*name*
optional	0	1	*name?*
optional and repeatable	0	unbounded	*name**
required and repeatable	1	unbounded	*name+*

In the following example, the first name is optional, the middle name is both optional and repeatable, and the last name is required but not repeatable:

```
<sequence>
  <element ref="DOC:first" minOccurs="0"
                           maxOccurs="1" />
  <element ref="DOC:middle" minOccurs="0"
                            maxOccurs="unbounded" />
  <element ref="DOC:last"   />
</sequence>

<!-- DTD EQUIVALENT:
     <!ELEMENT name (first?, middle*, last)> -->
```

All of the following examples conform to this model:

```
<name><last>...</last></name>

<name><first>...</first><last>...</last></name>

<name>
  <middle>...</middle>
  <middle>...</middle>
  <last>...</last>
</name>
```

It should be immediately obvious that these two attributes provide a very flexible way of constraining the number of occurrences, going far beyond the capabilities of DTDs. For example, it is possible to specify a minimum occurrence of '5' and a maximum of '9', or a minimum of '500' and a maximum of '900'.

Choices

Sometimes, a 'choice' of sub-elements may be needed. This is represented by the **Choice** element (instead of the Sequence element). In the following example, a Name element can either contain a personal name, or a company name:

```
<element name="name">
  <complexType>
    <choice>
      <element ref="DOC:personal" />
      <element ref="DOC:company" />
    </choice>
  </complexType>
</element>

<!-- DTD EQUIVALENT:
     <!ELEMENT name (personal | company)> -->


    <name><personal>...</personal></name>

    <name><company>...</company></name>
```

Group occurrence options

Just as it is possible to specify that a particular element is optional, required or repeatable, it is also possible to make a sequence or choice group optional and repeatable. The same two occurrence attributes that can be used on individual element references can also be used on the Sequence and Choice elements.

When the **MinOccurs** attribute is given a value of zero, all of the elements in a sequence group can be omitted:

```
<sequence minOccurs="0">
  <element ref="DOC:first"/>
  <element ref="DOC:middle"/>
  <element ref="DOC:last"/>
</sequence>

<!-- DTD EQUIVALENT: ... (first, middle, last)? ... -->


    <personal><!-- EMPTY --></personal>
```

Similarly, none of the elements need to be selected in a choice group:

```
<choice minOccurs="0">
  <element ref="DOC:para"/>
  <element ref="DOC:list"/>
  <element ref="DOC:table"/>
</choice>

<!-- DTD EQUIVALENT: ... (para | list | table)? ... -->


    <chapter><!-- EMPTY --></chapter>
```

When the **MaxOccurs** attribute is given a value greater than one, an entire sequence in a sequence group can be repeated:

```
<sequence maxOccurs="unbounded">
  <element ref="DOC:first"/>
  <element ref="DOC:middle"/>
  <element ref="DOC:last"/>
</sequence>

<!-- DTD EQUIVALENT: ... (first, middle, last)+ ... -->
```

The following example demonstrates this model:

```
<personalNames>
  <first>...</first><middle>...</middle><last>...</last>
  <first>...</first><middle>...</middle><last>...</last>
  <first>...</first><middle>...</middle><last>...</last>
</personalNames>
```

It is also possible to select more than one of the options in an option group, yet never select some of the others, and even select a particular option more than once:

```
<choice maxOccurs="unbounded">
  <element ref="DOC:para"/>
  <element ref="DOC:list"/>
  <element ref="DOC:table"/>
</choide>

<!-- DTD EQUIVALENT: ... (para | list | table)+ ... -->
```

This kind of model is ideal for narrative text flows (such as this book), where paragraphs, lists, tables and other structures are mixed in an unpredictable order:

```
<chapter>
  <para>...</para>
  <para>...</para>
  <table>...</table>
</chapter>
```

Embedded groups

The **Choice** and **Sequence** elements can contain each other, instead of (or as well as) directly containing element references. This is essential when there is a need to embed a sequence group as one option of many, or, conversely, to have a set of options within a larger sequence. In the following example, the outer sequence begins with a required title, then any combination of paragraphs, lists and tables:

```
<sequence>
  <element ref="DOC:title"/>
  <choice minOccurs="0" maxOccurs="unbounded">
    <element ref="DOC:para"/>
    <element ref="DOC:list"/>
    <element ref="DOC:table"/>
  </choice>
</sequence>

<!-- DTD EQUIVALENT: (title, (para | list | table)*) -->
```

There are no limitations on either the depth to which these models can be embedded within each other, or to the number of occurrences of one or both model types within another.

Mixed content

To allow text to appear in the content model, the **Mixed** attribute is given the value 'true' (the default value is 'false'). Typically, mixed content involves the unconstrained ordering of inter-mixed sub-elements and, because such elements are usually repeatable, the entire choice group is generally made optional and repeatable:

```
<element name="para">
  <complexType mixed="true">
    <choice minOccurs="0" maxOccurs="unbounded">
      <element ref="DOC:emph" />
      <element ref="DOC:name" />
    </choice>
  </complexType>
</element>

<!-- DTD EQUIVALENT:
     <!ELEMENT para (#PCDATA | emph | name)*> -->


    <para>Are <emph>you</emph> going
    to <name>Scarborough</name> fair?</para>
```

Note the words 'typically' and 'generally' in the paragraph above. Unlike DTD models, it is not necessary for the group to be an option group, and it is also not necessary to make the group optional and repeatable. For example, it is possible to make the whole group both required and not repeatable (by omitting the occurrence attributes), and then make a single embedded element reference required. This would ensure that the given sub-element is always present (though this technique would not work if other sub-elements could also occur, because the group would need to be repeatable):

```
<complexType mixed="true">
  <choice> <!-- required and not repeatable -->
    <element ref="name" /> <!-- REQUIRED ELEMENT -->
  </choice>
</complexType>


    <person><name>John Smith</name></person>

    <person>The famous <name>John Smith</name>.</person>

    <person>John Smith.</person>   <!-- ERROR -->
```

Note that the text around sub-elements is always optional, regardless of the minOccurs attribute value on the group.

However, 'mixed' content does not have to involve any element content at all. It could consist of just text (strictly speaking, rendering the name 'mixed' meaningless. For example, while a Paragraph element might be allowed to contain names and emphasized text, it would typically be allowed to not have either:

```
<para>Are you going to Scarborough fair?</para>
```

Attributes

Attributes are created and referenced in essentially the same way as elements. The **Attribute** element is used to create an attribute, and the name of the attribute is provided by the **Name** attribute. The **Type** attribute can be used, just as in element definitions, to specify the type of value it can contain. This declaration can appear at the end of a complex type definition. In the following example, the Security attribute is added to the Chapter element:

```
<element name="chapter">
  <complexType>
    ...
    <attribute name="security" type="string" />
  </complexType>
</element>

<!-- DTD EQUIVALENT:
    <!ATTLIST chapter security CDATA #IMPLIED> -->
```

Attribute Type values must always be simple data types, such as the 'string' type, and never complex types, because attributes cannot contain either element tags or sub-attributes.

Attributes on simple elements

When an element has simple content, it does not normally require the ComplexType element to help define it. While the next chapter explores a sophisticated way to enhance simple data types, such as 'string', to allow attributes to be added, a simpler technique involves ignoring the 'string' type, and instead uses 'mixed' content, as described above. But in this case there are no sub-elements for the text to be mixed with:

```
<element name="para">
  <complexType mixed="true">
    <attribute name="security" type="string" />
  </complexType>
</element>
```

```
<!-- DTD EQUIVALENT:
    <!ELEMENT para (#PCDATA)>
    <!ATTLIST para security CDATA #IMPLIED> -->


<para security="secret">Are you going to
Scarborough fair?</para>
```

Warning: As already stated, this concept seems not to be supported by some early versions of schema-sensitive parsers, perhaps due to different interpretations of the specification.

Required attributes

By default, attributes are optional. They do not have to be present in every element instance, or indeed in *any* instance. But the schema author can make sure that a document author adds the attribute to every occurrence of the element it belongs to. The **Use** attribute makes an attribute essential when given the value 'required' (the other options are 'prohibited' and 'optional' (the default value)):

```
<attribute name="security" type="string" use="required"/>

<!-- DTD EQUIVALENT:
    <!ATTLIST chapter security CDATA #REQUIRED> -->
```

DTD-compatible attribute value types

An attribute value can be constrained in various ways, by specifying a data type it must conform to. The example above shows the least restrictive option possible: 'string' (and many more are discussed in the next chapter). Other types include those inherited from the DTD scheme:

- NMTOKEN (name token)
- NMTOKENS (name tokens)
- ID (a unique value that can be referenced from IDREF values)
- ID (a reference to an ID value)
- IDREF (a number of IDREF values)
- NOTATION (a reference to a notation)
- ENTITY (a reference to an entity)
- ENTITIES (a reference to several entities).

These types can also be used to restrict element content, but are not recommended for this purpose as they were only included in the standard to provide backward compatibility with DTDs, which only use them for attribute value types. Each type is explained briefly below (but they are all more fully discussed in Chapter 5). Also note that 'CDATA' is not one of the options; the new 'string' type is equivalent.

The **NMTOKEN** data type constrains the value to a single word, consisting of alphabetic letters, digits, '_', ':', '.' and '-' characters. Unlike element and attribute names (and some of the other data types described below), the token can begin with any of these characters. Most significantly, spaces are forbidden in name token values. Examples of possible name token values include '132', '-123abc', 'x' and even '...'.

Three of the data types listed above are divided into singular and plural forms, for example NMTOKEN and **NMTOKENS**. The plural form indicates a series of values that conform to the same restrictions as the singular form. Spaces are considered to be token separators. A NMTOKEN attribute may contain '123abc', but a NMTOKENS attribute may contain '123abc 987xyz thirdToken', which represents three distinct tokens.

The **ID** type specifies that the value must be unique, so that it can be made the single target of a hypertext link. The **IDREF** type identifies a reference to an ID value. A parser should check that ID values are unique, and that IDREF values refer to existing ID values (but only in the same document). Both of these types are constrained in the same way as element and attribute names. A single element can refer to many target elements using the **IDREFS** type. Some XML browsers are sensitive to attributes that have these types, and will create hypertext links between referencing elements and targeted elements accordingly.

Though now not a very popular technique for referencing non-XML data, a combination of notation declarations, entity declarations and entity references identify the data format used for 'unparsable' data, the name of a file that contains the data, and the location in the document where the content of this file should appear when it is presented (Chapter 4 discusses these concepts in greater detail). The NOTATION and ENTITY attribute types are used to reference notation and entity declarations that are held in (or referenced from) the document. Although a DTD is not involved (when using XML Schema models) the document could still include a parameter entity that references an external document containing the notation and entity declarations, or just include them directly. The **NOTATION** type references a notation definition. The value must conform to normal name constraints (the alphabetical letters, digits, '_', ':', '.' and '-', but starting with a letter, '_' or ':' only). Such an attribute identifies the element it belongs to as being a container for notational data. The **ENTITY** type specifies that the value is the name of an external, unparsed entity. The element the attribute is attached to is replaced by the content of the specified entity. A single element may refer to several entities at once using the **ENTITIES** type.

List of possible values

It is possible to specify that an attribute value should match one of the values given in a pre-defined list of valid options. This is done by specifying that the value is basically a NMTOKEN value, but then restricting the value further, to one of a set of explicit token values. Although the following construct appears clumsy, it is actually justified because this is a minor example of a sophisticated feature of the standard (the SimpleType, Restriction and Enumeration elements are explained in the next chapter):

```
<element name="chapter">
  <complexType>
    ...
    <attribute name="security">
      <simpleType>
        <restriction base="NMTOKEN">
          <enumeration value="normal"/>
          <enumeration value="secret"/>
          <enumeration value="topSecret"/>
        </restriction>
      </simpleType>
    </attribute>
  <complexType>
</element>

<!-- DTD EQUIVALENT:
    <!ATTLIST chapter
      security (normal|secret|topSecret) #IMPLIED > -->
```

Default values

When an attribute is declared it can be given a default value. The value specified within the **Default** attribute is applied when the attribute is not physically present on the element it should be attached to (the Use attribute must have a value of 'optional', or simply be absent for this to work):

```
<attribute name="security" type="string"
                         default="secret" />

<!-- DTD EQUIVALENT:
    <!ATTLIST chapter security CDATA  "secret" > -->

    <chapter>...</chapter>       <!-- SECRET -->
    <chapter security="secret">
      ...
    </chapter>
    <chapter>...</chapter>       <!-- SECRET -->
    <chapter security="normal">
      ...
    </chapter>
    <chapter>...</chapter>       <!-- SECRET -->
```

Fixed values

It is possible to specify a value for the attribute that can never be changed. A 'fixed' attribute value is provided by the **Fixed** attribute:

```
<attribute name="security" type="string"
                           fixed="secret"/>

<!-- DTD EQUIVALENT:
    <!ATTLIST secretChapter
                        security  #FIXED  "secret" > -->


<secretChapter>...                          <!-- SECRET -->
<secretChapter security="secret">... <!-- SECRET -->
<secretChapter security="normal">... <!-- ERROR -->
```

Because the value is always present or implied, a Use attribute value of 'optional' does not apply, and neither does the Default attribute.

Note that default and fixed values can be applied to element content, as well as to attribute values (a topic that is explored further in the next chapter).

Namespaces and schema references

The Namespaces standard (see Chapter 10) can rarely be ignored when using XML Schemas. Namespaces must be considered both when using certain techniques within the schema model (the impact of namespaces on references to data types has already been demonstrated), and also when validating documents that use namespaces.

Schema document namespaces

The productivity techniques described later rely upon the ability of a schema author to create new data types that can be shared across several element or attribute definitions. In order to avoid confusing custom data types with built-in types, it is necessary to use two namespaces. When the XML documents to be validated do *not* use namespaces, a namespace prefix must *not* be used for the data types defined by the schema author. Inevitably, this means that they *must* be used for XML Schema elements instead. It is then important to remember to also add the same prefix to the simple data types defined in the standard, for example, 'xsd:string' instead of 'string'. Note the user-defined type 'string' below, which is unambiguously distinguished from 'xsd:string' (the SimpleType element is described in the next chapter):

```
<xsd:schema xmlns:xsd="http://www.w3.org/2001/XMLSchema">
   . . .
   .  <!-- REFERENCE XML SCHEMA DEFINED 'string' TYPE -->
   <xsd:element name="comment" type="xsd:string" />
   . . .
   . . .       <!-- CREATE 'string' TYPE -->
   <xsd:simpleType name="string">...</xsd:simpleType>
   . . .
   . . .   <!--REFERENCE USER DEFINED 'string' TYPE -->
   <xsd:element name="special" type="string" />
</xsd:schema>
```

Document issues

The XML Schema standard can be used to validate documents that do not use namespaces, and documents that do use namespaces. However, this distinction is important, and affects the way that a schema is built. While DTDs, which are not namespace-sensitive, can be used for both kinds of document, simply by treating pre-defined namespace prefixes as part of the element name, it is not possible to use this simple technique in schema models.

Documents without namespaces

The outer-structures of an XML document, or indeed the entire document, may not refer to a namespace at all. In this scenario, the XML processor must use some mechanism (such as explicit user selection, or a reference within the document to the schema it claims conformance with) to determine which schema to apply to the document.

When validating such a document, the schema must *not* specify a target name-space. By *omitting* the **TargetNamespace** attribute (explained below), all of the definitions in the schema are deemed to be 'unqualified' definitions that will be used to validate 'unqualified' elements and attributes in the document.

In the following example, within the 'quoteSchema' schema, the element 'quotation' does not belong to any namespace:

quoteSchema.xsd

```
<xsd:schema
      xmlns:xsd="http://www.w3.org/2001/XMLSchema">
   <xsd:element name="quotation" ... />
</xsd:schema>
```

A document that does not conform to a namespace can reference this schema using the **NoNamespaceSchemaLocation** attribute, which contains a URL reference. This attribute belongs to the http://www.w3.org/2001/XMLSchema-instance namespace:

```
<quotation
      xmlns:xsi="http://www.w3.org/2001/XMLSchema-instance"
      xsi:noNamespaceSchemaLocation=
                    "file:///d:/schemas/quoteSchema.xsd">
   ...
</quotation>


   <!-- DTD EQUIVALENT:
      <!DOCTYPE quotation SYSTEM "quoteSchema.dtd"> -->
```

Documents with namespaces

The XML Schema standard is designed to work effectively with XML documents that use namespaces. A schema-sensitive XML processor detects the namespace or namespaces used in the document instance, and applies appropriate schema definitions as required. If a document generally conforms to one namespace, but includes a fragment from another, the processor is able to switch schemas to validate the fragment (using features described below).

An XML document author may decide that the document conforms to a given namespace, such as 'file:///d:/ns/quoteNamespace'. In the following example, this is made the default namespace:

```
<quotation xmlns="file:///d:/ns/quoteNamespace"
              ...>
   ...
</quotation>
```

But, without any other changes to the schema shown above, a parser would report errors when applying the schema to this document. Modifications are required to both the schema reference and to the declarations in the schema document.

First, the NoNamespaceSchemaLocation attribute must be replaced by the **SchemaLocation** attribute. This attribute tells the parser where to find a schema, as before, but it contains value pairs instead of a single value. In each pair, the first value is the namespace for which a schema needs to be sought, and the second value is a URL reference that locates the schema. In the following simple example, involving a single pair of values, the 'quoteNamespace' namespace (applicable to the document as a whole) can be validated by the schema 'quoteSchema.xsd':

```
<quotation
    xmlns="quoteNamespace"
    xmlns:xsi="http://www.w3.org/2001/XMLSchema-instance"
    xsi:schemaLocation="file:///d:/ns/quoteNamespace
                        file:///d:/schemas/quoteSchema.xsd" >
  ...
</quotation>
```

But, even with this modification, errors will still occur. For example, the parser will report that the 'quotation' element is not declared. This error occurs because the declarations in the schema document declare elements that do not belong to any namespace, but the 'quotation' element in the document belongs to the 'quoteNamespace' namespace.

To avoid this error, it is necessary to add the **TargetNamespace** attribute to the schema. This attribute provides the URL that identifies the namespace to which the model will apply. It 'targets' its model definitions at the documents, document fragments or attributes that conform to the given namespace. In the example below, the Quotation element now belongs to the correct namespace:

```
<schema xmlns="http://www.w3.org/2001/XMLSchema"
        targetNamespace="file:///d:/ns/quoteNamespace">
  <element name="quotation" ... />
  ...
</schema>
```

In addition, it is also necessary to identify the same namespace in the schema, and, if this namespace reference uses a prefix, then references to elements and data types must include this prefix (as shown in almost all of the earlier examples):

```
<schema xmlns="http://www.w3.org/2001/XMLSchema"
        targetNamespace="file:///d:/ns/quoteNamespace"
        xmlns:Q="file:///d:/ns/quoteNamespace">
  <element name="quotation">
    <element ref="Q:quoteText" ... />
    <element ref="Q:citation" ... />
  </element>

  <element name="quoteText" ... />

  <element name="citation" ... />
</schema>
```

Alternatively, the target namespace can be made the default namespace, and the schema namespace is then given an explicit prefix:

```
<xsd:schema xmlns:xsd="http://www.w3.org/2001/XMLSchema"
            targetNamespace="file:///d:/ns/quoteNamespace"
            xmlns="file:///d:/ns/quoteNamespace">
  <xsd:element name="quotation">
    <xsd:complexType>
      <xsd:element ref="quoteText" ... />
      <xsd:element ref="citation" ... />
    </xsd:complexType>
  </xsd:element>

  <xsd:element name="quoteText" ... />

  <xsd:element name="citation" ... />
</xsd:schema>
```

Multiple-namespace documents

When a document contains elements from multiple namespaces, it can be fully validated using multiple schemas. Consider the possibility that a quotation could
include an HTML fragment. An appropriate 'EmbeddedHTML' element is added
to the document instance as follows, and the schema that can validate its contents
is added to the SchemaLocation attribute value, as a second pair of tokens:

```
<quotation
    xmlns="file:///d:/ns/quoteNamespace"
    xmlns:H="http://www.w3.org/1999/xhtml"
    xmlns:xsi="http://www.w3.org/2001/XMLSchema-instance"
    xsi:schemaLocation="
                    file:///d:/ns/quoteNamespace
                    file:///d:/schemas/quoteSchema.xsd

                    http://www.w3.org/1999/xhtml
                    file:///d:/schemas/HTMLSchema.htm">
  <quoteText>
    <embeddedHTML>
      <H:P>To be, or <H:B>not</H:B> to be...</H:P>
    </embeddedHTML>
  </quoteText>
</quotation>
```

The schema needs to be updated to include the EmbeddedHTML element, and also
to specify that its contents belong to another namespace, and so need to be validated (if validated at all) using a different schema. This is done using the **Any** element. This element contains a **Namespace** attribute to identify the namespace that
its contents should conform to:

```
<element name="embeddedHTML">
  <complexType>
    <sequence>
      <any namespace="http://www.w3.org/1999/xhtml" />
    </sequence>
  </complexType>
</element>
```

Validation and occurrence options

By default, the content is validated in a 'strict' fashion, meaning that the schema model should be found and applied in order to validate it fully. However, using the **ProcessContents** attribute, the parser can be told to ignore any elements or attributes that it cannot find a schema for, and to check these constructs only for well-formed conformance ('lax'), or to simply check all markup, regardless of the existence of referenced schemas, for well-formed conformance ('skip').

Also by default, a single 'root' element from the other namespace is expected to be found, but other requirements can be specified using the usual **MinOccurs** and **MaxOccurs** attributes.

In the following example, there must be at least one 'root' element within the EmbeddedHTML element, but there can be more, and there is also no requirement to validate the content against the HTML schema:

```
<any namespace="http://www.w3.org/1999/xhtml"
     minOccurs="1" maxOccurs="unbounded"
     processContents="skip" />


<embeddedHTML>
  <H:P>...</H:P>
  <H:P>

    . . .

    <H:XYZ><!-- NOT DEFINED, BUT OK! --></H:XYZ>
    . . .
  </H:P>
</embeddedHTML>
```

Multiple namespace references can appear in the Namespace attribute, separated by spaces, allowing elements from all of these namespaces to be present. The keyword '##targetNamespace' can appear in this list, and represents the target namespace (in this case, 'file:///d:/ns/quoteNamespace'). But it is not necessary to specify a particular namespace for the content. The reserved value '##any' can be used in the Namespace attribute to indicate that elements from any namespace (that are declared in the XML document, and possibly also referenced in the SchemaLocation attribute) may be inserted. When more than one 'root' element is allowed, these elements can even be from different namespaces. However, this option includes the namespace of the enclosing element too; if elements from this namespace are to be excluded, the value '##other' can be used instead. Finally, the '##local' option specifies that the element can only contain elements that do not belong to any namespace at all.

Attribute qualification

Normally, and by default in schemas, attributes that belong to the same namespace as the elements they are attached to are not qualified, and are just assumed to belong to the same namespace as the element (rather than to a possible default namespace). The **AttributeFormDefault** attribute on the Schema element has an implied value of 'unqualified'. This can be explicitly changed to the alternative value of 'qualified', and attributes are then expected to have a prefix:

```
<para ATTR:security="secret">...</para>
```

This setting can be overridden for individual attributes, using the **Form** attribute on the Attribute element, which takes the same two possible values:

```
<attribute name="security" form="unqualified" ... />


<para security="secret">...</para>
```

Any attribute

The schema may allow attributes from other namespaces to occur within an element. For example, it is common for the HTML Href attribute, which holds a URL reference to create links to external resources, to be utilized in other document models:

```
<publisherLink xmlns:X="http://www.w3.org/1999/xhtml"
               X:href="www.aw.com" />
```

This feature is supported by the **AnyAttribute** element. Just like the Any element, it has a **Namespace** attribute and a **ProcessContents** attribute, with the same purposes and possible values, but does not have the occurrence attributes (because attributes can only be optional or required).

This element may contain an annotation element, and can only be used once, at the end of a complex type definition (following any attribute definitions):

```
<element name="publisherLink">
  <complexType>
    <!-- CONTENT MODEL DEFINITIONS -->
    ...
    <!-- ATTRIBUTE DEFINITIONS -->
    ...
    <anyAttribute processContents="strict"
            namespace="http://www.w3.org/1999/xhtml">
      <annotation>
        <documentation>ALLOW ANY HTML ATTRIBUTE
          IN THE PUBLISHER LINK ELEMENT</documentation>
      </annotation>
    </anyAttribute>
  </complexType>
</element>
```

It is not possible to constrain the model to specific attributes from the given name-space, or to a specific number of attributes. In the example above, any HTML attribute, and any number of different HTML attributes, can be added to an instance of the PublishLink element.

Including other models

Within DTDs, parameter entities are often used to reference external document model components. For example, a commonly used table model, such as the CALS or HTML model, is often referenced from numerous document models that need to include tables. While general entities (see Chapter 4) can be used in all XML documents, and therefore in XML Schema documents, it is not necessary to rely upon this feature. The XML Schema standard has its own capabilities for sharing models.

Schema-switching

As already described, it is possible to let the XML processor do all of the work of including other models, using namespaces and the Any element (or the AnyAttribute element) to identify the namespace of the other model, and the valid locations where elements (or attributes) from this model may be used. However, when namespaces are not being used, it becomes necessary to copy one model's definitions into another model.

Including another schema

The **Include** element references a schema file, using a URL reference in the **SchemaLocation** attribute, the contents of which are to be included in the main file:

```
<include schemaLocation="tables.xsd" />
```

This element must occur before any element, attribute or complex definition. The schema to be included must also have the same target namespace (or the same absence of a target namespace). Consequently, this mechanism cannot be used to share model fragments among numerous models, when the models concerned target different namespaces.

Although the file to be included must be a complete schema document in its own right, capable of being used in isolation, typically it will only be used by reference from other schema documents, and never directly from an XML instance document. A schema-sensitive processor is expected to be able to call in the document whenever it is referenced by another schema document, and treat its contents as if they had existed in the primary file. The effect should be the same as using the XInclude standard (see Chapter 12) to embed the contents of the root element, before attempting to interpret the model, but with the additional refinement of ensuring that the schema content model remains valid.

Importing definitions

A schema author can reference definitions in other schemas, and has the choice of whether to use original element and attribute names, or to override them. This approach depends upon the author of the other schema document creating named data types (introduced below), rather than simply creating element and attribute definitions (and importing is discussed in more detail in the next chapter).

Efficiency shortcuts

Parameter entities are often used in DTDs to avoid unnecessary duplication, to clarify content models, and to generally make maintenance of the DTD easier. Although parameter entities cannot be used in XML Schema documents (or indeed any XML document), it is possible to use general entities instead. However, the XML Schema standard includes its own (arguably simpler) mechanisms to achieve the same aims, so avoiding the need for entities of any kind.

Shared content models

When a number of element content models are identical, it is not efficient to replicate the model in each element definition (and document model clarity and ease of future maintenance also suffers). Instead, the complex model can be created in isolation, using the **ComplexType** element, but this time given a name using the **Name** attribute. This name can be referenced from within each relevant element declaration, using the same **Type** attribute that is used to reference simple data types:

```
<complexType mixed="true" name="MixedInline">
  <choice minOccurs="0" maxOccurs="unbounded">
    <element ref="emph" />
    <element ref="name" />
  </choice>
</complexType>

<element name="title" type="DOC:MixedInline />

<element name="para" type="DOC:MixedInline />

<!-- DTD EQUIVALENT:
    <!ENTITY % MixedInline "(#PCDATA | emph | name)*" >
    <!ELEMENT para   (%MixedInline;)>
    <!ELEMENT title  (%MixedInline;)> -->
```

Note: The Ref and Type attributes should not be confused. The Ref attribute is always used to refer to an object of the same kind as the element it is in. It is used, for example, by an element (reference) to refer to another element (definition), or by an attribute (reference) to refer to another attribute (definition). The Type attribute, however, is used to reference a simple data type, such as 'string', or a complex data type, such as the model above.

This technique achieves much more than simply providing the means to share content models. It creates a new, custom complex data type that can be referenced and exploited in a number of ways (mostly covered by features described in the next chapter).

Groups

When only part of the content model is common to a number of element definitions, a variant of the technique described above uses the **Group** element, instead of the ComplexType element. This element has both a **Name** attribute and a **Ref** attribute. When it is used to define a common group, it may contain either a Choice group or a Sequence group (or a third option that is described in the next chapter). When this element is used as a reference, the **MinOccurs** and **MaxOccurs** attributes may be used:

```
<group name="Reference">
  <choice>
    <element ref="WebSite" />
    <element ref="book" />
  </choice>
</group>

<element name="citation">
  <complexType>
    <sequence>
      . . .
      <group ref="DOC:Reference" minOccurs="0"
                               maxOccurs="unbounded"/>
      . . .
    </sequence>
  </complexType>
</element>

<!-- DTD EQUIVALENT:
  <!ENTITY % Reference "(WebSite | book)" >
  <!ELEMENT citation  (... , (%Reference;)* , ...)> -->
```

Shared attribute declarations

Just as content models can be defined in isolation, then referenced from within element definitions, attributes can also be referenced in the same way (at the end of a ComplexType definition), using the **Ref** attribute. The **Use** attribute is used in references (just as the occurrence attributes are used in element references):

```
<attribute name="security" ... />

<element name="chapter">
  <complexType>
    ...
    <attribute ref="DOC:security" use="required"/>
  </complexType>
</element>

<element name="para">
  <complexType>
    ...
    <attribute ref="DOC:security" use="optional"/>
  </complexType>
</element>
```

Note that the Use attribute has no meaning in the isolated declaration, but can be used in each reference, and given a different value in each case.

Warning: This technique (when applied to attributes rather than to elements) is not as useful as it first appears, because it creates attributes that belong to a specific namespace, rather than directly to the element. This means that the attribute must always have a suitable namespace prefix when used in an element instance, even though the namespace this prefix maps to will be the same as the default or explicit namespace that the whole element maps to (the next technique, using attribute groups, is usually more appropriate):

```
<B:book xmlns:B         = "file:///d:/ns/myBookNamespace"
        xmlns:ATTRIBUTE = "file:///d:/ns/myBookNamespace">
  ...
  <B:chapter ATTRIBUTE:security="normal">...</B:chapter>
  ...
</B:book>
```

Attribute groups

When a number of element types require the same set of attributes, it is possible to pre-define and name a group of attributes, then refer to this group in each element definition. The **AttributeGroup** element has the usual **Name** and **Ref** attributes, and contains any number of attribute definitions and attribute references. When used as a reference, it appears at the end of a ComplexType declaration:

```
<attribute name="security" ... />

<attributeGroup name="standardAtts">
  <attribute name="id" type="ID" use="required"/>
  <attribute name="indentLevel" type="string" />
  <attribute ref="DOC:security" />
</attributeGroup>

<element name="chapter">
  <complexType>
    ...
    <attributeGroup ref="DOC:standardAtts" />
  </complexType>
</element>

<element name="para">
  <complexType>
    ...
    <attributeGroup ref="DOC:standardAtts" />
  </complexType>
</element>

<!-- DTD EQUIVALENT (apart from attribute name and
     Security attribute referencing issue):
  <!ENTITY % security     "security    CDATA #IMPLIED">
  <!ENTITY % standardAtts "id          ID    #REQUIRED
                           indentLevel CDATA #IMPLIED
                           %security;" >

  <!ATTLIST chapter  %standardAtts; >
  <!ATTLIST para     %standardAtts; > -->
```

An attribute group can also contain references to other attribute groups.

This technique should also be used for single attributes that need to be shared, as it overcomes the namespaces issue raised above concerning global single attribute definitions (a problem that still occurs with the Security attribute in the example above).

Also note that if all of the elements concerned will have identical content models, as well as identical attributes, it is possible to define a named complex type definition that includes both the model and the attributes needed. In addition, there is nothing to prevent this complex type definition from referencing attribute groups.

15. Advanced XML Schemas

The XML Schema standard is a very sophisticated modelling language that has a number of capabilities beyond those discussed in the previous chapter. This chapter describes the advanced features of the XML Schema standard, with little reference to the 'core' features already covered, so Chapter 14 should be read first.

Introduction

Beyond the basic concepts that replicate the well-known modelling features inherited from XML DTDs, the XML Schema standard includes several entirely new features, and resurrects some of the advanced features found in SGML DTDs. These features give the schema author the ability to:

- define default and fixed element content values
- define a content model that requires all of the referenced elements to be present, but does not dictate the order in which they can occur
- add attributes to simple element types
- explicitly identify element instances that have no value
- define context-specific elements within other elements, possibly with non-unique names, but with different content models and attributes
- specify that elements must have unique identifier values, possibly involving combinations of element content and attribute values
- define unique keys from attribute values, element content or combinations of attributes and elements, and validate that specific instances exist from references elsewhere in the same document
- choose a data type for an attribute value or for element content, from a large range of options
- reference data type libraries
- create new simple data types from existing types

- use complex 'patterns' to precisely control attribute and element values
- create new complex data types from existing complex data types
- restrict derivations of data types and usage of base or derived types
- re-define definitions in external schema documents, and use definitions created for other target namespaces.

Default and fixed element values

The concept of default and fixed values has traditionally been applicable only to attribute values, and can still be applied to attributes using a schema model (as explained in the previous chapter). However, it is now possible to apply these concepts to element content as well.

Default element content

An element type can be assigned a default content value that is to be inserted automatically when the element is present, but empty. The same **Default** attribute used in attribute definitions can also be used in element definitions for this purpose:

```
<element name="companyName" type="string"
                        default="ACME Corp" />
```

The following examples are then equivalent:

```
<companyName/>
<companyName></companyName>
<companyName>ACME Corp</companyName>
```

But there is a subtle difference between the way element defaulting works and the way attribute defaulting works. With attributes, the default only applies when the attribute is not present. With elements, the default only applies when the element is empty, but present. When the element is omitted, the default does not apply.

Caution: While the standard makes it clear in the text that an omitted element has no default value, elsewhere in the specification it is implied that it does, but only when the element is allowed to occur at most once.

Fixed element content

The content of an element can be 'fixed in stone', meaning that a document instance author cannot change its value. While it may be possible for the element to be absent, when it is present it must hold the value specified. The **Fixed** attribute, used to create fixed values for attributes, is again used in element definitions for this purpose:

```
<element name="companyName" type="string"
                         fixed="ACME Corp" />
```

The following examples show some legal and illegal instances:

```
<companyName/>                          <!-- ERROR -->
<companyName></companyName>             <!-- ERROR -->
<companyName>ACME Corp</companyName>    <!-- OK -->
<companyName>My Corp</companyName>      <!-- ERROR -->
```

Caution: Just as for default values, while the standard makes it clear in the text that an omitted element has no fixed value, elsewhere in the specification it is implied that it does, but only when the element is allowed to occur at most once.

All groups

It is entirely possible that both the Choice and Sequence elements will be inadequate to accurately model a required structure. Consider the need for a book cover to contain a title, author name and publisher name, but for the order of these three items to be unconstrained, so that a document instance author can decide which should appear first and last. The Sequence element would be too restrictive, and the Option element, which would need to be allowed to repeat, would not be restrictive enough (it would, for example, allow two titles to appear). What is needed is a construct that specifies a list of required elements, but does not dictate the order in which they should occur, and the **All** element is designed for this purpose:

```
<complexType>
  <all>
    <element ref="DOC:bookTitle" />
    <element ref="DOC:authorName" />
    <element ref="DOC:publisher" />
  </all>
</complexType>

<!-- SGML EQUIVALENT
    <!ELEMENT entry - - (bookTitle & authorName &
                        publisher)> -->
```

The examples below both conform to this rule:

```
<cover>
  <bookTitle>...</bookTitle>
  <authorName>...</authorName>
  <publisher>...</publisher>
</cover>
```

```
<cover>
  <authorName>...</authorName>
  <publisher>...</publisher>
  <bookTitle>...</bookTitle>
</cover>
```

Note that the very nature of this group type makes the order in which elements are defined or referenced within the group irrelevant (just as they are in optional groups).

There are some tight constraints on the use of this kind of content model, both in terms of where it can be used, and in terms of what it can contain.

Content limitations

A group of this kind cannot directly contain text. However, the elements in the group may do so, and the **Mixed** attribute can still be used on the ComplexType element. When in a mixed content model, the containing element can contain text before, between and after the sequence of elements. If the group is also made optional, then it is possible that only text will occur:

```
<complexType mixed="true">
  <all minOccurs="0" maxOccurs="1" >
    <element ref="DOC:bookTitle" />
    <element ref="DOC:authorName" />
    <element ref="DOC:publisher" />
  </all>
</complexType>


  <cover>This book cover is not defined yet!</cover>

  <cover>
    TITLE: *<bookTitle>...</bookTitle>*
    AUTHOR: *<authorName>...</authorName>*
    PUBLISHER: *<publisher>...</publisher>*
  </cover>
```

Unlike the other grouping types, this group type cannot contain embedded groups of any type. It can only contain annotations, then element definitions and element references.

Also note that the other group types cannot contain this kind of group; it must be the top and only level of a content model.

Occurrence options

By default, as usual, this content model is not optional and not repeatable. But, as with the other two group types, the All element may contain the **MinOccurs** and **MaxOccurs** attributes. However, the MaxOccurs attribute appears to be superfluous, as it cannot hold a value greater than '1' in this context, and clearly should not hold a value of '0' either (except in very special circumstances, concerned with derived data types, as explained later). It therefore follows that the MinOccurs attribute can only contain '0' or '1' (the default value). When set to '0', the whole model is optional; either all elements must be present (with one exception discussed below), or none of them are allowed to be present:

```
<all minOccurs="0" maxOccurs="1" >
  <element ref="DOC:bookTitle" />
  <element ref="DOC:authorName" />
  <element ref="DOC:publisher" />
</all>
```

```
  <cover></cover>
```

Content element occurrences

The elements defined or referenced in the model must have occurrence values of zero or one, which simply means that some or all elements can be made optional. In the following example, the Publisher element is optional (the author may have self-published the book):

```
<all>
  <element ref="DOC:publisher"  minOccurs="0" />
  <element ref="DOC:bookTitle" />
  <element ref="DOC:authrName" />
</all>
```

```
  <cover>
    <bookTitle>...</bookTitle>
    <authorName>...</authorName>
    <publisher>...</publisher>
</entry>
```

```
  <cover>
    <authorName>...</authorName>
    <bookTitle>...</bookTitle>
    <!-- NO PUBLISHER -->
  </cover>
```

Simple types with attributes

When an element has simple content, but also has attributes, it cannot simply refer to a data type, such as 'string'. Instead, it must include the ComplexType element, so that attribute declarations can be made. However, there remains the problem of how to specify the simple data type of the element content. The **SimpleContent** element is used to indicate that the complex element will actually be based on a simple data type. The **Extension** element is employed, both to specify the data type of the element in its **Base** attribute, and to extend the type by adding the required attribute:

```
<complexType>
  <simpleContent>
    <extension base="string">
      <attribute name="security" type="string" />
    </extension>
  </simpleContent>
</complexType>
```

Nil values

Consider the following XML fragment. The first, middle and last names of a person are given:

```
<name>
  <first>John</first><middle>W</middle><last>Smith</last>
</name>
```

Now consider the following similar fragments. In all of these examples, there is no middle name. In the first case, the Middle element is absent. In the second case, it is present but happens to have no content. In the third case, an empty element tag has been used:

```
<name>
  <first>Peter</first><!-- NO MIDDLE --><last>Jones</last>
</name>

<name>
  <first>Peter</first><middle></middle><last>Jones</last>
</name>

<name>
  <first>Peter</first><middle/><last>Jones</last>
</name>
```

The XML standard provides no hints as to how to interpret these alternatives. Perhaps the absence of the Middle element means that there is no middle name. Perhaps its presence, but with no content, means that there *is* a middle name, but it is not known. There is simply no way to tell.

The XML Schema standard introduces the concept of a 'nil' value to indicate that there is no value. An element can be explicitly given a nil value without ambiguity. The element is present, but has a value that states that there is no value. The standard suggests one typical use of this mechanism: to carry 'null' entries from database fields.

Typical values, such as 'null', 'nil' or 'false', cannot be used for this purpose, as they may already have specific meaning within a particular XML application. Instead, the http://www.w3.org/2001/XMLSchema-instance namespace is employed to identify a **Nil** attribute, which can take the value 'true' or 'false':

```
<names
   xmlns:xsi="http://www.w3.org/2001/XMLSchema-instance"
   <name>
     <first>Sam</first>
     <middle xsi:nil="true"></middle>
     <last>Smith</last>
   </name>
</names>
```

Some might argue that this is still not totally clear. For example, while a database may have a 'null' entry for the middle name, this still does not clarify whether or not the person *has* a middle name. Maybe it was just not known to the input operator. But this feature does at least make it clear that the information was not omitted by accident.

The schema author is able to state which elements can have 'nil' values. This is done by adding the **Nillable** attribute to the Element element, and giving it the value 'true':

```
<element name="middle" nillable="true" ... />
```

Note that a 'nil' element can still carry attributes.

Local element definitions

It is not necessary to define an element in one place, then refer to this definition in the content model of another element definition. When the element concerned is only used within the model of one other element, it is more efficient to simply define the sub-element *in situ* within the model of the outer element. The embedded element definition uses the **Name** attribute instead of the Ref attribute. Sub-elements of these inserted definitions can also be defined locally. In the following example, the Book element definition includes the Chapter element definition, and the Chapter element in turn defines the Paragraph element:

```
<element name="book">
  <!-- BOOK DEFINITION -->
  <complexType>
    <sequence>
      <element ref="DOC:title" />

      <!-- CHAPTER DEFINITION -->
      <element name="chapter" maxOccurs="unbounded">
        <complexType>
          <sequence>
            <element ref="DOC:title" />

            <!-- PARAGRAPH DEFINITION -->
            <element name="para" type="string" />

          </sequence>
        </complexType>
      </element>

    </sequence>
  </complexType>
</element>
```

Note that both the outer and inner models refer to the 'global' Title element definition. This demonstrates that it is possible to mix element definitions and element references.

Local limitations

The elements defined within the Book element above are known as 'local' elements because they have no existence beyond the location where they are defined. They cannot be referenced from other content models. Also, they can never be the root element of a conforming document (because there would be no context ancestor elements to unambiguously identify them).

Re-defining elements

Using local definitions, it is possible for the schema model to include several, context-specific element definitions that have the same name, but different content models or attributes. For example, within a Person element it may be desirable to have a Title element that is restricted to a few possible values, such as 'Mr', 'Mrs', 'Miss' and 'Ms'. A local definition overrides a global definition with the same name, and is also clearly distinct from any other definitions that are local to other element models:

```
<element name="title" type="string" />

<element name="chapter">
  <complexType>
    <sequence>
      <element name="title">...</element>
      ...
    </sequence>
  </complexType>
</element>

<element name="person">
  <complexType>
    <sequence>
      <element name="title">...</element>
      ...
    </sequence>
  </complexType>
</element>
```

Namespace prefix issues

This concept raises the issue that, within a compliant document, it is no longer sufficient to rely upon namespaces to specify exactly which element is being referenced. The context must also be taken into account. Apparently contrary to the Namespace specification, it is possible to specify in a schema that locally defined elements *must* be qualified (given a prefix, or assume the default namespace), or *must not* be qualified. This is a controversial concept, disparaged by many experts in the use of namespaces. It is particularly controversial because the latter option is the default mode. Consider the following example:

```
<listOfPeople>
  <title>This is a list of people</title>
  <P:person xmlns:P="...">
    <title>Mr</title>
    ...
  </P:person>
  ...
</listOfPeople>
```

In this example, the first Title element does not belong to any namespace. A namespace-sensitive parser will assume that the second title also does not belong to any namespace, because there is no default namespace declaration. The same problem would arise if the whole document belonged to a default namespace. Yet this title is defined within the same document model as the Person element containing it, so it really needs to be interpreted as belonging to the same namespace as the Person element. It should have the namespace prefix 'P:', and will therefore be misinterpreted by applications that are not schema-sensitive.

The other problem with this approach is that the document author needs to know which elements are forced to have a prefix, and which are forced to not have one (though a schema-sensitive XML editor could help considerably).

To overcome this issue, it is possible to specify that a prefix (or implied prefix, if the default namespace is in effect) must be present on local elements in the instance document. The **ElementFormDefault** attribute on the Schema element can be set to 'qualified' (from the default value of 'unqualified'). The example above would then need to be modified as shown below:

```
<listOfPeople>
  <title>This is a list of people</title>
  <P:person xmlns:P="...">
    <P:title>Mr</P:title>
    ...
  </P:person>
  ...
</listOfPeople>
```

The **Form** attribute on the Element element serves the same purpose, and has the same possible values, but specifies a setting for that element only (the Attribute element also has the Form attribute).

Unique values

Going far beyond the DTD concept of using a special attribute type (the ID type) to uniquely identify a single element within the whole document, this standard allows a set of selected elements to form a group, within which each element must have a unique value somewhere within it, though not necessarily an attribute value, and possibly a combination of values.

Unique elements

The **Unique** element can appear at the end of an Element definition, after the optional ComplexType or SimpleType sub-element. If the test is to be applied to the whole document instance, then this element should be placed in the definition of the root element, as in the Book element definition here (placement elsewhere is discussed later):

```
<element name="book">
  <complexType>...</complexType>
  <unique name="...">...</unique>
</element>
```

The Unique element also has a **Name** attribute, which can be used in 'key' references (described below).

The Unique element may first contain an Annotation element, then contains further elements that identify the structures that must be unique, and the values within these structures that should make them uniquely identifiable.

Element structure selectors

An XPath expression (see Chapter 13) identifies the elements that form a set of unique items. The **Selector** element has an **XPath** attribute, which has an implied path starting point of the element the Unique element is defined within (in this case the whole book, as represented by the Book element). In the following example, only the Chapter element children of the Book element are being considered:

```
<element name="book">
  <unique name="MyUniqueChaptersInBook">
    <annotation>
      <documentation>CHAPTERS ARE UNIQUE</documentation>
    </annotation>
    <selector xpath="chapter">
      <annotation>CHAPTER ELEMENTS IN BOOK</annotation>
    </selector>
    ...
  </unique>
</element>


  <book>
    <intro>...</intro>
    <chapter>...</chapter>
    <chapter>...</chapter>
    <chapter>...</chapter>
    <appendix>...</appendix>
  </book>
```

There are some limitations on the XPath expressions that can be used. The most significant thing to note is that it is not possible to navigate up the document structure, and that an attribute cannot be selected. The XPath expression can still have optional components, separated by '|' symbols, but each component is limited to starting with './/', '.', a qualified element name (such as 'ACME:chapter' or 'chapter'), the wildcard symbol ('*') or any element from a given namespace ('ACME:*'), and thereafter consists of '/' separated steps. The 'child::' prefix may also be used.

The XPath expression is namespace-sensitive; the relevant prefix defined in the schema document is used in the expression, but is mapped to the appropriate local document prefix when the document is being validated.

Unique identifier selectors

It is necessary to specify which attribute value or element content value forms the unique identifier. This is done using a **Field** element, which also has an **XPath** attribute, but this time the path it contains identifies the objects containing the unique values, and also assumes that the target object has already been selected, so the expression is relative to this position.

The XPath expression is the same as for selectors, as described above, except that it is possible to select attribute values. For example, if each chapter has an Id attribute, then the path '@id' selects the Id attribute of each Chapter element:

```
<unique name="MyUniqueChapters">
  <selector xpath="chapter" />
  <field xpath="@id" />
</unique>


  <book>
    <chapter id="Chapter1">...</chapter>
    <chapter id="Chapter2">...</chapter>
    <chapter id="Chapter3">...</chapter>
  </book>
```

Alternatively, the chapters could all have a unique Title child element:

```
<unique name="MyUniqueChapters">
  <selector xpath="chapter" />
  <field xpath="title" />
</unique>
```

```
<chapter>
  <title>Chapter One</title>
  ...
</chapter>
<chapter>
  <title>Chapter Two/title>
  ...
</chapter>
<chapter>
  <title>Chapter Three</title>
  ...
</chapter>
```

However, there can be one or more instances that have no value at all, without causing any errors. This is an important distinguishing feature between this feature and the 'key' feature (described later).

Compound values

There may be situations when a single attribute value or element content value is not guaranteed to be unique, but a combination of values would be.

For example, in a catalogue an item of clothing might be identified by a combination of its product code, its size and its colour. Multiple **Field** elements identify each piece of the unique value:

```
<unique name="UniqueClothesItem">
  <selector xpath="item" />
  <field xpath="@X123"/>
  <field xpath="size"/>
  <field xpath="colour"/>
</unique>
```

```
  <item code="X123">
    <title>Summer Dress</title>
    <size>10</size>
    <colour>red</colour>
    <price>...</price>
    <description>...</description>
  </item>
```

The document is invalid if the combined value is not unique. For example, if there are two items in the catalogue that have a code of 'X123', a size of '10' and a colour of 'red', then an error is reported.

Partial document coverage

The scope of the uniqueness test is limited to each instance of the element type that contains the definition. When defined in an element that is not the root element of a particular instance, the test is reapplied within each instance of that element.

For example, when specified within the Chapter element definition it applies separately to each chapter. So the Section element identifiers are considered unique in the example below, even though they are not unique within the book as a whole:

```
<element name="chapter">
  ...
  <unique name="SectionIDs">
    <selector xpath="section" />
    <field xpath="@id" />
  </unique>
</element>


    <book>
      <chapter>
            <!-- THIS IS UNIQUE -->
        <section id="SEC1">...</section>
        <section id="SEC2">...</section>
        <section id="SEC3">...</section>
      </chapter>

      <chapter>
            <!-- THIS IS UNIQUE -->
        <section id="SEC1">...</section>
        <section id="SEC2">...</section>
        <section id="SEC3">...</section>
      </chapter>

      <chapter>
            <!-- THIS IS UNIQUE -->
        <section id="SEC1">...</section>
        <section id="SEC2">...</section>
        <section id="SEC3">...</section>
      </chapter>
    </book>
```

Unique keys

It may be a requirement that for each element of a particular type in one part of the document, there needs to be another element elsewhere in the document that is related to it. The XML standard provides a crude scheme for validating that such a relationship exists, using the ID and IDREF attribute types. Each attribute of type IDREF has a value that serves as a reference to the value of another element that has an attribute of type ID. Although used primarily to support hypertext linking features, this mechanism can be used purely to validate that each referencing object does in fact point to another real object in the same file. A parser reports an error if the value in an attribute with a type of IDREF cannot also be found in any other attribute of type ID.

There are two points of interest in the XML ID/IDREF scheme. First, ID values must be unique. Second, IDREF values do not have to be unique (there can be many references to the same object). But the XML scheme is limited in several ways:

- the target object can only be a single value, restricted to specific characters, and must not include spaces
- the target object must be an element that holds the identifier value in one of its attributes
- the referencing object must be an element that directly holds the reference value in one of its attributes
- there is only one 'namespace' for identifiers, regardless of how many ways references are used, in different element structures, for very different purposes.

All of these limitation are addressed by the XML Schema standard, which provides an alternative, more powerful way to validate associations.

Keys

The discussion in the previous section concerning unique values is of relevance to this problem. The target object, or 'keyed' object, must be unique, so it should not be surprising that the **Key** element has the same content model and attributes as the Unique element (described above). The **Selector** sub-element again identifies the elements to be grouped and identified within a particular 'namespace', and the **Field** sub-element again identifies the key value or values. In addition, the **Name** attribute must be used to give the key an identifier that can be referred to later:

```
<element name="employees">
  ...
  <key name="PersonKeys">
    <selector xpath="person" />
    <field xpath="employeeNum" />
  </key>
</element>


  <employees>
    <person>
      <employeeNum>1234</employeeNum><name>J Smith</name>
    </person>
    <person>
      <employeeNum>9876</employeeNum><name>P Jones</name>
    </person>
  </employees>
```

Key references

A reference can only be made to a key if the referencing object holds a copy of the key value or values. To refer to one of the objects in the example above, it must already have an employee number, such as '1234'.

The **Keyref** element has an equivalent structure to the Key element, as it requires the **Selector** and **Field** elements to identify the referring object, and its copy of the key value. But it also has a **Refer** attribute, which is used to refer to the key name:

```
<element name="department">
  ...
  <keyref name="PersonKey">
    <selector xpath="person" />
    <field xpath="@employeeNum" refer="PersonKeys" />
  </keyref>
</element>


  <department>
    <person employeeNum="1234" />
    <person employeeNum="9876" />
  </department>
```

Note that the values do not have to be held in the same form. In the example above, the employee number is element content in the key objects, and attribute value content in the referencing objects. However, the values in each place must belong to the same data type, such as 'string' or 'integer'. Also, when multiple Field elements are needed, they must be arranged in the same order, though the actual values may be present in a different order within the two structures.

A reference can also be made to **Unique** elements, which also have a **Name** attribute. This option is needed to cater for the possibility that some of the target structures have no key values. Note that the **Keyref** element itself also has a **Name** attribute, but it is not clear what purpose it serves (nothing references this element).

Data types

The XML Schema standard includes a large number of data types (beyond those introduced in the previous chapter, needed for backward compatibility with DTDs). The following table shows all of the simple types, whether or not they are ordered types that have minimum and maximum possible values (leading and trailing '...' indicates no specified limits), and an example of the type in use:

Simple type	Ordered type	Min and max values	Examples

string	-	-	`<note>`
			
			`this    is    a`
			
			`string    </note>`

normalizedString	-	-	`name="J Smith"`
token	-	-	`colour="red"`
byte	Y	-128 -127 ... -1 0 1 ... 126 127	`-13   or   99`
unsignedByte	Y	1 2 ... 254 255	`age="77"`
base64Binary	-	-	`GpM7`
hexBinary	-	-	`<image>FF008B7C22F6</` `image>`
integer	Y	.... -2 -1 0 1 2 ...	`hourFromUTC="-2"`
positiveInteger	Y	1 2 3 ...	`age="3"`
negativeInteger	Y	... -3 -2 -1	`<debt goldBars="-3"/>`
nonNegativeInteger	Y	0 1 2 ...	`<score>0</score>`
nonPositiveInteger	Y	... -2 -1 0	`countdown="-5"`
int	Y	-2147483648 ... 2147483647	
unsignedInt	Y	0 1 2 ... 4294967295	
long	Y	-9223372036854775808 ... -1 0 1 ... 9223372036854775807	
unsignedLong	Y	0 1 2 ... 18446744073709551615	
short	Y	-32768 ... -1 0 1 ... 32767	
unsignedShort	Y	0 1 2 ... 65534 65535	
decimal	Y	... -1 ... -0.1 ... -00000.00001 0 00000.00001 ... 0.1 ... 1 ...	`<width>0.0013</width>`
float	Y	$E\ 2^{24\ -149\ ...\ 104}$ (IEEE 754-1985)	`<salary>123E99</salary>`

double	Y	E 2^{53} $^{-1075}$ ... ^{970} *(IEEE 754-1985)*	`<salary>45E876</salary>`
boolean	Y	false .. true *or* 0 ... 1	
time	Y	00:00:00.000 ... 23:59:59.999 *with possible suffix offset from UTC of* -01:00 ... -12:00 *or* 01:00 ... 12:00 *(ISO 8601)*	`maratho-nEnd="11:02:45.123"`
dateTime	Y	0001-01-01T00:00:00.000 ... 2999-12-31T23:59:59.999 ... *with possible '-' prefix offset from UTC of 'Z' (UTC) or* -01:00 ... -12:00 *or* 01:00 ... 12:00 *(ISO 8601)*	`countdown="-5"`
duration	Y	P*n*Y*n*M*n*DT*n*H*n*M (Y=Years/M=Months/D=Days/T=Time/H=Hours/M=Minutes)	`dura-tion="P1Y2M3DT10H30M"` *(1 year, 2 months, 3 days, 1 hour and 3 minutes)*
date	Y	0001-01-01 ... 2000-01-01 ... 2999-12-31 ... *with possible '-' prefix offset from UTC of 'Z' (UTC) or* -01:00 ... -12:00 *or* 01:00 ... 12:00 *(ISO 8601)*	`publish="2002-05-17Z"`
gMonth	Y	--01-- ... --12--	`<publishMonth>--05--</publishMonth>`
gYear	Y	0001 ... 2000 ...	`<publishYear>2002</publishYear>`
gYearMonth	Y	0001-01 ... 2000-12 ...	`<YearMonth>2002-05</YearMonth>`
gDay	Y	---01 ... ---31	`<publishInMay>---17</publishInMay>`
gMonthDay	Y	--01-01 ... --12-31	`<publishIn2002>--05-17</publishIn2002>`
Name	Y	-	`My:Name:Tag`
QName	Y	-	`ACME:MyName`
NCName	Y	-	`MyName`
anyURI	Y	-	`www.bradley.co.uk`
language	Y	-	`en`
ID*	Y	*see Chapter 5*	-
IDREF*	Y	*see Chapter 5*	-
IDREFS*	Y	*see Chapter 5*	-

ENTITY*	Y	*see Chapter 5*	-
ENTITIES*	Y	*see Chapter 5*	-
NOTATION*	Y	*see Chapter 5*	-
NMTOKEN*	Y	*see Chapter 5*	-
NMTOKENS*	Y	*see Chapter 5*	-

* included for backward compatibility with XML DTD attribute types, and for this reason should only be used for attribute values.

Type hierarchy

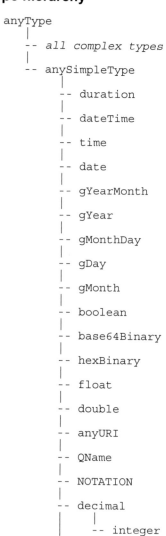

```
anyType
  |
  -- all complex types
  |
  -- anySimpleType
        |
        -- duration
        |
        -- dateTime
        |
        -- time
        |
        -- date
        |
        -- gYearMonth
        |
        -- gYear
        |
        -- gMonthDay
        |
        -- gDay
        |
        -- gMonth
        |
        -- boolean
        |
        -- base64Binary
        |
        -- hexBinary
        |
        -- float
        |
        -- double
        |
        -- anyURI
        |
        -- QName
        |
        -- NOTATION
        |
        -- decimal
        |      |
        |      -- integer
```

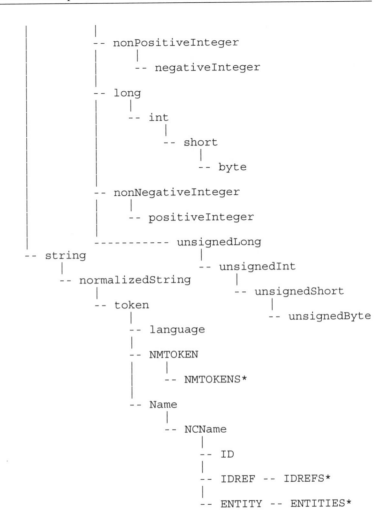

```
              |
              -- nonPositiveInteger
      |       |
      |          -- negativeInteger
      |       |
      |    -- long
      |       |
      |          -- int
      |       |      |
      |              -- short
      |                     |
      |                        -- byte
      |       |
      |    -- nonNegativeInteger
      |       |
      |          -- positiveInteger
      |       |
      |       ---------- unsignedLong
 -- string            |
      |                 -- unsignedInt
      -- normalizedString    |
             |                 -- unsignedShort
          -- token             |
             |                   -- unsignedByte
             -- language
             |
             -- NMTOKEN
             |     |
             |        -- NMTOKENS*
             |
             -- Name
                   |
                      -- NCName
                            |
                            -- ID
                            |
                            -- IDREF -- IDREFS*
                            |
                            -- ENTITY -- ENTITIES*
```

Type library

Many commonly required data types are pre-defined in the 'type library' provided with the standard, ftp://www.w3.org/2001/03/XMLSchema/TypeLibrary.xsd. This library includes such types as:

- text (TypeLibrary-text.xsd)
- arrays (TypeLibrary-array.xsd)
- lists (TypeLibrary-list.xsd)
- mathematics (TypeLibrary-math.xsd)
- quantity test (TypeLibrary-quantity.xsd).

Simple type derivations

A major feature of this standard is the ability it gives schema authors to create new simple data types that are specific to the document model being defined. A new data type is 'derived' from an existing type by first referencing an existing simple data type, then creating a new one that is either a restricted version or an extended version of that type (later it is shown how complex types can also be derived).

For example, it is possible to create a new numeric type that is based on the 'integer' type, but is constrained to a value between '5' and '50'. Conversely, the original type can be extended to allow lists of values, or by allowing the value to conform to one of several possible types. Once created, the new type can be referenced in the usual way from element and attribute definitions. In the following example, the element Score will hold a value of type 'scoreRange', which is a restricted or extended version of a simpler data type, such as 'integer':

```
<element name="score" type="DOC:scoreRange" />
```

Because 'scoreRange' is not a built-in data type, it has the namespace prefix of the target namespace, in this case 'DOC:', or would have no prefix if the default namespace was in use.

The creation of new simple data types is not limited to the creation of custom types from those types built in to the standard. It is also possible to create new types from other custom types. There is also a way to prevent this from happening, either at all, or in specific ways (using techniques described toward the end of this chapter).

Simple type definitions

New simple data types are created using the **SimpleType** element, and named using a **Name** attribute. In the following example, a new type called 'scoreRange' is being defined:

```
<simpleType name="scoreRange">...</simpleType>
```

This element can initially contain an Annotation element, then can either define a list type, create a new type that is a combination of two or more existing types (a 'union') or create a restricted version of an existing data type.

Lists

The **List** element is used to create lists of values of a given type. The **ItemType** attribute identifies the data type that the values in the list must conform to:

```
<simpleType name="scoresList">
  <list itemType="integer" />
</simpleType>
```

Spaces separate each item in a list. The following example shows multiple integer values in a Scores element that has adopted the type defined above:

```
<scores>57 123 19 87</scores>
```

It follows that it would be dangerous to base a list type on the 'string' data type, because strings can contain spaces. It would not be possible to distinguish between embedded spaces and item-separating spaces. A string with one space in it would be treated as two list items.

As an alternative to referencing an existing data type, the List element can contain a complete simple type definition, including unions and restrictions:

```
<simpleType name="scores">
  <list><simpleType>...</simpleType></list>
</simpleType>
```

The List element may have a **Fixed** attribute which, if set to 'true', indicates that no derived types can later be defined with this type as its base.

Unions

It is possible to create a new data type that is an amalgamation of two or more existing types. Values are considered valid when they conform to the constraints of any of the types concerned. The **Union** element refers to two or more data types, possibly using the **MemberTypes** attribute to refer to the types to be included. The following example creates a new data type called 'ScoreOrNoScore', from a union of the 'integer' type and the 'NoScore' type (the 'enumeration' element is discussed later):

```
<!-- value is 'none' only -->
<simpleType name="NoScore">
  <restriction base="NMTOKEN">
    <enumeration value="none"/>
  </restriction>
</simpleType>

<!-- value is either 'none', or a number -->
<simpleType name="ScoreOrNoScore">
  <union memberTypes="integer DOC:NoScore" />
</simpleType>
```

A Score element that adopts this type can have values such as:

```
<score>44</score>
<score>none</score>
<score>9</score>
```

But it is not necessary to reference existing data types. Instead, one or more of the types to be merged can be created within the Union element itself. This approach requires another, embedded **SimpleType** element, usually containing a Restriction element to create a restricted version of an existing data type (described later).

Combinations of unions and lists

A list can be created from a union type. For example:

```
<!-- value is either 'none' or a number, and
     is repeatable -->
<simpleType name="ScoreOrNoScoreList">
  <list itemType="DOC:ScoreOrNoScore" />
</simpleType>
```

A Scores element that adopts this type could have a value as follows:

```
<scores>44 none 9</scores>
```

Conversely, a union can include a list as one (or more) of its components. In the following example, the scores list type is combined with a simple boolean type:

```
<simpleType name="ScoreOrGamePlayed">
  <union memberTypes="DOC:ScoreOrNoScoreList boolean" />
</simpleType>
```

But this construct can be confusing. It it important to understand that it does not allow the two component types to be mixed within a single value, just because one of the component types happens to be a list type. Instead, it is only possible to have a list of values from the list type, or to have a single value from the other type. An element called ScoresOrGamePlayed that adopted this type could have the following values:

```
        <!-- game was played -->
<scoresOrGamePlayed>true</scoresOrGamePlayed>

        <!-- game was not played -->
<scoresOrGamePlayed>false</scoresOrGamePlayed>

    <!-- game way played, and here are the scores -->
<scoresOrGamePlayed>44 none 9</scoresOrGamePlayed>
```

Restrictions

A simple way to form a new data type is to create a restricted version of an existing type. The previous chapter briefly showed how this concept is used to restrict an attribute value to one of a pre-defined set of possible values. In this example, the Attribute definition must modify a simple type (attributes cannot contain complex types). This is done by embedding a SimpleType element (or possibly referencing one defined elsewhere). Within this element, a **Restriction** element is used to first identify, in its **Base** attribute, the existing data type that is to be the basis of the new, more restricted type (in this case, 'NMTOKEN'), then hold Enumeration elements to identify each possible value:

```
<attribute name="security">
  <simpleType>
    <restriction base="NMTOKEN">
      <enumeration value="normal"/>
      <enumeration value="secret"/>
      <enumeration value="topSecret"/>
    </restriction>
  </simpleType>
</attribute>
```

Note that, because this attribute is defining its own data type, it must not include either a Type attribute or a Ref attribute (it is creating the type, not referring to an existing one, and also not referencing an attribute declaration elsewhere).

Facets

As shown above, a restriction is created by first identifying an existing data type, then specifying the constraints to be applied to this data type in order to form the new data type. These constraints are known as **facets**. The facets available vary somewhat, depending on the data type. For example, the 'NMTOKEN' type has an 'enumeration' facet, and indeed this facet applies to all data types except for the 'boolean' type. Other facets are less ubiquitous. For example, the 'length' facet cannot be used with the number-based types, such as the 'integer' facet.

The most basic facet types are:

- length ('length')
- minimum length ('minLength')
- maximum length ('maxLength')
- pattern ('pattern')
- enumeration ('enumeration')
- whitespace ('whiteSpace').

Simple type	length	min-Length	max-Length	pattern	enumera-tion	white-Space
string	Y	Y	Y	Y	Y	Y
normalizedString	Y	Y	Y	Y	Y	Y
token	Y	Y	Y	Y	Y	Y
byte				Y	Y	Y
unsignedByte				Y	Y	Y
base64Binary	Y	Y	Y	Y	Y	Y

hexBinary	Y	Y	Y	Y	Y	Y
integer				Y	Y	Y
positiveInteger				Y	Y	Y
negativeInteger				Y	Y	Y
nonNegativeInteger				Y	Y	Y
nonPositiveInteger				Y	Y	Y
int				Y	Y	Y
unsignedInt				Y	Y	Y
long				Y	Y	Y
unsignedLong				Y	Y	Y
short				Y	Y	Y
unsignedShort				Y	Y	Y
decimal				Y	Y	Y
float				Y	Y	Y
double				Y	Y	Y
boolean				Y		Y
time				Y	Y	Y
dateTime				Y	Y	Y
duration				Y	Y	Y
date				Y	Y	Y
gMonth				Y	Y	Y
gYear				Y	Y	Y
gYearMonth				Y	Y	Y
gDay				Y	Y	Y
gMonthDay				Y	Y	Y
Name	Y	Y	Y	Y	Y	Y
QName	Y	Y	Y	Y	Y	Y
NCName	Y	Y	Y	Y	Y	Y
anyURI	Y	Y	Y	Y	Y	Y
language	Y	Y	Y	Y	Y	Y
ID	Y	Y	Y	Y	Y	Y
IDREF	Y	Y	Y	Y	Y	Y
IDREFS	Y	Y	Y	Y	Y	Y

ENTITY	Y	Y	Y	Y	Y	Y
ENTITIES	Y	Y	Y	Y	Y	Y
NOTATION	Y	Y	Y	Y	Y	Y
NMTOKEN	Y	Y	Y	Y	Y	Y
NMTOKENS	Y	Y	Y	Y	Y	Y

Enumerated types have additional facets. These types can be constrained to a specific range of values, using a minimum and maximum setting, and the total number of digits in the value, or in just the fractional part of the value, can also be specified. The additional facets are:

- maximum inclusive ('maxInclusive')
- maximum exclusive ('maxExclusive')
- minimum inclusive ('minInclusive')
- minimum exclusive ('minExclusive')
- total digits ('totalDigits')
- fractional digits ('fractionDigits').

The following table shows which enumerated types can have these facets:

Simple type	max-Inclusive	max-Exclusive	min-Inclusive	min-Exclusive	totalDigits	fraction-Digits
byte	Y	Y	Y	Y	Y	Y
unsignedByte	Y	Y	Y	Y	Y	Y
integer	Y	Y	Y	Y	Y	Y
positiveInteger	Y	Y	Y	Y	Y	Y
negativeInteger	Y	Y	Y	Y	Y	Y
nonNegativeInteger	Y	Y	Y	Y	Y	Y
nonPositiveInteger	Y	Y	Y	Y	Y	Y
int	Y	Y	Y	Y	Y	Y
unsignedInt	Y	Y	Y	Y	Y	Y
long	Y	Y	Y	Y	Y	Y
unsignedLong	Y	Y	Y	Y	Y	Y
short	Y	Y	Y	Y	Y	Y
unsignedShort	Y	Y	Y	Y	Y	Y
decimal	Y	Y	Y	Y	Y	Y

float	Y	Y	Y	Y		
double	Y	Y	Y	Y		
time	Y	Y	Y	Y		
dateTime	Y	Y	Y	Y		
duration	Y	Y	Y	Y		
date	Y	Y	Y	Y		
gMonth	Y	Y	Y	Y		
gYear	Y	Y	Y	Y		
gYearMonth	Y	Y	Y	Y		
gDay	Y	Y	Y	Y		
gMonthDay	Y	Y	Y	Y		

A separate element represents each facet. These are the **Length**, **MinLength**, **MaxLength**, **Pattern**, **Enumeration**, **Whitespace**, **MaxInclusive**, **MaxExclusive**, **MinInclusive**, **MaxInclusive**, **TotalDigits** and **FractionDigits** elements. All of these elements are empty apart from an optional Annotation element, and all have a **Value** attribute to specify a constraint for that particular type. For example, the 'length' facet may be used to constrain a value to 13 characters:

```
<length value="13" />
```

```
<length value="13"><annotation>...</annotation></length>
```

The **Fixed** attribute can be set to 'true' in order to ensure that any data type that uses the current data type as a base cannot override the facet value (except on the Enumeration and Pattern elements, where this attribute is not permitted):

```
<length value="13" fixed="true"/>
```

Length facets

The 'length' facet constrains the value to a set number of characters. The 'minimum length' and 'maximum length' facets merely constrain the value to a minimum and maximum number of characters respectively. These two facets can be used together, but it would not make sense to use either along with the 'length' facet (which already specifies a minimum and (identical) maximum value). The **Length**, **MinLength** and **MaxLength** elements are used:

```
<restriction type="string>
  <length value="13" />
</restriction>
```

```
<restriction type="string>
  <minLength value="13" />
  <maxLength value="13" />
</restriction>
```

Pattern facet

The 'pattern' facet defines a pattern of characters (a template), against which a value is compared. For example, a pattern can be used to specify that a value must begin with three letters, followed by four digits. A value of 'abc1234' would match this pattern, and so would 'xyz9876', but 'ab12345' would fail to match because it has too few letters and too many digits. Patterns can be much more complex, however. For example, 'ab?c(x\^x|[d-w-[m]]|zz\p{IsGothic})+' is a valid pattern (and the pattern language is explained in detail below). The **Pattern** element is used:

```
<pattern value="ab?c(x\^x|[d-w-[m]]|zz\p{IsGothic})+"/>
```

Enumeration facet

The 'enumeration' facet defines a fixed value. Typically, there will be several Enumeration elements, between them defining a range of options. Note that an enumeration value can have a space in it (unlike a DTD enumerated type), but this is not advisable if there is a possibility that a new list type will be derived from this type, because spaces are used in list types to separate the items. The **Enumeration** element is used:

```
<restriction base="string"> <!-- abc or def -->
  <enumeration value="abc" />
  <enumeration value="def" />
</restriction>


  <code>abc</code>
  <code>def</code>
  <code>abcdef</code> <!-- NOT VALID -->
  <code>xyz</code>    <!-- NOT VALID -->
```

Whitespace facet

The 'whitespace' facet affects the whitespace characters (space, tab, line-feed and carriage-return) in a value, and can be used to 'replace' line-feed, carriage-return and tab characters with space characters, or go further and 'collapse' such a value by then also removing leading, trailing and multiple-embedded spaces. The value 'collapse' is assumed and fixed for data types that are not string-based. The same is true for all list types. At the other extreme, the value 'preserve' is assumed and fixed for the 'string' data type. But for all types derived from 'string', the **Whitespace** element can be used to set any of the options (the default being 'preserve').

Note that, uniquely, this facet type is not used to validate a target value, but to modify that value (though the standard seems to be confused on this point, as it also suggests that it is used to create the 'normalizedString' type from the 'string' type, and therefore acts as a validation rather than a transformation instruction):

```
<!-- ORIGINAL -->
 <para> This is a
     paragraph.  </para>

<restriction base="string">
  <whitespace value="replace" />
</restriction>

  <!-- REPLACED -->
  <para> This is a   paragraph.  </para>

<restriction base="string">
  <whitespace value="collapse" />
</restriction>

  <!-- COLLAPSED -->
  <para>This is a paragraph.</para>
```

Numeric value limitation facets

The 'minimum inclusive' facet specifies a minimum allowed value, such as '15'. For a value to be legal, it must be at least this amount. The term 'inclusive' means that the specified value is allowed, as well as all higher values. A 'minimum exclusive' value, on the other hand, excludes the specified value. A value of '15' means that the actual value must be higher than this. How close it can get to this value depends on the data type. For an integer type, the lowest possible value would be '16', but for a decimal type it could be lower than '15.0000000001'.

The **MinInclusive**, **MinExclusive**, **MaxInclusive** and **MaxExclusive** elements are used to set these limits on values:

```
<!-- 1 - 99 -->
<restriction base="integer">
  <minInclusive value="1" />
  <maxInclusive value="99" />
</restriction>

<!-- 0.00001 - 0.99999 -->
<restriction base="decimal">
  <minExclusive value="0" />
  <maxExclusive value="1" />
</restriction>
```

Number of digits facets

The 'total digits' facet specifies the maximum number of digits in a numeric value. This is not the same as the length constraint, as other symbols may appear in a number, such as a leading '+' or '-' sign, and a decimal point. The value '6' simply states that there may be no more than six digits in the value. It is further possible to control the number of these digits that follow a decimal point, using the 'fraction digits' facet. The value of this facet type is the maximum number of digits allowed in the fractional part of a decimal number. The **TotalDigits** and **FractionDigits** elements are used:

```
<restriction base="decimal">
  <totalDigits value="4"/>
  <fractionDigits value="2"/>
</restriction>
```

```
<amount>1</amount>
<amount>1.2</amount>
<amount>12.3</amount>
<amount>12.34</amount>
<amount>123.45</amount> <!-- TOO MANY DIGITS -->
<amount>1.234</amount>  <!-- TOO MANY FRACTION DIGITS -->
<amount>12.345</amount> <!-- BOTH CONSTRAINTS BROKEN -->
```

Facets in list types

List data types can be constrained using the following facets:

- length
- minLength
- maxLength
- enumeration.

The three length-related facets are, in this case, used to constrain the number of items in the list, rather than the length of each of these items:

```
<!-- value is either 'none', or a number and
     is repeatable -->
<simpleType name="ScoreOrNoScoreList">
  <list itemType="DOC:ScoreOrNoScore" />
</simpleType>

<!-- no more than 10 scores in list -->
<simpleType name="ScoreOrNoScoreListLimits">
  <restriction base="DOC:ScoreOrNoScoreList">
    <maxInclusive value="10" />
  </restriction>
</simpleType>
```

The 'enumeration' facet restricts the items that can appear in the list to the given values.

Facet usage limitations

While the **Pattern** and **Enumeration** elements may repeat, in order to define over-lapping restrictions, and to define a list of options, it is not possible to repeat any of the other facets. It makes no sense, for example, to specify two lengths, or two minimum values.

Many combinations of facets make no sense, and are therefore mutually exclusive. For example, it is not possible to set a minimum inclusive value while also setting a minimum exclusive value.

Patterns

The 'pattern' facet clearly requires more explanation than the brief description above. This XML Schema feature is based on the **regular expression** capabilities available in the Perl programming language, and is therefore very powerful, but also consequently quite complex.

Simple templates

The **Pattern** element holds a pattern in its **Value** attribute. The simplest possible form of pattern involves a series of characters that must be present, in the order specified, in each element or attribute definition that uses it. The following pattern restriction specifies that the value must be 'abc':

```
<pattern value="abc" />
```

In this simple form, a pattern is similar to an enumeration. Just as a restriction can contain multiple Enumeration elements, it can also contain multiple Pattern elements. The element or attribute instance is valid if it matches any of the patterns:

```
<restriction base="string">
  <pattern value="abc"/>
  <pattern value="xyz"/>
</restriction>


  <code>abc</code>
  <code>xyz</code>
  <code>acb</code> <!-- ERROR -->
  <code>xzy</code> <!-- ERROR -->
  <code>abcc</code> <!-- ERROR -->
```

Alternatively, a single pattern may contain multiple 'branches'. Each branch is essentially a separate expression, separated from surrounding branches using 'I' symbols. Again, the pattern test succeeds if any one of the branches matches the target value, so the 'I' symbol is performing a similar function to its use in DTD content models. The following example is therefore equivalent to the multi-pattern example above:

```
<restriction base="string">
  <pattern value="abc|xyz"/>
</restriction>
```

Note that, although branches are an optional technique at this level, they are the only way to achieve this effect in the later discussion on sub-expressions.

Atoms

Each branch of an expression (or the whole expression, if it is not divided into branches) consists of a number of 'atoms'. In the examples above, the single letter 'a' is an atom, and 'b' is another. Apart from individual characters, an atom can also be a 'character class' (an escape sequence, or a selection from a pre-defined or user-defined group of characters), or a complete sub-expression (as explained further below).

Each atom validates one portion of the value the pattern is being compared to, in sequential order from left to right. This is why the first atom, 'a', is expected to match the first character of the value. If the value does not begin with an 'a' character, the value has already failed to match the pattern. If the value *does* begin with 'a', then the next atom, 'b', is compared with the next character in the value.

Quantifiers

A 'quantifier' can be added to an atom to specify how frequently the atom may occur. The examples above have no quantifier. In these cases, an implied quantifier specifies that the atom must occur exactly once. The expression 'abc' therefore specifies that the content of the element or attribute must be exactly 'abc'. There must be one 'a' character, followed by one 'b' character, followed by one 'c' character. The values 'ab', 'bc' and 'abcc' would not be valid.

Explicit quantifiers include the symbols '?', '+' and '*' (which have meanings that will be unsurprising to those familiar with DTD content models), and 'quantities' that allow any number of occurrences to be precisely specified.

The explicit quantifier '?' indicates that the atom is optional. The expression 'ab?c' makes the 'b' atom optional, so legal values include 'abc' and 'ac'.

The explicit quantifier '+' indicates that the atom is repeatable. The expression 'ab+c' makes the 'b' atom repeatable, so legal values include 'abc' and 'abbbc'.

The explicit quantifier '*' indicates that the atom is both optional and repeatable. The expression 'ab*c' makes the 'b' atom optional and repeatable, so legal values include 'ac', 'abc' and 'abbbc'.

The following example includes all three quantifiers, and all of the following target Code elements are valid according to this pattern:

```
<pattern value="a+b?c*" />


    <code>a</code>
    <code>ab</code>
    <code>abc</code>
    <code>aaa</code>
    <code>aaab</code>
    <code>aaabc</code>
    <code>aaabccc</code>
```

Quantities

A 'quantity' is a more finely-tuned instrument for specifying occurrence options than the qualifiers described above. Instead of a single symbol, such as '+', a quantity involves one or two values, enclosed by curly brackets, '{' and '}'.

The simplest form of quantity involves a single value, such as '{3}' or '{123}', which specifies how many times the atom must occur. For example, 'ab{3}c' specifies that the value must be 'abbbc'.

A quantity range can have two values, separated by a comma, such as '{3,7}'. A value can include any number of occurrences of the atom between, and including, these two extremes. For example, 'ab{3,4}c' specifies that the value must be either 'abbbc' or 'abbbbc'.

It is also possible to specify just a minimum number of occurrences. If the second value is absent, then only a minimum is being specified, so '{3,}' means 'at least 3'. But the comma must still be present. For example, 'ab{2,}c' allows for everything from 'abbc' to 'abbbbbbbbbc' and beyond.

Escape characters

A number of significant symbols have now been introduced, such as '*' and '{'. These symbols cannot be used within an expression as atoms, because they would be misinterpreted as significant pattern markup. It is therefore necessary to escape them, in the same way that '&' and '<' must be escaped in XML documents. Instead of the '&' character, however, the '\' symbol is used in a pattern. Again, just as an '&' is needed in XML documents to use the escape character itself as a data character, the '\' symbol must also be escaped in patterns, giving '\\' (this should be familiar to C and Java software developers). The characters that need to be escaped are '.' '\', '?', '*', '+', '{', '}', '(', ')', '|', '[' and ']'. For example, '?' is escaped as '\?':

```
\\ (the escape character)
\| (branch separator)
\. (not-a-line-end character)
\- (range separator) (character class subtraction)
\^ (used at start of negative character group)
\? (optional indicator)
\* (optional and repeatable indicator)
\+ (required and repeatable)
\{ (quantity start)
\} (quantity end)
\( (sub-group start)
\) (sub-group end)
\[ (range group start)
\] (range group end)
```

In some circumstances, the '-' and '^' characters must also be escaped:

```
\- (range separator)
\^ (negative group indicator)
```

In addition, escape characters are used to include whitespace characters that would otherwise be difficult or impossible to add, such as the tab character:

```
\n (newline)
\r (return)
\t (tab)
```

Character groups

Atoms (quantified or otherwise) do not have to be single characters. They can also be escape sequences, so an escaped character can be quantified, such as '\++', which states that the '+' character is required and repeatable. In addition, they can also be 'character groups', a feature that allows a particular character in the target value to be one of a number of pre-defined options.

It could be imagined that a product code needs to start with exactly three letters, and end with between two and four digits. While 'abc123' and 'wxy9876' would both be valid, 'ab123' and 'wxy98765' would not (the first has too few letters, and the second has too many digits). This requirement could be achieved using a very large number of branches, such as 'aaaa00 | aaaa000 | aaaa0000 | ... |' (and so on), but this is clearly impractical. Instead, a 'character class' expression is enclosed by square brackets, '[' and ']'. For example, '[abc]' means that, at this position, the letters 'a', 'b' or 'c' may appear.

When the first character is '^', the group becomes a 'negative character group', reversing the meaning, so that any character *except* those in the group can be matched. For example, '[^abc]' specifies that any character except 'a', 'b' or 'c' can be included. The '^' symbol can be used later in the group without having this significance, so '[a^b]' simply means that the character must be 'a' or '^' or 'b'.

Quantifiers can be used on groups as well as individual characters. For example, '[abc]+' specifies that at least one of the letters 'a', 'b' and 'c' must appear, but then additional characters from this set may also appear, so 'abcbca' would be a valid match.

Character ranges

It is not always efficient to have to specify every possible character in a group. For example, '[abcdefghijklmnopqrstuvwxyz]' is a verbose way to specify that any lower-case letter can occur. When a large set of options have sequential ASCII values, as in this example, a 'range' can be specified instead, using a '-' separator between the first character in the range and the last character in the range. The more succinct equivalent of the example above is therefore '[a-z]'. The expression '[a-zA-Z0-9]' allows all normal letters and digits to occur.

If the '-' character is to be matched, within a group, it must be escaped using '\-', but it is not necessary to do this outside of a group. For example, 'a-b[x\-y]+' matches 'a-bxxx---yyy'.

An XML character reference can be included in a range, such as '{' or 'ª'. This is particularly useful for representing characters that are difficult, or even impossible, to enter directly from a keyboard.

This approach can still be used when some of the characters in the range are not wanted. Individual items can be selectively removed from the range, using a 'sub group', with a '-' prefix, as in '[a-z-[m]]', which removes 'm' as a valid option.

Sub-groups

An entire expression can be created within another expression, with the embedded expression enclosed by brackets, '(' and ')'. This is useful when several options are required at a particular location in the pattern, because a complete expression can contain branches, such as '1|2|3'. Therefore, 'abc(1|2|3)d' matches 'abc1d', 'abc2d' and 'abc3d'.

The simple example above, with only a single character in each option, is just another interpretation of the more succinct 'abc[123]*d' expression. However, the simpler technique cannot work for multi-character alternatives, such as '[abc(XX|YY|ZZ)d]'.

A quantifier can be assigned to a sub-group. In the following example, there can be any number of the given strings embedded within the value:

```
<pattern value="abc(XX|YY|ZZ)*d" />


<code>abcd</code>
<code>abcYYd</code>
<code>acbZZYYXXXXd</code>
```

Character class escapes

There are various categories of 'character class escape':

- single character escapes (discussed above)
- multi-character escapes (such as '\s' (non-whitespace) and '.' (non-line-ending))
- *general* category escapes (such as '\p{L}' and '\p{Lu}') and complementary *general* category escapes (such as '\P{L}' and '\P{Lu}')
- *block* category escapes (such as '\p{IsBasicLatin}' and '\p{IsTibetan}') and complementary *block* category escapes (such as '\P{IsBasicLatin}' and '\P{IsTibetan}').

A 'single category escape' is an escape sequence for a single character, such as the '{' character, which has a significant role in expressions (they are listed and discussed in more detail above).

Multi-character escapes

For convenience, a number of single character escape codes are provided to represent very common sets of characters, including:

- non-line-ending characters
- whitespace characters and non-whitespace characters

- initial XML name characters (and all characters except these characters)
- subsequent XML name characters (and all characters except these characters)
- decimal digits (and all characters except these digits).

The '.' character represents every character except a new-line or carriage-return character. The expression '. . . . .' therefore represents a string of five characters that are not broken over lines.

The remaining multi-character escape characters are all escaped in the normal way, using a '\' symbol. They are all defined in pairs, with a lower-case letter representing a particular common requirement, and the equivalent upper-case letter representing the opposite effect.

The escape sequence '\s' represents any whitespace character, including the space, tab, new-line and carriage return characters. The '\S' sequence therefore represents any non-whitespace character.

The escape sequence '\i' represents any initial name character ('_', ':' or a letter). The '\I' sequence therefore represents any non-initial character. Similarly, the escape sequence '\c' represents any XML name character, and '\C' represents any non-XML name character.

The escape sequence '\d' represents any decimal digit. It is equivalent to the expression '\p{Nd}' (see below). The '\D' sequence therefore represents any non-decimal digit character.

The escape sequence '\w' represents all characters except for punctuation, separator and 'other' characters (using techniques described below, this is equivalent to '[&#x0000;-&#x10FFFF;-[\p{P}\p{Z}\p{C}]]'), whereas the '\W' sequence represents only these characters.

Category escapes

The escape sequence '\p' or '\P' (reverse meaning) introduces a 'category escape' set. A category token is enclosed within following curly brackets, '{' and '}'. These tokens represent pre-defined sets of characters, such as all upper-case letters or the Tibetan character set.

General category escapes

A 'general category escape' is a reference to a pre-defined set of characters, such as all of the upper-case letters, or all punctuation characters. These sets of characters have special names, such as 'Lu' for upper-case letters, and 'P' for all punctuation. For example, '\p{Lu}' represents all upper-case letters, and '\P{Lu}' represents all characters except upper-case letters.

Single letter codes are used for major groupings, such as 'L' for all letters (of which upper-case letters are just a subset). The full set of options are:

L		All letters
	Lu	uppercase
	Ll	lowercase
	Lt	titlecase
	Lm	modifier
	Lo	other
M		All Marks
	Mn	nonspacing
	Mc	spacing combination
	Me	enclosing
N		All Numbers
	Nd	decimal digit
	Nl	letter
	No	other
P		All Punctuation
	Pc	connector
	Pd	dash
	Ps	open
	Pe	close
	Pi	initial quote
	Pf	final quote
	Po	other
Z		All Separators
	Zs	space
	Zl	line
	Zp	paragraph
S		All Symbols
	Sm	math
	Sc	currency
	Sk	modifier
	So	other

C		All Others
	Cc	control
	Cf	format
	Co	private use

These concepts are defined at http://www.unicode.org/Public/3.1-Update/UnicodeCharacterDatabase-3.1.0.html.

Block category escapes

The Unicode character set is divided into many significant groupings, such as musical symbols, Braille characters and Tibetan characters. A keyword is assigned to each group, such as 'MusicalSymbols', 'BraillePatterns' and 'Tibetan'.

In alphabetical order, the full set of keywords is:

AlphabeticPresentationForms	Dingbats	LetterlikeSymbols
Arabic	EnclosedAlphanumerics	LowSurrogates
ArabicPresentationForms-A	EnclosedCJKLettersand-Months	Malayalam
ArabicPresentationForms-B	Ethiopic	MathematicalAlphanumeric-Symbols
Armenian	GeneralPunctuation	MathematicalOperators
Arrows	GeometricShapes	MiscellaneousSymbols
BasicLatin	Georgian	MiscellaneousTechnical
Bengali	Gothic	Mongolian
BlockElements	Greek	MusicalSymbols
Bopomofo	GreekExtended	Myanmar
BopomofoExtended	Gujarati	NumberForms
BoxDrawing	Gurmukhi	Ogham
BraillePatterns	HalfwidthandFullwidthForms	OldItalic
ByzantineMusicalSymbols	HangulCompatibilityJamo	OpticalCharacterRecognition
Cherokee	HangulJamo	Oriya
CJKCompatibility	HangulSyllables	PrivateUse (3 separate sets)
CJKCompatibilityForms	Hebrew	Runic
CJKCompatibilityIdeographs	HighPrivateUseSurrogates	Sinhala
CJKCompatibilityIdeographsSupplement	HighSurrogates	SmallFormVariants

CJKRadicalsSupplement	Hiragana	SpacingModifierLetters
CJKSymbolsandPunctuation	IdeographicDescriptionChar- acters	Specials (two seperate sets)
CJKUnifiedIdeographs	IPAExtensions	SuperscriptsandSubscripts
CJKUnifiedIdeographsExten- sionA	Kanbun	Syriac
CJKUnifiedIdeographsExten- sionB	KangxiRadicals	Tags
CombiningDiacriticalMarks	Kannada	Tamil
CombiningHalfMarks	Katakana	Telugu
CombiningMarksforSymbols	Khmer	Thaana
ControlPictures	Lao	Thai
CurrencySymbols	Latin-1Supplement	Tibetan
Cyrillic	LatinExtended-A	UnifiedCanadianAboriginal- Syllabics
Deseret	LatinExtended-B	YiRadicals
Devanagari	LatinExtendedAdditional	YiSyllables

A reference to one of these categories involves a keyword that begins with 'Is...', followed by a name from the list above, such as 'Tibetan'. For example, '\p{IsTibetan}'.

Complex type derivations

Just as it is possible for the schema author to derive new simple data types from existing simple types, it is also possible to create new complex types from existing complex types. Again, this can be done either by extending or by restricting the base type, though the precise techniques are necessarily different (there are no list and union constructs, and no facets to consider).

A major apparent difference between deriving complex types and deriving simple types is that there are no complex types built in to the XML Schema standard. The usual reason for creating new simple types is to create types that deal with specific document model requirements, but it seems that the same argument cannot be made for complex types: an original complex type should have already been crafted for the intended purpose. Yet there are some good reasons for the presence of this feature, including the ability to create (and later validate) a hierarchy of increasingly refined data types.

Complex content

The **ComplexContent** element is used within the **ComplexType** element to indicate that the content will be a derivation of another complex data type. The **Mixed** attribute may be used on the ComplexContent element, and overrides any setting for this attribute on the ComplexType element.

```
<complexType>
  <complexContent mixed="false">
    ...
  </complexContent>
</complexType>
```

Extensions

As with simple types, an extension of a base type is defined using the **Extension** element. The new model is created by appending any new definitions, as if the original and new definitions were enclosed in a sequence group:

```
<sequence>
  <!-- ORIGINAL DEFINITIONS -->
  <!-- NEW DEFINITIONS -->
</sequence>
```

The original definitions are not repeated. For example, consider a base type that defines a book cover page structure:

```
<complexType name="BookCover">
  <sequence>
    <element ref="DOC:title" />
    <element ref="DOC:publisher" />
    <element ref="DOC:authorName" />
  </sequence>
</complexType>
```

Then consider an extension that adds a Date element. The comments in the example below enclose the implied content, including the conceptual outer-sequence element:

```
<complexType name="BookCoverWithDate">
  <!--
  <sequence>
    <sequence>
      <element ref="DOC:title" />
      <element ref="DOC:publisher" />
      <element ref="DOC:authorName" />
    </sequence>
    -->
    <sequence>
      <element ref="DOC:date" />
    </sequence>
  <!--
  </sequence>
  -->
</complexType>
```

Restrictions

Just as simple types can be restricted, it is also possible for complex types to be restricted. However, there are no facets to be applied in this case. Instead, restrictions are created by reproducing the original complex type definition, but with more limited options. For example, an original occurrence range can be narrowed, in the following case from a minimum of zero participants to a minimum of one participant:

```
<complexType name="ParticipantsType">
  <element ref="DOC:participant" minOccurs="0"
                                  maxOccurs="100">
</complexType>

<complexType name="AtLeastOneParticipantType">
  <complexContent>
    <restriction base="DOC:ParticipantsType">
      <element ref="DOC:participant" minOccurs="1" />
    </restriction>
  </complexContent>
</complexType>
```

Other ways of restricting a complex base type include:

- setting a default value for an element or attribute that previously had no default value
- setting a fixed value for an element or attribute that previously had no fixed value
- omitting an element or attribute reference when that item was previously optional (in the case of an element, just making the maximum occurrence zero, and in the case of an attribute, setting the Use attribute value to 'prohibited').

Any instance document structure that conforms to the restricted model should also conform to the original base model. This is why, for example, an element can only be omitted if it was originally optional. A schema-sensitive parser should also find nothing in a restricted model that is new.

It has been argued that the need to reproduce the definition in the derived restricted type makes the whole concept inefficient, and potentially redundant. After all, it would be just as easy to create the new type from scratch, without any reference to the type it is based on, and validation of document instances would not be affected in any way. But this approach would not allow for the feature described next (derivation selection from within instance documents), and would not permit the schema-sensitive parser to detect any changes to the base type that had not been copied into the derived types.

Selection from instance documents

While derived simple types and complex types can be referenced from element definitions, like any other type, they can also be used in a more flexible way that echoes techniques available to software developers using object-oriented programming languages.

An attribute in a document instance is used to reference a derived type. Essentially, the same **Type** attribute is used, but this time in the document instance instead of in the schema document. It therefore must belong to the 'http://www/w3/org/2001/XMLSchema-instance' namespace.

In the following example, an extension of the book cover model that allows for a date to be added is selected (but the Cover element that refers to the original cover type still appears in the document):

```
<book xmlns="..."
      xmlns:X="http://www.w3.org/2001/XMLSchema-instance">
   ...
   <cover X:type="twoAuthors">
      <bookTitle>...</bookCover>
      <publisher>...</publisher>
      <authorName>...</authorName>
      <date>...</date>
   </cover>
   ...
</book>
```

The Cover element would normally not allow the date to be present, but the Type attribute selects a derived type that allows it. There may, or may not, also be an element definition for this extended model, but when using this technique it is irrelevant.

Note that one very good reason for defining a complex type separately from a single element definition that needs it is to allow the type to be sub-classed in this way.

Constraining derivations

It is not always healthy for derived simple and complex data types to be used in document instances directly, or even for complex types (and derived simple types) to be derived in the first place; this is especially important when a schema author is creating a type library that will be utilized by other schema authors, and it is felt that some of these other authors might be tempted to created derived types in ways that the original author would find unacceptable.

There are therefore a number of techniques for preventing derivations and usage of derivations. Conversely, there is even an option to prevent usage of the original data type, so forcing the use of derived types.

Blocking derivation creation

The **Final** attribute can be added to the ComplexType and SimpleType elements, and is used to prevent derivation by 'extension' or by 'restriction', or even to prevent both kinds of modification using the keyword '#all'.

A default constraint can be assigned to all types that do not explicitly set a constraint. The Schema element has a **FinalDefault** attribute that can take the same three values. When set to 'restriction', for example, all types that do not have the Fixed attribute in their definitions are automatically constrained in this way.

Blocking derivation in instance documents

As an alternative to preventing data types from being extended or restricted, it is possible to allow this, yet prevent some or all of the derived types from being directly selected from document instances.

It could be envisaged that a data type would be extended, for example, so that the extended types can be assigned to various element types in the document model, but that these derived types would be inappropriate substitutes for the original type within an element that refers to that original type. Normally, a document instance author would, nevertheless, be able to select one of the derived types.

This can be prevented using the **Block** attribute on the ComplexType element (but, for some reason, not on the SimpleType element). This attribute takes the same value options as the Final attribute described above: 'extension', 'restriction' or '#all'.

In addition, a default setting can be specified in the **Schema** element, this time using the **BlockDefault** attribute.

Facet derivation control

Simple data type derivations can be controlled in a more subtle way than the techniques described above. It is possible to put constraints on individual facets, such as the length of a value, while allowing other facets to be added or modified in derived restricted types.

The **Fixed** attribute can be used on most facets, including all the facet types except those represented by the **Pattern** and **Enumeration** elements (presumably because they can repeat, so it would not be clear which one is being re-defined). When set to 'true' (from the default value of 'false), a derived type will not be able to change this setting, and should not even bother to incorporate the element concerned (it will be inherited as is). A type derived from the following simple 'code' type must also have a minimum length of '1', but could change the maximum length:

```
<simpleType name="code">
  <restriction base="string">
    <minLength value="1" fixed="true" />
    <maxLength value="100" />
  </restriction>
</simpleType>
```

Blocking original type usage

Contrary to the techniques above, it is sometimes desirable to allow the use of derived types, but to prevent the use of the original, base type. This can be achieved only for complex types, not simple types, using the **Abstract** attribute (also used on the Element element). This attribute is given the value 'true' (from the default value of 'false') to ensure that this type cannot be used, but that types derived from it can (assuming that they do not also use this attribute). In the following example, the AbstractBaseName type is defined only to help create the other two name types, and is never intended to be used in document instances:

```
<complexType name="AbstractBaseName" abstract="true">
  <complexContent>
    <extension base="Name">...</extension>
  </complexContent>
</complexType>

<complexType name="PersonalName">
  <complexContent>
    <extension base="AbstractBaseName">...</extension>
  </complexContent>
</complexType>

<complexType name="CompanyName">
  <complexContent>
    <extension base="AbstractBaseName">...</extension>
  </complexContent>
</complexType>
```

Element restrictions

The **Element** element has **Final** and **Block** attributes. The Final attribute determines whether or not the element can be used as the head of a substitution (see below). The Block attribute determines whether or not the element can be substituted in a document instance.

Substitutions

There may be times when a number of alternative elements could be used at a specific location in a document model. Of course, this group of elements could just be referenced in each location that it can be used (achieved using a non-repeating choice group), and the Group or ComplexType elements could even be used to make the relationships more obvious, and to make management of the group easier. However, another technique is available that offers some advantages.

Head element

In any 'substitution group', one element definition is known as the 'head' element. All remaining elements in the group are possible substitutions for this element. The head element is defined in the normal way, and must be a global element (not locally defined within another element definition). For example, the following element definition has no distinguishing features, but is nevertheless a head element for substitution elements that will be shown later:

```
<element name="name" type="string" />
```

Actually, the lack of any hints as to its role in a substitution is a concern (addressed below).

Substitute elements

The Name element defined above is perhaps too general in nature. It may be necessary, sometimes, to distinguish between personal names and company names. Two new elements could be defined to make this distinction. References to these two elements could then be added to the schema, at every point where a reference to the Name element already exists. Alternatively, they could be identified as substitution elements for the Name element, using the **SubstitutionGroup** attribute, which refers to the head element by name:

```
<element name="personalName" type="string"
        substitutionGroup="DOC:name" />

<element name="name" type="string"
        substitutionGroup="DOC:name" />
```

The advantage of this technique is that there is no need to modify the content models of the elements that can contain elements from the group (though the use of entities, Group elements or external type definitions will also achieve this aim). However, this is also the only disadvantage to this approach (that the other techniques do not share). It is not obvious, when studying such a content model, that in fact there are other elements that could legally appear at the same location. The other elements in the group are not referenced in any way from the head element.

Therefore, either a comment should be added to the model, or a schema presentation tool should do the work of finding and displaying the alternative element names (though the following technique also makes it clear that an element referenced in the model is a head element).

Abstract head elements

Sometimes, the head element only exists to form a focus for a number of interchangeable elements, and should not itself ever be used. This can be forced by adding the **Abstract** attribute to the head element, and giving it the explicit value 'true' (just as data types can be made abstract, using the same attribute). In the following example, the Name element can no longer be used in a document instance (only the personal and company name variants can):

```
<element name="name" type="string" abstract="true" />
```

It is an error (and indeed meaningless) to create an abstract element, then not create any substitutions for this element.

It is important to remember that when the head element is abstract, it is still referenced in the content model or models where its substitution elements are allowed to occur, and that references to these substitutes should still not be made in such models. As strange as it sounds, the model refers to the one and only element in the group that the document instance author is *not* allowed to select.

Relationships with data types

Substitution elements must have the same data type as the head element, or have a data type that is derived from this type. The following diagram shows some legal relationships between elements and types:

It would not be legal for 'element 2' and 'element 3' to refer to either 'type A' or 'type B'.

If a substitute element refers to an abstract data type, then the document instance must refer to a substitute data type. Due to the nature of these relationships, it is possible that a substitute element refers to an abstract data type, while the head element does not.

One key advantage of this technique over purely using derived data types is that the document author selects an appropriate element, rather than adds a Type attribute and selects the data type required. This is arguably simpler and more intuitive, and almost certainly easier for authoring tools to support.

Re-defining external definitions

When part of a schema is stored in an external schema file, it can be included as described previously. But when defining a new type, based on a type in the included file, it is necessary to give the new type a different name. This may be inconvenient, and is avoided by using a 'redefinition' instead. The **Redefine** element contains a **SchemaLocation** attribute, which holds a URL reference that points to the schema file to be included. This element then contains any mixture of Annotation, SimpleType, ComplexType, AttributeGroup and Group elements to override definitions in the referenced file.

A feature of this approach is that external definitions in a file that has no target namespace can both be re-defined and be associated with the current target namespace, in a single step. This is a reasonable technique for re-using schema components that are needed in many schemas that have different target namespaces:

```
<!-- COMMON.XSD -->
<schema xmlns="...">
  <!-- no target namespace -->
  <simpleType name="name" ... />
</schema>


<schema xmlns="..." targetNamespace="...">
  <redefine
         schemaLocation="file:///d:/schemas/common.xsd">
    <simpleType name="name" ... >
      <extension base="DOC:name"> <!-- 'name' already in
                                        target namespace -->
        <!-- NO ADDITIONS, JUST COPIED TO
             THIS NAMESPACE -->
      </extension>
    </simpleType>
  </redefine>
  ...
</schema>
```

However, this technique can also be dangerous. Some existing derivations of the Name type may be copied across unchanged, but would now have to assume the new definition of this type as its base. Yet a change in the re-definition may conflict with one in the derived type. For example, if a derivation in the external file added an Age attribute, but the re-definition also added this same attribute, then there would be a conflict that would cause an error. Schema authors must be very careful to avoid such problems arising.

Imports

A schema can 'import' definitions from other schemas. Unlike the inclusion and re-definition features described above, this technique copes well with external schema documents that have different target namespaces.

The **Import** element calls in the other schema, using the **Namespace** attribute to identify the namespace targeted by the other schema and the **SchemaLocation** attribute to physically locate the other schema file (using a URL reference):

```
<import namespace="file:///d:/ns/namesSchema"
        schemaLocation="file:///d:/schema/names.xsd" />
```

The SchemaLocation attribute is optional, because the XML Schema parser may have other ways to locate other schemas. The Namespace attribute is also optional, because the schema may not have a target namespace. It is less clear, however, how to refer to remote elements and types in this case, as there will be no namespace prefix. While it might seem appropriate to simply not use a prefix, the first generation of schema-sensitive parsers gives varying results, with some reporting errors.

In order to be able to reference objects from the other schema, a namespace prefix is needed. The namespace concerned is defined in the Schema element, and note that this is always the same namespace that appears in the Namespace attribute of the Import element:

```
<schema ... xmlns:NAMES="file:///d:/ns/namesSchema"
   <import namespace="file:///d:/ns/namesSchema"
        schemaLocation="file:///d:/schemas/names.xsd" />
   ...
</schema>
```

Adopting foreign elements

It is very simple to adopt (copy into the current namespace) an element definition from the remote schema. This is done by referring directly to the element, as usual, but using the foreign schema namespace prefix instead of the local one:

```
<element ref="NAMES:personalType" />
```

This only works for elements defined globally (at the top level) in the foreign schema. Local element definitions are not guaranteed to be unique, so could not be referenced unambiguously.

It is important to remember that this reference essentially creates a new, local definition, meaning that it is now in the current target namespace. Document instance authors need never be aware that it was originally defined elsewhere.

Using foreign data types

It is also quite simple to refer to data types defined in the other schema. For example:

```
<element name="personalName" type="NAMES:personalType" />

<element name="companyName" type="NAMES:companyType" />
```

Foreign data types can also be derived locally:

```
<complexType name="RestrictedCompanyName">
  <complexContent>
    <restriction base="NAMES:CompanyName">
      ...
    </restriction>
  </complexContent>
</complexType>
```

16. Processing XML data

Issues involved in developing software to read and write XML documents are covered in this chapter, as well as the circumstances that determine when it is necessary to process a DTD in order to accurately interpret the markup in a document. It also introduces concepts that led to the development of the SAX and DOM standards, and highlights the difference between these approaches.

Writing XML

XML documents can be hand-written using one of many editing tools now available. But the new uses to which XML markup is being put, including data interchange, increasingly require XML data to be generated automatically.

Outputting markup

Fortunately, getting software to write XML data is quite straightforward, and involves little more than including XML tags in the strings to be output:

```
PRINT #FileNum "<para>A paragraph.</para>"

fprintf(stdout, "<para>A paragraph.</para>\n");

System.out.println( "<para>A paragraph.</para>\n");

Clib.puts( "<para>A paragraph.</para>\n");
```

Escaping special characters

But it is very important to remember that some characters must be 'escaped' as entity references. Writing the '&', '<' or '>' characters out as data would create invalid XML.

```
PRINT #FileNum "<company>Smith &amp; Son</company>"
```

Within attribute values, quotation marks may also need to be escaped with '"' or '''.

Creating lines

One decision that has to be made is whether to output line-end codes, as in the examples above, or whether to omit them. In many respects it is simpler and safer to omit line-end codes. But if the XML document is likely to be viewed or edited using tools that are not XML-sensitive, this approach makes the document very difficult to read. Some text editors will only display as much text as will fit on one line in the window:

```
<book><front><title>The Book Title</title><author>J...
```

Although some editors are able to display more text by creating 'soft' line breaks at the right margin, the content is still not very legible:

```
<book><front><title>The Book Title</title><author>J.
Smith</author><date>October 1997</date></front><body>
<chapter><title>First Chapter</title><para>This is the
first chapter in the book.</para><para>This is the ...
....
```

It would seem to be more convenient to break the document into separate lines at obvious points in the text, as in the example below. However, there may be a problem for the recipient application in determining which line-end codes are present only to make the XML data file more legible, and which form a crucial part of the enclosed document (this issue is covered in detail in Chapter 8):

```
<book>
<front>
<title>The Book Title</title>
<author>J. Smith</author>
<date>October 1997</date>
</front>
<body>
<chapter>
<title>First Chapter</title>
<para>This is the first chapter in the book.</para>
<para>This is the ...
```

Another good reason for breaking up XML documents into lines of text is to assist with the detection of any validation errors in the document. Most XML parsers are able to report the line number of the line containing the error.

Reading XML

While software *can* be used to write XML data, software is *always* required to read it. XML markup is never intended to be viewed by humans, except in extreme circumstances, such as to correct an invalid file. Unfortunately, reading XML is a much more difficult task than writing it.

Reading XML

Reading an XML document can be complicated by a number of issues and features of the language. The various ways in which whitespace can be used to format the data file may cause problems of interpretation. It may be necessary for entities to replace all references to them, and for attribute values to be processed. Finally, the DTD may need to be processed, either to add default information, or to compare against the document instance in order to validate it.

The XML specification provides all the information necessary for software developers to write programs that can read and interpret any XML document, and the specification is far simpler than its older brother, SGML. But writing such software is still far from trivial. Even programmers experienced in similar languages could expect to spend months on the task. The only feasible reason for writing a parser now is to work in a computer language, or on a computer platform, that currently has no XML support.

Most programming languages have the capability to incorporate software libraries, and a number of XML libraries already exist. Programmers wishing to read XML data files need an XML-sensitive processing module, termed an **XML processor**. The XML processor is responsible for making the content of the document available to the application, and will also detect problems such as file formats that the application cannot process, or URL references that do not point to valid resources.

XML processors

Programmers who wish to concentrate on their application, rather than on the details of XML syntax, will always adopt an existing XML processor for the task.

Note: Although the term 'parser' is generally used in place of 'XML processor' (in this book and elsewhere), it is necessary here to use formal terminology, because parsing is just part of the operation of an XML processor.

The XML processor hides many complications from the application using it. An XML processor has at least one sub-unit, termed the **entity manager**, which is responsible for locating fragments of the document held in entity declarations or in other data files, and handling replacement of all references to them.

Most XML processors also include an integrity checker, or **parser**. The parser interprets the XML markup, checks for conformity with well-formed structures, and perhaps compares the document against a document model.

XML processors have been written in numerous programming languages, and many are freely available. Most have now existed for a number of years, and have proved reliable.

The XML processor ultimately delivers data to the application, but there are at least two distinct ways in which this can be done. These are termed the **event-driven** and **tree-walking** approaches. Each is discussed in more detail below, and each has an associated, well-supported standard to make applications less reliant on particular XML processors, and skills transfer much simpler.

Application developers should be able to incorporate pre-packaged software libraries that perform event-driven or tree-manipulation processing. There are already a number of such packages. The application must communicate with one of these libraries through an API (an *Application Programmers Interface*), but the developer may find it difficult to adopt newer and better products from different vendors if the API differs each time. Standards have therefore been developed for both the event-driven and tree-walking approaches, called **SAX** and **DOM** respectively.

A third approach that has been discussed, but for which there is little support at the time of writing, could be termed the **pull-data** approach. In this scenario, the application simply requests the next piece of the XML data stream or file (the next piece being a start-tag, attribute, chunk of text, end-tag, comment or processing instruction).

Event processing

Almost all XML processors support event-based parsing. This is arguably the simplest method for information to be passed from the processor to the application. The application responds to 'events' in the data stream. It reacts to information contained in XML markup as it is encountered in the data stream by the XML processor.

A general-purpose programming language, such as 'C' or Java, may be used. The application would include functions to deal with specific kinds of markup, such as 'ProcessOpenTag' to intercept all the start-tags. If contextual processing is required, the current location in the document structure may be tracked using variables to indicate which elements are currently open.

In the following example, the first test detects paragraph elements, then sets a global flag to indicate to later events that a paragraph is currently being processed. Similar flags are tested to determine if the paragraph is within a chapter or appendix, and if not, further activity is undertaken:

```
void ProcessOpenTag( char tagname[] )
{
  if ( ! strcmp( tagname, "para" ) )
  {
    inPara = TRUE;
    if (( inChapter == FALSE ) && ( inAppendix == FALSE))
    {
      /* must be in Introduction - copy content to
         new summary book */
      ...
    }
  }
}
```

Single-pass limitations

If out-of-sequence processing is required, such as needing to collect all the titles in a document for insertion at the start of the document as a table of contents, then a 'two-pass' process is needed. In the first pass, the titles are collected. In the second pass, they are inserted where they are required. Readers familiar with the CALS or HTML 4.0 table models may have wondered why the element representing the footer section appears before the body section element. The answer is that this design avoids the necessity for two-pass processing; the footer text is read first, so it can be printed at the bottom of each page that contains a reference to it, or permanently displayed beneath a scrollable pane that contains the body rows.

Simple API for XML (SAX 1.0)

There are several good reasons why all parsers should supply an API that conforms to an independent standard, including the ready availability of documentation, and the contribution of many experts in the field into its design. But the main advantages are that an application is not as dependent on a particular parser, and can switch to a another supplier at any time, and application developers can transfer their skills more easily.

The **SAX** standard (standing for *Simple API for XML*) has not been developed by an official standards body, but has nevertheless emerged as a *de facto* standard, and is free for commercial use (see Chapter 18 and Chapter 19). It was developed for object-oriented languages such as Java.

Tree manipulation

Most XML processors support the tree-walking approach to provide access to the document in a 'random-access' method (by 'tree-walking' the document structure). The XML processor first reads the entire document into memory, before allowing the application instant access to any part of it. There is no need for multi-pass parsing. The processor therefore organizes the content so that it can be easily found and manipulated. Applications that benefit from this approach include XML-sensitive document editors and transformation tools (including XSLT engines).

But, as this is a more sophisticated technique than the event-driven approach described above, there are some concepts and associated terminology that need to be understood.

Nodes

As the XML processor reads the XML document, each component is stored as a separate object in memory. These objects are called **nodes**. Each node is an object of a specified type, such as an element node or a comment node. The XML processor gives the main application access to these nodes.

The concept of nodes appears in a number of standards, including the **Grove** (**Graph Representation Of Property ValuEs**) scheme devised for use with SGML. Some of the examples below are taken from this standard, though a newer, XML-based standard has also emerged and is discussed later.

Properties

Each node contains information about itself, in a manner similar to the way that elements contain attributes. Each kind of node has a pre-defined **property**, and each property has a name and a value. For example, a node that describes a person may have a property called 'age' which holds the value representing the age of an individual:

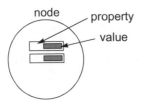

One property is particularly significant to every node. This property identifies what kind of node it is. In the Grove standard, this property is called 'type'. When the type property has a value of 'element', another property is used to determine what kind of element it represents. This property is called 'gi' (Generic Identifier). The following node represents a Paragraph element:

Connected nodes

A node may also contain properties that refer to other nodes, and this connection between nodes is known as an arc. A single property may refer to a single other node, or contain a list of references to other nodes. For example, an element node may refer to several attribute nodes:

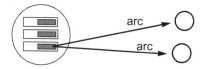

In the Grove scheme, the arc is labelled according to the name of the property, and may be one of three possible relationship types: 'subnode' (child node), 'irefnode' (internal reference node) or 'urefnode' (unrestricted/external reference node).

Hierarchical structures

Arcs may be used to organize nodes into tree structures that are suitable for describing the hierarchical nature of XML documents. This technique allows an application to 'drill down' into a document to find a required element. It also becomes possible to delete document fragments (branches), or move or copy them to other locations.

However, it is still possible to extract the content of an element (or the entire document, when starting at the root element) in sequential order, though the technique is more complex than for simple event-driven processing. It is necessary to use recursive iteration techniques to traverse nodes that represent all the descendants:

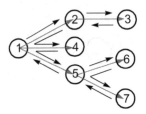

Non-hierarchical structures

In the Grove standard, arcs between nodes do not have to follow a tree-like structure. It is possible for a node to refer to any other node, regardless of its position in the tree, providing that it is an irefnode type. As groves may be multi-directional, even cyclic, they can also represent a DTD structure that includes nested element models.

For example, a node that represents a List element declaration points to other nodes describing the elements that the list may contain. Assuming this is only an Item element, there will be an arc from the List node to the Item node. But assuming that the Item element may also be able to contain a complete list, the Item node will also contain an arc back to the List node (as well as to other elements):

```
<!ELEMENT list (item+)>
<!ELEMENT item (list|para)*>
```

Document Object Model (DOM 1.0)

For exactly the same reasons why it is desirable to have a standard API for event-driven processing, it is equally desirable for a standard to exist for tree-walking access to a parser.

Such an API has been developed for object-oriented languages such as Java, for HTML as well as XML documents. The **DOM** (*Document Object Model*) standard has been developed for this purpose, and is free for commercial use (see Chapter 20 and Chapter 21).

Processing approach decisions

Many parsers supply at least two basic methods for accessing XML documents, and the application developer must then choose from the available choices. Some of the key decision factors are discussed below.

Pull method

Programming languages that do not support a call-back technique to get software libraries to pass events back to the main application cannot make use of the SAX standard. If the DOM approach is ruled out, for reasons given below, the only remaining practical option is to adopt a parser that provides a pull-based alternative. In this scenario, the application simply calls methods/functions in the XML processor to retrieve the next piece of the document.

Unfortunately, there are no standards for this approach as yet. It is necessary to learn how the individual parser supports this method.

Event or DOM

If a parser that supports both event-driven and tree-walking approaches is chosen, then the SAX and DOM standards will almost certainly be supported. The application developer may ponder which approach to choose in a given circumstance, and a number of factors can influence this decision.

Event benefits

With the event-driven approach, the parser does not have to hold much information about the document in memory. Each piece is extracted from the document and passed immediately to the application, after which it can be discarded. There is no danger of the parser running out of memory while parsing large documents. In addition, the document structure does not have to be managed in memory, either by the parser or, depending on what it needs to do, by the application. This can make parsing very fast.

However, it should be noted that some parsers provide access to the document via a SAX API, but only after parsing the whole document and building the tree model in memory. While this can still be useful, the memory usage and speed advantages are lost:

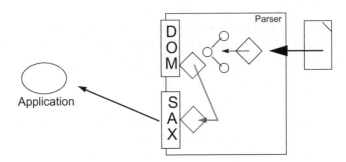

The fact that the application receives pieces of the document in the order in which they were encountered means that it does not have to do anything special in order to process the document in a simple linear fashion, from start to end.

However, it should also be noted that the linear processing issue in the tree-walker approach can be largely overcome if the parser has a convenient sequential tree-walking class (as most now have).

Tree-walking benefits

Some data preparation tasks require access to information that is further along the document. For example, to build a table of contents section at the beginning of a book, it is necessary to extract all the chapter titles that occur later. With the entire document held in memory, the document structure can be analysed several times over, quickly and easily.

When an application needs to reorder document components, or needs to build a new document but in a non-linear fashion, a data structure management module may be profitably utilized by the application to manage the document components on its behalf.

With this approach, the entire document can be validated as well-formed, and possibly also conformant to a particular DTD, before passing any of the document to the application. A document that contains errors can be rejected before the application begins to process its contents, thereby eliminating the need for messy roll-back routines.

Transformation tools

When the intent is simply to change an XML document structure into a new structure, there are often simpler ways to do this than to develop an application that reads in the source data, performs the transformation, then writes out the new structure. Providing that the transformations required are not too ambitious, there are existing tools on the market that can perform them. They are configured using scripting languages of various kinds.

The following example uses a popular scripting language to convert Para elements into either P or H2 elements, depending on what the parent element is (creating HTML output from the source XML document):

```
<intro>
  <para>Introduction</para>
</intro>
<description>
  <para>Description.</para>
</description>
```

```
element para
  do when parent is description
    output "<P>%c</P>"
  else when parent is intro
    output "<H2>%c</H2>"
  done
```

```
    <P>Introduction</P>
    <H2>Description.</H2>
```

These tools can usually do much more advanced things, such as changing the order of elements, sorting them, and generating new content automatically.

Although initially designed to assist XSL in the processing of data for formatting and presenting, the XSLT language can also be used purely to transform one XML document into another XML document, or (due to its similarity to XML) into an HTML document. The following example performs the same operation as the script above:

```
<xsl:template match="intro/para">
 <H2><xsl:apply-templates/></H2>
</xsl:template>

<xsl:template match="description/para">
 <P><xsl:apply-templates/></P>
</xsl:template>
```

See Chapter 17 for details on XSLT.

17. Transformations (XSLT)

use XSLT instead of css.

XSLT is a popular standard for transforming XML documents into other forms, including XML-based formatting languages (such as XSL, XHTML and WML) and other formatting languages (including HTML and RTF). It is also widely used to re-work XML documents to conform with alternative DTDs and schemas, so enabling the smooth exchange of data between systems and organizations.

Overview

The **XSLT** (*XSL Transformations*) standard defines an XML document transformation language.

An **XSLT processor** takes an existing XML document as input, and generates a new document as output. The output document may also be an XML document, but does not have to be (and HTML output is currently a popular choice).

When the output is an XML document, the new document typically conforms to a different document model to the input. One major application of XSLT is therefore to convert documents from one model to another, usually to enable communication of information between systems or organizations.

Transformations to be performed are specified using a **stylesheet** that conforms to the XSLT standard:

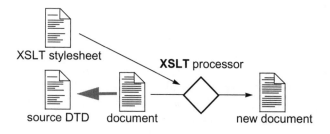

Transformations are performed in accordance with **template** rules embedded in the stylesheet. Templates are matched to elements in the source document using XPath expressions (see Chapter 13). The original element tags are removed in the process, and typically replaced with new 'output' tags:

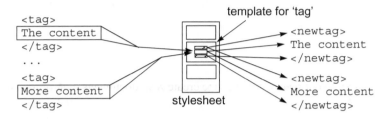

With XSLT, it is possible to:

- add prefix or suffix text to element content
- remove, create, reorder and sort element content
- convert element content to attribute values, and vice versa
- present the content of elements situated elsewhere in the document
- replace source elements with new output elements.

XSLT and XSL

The term 'XSL' and the term 'XSLT' are easily confused, and sometimes wrongly used interchangeably.

XSL

The XSL format was originally designed to fill a void between the simple CSS and complex DSSSL standards, and has features that are derived from both. The main structure of the language was derived from DSSSL, but the styling characteristics were inherited from CSS.

XSLT extracted from XSL

XSLT was previously just one part of the draft XSL standard, but has now been extracted into a separate standard of its own. The reason for this follows from a widespread belief that XSL was attempting to do two very different things, and that the first of these things – the manipulation of XML structures – while useful for reordering information, adding template text and building content lists, is also equally appropriate for many non-publishing applications.

Confusingly, the other half of the original specification, which deals with identifying the format to apply to the text, retains the name 'XSL', despite the fact that the 'S' stands for 'Stylesheet'. That standard no longer includes a stylesheet concept; XSL is really just a typesetting language that happens to use XML syntax.

XSLT and XSL together

Despite the separation of standards, XSLT and XSL will continue to be closely associated, and they work together to provide an effective XML publishing solution. An XSLT stylesheet can be used to create XSL documents (conforming to the XSL DTD), ready to be processed to create pages:

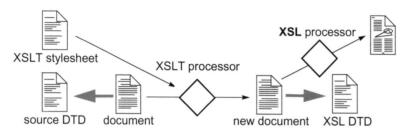

The following example shows a single XSLT rule, specifying in XSL format that emphasized text should be presented in-line and styled in bold:

```
                          An <emph>emphasized</emph> word.
    <template match="emph">
      <fo:inline font-weight="bold">
          <apply-templates/>
      </fo:inline>
    </template>                     An emphasized word.
```

XSLT DTD

An XSLT stylesheet document is identified by the namespace 'http://www.w3.org/XSL/Transform/1.0'. This format is defined by a DTD in an appendix to the standard. The DTD describes the 35 elements, and their attributes, that constitute the XSLT language. Most of these elements are used only to support complex requirements, and it is typically possible to build a useful stylesheet using just three of them (see Chapter 33 for the full list).

Note that, for the sake of clarity, examples in this chapter generally use the default namespace. In the standard itself, the prefix 'xsl:' is used in the examples, but this is simply a matter of preference.

General structure

The root element is named **Stylesheet**:

```
<stylesheet xmlns="http://www.w3.org/XSL/Transform/1.0">
  ...
</stylesheet>
```

The element name **Transform** may be used as an alternative to Stylesheet. These two element names are totally synonymous, and simply reflect the two purposes for which this standard can be utilized (though in practice the Transform element is rarely used):

```
<transform xmlns="http://www.w3.org/XSL/Transform/1.0">
  ...
</transform>
```

The Stylesheet element may be embedded within a larger XML document. This is appropriate when the stylesheet only applies to the document containing it. The processing instruction used in the document to identify a stylesheet simply refers to the embedded sheet, using an XPointer expression (see Chapter 28). The Stylesheet element must have an **Id** attribute for this to work:

```
<?xml-stylesheet type="text/xsl" href="#MyStyles" ?>
<X:book>
  <stylesheet id="MyStyles" ...>
    ...
  </stylesheet>
  ...
</X:book>
```

Templates

The body of the stylesheet consists of at least one transformation rule, as represented by the **Template** element:

```
<template ... >
  ...
</template>
```

In practice, a stylesheet typically contains a large number of rules, each one defining the transformation to be applied to a specific element in the source document, using the **Match** attribute, which contains an XPath expression. The following example demonstrates two rules: one for all Paragraph elements, and one for Emphasis elements:

```
<template match="para">
  ...
</template>

<template match="emph">
  ...
</template>
```

Multiple element template

When the same transformation rules apply to a number of elements, it is convenient to be able to use the same template for all the elements concerned. This saves space, and simplifies stylesheet maintenance. All the element names are included in the Match attribute, separated by 'I' symbols:

```
<template match="name | emph | foreign">
  <!-- PROCESS NAME, EMPH AND FOREIGN IDENTICALLY -->
  ...
</template>
```

A rule can be applied to every element type, without having to name them all. The wildcard '*' character is used to represent all elements:

```
<template match="*">
  <!-- PROCESS ALL ELEMENTS -->
  ...
</template>
```

Context

Sometimes, the content of an element may need to be processed differently, depending on where it is in the document. More specific rules can be defined by exploiting the full power of the XPath scheme (described in Chapter 13). The following template formats paragraphs that are directly contained within a Warning element:

```
<template match="warning/para">
  ...
</template>
```

Recursive processing

Typically, it is necessary to process all elements in a document, starting with the root element, then working through its children, but processing the descendants of each child before proceeding to the next (in the same manner as shown for linear processing of a tree structure, as discussed in Chapter 16). In XSLT, this does not happen automatically.

Applying templates

 The **Apply Templates** element must be used to indicate that children of the current element are to be processed. In the example below, the Emphasis element rule is only triggered if the Paragraph rule contains this instruction, and the text within the Emphasis element is only processed (presented) if the same instruction is included:

```
<para>An <emph>emphasized</emph> word.</para>
```

```
<template match="para">
  <apply-templates/>
</template>

<template match="emph">
  <apply-templates/>
</template>
```

Default template

However, this is not sufficient on its own. Normally, a stylesheet author would not bother to create templates for elements that do not need to be formatted or translated differently to their ancestor elements. Yet some of these 'ignored' elements may themselves contain further elements that *do* require such attention. A rule is therefore needed to act as a 'catch-all', representing the elements not covered by explicit formatting rules.

All XSLT processors should include an implied rule that acts as if the following explicit rule were present. Following XPath standard conventions, this rule uses the wildcard operator, '*', to represent all elements, and the '/' symbol to represent the root of the document. This rule is less important than others (see below for importance rules), so will only be activated for elements that are not dealt with by explicit templates:

```
<template match="/|*">
  <apply-templates/>
</template>
```

Although this is an implied rule, it can also be included explicitly, so allowing its default action to be modified. For example, the Apply Templates element could be removed, in which case the content of elements that do not have an associated rule will not be processed.

Text processing default

Similarly, a built-in rule is needed to present the text content of every element. This rule uses the '**text()**' function to achieve this (the content of this template is explained later):

```
<template match="text()">
  <value-of select="."/>
</template>
```

PIs and comments

Note that comments and processing instructions are by default not processed. Explicit rules similar to the one above, but using the '**processing-instruction()**' or '**comment()**' functions, must be included to process these items.

Selective processing

Using the Apply Templates element as described above, it is a rather blunt instrument that performs a useful but simple task. However, it can be made much more flexible. It can be used to select specific elements to be processed, not just descendents of the current element.

Specific children

The Apply Templates element can take a **Select** attribute, which overrides the default action of processing all children. Using XPath patterns, it is possible to select specific children and to ignore others. In the following example, the rule that matches a list of names targets only the embedded Name elements with a Type attribute value of 'company':

```
<template match="names">
  <apply-templates select="name[@type='company']"/>
</template>
```

When the Select attribute is not present, it is implied, and has the value '**node()**' to represent all children of the current element.

Specific descendants

The idea of selecting the elements to process can be taken much further than merely selecting specific child elements. Using XPath patterns, it is also possible to select specific elements at any deeper level. In the following example, all titles within a book are selected, possibly to create a table of contents:

```
<template match="book">
  <apply-templates select=".//title" />
  ...
</template>
```

Specific elements elsewhere

Template selection is not even restricted to the contents of the current element. It is possible to select elements that are located elsewhere in the document. The '..' operator is used to select the parent, and the '/' operation at the beginning of an expression selects the whole document, from where it is possible to zero in on the required information. The following example inserts chapter titles into the introduction of a book:

```
<book>
  <intro/>   <!-- COPY TITLES TO HERE -->
  ...
  <chapter><title>Introduction</title>...</chapter>
  <chapter><title>Details</title>...</chapter>
  <chapter><title>Summary</title>...</chapter>
</book>


<template match="intro">
  <apply-templates select="//chapter/title"/>
</template>
```

Multiple passes

The Apply Templates element can be used more than once in a template. In the following example, chapter titles are inserted into the introduction, but only after the content of the Introduction element itself:

```
<template match="intro">
  <apply-templates/>
  <apply-templates select="/book/chapter/title"/>
</template>
```

Priorities

When an XSLT processor attempts to find a matching rule for an element in the source document, it may find more than one template that matches. For example, a paragraph in a Warning element would match both 'para' and 'warning/para' XPath expressions, and consequently would appear to select two templates if they held these expressions. But this cannot be allowed, as it would not be possible to apply conflicting transformation instructions. The problem is avoided by making some templates more important than others, and ensuring that only the most important template is selected when such a conflict arises.

Default weightings

Each match rule is given a default priority value, between '-0.5' and '0.5'.

A test for a node, 'node()' has the lowest priority of all. It is given a priority weighting of '-0.5'. Also at this level is the wildcard, '*', and such general functions as 'text()' and 'processing-instruction()'.

Only slightly more significant are simple element and attribute names, such as 'title' and '@id'. These are given a priority weighting of just '-0.25'.

Rules that name an element belonging to a given namespace have a priority value of '0'. The name 'acme:title' is therefore more significant than just 'title'. Processing instructions with target names, such as 'processing-instruction('ACME')' are also at this level of significance.

Rules that are more specific than any of the above scenarios, such as 'warning/para', have a default priority value of '0.5'.

Overriding

When more than one complex rule matches the current element, it is necessary to explicitly give one rule a higher priority than the others. This can be done using the **Priority** attribute. Because all the default weightings are below '1', any template given a priority of '1' sets it above the rest. For example, it may be appropriate to specify that a paragraph in a Warning element is more specific than one in a Chapter element, if all warning paragraphs (within a chapter or not) are to be formatted in the same way:

```
<template match="para">     <!-- priority  -0.25 -->
  ...
</template>
<template match="chapter//para"> <!-- priority 0.5 -->
  ...
</template>
<template match="warning//para" priority="1">
  ...
</template>
```

Still higher priority values are needed to rank a number of conflicting complex rules.

If the Priority attribute is not used when a conflict occurs, or fails to isolate a single most important template, then the XSLT processor should report an error. However, it may choose to continue processing, and simply select the last rule it detects (the rule nearest to the end of the stylesheet file).

Output

In the examples above, the content of each element in the source document is identified and processed, and the text content is output, but no formatting is applied to this text. The element tags from the source document are also discarded during this process. But an XSLT transformation tool is typically required to write out a new document with meaningful tags (XML, HTML or some other recognized document or data-exchange format).

Direct element output

One way to write out XML elements is simply to insert the appropriate output element tags into the templates. The Namespaces standard (see Chapter 10) is applied in XSLT to distinguish these elements from XSLT elements. For example, to enclose the content of a Paragraph element in HTML P (Paragraph) elements, the start-tag and end-tag surround the Apply Templates element:

```
<template match="para">
  <html:P><apply-templates/></html:P>
</template>
```

This is an interesting approach that has both strengths and weaknesses. One major weakness concerns the building of an XSLT DTD for guided authoring and validation of stylesheets, and this issue is discussed later. The other major problem is that the stylesheet must be a properly well-formed XML document, so it is not easy to alter the hierarchical structure of the output document from that of the source document. For example, a source document may contain a list of 'firstName' and 'secondName' elements, with each pair *not* directly enclosed by an element that represents the whole name:

```
<firstName>John</firstName>
<lastName>Smith</lastName>
<firstName>Susan</firstName>
<lastName>Jones</lastName>
```

In the output document, an enclosing element may be needed, but it would *not* be possible to achieve this effect in the following way:

```
<!-- ERROR (overlapping structures) -->
<template match="firstName">
  <html:P><apply-templates/>
</template>
<template match="lastName">
  <apply-templates/></html:P>
</template>
```

However, this constraint does ensure that the output document will be well-formed, as a side effect of the whole stylesheet needing to be well-formed. It is also possible to overcome this constraint using the Text element (explained later).

Ignoring extension elements

Another issue this approach raises is that the XSLT processor needs to be able to distinguish output elements from other elements that the XSLT processor vendor may have added as extensions to XSLT. Such a vendor would not be able to use the XSLT namespace, so would create a new namespace for these extension elements.

An XSLT processor can be informed that an element is an extension element, added by an XSLT processor vendor, by registering its namespace as an extension namespace. The **Extension Element Prefixes** attribute may be used on the Stylesheet element, and it holds a space-separated list of namespace prefixes used for extension elements:

```
<stylesheet ... extension-element-prefixes="acme" >
  ...
  <template match="scrambleText">
    <html:P>SCRAMBLE THIS: <acme:scramble select="."/>
    </html:P>
  </template>
  ...
</stylesheet>
```

The keyword '#default' can be entered in this attribute if the extension elements use the default namespace.

Namespace aliases

Sometimes it is convenient, or even essential, that the namespace prefix of output elements appearing in the stylesheet should be different to the normal prefix used. For example, a stylesheet that creates output stylesheets should not use 'xsl:' for both instruction and output elements, as this would be confusing to the processor. It is therefore possible to use an alias prefix such as 'xsl2:' in the stylesheet, yet still ensure that when output these elements have the normal 'xsl:' prefix. The **Namespace Alias** element uses the **Stylesheet Prefix** attribute to identify the alias used in the stylesheet, and the **Result Prefix** attribute to specify the prefix to use when the elements are output:

```
<namespace-alias stylesheet-prefix="xsl2"
                 result-prefix="xsl" />
```

Comments and processing instructions

Comments and processing instructions can be inserted into an XML output document using the **Comment** and **Processing Instruction** elements. The Comment element simply contains the text to be output as the content of an XML comment tag. The Processing Instruction element works in the same way, but has a **Name** attribute to hold the target application name for the processing instruction:

```
<template match="book">
  <processing-instruction name="ACME">
    INSERT_TOC
  </processing-instruction>
  <comment>This is the HTML version</comment>
  <html:BODY><apply-templates/></html:BODY>
</template>
```

```
        <?ACME INSERT_TOC?>
        <!--This is the HTML version-->
        <BODY>...</BODY>
```

Prefix and suffix text

A template can also contain text that needs to be added to the content of the given element (often termed 'boilerplate' text). If this text appears before the Apply Templates element, it becomes a prefix to the content. If this text appears after the Apply Templates element, it becomes a suffix. The following example inserts the prefix 'NOTE:' and suffix ']' around the content of a Note element:

```
<note>This is a note.</note>
```

```
<template match="note">
  <html:P>NOTE: <apply-templates/> ]</html:P>
</template>
```

```
  <P>NOTE: This is a note. ]</P>
```

Reserved characters

A problem that can easily arise with added text is that it may need to include characters that are significant in XML documents. This issue is resolved using the usual entity references: '<', '>' and '&'. However, this only works for XML and HTML output. When writing data out to other data formats, such as RTF, it is important to avoid the usual 'escaping' of these characters.

The first way this can be achieved is to use the **Disable Output Escaping** attribute, and give it the value 'yes'. As its name suggests, this attribute switches off the normal escaping of the significant characters during output, so the output contains '<', '>' and '&' characters. This attribute can be used in the **Text** element and the **Value Of** element:

```
<template match="note">
  <text disable-output-escaping="yes">NOTE&gt; </text>
  <apply-templates/>
</template>
```

```
  NOTE> This is a note.
```

Note that for the stylesheet to be valid these characters must still be present in the escaped form. The references are converted into real characters as the stylesheet is parsed, so the Disable Output Escaping attribute simply prevents them from being re-converted back to entity references later.

Having dealt with reserved characters in the stylesheet template, it is also necessary to deal with the same characters when they occur in the source XML document. This can be done by overriding the built-in template for processing text nodes as follows:

```
<template match="text()">
    <value-of select="."
        disable-output-escaping="yes"/>
</template>
```

CDATA sections

Another way to avoid the need for escaped characters in text is to output CDATA sections. It is possible to name output elements that must directly contain such a section. The **CDATA Section Elements** attribute on the **Output** element holds the names of the output elements that will directly contain a CDATA section. If this attribute contained the name 'code', then the output would consist of '`<code><![CDATA[...]]></code>`' each time the Code element is output.

Text mode output

The tortuous methods of dealing with non-XML output described above can all be avoided. Although it is not an obligatory feature of XSLT, most implementations should support a mode of operation that assumes non-XML output, and therefore never escapes any of the reserved characters. The **Output** element may include the **Method** attribute, which has a default value of 'xml', but can be assigned the value 'text':

```
<output ... method="text" />
```

Note that anything that looks like an XML tag is not output at all in this mode. Instead of '`Press <ENTER> to proceed`', for example, it is necessary to use '`Press &lt;ENTER&gt; to proceed`'.

HTML mode output

HTML document markup is slightly different to XML. The main difference is that empty elements are just like XML start-tags (the end-tag is simply missing). The **Method** attribute can be given a value of 'html' to ensure that empty elements are written correctly:

```
<output ... method="html" />
...
<template match="break"><html:BR/></template>
```

```
<BR>
```

Note that this mode is selected automatically if the root output element name is 'html'.

The **Version** attribute, in this context, specifies the version of HTML to output. The current version of HTML is '4.0', though version '3.2' is still the most universally supported.

Media type

The **Media Type** attribute on the **Output** element specifies the Internet MIME type of the output document. This should be 'xml/text' or 'xml/application' for XML documents. It has no effect on the output document itself, but could be used by an application that first transforms the document, then transmits it to another location using Internet technologies.

In HTML output, this value is placed in the 'content type' META tag:

```
<META HTTP-EQUIV="Content-Type"
      CONTENT="text/html" ... >
```

Breaking well-formed constraints

The problem outlined above concerning output tags needing to comply with the well-formed nature of the stylesheet document can be solved using the **Disable Output Escaping** attribute:

```
<template match="firstName">
  <text disable-output-escaping="yes">&lt;html:P&gt;
  <apply-templates/>
</template>

<template match="lastName">
  <apply-templates/>
  <text disable-output-escaping="yes">&lt;/html:P&gt;
</template>
```

Whitespace

When processing the source document, an XSLT processor creates a tree of nodes (possibly using a DOM tree: see Chapter 20), including nodes for each text string within and between the markup tags. If the source document contains only whitespace characters between two markup constructs, a text node may be created. But nodes that contain only whitespace will by default then be discarded. In the following example, text nodes will not be created before and after the Para element:

```
<book>   <para>A paragraph.</para>
   </book>
```

But it can be desirable to preserve such spaces in some circumstances.

Preserve space

Individual elements can be added to an (initially empty) list of whitespace preserving elements, using the **Preserve Space** element, and then removed from the list using the **Strip Space** element. In both cases, the **Elements** attribute contains a list of space-separated element names. In the following example, only the Preformatted and Poetry elements preserve whitespace:

```
<stylesheet ... >
  <preserve-space elements="pre poetry" />
  ...
</stylesheet>
```

The wildcard character, '*', may be used to include all elements. This is useful when space is to be preserved in most elements. The Strip Space element then overrides this instruction for the few elements where this is not wanted:

```
<preserve-space elements="*" />
<strip-space elements="title para" />
```

Indentation

The **Indent** attribute can be used on the **Output** element to ensure that the output data file contains indents to reveal the hierarchical structure of the document:

```
<output ... indent="yes" />
```

```
<book>
  <title>The Title</title>
  <chapter>
    <title>The Chapter Title</title>
    <para>The only paragraph.</para>
  </chapter>
</book>
```

The default value is 'no':

```
<output ... indent="no" />
```

```
<book>
<title>The Title</title>
<chapter>
<title>The Chapter Title</title>
<para>The only paragraph.</para>
</chapter>
</book>
```

Stylesheet space

When the XSLT processor reads the stylesheet, ignorable whitespace is stripped from all elements, except from within the **Text** element. This element is primarily used to ensure that whitespace is not removed, as in the following example, where a single space must be preserved between the presentation of an attribute value and the presentation of the content of the element:

```
<value-of select="@security" />
<text> </text>
<apply-templates/>
```

Sorting elements

When the source document contains a list of items that are not arranged in any order, but need to be output in alphabetical or numerical order, it is possible to sort these items. The **Sort** element is used within the Apply Templates element to sort the elements it selects:

```
<list>
  <item>Zimbabwe</item>
  <item>Morocco</item>
  <item>Zaire</item>
  <item>Algeria</item>
</list>
```

```
<template match="list">
   ... <apply-templates><sort/></apply-templates> ...
</template>
```

Algeria
Morocco
Zaire
Zimbabwe

Note that, contrary to the impression given by earlier examples, the Apply Templates element is not always an empty element, and other scenarios covered later also require this element to be present as a container element.

Basic sorting

In the simple default form shown above, the sort key is the content of the child elements. The item 'Algeria' will therefore appear first in the output document. By adding a **Select** attribute to the Sort element, it is possible to be more explicit. For example, the Item element may contain an attribute which is to serve as the sort key:

```
<list>
   <item sortcode="Z">...</item>
   <item sortcode="M">...</item>
   <item sortcode="A">...</item>
</list>
```

```
<sort select="@sortcode"/>
```

Secondary sorting

It is possible to create secondary sort keys simply by adding more Sort elements. The second occurrence of the Sort element indicates a sub-key. For example, a list of names may need to be sorted by last name, then, within each group, by first name as well:

```
<template...>
   <sort select="secondName"/>
   <sort select="firstName"/>
</template>
```

Bergman, **Ingm**ar
Bergman, **Ingr**id
...
Monroe, James
Monroe, **Mari**lyn

Sort options

Sorting order is also affected by the optional **Order** attribute, which takes a value of 'ascending' (the default) or 'descending', and possibly also by the **Lang** attribute, which identifies the language of the text.

In addition, the **Data Type** attribute, which has a default value of 'text', can be given a value of 'number', specifying that the items should be sorted by numeric value. For example, '12' would normally appear before '7', because the first digit of '12' has a lower ASCII value than '7', but in number mode '7' is obviously a smaller value than '12', so appears first.

Finally, the **Case Order** attribute specifies whether 'a' appears before 'A' ('lower-first') or the other way around ('upper-first').

Automatic numbering

In many XML documents, list items are not physically numbered in the text. This approach makes it easy to insert, move or delete items without having to edit the prefix of all the other items. In such circumstances, the stylesheet must add the required numbering. In the simplest case, a list of item numbers is added by insert-ing the **Number** element at the appropriate position relative to the content:

```
<template match="item">
  <html:P><number/>) <apply-templates/></html:P>
</template>


    <P>1) item one</P>
    <P>2) item two</P>
    <P>3) item three</P>
```

Simple numbering

In the simple case shown above, each Item element is assigned a number based on its sequential position among other elements of the same type. Elements of differ-ent types are ignored, and numbering restarts within each parent element (in this case, within each list).

This default action is equivalent to using the **Level** attribute, with a value of 'single' (this is single level numbering). Explicitly changing this value to 'any' dictates that numbering does not reset, so the items in each list simply continue in one large sequence throughout the entire document. This option is useful for such things as sequentially numbering all the tables or images in a book.

The optional **Lang** attribute specifies a language code, such as 'en' or 'fr', that identifies a general number format to use for the given language.

Re-start numbering

The **From** attribute can be used to specify an element from which numbering must start, and is particularly useful when the level is set to 'any'. In the following example, all Table elements are numbered sequentially within each chapter, regardless of how many other intermediate structures surround any particular table:

```
<template match="table">
  <number level="any" from="chapter"/>) <apply-templates/>
</template>
```

Multi-part numbering

More complex numbering is provided using the value 'multiple' in the **Level** attribute. This option indicates that the number will consist of several parts, possibly separated by punctuation.

The **Format** attribute indicates the type of numbering to use at each level, and the punctuation that appears between levels. For example, '1. A.' indicates numbering of the larger items using digits, and the second level items using letters, with full-point characters after each part.

The token 'A' represents alphabetical ordering, with 'AA', 'AB', 'AC' following on from 'Z' in the output. The token 'a' represents the lower-case equivalent. Leading zeros in a numeric token add the given amount of padding to each value. For example, '001' indicates a sequence of '001', '002', '003' and '099', '100', '101'. Upper- and lower-case roman numerals are represented by the tokens 'I' and 'i' respectively.

The **Count** attribute lists the elements that are to be included in the multi-part count, with vertical bars separating the element names (and the current element does not have to be one of them, as demonstrated in the example below).

Putting all this together, it is possible to number the title of a section (using a letter) in such a way that it also includes the number of the chapter (using a digit) that it is in:

```
<chapter>
  <section>
    <title>First Section of Chapter One</title>
```

```
<template match="section/title">
  <number level="multi"
          count="chapter|section"
          format="1.A"/>
  <apply-templates/>
</template>
```

1.A First Section of Chapter One
...
2.C Third Section of Chapter Two

Advanced formatting

In large numbers, groups of digits are often separated using a comma or full point character. The **Grouping Separator** attribute specifies which symbol to insert between groups, such as ',', and the **Grouping Size** attribute indicates how many digits to place in each group (and is typically set to '3'):

```
<number ... grouping-separator=","
            grouping-size="3"
            format="1"/>
```

999,999 Large item
1,000,000 Even larger item

In some languages, there is more than one way to create a sequence that does not use digits. In English, this applies to the alphabetical sequence 'a, b, c, d' and the alternative roman numeral sequence 'i, ii, iii, iv'. It is easy to distinguish between these two sequences because they start with a different letter: 'a' and 'i' (or 'A' and 'I'). But this may not be the case with some other languages. To assist with this distinction, the **Letter Value** attribute can be used. It takes a value of 'alphabetic' ('a, b, c' in English) or 'traditional' ('i, ii, iii, iv') in English. The following example selects a Greek character sequence, but ensures that the sequence uses 'classical' Greek characters:

```
<number format="&#x03B1" letter-value="traditional" />
```

Sorted output numbering

When numbering elements that are also sorted, the numbering is applied first. Using the techniques described above, the numbers will therefore not be presented in the correct sequence. In some cases, this may be the desired result. But if this effect is not wanted, it is necessary to sequentially number the elements in their final order. This can be achieved using the **Value** attribute, which calculates the number from the expression it holds. The most obvious use of this attribute is to hold the 'position()' function, which returns the sequential position of the element in the sorted node set:

```
<number value="position()" format="1)" />
```

Modes

Typically, information that is copied and reused elsewhere must also be styled in a different way (the chapter titles in this book are not as large in the table of contents as they are at the top of each chapter). This can be achieved using 'modes' to create templates that are only used in specific circumstances.

The **Mode** attribute is added to the Template element, and assigned a meaningful name to represent the mode this template belongs to. This attribute is also used in the Apply Templates element, but this time to select a template only from those that have a matching mode name.

All the examples above used the default mode, which does not require specific identification, but a second mode requires a unique name to identify it.

In the following example, chapter titles are normally translated into HTML H1 elements (large headings), but when reused in the Introduction element, they are rendered in H3 elements (smaller headings):

```
<template match="intro">
  <apply-templates
          select="//chapter/title" mode="TOC" />
</template>

<template match="chapter/title">
  <html:H1>
    <apply-templates/>
  </html:H1>
</template>

<template match="chapter/title" mode="TOC">
  <html:H3>
    <apply-templates/>
  </html:H3>
</template>


  <HTML>
    <H3>Chapter One</H3>
    <H3>Chapter Two</H3>
    <H3>Chapter Three</H3>
    . . .
    <H1>Chapter One</H1>
    . . .
    <H1>Chapter Two</H1>
    . . .
    <H1>Chapter Three</H1>
    . . .
  </HTML>
```

Variables and named templates

A stylesheet often contains a number of templates that produce identical or very similar output. XSLT includes some mechanisms for avoiding such redundancy.

Variables

A 'variable' is a container of information that has a name. Whenever the variable is referenced in the stylesheet, the reference is replaced by the value of the variable.

Variables are declared using the **Variable** element. The name of the variable is given in the **Name** attribute, and the value of the variable may be the content of the element. The following example creates a variable called 'Colour', and gives it the value 'red':

```
<variable name="Colour">red</variable>
```

Alternatively, the value can be generated from an expression using a **Select** attribute. The Variable element must then be empty.

Note that variables are not actually 'variable', as they are in programming and scripting languages. The value of a particular variable cannot be changed. However, a variable can be temporarily overridden by another variable with the same name, defined within a sub-structure of the stylesheet. For example, 'global' variables defined within the Stylesheet element can be replaced within a particular Template element. Similarly, the same variable can have different values within each iteration of a For Each element loop (see below).

A variable is used by inserting a variable reference into an attribute. A variable reference is identified by a leading '$' symbol.

In order to insert the value into output text, the variable can be placed in the **Select** attribute of the **Value Of** element:

```
<html:H1>The colour is
        <xsl:value-of select="$Colour"/>.</html:H1>
```

> The colour is **red**.

A variable can also be referenced in output elements. In the following example, a variable is used to specify the border width. However, note that in this case it is necessary to enclose the variable in curly brackets, '{' and '}'. Without the brackets, the variable would not be recognized:

```
<variable name="Border">3pt</variable>
...
...<fo:block border-width="{$Border}">...
```

The brackets shown above actually enclose any string expression. In order to use curly brackets as normal in an attribute value, they must be escaped by repeating the character. The sequence '{{' represents '{', and '}}' represents '}'. As shown above, string expressions may include variable references, but in addition they may contain literal text (enclosed by quotes), and XPath expressions.

Named templates

When the same formatting is required in a number of places, it is possible to simply reuse the same template. Instead of a Match attribute, a **Name** attribute is used to give the template a unique identifier. Elsewhere, within other templates, the **Call Template** element is used to activate the named template, also using a **Name** attribute to identify the template required:

```
<template name="CreateHeader">
  <html:hr />
  <html:h2>***** <apply-templates/> *****</html:h2>
  <html:hr />
</template>

<template match="title">
  <call-template name="CreateHeader" />
</template>

<template match="head">
  <call-template name="CreateHeader" />
</template>
```

However, in such a simple case it is probably easier simply to include all the element names in the Match attribute of a single template.

Template parameters

The named template mechanism is more useful when the action performed by the named template can be modified, by passing parameters to it that override default values. To assist with this, a special type of variable can be used. The **Parameter** element defines a variable, using the **Name** attribute to give it an identity, but differs from other variables in that the element content is only the default value:

```
<param name="Prefix">%%%</param>
```

The default value can be overridden by a parameter value. Parameters can be passed to a named template by use of the **With Parameter** element, which names the parameter in its **Name** attribute, and gives the parameter an override value in its content (or its **Select** attribute expression):

```
<with-param name="SecurityLvl">3</with-param>
```

The With Parameter element is placed within the **Call Template** element in order
to pass the parameter name and value to the template that is being called:

```
<call-template name="CreateHeader">
  <with-param name="Prefix">%%%</with-param>
  <with-param name="SecurityLvl">3</with-param>
</call-template>
```

The following example shows that the named template holds the default values for
these parameters, how these parameters are used, and what is presented if the
parameters shown above are passed to the template:

```
<template name="CreateHeader">
  <param name="Prefix">*****</param>
  <param name="SecurityLvl">0</param>
  <html:HR />
  <html:H2>
    <value-of select="$Prefix" />
    Security = <value-of select="$SecurityLvl" />-
    <apply-templates/>
    *****</html:H2>
  <html:HR />
</template>
```

%%%Security = **3**-The Header To Present *****

Parameters can be passed, in exactly the same manner, with the Apply Templates
element in order to send values to the templates that are activated by the presence
of child (or other) elements. Parameters can also be passed to the stylesheet from
the XSLT processor (obviously, the With Param element has no role in this scenario):

```
<stylesheet ...>
  ...
  <param name="ExternalParam1">DEFAULT1</param>
  <param name="ExternalParam2">DEFAULT2</param>
  ...
  <template match="...">
    <apply-templates>
      <with-param name="PASS_DOWN1">X</with-param>
      <with-param name="PASS_DOWN2">Y</with-param>
    </apply-templates>
  </template>
  ...
  <template match="...">
    <param name="PASS_DOWN1">DEFAULT1</param>
    <param name="PASS_DOWN2">DEFAULT2</param>
    ...
  </template>
  ...
</stylesheet>
```

Using attribute values

Attribute values in the source document may be copied to appropriate attributes in the output document, and may also be inserted into element content for display. Attributes are identified by the '@' prefix.

To simply copy the value into an output attribute, an expression is used. The following example shows how to copy a name from the Fullname element, containing a First and Second attribute, into a Person element that contains a single Name attribute:

```
<fullName first="John" second="Smith"/>
```

```
<template match="fullName">
  <X:person name="{@first} {@second}"/>
</template>
```

```
<person name="John Smith"/>
```

To copy the value into element content text, the **Value Of** element is needed:

```
<fullName first="John" second="Smith"/>
```

```
<template match="fullName">
  <X:person>
    <value-of select="@first"/>
    <value-of select="@second"/> -
    <apply-templates/>
  </X:person>
</template>
```

```
<person>John Smith - ... </person>
```

Creating and copying elements

Perhaps the most significant task a stylesheet performs is the generation of XML output, including element tags. XSLT includes further methods for creating elements, and for copying elements from the source document directly to the output document.

Create element

An element can be created in the output document using the **Element** element, with the element name specified using the **Name** attribute, and an optional namespace specified using the **Namespace** attribute. At first, there appears to be little point to this, as the following two examples are equivalent, and the first is easier to create and interpret:

```
<template match="section">
  <html:H3>
    <apply-templates/>
  </html:H3>
</template>


<template match="section">
  <element namespace="html" name="H3">
    <apply-templates/>
  </element>
</template>
```

However, one strength of this construct is the Name attribute, which can take an expression instead of just a pre-defined name. In this way, the name of the element can be modified by a variable. For example, a parameter passed to a named template may specify the header level to output in an HTML document. The named template below by default creates an H3 element, but a parameter passed to it may change this, perhaps to an H5 element:

```
<template name="CreateHeader">
  <param name="HeaderLvl">3</param>
  <element namespace="html" name="H{$HeaderLvl}">
    <apply-templates/>
  </element>
</template>


    <H3>the default header</H3>
```

The other benefit to using the Element element is that it makes it much simpler to create an XSLT DTD that is applicable to any number of output formats (because namespaces and additional, output-specific elements are not needed).

Copy element

Elements can also be created that are copies of elements in the source document, using the **Copy** element. This element is simply replaced by the original element that triggered the template. For example, to add a prefix to all HTML header elements, the following template would suffice:

```
<template match="H1|H2|H3|H4|H5|H6|H7">
  <copy>
    Header: <apply-templates/>
  </copy>
</template>
```

Note that attributes attached to the source element are not preserved when the Copy element is used, but a solution to this problem is outlined below.

Attaching attributes

In order to attach attributes to elements created using the Element or Copy elements, the **Attribute** element can be used. This element takes a **Name** attribute to hold the name of the attribute to be created, and optionally a **Namespace** attribute to hold the namespace prefix. The content of this element is the attribute value. In the following example, a Style attribute is added to the headers:

```
<template match="H1|H2|H3|H4|H5|H6|H7">
  <copy>
    <attribute name="STYLE">color: red</attribute>
    Header: <apply-templates/>
  </copy>
</template>
```

As noted above, the Copy element does not preserve its original attributes. It is possible to resurrect source attribute values using the Attribute element along with the Value Of element, which is used to select and insert the original value of the attribute:

```
<attribute name="STYLE">
  <value-of select="@STYLE"/>
</attribute>
```

All the original attributes can be copied to the output element as follows:

```
<copy>
  <apply-templates select="@*" />
  ...
</copy>
```

Attribute sets

Sets of attributes can be defined within the **Attribute Set** element, which is given a name using the **Name** attribute. These sets can be used in various places, including within the Copy element, using the **Use Attribute Sets** attribute:

```
<attribute-set name="class-and-colour">
    <attribute name="style">color:red</attribute>
    <attribute name="class">standard</attribute>
</attribute-set>
```

```
<template match="H1|H2|H3|H4|H5|H6|H7">
  <copy use-attribute-sets name="class-and-color" />
    Header: <apply-templates/>
  </copy>
</template>
```

Note that this attribute can also be used on the Element and Attribute elements, and on the Attribute Set element itself (to merge sets).

Copy document fragment

Source document elements can also be selected and copied out to the destination document using the **Copy Of** element, which uses a **Select** attribute to identify the document fragment to be reproduced at the current position. In addition, attributes and all descendant elements and attributes are retained (unlike using the Copy element described above). For example, if the source document contains numerous H1 and H2 header elements, it would be possible to reproduce them at the start of an HTML output document as follows:

```
<template match="BODY">
  <html:BODY>
    <copy-of select="//html:H1 | //html:H2" />
    <apply-templates/>
  </html:BODY>
</template>
```

```
<BODY>
    <H1 ID="intro">Introduction</H1>
    <H2>Secondary header</H2>
    <H1><B>Main Text</B></H1>
    ...
</BODY>
```

This technique can also be used to copy the current element to the output, while retaining its attributes and contents. An earlier example demonstrates adding a prefix to a header. This example can be reformulated, replacing the Copy and Apply Templates elements with the Copy Of element. All attributes are taken care of, but any elements that may be embedded within the headers will not be processed (they will be output just as they are):

```
<template match="H1|H2|H3|H4|H5|H6|H7">
  <html:P>Header:</html:P><copy-of select="."/>
</template>
```

XML output headers

The ability to output XML documents, including XSL and XHTML files, is very important. There are a number of features in XSLT for controlling how these files are identified by their initial markup constructs, as in the following example:

```
<?xml version="1.0" encoding="ISO-8859-1"
                                      standalone="yes"?>
<!DOCTYPE book PUBLIC "-//myCorp//DTD My DTD//EN"
                       "book.dtd" >
```

The **Output** element has a number of attributes that control whether or not these tags are output, and what values their respective parameters will take.

XML declaration

The **Omit XML Declaration** attribute can be given the value 'yes' to prevent the declaration being created in the output file. When this attribute is not used (or is explicitly given the value 'no'), the declaration is output, and three other attributes are used to set its parameter values. The **Version** attribute needs to be given the value '1.0' for XML output. The **Encoding** attribute holds the character set encoding, such as 'ISO-8859-1'. Finally, the **Standalone** attribute holds the value 'yes' or 'no':

```
<output method='xml' version='1.0' encoding='ISO-8859-1'
                                   standalone='yes' />
```

Document type declaration

If the output document conforms to an externally held DTD, then the document type declaration needs to contain either a public identifier, a system identifier or both. The **Doctype Public** and **Doctype System** attributes hold the respective parameter values:

```
<output type='xml' ...
        doctype-public='-//myCorp//DTD My DTD//EN'
        doctype-system='book.dtd' />
```

Repeating structures

When creating tabular output from source elements, or some other very regular structure, a technique is available that reduces the number of templates needed, and in so doing improves the clarity of the stylesheet. For example, consider the need to transform the following structure into a tabular format:

```
<countries>
  <country>
    <name>United Kingdom</name>
    <capital>london</capital>
  </country>
  <country>
    <name>United States</name>
    <capital>Washington</capital>
    <borders>Canada</borders>
    <borders>Mexico</borders>
  </country>
</countries>
```

To create an HTML table for this data, with one row for each country, the following four templates could be defined:

```
<template match="countries">
  <html:TABLE><apply-templates/></html:TABLE>
</template>

<template match="country">
  <html:TR><apply-templates/></html:TR>
</template>

<template match="name">
  <html:TH><apply-templates/></html:TH>
</template>

<template match="capital | borders">
  <html:TD><apply-templates/></html:TD>
</template>
```

It would require some study to deduce the exact nature of the conversion to be applied. To clarify this example, the output would be as follows:

```
<TABLE>
  <TR><TH>United Kingdom</TH>
      <TD>London</TD>
  </TR>
  <TR><TH>United States</TH>
      <TD>Washington</TD>
      <TD>Canada</TD>
      <TD>Mexico</TD>
  </TR>
</TABLE>
```

Using the **For Each** element, the entire transformation can be accomplished with a single template. The **Select** attribute applies the enclosed template to each occurrence of the matching element. This mechanism is particularly useful when there are multiple levels of structures, as in the variable number of bordering countries in this example:

```
<template match="countries">
  <html:TABLE>
  <for-each select="country">
    <html:TR>
    <html:TH><apply-templates select="name"/></html:TH>
    <html:TD><apply-templates select="capital"/>
    </html:TD>
    <for-each select="borders">
      <html:TD><apply-templates/></html:TD>
    </for-each>
    </html:TR>
  </for-each>
  </html:TABLE>
</template>
```

Conditions

It is possible to vary the output of a template depending on certain conditions. In the simplest case, part of the formatting can be optional, and only instantiated when a specific condition is true.

Simple test

The **If** element encloses optional formatting instructions, and uses a **Test** attribute to determine whether or not the content is to be made an active part of the transformation. The test is an XPath expression. When the Test attribute contains only an element name or attribute name, the test returns 'true' when the element is present as a child of the current element, or the attribute is attached to the current element:

```
<if test="secret">
  <X:title>THIS ELEMENT CONTAINS A SECRET ELEMENT</X:title>
</if>
```

This feature can be used to reduce the number of templates needed. For example, if alternating paragraphs are to be coloured differently, the first template below produces the same effect as the following two. Note that, to keep the example well-formed, it is necessary to specify the HTML open tag once, then use the Attribute element to add an appropriate attribute value to this element (the attribute is not added to the If element, but to the nearest output element, which in this case is the P element):

```
<template match="para">
  <html:P>
    <if test="position() mod 2 = 0">
      <attribute name="STYLE">color: red</attribute>
    </if>
    <if test="not(position() mod 2 = 0)">
      <attribute name="STYLE">color: blue</attribute>
    </if>
    <apply-templates/>
  </html:P>
</template>


<!-- VERBOSE ALTERNATIVE -->

<template match="para[position() mod 2 = 0]">
  <html:P STYLE="color: red">
    <apply-templates/>
  </html:P>
</template>

<template match="para[not(position() mod 2 = 0)]">
  <html:P STYLE="color: blue">
    <apply-templates/>
  </html:P>
</template>
```

The saving can be more significant. In the following example an attribute can take a number of possible values, each one producing a different format:

```
<para type="normal">A normal paragraph</para>
<para type="secret">A secret paragraph</para>
<para type="optional">An optional paragraph</para>
```

```
<template match="para">
  <html:P>
  <if test="@type='normal'">
    <attribute name="STYLE">color: black</attribute>
  </if>
  <if test="@type='secret'">
    <attribute name="STYLE">color: red</attribute>
  </if>
  <if test="@type='optional'">
    <attribute name="STYLE">color: green</attribute>
  </if>
  <apply-templates/></html:P>
</template>
```

```
<P STYLE="color: black">A normal paragraph</P>
<P STYLE="color: red">A secret paragraph</P>
<P STYLE="color: green">An optional paragraph</P>
```

However, this technique can still be quite clumsy. It does not prevent two or more tests from succeeding, and does not provide for a catch-all condition to be activated in the event that all the tests fail.

Choice and default

The **Choose** element is more flexible than the If element. It contains **When** elements for each case, and an **Otherwise** element that is activated when none of the explicit cases apply. The When element has a **Test** attribute, which works as described for the If element:

```
<template match="para">
  <html:P>
  <choose>
    <when test="@type='normal'">
      <attribute name="STYLE">color:black</attribute>
    </when>
    <when test="@type='secret'">
      <attribute name="STYLE">color:red</attribute>
    </when>
    <when test="@type='optional'">
      <attribute name="STYLE">color:green</attribute>
    </when>
    <otherwise>
      <attribute name="STYLE">color:yellow</attribute>
    </otherwise>
    . . .
  </choose>
  <apply-templates/>
  </html:P>
</template>
```

Only the first successful test is chosen; the remaining tests are ignored. Only if none of the tests succeed does the content of the Otherwise element become active.

Keys

The XML linking system, using the ID and IDREF special attribute types, is quite limited in a number of respects. First, without a DTD it is not possible to identify these attributes. Second, there is only one set of identifiers, which means that every identifier in the document must be totally unique. Third, the name of the identifier must conform to the constraints of XML names (for example, spaces are not allowed in these identifiers). Fourth, an element can have only one identifier. Finally, the identifier must take the form of an attribute value.

XSLT 'keys' avoid all these limitations. However, unlike ID/IDREF identifiers, keys are not validated (by the XSLT processor) so are only used to make processing more efficient.

Key element

XSLT allows keys to be defined and associated with particular elements. Every key has a name, a value and a node with which it is associated. A set of keys is defined using the **Key** element:

```
<key ... />
```

The **Name** attribute provides a name for a set of identifiers in an 'identifiers name-space'. When only one set is needed, a name such as 'global' may be considered.

The **Match** attribute specifies the elements to be included in this set of identifiers using an XPath pattern. For a global set, this would be '*' (representing all elements).

The **Use** attribute is an XPath expression that identifies the location of the identifier values. If the identifier is in an attribute called 'id', then the expression would be '@id':

```
<key name="global" match="*" use="@id" />


<book id="book">
  <chapter id="chap1">...</chapter>
  <chapter id="chap2">...</chapter>
</book>
```

The following example creates a set of keys specifically for Name elements, where the unique key values are taken from the content of the embedded Employee Number elements. Note that the values in this example would not be valid XML ID names, as they begin with digits and have spaces in them:

```
<key name="nameKeys"
     match="name"
     use="employnum/text()" />


<name>
  <first>John</first><second>Smith</second>
  <employnum>12345 X12</employnum>
</name>
<name>
  <first>Peter</first><second>Jones</second>
  <employnum>18887 X12</employnum>
</name>
```

Key function

A function called '**key()**' has been added to those provided by XPath. It works in a similar fashion to the 'id()' function, but this function takes two parameters. The first parameter identifies a key set to use, such as 'global' or 'nameKeys', and the second may be the value to locate:

```
key("global", "chap2")/para[3]
key("names", "18887 X12")/first
```

Of course, it is possible to create similar expressions that do not rely upon the use of keys, as the following equivalent examples demonstrate:

```
/book/chapter[id="chap2"]/para[3]
//name[employnum="18887 X12"]/first
```

However, it is expected that processing will be much more efficient when keys are used, as the processor can create a list of key values in advance of template processing for quick look-up.

Messages

The stylesheet is able to pass a message to the XSLT processor, which should provide some means to further pass on this message to the user, perhaps in a pop-up window or as output to the command line.

The **Message** element contains the XML fragment to be displayed. This element cannot be used at the top level of the stylesheet, only within templates and other structures.

Its most obvious purpose is to assist with debugging:

```
<template match="weird-element">
  <message>The WEIRD element has occurred</message>
  <html:P><apply-templates/></html:P>
</template>
```

Serious problems may require more drastic action than simply displaying a message. When reporting a serious error, it may be appropriate to halt the styling process as well. The **Terminate** attribute has a default value of 'no', but this can be changed to 'yes':

```
<template match="weird-element">
  <message terminate="yes">The WEIRD element
    should not be present! HALTING PROCESS.</message>
</template>
```

Imports and inclusions

Multiple stylesheets may share some definitions. To avoid unnecessary repetition, common sets of rules may be placed in a separate stylesheet, and referenced from others:

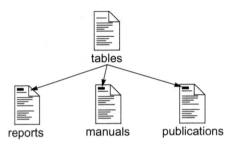

Import

Sets of rules can be imported using the **Import** element. They must all occur before the style rules. This element may be used repeatedly, to import a number of other resources, and has an **Href** attribute that identifies a file to import by its URL:

```
<stylesheet ...>
  <import href="tables.xsl" />
  <import href="colours.xsl" />
  <template ...>...</template>
```

Imported rules are not considered to be as important as other rules, which can affect selection of a rule when conflicts occur. Normally, a template in the main stylesheet file will be considered more important than an imported template, and will simply override it. However, it is possible to 'inherit' the behaviour of the imported template instead. The behaviour given in that template is enacted using the **Apply Imports** element (usually in place of the Apply Templates element).

For example, if the imported template were to wrap the contents in a simple Paragraph element, then the overriding template below would add a prefix, before passing control to the imported template:

```
<!-- MAIN STYLESHEET TEMPLATE (OVERRIDING IMPORTED ONE) -->
<template match="para">
  <html:P>PARA FOLLOWING:</html:P>
  <apply-imports/>
</template>
```

Include

Rules in other files can also be inserted. This is a similar concept to importing, except that the **Include** element can be used anywhere (after the Import elements), and included rules are not considered to be less important than other rules. It also uses an **Href** attribute to locate the file to be included:

```
<include href="tables.xsl" />
```

Extended functions

Apart from the functions XSLT inherits from XPath (described in Chapter 13), this standard adds a few more that are particularly useful to this application. The key() function has already been discussed, and the next section discusses the format-number() function. The remaining new functions are introduced here.

Current function

The **current()** function identifies the current node. In many circumstances, it refers to the same node that '.' does. However, the exact meaning of '.' depends on where it is used within a location path expression. This function, though, always refers to the node that triggered the template, regardless of where it is used in an expression.

Document function

The **document()** function allows the content of other documents to be accessed. For example, to access the name of an author of a remote document:

```
The author of the other document is [ <value-of
    select="document('other.xml')/book/authorName"/> ].
```

The parameter is actually a URL, and this URL can be represented by a node instead of a string, so allowing the name of the remote document to be found in element content, or in an attribute value:

```
The author of the other document is [ <value-of
    select="document(@docRef)/book/authorName"/> ].
```

If the parameter is a relative URL reference, then the absolute address of the remote document is calculated from the location of the stylesheet. However, it is possible to override this by passing a new base location as the second parameter:

```
document(@docRef, "file:///D:/XML/otherdocs")
```

Generate ID function

The **generate-id**() function returns a unique identifier that can be assigned to an output element:

```
<html:DIV ID="{generate-id(.)}">...</html:DIV>
```

If the same function is used again, elsewhere, and refers to the same element, then it will return the same value. This makes it possible to reliably create references to the element:

```
A <html:A HREF="#{generate-id(/book/chapter[1])}">
reference</html:A> to the first chapter.
```

System function

It is possible to discover the version of XSLT that the processor supports, the name of the vendor of the processor, and a URL reference to the vendor's organization, using the **system-property**() function. A string parameter passed to the function determines what information is being requested. The standard parameter names are '**xsl:version**', '**xsl:vendor**' and '**xsl:vendor-uri**'. For example:

```
<text>XSLT version: </text>
<value-of select="system-property( xsl:version )" />

XSLT version: 1.2
```

A particular processor may also provide access to additional information.

Unparsed entity URI function

An attribute value in the source file may be the name of an external unparsed (binary) entity, yet the output element content or attribute value typically needs to reference the file directly instead. This can be accomplished using the **unparsed-entity-uri**() function. It is used to obtain the system identifier of the given entity. Consider the following example:

```
<!ENTITY MyBoat SYSTEM "/images/boat.GIF" NDATA GIF>
...
<!ATTLIST image name ENTITY #REQUIRED>
...
<image name="MyBoat" />

<template match="image">
  <html:IMG HREF="{unparsed-entity-uri(@name)}" />
</template>

<IMG HREF="/images/boat.GIF">
```

Vendor extensions

The **Fallback** element can be used within vendor-specific instructions to hold normal XSLT instructions that should be enacted if the XSLT processor cannot understand the vendor-specific instruction. If the processor does not understand the instruction, it implements the instructions embedded within the Fallback element instead:

```
<acme:scramble select=".">
  <fallback>The following text should
    have been scrambled: [<apply-templates/>]
  </fallback>
</acme:scramble>
```

Multiple Fallback elements can be used, but are normally only needed when further extension instructions are also embedded within the main instruction.

The Fallback elements and their contents are all ignored if the processor recognizes the extension instruction.

Element available

When an XSLT processor does not support a particular extension element, it can detect it and avoid it. Unknown instructions can be avoided by first asking the processor if it understands the instruction, then stepping over the instruction if the processor says that it does not. The function **element-available()** returns 'true' if the element name passed to it is supported by the XSLT processor:

```
<if test="element-available('acme:scramble')" >
  <acme:scramble select="." />
</if>
```

Number formatting

Format-number function

Using the **format-number()** function, numeric values can be formatted as required. The first parameter is the string containing the number to be formatted. The second parameter is a template to be used to format this number.

In the following example, the template ensures that the price has two digits after the decimal point:

```
<price val="3.5"/>
```

```
Price: <value-of select="format-number(@val, '0.00')"/>.
```

3.50

The template may contain a number of significant symbols. As indicated above, '0' indicates that a digit must appear at this position, and the '.' symbol indicates the position of the decimal point. In addition, the '#' symbol indicates the position of possibly absent digits, and is used in conjunction with commas, which specifies where grouping separators should appear. When used after a decimal point, the '#' symbol is used to restrict the number of digits output. For example, the template '###,###,#00.0#' would create '132,456,789.12' from the value '123456789.1234'. The semicolon character separates two templates, the second being for negative numbers. The '%' symbol indicates a percentage value (fractions such as '0.2' are converted to '%20'). In the same way, the '?' symbol represents 'per mille' (per thousand). Finally, the international currency symbol stands in for an appropriate local currency symbol, such as '$'.

Format element

The formatting template described above makes some assumptions that are not always relevant. The full point and comma characters are not universally used in numbers, or their roles may be different. The **Decimal Format** element may be used to specify alternative symbols to be used in both the formatting template and the output. For example, in France the full point and comma character roles are reversed. The **Decimal Separator** and **Grouping Separator** attributes specify the character to use for each role:

```
<decimal-format decimal-separator=","
                grouping-separator="." ... >
```

This element has a **Name** attribute, and its value is referenced from the function that wishes to use these settings:

```
<decimal-format name="France" ... />
<value-of select="format-number(@val, '0,00', France)" />
```

3,50

In some languages, '-' is not used as a minus sign, '%' is not used for percentages, and '0' is not used for zero digits. The **Minus Sign**, **Percent**, **Per Mille** and **Zero Digit** attributes are used to override these defaults:

```
<decimal-format ... minus-sign="M" percent="P"
                    per-mille="?" zero-digit="Z" />
```

Stylesheet DTD issues

In theory, one of the most obvious benefits of using the XML data format for XSLT stylesheets is that an XML editor can be used to assist in the construction of stylesheets. Such editors can prevent errors from occurring in the markup, ensure that the stylesheet conforms to the constraints of the XSLT standard, and help the author by indicating which elements and attributes are available in the current context. But these benefits are only realized if a DTD or schema exists, and this requirement raises some issues.

The XSLT standard includes a DTD that defines the XSLT elements and attributes. But this DTD alone may not be sufficient. The fact that XSLT markup can be mixed with output markup means that a DTD may need to be defined that includes both sets of elements.

For example, a stylesheet that produces XSL output would be different to one (even for the same source data) that produces HTML output, and the DTDs should differ accordingly. For this reason, the XSLT DTD includes a parameter entity, called **Result-Elements**. The following examples illustrate different definitions for this entity:

```
<!ENTITY % result-elements "fo:block | fo:inline | ... ">

<!ENTITY % result-elements "html:P | html:B | ... ">
```

The DTD must also contain the definitions for the elements concerned (see Chapter 10 for details on general namespace modelling issues). While an early draft of the XSL specification included a DTD for XSL elements, unfortunately it did not accurately describe the attributes allowed on each element (instead, it included only attributes which represent properties that apply to the object, not those that can be used to set inherited properties, though this may not be true when the standard is finally released). For example, the Inline element only contains an Id attribute, yet in reality is used to specify a number of inherited properties, so needs to be able to include such attributes as Font Weight. Hopefully, the final standard will include a DTD that can be merged with the XSLT DTD to provide a single DTD for creation of XSL-based stylesheets (though the latest draft does not include a DTD at all).

This problem can be avoided entirely using Element and Attribute elements throughout the stylesheet. In this scenario, the XSLT DTD is sufficient for all needs; though in its simplest form it does not contain any constraints on the possible names of output elements, or indeed the attributes allowed in each element. But the stylesheet will also be harder to read. The second example below is not as easy to interpret as the first:

```
<template match="book">
  <html:HTML>
    <html:HEAD>
      <html:TITLE>The Document</html:TITLE>
    </html:HEAD>
    <html:BODY STYLE="color:blue">
      <apply-templates/>
    </html:BODY>
  </html:HTML>
</template>


<template match="book">
  <element name="HTML" ns="html">
    <element name="HEAD" ns="html">
      <element name="TITLE" ns="html">
       The Document
      </element>
    </element>
    <element name="BODY" ns="html">
      <attribute name="STYLE">color:blue</attribute>
      <apply-templates/>
    </element>
  </element>
</template>
```

18. SAX 1.0

SAX is a standard software interface for event-driven processing of XML data, allowing parsers to deliver information to applications in digestible chunks. This chapter describes the SAX 1.0 standard in detail, and illustrates its use with a popular Java-based parser. SAX has been designed primarily to work with Java, though other language versions have been developed, or are in development, including VB, C++ and C# versions.

Although SAX 1.0 has now been superseded by SAX 2.0 (see Chapter 19), this is still the most universally supported version of the standard. It remains relevant, and SAX 2.0 processors retain backward compatibility with this version. Readers interested in SAX 2.0 should read this chapter first, as it covers the concepts and features common to both.

Background

SAX (*Simple API for XML*) Version 1.0 was released in May 1998, and is free for both private and commercial use. The standard is available from www.megginson.com/SAX/index.htm.

SAX is an API for event-driven processing of XML (the general nature and benefits of this approach are explored in Chapter 16).

A large number of SAX-compliant parsers have been developed, in an increasing number of computer languages, and most are freely available from the Web. But SAX has its origins as a Java-based technology. Most of the SAX-compliant parsers are Java applications, and this language has therefore been chosen for the examples that follow.

Call-backs and interfaces

Call-backs

The application instantiates a parser object, supplied by the parser developer (in this case the open-source Apache Software Foundation (www.apache.org) parser called Xerces), and instructs it to parse a specified XML document or data stream. As the parser processes the XML data, it detects significant items, such as an element start-tag, or a comment. But the parser also needs to send all this information back to the main application.

The SAX API is mainly concerned with the means by which the parser is able to return information to the application, using a 'call-back' mechanism. The parser must be given access to methods in objects created by the main application, so that it can pass-on information as it reads it from the XML document.

Event handlers

Depending on the need, the application creates one or more objects that contain methods that the parser must call when appropriate events occur.

The application may only wish to be informed of document markup: the element start-tags, end-tags and text content (as well as any whitespace), the comments and processing instructions, and the document start and end. But it may also wish to be informed of calls to external unparsed entities, and declarations of notations. Or it may also wish to be informed of errors. When errors occur, it may need to be able to determine the location of these errors. Finally, it may wish to be informed of all calls to external entities, and be given the opportunity to intercept and redirect these calls.

The application passes references to these 'handler' objects to the parser, so that it can call the methods in them when appropriate.

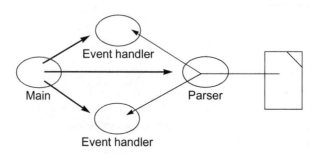

SAX interfaces

So that the parser can accept the handler objects created by the application, they must belong to a class that defines one or more of the SAX interfaces (located at **'org.xml.sax.*'**). The parser can then be certain that the necessary methods are present, and call them when appropriate events occur.

The SAX interfaces are:

- Parser (implemented by the parser itself) (deprecated in SAX 2.0)
- DocumentHandler (deprecated in SAX 2.0)
- AttributeList (deprecated in SAX 2.0)
- ErrorHandler
- EntityResolver
- Locator
- DTDHandler.

Note that the first three interfaces in this list have been deprecated in SAX 2.0, but are still present in the later version of the standard. However, it is expected that they will become obsolete if yet another version is ever released.

These interfaces are discussed in detail below.

Java Xerces implementation

There are some important activities involved in parsing, navigating and processing documents that the SAX standard does not cover. For example, writing out a structure into XML format is outside the scope of the standard. These features, if implemented at all, will differ in operation between parsers. For the sake of providing working examples, therefore, a specific parser has been chosen. In this case, the Xerces Java parser (available from xml.apache.org) is used throughout.

To use the Xerces parser, the following import statements are required:

```
import org.xml.sax.*;

import org.apache.xerces.parsers.SAXParser;
```

Apache provides classes for parsing an XML file or data stream, including one called 'SAXParser'. This class implements the first interface discussed below (parser in SAX 1.0, SAXParser in SAX 2.0). It has a 'setFeature' method that can be used to switch on validation against a DTD (which is actually part of the SAX 2.0 standard):

```
SAXParser mySAXParser = new SAXParser();

try
{
  mySAXParser.setFeature("http://xml.org/sax/
                          features/validation", true);
}
catch (SAXException e){ ... }
...
try
{
  myParser.parse("myDocument.xml");
}
catch( IOException err ) { ... }
catch( SAXException err ) { ... }
```

This example shows the simplest variant of the parse method, which takes a URL reference locating a data file. When the data is not stored in a file, a more complex variant is used. This variant is described later.

Note: This Xerces parser is actually a fully compliant SAX 2.0 parser, but because this version is backward-compatible, only the 1.0 functionality is described in this chapter. The next chapter shows the same parser in use as a SAX 2.0 parser.

The parser

The parser developer creates a class that parses the XML document or data stream. This parser class implements the **Parser** interface, which defines the following methods:

```
void  parse(InputSource src)
                throws SAXException, IOException;
void  parse(String src)
                throws SAXException, IOException;

void  setDocumentHandler(DocumentHandler doch);
void  setErrorHandler(ErrorHandler errh);
void  setDTDHandler(DTDHandler dtdh);
void  setEntityResolver(EntityResolver entres);
void  setLocale(Locale loc) throws SAXException;
```

Note that in SAX 2.0, while this interface is still available, it is superseded by the XMLReader interface, which mainly adds a standard model for getting and setting parser features and properties.

These methods fall into two groups. The larger group of 'set...' methods is used by the application to register classes that conform to other interfaces. This is needed to enable the parser to make the call-backs. Most of these methods are described later, as the interfaces they register are discussed. The only one remaining to discuss now is the **setLocale** method, which is used to tell the parser what language to use for error messages and warnings, which the parser may ignore (and this method is absent from SAX 2.0).

After registering one or more of these objects with the parser, the application will call the **parse** method, as demonstrated above.

The parser begins to read the XML source data, but as soon as it encounters a meaningful object, such as the start-tag of an element, it stops reading, sends the information to the main application by calling an appropriate method in one of the objects registered with the parser, and waits for this method to return before continuing.

Document handlers

In order for the application to receive basic markup events from the parser, the application developer must create a class that implements the **DocumentHandler** interface. This interface defines methods that handle different kinds of event:

```
void   startDocument() throws SAXException;
void   endDocument() throws SAXException;
void   startElement(String name, AttributeList atts)
                                      throws SAXException;
void   endElement(String name) throws SAXException;
void   characters(char ch[], int start, int length)
                                      throws SAXException;
void   ignorableWhitespace(char ch[], int start, int length)
                                      throws SAXException;
void   processingInstruction(String target, String data)
                                      throws SAXException;
void   setDocumentLocator(Locator myLoc);
```

Note that in SAX 2.0, while this interface is still available, it is superseded by the ContentHandler interface, which adds namespace support to element handling.

Note that comments are not handled by SAX (even in the next version). There is no method defined for receiving comment events.

Some of these methods are included in the diagram below, which shows the application creating an object belonging to a class that implements the DocumentHandler interface (containing the methods listed above), then creating the parser object (which implements the Parser interface, so contains the parse method), which is then told to begin reading the XML data file, and in turn triggers appropriate methods in the first object as notable items are encountered:

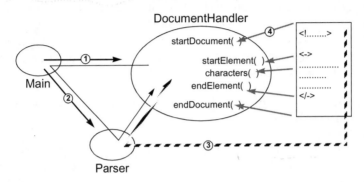

Registration

In order for this to work the parser object needs to be given a reference to the DocumentHandler object. The main application passes such a reference to the parser by calling its **setDocumentHandler** method:

```
SAXParser myParser = new SAXParser();

myDocHandlerClass myDoc = new myDocHandlerClass();

myParser.setDocumentHandler(myDoc);

// now begin parsing...
```

Note that it is common practice for a single object to be developed that handles all the events that the parser will activate, and also creates and activates the parser itself. In this case, each 'set...' method is simply passed the word 'this' (a reference back to the current object):

```
class MyClass implements DocumentHandler {
...
myParser.setDocumentHandler(this);
```

Start and end document events

The first method called is always the **startDocument** method, and the last called is always the **endDocument** method. These methods are useful for general housekeeping, such as initializing variables and opening and closing files:

```
public void startDocument ()
{
  inChapter = false;
  inChapterTitle = false;
  nextTitle = 1;
}
```

The **startElement** method is called when an element start-tag is encountered in the data stream. It is passed the name of the element and its attributes (using another class that is described below). The **endElement** method is called when an end-tag is encountered, and is also passed the name of the element (as all element end-tags must be present in XML, this information is potentially redundant, but convenient nevertheless).

The examples below set flags that are used to identify a title inside a chapter. A later example shows how this information is used to extract all the chapter titles:

```
public void startElement(String name, AttributeList atts)
{
  if ( name.equals("chapter") ) inChapter = true;
  if (( name.equals("title") && ( inChapter == true ))
  {
    inChapterTitle = true;
    chapterTitle = ""; // append to this later
  }
}
```

```
public void endElement(String name)
{
  if ( name.equals("chapter") ) inChapter = false;
}
```

Characters found event

The 'characters' method is called when a string of text is encountered. It is passed as a character array, but it is not assumed that the string completely fills this array, nor that it starts at the beginning of the array, so start and length values are also supplied.

The example below shows how to convert this information into a simple string:

```
public void characters(char ch[], int start, int length)
{
  String chars = new String( ch, start, length );

  if ( inChapterTitle == true )
                chapterTitle = chapterTitle + chars;
}
```

It cannot be guaranteed that the parser will always pass the entire text content of an element in one call to this method. Much depends on the approach taken by the parser to read the source XML data. The examples above show the safe way to store this text in a variable. In the start-tag event, the variable is set to an empty string. In the characters event, the value passed is appended to this string. If the text is passed in multiple events, nothing is lost.

Ignorable whitespace event

The **ignorableWhitespace** method is called when a string of ignorable whitespace characters is encountered. This is whitespace that appears in elements that are only allowed to contain elements.

Note that when a DTD is not in use, this method is unlikely to be called at all, because it is not possible for the parser to distinguish between elements that can contain text, and elements that can only contain other elements. The parameters are the same as for the characters method.

Processing instruction event

The **processingInstruction** method is called when a processing instruction is encountered, and is passed both the target application name and the actual instruction:

```
public void processingInstruction(String target,
                                  String data)
{
  if ( target.equals("ACME") )
  {
    // target is ACME processor

    if ( data.equals("new_page") )
    {
      // page break here
    }

  }
}
```

Attribute lists

When a parser informs the application that an element start-tag has been encountered, it calls the startElement method, as described above. However, a start-tag may contain one or more attributes. It would not be possible to pass details of each attribute as individual parameters, because it is unknown in advance how many there could be. There is no theoretical limit to the number of attributes an element can contain.

The solution is for the parser to create a 'wrapper' object for all attribute details. This object must implement the **AttributeList** interface, which defines the following methods:

```
int      getLength();
String   getName(int i);
String   getType(int i);
String   getType(String name);
String   getValue(int i);
String   getValue(String name);
```

Note that in SAX 2.0, while this interface is still available, it is superseded by the Attributes interface, which adds support for namespaces.

Limitations

An attribute value may not be physically present in the start-tag, but may be supplied as a default value from the DTD instead. There is no way to distinguish between attributes defined explicitly and those that are supplied by the DTD. Also, the parser does not hold any information on attributes defined in the DTD that are both implied and happen not to appear in the start-tag.

It is therefore not possible, using the SAX API, to reconstruct a DTD from analysis of documents that conform to it.

Number of attributes

To ascertain how many attributes are present in this object, the **getLength** method is called. This method returns an integer value representing the number of attributes present (and a value of zero indicates that there are no attributes). Each attribute is identified by a simple index value. The first attribute has an index value of zero. It follows that the last attribute has an index value one less than the number returned by the getLength method.

Attribute name

To discover the name of one of the attributes, the **getName** method is called, along with its index value. This example retrieves the name of the last attribute:

```
String lastAttribute = null;
int totalAtts = atts.getLength();

if ( totalAtts > 0 )
      lastAttribute = atts.getName(totalAtts - 1);
```

Attribute value

Similarly, to get the value of an attribute, the **getValue** method is called. Unsurprisingly, the attribute value with a given index number matches the attribute name with the same index number.

The following example retrieves the value of the attribute with the name extracted in the previous example:

```
lastAttValue = atts.getValue(totalAtts - 1);
```

Attribute type

When a DTD is in use, each attribute is assigned a data type, such as CDATA, ID or NMTOKEN. The **getType** method returns this information. If the parser is unable to get this information from the DTD, perhaps because it is not a validating parser, then it substitutes the default type, 'CDATA'.

The following example partially reconstructs the original attribute list declaration (but makes a few unjustifiable assumptions about default values and requirement status):

```
public void startElement(String name, AttributeList atts)
{
  System.out.print( "<!ATTLIST " + name + " " );

  for( int i = 0; i < atts.getLength(); i++ )
  {
    System.out.print( atts.getName(i) + " " +
                      atts.getType(i) + " " +
                      "#IMPLIED \"" +
                      atts.getValue(i) + "\" \n");
  }

  System.out.print( "> \n" );
}
```

Direct value access

When the application is only interested in a specific attribute, a simpler mechanism is provided for ascertaining its value. Instead of stepping through the attributes in sequence, looking for the one with the correct name, it is possible to simply request the value of a named attribute.

If the attribute is not present, a null value is returned.

The following example extracts the value of the Id attribute, regardless of which element is being processed:

```
public void startElement(String name, AttributeList atts)
{
    String ID = atts.getValue("Id");
}
```

The type of a named attribute can be discovered in the same way, though this seems to be a much less valuable feature. If the application already knows the name of the attribute it wants, it probably knows what data type its values conform to as well.

Error handlers

If the application wishes to be informed of warnings and errors, then it can implement the **ErrorHandler** interface. This interface includes the following methods for intercepting warnings and errors. These methods all work in the same way, but react to problems of various levels of seriousness:

```
void  warning(SAXParseException err) throws SAXException;
void  error(SAXParseException err) throws SAXException;
void  fatalError(SAXParseException err)
                                      throws SAXException;
```

Note that this interface is unchanged in SAX 2.0.

Registration

Typically, the same object that handles normal document events will also handle error events. These methods then just become additional event handlers in the main event-handling object. To inform the parser where to send error events, the object must be registered in the same way that the document handler is, but using the **setErrorHandler** method instead:

```
class MyClass implements DocumentHandler, ErrorHandler {
...
myParser.setDocumentHandler( this );
myParser.setErrorHandler( this );
```

Example

The following example simply displays a message each time a warning is triggered by the parser:

```
public void warning(SAXParseException err)
{
  System.out.println( "WARNING: " + err );
}
```

SAXParseException

It should be noted that it is not a string that is passed to the methods described above, but an object that implements the **SAXParseException** interface. In the example above, the string value of this object is printed. This would be a message that represents the type of error or warning that occurred. But this object has much more useful information within it (and is described in detail in the next section).

SAX Parse exception

An error message is not particularly helpful when no indication is given as to where the error was detected in the XML document. To a greater or lesser extent, depending on the type of error concerned, all errors could be traced to an exact point in the data, and this information is often of vital assistance for correcting such errors.

Line and character position

Most parsers count linefeed characters as the document is parsed, so can report which line of text the error occurred on (note that this feature alone supplies a very good reason for including linefeeds in the text when writing XML data).

Some parsers may even keep track of the number of characters they have read from the current line, so can provide even more precise information:

```
ERROR: Line 35, Char 92 - missing end-tag '</Para>'
```

Entity containing error

To complicate matters, a single XML data stream may be derived from a number of data sources (which reference each other using external entities), and the line number alone is not sufficient in these cases. It is necessary to know which source file or stream the parser was working through at the time.

For example, an error reported to be on line 53 could have occurred in any of the entities used in a document that has at least this many lines. Without the name of the entity concerned, it would be necessary to look at them all for the error.

SAXParse interface

The parser can tell the application the entity, line number and character number of the warning or error using an object that implements the **SAXParseInterface**. This interface defines the following methods:

```
int       getLineNumber();
int       getColumnNumber();
String    getSystemId();
String    getPublicId();
```

Note that this interface is unchanged in SAX 2.0.

Most of these methods are self-explanatory, given the discussion above. The **get-LineNumber** method returns the line number of the error ('-1' if this information is not available). The **getSystemId** and **getPublicId** methods return their respective source location information types. The **getColumnNumber** method returns the number of the column where the error occurred (again, '-1' if not available). The term 'column' is used here to mean the character position within the line (which can be thought of as a 'row').

Example

The following example shows this information being used to provide a more informative error message:

```
Locator myLocator;
...
public void error(SAXParseException err)
{
  int ln = err.getLineNumber();
  int ch = err.getColumnNumber();
  String ent = err.getSystemID();

  System.out.println( "ERROR (" + err + ")" +
                      " at " + ln + ":" + ch +
                      " in file " + ent );
}
```

Locators

Although it is very important for an application to know where the parser has got to in a document when an error occurs, as discussed above, it may also wish to know this information at other times.

Locator interface

The parser can tell the application the entity, line number and character number of current event, by instantiating an object that belongs to a class that implements the **Locator** interface, then giving the application a reference to this object. The Locator interface defines the following methods:

```
int      getLineNumber();
int      getColumnNumber();
String   getSystemId();
String   getPublicId();
```

Note that this interface is unchanged in SAX 2.0.

Most of these methods are self-explanatory, given the discussion above, and they are the same as the methods with the same names in the SAXParseException interface. The **getLineNumber** method returns the line number of the error ('-1' if this information is not available). The **getSystemId** and **getPublicId** methods return their respective source location information types. The **getColumnNumber** method returns the number of the column where the error occurred (again, '-1' if not available).

Registration

The parser will continue to update an object that implements this interface each time it finds an error. But the main application needs access to it, so that it can use the methods described above to discover the current location.

It should be recalled that the DocumentHandler interface includes a method called **setDocumentLocator**. This method is used by the application to obtain a reference to this object:

```
Locator myLocator;
...
public void setDocumentLocator(Locator aLocator)
{
   myLocator = aLocator;
}
```

However, it must be stressed again that this slightly cumbersome process is not required for detecting the location of errors. The SAXParseException object supplies the same information without the need for accessing and maintaining another object.

Example

The following example shows the locator being used to specify where the parser is in the XML data file when it detects each start-tag event:

```
Locator myLocator;
...
public void startElement( ... )
{
   int ln = myLocator.getLineNumber();
   int ch = myLocator.getColumnNumber();
   String ent = myLocator.getSystemID();

   System.out.println( "START-TAG "
                       " at " + ln + ":" + ch +
                       " in file " + ent );
}
```

DTD handlers

External entity data that does not conform to the XML syntax cannot be processed by the parser, so it is not passed on to the application. The application would therefore not know of its existence. To overcome this limitation, a mechanism is provided for the parser to tell the application about any binary entity declarations it encounters, as well as any notation declarations (which the entity declarations reference).

Using this information, the application can locate the binary entities, and perhaps call other applications that can handle them on its behalf.

The **DTDHandler** interface is implemented by a class in the main application. The class that implements this interface must include the following methods:

```
void notationDecl(String name, String publicId,
                  String systemId ) throws SAXException;

void unparsedEntityDecl(String name, String publicID,
                  String systemID,
                  String notationName)
                            throws SAXException;
```

Registration

Then an object instantiated from this class needs to be passed to the parser, in the now familiar way, this time using the **setDTDHandler** method. Once again, an application would typically implement this interface in the same class as the event-handler methods:

```
class MyClass implements DTDHandler {
...
myParser.setDTDHandler(this);
```

Note that this interface is unchanged in SAX 2.0.

Unparsed entities

The final parameter of the **unparsedEntityDecl** method provides the name of a notation. The details of this notation should have already been passed to the **notationDecl** method.

Input sources

While it is possible to parse documents by passing the **parse** method a string representing a file or other data source identified by a URL, it is also possible to specify a byte stream or a character stream instead. This is very useful when the application is reading data directly from another application, perhaps over a network.

Input sources

The **InputSource** class contains methods that specify the exact nature of the data source. An InputSource object can be passed to the parser when parsing is ready to commence (instead of the string that gives the parser a URL), and has further uses that are described later. This class includes the following methods:

```
InputSource();
InputSource( String systemID );
InputSource( InputStream byteStream );
InputSource( Reader characterStream );

void   setPublicId( String publicId );
void   setSystemId( String systemId );
void   setByteStream( InputStream byteStream );
void   setCharacterStream( Reader characterStream );
void   setEncoding( String encoding );

String         getPublicId();
String         getSystemId();
```

```
InputStream   getByteStream();
Reader        getCharacterStream();
String        getEncoding();
```

There are a large number of methods in this class. However, most of the 'set...' methods are just alternative means to using the constructor to define the input source, and the various 'get...' methods are normally only used by the parser, to extract the information supplied by the application.

Example

The following example demonstrates using this object to pass a string containing XML markup to the parser:

```
String text = "<note>This is a note</note>";

StringReader myReader = new StringReader( text );

InputSource myInputSource = new InputSource();
myInputSource.setCharacterStream( myReader );

myParser.parse( myInputSource );
```

Entity resolvers

Using only the interfaces and classes discussed so far, the application remains unaware of the physical structure of the XML data. An XML document may be a single data file, or composed from a number of files that are managed as external entities. The parser contains an entity manager that hides this complexity from the application.

However, it has already been shown that it can be useful to know more about each entity, if only to be able to provide useful error reports when problems are encountered within them. It would also be useful to be able to intercept an entity reference, and redirect the parser to another resource, or simply to a local copy of the named resource.

Entity resolver interface

It is possible to intercept references to entities using the **EntityResolver** interface. The application needs to create a class that implements this interface, which defines the following single method:

```
InputSource resolveEntity( String publicId,
                           String systemId );
```

Note that this interface is unchanged in SAX 2.0.

Each time the parser encounters an entity reference that resolves to an external entity (but not to a binary entity), it stops and passes the system identifier (and public identifier, if present) to the **resolveEntity** method. It waits for the method to return, either with a null value, which signifies that the parser should continue as normal, or alternatively with a replacement data file or data stream to process.

This method returns an **InputSource** object. The following example shows how to return a locally valid system identifier, to a file called 'disc.xml' in the 'xml' directory, whenever an entity is encountered that has a system identifier of 'Disclaimer', or a public identifier of '-//MyCorp//TEXT Disclaimer//EN':

```
public InputSource resolveEntity( String publicID,
                                   String systemID)
{
   if ( systemID.equals("Disclaimer") ||
      publicID.equals("-//MyCorp//TEXT Disclaimer//EN") )
         return ( new InputSource( "file:///xml/disc.xml") );

   return null; // entity reference not intercepted
}
```

Catalogues

An application could implement a catalogue feature using this feature (assuming that the parser does not already have such a facility). For example, it could resolve public identifiers into local system identifiers (or URNs into URLs).

Handler bases

When the application only needs to do something very simple with the XML source data, implementing all the interfaces described above may seem like too much effort. It would be useful if there were a ready-made class that implemented all the interfaces, providing some sensible default behaviour for each event, which could be subclassed to add application-specific functionality.

The SAX API therefore includes a class called **HandlerBase** that does just this. However, it is still necessary to locate and activate the parser, and pass this class to the parser as the handler of the various interfaces.

Note that in SAX 2.0, while this class is still available, it is superseded by the DefaultHandler class.

Example

The following example demonstrates a very simple application that just reads processing instructions and presents their contents. This application ignores all other events, and assumes that the underlying base handler will do sensible things when they are encountered:

```
import org.xml.sax.HandlerBase;
    ...
public class myHandler extends HandlerBase( ) {
{
  public void myHandler()
  {
    ...
  }

  public void processingInstruction(String target,
                                    String content)
  {
    System.out.println( target + "\t" + content );
  }
}
```

Helper classes

A parser developer may choose to write classes that implement the interfaces described above, and also add further useful methods. But this kind of support is optional. The standard includes some recommendations for helper classes, and specifies that they appear in the following package:

```
org.xml.sax.helpers
```

Attributes list implementation

The **AttributesListImpl** helper class has the following constructors and methods. It implements the AttributesList interface, and adds methods for adding and removing attributes. It could be used by application developers to persistently store and manage attributes.

Constructors:

```
AttributeListImpl();

AttributeListImpl(AttributeList atts);
```

Methods:

```
int      getLength();
String   getName(int i);
String   getType(int i);
String   getType(String name);
String   getValue(int i);
String   getValue(String name);

void     setAttributeList(AttributeList atts);
void     addAttribute(String name, String type,
                         String value);
void     removeAttribute(String name);
void     clear();
```

Note that SAX 2.0 deprecates this class and introduces a replacement called AttributesImpl.

Locator implementation

The **LocatorImpl** helper class implements the Locator interface, and adds methods for setting its properties, so would be most likely to be used by the parser rather than the application itself. It has the following constructor and methods.

Constructor:

```
LocatorImpl(Locator locator);
```

Methods:

```
int      getLineNumber();
int      getColumnNumber();
String   getSystemId();
String   getPublicId();

void     setColumnNumber(int columnNumber);
void     setLineNumber(int lineNumber);
void     setPublicId(String publicId);
void     setSystemId(String systemId);
```

Parser factory

The **ParserFactory** helper class has the following constructors. It is used to dynamically create a parser at run-time, so that application can be coded to cope with any compliant SAX parser without recompiling.

Constructors:

```
static Parser makeParser();
                    throws ClassNotFoundException,
                           IllegalAccessException,
                           InstantiationException,
                           NullPointerException,
                           ClassCastException;

static Parser makeParser(String className)
                    throws ClassNotFoundException,
                           IllegalAccessException,
                           InstantiationException,
                           ClassCastException;
```

There are no other methods.

The constructor with no parameter is used when the 'org.xml.sax.parser' system property holds the name of the parser.

Consider the following example:

```
import java.io.IOException;
import org.xml.sax.*;
import org.xml.sax.helpers.ParserFactory;
...
String pClass = "org.apache.xerces.parsers.SAXParser";

// CREATE PARSER

try
{
  Parser mySAXParser = ParserFactory.makeParser(pClass);
}
catch (SAXException err) { ... }
catch (NullPointerException err) { ... }
catch (ClassCastException err) { ... }

// REGISTER HANDLERS

mySAXParser.setDocumentHandler( this );
mySAXParser.setErrorHandler( this );
mySAXParser.setEntityResolver( this );

// PARSE DOCUMENT

try
{
  mySAX2Parser.parse("file:///TestFile.xml");
}
catch (SAXException err) { ... }
```

19. SAX 2.0

While SAX 1.0 is extremely well supported by a number of XML parsers, it was recognized from the start that this API supplied the minimum requirements for a 'push-based' parsing technique. The need for rapid development and release of the standard, coupled with the need for widespread consensus, made this fact inevitable. Since its release, however, there has been time to define a more comprehensive interface. The need to support the Namespaces standard was also recognized. SAX 1.0 should be fully understood before reading this chapter.

Changes from 1.0

There are many changes to SAX in version 2.0, including core classes and interfaces, as well as the helper classes.

Core classes and interfaces

As far as practically possible, SAX 2.0 is backward-compatible with the original release. The following interfaces remain unchanged:

- DTDHandler interface
- EntityResolver interface
- ErrorHandler interface
- Locator interface.

Where changes have had to be made in other interfaces to improve functionality, the original interface is retained as an alternative mechanism to support the feature in question.

However, the 'old' interfaces and classes are now deprecated, and likely to be omitted from future versions of the standard. The following interfaces and classes are therefore still available, but not recommended for use:

- Parser interface (superseded by XMLReader interface)
- DocumentHandler interface (superseded by ContentHandler interface)
- AttributeList interface (superseded by Attributes interface)
- HandlerBase class (superseded by DefaultHandler class).

The following interfaces and classes are new to SAX 2.0:

- XMLReader interface (use instead of Parser interface)
- ContentHandler interface (use instead of DocumentHandler interface)
- Attributes interface (use instead of AttributeList interface)
- XMLFilter interface
- SAXNotSupportedException class
- SAXNotRecognizedException class.

The XML reader adds standardized configurability to the parser. The ContentHandler and Attributes interfaces add support for namespace-related information. ContentHandler also adds a callback for skipped entities, and Attributes adds the capability to discover an attribute's index by name. Finally, the new exception classes are used by the configurable feature to report problems

Helper classes

For Java developers specifically, there are a number of helper classes. In fact, version 1.0 also includes three such classes. However, there is a major change in that all helpers are now to be found in a single location: 'org.sax.xml.helpers'.

The following are still available, but not recommended (and are also now duplicated in the 'helpers' package):

- org.xml.sax.helpers.ParserFactory
- org.xml.sax.helpers.AttributeListImpl (now use AttributesImpl)
- org.xml.sax.HandlerBase (now use DefaultHandler).

The following are new to SAX 2.0:

- org.xml.sax.helpers.AttributesImpl (use instead of AttributeListImpl)
- org.xml.sax.helpers.DefaultHandler (use instead of HandlerBase)
- org.xml.sax.helpers.NamespaceSupport
- org.xml.sax.helpers.XMLFilterImpl
- org.xml.sax.helpers.ParserAdapter
- org.xml.sax.helpers.XMLReaderAdapter.

The **AttributesImpl** class directly replaces the AttributesListImpl class, because it implements the Attributes interface (instead of the AttributeList interface).

The **DefaultHandler** class directly replaces the HandlerBase class of SAX 1.0 (confusingly, to be found in org.xml.sax rather than org.xml.sax.helpers), and implements the newer interfaces.

The **NamespacesSupport** class is available for use by parser developers, and is probably not useful beyond this purpose.

The **XMLFilterImpl** class sits between an XMLReader and the client application, and does nothing until it is subclassed. It simply passes requests to the reader, and events on to the handlers. But this class can be subclassed to override specific methods, and modify the event stream or the configuration requests as they pass between the application and the parser.

The **ParserAdapter** class makes a SAX 1.0 Parser pretend to be a SAX 2.0 XML-Reader. The **XMLReaderAdapter** class, on the other hand, makes a SAX 2.0 XML reader behave as a SAX 1.0 Parser. These two classes are intended to ease the transition from SAX 1.0 to SAX 2.0; allowing SAX 1.0 drivers and clients to coexist with SAX 2.0 drivers and clients within the same application.

XML Reader

The XMLReader interface replaces the Parser interface. The parser must implement this interface, and the methods below are therefore guaranteed to be accessible to the application.

The following methods are unchanged from SAX 1.0, except for the name of one of them:

```
void   parse(InputSource src)
                  throws SAXException, IOException;
void   parse(String src)
                  throws SAXException, IOException;
void   setContentHandler(ContentHandler handler);
void   setDTDHandler(DTDHandler handler);
void   setEntityResolver(EntityResolver resolver);
void   setErrorHandler(ErrorHandler handler);
```

The following methods are new:

```
void     setFeature(String name, boolean value)
             throws SAXNotRecognisedException,
                    SAXNotSupportedException;
boolean  getFeature(String name)
             throws SAXNotRecognisedException,
```

```
                              SAXNotSupportedException;
   void        setProperty(String name, Object value)
                   throws SAXNotRecognisedException,
                              SAXNotSupportedException;
   Object      getProperty(String name)
                   throws SAXNotRecognisedException,
                              SAXNotSupportedException;

   ContentHandler      getContentHandler();
   DTDHandler          getDTDHandler();
   EntityResolver      getEntityResolver();
   ErrorHandler        getErrorHandler();
```

Note that the setLocale method is now absent.

The differences are the change from setDocumentHandler to **setContentHandler** (in order to pass an object that implements the new ContentHandler interface), the new 'get...' methods, and the new standard means to see and modify parser properties and features.

The new **getFeature** and **setFeature** methods are used to standardize the way in which applications can discover what features are supported, and in some cases allow the application to enable or disable certain optional features. Similarly, the **getProperty** and **setProperty** methods allow investigation and modification of properties.

Features

This version of SAX formally introduces a single way for optional parser features to be controlled from the application. All features work in the same way. The SAX standard includes some recommended features, and parser developers are encouraged to support them. They may also add their own features.

This technique has already been seen in the previous chapter (the Xerces parser implemented this technique in advance of the SAX 2.0 release), where this mechanism was used to tell the parser to validate documents against a DTD or XML Schema.

Feature names

The feature name is a reference to a URL. This approach is taken for the same reason that the Namespaces standard uses URLs to avoid conflicts. Only complete URLs, including domain names, are used. This ensures that features provided by different parser developers will not have the same name.

Core features

The standard includes a small number of features that parser developers are encouraged to support, including namespace support, optional validation and inclusion or exclusion of general and parameter entities:

```
http://xml.org/sax/features/namespaces
http://xml.org/sax/features/namespace-prefixes
http://xml.org/sax/features/validation
http://xml.org/sax/features/string-interning
http://xml.org/sax/features/external-general-entities
http://xml.org/sax/features/external-parameter-entities
```

Get and set feature

It is possible to ask the parser in a standard way what features it has, using the **get-Feature** method. This method returns a boolean value, indicating whether the feature is supported ('true') or not supported ('false'):

```
boolean canValidate =
     mySAXParser.getFeature( featureURL );
```

The **setFeature** method is called with two parameters. The first parameter names a feature. The second parameter switches the feature on or off using a boolean value ('true' equals 'on', 'false' equals 'off'):

```
mySAXParser.setFeature( "featureURL", trueOrFalse );
```

Essential namespace features

There are two features that all parsers are required to support, both concerning namespaces. All parsers must recognize the http://xml.org/sax/features/namespaces and the http://xml.org/sax/features/namespace-prefixes features.

When the http://xml.org/sax/features/namespaces feature is successfully set to 'true', the parser is guaranteed to pass namespace names, and support the **start-PrefixMapping** and **endPrefixMapping** methods.

When the http://xml.org/sax/features/namespace-prefixes feature is successfully set to 'true', qualified names are guaranteed to be passed to the application, and attributes with names beginning 'xmlns...' are not suppressed.

All parsers must support a 'true' value for the namespaces feature, and a 'false' value for the namespace-prefixes feature. This combination ensures that namespaces are processed, and that namespace declarations are not treated as other attributes, and placed in attribute lists (the application does not need to know about them because the parser itself is dealing with them).

Parsers are not obliged to support the alternative values for each feature, in which case they might not bother to include these features at all.

The standard does not clarify exactly what will happen if the namespaces feature is set to 'false', though it does make it clear that, if the namespace-prefixes feature is set to 'true', then attributes that act as namespace declarations will be treated like any other attribute.

Parsers are not required to recognize or support any other features or any properties, including the core ones described below.

Validation feature

By default, the parser is not asked to perform validation against a DTD or XML Schema. It can be instructed to perform validation using the http://xml.org/sax/features/validation feature:

```
SAXParser mySAXParser = new SAXParser();
try
{
  mySAXParser.setFeature("http://xml.org/
                          sax/features/validation", true);
}
...
```

Note that when validation is switched on, it is an error for a document not to reference a DTD or XML Schema. This can be inconvenient when the same parser needs to be used to validate well-formed documents as well (the Xerces parser has a more flexible variant, which is described below).

External entities features

General and parameter entities can be processed or ignored by the parser, using the http://xml.org/sax/features/external-general-entities   and   http://xml.org/sax/features/external-parameter-entities features, which both default to 'true' (all entities are processed):

```
http://xml.org/sax/features/external-general-entities
```

```
http://xml.org/sax/features/external-parameter-entities
```

Parameter entity processing includes external DTD subset processing.

Vendor features

Apart from some core features, each parser vendor can add their own, without danger of using the same name for different features. For example, the developers of the Xerces parser have the domain name 'apache.org':

```
http://apache.org/xml/features...
```

If an application is developed to work with several parsers, there is nothing to prevent the application from attempting to read or set features using each vendor's specific features. The parser will ignore features it does not recognize (though it may throw an exception that the application may ignore).

For example, the Xerces parser includes a feature which specifies that validation should be performed, but that an error should not be raised if there is no DTD or XML Schema to validate against. This feature is called http://apache.org/xml/features/validation/dynamic:

```
SAXParser mySAXParser = new SAXParser();

try
{
  mySAXParser.setFeature("http://apache.org/
              xml/features/validation/dynamic", true);
}
...
```

Another feature from the same supplier, http://apache.org/xml/features/validation/warn-on-duplicate-attdef, allows duplicate attribute definition warnings to be switched off. In this case, the default value is 'true', so the feature is only used to disable such warnings:

```
SAXParser mySAXParser = new SAXParser();

try
{
  mySAXParser.setFeature("http://apache.org/xml/
     features/validation/warn-on-duplicate-attdef", false);
}
...
```

Exceptions

If an application attempts to query or set a feature that the XML reader does not recognize, the XML reader throws a **SAXNotRecognizedException**.

If the application attempts to set a feature state or property value that the XML reader cannot support at that time, or attempts to modify a feature or property when it is read-only, the XML reader throws a **SAXNotSupportedException**.

Properties

Properties are in many ways similar to features, and there are equivalent methods for getting and settings properties. The subtle difference is that properties are changing characteristics, such as the current text string that triggered the latest event. They are mostly read-only, and the properties can be accessed as strings or objects.

Get and set properties

It is possible to ask the parser in a standard way what properties it has, using the **getProperty** method. This method returns an object that represents the property:

```
Object property = mySAXParser.getProperty( URL );
```

The **setProperty** method is called with two parameters. The first parameter names a property. The second parameter switches the feature on or off using a boolean value ('true' equals 'on', 'false' equals 'off').

```
mySAXParser.setProperty( URL, boolean );
```

Core properties

There are only two core properties:

```
http://xml.org/sax/properties/xml-string
```

```
http://xml.org/sax/properties/dom-node
```

XML string property

The xml-string property is the string of characters that caused the event. For example, an end-tag event would be triggered by the characters '`</para>`':

```
public void endElement(String name)
{
  ...
  String endTag =
    (String)mySAXParser.getProperty(
            "http://xml.org/sax/properties/xml-string");
  ...
}
```

If supported, this feature could be used to supply meaningful context in error messages, or to feed through the data (modified in some way) to an output file in a more convenient fashion than having to rebuild the markup within the application.

DOM node property

The first of the core properties allows the application access to the nodes in an underlying DOM (see Chapter 20). This assumes that the document has first been parsed into a DOM structure, and SAX is merely being used as a convenient way to read data from the DOM in a linear fashion. The current node is accessible through the http://xml.org/sax/properties/dom-none property:

```
Node myNode =
   (Node)mySAXParser.getProperty(
              "http://xml.org/xml/properties/dom-node");
```

If used before parsing begins, it returns the root node, and this node (and whole document) can be modified prior to parsing. Otherwise, it is read-only.

Vendor properties

Apart from some core properties, each parser vendor can add their own, without danger of using the same name for different properties:

```
http://apache.org/xml/properties...
```

Namespace support

The increasing adoption of the Namespaces standard (see Chapter 10) highlighted a weakness in the original SAX standard, which was developed before the concept of namespaces was solidified into a standard. SAX 1.0 can be said to be 'namespace-insensitive'.

Readers unaware of either the intent or details of the Namespaces standard are strongly advised to read Chapter 10 before continuing.

The issue

A namespace-sensitive application using the SAX interface to read XML documents that use namespaces has a single but significant problem to overcome. When using namespaces, an element name or attribute name is not as informative as would otherwise be the case. The first part of each element and attribute name is a prefix that has been defined by the DTD or document author, and will not mean anything to the application. Only the URL that the prefix has been mapped to is significant, and this mapping is found in a namespace declaration, which may be defined on another element (often the root element).

SAX 1.0 approach

It is certainly possible to develop a namespace-sensitive application using SAX 1.0, but the application would need to perform a number of operations.

First, it would need to analyse every element for namespace declarations, find the attributes beginning 'xmlns' and extract the values (the URLs) and the rest of the attribute names (the local mappings).

Second, the application would need to maintain a list of currently active namespace mappings.

Third, it would need to observe the scope of the declaration by counting descendant elements in order to find the matching end-tag. At this point, any previous, enclosing declaration with the same prefix name needs to re-assert itself.

Fourth, when wishing to react to the presence of particular elements or attributes from a given namespace, it would need to look up the currently active prefix (or prefixes) used for this namespace, and compare this string with the first part of each element or attribute name.

This is a lot of work that could be delegated to the parser. It should be possible for the parser to keep track of mappings and the scope of these mappings. All that is then needed is for the SAX interface to provide this additional information in the most convenient form possible. That is what the SAX 2.0 standard does, via the new ContentHandler interface and Attributes interface.

ContentHandler

The **ContentHandler** interface is a direct replacement for the original DocumentHandler interface. It provides the same functionality, but adds support for namespaces.

The following methods are unchanged from SAX 1.0:

```
void  startDocument() throws SAXException;
void  endDocument() throws SAXException;
void  characters(char[] ch, int start, int length)
                                    throws SAXException;
void  ignorableWhitespace(char[] ch, int start,
                          int length) throws SAXException;
void  processingInstruction(String target, String data)
                                    throws SAXException;
void  setDocumentLocator(Locator myLoc);
```

The following methods have changed to handle namespaces properly, and to pass attributes in objects that implement the new Attributes interface:

```
void   startElement(String namespaceURI,
                    String localName, String qName,
                    Attributes atts)
                              throws SAXException;
void   endElement(String namespaceURI,
                  String localName, String qName)
                              throws SAXException;
```

The following methods are new:

```
void   endPrefixMapping(String prefix)
                    throws SAXException;
void   startPrefixMapping(String prefix, String uri)
                    throws SAXException;
void   skippedEntity(String name) throws SAXException;
```

Namespaces

The **startElement** and **endElement** methods have been updated to pass namespace information to the application.

When namespace processing is performed, complete element names are called qualified names. The colon becomes very significant, as it separates the local name from the prefix. The prefix is not considered relevant, because it maps to a URL, which is far more significant, and is supplied in the first parameter. The local name is supplied in the second parameter:

```
startElement( namespace, localName, qName, atts)
{
  System.out.println( "Found element " + localName );
  System.out.println( "belonging to URL " + namespace );
}
```

The third parameter may hold the qualified name, if the parser is willing to pass this value, but will otherwise be an empty string. This parameter, if given a value, is equivalent to the simple element name parameter in SAX 1.0, and is the only direct way to discover the actual prefix on the name.

By default, an XML reader will report a Namespace URI and a local name for every element, in both the start and end handler. Consider the following example:

```
<html:HTML xmlns:html="http://www.w3.org/1999/xhtml"/>
...
</html:HTML>
```

On encountering an embedded Paragraph element, the following would be reported:

```
<html:P>HTML paragraph.</html:P>
```

```
Found element P
belonging to URL http://www.w3.org/1999/xhtml
```

The XML reader might also report the original qualified name 'html:P', but that parameter might simply be an empty string.

Mapping scope

The **startPrefixMapping** and **endPrefixMapping** methods between them indicate the scope of a prefix mapping, should the application be interested in this information, though it is not essential in most cases.

The startPrefixMapping method is triggered before the event for the start-tag of the element that contains the declaration attribute. This is because the element itself is in the scope of the declaration (and may have the prefix it defines):

```
startPrefixMapping( String prefix, String URI )
{
  System.out.println( "Start scope of " + prefix );
}
```

The endPrefixMapping method is triggered after the event for the end-tag of the element that contains the declaration attribute. Again, this is because the element itself is in the scope of the declaration:

```
endPrefixMapping( String prefix )
{
  System.out.println( "End scope of " + prefix );
}
```

The URI is not passed to this method, as the mapping is already known to the application (from the call to startPrefixMapping with the same prefix name).

Skipped entities

The only significant change to this interface that does not relate to namespaces is the **skippedEntity** method. This method tells the application when the parser has skipped a non-XML entity, and passes the name of this entity to the application.

This method should be activated for all binary entities, and also for parameter entities or text entities if the parser is told not to process them.

Attributes

The **Attributes** interface replaces the AttributeList interface. Again, the principal reason for this new interface is to support namespaces.

The methods are largely the same as before, but note that **getQName** replaces get-Name, as element and attribute names are now called as they appear in tags (regardless of whether or not they include colons, and even then whether the colons are significant):

```
int      getLength();
String   getQName(int index);
String   getValue(int index);
String   getValue(String qName) ;
String   getType(int index);
String   getType(String qName);
```

The following new methods are equivalent to the ones above, but support name-spaces. Attribute names, values and types can be found without knowing the prefix used in the document for the given namespace:

```
int      getIndex(String qName);
int      getIndex(String uri, String localPart);
String   getURI(int index);

String   getLocalName(int index);
String   getValue(String uri, String localName);
String   getType(String uri, String localName);
```

Get index

The new **getIndex** method allows the application to discover the sequential position of an attribute within the Attributes object.

Finding attributes

The SAX 1.0 method getName has been replaced by three new methods, **getQName** (the new equivalent method), **getURI** and **getLocalName**. The getURI method returns the URI for the attribute. The getLocalName method returns the element name without the prefix.

Consider the following example:

```
<html:IMG html:SRC="boat.gif" html:ALT="a boat"/>
```

Both the SRC and ALT attributes belong to the 'html' namespace:

```
for( int i = 0 ; i < atts.getLength() ; i++ )
{
  String URI = atts.getURI( i );
  String localName = atts.getLocalName( i );
  String qualifiedName = atts.getQName( i );

  System.out.println( "Attribute " + i + " name:" );
  System.out.println( "   URI = " + URI );
  System.out.println( "   local = " + localName );
  System.out.println( "   qualified = " + qualifiedName );
}
```

For the example fragment above, this code will produce the following output:

```
Attribute 1 name:
  URI = http://www.w3.org/1999/xhtml
  local = SRC
  qualified = html:SRC

Attribute 2 name:
  URI = http://www.w3.org/1999/xhtml
  local = ALT
  qualified = html:ALT
```

Some parsers may opt not to supply anything but an empty string in the qualified parameter.

Finding specific attribute value

It should not be necessary to loop around all the attributes in an element to find one. An updated version of the **getValue** method can be used to find the value of a specific attribute, without knowing which namespace prefix has been assigned to it. The URL is passed to the method, along with the local name:

```
String URI = "http://myNamespace/definition";

String value = atts.getValue( URI, "myAttribute" );
```

By default, an attribute name beginning 'xmlns...' is not included in the attribute list, because the application need not be directly concerned with this type of attribute. However, such attributes can be included using one of the SAX features. The http://xml.org/sax/features/namespace-prefixes feature needs to be set to 'true'.

If the namespace-prefixes feature (see above) is false, access by qualified name may not be available. If the http://xml.org/sax/features/namespaces feature is false, access by Namespace-qualified names may not be available.

Helper classes

A parser developer may choose to write classes that implement the interfaces described above, and add further useful methods. As before, the standard includes some recommendations for helper classes. All the helpers defined for SAX 1.0 are retained for backward compatibility, but several new ones have been added to support the new interfaces.

Attributes implementation

The **AttributesImpl** helper class has the following constructors and methods. It implements the **Attributes** interface and adds methods for creating, removing and changing the name, value or type of an attribute.

Constructors:

```
attributesImpl();

attributesImpl(Attributes atts);
```

Additional methods:

```
void     setAttribute(int index, String uri,
                      String localName, String qName,
                      String type, String value);
void     setAttributes(Attributes atts);
void     addAttribute(String uri, String localName,
                      String qName, String type,
                      String value);
void     clear();
void     removeAttribute(int index);
void     setLocalName(int index, String localName);
void     setQName(int index, String qName);
void     setType(int index, String type);
void     setURI(int index, String uri);
void     setValue(int index, String value);
```

Default handler

The **DefaultHandler** helper class replaces the HandlerBase helper class, and implements the **DTDHandler**, **EntityResolver**, **ContentHandler** and **ErrorHandler** interfaces. It has the following single constructor:

```
DefaultHandler();
```

As with the class it replaces, this class is useful for subclassing in order to avoid much of the complexity of setting up default handlers (for the many events the four interfaces it implements include).

Namespace support

The **NamespaceSupport** helper class is useful for storing and managing prefix-to-URL mappings, and would be used in conjunction with the **startPrefixMapping** and **endPrefixMapping** methods.

However, there appears to be little reason for using this helper class, as the parser itself would use it (or something similar) to perform all the namespace management required.

This class has the following constructors and methods.

Field:

```
String XMLNS;
```

Constructor:

```
NamespaceSupport();
```

Methods:

```
boolean       declarePrefix(String prefix, String uri);
Enumeration   getDeclaredPrefixes();
String        getPrefix(String uri);
Enumeration   getPrefixes();
Enumeration   getPrefixes(String uri);
String        getURI(String prefix);
void          popContext();
String[]      processName(String qName, String[] parts,
                          boolean isAttribute);
void          pushContext();
void          reset();
```

Parser adaptor

The **ParserAdaptor** class sits on top of a SAX 1.0 parser and provides SAX 2.0 support to the application. It therefore adds namespace support (possibly by including the NamespaceSupport class described above). However, because SAX 1.0 parsers cannot report on skipped entities, there will be no **skippedEntity** events.

This class implements the **XMLReader** and **DocumentHandler** interfaces, and has the following constructors:

```
ParserAdaptor();

ParserAdaptor(Parser parser);
```

XML filter implementation

The **XMLFilterImpl** class sits between an XMLReader and the client application, and does nothing at all. It simply passes requests from the application on to the reader, and events from the parser on to the handlers. But this class can be subclassed to override specific methods, and modify the event stream or the configuration requests as they pass between the two.

This helper class implements the **XMLFilter, EntityResolver, DTDHandler, ContentHandler** and **ErrorHandler** interfaces, and has the following constructors:

```
XMLFilterImpl();

XMLFilterImpl(XMLReader parent);
```

XML reader adaptor

The **XMLReaderAdaptor** helper class performs the exact opposite function of the ParserAdaptor class described above. It sits on top of a SAX 2.0 parser to create a SAX 1.0 parser for the application. It therefore cripples the functionality of the underlying parser, so as to support applications that can only deal with SAX 1.0 functionality.

The XMLReader must support a 'true' value for the http://xml.org/sax/features/ namespace-prefixes feature. This feature is activated to ensure that namespace declarations are passed to the application (as any other attribute would be), and that qualified names are available (so that they can be passed through to the application).

This class implements the **Parser** and **DocumentHandler** interfaces, and has the following constructors :

```
XMLReaderAdapter();

XMLReaderAdapter(XMLReader xmlReader);
```

XML reader factory

The **XMLReaderFactory** helper class replaces the ParserFactory helper, and has the following constructors:

```
static XMLReader CreateXMLReader();

static XMLReader CreateXMLReader(String className);
```

The following example echoes the factory method of dynamically creating a parser introduced in the previous chapter, but uses the new interfaces to link to any parser (in this case, the Xerces SAX parser). It also uses the new features and properties methods. The essential changes from SAX 1.0 are highlighted:

```
import java.io.IOException;
import org.xml.sax.*;
import org.xml.sax.helpers.XMLReaderFactory;
...
String pClass = "org.apache.xerces.parsers.SAXParser";

try
{
    XMLReader mySAX2Parser =
                XMLReaderFactory.createXMLReader(pClass);
}
catch (SAXException err) { ... }
catch (NullPointerException err) { ... }
catch (ClassCastException err) { ... }

try
{
    mySAXParser.setFeature("http://xml.org/
        sax/features/external-general-entities", false );
    mySAXParser.setFeature("http://apache.org/
        xml/features/validation/dynamic", true );
}
catch (SAXException err) { ... }

mySAXParser.setContentHandler( this );
mySAXParser.setErrorHandler( this );
mySAXParser.setEntityResolver( this );

try
{
    mySAX2Parser.parse("file:///TestFile.xml");
}
catch (IOException err) { ... }
catch (SAXException err) { ... }
```

Note that fewer exceptions are thrown when creating the parser than is the case in the SAX 1.0 version.

20. DOM Level 1

The DOM is an API for accessing the components of an XML document, allowing an application to navigate through a tree of nodes representing elements, attributes, comments and other structures, in any order. As such, it is a very different API to the SAX standard covered previously.

Chapter 21 discusses the latest version of this standard, DOM Level 2. But it is necessary to read this chapter first, Chapter 21 only discusses changes and additions.

See Chapter 33 for a list of all DOM methods.

Background

Most XML parsers are able to build a tree model of an XML document as it is parsed, then allow the main application access to this model through an API. The arguments for using a standard API are the same as for the SAX approach, but in addition the major Web browser developers agreed that there was a need to provide a similar capability for accessing HTML elements from scripts in a Web page. **DOM** (the *Document Object Model*) was developed by the W3C, primarily to specify how Web browsers and embedded scripts should access HTML and XML documents. But the DOM is equally suited to more general software processing of XML documents, and the generation of new documents.

There is a core standard that applies to both HTML and XML documents (available from http://www.w3.org/TR/REC-DOM-Level-1/), and is concerned with defining an interface to document instance constructs common to both (elements, attributes, comments, processing instructions and text content). While there are extensions for more specific HTML processing, they are not described in this chapter.

Implementing a DOM

The DOM has an object design that assumes the use of object-oriented programming and scripting languages, such as C++, Java and JavaScript. The following examples are all Java code fragments, but the principles are the same for other languages.

The DOM standard is composed of a number of interfaces. In Java, these interfaces are defined in the package org.w3c.dom. Typically, a parser developer will implement these interfaces, and replace them with classes that have the same names. The application developer then only needs to import this package and use these classes. The following examples assume this scenario.

There are some important activities involved in parsing, navigating and processing documents that the DOM standard does not cover. Tree-walking a DOM structure, and writing out a structure into XML format, are both outside the scope of the standard (though DOM Level 2 covers more functionality). These features, if implemented at all, will differ in operation between parsers.

Specific parser

The following example reads a document called 'test.xml' into a DOM tree using the Xerces parser (see http://www.xml.apache.org/). The root element is accessed from the DOM tree, and its name is printed (note that this parser requires the SAX API to be included, even when using the DOM instead):

```java
import java.io.*;
import org.w3c.dom.*;
import org.apache.xerces.parsers.DOMParser;
import org.xml.sax.*;
import org.xml.sax.SAXException;
...
DOMParser parser = new DOMParser();

try
{
  parser.parse("test.xml");
}
catch (SAXException se) { ... }
catch (IOException ioe) { ... }

Document myDoc = parser.getDocument();
Element rootElement = myDoc.getDocumentElement();
System.out.println( "ROOT ELEMENT: " +
                    rootElement.getTagName() );
```

Nodes

The DOM standard defines interfaces that are used to manage **nodes**. Nodes represent elements, text, comments, processing instructions, CDATA sections, entity references and declarations, notation declarations and even entire documents. Nodes are also used to represent attributes, though these nodes are not strictly part of the document tree. There are also some additional node types defined for ease of managing groups of nodes, including two that hold lists of nodes, and one that is useful for transferring nodes to another part of the document tree.

The API allows an object to represent a node. The software can interrogate the node object for information about the node, and about the other nodes it is attached to.

The **Node** interface is at the heart of the DOM scheme. In fact, this is practically the only interface that is needed, though several others subclass it to provide additional, more specific functionality, depending on the type of object the given node represents. All of the interfaces shown in this diagram are discussed in detail later:

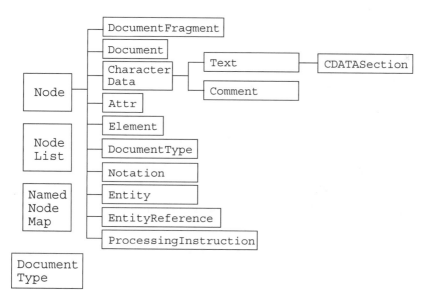

The Node interface defines a number of methods that can be divided into three broad categories. First, each node has characteristics, such as its type, name and value. Each node also has a contextual location in the document tree, and provides access to its relatives (its parent, siblings and children). Finally, each node has the capability to modify its contents (the nodes that represent its children).

Node characteristics

Each node carries some important information about itself, including its type and its name, but possibly also its value, contained attributes and contextual location. The following methods are supplied to provide access to this information:

```
short         getNodeType();
String        getNodeName();
String        getNodeValue() throws DOMException;
void          setNodeValue(String nodeValue)
                                  throws DOMException;
boolean       hasChildNodes();
NamedNodeMap  getAttributes();
Document      getOwnerDocument();
```

Note that attribute handling methods are discussed later.

Get node type

As a node can represent any XML object, it is often necessary to determine what it *actually* represents before performing other operations on it. The **getNodeType** method is used to determine its type. A short integer value is returned, which matches one of the following constants:

```
ELEMENT_NODE = 1
ATTRIBUTE_NODE = 2
TEXT_NODE = 3
CDATA_SECTION_NODE = 4
ENTITY_REFERENCE_NODE = 5
ENTITY_NODE = 6
PROCESSING_INSTRUCTION_NODE = 7
COMMENT_NODE = 8
DOCUMENT_NODE = 9
DOCUMENT_TYPE_NODE = 10
DOCUMENT_FRAGMENT_NODE = 11
NOTATION_NODE = 12
```

The following example shows how to use this information to detect that a node represents an element:

```
if ( myNode.getNodeType() == Node.ELEMENT_NODE )
{
  // process element
}
```

Get node name

Every node has a name. In some cases, a fixed name is used, such as '#comment' in all comment nodes. In the case of nodes that represent elements, this is the element name, such as 'para'. The **getNodeName** method returns the name of the node:

```
if ( myNode.getNodeName().equals("#comment"))
{
  // process comments
}
if ( ( myNode.getNodeName().equals("para") ) &&
     ( myNode.getNodeType() == Node.ELEMENT_NODE ) )
{
  // process paragraph element
}
```

It should be obvious from this that the node name is not a unique node identifier, as there would typically be many nodes with a name like 'para' in a document. An individual node can only be uniquely identified by its location in the document tree.

Get node value

The **getNodeValue** method returns the value of the node. The value for some node types will always be 'null'. For example, elements never have a value (they have content instead). But attributes, character data sections, comments and processing instructions all have values. The value of nodes that represent these items within is the text itself:

```
String myComment = myCommentNode.getNodeValue();
```

Set node value

The value of a node can be replaced using the **setNodeValue** method. A string is passed to this method, representing the text to use as the value. In this way, the content of a text string, attribute, comment, processing instruction (instruction part only) and CDATA section can be modified:

```
// Create <!-- this is a comment -->
try
{
  myCommentNode.setNodeValue(" this is a comment ");
}
catch (DOMException err) { ... }
```

Names and values by type

The following table shows, for each node type, the values returned by the two methods described above:

Type	Interface name	Name	Value
ATTRIBUTE_NODE	Attr	*attribute name*	*attribute value*
DOCUMENT_NODE	Document	#document	*NULL*

Type	Interface name	Name	Value
DOCUMENT_FRAGMENT_NODE	DocumentFragment	#document-fragment	*NULL*
DOCUMENT_TYPE_NODE	DocumentType	*DOCTYPE name (root element name)*	*NULL*
CDATA_SECTION_NODE	CDATASection	#cdata-section	*CDATA content*
COMMENT_NODE	Comment	*entity-name*	*content string*
ELEMENT_NODE	Element	*tag name*	*NULL*
ENTITY_NODE	Entity	*entity name*	*NULL*
ENTITY_REFERENCE_NODE	EntityReference	*entity name*	*NULL*
NOTATION_NODE	Notation	*notation name*	*NULL*
PROCESSING_INSTRUCTION_NODE	ProcessingInstruction	*target string*	*content string*
TEXT_NODE	Text	#text	*text string*

Node has children

Most types of node cannot have children. For example, it makes no sense to talk about the child of a comment node. The only nodes that can have children are the Element, Document and DocumentFragment node types. There is a simple method to determine whether or not a node has children. The **hasChildNodes** method returns a boolean value of true if it has:

```
if ( myNode.hasChildNodes() )
{
    // process children of myNode
}
```

Get all attributes

When a node has attributes, they can be accessed using the **getAttributes** method, which returns an object of type NamedNodeMap (described later). In practice, only Element nodes can have attributes (and the Element interface includes some alternative ways to process attached attributes in a simpler way):

```
NamedNodeMap myNodeMap = myNode.getAttributes();
```

Node navigation

Every node has a specific location in the document hierarchy. When processing a document via the DOM interface, it is usual to use nodes as stepping-stones from one location to another. Each node therefore has methods that return references to surrounding nodes:

```
Node        getFirstChild();
Node        getLastChild();
Node        getNextSibling();
Node        getPreviousSibling();
Node        getParentNode();
NodeList    getChildNodes();
```

Using only two of these methods (**getFirstChild** and **getNextSibling**) it is always possible to traverse the entire tree. However, this would only be possible if references to all ancestor nodes were retained by the application while sub-element nodes were being processed. The other four methods offer more convenient ways to go back to the first sibling (**getFirstChild**), travel back up the tree structure (**getParentNode**), go backward through the list of siblings (**getPreviousSibling**), and iterate through all children (**getChildNodes**):

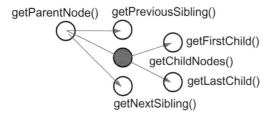

In the following example, after testing that a given node has children, references to the first and second child are obtained. The second reference will be 'null' if the given node has only one child:

```
if ( myNode.hasChildNodes() )
{
  Node firstChild = myNode.getFirstChild();
  Node secondChild = firstChild.getNextSibling();
}
```

Although the main benefit of using the DOM (over the SAX approach) is that it provides a way to process an XML document in a random order, the ability to process the tree in sequential order is often still important. In practice, this means traversing the nodes in a very specific manner that is often termed 'tree-walking'. Using the navigation methods described previously, tree-walking is a difficult process. A recursive set of steps is required to process all the children of each node before continuing on to the next sibling of that node:

- if there are children, move to the first child, otherwise...
- if there are further siblings, move to the next sibling, otherwise...
- move to the nearest ancestor that has further siblings, and on to its next sibling, otherwise...
- stop.

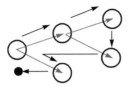

In DOM Level 2 there is a standard way to achieve this. But even DOM Level 1 parsers may include parser-specific methods of traversing the tree. A method may be included that simply returns a reference to the next node in the tree, effectively hiding the complexities described above.

Node manipulation

Structures in a DOM tree can be edited. A node has methods that allow its children to be modified. Child nodes can be removed, added, replaced and copied:

```
Node   removeChild(Node oldChild) throws DOMException;
Node   insertBefore(Node newChild, Node refChild)
                                    throws DOMException;
Node   appendChild(Node newChild) throws DOMException;
Node   replaceChild(Node newChild, Node oldChild)
                                    throws DOMException;
Node   cloneNode(boolean deep);
```

Remove child node

A child node can be detached from its location in the tree by use of the **removeChild** method. The removed node still exists, and a reference to it is returned, but it no longer has a location in the tree. Other methods that are described below may be used to reattach it to another part of the document.

In the following example, the first child of a given node is first accessed, then this object is used as a reference to remove itself from the parent (but it still exists, outside of the document, in the variable removedNode):

```
Node firstChildNode = myParentNode.getFirstChild();

try
{
   Node removedNode =
            myParentNode.removeChild(firstChildNode);
}
catch ( DOMException err ) { ... }
```

Append new child node

New nodes can be appended to the child list of a given node. These new nodes may be existing nodes already detached from another part of the tree (as described above), or may be manufactured using 'factory' methods in the Document interface.

The **appendChild** method is used to pass a reference to the new node. Another reference to the new node is returned by this method. The reason for doing this is to allow for the case where no reference exists until after the node has been added, as in the following example (which uses a 'factory' method of the Document interface, as discussed later):

```
try
{
  Node addedNode =
      theParent.appendChild(doc.createElement("para"));
}
catch ( DOMException err ) { ... }
```

Insert new child node

A new node may need to be inserted between existing nodes in the child list (instead of just appended to the end). In this case, it is necessary to identify the location, and this is done by referring to the node that the new node must precede:

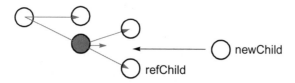

The **insertBefore** method therefore takes two parameters: first, the reference to the new child node, and second, a reference to the existing node in the list. In the following example, a paragraph node is appended to the list, then a Note element is inserted before the paragraph:

```
Node paraNode =
  theParent.appendChild(myDoc.createElement("para"));

try
{
  theParent.insertBefore( myDoc.createElement("note"),
                          paraNode );
}
catch ( DOMException err ) { ... }
```

Replace node

Using the methods described above, it is of course possible to replace one node with another. The original can be removed, then the replacement can be inserted before its next sibling (or appended, if the original was the final node in the list), as in the following example:

```
Node newNode = myDoc.createElement("para");
theParent.removeChild( oldNode );
theParent.insertBefore( newNode, refNode );
```

But this process can be simplified using the **replaceChild** method. This method takes two parameters, the first being a reference to the new node, the second being a reference to the node to be removed. The method returns a reference to the replaced node:

```
Node newNode = myDoc.createElement("para");
try
{
  theParent.replaceChild( newNode, refNode );
}
catch ( DOMException err ) { ... }
```

Clone a node

When editing a document, it may be necessary to create copies of existing nodes, or whole branches of the tree, for use elsewhere. The **cloneNode** method creates a new node that has the same type, name and value as the given node. This method takes a boolean value which, when set to 'true', indicates that copies should also be made of all the children of the node, and all descendants of those children. In this way, entire branches of the tree can be copied. When set to 'false', only the selected node is copied, and the new copy therefore has no children. These two modes are known as 'deep' and 'shallow' cloning:

```
Node shallowClone = myNode.cloneNode( false );
Node deepClone = myNode.cloneNode( true );
```

Documents

An entire XML document is represented by a special type of node. An important concept to appreciate at this point is that the root element of an XML document is not the root node of the DOM. If it were, it would not be possible for the DOM to contain nodes that represent markup around the root element, such as a preceding comment or following processing instruction. The **Document** interface extends the Node interface, adding a number of methods. The first four of these methods obtain information about the document. The remainder are 'factory' methods, used to create new objects to put in the document:

```
DocumentType        getDoctype();
DOMImplementation   getImplementation();
Element             getDocumentElement();
NodeList            getElementsByTagName(String tagName);

Element             createElement(String tagName)
                            throws DOMException;
DocumentFragment    createDocumentFragment();
Text                createTextNode(String data);
Comment             createComment(String data);
CDATASection        createCDATASection(String data)
                            throws DOMException;
ProcessingInstruction
        createProcessingInstruction(String target,
                            String data)
                            throws DOMException;
Attr                createAttribute(String name)
                            throws DOMException;
EntityReference     createEntityReference(String name)
                            throws DOMException;
```

Note that DOM Level 2 adds seven more methods to this interface, mostly for handling elements and attributes that use namespaces.

Get document type

The **getDoctype** method provides access to information about the document, such as the DOCTYPE name (the name of the root element), and lists of entity declarations and notation declarations, through a DocumentType interface object (explained later):

```
DocumentType myDocType = myDoc.getDoctype();
```

Get implementation

The **getImplementation** method provides access to information concerning the capabilities of the DOM-compliant package. It returns a reference to an object that can be queried for information on whether or not a specific feature is supported.

For example, it can be asked whether or not HTML extensions are available. The DOMImplementation interface is discussed in detail later:

```
DOMImplementation myDOMImpl =
                    myDoc.getImplementation();
```

Get document element

The **getDocumentElement** method returns a reference to the node that represents the root element:

```
Element myRootElem = myDoc.getDocumentElement();
```

This method returns an object of type Element (described later).

It should be noted at this point that the node representing the entire document has child nodes, including one that represents the root element. Other nodes are present if the root element is surrounded by markup, such as comments and processing instructions. It is therefore possible to gain a reference to the root element by searching through the document's children for the first (and only) node that represents an element, although this method is not as efficient as simply asking for the root element directly, as shown above.

Get descendant elements

A document may need to be searched for all occurrences of a specific element. For example, an application could extract the content of all title elements in order to construct a contents list for the document. The **getElementsByTagName** method returns a reference to an object that holds a list of matching element nodes:

```
NodeList myList = myDoc.getElementsByTagName("title");
```

The NodeList interface is discussed later.

Factory methods

When reading an XML document into a DOM structure, all the nodes are created by the parser. However, the DOM can be used to create new documents, or to add new structures to an existing document. It must therefore be possible for the application to create new nodes as they are needed, before attaching them to the tree (using the append or insert methods described previously).

The Document interface contains a number of so-called 'factory' methods for this purpose, including **createElement**, **createDocumentFragment**, **createText-Node**, **createComment**, **createCDATASection**, **createProcessingInstruction**, **createAttribute** and **createEntityReference**. Most of these methods take a single string parameter, giving the name to assign to the new object of the given type. The createProcessingInstruction method is one exception, as it requires two parameters (to set the target name and the instruction text). The other exception is the create-DocumentFragment method, which takes no parameters. Some of the methods also throw an exception if the parameters are incorrect in any way:

```
try
{
  Element myElem = myDoc.createElement("para");
}
catch (DOMException err) { ... }

DocumentFragment myFragment =
      myDoc.createDocumentFragment();

TextNode myText = myDoc.createTextNode("a paragraph.");

Comment myComment =
      myDoc.createComment("edit this document");

try
{
  CDATASection myCDATASect =
      myDoc.createCDATASection("Press <ENTER>");
}
catch (DOMException err) { ... }

try
{
  ProcessingInstruction myPI =
      myDoc.createProcessingInstruction("ACME",
                                        "page-break");
}
catch (DOMException err) { ... }

try
{
  Attr myAttribute = myDoc.createAttribute("Author");
}
catch (DOMException err) { ... }

try
{
  EntityReference myEntityRef =
      myDoc.createEntityReference("company");
}
catch (DOMException err) { ... }
```

These methods return references to nodes of various types. These node types are discussed in detail later.

Document types

Information about a document (beyond the actual content hierarchies and text) is encapsulated in an object of type **DocumentType**, which is returned by the **get-Doctype** method.

This interface contains the following methods:

```
String        getName();
NamedNodeList getEntities();
NamedNodeList getNotations();
```

The **getName** method returns the name of the document, which is the word appearing after the DOCTYPE keyword, and is also the name of the root element.

The **getEntities** and **getNotations** methods return an object that contains a list of nodes that represent general entities (either internal or external) or notations declared in the document and DTD.

Note that DOM Level 2 adds methods for accessing the declarations that create the document type model.

Elements

Nodes that represent elements are often the most common type of node to be found in a document tree structure. The DOM standard includes an **Element** interface that extends the Node interface to add element-specific functionality. Most of these methods are used to manage attributes, but the first three are more generalized in nature:

```
String    getTagName();
NodeList  getElementsByTagName( String name );
void      normalize();

String    getAttribute( String name );
void      setAttribute( String name, String value )
                                throws DOMException;
void      removeAttribute( String name )
                                throws DOMException;

Attr      getAttributeNode( String name );
void      setAttributeNode( Attr newAttr )
                                throws DOMException;
void      removeAttributeNode( Attr OldAttr )
                                throws DOMException;
```

The 'get...' and 'set...' methods have namespace-aware versions in DOM Level 2.

Get element tag name

The **getTagName** method returns a string that holds the element name. This method is identical in function to the underlying getNodeName method. It is simply more descriptive within this context.

Get elements by tag name

The **getElementsByTagName** method returns a list of all descendant elements that have the given name. This is the same method as the method with the same name in the Document interface, but lists only elements found under the source element node, rather than across the entire document.

Normalize text

When editing text, an application may split, delete, rearrange and create new Text nodes. These operations tend to lead to multiple adjacent Text nodes. While this is not illegal, and would not be noticed if the next task was simply to write out the text to an XML file, it is nevertheless undesirable.

There are good reasons why it is useful to be able to tidy up the structure. The **Normalize** method cleans up the fragment of the tree within the element, by merging adjacent Text nodes together:

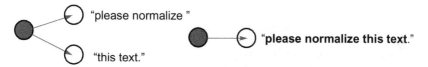

Perhaps the most important reason for normalizing the text is to avoid confusing an advanced hypertext linking system that identifies a range of text by its absolute location in the tree, or by counting adjacent nodes (see the XPointer standard).

Note that this method has been moved into the Node interface in DOM Level 2.

Attribute management

Elements may contain attributes. The getAttributes method in the Node interface, briefly shown earlier, can be used to gain access to all the attributes of an element, and provides all the functionality necessary. But it is an unwieldy device when only simple operations are needed, and it is for this reason that additional methods have been defined in the Element interface to do simple things with attributes.

Get attribute

The value of a given attribute can be retrieved as a string value using the **getAttribute** method. If the named attribute is not present in the element (and also not defined with a default value in the DTD), then an empty string is returned:

```
String titleAttr = myElemNode.getAttribute("title");
```

An alternative form of this method, **getAttributeNode**, returns a node instead of a string. The Attr node type is discussed below. This node is null if the attribute is not present:

```
Attr titleAttrNode =
            myElemNode.getAttributeNode("title");
```

Set attribute

The value of a specific attribute can be changed by naming the attribute and supplying the replacement value. The **setAttribute** method therefore takes two string parameters. The name of the attribute is followed by the value to be assigned to it. The named attribute is created if not already present. Again, there is a variant of this method that takes an Attr type node instead of two string parameters, called **setAttributeNode**:

```
try
{
  myElemNode.setAttribute("title", "The Title");

  myElemNode.setAttributeNode( titleAttrNode );
}
catch (DOMException err) { ... }
```

Remove attribute

An attribute can be removed using the **removeAttribute** methods:

```
try
{
  myElemNode.removeAttribute("title");
}
catch (DOMException err) { ... }
```

As before, there is a variant of this method, called **removeAttributeNode**, that takes an Attr type node instead of two string parameters:

```
try
{
  myElemNode.removeAttributeNode( titleAttrNode );
}
catch (DOMException err) { ... }
```

Complex attribute operations

These simple methods cannot supply all the information that might be necessary. They are inadequate when the name of the required attribute is not known, or when it is necessary to distinguish between values explicitly added to the element by a document author, and values that have been supplied by a default in the DTD. They also cannot determine the type of an attribute. To do these, and other complex things, it is necessary to use the underlying **getAttributes** method and work with NamedNodeMap and Attr objects, which are described below:

```
NamedNodeMap myAtts = myElemNode.getAttributes();
```

Attributes

Some of the methods in the Element interface return objects of type **Attr**. This interface is used to hold information on individual attributes. The following methods are available:

```
String  getName();
String  getValue();
void    setValue( String value );
boolean getSpecified();
```

Get name and value

The **getName** and **getValue** methods are exactly the same as the underlying getNodeName and getNodeValue methods:

```
String attributeName = myAttrNode.getName();
String attributeValue = myAttrNode.getValue();
```

Set value

The value of an attribute can be changed using the **setValue** method. The string passed to this method replaces its existing value. Again, this is the same as SetNodeValue in the underlying Node interface:

```
myAttrNode.setValue( "the new value" );
```

Specified in DTD or document

It is possible to discover if the attribute value originated from the start-tag of the element, or was supplied as a default by the DTD. If the **getSpecified** method returns a value of 'true', this means that the attribute was defined in the start-tag. A value of 'false' means that the attribute was not present, but the DTD provided the default:

```
if ( myAttrNode.getSpecified() )
{
  // attribute specified in document
  . . .
}
else
{
  // attribute specified as DTD default
  . . .
}
```

Attribute node children

An Attr node can have child nodes. These nodes represent the value of the attribute in a more complex form than that returned by the getValue method.

In the simplest case, there is a single child node, of type Text (described later). Using getNodeValue on this object returns the same value as does getValue on the parent Attr object. This is of minor benefit, but could be useful if the intention is to extract an attribute value and convert it to element content, because the Text node can simply be moved to its new location.

But the real benefit of this approach becomes apparent when the attribute value includes one or more entity references. In this case, each entity reference is represented by an EntityReference node, and each block of text between entity references is represented by a Text node. EntityReference nodes also have children that contain the replacement value for the reference. Using this scheme, it is possible to see which parts, if any, of an attribute value are entity replacement text:

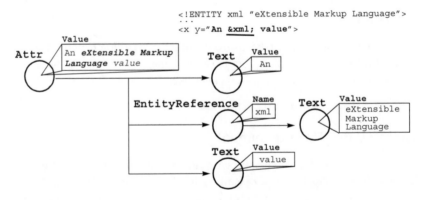

Note that some parsers that claim DOM compliance nevertheless neglect to implement this feature.

Creating attributes

An Attr node can be created using the **createAttribute** factory method defined in the Document interface. The name of the attribute to create is passed to this method. In the following example, a new attribute is first created with the name 'status'. It is then given the value 'secret'. Finally, the new attribute is attached to an existing paragraph element:

```
// <para status="secret">
Attr newAttribute = myDoc.createAttribute( "status" );
newAttribute.setValue( "secret" );
myParaElement.setAttributeNode( newAttribute );
```

Character data

Many of the node types still to be discussed have textual content of some kind. The **CharacterData** interface described here is not used directly, but extends the Node interface, adding a number of useful text processing methods, and is then further extended by other node types. The reason for this arrangement is that all text-based node types have some common requirements for text handling. For example, it should be possible to delete a range of characters, insert new text at a given position in the string, and determine the length of the string.

The CharacterData interface contains the following methods:

```
String   getData() throws DOMException;
void     setData( String data ) throws DOMException;
int      getLength();
void     appendData( String arg ) throws DOMException;
String   substringData( int offset, int count )
                                        throws DOMException;
void     insertData( int offset, String arg )
                                        throws DOMException;
void     deleteData( int offset, int count)
                                        throws DOMException;
void     replaceData( int offset, int count, String arg )
                                        throws DOMException;
```

Reading and writing

The **getData** method is directly equivalent to the underlying getNodeValue method. The text value can be changed using the **setData** method (which is equivalent to setNodeValue):

```
String text = myText.getData();

myText.setData("The DOM is a good thing.");
```

Length of text

The number of characters in the string can be obtained by calling the **getLength** method:

```
int numOfChars = myText.getLength();
```

Append to text

New text can be added to the end of the existing string using the **appendData** method:

```
// add ' Is it not?' to 'the DOM is a good thing.'
String sub = myText.appendData(" Is it not?");
```

Value editing

The remaining methods all involve processing only part of the text string, so must be passed a value that represents the position of the first character to be affected, and in most cases also a value that represents the number of characters involved. The offset parameters are integer values, with the value zero representing the first character in the string:

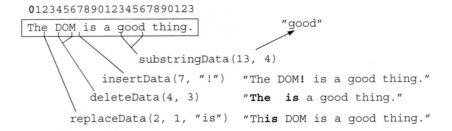

Get part of text

A fragment of the text can be obtained using the **substringData** method. An offset to the start of the text must be provided, as well as a count of the number of characters required. The character at the offset position is included in the extracted string, and is counted as the first character in the range:

```
String subString = myText.substringData(13, 4);
```

Insert string into text

Text can be inserted into the string using the **insertData** method. The first parameter indicates where to insert the new text. The character currently at this position, and all remaining characters, will be moved to the right to make room for the new text:

```
myText.insertData(4, "!");
```

Delete part of text

Text can be deleted from the string using the **deleteData** method. The first para-meter indicates the location of the first character to be deleted, and the second parameter indicates how many characters to remove:

```
myText.deleteData(4, 3);
```

Replace part of text

Replacing a segment of the text is a common requirement that can be achieved using the delete and insert methods. But a more convenient method, called **replaceData**, is included to achieve this operation in a single step. The first two parameters work exactly as described for deleting text, and the third parameter is the replacement string. Note that the replacement string does not have to be the same length as the original.

The two examples below are equivalent:

```
// two-step replace

myText.deleteData(2, 1);
myText.insertData(2, "is");

// one-step replace

myText.replaceData(2, 1, "is");
```

Text

Next to Element nodes, **Text** nodes are likely to be the most common in the aver-age DOM tree. They tend to be children of Element nodes, and are always leaf nodes. The Text interface extends the CharacterData interface, so that the content of a Text node can be modified using the methods described above, but also adds the following single method:

```
Text  splitText( int offset ) throws DOMException;
```

Split text into two nodes

The **splitText** method is used to split one Text node into two adjacent Text nodes, at the location in the string given in the parameter.

The first part is considered to be the original node. The second part is a new node, and a reference to this new node is returned by the method:

```
try
{
  Text myTextNode = aTextNode.splitText( 15 );
}
catch (DOMException err) { ... }
```

This is useful for inserting other nodes into the text, such as a comment or entity reference node.

Create text node

A new Text node can be created using the **createTextNode** factory method defined in the Document interface.

The following example creates a Text node, then appends it to the content of an element:

```
Text newTextNode = myDoc.createTextNode( "the text" );

anElement.appendNode( newTextNode );
```

Character data sections

Ranges of text, possibly containing reserved markup characters that are not to be interpreted as markup, can be enclosed in a character data section. A **CDATASection** node represents such a text range.

This interface extends the CharacterData interface, and adds no further methods. It is therefore simply used to identify character data nodes. When the value of a CDATASection node is written out to XML, the delimiter markup, '<![CDATA[' and ']]>' is added.

Creating CDATA sections

A new CDATASection node can be created using the **createCDATASection** factory method defined in the Document interface:

```
// <![CDATA[press <ENTER>]]>

CDATASection newCDATANode =
        myDoc.createCDATASection( "press <ENTER>" );
```

Comments

Comments are represented by **Comment** nodes. This interface extends Character-Data and does not add any further methods. It is simply used to identify nodes that represent comments.

When the value of a comment node is written out to XML the delimiter markup, '<!--' and '-->', is added.

Creating comments

A new Comment node can be created using the **createComment** factory method defined in the Document interface. The following example shows a new comment being created with the value ' my comment ' (note the surrounding spaces, which are used to make the comment easier to read within delimiter markup), then the comment being attached to the end of the document:

```
// <!-- The End -->

Comment newCommentNode =
            myDoc.createComment( " The End " );

myDoc.appendChild( newComment );
```

Processing instructions

Processing instructions are represented by **ProcessingInstruction** nodes. The name of this type of node is the name of the target application (the first word in the tag). The value of this type of node is the instruction data that occupies the body of the tag.

The whitespace between the target and the instruction is implied, and parsers will insert a single space between them when writing out to XML format. The methods defined by this interface are:

```
String  getTarget();
String  getData();
void    setData(String data);
```

Consider the following example, which is referred to below. It consists of a target name of 'ACME' and an instruction of 'page-break':

```
<?ACME page-break ?>
```

Get target or data

The **getTarget** method returns the target application. From the example above, this method would return 'ACME':

```
String targetName = myPI.getTarget();
```

The **getData** method returns the processing instruction itself. From the example above, the method would return 'page-break':

```
// get 'page-break' or other instruction

String instruction = myPI.getData();
```

Set data

Although it is not possible to change the target name, it is possible to replace the instruction using the **setData** method:

```
// change 'page-break' to 'column-break'

try
{
  myPI.setData("column-break");
}
catch ( DOMException err ) { ... }
```

An exception is thrown if the node is read-only.

Creating PIs

The **createProcessingInstruction** factory method defined in the Document inter-face can be used to create new processing instruction nodes. It takes two param-eters, the target name then the instruction:

```
// <?ACME page-break?>

ProcessingInstruction myProc =
   myDoc.createProcessingInstruction( "ACME",
                                      "page-break" );
```

Entities and notations

XML documents may include entities (some of them perhaps including references to notations) and references to these entities embedded in the text. The DOM there-fore includes interfaces for handling notations, entities and references to entities.

Entity references

When parsable entity references appear in an XML document, the parser will either replace the references with the content of the entity before building the DOM tree, or will leave the entity references in place. In the former case, the application reading from the DOM simply never knows that they existed. But when the references are left in the text, they are represented by **EntityReference** nodes (rather than ignored and left as embedded character sequences in the text). This interface does not define any additional methods.

The name property reflects the name of the entity, but the value property is not used. Instead, an EntityReference object has children that represent the replacement content of the entity. At a minimum, this would be a single Text node that contains the string as its value:

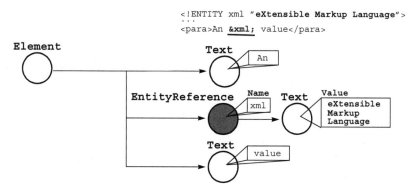

Entities

As stated above, the parser may replace entity references, or create EntityReference nodes. Either way, it can be argued that the original entity declarations are now redundant, so can be discarded. Some parsers may do this. However, external binary data cannot be inserted into a DOM tree, so it is important that the original entity definitions for such data be accessible to the application. The application would not otherwise know of the existence of these entities.

The **Entity** interface extends the Node interface, and adds the following methods:

```
String    getPublicId();
String    getSystemId();
String    getNotationName();
```

Get details

The **getSystemId** and **getPublicId** methods allow location information to be extracted. An Entity object can represent any kind of entity, but for non-parsable (binary) entities it allows the name of the notation to be obtained using the **getNotationName** method:

```
// <!ENTITY MyBoat PUBLIC "BOAT" SYSTEM "boat.gif"
//                                       NDATA GIF>

String pub = ent.getPublicId();      // BOAT
String sys = ent.getSystemId();      // boat.gif
String nota = ent.getNotationName(); // GIF
```

A node representing a parsable entity may have child nodes that represent the replacement value of the entity. If present, these should exactly match the child nodes of each EntityReference node with the same name:

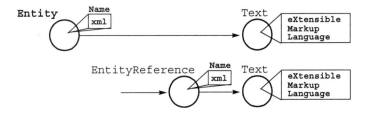

All the entities in a document can be accessed using the **getEntities** method in the DocumentType object.

Changing entity values

It should be noted that the children of an Entity node cannot be edited, and that even if they could be edited the changes would not be dynamically reflected in each reference. Once the DOM has been constructed, there is no connection between references and declarations. To make matters even worse, the children of EntityReference nodes cannot be edited either.

So, to make a change, it is necessary to replace each reference with clones of the children of the Entity node. The inserted nodes can then be edited at each location.

This process is likely to create adjacent Text nodes, so it may be appropriate to call the Normalize method after making all of the edits.

Notations

Having retrieved the name of the notation that a non-parsable entity complies with, it may be necessary to discover more about that notation. Each notation declaration in the document can be represented by an object that implements the **Notation** interface. This interface extends the Node interface, and adds the following methods:

```
String    getPublicId();
String    getSystemId();
```

These methods are the same as for the Entity interface. The **getPublicId** method returns the content of the public identifier (if there is one), and the **getSystemId** method returns the content of the system identifier.

It is possible that the system identifier locates an external application that is able to display or process all the entities that conform to that notation. For example, it may reference a GIF image viewer.

All the notations in a document can be accessed using the **getNotations** method in the DocumentType object.

Node lists

Some of the operations described above return lists of nodes that match some criteria. For example, getElementsByTagName returns all the element nodes that have a given name, and getChildNodes returns all the children of a given node. For convenience, a single **NodeList** object is returned. This object acts as a wrapper for the returned nodes. The nodes contained in this object are organized into a logical, linear sequence. For example, the getChildNodes method returns all the children nodes, in their original order of appearance, so that they can be easily processed in correct document order. The NodeList interface defines the following two methods:

```
Node   item(int index);
int    getLength( );
```

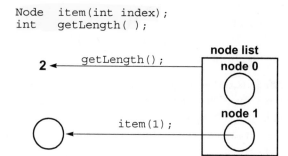

Get node from list

A reference to a node in the list is obtained by calling the **item** method, and providing it with the sequential number of the required node. The first node in the list is assigned the number zero, so to obtain the fourth node it is necessary to request node three:

```
Node myNode = myNodeList.item(3);
```

Get length of list

In order to access all the nodes in a list, or simply to avoid asking for a node that does not exist, it is important to be able to ask the list how many nodes it contains. The **getLength** method returns an integer value that represents the total number of nodes. However, because the first node in the list is numbered zero, the value returned by this method will always be one higher than the number of the last node in the list. The following example presents the names of all element children of the root element:

```
Node aChildNode;
NodeList rootsChildren = rootElement.getChildNodes();
for( int i = 0; i < rootsChildren.getLength(); i++ )
{
  aChildNode = rootsChildren.item(i);
  if ( aChildNode.getNodeType() == Node.ELEMENT_NODE )
  {
    System.out.println( aChildNode.getNodeName() );
  }
}
```

Named node maps

In some circumstances, a set of nodes that have no particular ordering significance need to be grouped together. This applies to attributes and to entity and notation declarations. Attributes do have a real location, in the sense that they belong to a specific element instance, but their order of appearance within the start-tag is not significant. Likewise, entity declarations have an order in the data stream, but this order is not significant (beyond the fact that only the first occurrence of duplicate declarations is acted upon). While the location is not significant in these instances, the names of these items certainly *is* significant. Unique names are essential.

The **NamedNodeMap** interface is designed to contain nodes, in no particular order, that can be accessed by name. For this reason, the names must be unique within a NamedNodeMap object. This can be used to hold a set of attributes that belong to a given element, and sets of entity and notation declarations that belong to a document, as the following examples demonstrate:

```
NamedNodeMap elemAttributes = myElement.getAttributes();

NamedNodeMap docEntities = myDoc.getEntities();

NamedNodeMap docNotations = myDoc.getNotations();
```

The methods defined in this interface are:

```
Node   item(int index);
int    getLength( );
Node   getNamedItem(String nodeName);
Node   setNamedItem(Node theNode) throws DOMException;
Node   removeNamedItem(String nodeName)
                                throws DOMException;
```

For example:

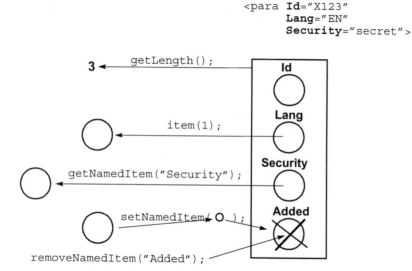

Extracting by name

Because nodes in these lists are distinguished by name, a method called **get-NamedItem** is included. The following example extracts the security status of an element (the node is 'null' if the attribute is not present):

```
NamedNodeMap myMap = myElement.getAttributes();

Attr security = (Attr) myMap.getNamedItem("Security");
```

Removing and adding items

Nodes can be removed from and added to the list.

The **removeNamedItem** method removes the node with the given name from the list. However, it does not actually delete the node, but returns a reference to it for possible reuse elsewhere.

The **setNamedItem** method adds a given node to the list, but despite its name passes a node reference to the list, not the node name. This method is probably so named as a reminder that the operation will not succeed if there is a node with the same name already present in the list.

The following example demonstrates both methods, by first removing the Security attribute, then reinserting it into the list:

```
Node temp = myMap.removeNamedItem("Security");

myMap.setNamedItem(temp);
```

The setNamedItem method also returns a reference to the node just added, which can be useful when the node is added at the same time as it is created:

```
Node newNode =
    myMap.setNamedItem(myDoc.createAttribute("Added"));
```

Extracting without name

Although NamedNodeMap objects have an **item** method that works in the same way as in the NodeList interface, there is no equivalent significance to the item number. The **getLength** and item methods are included so that nodes can be selected even when their names are not known.

In the following example, all attributes are accessed, and their names are displayed:

```
Node aNode;

NamedNodeMap atts = myElement.getAttributes();

for( int i = 0; i < atts.getLength(); i++ )
{
  aNode = atts.item(i);

  System.out.println( aNode.getNodeName() );
}
```

Document fragments

A fragment of the document can be attached temporarily to a 'lightweight' object, formally called a **DocumentFragment** node. This can also be thought of as a 'scratchpad' or 'clipboard'.

The most interesting characteristic of this node is that it dissolves when it is attached to another node as a child. Its children are promoted to be direct children of the node that it became (temporarily) attached to:

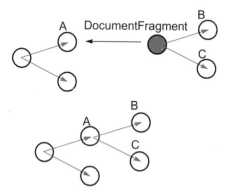

However, if the final location is already known, it is perhaps easier just to move each node directly to its intended location. This node type is probably only relevant when the application really does not know the ultimate destination of the nodes at the time they are removed from the document tree. It is therefore very useful when the application is interactive, supporting an XML editing environment that provides a 'cut and paste' option for authors.

DOM implementation

The **DOMImplementation** interface defines a single method, called **hasFeature**, which is used to determine the extent of DOM support that the application/parser has. This method returns a boolean value, with 'true' indicating support for the given feature:

```
boolean hasFeature( String feature, String version);
```

It can be called a number of times, each time testing for support for a particular feature, or 'module'. The name of the module is passed as the first parameter. In DOM Level 1, this method can be called to test for support for 'Core' DOM features, and for additional 'XML' or 'HTML' features.

It is also necessary to check which version of the DOM is supported in each case, and the DOM version is therefore passed as the second parameter. For the version described in this chapter, DOM Level 1, the string '1.0' is used. For DOM Level 2 (see Chapter 21), the string '2.0' is used. DOM Level 2 has more modules, and also more powerful capabilities in some of the existing modules ('Core' support in Level 2 is more sophisticated than 'Core' support in Level 1).

The following example tests for DOM Level 1 support for XML additional features (CDATA sections, document types, notations, entity references and processing instructions):

```
if ( theParser.hasFeature( "XML", "1.0" )
{
  // DOM Level 1 (1.0) support for XML is available
  ...
}
```

The following table shows all the interfaces, and the modules they are found in. Note that a number of Core interfaces are optional, in the sense that they are not needed if working with HTML instead of XML. To ensure that these are present, the test for XML support must be carried out:

Exception or Interface	Core	XML	HTML
DomException	Yes		
DocumentFragment	Yes		
Document	Yes		
Node	Yes		
NodeList	Yes		
NamedNodeMap	Yes		
CharacterData	Yes		
Attr	Yes		
Element	Yes		
Text	Yes		
Comment	Yes		
CDATASection	Optional	Yes	
DocumentType	Optional	Yes	
Notation	Optional	Yes	
Entity	Optional	Yes	
EntityReference	Optional	Yes	
ProcessingInstruction	Optional	Yes	

Exception or Interface	Core	XML	HTML
HTMLDomImplementation			Yes
HTMLCollection			Yes
HTMLDocument			Yes
HTMLElement			Yes
HTMLAnchorElement			Yes
HTMLAppletElement			Yes
HTMLAreaElement			Yes
HTMLBaseElement			Yes
HTMLBaseFontElement			Yes
HTMLBodyElement			Yes
HTMLBRElement			Yes
HTMLButtonElement			Yes
HTMLDirectoryElement			Yes
HTMLDivElement			Yes
HTMLDListElement			Yes
HTMLFieldElement			Yes
HTMLFontElement			Yes
HTMLFormElement			Yes
HTMLFrameElement			Yes
HTMLFrameSetElement			Yes
HTMLHeadElement			Yes
HTMLHeadingElement			Yes
HTMLHRElement			Yes
HTMLHtmlElement			Yes
HTMLIFrameElement			Yes
HTMLImageElement			Yes
HTMLInputElement			Yes
HTMLIsIndexElement			Yes
HTMLLabelElement			Yes
HTMLLegendElement			Yes
HTMLLIElement			Yes
HTMLLinkElement			Yes

Exception or Interface	Core	XML	HTML
HTMLMapElement			Yes
HTMLMenuElement			Yes
HTMLMetaElement			Yes
HTMLModElement			Yes
HTMLObjectElement			Yes
HTMLOListElement			Yes
HTMLOptGroupElement			Yes
HTMLOptionElement			Yes
HTMLParagraphElement			Yes
HTMLParamElement			Yes
HTMLPreElement			Yes
HTMLQuoteElement			Yes
HTMLScriptElement			Yes
HTMLSelectElement			Yes
HTMLStyleElement			Yes
HTMLTableCaptionElement			Yes
HTMLTableCellElement			Yes
HTMLTableCollElement			Yes
HTMLTableElement			Yes
HTMLTableRowElement			Yes
HTMLTableSectionElement			Yes
HTMLTextAreaElement			Yes
HTMLTitleElement			Yes
HTMLUListElement			Yes

21. DOM Level 2

Although the original DOM standard is a successful, well-established technology, it has been perceived to have some unnecessary limitations, and in particular does not support the Namespaces standard (see Chapter 10).

The DOM Level 2 standard is now in widespread use, but should not be considered if there is any possibility of using software that does not support this version. This chapter covers the core standard, the optional tree-walking and range selection components, but not the optional event-handling and styling components.

Namespace support

The primary enhancement to the DOM standard provided by this release concerns its support for namespaces. A number of new methods have been added to access and create elements and attributes that use the Namespaces standard. This support also ensures that elements that are moved from one part of a DOM structure to another part of the structure retain their namespace identity. Methods with names ending '...NS' are used to create, access and modify elements and attributes without needing to know the namespace prefixes used.

Consider the following document fragment, which declares the prefix 'H' for the HTML 4.0 namespace, and includes a Span element with a Style attribute. This fragment is referenced in numerous examples below, which focus on the embedded Span element and Style attribute:

```
<H:html xmlns:H="http://www.w3.org/TR/REC-html40">
   ... <H:span H:style="color:red">...</H:span> ...
</H:html>
```

Node extensions

All the existing methods in the **Node** interface are still available. The following methods are described in the previous chapter:

```
short        getNodeType();
String       getNodeName();
String       getNodeValue() throws DOMException;
void         setNodeValue(String nodeValue)
                                   throws DOMException;
boolean      hasChildNodes();
NamedNodeMap getAttributes();
Document     getOwnerDocument();

Node    getFirstChild();
Node    getLastChild();
Node    getNextSibling();
Node    getPreviousSibling();
Node    getParentNode();
NodeList getChildNodes();

Node    removeChild(Node oldChild) throws DOMException;
Node    insertBefore(Node newChild, Node refChild)
                                   throws DOMException;
Node    appendChild(Node newChild) throws DOMException;
Node    replaceChild(Node newChild, Node oldChild)
                                   throws DOMException;
Node    cloneNode(boolean deep);
```

But a number of attributes, methods and types have been added, mostly concerned with namespace support and extended support for document models. The new methods are:

```
String       getLocalName();
String       getPrefix();
String       getNamespaceURI();
void         setPrefix(String prefix)
                                   throws DOMException;
boolean      supports(String feature, String version);
boolean      hasAttributes();
void         normalize();
Document     getOwnerDocument();
```

Changes to this interface to support namespaces involves the addition of three new methods for obtaining the name of an element or attribute node.

Get local name

The **getLocalName** method returns the local name of the node. It is applicable to element and attribute node types. In the example above, the string 'span' would be returned:

```
// get 'span' from 'H:span'

String localName = myNode.getLocalName();
```

Get prefix

The **getPrefix** method returns the namespace prefix. It is applicable to element and attribute node types. In the example above, the string 'H' would be returned:

```
// get 'H' (or whatever prefix is in use) from 'H:span'

String nodePrefix = myNode.getPrefix();
```

Get namespace URI

The **getNamespaceURI** method returns the URI that the prefix maps to (in this case, http://www.w3.org/TR/REC-html40):

```
// get http://www.w3.org/TR/REC-html40 from 'H:span'

String nodeURL = myNode.getNamespaceURI();
```

Set prefix

Only the prefix can be changed by this interface, using the **setPrefix** method. Changing the prefix does not change the URI mapping, so the namespace does not change, only the prefix it is mapped to. If the XML data were then saved to a file, an extra declaration would be generated on the current element to map the new prefix to the namespace:

```
// change to <Html:span>...</Html:span>

try
{
   myNode.setPrefix("Html");
}
catch ( DOMException err ) { ... }
```

Errors are thrown if there is no URL to map the prefix to (it is 'null'), or if the prefix does not conform to XML syntax constraints.

Supported features

The **supports** method has been added, and is used to discover whether or not a given DOM feature is supported by the parser. It returns a boolean value of 'true' if the given feature is present, and 'false' otherwise.

The feature is passed to the parser in the first parameter. The features list is the same as the list given for HasFeatures on the DOMImplementation interface ('Core', 'XML' and 'HTML', with versions '1.0' or '2.0', and the additional 'Navigate', 'Span' and 'Events' modules in Level 2):

```
if ( myNode.supports("XML", "1.0") )
{
  // this node supports the DOM Level 1 (1.0) XML module
  ...
}
```

This method works in exactly the same way as the hasFeature in the DOMImplementation interface, except that it is targeted at support within the current node. The standard does not make it clear how support for modules like the XML or HTML modules can change between nodes. Possibly, some parsers might support some DOM 2.0 XML functionality, such as the improved Element interface, but not others, such as the improved Attr interface. In this scenario, support for this module would depend on whether the current node is of type Element or of type Attr. However, this variable level of support would mean that any response given by the hasFeature method for the whole document would be only partially true.

Attributes present

The **hasAttributes** method returns the boolean value 'true' if the node is an element, and this element has attributes attached to it. It returns 'false' in all other circumstances. This method can be used as a test to decide whether it is worthwhile trying to obtain and cycle through a list of attributes:

```
if ( myNode.hasAttributes() )
{
  // This is an element, and it has attributes

  NamedNodeMap theAttributes = myNode.getAttributes();
  ...
}
```

Normalization

The **Normalize** method has been moved into this interface from the Element interface, but its purpose and scope are unchanged. This change has only been made to make this feature available when avoiding use of the Node interface subclasses, including the Element interface.

Owner document

The **getOwnerDocument** method now has a value of 'null' when the node is a DocumentType that has not yet been referenced from any Document.

Document extensions

The **Document** interface retains all the existing methods:

```
DocumentType        getDoctype();
DOMImplementation  getImplementation();
Element            getDocumentElement();
NodeList           getElementsByTagName(String tagName);

Element            createElement(String tagName)
                                    throws DOMException;
DocumentFragment   createDocumentFragment();
Text               createTextNode(String data);
Comment            createComment(String data);
CDATASection       createCDATASection(String data)
                                    throws DOMException;
ProcessingInstruction
        createProcessingInstruction(String target,
                                    String data)
                                    throws DOMException;
Attr               createAttribute(String name)
                                    throws DOMException;
EntityReference    createEntityReference(String name)
                                    throws DOMException;
```

But a number of methods have also been added. Mostly, they handle namespaces, but other useful functions have also been added:

```
Element   createElementNS(String namespaceURI,
                          String qualifiedName)
                                    throws DOMException;
Attr      createAttributeNS(String namespaceURI,
                          String qualifiedName)
                                    throws DOMException;
NodeList getElementsByTagNameNS(String namespaceURI,
                          String localName);

Element  getElementById(String elementId);
Node     importNode(Node importedNode, boolean deep)
                                    throws DOMException;
```

Create element with namespace

The **createElementNS** method creates (and returns a reference to) a new element, and is based on the original **createElement** method. It is given the URL for the namespace it belongs to, and the qualified name of the element:

```
try
{
  Element myElement =
      myDoc.createElementNS("http://www.w3.org/
                          TR/REC-html40", "H:span");
}
catch ( DOMException err ) { ... }
```

This method throws a DOMException exception if the qualified name contains an illegal character, or if the qualified name is malformed. Also, if the qualified name has a prefix and the namespaceURI is 'null' or is an empty string, and finally if the qualified name has a prefix that is 'xml' and a namespaceURI that is not 'http://www.w3.org/XML/1998/namespace' (because this prefix is reserved for that namespace).

Create attribute with namespace

The **createAttributeNS** method works in exactly the same way as the createElementNS method, and is based on the original **createAttribute** method:

```
try
{
  Attr myAttribute =
      myDoc.createAttributeNS("http://www.w3.org/
                              TR/REC-html40", "H:style");
}
catch ( DOMException err ) { ... }
```

Get elements by tag name with namespace

The **getElementsByTagNameNS** method is based on the original **getElementsByTagName** method, but again takes two parameters. In this case, though, the second parameter is just the local name. The application does not need to know what prefix the URL was mapped to in order to find the elements:

```
// get acme:id (or whatever prefix is in use)

NodeList myIdElements =
       myDoc.getElementsByTagNameNS("http://www.w3.org/
                                    TR/REC-html40", "span");
```

The '*' character can be used as a wildcard, standing for all elements that belong to the given namespace.

Get elements by identifier

The **getElementById** method returns a reference to the element with the supplied identifier:

```
// get H:a (or whatever prefix is in use)

Element myElements = myDoc.getElementById("Anchor123");
```

This does not search for attributes with the name 'Id', unless this is unambiguously defined somehow. It is assumed that the parser can discover which attributes act as identifiers from an associated DTD or XML Schema. In the case of the HTML example, this would probably be the Anchor element, which uses the Name attribute to hold the unique identifier.

Import node

The **importNode** method allows nodes from other documents to be copied into the current document. The first parameter is the node to copy to the current document. The second parameter specifies whether to copy descendant nodes as well ('true') or not ('false'):

```
try
{
  Element otherDocNodeElement =
                  otherDoc.getElementById("Anchor123");

  currentDoc.importNode( otherDocNodeElement, true );
}
catch ( DOMException err ) { ... }
```

The original node in the other document is not affected by this operation. It is simply copied into the current document. This is therefore very similar to the cloning method, and the boolean 'deep' or 'shallow' copying mode option is the same.

When an element is imported, the attached attributes are also copied. However, default attributes are not copied, but defaults that apply to the current document may be added (when both documents use the same DTD, this means that these attributes can be thought of as being copied, since the end result is the same). Descendant elements (and their attributes) are also copied.

When an attribute is imported, the descendants of the source attribute are also imported. The second parameter does not apply to these nodes, as 'deep' ('true') copying is always assumed. Embedded entity references remain intact.

When importing an entity reference, only the reference itself is copied, regardless of the second parameter value. The current document will have its own, possibly different, definition for the entity.

When importing a document fragment, a boolean value of 'true' on the second parameter ensures that the contents of the fragment are imported. If set to 'false', an empty fragment is created.

Note that Entity nodes and Notation nodes can also be imported, but cannot be added to a DocumentType object, because in DOM Level 2 this is a read-only object. Also note that Document and DocumentType nodes cannot be imported at all.

Document type extensions

The original methods of the **DocumentType** interface are still available:

```
String          getName();
NamedNodeList getEntities();
NamedNodeList getNotations();
```

In addition, a small number of methods have been added to obtain information about the document model:

```
String getInternalSubset();
String getPublicId();
String getSystemId();
```

Note that a new object which implements this interface can be created using the new createDocumentType method in an object that implements the DOMImplementation interface (see below).

Internal subset

The contents of the internal subset of a document are returned as a single string using the **getInternalSubset** method. This string will therefore contain all the notation, entity, element and attribute declarations that may be present in this subset:

```
<!DOCTYPE myDoc [
<!NOTATION GIF SYSTEM "gifeditor.exe">
<!ENTITY boat SYSTEM "boat.gif" NDATA GIF>
]>
```

```
    <!NOTATION GIF SYSTEM "gifeditor.exe"><!ENTITY
    boat SYSTEM "boat.gif" NDATA GIF>
```

The application would still need to parse these declarations to make any sense of the information supplied.

Public and system identifiers

The public and system identifiers for the external subset are now available using the **getPublicId** and **getSystemId** methods. Once obtained, it is possible for the application to access the file and read the declarations it contains. The entire model can be read using these methods, along with the getInternalSubset method described above, though the application may have to access further files from parameter entity references embedded in either subset.

Element extensions

The **Element** interface retains the original methods:

```
String    getTagName();
NodeList getElementsByTagName( String name );
void      normalize();

String    getAttribute( String name );
void      setAttribute( String name, String value )
                                    throws DOMException;
void      removeAttribute( String name )
                                    throws DOMException;

Attr      getAttributeNode( String name );
void      setAttributeNode( Attr newAttr )
                                    throws DOMException;
void      removeAttributeNode( Attr OldAttr )
                                    throws DOMException;
```

A number of new methods have been added to handle namespaces, and one other has been added to discover if a particular attribute is present:

```
boolean    hasAttribute(String name);

boolean    hasAttributeNS(String namespaceURI,
                          String localName);
String     getAttributeNS(String namespaceURI,
                          String localName);
Attr       getAttributeNodeNS(String namespaceURI,
                              String localName);
Attr       setAttributeNodeNS(Attr newAttr)
                                    throws DOMException;
void       setAttributeNS(String namespaceURI,
                          String qualifiedName,
                          String value);
NodeList   getElementsByTagNameNS(String namespaceURI,
                                  String localName);
void       removeAttributeNS(String namespaceURI,
                             String localName)
                                    throws DOMException;
```

In addition, the Normalize method is now inherited from the Node interface.

Element has specific attribute

The **hasAttribute** method returns 'true' if the given string is the name of an attribute that the element has (whether specified directly or defaulted from a DTD). But note that this method is not sensitive to namespaces, so the full, unqualified name is required if the attribute happens to have a namespace prefix:

```
if ( myElement.hasAttribute("H:style") )
{
  // This element has an 'H:style' attribute
  ...
}
```

However, there is also a namespace-aware version of this method called **hasAttributeNS**. In this version, the URL and local name part is passed, so the application does not have to know what prefix might have been assigned to it in the document:

```
if ( myElement.hasAttributeNS("http://www.w3.org/
                              TR/REC-html40", "style") )
{
  // This element has an HMTL 'style' attribute
  ...
}
```

Get attribute using namespace

The **getAttributeNS** and **getAttributeNodeNS** methods are equivalent to the original **getAttribute** and **getAttributeNode** methods, except that with these methods it is not necessary to know what prefix the attribute has. Instead, the URL the prefix is mapped to is supplied as the first parameter:

```
String styleAttr =
  myElement.getAttributeNS("http://www.w3.org/
                            TR/REC-html40", "style");

Node styleAttr =
  myElement.getAttributeNodeNS("http://www.w3.org/
                                TR/REC-html40", "style");
```

The first method returns a 'null' string if the required attribute is not present, although there seems to be no logical reason for this, since the getAttribute method returns an empty string in this circumstance. The second method also returns 'null' if the attribute is not present (and in this case the behaviour is the same as for the original getAttributeNode method).

Set attribute using namespace

The **setAttributeNS** and **setAttributeNodeNS** methods are equivalent to the original **setAttribute** and **setAttributeNode** methods, except that with these methods it is not necessary to know what prefix the attribute has. Instead, the URL the prefix is mapped to is supplied as the first parameter:

```
// add style="traditional" to element
try
{
  String styleAttr =
    myElement.setAttributeNS("http://www.w3.org/
                   TR/REC-html40", "style", "color:red");
}
catch ( DOMException err ) { ... }

try
{
  Attr replacedAttr =
    myElement.setAttributeNodeNS( myAttributeNode );
}
catch ( DOMException err ) { ... }
```

Note that the second method returns the attribute that the new one replaced, if there was already an attribute in the element with the same name (the same namespace and local part). Otherwise, it returns 'null'. Also, an error is thrown if the attribute to be added is already attached to another element.

Get child elements with namespace

The **getElementsByTagNameNS** method is a namespace-aware version of the **getElementsByTagName** method. The first parameter is the namespace, and the second is the local element name. The application does not need to know what prefix is used in the document:

```
NodeList mySpanElements =
    myElement.getElementsByTagNameNS("http://
        www.w3.org/TR/REC-html40", "span");
```

The wildcard character, '*', can be used in both parameters. In the first parameter, it represents all namespaces. In the second parameter, it represents all elements in the given namespace. Using a wildcard, it is therefore possible to select all elements that belong to a given namespace, such as all HTML elements, or to select all elements with a given local name, such as 'span', regardless of which namespace they belong to.

Remove attribute with namespace

The **removeAttributeNS** method is the namespace-aware version of the **removeAttribute** method. The application passes the URL and local name, so does not need to know what prefix is used:

```
try
{
  myElement.removeAttributeNS("http://www.w3.org./
                    TR/REC-html40", "style");
}
catch ( DOMException err ) { ... }
```

Attribute extensions

The **Attr** interface retains the original methods:

```
String  getName();
String  getValue();
void    setValue( String value );
boolean getSpecified();
```

The only addition is the **getOwnerElement** method:

```
Element getOwnerElement();
```

This method returns a node representing the element that contains the attribute:

```
Element owner = myAttribute.getOwnerElement();
```

Note that the Attr interface is not affected by the need to cope with namespaces. The objects that implement the Element and NamedNodeMap interfaces are affected instead, because they are used to access attributes.

Named node map extensions

The **NamedNodeMap** interface retains the original methods:

```
Node  item(int index);
int   getLength( );
Node  getNamedItem(String nodeName);
Node  setNamedItem(Node theNode) throws DOMException;
Node  removeNamedItem(String nodeName)
                                   throws DOMException;
```

Three new methods have been added to handle elements and attributes by reference to the namespace URL rather than the prefix:

```
Node  getNamedItemNS(String namespaceURI,
                     String localName);
Node  removeNamedItemNS(String namespaceURI,
                        String localName)
                                    throws DOMException;
Node  setNamedItemNS(Node arg) throws DOMException;
```

These methods are variants of existing methods to get and remove nodes in the list, and to add nodes to the list. In the first two cases, the variant is simply the addition of an extra parameter that gives the URL of the required attribute. The application does not need to know the prefix it was mapped to when using the **getNamedItemNS** method and **removeNamedItemNS** method.

At first sight, the **setNamedItemNS** method appears to be identical to the original **setNamedItem** method. In both cases, a node is added to the list by passing a reference to that node to the NamedNodeMap object. The subtle difference is that the added node will replace an existing node if they share the same local name and namespace URL, even if they have different prefixes. This contrasts with the original behaviour, where the prefix, colon and local name would be compared as a single name string.

DOM implementation extensions

The **DOMImplementation** interface continues to hold the original method for checking for the presence of features supported by the parser:

```
boolean hasFeature( String feature, String version);
```

But the **createDocumentType** and **createDocument** methods have been added, allowing new document types and individual documents to be created from scratch within the DOM:

```
Document        createDocument(String namespaceURI,
                               String qualifiedName,
                               DocumentType doctype);
DocumentType createDocumentType(String qualifiedName,
                                String publicId,
                                String systemId);
```

For example, the Xerces parser implements this interface in a class called DOMImplementationImpl:

```
import org.apache.xerces.dom.DOMImplementationImpl;
...
DOMImplementationImpl myDOMImpl =
                    new DOMImplementationImpl();
```

Using this parser, the examples below first create a new document type, then a new document which uses the created document type.

Create document type

The **createDocumentType** method creates a new set of document type details that can later be attached to a document. These details are essentially the components of a document type declaration. The root element name, and the public and system identifiers of the external DTD subset, are all passed as string parameters:

```
import org.w3c.dom.DocumentType;
import org.w3c.dom.DOMException;
...
try
{
  DocumentType myDocType =
    myDOMImpl.createDocumentType( "H:html",
        "-//W3C//DTD HTML 4.0 Final/EN", "html.dtd" );
}
catch ( DOMException err ) { ... }
```

This example would create the instruction below:

```
<!DOCTYPE H:html   PUBLIC "-//W3C//DTD HTML 4.0 Final/EN"
                          "html.dtd" >
```

Create document

The **createDocument** method creates a new XML document from scratch. To do this, it needs the public and system identifiers that identify the DTD it belongs to, and the document type object (giving the system identifier of the external DTD, plus any notations and entities) the document belongs to:

```
import org.w3c.dom.Document;
...
try
{
  DocumentType myDocType =
    myDOMImpl.createDocumentType( "H:html",
        "-//W3C//DTD HTML 4.0 Final/EN", "html.dtd" );

  // create new document (attach document type to it)
  Document myDocument =
    myDOMImpl.createDocument("http://www.w3.org/
                TR/REC-html40", "H:html", myDocType);
}
catch ( DOMException err ) { ... }
```

The following document element would be created:

```
<!DOCTYPE H:html   PUBLIC "-//W3C//DTD HTML 4.0 Final/EN"
                   "html.dtd" >
<H:html xmlns:H="http://www.w3.org/TR/REC-html40">
</H:html>
```

If the first parameter is 'null', the document will not use namespaces.

If the final parameter is 'null', there will be no document type declaration.

Unchanged interfaces

The remaining interfaces are unchanged from the previous release of this standard. The **CDATASection** interface, **Comment** interface and the **DocumentFragment** interface have all remained unchanged. They still do not have any specific methods, but simply inherit from underlying interfaces. The following sections review the other unchanged interfaces, showing the original methods as defined in DOM Level 1.

CharacterData interface

```
String   getData() throws DOMException;
void     setData( String data ) throws DOMException;
int      getLength();
void     appendData( String arg ) throws DOMException;
String   substringData( int offset, int count )
                                       throws DOMException;
void     insertData( int offset, String arg )
                                       throws DOMException;
void     deleteData( int offset, int count)
                                       throws DOMException;
void     replaceData( int offset, int count, String arg )
                                       throws DOMException;
```

Text interface

```
Text   splitText( int offset ) throws DOMException;
```

ProcessingInstruction interface

```
String   getTarget();
String   getData();
void     setData(String data);
```

Entity interface

```
String     getPublicId();
String     getSystemId();
String     getNotationName();
```

Notation interface

```
String     getPublicId();
String     getSystemId();
```

NodeList interface

```
Node   item(int index);
int    getLength( );
```

Iteration and tree-walking

The concept of tree-walking (discussed in Chapter 16) is a useful concept when working with a DOM structure. DOM Level 2 supports this concept in a standard way. A new optional package for convenient traversal of document trees has been introduced in this version of the standard. This package includes four interfaces: DocumentTraversal, TreeWalker, Iterator and NodeFilter.

Document traversal interface

There are two ways of traversing a document tree, one more sophisticated than the other. Objects that implement these two approaches can be created on behalf of the application using an object that implements the **DocumentTraversal** interface.

For example, the Xerces parser includes a class called DocumentImpl that implements this interface:

```
import org.apache.xerces.dom.DocumentImpl;

DocumentType myDoctype = document.getDoctype();

DocumentImpl myDocImpl =
                new DocumentImpl( myDoctype );
```

This interface enables the creation of a node iterator or a tree-walker, using the following methods:

```
NodeIterator createNodeIterator(Node root,
                              int whatToShow,
                              NodeFilter filter,
                    boolean entityReferenceExpansion);

TreeWalker createTreeWalker(Node root,
                          int whatToShow,
                          NodeFilter filter,
                boolean entityReferenceExpansion);
```

The parameters are identical in these two methods. The first parameter is the node to start iterating or tree-walking from. The next parameter is a value that can be dissected to provide information on which types of node are to be skipped over. The third parameter is a filter object ('null' if there is no filter). The final parameter specifies whether entity references should be expanded (replaced by their content) or not ('true' or 'false'):

The **createNodeIterator** method returns an object that allows iteration to take place over the document tree.

```
NodeIterator myIterator =
    myDocImpl.createNodeIterator( theRootNode,
                                7, null, true);
```

The **createTreeWalker** method returns an object that allows tree-walking to take place over the document tree:

```
TreeWalker myTreeWalker =
     myDocImpl.createTreeWalker( theRootNode,
                                 7, null, true);
```

What to show

The second parameter in both these methods specifies what types of nodes are of interest to the application. Other node types are to be ignored, just as if they did not exist at all in the document. For example, the application may only be interested in elements and attributes, or may only be interested in comments and processing instructions.

A single value is able to supply this information because it is built from 16 binary 'switches' (of which only 12 are used). Each node type has a value that is a different multiple of two. To specify a particular combination of required node types, it is necessary to add together their values (such as '1' plus '4' plus '16' gives '21', which represents a requirement to ignore all but the element, text and entity reference node types).

It is not necessary to learn and memorize these values, as they are all defined in the NodeFilter interface:

```
static int SHOW_ELEMENT = 1;
static int SHOW_ATTRIBUTE = 2;
static int SHOW_TEXT = 4;
static int SHOW_CDATA_SECTION = 8;
static int SHOW_ENTITY_REFERENCE = 16;
static int SHOW_ENTITY = 32;
static int SHOW_PROCESSING_INSTRUCTION = 64;
static int SHOW_COMMENT = 128;
static int SHOW_DOCUMENT = 256;
static int SHOW_DOCUMENT_FRAGMENT = 1024;
static int SHOW_DOCUMENT_TYPE = 512;
static int SHOW_NOTATION = 2048;
static int SHOW_ALL = FFFFFFFF;
```

In the following example, the values '1' and '4' are added together, to supply the value '5' to one of the methods discussed below:

```
... , NodeFilter.SHOW_ELEMENT + NodeFilter.SHOW_TEXT , ...
```

Note that providing access to these definitions is not the main purpose of the NodeFilter interface, which is discussed in more detail elsewhere.

Xerces implementation

First, for any Java implementation, it is necessary to add some important class paths. The first one below is needed to find the traversal-oriented interfaces. The second is needed to find the Xerces class that implements the interface described above:

```
import org.w3c.dom.traversal.*;
import org.apache.xerces.dom.DocumentImpl;
```

The Xerces parser implements the DocumentTraversal interface in its Document-Impl class (which also implements the Document interface). The DocumentType object is passed to it, so that it has a reference to the tree it will be traversing:

```
DocumentImpl myDocImpl =
                new DocumentImpl( myDocumentType );
```

Recall that this object contains a reference to the Document object it belongs to (and is extracted from the Document object using the getDoctype method):

```
Document myDoc = parser.getDocument();
DocumentType myDoctype = myDoc.getDoctype();

DocumentImpl myDocImpl = new DocumentImpl( myDoctype );
```

This Xerces class includes the methods listed above to create objects that support the tree-walking and iteration interfaces. Before using either of these methods, though, a node is required to start iterating from. Typically, the root element node of the document is used to traverse the entire document:

```
Element rootElement = myDoc.getDocumentElement();
```

Common features

Before discussing the individual features of the **NodeIterator** and **TreeWalker** interfaces, it should be noted that they have a number of methods in common. These methods work in the same way in both interfaces:

```
NodeFilter  getFilter();
int         getWhatToShow();
boolean     getExpandEntityReferences();
Node        getRoot();
```

The **getFilter**, **getWhatToShow** and **getExpandEntityReferences** methods return the settings used to configure the object. From the example above, they would return 'null', the value '7', and 'true' respectively:

```
NodeFilter myNodeFilter = myWalker.getFilter();
int whatToShow = myWalker.getWhatToShow();
boolean expandEnts =
            myWalker.getExpandEntityReferences();
```

The **getRoot** method returns a reference to the node at the root of the tree being traversed. This is the same node as the one passed to the method to begin traversing:

```
Node theRootNode = myWalker.getRoot();
```

Note that other methods in each interface have a passing resemblance, but are subtly different.

Node iteration

Although the TreeWalking interface has an appropriate name, it is the **NodeIterator** interface that provides the simple tree-walking functionality discussed previously. When implemented, this interface gives the application the ability to easily step through document nodes in the correct order.

Using the Xerces package, a class called NodeIteratorImpl is used to implement this interface:

```
NodeIteratorImpl myNodeIterator =
     (NodeIteratorImpl) myDocImpl.createNodeIterator
                                ( rootElem, 7, null, true );
```

This interface defines the following methods (beyond the common ones described above):

```
Node   nextNode() throws DOMException;
Node   previousNode() throws DOMException;
void   detach();
```

The **nextNode** method returns a reference to the next node in the document. When there are no more nodes in the document, it returns 'null'. This method is at the heart of the whole concept of tree-walking. The following example outputs the name of every node in the document:

```
Node nextNode = null;

do
{
  try
  {
    nextNode = myNodeIterator.nextNode();

    System.out.println( "Next Node: " +
                           nextNode.getNodeName() );
  }
  catch ( DOMException err ) { ... }
}
while ( nextNode != null );
```

The **previousNode** method returns a reference to the previous node, giving the application the opportunity to work backwards through the document.

While iterating through the document, there is always a 'current position', which is between two nodes. When one of the methods is called, the current position moves to the next gap between nodes in the relevant direction, and the method returns the node that is passed along the way:

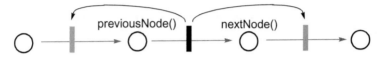

Before commencing iteration, the current position is before the first node. On completion, it follows the last node.

The **detach** method detaches the iterator from the document tree. Any attempt to use either the nextNode or previousNode method after this one causes an error.

Tree-walking

The **TreeWalker** interface is more sophisticated than the node iterator described above. While duplicating the ability of the more primitive interface, it also offers more features. This interface defines the following methods (beyond the common ones described above):

```
Node   nextNode();
Node   previousNode();
Node   getCurrentNode();
Node   setCurrentNode() throws DOMException;

Node   parentNode();
Node   nextSibling();
Node   previousSibling();
Node   firstChild();
Node   lastChild();
```

The **nextNode** method is probably the most significant one, and returns the next node in the tree. Nodes are returned in document order. However, it is also possible to re-trace the steps taken in reverse order by selecting the **previousNode** method. These two methods work in the same way as described for the methods with the same names in the NodeIterator interface, except that they never trigger an error. The other subtle difference is that there is always a 'current node'. The **getCurrentNode** method simply returns a reference to this node (should a reference to it be lost for any reason):

There is no current node before tree-walking commences, or after the last node is passed.

The remaining methods allow the application to interrupt the normal order of node processing by jumping up to the parent node (**parentNode**), the next or previous sibling (**nextSibling** and **previousSibling**), or to the first or last child of the current node (**firstChild** and **lastChild**). Alternatively, the **setCurrentNode** method selects the given node.

This interface is implemented by the Xerces **TreeWalkerImpl** class. The **createTreeWalker** method is then used to get a tree walker, passing to it first the root element node, then the value '7' (elements, attributes and text nodes only), indicating that all node types are to be included as steps through the tree. A NodeFilter object is not needed, so 'null' is passed as the third parameter. Finally, the boolean value 'true' indicates that entities are to be expanded (replaced):

```
import org.apache.xerces.dom.TreeWalkerImpl;

TreeWalkerImpl myTreeWalker =
        myDocImpl.createTreeWalker( rootElement, 7,
                                    null, true );
```

Filter interface

It has been shown how iterators and tree-walkers can be created that ignore nodes of certain types, and how the **NodeFilter** interface provides assistance through the use of a number of constants that represent the values of each type of node. But this interface is at the heart of a more powerful concept. Applications that implement this interface can define much more complex constraints on acceptable nodes. The class that implements this interface can be programmed in any way imaginable. For example, it could detect and reject all processing instructions with an application code of 'ACME', or all elements with the name 'Span' and a Style attribute value that contains the word 'color'.

This interface has a single method, called **acceptNode**, which the parser calls to ask the object whether the next node it would normally return to the application should be stepped over instead. The parser passes a reference to the node, and receives a value that indicates what it should do:

```
public short acceptNode(Node n);
```

The three possible return values are defined as follows:

```
public static final short FILTER_ACCEPT = 1;
public static final short FILTER_REJECT = 2;
public static final short FILTER_SKIP   = 3;
```

The class that implements this interface should return the value '1' (FILTER_ACCEPT) when it decides that the node is not to be ignored by the parser. The distinction between 'rejecting' (FILTER_REJECT) and 'skipping' (FILTER_SKIP) is subtle but important. When a node is rejected, its children and other descendants should all be ignored as well. When a node is skipped, however, its children and other descendants should still be visited (though they may also be individually rejected or skipped too).

The application passes this object to the iterator or tree-walker as the third parameter, and pass 'null' instead if there is no filter object.

Dynamic update effects

Both the node-iteration and the tree-walking techniques discussed above should continue to work correctly even if the document structure is changed while the iteration or tree-walking operation is still in progress.

A tree-walker always involves a current node. Whatever edits are made to the document, the tree-walker remains attached to the current node. The tree-walker continues to operate even if the current node is moved to a location outside the scope of the original root node of the subtree being traversed.

An iterator has a less solid foundation, being attached to no specific current node. Instead, the concept of a 'reference node' is introduced in the standard. This is generally the last node returned by this technique (the node the iterator passed over in the previous step). When starting a new iterator, the reference node is the first node in the sequence. The iterator is associated with the reference node during editing of the document structure, and remains in its current position relative to this node (before or after it). If the reference node is deleted, then a new reference node is chosen, and then the iterator becomes attached to the next node in the direction of the original reference node (backward or forward).

Ranges

Modern word processors allow a range of text to be selected by clicking the mouse at the start-point, and dragging across and down to the end-point, leaving the selected area highlighted to show its scope. After selection, the user can select 'delete' or 'copy' from a menu. This concept can also be applied to DOM trees. The new Ranges module of the DOM standard provides a standard way to define and modify a range of data that may include nodes of various types, including text and element nodes.

Parser support

The **hasFeature** method can be used to discover whether or not a parser supports this module:

```
if ( myDOM.hasFeature("Range", "2.0") == true )
{
    // Ranges are supported
}
```

Range scope

A range is defined by a start-point and an end-point. Each of these points is defined by a location that is given by the node containing it, to which is added a character offset value. However, each point lies between characters (just as an on-screen editor selection starts and ends between characters). Offset '0' is a position that precedes the first character. In the following example, the start-point is in the Paragraph element, at offset '2', and the end-point is in the same element node, at offset '7':

```
<para>A range in this paragraph.</para>

     start-point    end-point
```

Note that it is not possible for the start-point to appear later in the document than the end-point. If this is attempted, the start-point is brought back to the position of the end-point (so that the range does not enclose anything).

A range can include element nodes. Child elements are treated as equivalent to a single character when specifying the offset position. In the example below, the start-point is at position '2' and the end-point is at position '3':

```
A <emph>range</emph> in this paragraph.

start-point                 end-point
```

A range can also include part of an element. This concept breaks the usual rules of well-formed nesting, and causes a few complications when editing the range (these issues are discussed in detail later):

```
A <emph>range</emph> in this paragraph.

    start-point           end-point
```

In the example above, the start-point is in offset position '2' within the Emphasis element, and the end-point is in offset position '6' of the enclosing paragraph. The embedded Emphasis element is treated as a single character (a single node) in this respect.

Java package

The following package is used:

```
package org.w3c.dom.ranges;
```

This package defines two interfaces and a single class for handling errors.

DocumentRange interface

The **DocumentRange** interface defines a single method for passing to the application an object that implements the Range interface (see below).

```
public Range    createRange();
```

The returned object is a range that has a start-point and an end-point initially both situated at the start of the document. Methods in the Range interface (see below) permit the application to move these points to the desired locations:

```
myRange =   myDocumentRange.createRange();
```

Xerces implementation

The Xerces parser does not implement the DocumentRange interface. Instead, in a more direct way it includes a RangeImpl class that implements the Range interface (see below), and a new object of this type can be created and passed to the object that implements the DocumentImplementation object, so that the range can be attached to the specified XML document:

```
import org.apache.xerces.dom.RangeImpl;

DocumentType myDoctype = document.getDoctype();
DocumentImpl myDocImpl =
                    new DocumentImpl( myDoctype );

RangeImpl myRange = new RangeImpl( myDocImpl );
```

As stated above, the range is initially an insertion point at the start of the document. Methods for specify a more useful range within the document are discussed below.

Range interface

The **Range** interface defines methods for setting the start-point and end-point of the range, collapsing the range, discovering where the range is, comparing two ranges, copying the contents of the range, inserting new items into a range, deleting the contents of the range and finally copying the range details (not the contents of the range):

```
public void    selectNode(Node refNode)
                    throws RangeException, DOMException;
public void    selectNodeContents(Node refNode)
```

```
                          throws RangeException, DOMException;
public void     setStartBefore(Node refNode)
                          throws RangeException, DOMException;
public void     setEndBefore(Node refNode)
                          throws RangeException, DOMException;
public void     setStartAfter(Node refNode)
                          throws RangeException, DOMException;
public void     setEndAfter(Node refNode)
                          throws RangeException, DOMException;
public void     setStart(Node refNode, int offset)
                          throws RangeException, DOMException;
public void     setEnd(Node refNode, int offset)
                          throws RangeException, DOMException;

public void       collapse(boolean toStart)
                                       throws DOMException;
public boolean   getCollapsed() throws DOMException;

public Node       getStartContainer() throws DOMException;
public Node       getEndContainer() throws DOMException;
public Node       getCommonAncestorContainer()
                          throws DOMException;
public int        getStartOffset() throws DOMException;
public int        getEndOffset() throws DOMException;

public short    compareBoundaryPoints(short how,
                              Range sourceRange)
                          throws DOMException;

public DocumentFragment    extractContents()
                          throws DOMException;
public DocumentFragment    cloneContents()
                          throws DOMException;
public String toString() throws DOMException;

public void     insertNode(Node newNode)
                          throws DOMException, RangeException;
public void     surroundContents(Node newParent)
                          throws DOMException, RangeException;

public void     deleteContents() throws DOMException;

public Range    cloneRange() throws DOMException;
public void     detach() throws DOMException;
```

There are eight methods dedicated to setting the range. These are discussed first.

Set range to node

The **selectNode** method sets the points to each side of the node:

```
try
{
   myRange.selectNode( emphNode );
}
catch ( RangeException err ) {...}
catch ( DOMException err ) {...}
```

```
<para>A <emph>range</emph> in this paragraph.</para>
```

Set range to node contents

The **selectNodeContents** method sets the points to the contents of the node:

```
try
{
   myRange.selectNodeContents( emphNode );
}
catch ( RangeException err ) {...}
catch ( DOMException err ) {...}
```

```
<para>A <emph>range</emph> in this paragraph.</para>
```

Set range to node range

The **setStartBefore** and **setEndBefore** methods set the respective points immediately before the given node. Similarly, the **setStartAfter** and **setEndAfter** methods set the respective points immediately after the given node:

```
try
{
   myRange.setStartBefore( emph1Node );
   myRange.setEndAfter( emph2Node );
}
catch ( RangeException err ) {...}
catch ( DOMException err ) {...}
```

```
A <emph>range</emph> in <emph>this</emph> paragraph.
```

Set range to text

The **setStart** and **setEnd** methods set the start-point and end-point using a reference to the container node, and an offset position:

```
try
{
  myRange.setStart( paraNode, 2);
  myRange.setEnd( paraNode, 7);
}
catch ( RangeException err ) {...}
catch ( DOMException err ) {...}
```

```
<para>A range in this paragraph.</para>
       2   7
```

Collapse and test collapse

The **collapse** method collapses the area to a single insertion point at the start or end of the original area. The boolean value is 'true' to collapse to the start of the area (the start-point). It is 'false' to collapse to the end of the area (the end-point). At any time, it is also possible to check if the range is currently collapsed using the **getCollapsed** method, which returns 'true' if the start-point and end-point are at the same position:

```
try
{
  myRange.collapse( true );

  boolean isCollapsed myRange.getCollapsed();
  if ( isCollapsed == false )
              System.out.println( "Did NOT collapse"
}
catch ( DOMException err ) {...}
```

Accessing relevant nodes

The nodes that contains the start-point, end-point or the nearest common ancestor can all be accessed using the **getStartContainer**, **getEndContainer** and **getCommonAncestorContainer** methods:

```
try
{
  Node startNode = myRange.getStartContainer();
  Node endNode = myRange.getEndContainer();
  Node commonNode = myRange.getCommonAncestorContainer();
}
catch ( DOMException err ) {...}
```

Accessing offsets

Once the node containing a start-point or end-point has been accessed, it is also possible to discover exactly where in the node the point resides using the **getStartOffset** and **getEndOffset** methods:

```
try
{
  int startOffset = myRange.getStartOffset();
  int endOffset = myRange.getEndOffset();
}
catch ( DOMException err ) {...}
```

Comparing two ranges

When comparing two ranges, the following constants are useful:

```
try
{
  short start-to-start-compare =
    myRange.compareBoundaryPoints(1, otherRange);
}
catch ( DOMException err ) {...}
```

The first parameter must be a value between '0' and '3'. These values have the following significance:

```
public static final short START_TO_START = 0;
public static final short START_TO_END = 1;
public static final short END_TO_END = 2;
public static final short END_TO_START = 3;
```

The value '0' compares the start-points of the two ranges. The value '1' compares the start-point of the range with the end-point of the other range. The value '2' compares the end-points, and '3' compares the end-point of the range with the start-point of the other range. These constants can be used as follows:

```
... myRange.compareBoundaryPoints(Range.END_TO_END, ...);
```

The return value is either '-1' (the specified point in the range is before the given point in the other range), '0' (the points are in the same place in the document) or '1' (the point is after the given point in the other range).

Extracting range contents

One of the main reasons for creating a range is to extract the contents of the range. This is equivalent to a 'cut' or 'copy' operation when using a text editor or word processor. There are three methods that are used for this purpose. The **extractContents** performs a 'cut' operation. It removes the content of the range from the document, and returns it wrapped in a document fragment object. The **cloneContents** method performs a 'copy' operation. It leaves the original contents untouched, and returns a copy of all the nodes as a document fragment. The **toString** method also copies the range, but this time returns a simple string constructed from any text nodes in the range:

```
try
{
   DocumentFragment myExtract = myRange.extractContents();
   DocumentFragment myClone = myRange.cloneContents();
   String stringContent = myRange.toString();
}
catch ( DOMException err ) {...}
```

Insert node

Document editing could continue while a range is in effect, and it is conceivable that a new node may need to be added to the content of a range. The **insertNode** method inserts the given node into the range, putting it at the start:

```
try
{
   myNode.insertNode( newNode );
}
catch ( DOMException err ) {...}
catch ( RangeException err ) {...}
```

Surround contents

The **surroundContents** method essentially performs a 'cut and paste' operation, moving the selected contents from the current position into the given node (as its child or children):

```
try
{
   myNode.surroundContents( newParent );
}
catch ( DOMException err ) {...}
catch ( RangeException err ) {...}
```

Delete range

The **deleteContents** method is equivalent to a 'delete' operation in a word processor. The contents of the selected area are removed:

```
try
{
   myNode.deleteContents();
}
catch ( DOMException err ) {...}
```

The start-point and end-point are moved to the same place (between the two nodes at each side of the original range).

Cloning a range

Details of a range can be copied to a new Range object using the **cloneRange** method. This does not affect the XML document in any way:

```
try
{
  Range otherRange = myRange.cloneRange();
}
catch ( DOMException err ) {...}
```

Detaching a range

The range can be detached from the document using the **detach** method. All of the
methods above would return exceptions if there is any attempt to use them after the
range is detached:

```
try
{
  myRange.detach();
}
catch ( DOMException err ) {...}
```

RangeException class

The **RangeException** class is passed to the application by a number of the
methods described above, and extends the RuntimeException class. It contains the
following single method, which is used by the parser to set the error message and
error type code:

```
public RangeException(short code, String message);
```

The code is one of the following:

```
public static final short BAD_BOUNDARYPOINTS_ERR = 1;
public static final short INVALID_NODE_TYPE_ERR = 2;
```

22. Document formatting

This chapter introduces the concept of XML formatting for presentation and publication, and also acts as an introduction to the next three chapters. It covers typical simple and complex formatting requirements, differences between output media technologies, the use and scope of stylesheet languages, a standard for referencing such stylesheets, and describes a number of markup and stylesheet languages.

Presenting XML

The emphasis that the XML philosophy places on content rather than formatting makes it suitable for many diverse applications, including data interchange. But the absence of formatting information in this philosophy is an issue when an XML document is intended for human consumption. Consider the following example XML fragment; only an XML expert should ever see the tags in this sample (and, even then, perhaps only to correct an error in the tagging):

```
<title>An example of style</title>
<intro>This example shows how important style is
to material intended to be read.</intro>
<para>This is a <em>normal</em> paragraph.</para>
<warning><para>Styles are important!</para></warning>
```

To present this sample, it is clearly not sufficient to simply select a suitable font and remove the markup:

An example of style This example shows how important style is to material intended to be read. This is a normal paragraph. Styles are important!

Many techniques are typically employed to make the text interesting to read and to highlight significant components of the document. These include:

- the use of margins, borders and padding around text blocks
- varying the font used and the size of the text

- adding styles such as bold, italic and underline
- making use of colour and other effects
- including hyphenation and well-positioned page-breaks
- creation of navigation aids, such as content lists and indexes.

Of course, the degree to which these and other features are used varies, depending on the nature of the publication, from relatively dull academic textbooks, legal documents and maintenance manuals, to visually attractive brochures and magazines.

Style-oriented markup languages

A number of **markup languages** have been developed, over several decades, specifically for the purposes for formatting documents. Unlike XML, these languages focus entirely on the appearance of the text.

Historical markup languages

In almost all older languages, the syntax of the language, as well as the commands it contains, have been vendor- or product-specific. In the following example, embedded markup is used to specify the start of a paragraph, and make one word in the paragraph appear in bold style:

```
\par This paragraph has a \bf bold \rm word in it.
```

This paragraph has a **bold** word in it.

Some of these languages are discussed in more detail later.

XHTML

It was perhaps inevitable that the XML standard would be co-opted as the base syntax for at least one formatting-based markup language, despite the obvious objections to this breaking of XML principles.

Those familiar with **XHTML** (the XML-compliant version of HTML 4.0) will appreciate that this application of XML uses formatting-oriented tags, such as P (Paragraph) and B (Bold) (see Chapter 23). XHTML is not alone in this approach. First, there are many variants of XHTML targeted at specific output devices, such as mobile telephones and electronic books. The example above can be represented in XHTML as follows:

```
<h1>An example of style</h1>
<h2><i>This example shows how important style is
to material intended to be read.</i></h2>
<p>This is a <b>normal</b> paragraph.</p>
<p><b>Styles are important!</b></p>
```

XSL

In addition, **XSL** (*Extensible Stylesheet Language*) is a more sophisticated formatting application of XML, though it is far less friendly as an authoring language, and is really not intended to be used as such (see *The XSL Companion* (Addison Wesley, ISBN 0-201-67487-4) for details). The example above can be formatted using XSL as follows:

```
<block font-size="14pt">An example of style</block>
<block font-size="12pt"><inline font-style="italic">This
example shows how important style is to material
intended to be read.</inline></block>
<block font-size="9pt">This is a
<inline font-weight="bold">normal</inline>
paragraph.</block>
<block font-size="9pt"><inline font-weight="bold">Styles
are important!</inline></block>
```

Drawbacks

Attempting to solve the formatting issue by adopting either the XHTML or XSL DTD document model would, however, be a huge backward step in most circumstances. The reason for the development of XML (and its older brother, SGML) was precisely to overcome the limitations of this approach.

Formatting instructions

If formatting-based applications of XML are seen as a distraction at best, and a dangerous idea at worst, then there is obviously a need for a mechanism by which the components of any self-describing XML document can be given appropriate formatting characteristics when it needs to be presented.

Unfortunately, it is not possible to rely upon computer software to make meaningful formatting decisions, such as deciding that the content of a 'CompanyPresident' element should be presented in a bold typeface. Instead, such mappings between information units and presentation styles must be made using human judgement, and through the creation of pre-defined **formatting instructions**.

For example, the formatting instruction 'font-weight:bold' could be applied to any element that needs to be presented in bold style.

For each element type, the following decisions typically need to be made:

- should the content be visible?
- should the content have a distinctive appearance?
- should its appearance depend upon the context in which the element is used?
- does the content need to be relocated, or duplicated elsewhere?

The same questions can be asked again each time the material needs to be presented on a different medium such as CD-ROM or paper, or delivered to a different audience such as children, the visually impaired or academics.

Using formatting instructions, the XML fragment above could be presented in the following format:

An example of style

This example shows how important style is to material intended to be read.

This is a ***normal*** paragraph.

> **WARNING: Styles are important!**

Embedded styles

A formatting instruction can often be attached directly to the element it applies to, and attributes are generally used for this purpose. In XHTML, the Style attribute contains formatting instructions:

```
<p style="color:red">DANGER: This is an Inline style</p>
```

The primary benefit of this approach is that the document author has complete and direct control over the appearance of every element instance.

But this is really just a hybrid approach, mixing descriptive markup with formatting markup. As such, it still requires the document author to understand formatting instructions, and forces him to apply them to every element instance.

Stylesheets

There are a number of reasons why it is useful to be able to separate formatting instructions from the elements they apply to, including authoring efficiency, gaining the ability to reuse the styles, and the creation of smaller documents.

Remote formatting instructions

In order to remove formatting instructions from the elements they apply to, it is necessary to create a **formatting rule** to hold them, and to map the rule back to *all* the elements it applies to by reference instead. The following examples map a rule to all Paragraph element instances (using two of the standards discussed later):

```
para { font-size:10pt ; color:black }
```

```
<xsl:template match="para">
  <fo:block font-size="10pt" color="black">
    <xsl:apply-templates/>
  </fo:block>
</xsl:template>
```

The XML document is smaller when using this approach, because the instructions only appear once, instead of being repeated in every element they apply to. It is also easier to change a style because a single edit made to a rule affects all the element instances it references.

Stylesheets

When formatting instructions are separated from the document content, and are grouped together as a number of formatting rules, these rules are said to comprise the content of a **stylesheet**.

The one disadvantage of this approach is that it is harder to apply a specific style to a specific element instance. However, this can often still be achieved simply by giving the unusual element a unique identifier (in an appropriate attribute), then mapping the formatting rule to this identifier.

Multiple stylesheets

A great benefit of the stylesheet approach is that the same XML document can be associated with many stylesheets. For example, an emphasized word may be printed using an italic style on paper, but, due to the current limitations of computer displays, may be styled in bold or in red on screen:

```
<title>This is a Title</title>
<p>This paragraph contains
a <em>highlighted</em> term.</p>
```

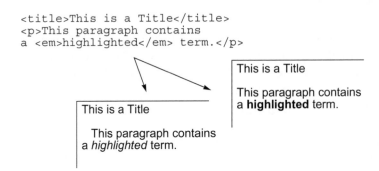

As another example, the visually impaired may require the document to be presented in larger type, or in Braille.

Embedded stylesheets

Depending on the technology used, it is sometimes possible for the stylesheet to be embedded within the document that it applies to. In an XHTML document, for example, a stylesheet is placed within the Style element:

```
<style>para { font-size:12pt ; color:black }</style>
```

An embedded stylesheet is naturally easy to manage. It is always available whenever it is needed. But this is not a practical approach when the document is likely to be styled in different ways for multiple purposes. Also, if many documents have identical stylesheets embedded within them, any change to the stylesheet specification requires modifications to be made to every document in the collection.

Stylesheet documents

The obvious way to support multiple output formats is to separate the stylesheet from the XML document. Another good reason for doing this is to allow the stylesheet to be associated with a number of XML documents. Edits made to the stylesheet are automatically applied to all the documents that reference it (the next time they are presented). In addition, document authors do not have to understand how to create formatting rules; professional stylesheet designers perform this task instead.

The link between the XML document and the stylesheet may be either implicit or explicit. An explicit link is created using a reference to the stylesheet in the document, as in the following example, which uses a processing instruction for this task:

```
<?xml-stylesheet href="mystyles.xsl" type="text/xsl" ?>
```

Transformations

Some rendering applications are able to accept an XML document and a stylesheet, and immediately present the content of the document using the formatting rules defined in the stylesheet. But many more formatting applications (mostly created before XML was invented) expect the input to be in a different markup language, of which the most well-known modern example is HTML.

Transformation stylesheets

In order to utilize the power of existing systems, some stylesheet languages focus on transforming XML documents into new documents that conform to the typesetting languages these systems can process.

Presently, such stylesheets are mostly used to convert XML documents into HTML documents, though alternatives such as WML, E-Book and XSL are quickly emerging, and it is possible to convert some documents into RTF (*Rich Text Format*), and older typesetting languages:

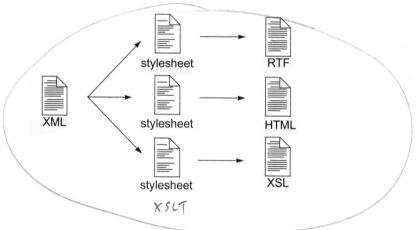

Non-formatting transformations

An interesting secondary benefit of the transformation approach is that the same technologies can be used to perform transformations that have nothing to do with creating a formatted document.

Stylesheets can be used to prepare documents for access by other software applications, and to convert XML documents into differently structured XML documents that conform to other document models:

This facility is particularly important when a number of organizations need to communicate similar or identical information, but use incompatible documents models.

DTD associations

Typically, a large number of XML documents are created to serve a particular purpose, and a DTD or schema is written to describe and control the model they should all adhere to. A stylesheet author may refer to the DTD or schema to discover which elements may occur, and the contexts within which they may be used, in order to ensure that the stylesheet to be created covers all legal document structure scenarios.

There is therefore a close relationship between the DTD and the completed stylesheet; they both apply to the same collection of related documents:

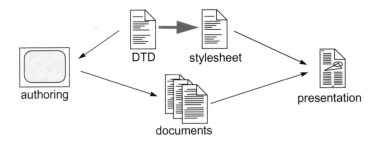

Stylesheet authors should understand enough about the nature, scope and syntax of the DTD or schema language used in order to be able to determine:

- which elements are allowed in the document (that may need to be formatted)
- which of these elements are optional (to avoid relying on their presence)
- the contexts within which these elements may be used (to detect contextual conflicts and context-specific formatting needs (see below))
- which attributes may affect formatting requirements.

Stylesheet features

Typically, stylesheets attempt to accomplish a number of tasks, including styling the text, adding template text, reordering and moving content, and styling text differently depending on the current context.

Style

The one thing that all stylesheets should be able to achieve is to apply stylistic information to the text of a document. This includes the shape of the characters (the font used), the size of the characters (the point size), style variants (including bold, italic and small caps), underlining and the use of colour.

In addition, they should be able to distinguish between **in-line styles** and **block styles**. An in-line object does not break the flow of words (the bold words in this paragraph are in-line styles). But when an element is identified as a block element, its contents are separate from surrounding blocks. Titles and paragraphs, for example, are separated from each other. Formatting instructions should be able to specify the size of the gaps between block objects, and perhaps allow border lines to be drawn around them.

Template text

When documents are encoded in XML, it is advisable to omit information that never varies. This can be described as 'template' text. For example, if every paragraph that would normally begin with the word 'CAUTION' is tagged using a Caution element, there is no need to include this word in the content of the element. Instead, it can be generated automatically when the Caution element is presented. This approach reduces the size of the document and the effort involved in data entry, but also gives the stylesheet developer more options. For example, in one rendition the word 'CAUTION' may be deemed redundant, because the warning text is to be presented in bold, italic lettering:

```
<caution>This is a caution</caution>
```

   This is a caution

In another rendition, the word may be added, and perhaps given a different style to the content:

   CAUTION: This is a caution

Whole document fragments may need to be inserted by the stylesheet, such as a standard preamble that describes the publishing organization. This also applies to header and footer text (such as 'The XML Companion' in this book).

Reordering and reusing

The order in which components of a document are to be presented may not always be the same as the order in which they were created. The needs of the ultimate readers of the document may be very different to those of the document authors and editors. In addition, information in documents aimed at different audiences may need to be omitted in some cases, or moved to a more (or less) prominent position in others. In the following example, the summary is moved to the top, and the secret paragraph is omitted from the presentation:

```
<para>This is the FIRST paragraph.</para>
<secret>Not everyone can read this.</secret>
<summary>This summary may appear first
in some cases.</summary>
```

> This summary may appear first in some cases.
> This is the FIRST paragraph.

When the XML philosophy has been rigorously applied, redundancy is avoided by omitting material that already appears elsewhere. Many stylesheet languages are able to copy information to other parts of the document presentation. For example, if a book review contains a number of keywords, marked up within the review text, it would be wasteful (and also error-prone) to repeat these keywords in a summary at the top:

```
<book>
   <review>This book covers <kw>XML</kw> and <kw>XSL</kw>,
   as well as the <kw>CSS</kw> styling language.</review>
   ...
</book>
```

> KEYWORDS: **XML**, **XSL**, **CSS**
>
> This book covers **XML** and **XSL**, as well as the **CSS** styling language.

The ability to reuse and sort information can also be very useful for building table of contents lists.

Context-specific formatting

The same element type may need to be presented in a number of different ways, depending on the location of each specific instance of that element within the document. For example, the content of a Paragraph element may need to be presented in larger text than normal if that instance of the element appears within an introduction section, or bolder if it occurs inside a Warning element. Most stylesheet languages can detect the current context and select the formatting that applies in that context.

However, conflicting context specifications may arise when the current element is deeper than two levels in the document hierarchy. For example, if there is a formatting rule for paragraphs in introductions, and another rule for paragraphs within Warning elements, then it is not clear what should happen when a paragraph appears in a Warning element that is inside an Introduction element:

```
<para>Normal paragraph. No context applies.</para>
<warning>
  <para>Paragraph in Warning.</para>
</warning>
<intro>
  <para>Paragraph in Introduction</para>
  <warning>
    <para>Paragraph in Warning and Introduction.</para>
  </warning>
</intro>
```

In order to avoid such conflicts, some rules need to be given a higher priority than others. Much of the effort and skill involved in developing stylesheets centres on ensuring that the correct rule is used in every circumstance.

Complex requirements

Stylesheet languages that deal only with straightforward textual concepts such as headers, paragraphs and lists can be complex enough, but long experience with SGML-based publishing systems has shown just how demanding the formatting task becomes when tables, graphics and mathematical formulae are also involved.

Tables

Tables are complex because they are divided into smaller components that do not follow a simple linear sequence; including rows, columns and cells. Rendering software needs to know which elements play specific roles in the structure of the table, and which attributes specify such things as column widths, text alignment within columns and individual cells, and cells that span across or down into adjacent cell spaces.

Due to the widespread need for tabular output, this problem was addressed very early in the history of both SGML and HTML. Indeed, the HTML table model is based on the *de facto* **CALS** standard developed initially for use with US Department of Defense documentation (and used to create the tables in this book). The XHTML DTD (described in Chapter 23) contains the XML-compatible version of the HTML table model:

```
<table>
  <tr><th>Header One</th><th>Header Two</th></tr>
  <tr><td>Cell One</td><td>Cell Two</td></tr>
</table>
```

Because XHTML is being adapted for various other uses, the model it contains is rapidly becoming the *de facto* XML table model, and it is well supported by authoring and publishing software.

Images

By their nature, many images cannot be easily represented by text-based languages such as XML. They are typically referenced from XML entities or by using URL references. However, the latest vector image format, called **SVG (*Standard Vector Graphics*)**, is an XML application. SVG commands can therefore easily be embedded in XML documents:

```
<figure>
  <title>A Circle</title>

  <svg:svg width="600" height="600"
           xmlns:svg="http://www.w3.org/2000/svg">
    <svg:circle cx="300" cy="400" r="50"
                style="fill:rgb(50%,75%,100%);
                       stroke:navy; stroke-width:2;
                       stroke-dasharray: 5 2" />
  </svg:svg>

</figure>
```

For more information on SVG see http://www.w3.org/Graphics/SVG/Overview.htm8.

Mathematical formulae

T$_E$X data has often been found embedded within SGML and XML documents, simply due to the lack of an agreed SGML or XML standard for mathematical formulae, and the lack of good rendering software for the many candidate standards that have arisen over time. This situation is now being rectified with the release of the widely supported **MathML** (now at version 2.0):

```
<reln>
  <eq/>
  <ci>A</ci>

  <matrix>
    <matrixrow>
      <ci>x</ci>
      <ci>y</ci>
    </matrixrow>
    <matrixrow>
      <ci>z</ci>
```

```
      <ci>w</ci>
    </matrixrow>
  </matrix>

</reln>
```

$$A = \begin{pmatrix} x & y \\ z & w \end{pmatrix}$$

It is noted in the standard that a priority in the design of MathML was the ability to convert T_EX mathematical input into MathML format.

For details see http://www.w3.org/Math/.

Arbitrary structures

Sometimes, established publishing practices involve structures that do not fall into any of the well defined categories described above. Consider the following example:

> XML is actually a combination and refinement of existing technologies and standards.
>
> The XML format is related to two previous standards: $\left\{ \begin{array}{l} \text{HTML} \\ \text{SGML} \end{array} \right.$

These effects are relatively easy to create when using DTP packages, but are much harder to reproduce with automated publishing tools. There are usually only two possible solutions: avoid the technique entirely and do something simpler, or use an image for the unusual structure. The first technique is always preferable, because it is more convenient to implement.

Document layout categories

A variety of technologies and techniques may be used to prepare, manage and publish material to paper. But most are only appropriate in specific circumstances, and the most significant factor that affects the choice of approach is the layout of the final document. The layout reveals underlying characteristics of the text itself, and documents can usually be classified as one of the following three types:

- designed
- templated
- structured.

It is necessary to understand what each of these terms means (but note that they are not used beyond this book), and what the technology implications are, especially in regard to the possible role of XML in the process.

Three categories

In a **designed document**, there is heavy emphasis on the layout of material on each page, and few if any pre-defined rules are detectable in respect to this layout. Human judgement is required to create the pages, and perhaps even to decide what material will fit on each page. Indeed, layout takes such precedence over content that text may be omitted or trimmed to make it fit a given space. In addition, the style of conceptually equivalent structures, such as article headers, may also differ in an apparently arbitrary fashion. Typical products of this type include leaflets, brochures and magazines. Many picture books and high-quality instruction books (such as cookery books) also fall into this category:

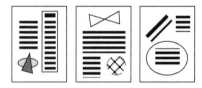

At the other extreme, a **templated document** is very strictly organized. Every page is almost exactly like every other page. Either each page is divided into pre-defined regions, each with a specific purpose, or the pages are composed of a simple series of blocks that are themselves so arranged. Typical products of this kind include directories and catalogues:

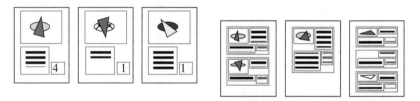

Somewhere between designed and templated documents there are **structured documents**. These documents have a narrative flow, often consisting of paragraphs, lists, tables and embedded images, and each construct has a pre-defined style (that could be defined in a stylesheet). Typical products include fiction and non-fiction books, including reference books (of which this book is an example), memos, reports and manuals:

Combinations

Note that in more complex cases, different sections of a document fall into different categories, though it is often possible to treat these sections as separate products in the production process, only bringing them together at the printing or binding stage.

XML for designed documents

XML is not the ideal storage format for designed documents. While it is theoretically possible for an XML document to carry the precise layout of each page, and the styling information of each component on the page, this is obviously not a key strength of XML.

Authors and document designers also need to work within an interactive environment, and these are already well provided by DTP packages. XML could play a role in supplying text for import into a DTP system. Traditionally, this role has often been played by low-cost word-processing packages.

But XML has an advantage if the text is not going to be edited in the DTP package. In this scenario, the XML document can also be used to provide alternative, simpler publishing outputs. It would be much harder to get clean, descriptive data out of DTP packages.

XML for templated documents

Template documents have long been published automatically, using **database publishing** techniques. The content is broken down into database records and fields. In simple cases, the form-printing features that many database vendors supply are adequate for the publishing task.

The roles that XML can play in this sphere are limited. It can be used to supply the raw data to the database, and to loosely connect the database to a remote typesetting system. XML would certainly make it easier to supply the data to multiple outputs, as a single database export is used, then the various outputs are created using XSLT.

While it would be possible to replace a traditional database technology with an XML database, these technologies are still considered by many to be more mature. Some would even argue that XML databases will never compete fully with database technologies that are highly tuned to the management of structured data.

XML for structured documents

SGML was invented for structured documents, and XML inherits its natural ability to handle such documents. XML can be used throughout the production process, from authoring to document management, and on to automated publication on any medium.

Publishing from XML

Publishers are increasingly viewing their narrative structured content as valuable assets that should be stored in an audience-neutral and publishing medium-neutral format. A flexible **content management system** holds these assets in XML format, and complementary formats (for images and database-held data), for delivery or publication in any required manner. Fragments from many XML documents can be extracted from such systems, assembled into a new document, and formatted in different ways for publication on paper, CD-ROM and over the Internet:

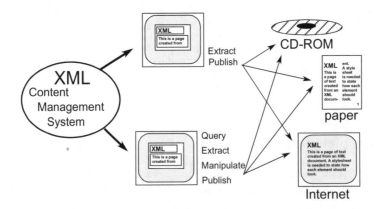

Yet each medium has its own demands, characteristics and quirks.

Publishing to CD-ROM

CD-ROM publishing was probably responsible, beyond all other factors, for the increasing popularity of SGML in the early 1990s. Many CD-ROM publishing products are SGML-based. Because XML is a subset of SGML, these products will accept XML documents. Often, the most significant task to perform is simply to merge large numbers of documents into a single 'import file'.

These packages usually support the ID/IDREF linking scheme, and the fact that documents are usually merged into a single large document makes these links more useful (because they do not work across multiple documents).

Publishing to the Web

Web publishing is really the simplest of the media types. Conversion of XML documents into HTML format is an almost trivial operation, often now undertaken using XSLT-based stylesheet processors. The most significant task is often the opposite to the one needed for CD-ROM publishing: a single XML document typically needs to be broken down into a number of Web pages. Unfortunately, XSLT version 1 is not capable of doing this, though the next version will be, and some vendors may have added this functionality in the form of extensions.

When images are initially prepared for paper publishing, an image transformation process is usually needed to downgrade images to GIF or JPEG formats, at resolutions suitable for on-screen presentation.

Printing to paper

Printing to paper has a long and complex history, and can be said to go back almost to the origins of writing itself. Over time it has developed and matured into an arcane and highly specialized craft. Expectations of quality are therefore very high, and for this reason automated typesetting (from XML or otherwise) is a particular challenge.

A number of steps are required to create printed publications from XML documents. Using a stylesheet, the XML data is first converted into a formatted representation.

The **pagination** process involves creation of multiple pages, with the text breaking over pages at appropriate points. A composition engine takes the page template (or templates), and flows the text into the regions it defines, to create the final pages. The exact content of each page may be affected by numerous factors, such as widow/orphan control (preventing a single line of a paragraph from appearing at the top or bottom of a page), keeping a heading on the same page as the following paragraph, repetition of the heading rows of large tables at the top of each page, and making room for footnotes. The final pages are held in a page description file format, such as **PostScript** or **PDF** (*Portable Document Format*). Finally, the page is printed using a **RIP** (*Raster Image Processor*), which renders the text and graphics at a resolution supported by the printing device:

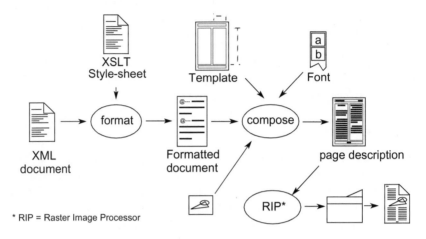

Increasingly, the same techniques are being used to generate PDF files instead of printed pages. These files can be made available for downloading from the Web (to be printed by end-users on personal printers).

Stylesheet languages

Some stylesheet languages described below are used to directly format the content. Others are really transformation languages that can be used to produce output in any of the formatting languages described in the next section.

DSSSL

The powerful **DSSSL** (*Document Style Semantics and Specification Language*) standard has been developed over many years for use with SGML. It was finally released as an ISO standard in 1996, but due to its complexity there is still little software support for it. Potential users of this sophisticated language have avoided it due to its complex syntax, which is derived from its origins as a Scheme-based language:

```
<para>This paragraph has a <emph>bold</emph> word in
it.</para>
```

```
(element para
  (make paragraph space-before: 12pt
                  font-size: 10pt
    (process-children-trim)
  )
)

(element emph
  (make sequence font-posture: 'bold
    (process-children-trim)
  )
)
```

CSS

The **CSS** (*Cascading StyleSheets*) language was developed in 1996 for use with HTML, in order to give document authors more control over presentation of Web documents (see Chapters 24 and 25 for details):

```
p { display: block ; margin-top: 12pt ; font-size:10pt }
...
<p>This paragraph has a <b style="color:red">bold</b> word
in it.</p>
```

CSS is a good styling language that has improved greatly in recent update releases, though the latest versions are still not well supported by software, and it is still a relatively weak formatting language beyond its core remit as a rendering technology for single page (scrollable) documents.

XSLT

XSLT largely replicates the transformation part of DSSSL (on which it is based), but adopts an XML syntax to utilize the many XML-based tools available for authoring, validating and presenting stylesheets.

It can be used for many purposes, such as converting XML documents into HTML or XHTML documents that could also contain in-line CSS styles, embedded CSS stylesheets, or externally referenced CSS stylesheets.

Interestingly, an XSLT stylesheet could even be developed to format and present any XSLT stylesheet (including itself).

Formatting languages

Some stylesheet languages (including XSLT) are really transformation languages that can be used to create output in a number of presentation formats, including the ones described below.

T$_E$X

T$_E$X is a very popular typesetting language (written by Donald E. Knuth):

```
\par This paragraph has a \bf bold \rm word in it.
```

Its particular strength is typesetting books and journals that contain mathematical formulae. See http://tug.ctan.org/tex-archive/info/gentle/gentle.pdf for an introduction to this language.

TROFF

The **TROFF** (*Text Run OFF*) language has long been a popular typesetting language on UNIX systems. Developed in 1973, it soon became a popular typesetter-independent text formatter. It has detailed page control, and sophisticated handling of typography:

```
.PP
This paragraph has a \fB bold \fR word in it.
```

See http://www.csc.liv.ac.uk/~ped/teachadmin/troff_intro.html for an introduction to this language.

RTF

A number of word processors and other packages can read and present material tagged in **RTF** (*Rich Text Format*). This format was developed by Microsoft. While very convenient as a desktop typesetting language, it is notoriously easy to create corrupted documents, and it is not easy to include images in the output:

```
\par\pard\plain\s1\fs18\sb160 This paragraph has
a \b bold \b0 word in it.
```

The latest version of this format (1.6) is described at http://msdn.microsoft.com/library/specs/rtfspec.htm.

HTML

Although the main purpose of **HTML** (*HyperText Markup Language*), developed in 1990, was originally to provide a system for creating hypertext links between documents, most of the markup defined by this language is actually used to format the document contents. The latest version of this language is XML-compatible, and is called **XHTML** (see Chapter 23):

```
<p>This paragraph has a <b>bold</b> word in it.</p>
```

For details see http://www.w3.org/MarkUp/.

XSL

XSL (*eXtensible Stylesheet language*) is the latest typesetting language to emerge, and uses XML as its underlying syntax. XSL is not intended as an authoring format (unlike HTML and XHTML), in part due to its complexity, but also because it deliberately and completely breaks the golden rule of XML documents: that they should not be focused on format (apart from the root element, all other elements and attributes are dedicated to formatting the content). At the moment, XSL documents are usually created as transformation output from other XML documents formats, typically using an XSLT stylesheet. In future, it may also become a standard export format from many DTP packages (from a menu option such as 'Save as XSL'):

```
<block>This paragraph has
a <inline font-weight="bold">bold</inline> word in
it.</block>
```

For details see http://www.w3.org/Style/XSL/.

XSL or CSS

XSL and CSS are often viewed as competing options, despite the fact that the first is a markup language and the second is a stylesheet language. However, neither is a transformation language, and XSLT or another transformation language is usually needed to create XSL documents.

Both XSL and CSS are strong candidates for styling XML documents, and at first sight they appear to compete with each other for dominance. But there is no reason why both standards should not continue to succeed, as they offer very different strengths.

Retaining self-descriptive markup

Because CSS is not a markup language, like HTML or XSL, using this standard does not involve the destruction of the self-describing markup in an XML document, and therefore permits intelligent document processing to occur *after* rendering. This is important because modern Web browsers are able to read XML documents into in-memory DOM tree structures (see Chapter 20), as well as apply CSS styles to display the document. Scripts can intelligently process the DOM tree after styling.

Scope and maturity

XSL attempts to do far more than CSS. It is the ideal language for formatting to paper output as it has features that control page flow and column flow, hyphenation and other features commonly found in professional paper-based output.

Conversely, CSS has been in existence far longer than XSL, and is well supported by popular Web browsers. It was initially used purely to enhance the formatting of HTML documents, but can now be equally well applied to XML documents.

Using XSLT and CSS together

CSS competes more with XSL than with XSLT. Indeed, CSS and XSLT complement each other very well, especially when the desired output format is HTML or XHMTL. XSLT can easily convert XML documents into HTML or XHTML documents that include CSS formatting instructions to improve the appearance of the resulting documents, and is equally adept at outputting in-line CSS styles, embedded stylesheets, or references to existing external CSS stylesheets.

Crossover concepts

The skills learned from using one language can be reused for using another, because XSL has adopted CSS property names and values for its attribute names and values. The colon and semicolon separators are simply replaced by an equals symbol and quotation marks around the value:

```
para { color:red }
```

```
<fo:block color="red">...</fo:block>
```

Standard stylesheet references

To ensure interoperability between all applications that can detect a reference to a stylesheet from within an XML document, a standard mechanism has been devised by the W3C. Version 1.0 of the '*Associating Style Sheets with XML documents*' standard was released in June 1999, and can be found at http://www.w3.org/TR/xml-stylesheet.

This approach uses a processing instruction with the target name '**xml-stylesheet**'. This processing instruction must occur before the root element:

```
<?xml-stylesheet ... ?>
```

Name and type

A number of parameters can be included, and each one resembles the format of an attribute appearing in a start-tag. The 'attribute' names, and the values each may take, are the same as those defined in the HTML and XHTML standards for true attributes of the Link element. The Href and Type parameters identify the stylesheet, and specify the kind of stylesheet it is by its MIME type:

```
<?xml-stylesheet href="mystyles.xsl" type="text/xsl" ?>
```

Multiple stylesheets

When a number of stylesheets are available, the processing instruction may be repeated. Each processing instruction should be given a suitable title so that a user can select the one they wish to apply (possibly from a menu). The default stylesheet should be easily identifiable, as all the others should include an Alternative pseudo-attribute with a value of 'yes':

```
<?xml-stylesheet  href="mystyles.xsl"
                  type="text/xsl"
                  title="default" ?>
<?xml-stylesheet  href="myBIGstyles.xsl"
                  type="text/xsl"
                  title="bigger font"
                  alternative="yes" ?>
```

Another reason for including multiple references is to associate the document with stylesheets conforming to various stylesheet languages, such as CSS and XSLT, so that a rendering engine can choose the one that it understands, or the one that it provides the most support for:

```
<?xml-stylesheet  href="mystyles.xsl"
                  type="text/xsl"
                  title="default" ?>
<?xml-stylesheet  href="mystyles.css"
                  type="text/css"
                  title="default" ?>
```

Implicit stylesheet references

A common approach to selecting a stylesheet is to simply state which stylesheet to use when it is needed. Many command-line or GUI-based tools allow a document to be formatted by specifying the source XML document, then the stylesheet to use, and finally the output file to be created. In the following example, the same XML document is formatted three times, to produce output suitable for different media:

```
>style  doc1.XML  paperOut.XSL  doc1.FO
>OK
>
>style  doc1.XML  webOut.XSL  doc1.HTM
>OK
>
>style  doc1.XML  wapOut.XSL  doc1.WML
>OK
```

In a professional publishing application, many XML documents conforming to the same DTD may be formatted together, in a 'batch process', with all the documents formatted using the same stylesheet.

The advantage of this approach over embedded references is that a single XML document may be formatted in many different ways, and it therefore makes no sense to specify within the document itself which stylesheet is to be applied to it. While a document may contain multiple stylesheet references, one of them needs to be chosen somehow. In addition, the document would need to be edited to add further references later as new output requirements are added. While this is not a problem for a single document, a large collection of documents could not be managed efficiently in this way.

The only disadvantages to implicit references are that the end-user has no choice in presentation, and an informed decision on which stylesheet to use must be made by software whenever the document is to be processed. However, the first problem can be overcome simply by making the output element contain references to appropriate 'secondary' stylesheets.

23. XHTML

Although this chapter describes XHTML, an application of XML that is being promoted as the successor to HTML 4.0, it can also be treated as a description of HTML 4.0 itself (with only minor differences). XHTML also serves as a template from which other, usually smaller, 'dialects' are defined (including WML and E-Book).

HTML

XHTML is derived from HTML, and it is useful to know some of the history of this language, in order to appreciate its current and possible future roles.

The concept of electronic links between documents stored on computer systems is an old one, and many **hypertext** systems have been developed, though most have been confined to linking texts stored on the same system, and have used proprietary technologies. It was only a matter of time before the Internet became an obvious candidate to support a hypertext system that spans systems and countries. With the infrastructure in place, it was only necessary to define two additional protocols: first, a new access protocol that would allow hypertext documents to be requested from a server (HTTP); and, second, a document markup language that would be used to both style the received document and locate and enable any embedded hypertext links. The **HTML** (*HyperText Markup Language*) protocol performs the second of these roles, and was devised in 1990.

Format not structure

The HTML markup language takes a position half-way between format and structure. It includes style tags, such as the Italic element, where the output format is explicitly stated, but it also includes generalized objects, such as the Emphasis element, where output format is left to the browser or to a stylesheet developer.

Linked pages

The core feature of HTML – the very reason for its existence – is its ability to let readers follow links to other HTML documents situated anywhere on the Internet (or local intranet). When a **URL** reference to another file is selected by the user, the browser extracts the reference and sends a further request to the server (or to another server) for another HTML document. Similarly, an HTML document may contain references to resources that conform to other data formats. In this way, image files and Java applets, amongst other objects, are downloaded to the browser and inserted into the presented version of the document.

HTML documents are also known as '**pages**'. The page first made available to users is known as the '**home page**', which usually has the default filename of 'index.html' (or 'index.htm').

HTML 4.0

HTML 4.0 is the latest version of HTML and was released in December 1997. It was released by the W3C in December 1997. Some of its features have long been available in at least one of the popular browsers. There is an SGML DTD for this standard (http://www.w3.org/TR/REC-html40/).

It is not possible for HTML 4.0 to be considered an application of XML as it cannot be accurately described by an XML DTD. It uses advanced features of SGML, such as element and attribute minimization, and adopts SGML conventions for representation of empty elements (see Chapter 32). A new standard was required to create an XML-compatible variant of HTML, and XHTML is the resulting XML variant of HTML 4.0.

Change of syntax

While based on HMTL, XHTML conforms to the XML standard. This requirement affects some of the markup conventions used.

Lower-case names

Element and attribute names are case-sensitive in XML, and for XHTML it was decided to use lower-case letters for all elements and attributes. In HTML it is possible to use 'meta', 'Meta' or 'META' (or any other combination) for the Meta element, but it must be 'meta' in XHTML.

Empty elements

All empty elements must end with '/>', and for compatibility with older Web browsers, it is recommended that there is a preceding space ('<... />'):

```
<area .../>
<base ... />
<basefont ... />
<br ... />
<col ... />
<frame ... />
<hr ... />
<img ... />
<isindex ... />
<link ... />
<meta ... />
<param ... />
```

Attribute minimization

Attributes must not be minimized. It is not permissible to omit the attribute name, or the quotation marks around the attribute value. Consider the following HTML example:

```
<INPUT TYPE=RADIO NAME=VEHICLE VALUE=CAR CHECKED>
  ...
</INPUT>
```

Quotation marks are required around all the values. In addition, terms like 'checked' have to be considered to be attribute values that belong to an attribute with the same name:

```
<input type="radio" name="vehicle" value="car"
       checked="checked">
  ...
</input>
```

Backward compatibility

It is very important that existing HTML-based Web browsers are able to process and present XHTML documents, and this can only be achieved by making an XHTML document pretend to be an HTML document. This requires a number of compromises to be made.

The first compromise made is in the standard itself. The root element is named 'html', not 'xhtml', for this reason.

Document authors or XHTML authoring tools need to ensure that there is a space before the '/>' markup in an empty element, as in '<br />'. Browsers will then ignore the '/' symbol.

Note that the lack of minimization features is irrelevant to this requirement, as browsers have always been able to accept non-minimized element and attribute markup.

Flavours of XHTML

The XHTML standard is defined by three different DTDs. One DTD defines the strict XHTML core standard. There is also a 'transitional' DTD that is closer to the current HTML standard, and should be phased out over time. Finally, the third DTD covers frame features. Frame-building elements are treated separately because frames are used to create the infrastructure of a Web site, rather than a document.

Identifying XHTML documents

The three parts or versions of XHTML must include a DOCTYPE declaration, with a public identifier that matches one of the following strings:

```
-//W3C//DTD XHTML 1.0 Strict//EN
-//W3C//DTD XHTML 1.0 Transitional//EN
-//W3C//DTD XHTML 1.0 Frameset//EN
```

A system identifier is still needed to reference the DTD. By default, these DTDs have names that reflect the three variants:

```
xhtml1-strict.dtd
xhtml1-transitional.dtd
xhtml1-frameset.dtd
```

For example:

```
<!DOCTYPE PUBLIC "-//W3C//DTD XHTML 1.0 Strict//EN"
               "xhtml1-strict.dtd" >
```

Note that the rest of this chapter discusses the strict version of XHTML, so omits material from HTML 4.0 that does not conform to this model, and focuses on document structures and formatting, rather than Web site construction (the 'frames' feature).

Example

The following is a complete, valid XHTML document:

```
<!DOCTYPE PUBLIC "-//W3C//DTD XHTML 1.0 Strict//EN"
                 "xhtml1-strict.dtd" >
<html>
   <head><title>STRICT DOCUMENT</title></head>
   <body><p>STRICT</p></body>
</html>
```

Basic document structure

An XHTML-conforming document has a document element called **Html**:

```
<html>...</html>
```

This element has a fixed attribute value, giving the default namespace the value 'http://www.w3.org/1999/xhtml'.

The Html element encloses a **Head** element and a main **Body** element. Both are required. The header must contain a **Title** element, which is presented in the title bar of the browser. The Body element may contain any of a number of other elements but will often begin with the title repeated in a first-level-header element, **H1**. An **Address** element encloses details of the author of the document, and may be inserted at the end of the document, where it is displayed in italic, possibly indented or centred:

```
<html>
   <head>
      <title>A Description of XHTML</title>
   </head>
   <body>
      <h1>This is XHTML</h1>
      ......
      <address>Neil Bradley
      (http://neil@bradley.co.uk)</address>
   </body>
</html>
```

The Head element holds the language identifier attributes described below, and in addition the **Profile** attribute, which is a URL that locates a document that (in human or machine-readable form) defines the meaning of link relationships (see the Meta, Link and Anchor element descriptions below).

Header elements

The following elements are used in the header section of an XHTML document. To these elements can be added the Object element, which is also used in the body of a document, and is described later.

Meta tags

The empty **Meta** element is of most interest to those involved in browser/server communication. The **Name** attribute provides the name of the meta-information (almost an attribute name in itself), and the **Content** attribute provides the current value for the named item. For example:

```
<meta name="Index"  content="cycle" />
```

This could be considered equivalent to an XML attribute such as 'Index="cycle"'. If more than one Meta element is present with the same Name attribute value, the various content values are accumulated into a comma-separated list, for example 'cycle, bus, car'.

The third attribute, **HTTP-Equiv**, allows the content to be inserted into an **HTTP** header field.

The **Scheme** attribute may be used to indicate what standard scheme the value adheres to. For example, the scheme might be 'isbn' if the value is an ISBN (an International Standard Book Number).

Linked resources

The **Link** element identifies other resources that are connected to this document, such as a stylesheet. To identify the resource, it has an **Href** attribute, and a **Type** attribute to identify the language used. The **Title** attribute holds a brief description of the resource:

```
<link title="big print" href="bigprint.css"
      type="text/css" />
```

Note that this usage is equivalent to the xml-stylesheet processing instruction, and should only be used for backward compatibility with HTML. A number of attribute may be present. The **Media** attribute is used when the link is to a stylesheet, and has values such as 'screen' and 'print' that specify when the stylesheet should be applied. The **Href Language (Hreflang)** attribute holds a language code conforming to the RFC 1766 specification (see the ISO 639 language codes table in Chapter 33). The **Charset** attribute explains which character set the document conforms to, as defined in RFC 2045.

Styles

The **Style** element encloses stylesheet instructions. The required **Type** attribute identifies the stylesheet language, such as 'text/css' or 'text/xsl'. The **Media** attribute identifies the type of media the stylesheet is aimed at, such as 'screen' (the default) or 'paper'. A **Title** attribute is also allowed to identify the stylesheet:

```
<style type="text/css" media="screen">
  p { color: green }
</style>
```

The XML Space attribute is also used, and fixed in the DTD to the value 'preserve', to prevent the stylesheet instructions from being reformatted (and possibly merged).

Scripts

The **Script** element is used to enclose or reference software scripts. A CDATA section is often required to allow significant characters such as '<' and '&' to appear in the script without escaping them.

The required **Type** attribute describes the scripting language used, such as 'text/javascript'. The **Src** attribute identifies a remote file containing the scripts, using a URL. When Src is used, the **Charset** attribute may also be used to identify the character set used in the file that contains the scripts. The **Defer** attribute takes a single possible value of 'defer' to indicate, when present, that the browser should defer executing the script (this is a hint that the script does not alter the document in any way, so the browser can go ahead and render the document). The XML Space attribute is also used, and fixed in the DTD to the value 'preserve', to prevent the scripts from being reformatted.

The **NoScript** element has been included to hold alternative information in case the browser is configured to prevent scripts from running or is not familiar with the scripting language used. Despite appearing in the header section of the document, it holds the block-level body elements described below to format the content.

Base URL locations

When relative paths are included in the URL, the starting point is normally the address of the page containing the link. The optional **Base** element is used to provide a new fixed point in the directory structure from which relative links should be calculated. It uses an **Href** attribute to specify the replacement path. Note that this element provides the same functionality as the new XML Base standard (see Chapter 11).

Paragraphs

Except in one special circumstance, a browser will not obey any line breaks in the ASCII text file that contains the XHTML document, but will instead reformat the text to break at the right-hand margin of the window (or sub-region of the window) in which it is being presented.

The most essential element is the **Paragraph** element (**P**), which defines a single paragraph in the text. The browser begins a new paragraph on a new line and creates gaps between paragraphs:

```
<p>This is a paragraph.</p>
<p>This is another paragraph.</p>
```

With the advent of CSS and some of the common attributes described later, it is possible to use this one tag for almost all block-level formatting, though a number of other tags were defined in early versions of HTML and are still widely used for identifying headings, lists and other structures.

Basic hypertext links

Without the concept of links in and between documents, the HTML language (and now the XHTML language) would not have been invented. The need for markup to identify the source and target of a link preceded the need for other markup to structure and format the text around this markup.

Anchors

The **Anchor** element (**A**) is used to locate both the source and target ends of a hypertext link. When used as a target element, the Anchor element usually contains the title of the referenced text (in order that it may be highlighted on completion of a link to that item). The **Name** attribute provides a unique identifier for the element:

```
<p><a name="details">The Details</a> are
here. ...</p>
```

When used as a source element, the Anchor contains a **Hypertext Reference** attribute (**Href**) which contains a **URL** reference:

```
<p>See <a href="#details">the details</a> for
the details</p>
```

A single Anchor may be both the source of a link and the target of a link:

```
<a name="summary" href="#details">See details</a>
```

When inserting links to other documents, the target document does not require an Anchor element, because the entire file is the target. However, it is possible to link to an anchored item in the other file by appending the hash symbol and item name:

```
<a href="../myfiles/detail.htm#part3">See
details, part 3</a>
```

A **Title** attribute can be used to hold a brief description of the target resource, to be displayed by the browser when the mouse is over the link.

Relationship indicators

The Anchor and Link elements may contain a **Relationship** (**Rel**) attribute, which identifies the relationship between the target object and the current page. The **Reverse Relationship** (**Rev**) attribute identifies the previous relationship when the link forms part of a chain. A browser could (in theory) style these links differently from others to indicate to the user that there is a preferred path to follow. These attributes are not widely used, but may be useful to Web search engines:

```
... go <a rel="historical perspective"
         href="history.xhtml">here</a> for more
details...
```

The **Type** attribute specifies the kind of link, such as a link to a table of contents, 'toc', though few types are well known and agreed.

As above, the **Hreflang** attribute identifies the language used in the resource, and the **Charset** attribute identifies the character set used.

Core attributes

Some useful attributes are available to almost every XHTML element. The most ubiquitous are four core attributes: **Style, Class, Title** and **Id**. However, none of these attributes are required to be present in any particular element. There are few elements that cannot use them, but they include the structural tags (Html, Head and Title), background scripts (Script, Style and Area), applet tags (Applet and Param) and meta-data (Base, Basefont and Meta).

Style

The **Style** attribute allows **CSS** in-line styles to be applied (see Chapters 24 and 25). These in-line styles consist of CSS properties and values, separated by semicolons:

```
<p style="color: yellow ; background-color: black">
This paragraph will be styled in yellow on a black
background.</p>
```

Note that this very flexible feature replaces many specific attributes that would otherwise have been inherited from HTML 4.0.

Element classes

The **Class** attribute adds a measure of the generalized markup concept to XHTML by allowing category names to be added to element instances. For example, some Paragraph elements may be more important than others:

```
<p>This is a normal paragraph.</p>
<p class="important">This is an IMPORTANT paragraph.</p>
<p>This is another normal paragraph.</p>
```

The most common use of this feature is to create categories of paragraph that are styled differently by a stylesheet, as in the following CSS example:

```
p:{ color: black ; font-size: 10pt }
p:important{ color: red ; font-size: 14pt }
```

Element identifiers

The **Identifier** (**Id**) attribute gives the element a unique name that may be used for various purposes, such as to provide a target for a hypertext link, to allow a style defined in a separate stylesheet to be applied to a specific element (as an alternative to using the Class attribute), or to be manipulated in a specific way by an ECMAScript procedure.

The following paragraph is given a red colour by the stylesheet and is also the target of a link:

```
p:#Scarborough { color: red }
. . .
<p id="Scarborough">This is a paragraph about
Scarborough, a seaside resort in the north of
England.</p>
. . .
... See <a href="#Scarborough">Scarborough</a>...
```

This technique is familiar to XML users and is certainly a less clumsy way to identify the target of a link than wrapping the paragraph text within an Anchor element (using the Name attribute to identify it). However, some of the currently popular browsers do not yet support this feature.

Element titles

The **Title** attribute allows a brief description of the content of the element to be included. Normally not visible, this text would only be revealed on user request. It could be used to build a simple table of contents, and it may be presented in the status bar:

```
<p title="XHTML document">This is a paragraph about
XHTML documents.</p>
```

International attributes

The following attributes are used on the same elements as the core attributes, with the exception of Bdo and Break Line, but in addition are used in the Html, Head, Title, Meta, Style and Map elements.

Language

The **Language (Lang)** attribute describes the human language used for the textual content of the element. It is included for backward compatibility with HTML:

```
<p lang="EN">This is an English paragraph.</p>
```

The XML equivalent attribute, **XML Lang**, should be used instead:

```
<p xml:lang="EN">This is an English paragraph.</p>
```

Direction

The **Direction (Dir)** attribute describes the direction of writing that is conventional for the human language concerned. It takes a value of 'ltr' (left to right) or 'rtl' (right to left):

```
<p lang="EN" dir="ltr">This is an English
paragraph read from left to right.</p>
```

Headers and divisions

Long texts are usually divided into smaller parts, such as chapters or sections, each having their own title.

Headers

Headers can be used to create crude section and sub-section divisions in the document. The heading elements, **H1** to **H6**, hold title text with varying degrees of highlighting. H1 is the most important, and is typically used only for the title of the document. At the other extreme, H6 is the least important header, and should only be used when six levels of heading are necessary.

Although no specific formatting style is indicated, typically the header elements are all displayed in bold typeface and the point size of the text varies, increasing with the level of importance:

```
<h1>The Document Title</h1>
<h2>A Section Title</h2>
<h3>A sub-section title</h3>
```

All the core attributes are allowed in these elements.

Divisions

The **Division** element (**Div**) surrounds any group of block-level elements that require specific formatting. The real power of this element becomes apparent when the Style or Class attribute is applied to it:

```
<div style="color: red">
  <h1>A red heading</h1>
  <p>A red paragraph.</p>
</div>
```

Horizontal rules

The **Horizontal Rule (Hr)** element draws a line across the screen. It is an empty element that can be used to highlight divisions of a large document:

```
<p>The next para is in another section</p>
<hr />
<p>New section of the document</p>
```

All the standard attributes may be used, including the Style attribute.

Lists

XHTML supports various types of list structure. In all cases, an element that expresses the type of list is used to enclose a number of other elements, each representing one item in the list.

Unordered and ordered lists

The most basic type of list is the **Unordered List (Ul)**. An unordered list is used when the items do not form a logical sequence of steps, and do not need to be separately referenced from elsewhere in the document. It contains a number of **List Item (Li)** elements. Each of these contains text, and is automatically preceded by a bullet, dash or other symbol:

```
<ul>
  <li>First Item</li>
  <li>Second Item</li>
  <li>Third Item</li>
</ul>
```

- First Item
- Second Item
- Third Item

The **Ordered List (Ol)** element is similar to the unordered list, but each item is preceded by a sequential, automatically generated number. It is used in preference to the Unordered List element when the items describe a series of steps, or are referred to individually elsewhere:

```
<ol>
  <li>Step 1</li>
  <li>Step 2</li>
  <li>Step 3 - Go To Step 1</li>
</ol>
```

1. Step 1
2. Step 2
3. Step 3 - Go To Step 1

Definition lists

Some lists consist of a keyword or term, followed by an explanation of that keyword or term. The **Definition List (Dl)** element contains a number of items (but *not* Item elements), each one consisting of two parts, a **Definition Term (Dt)** element and a **Definition Description (Dd)** element:

```
<dl>
  <dt>HTML</dt><dd>HyperText Markup Language</dd>
  <dt>DTD</dt><dd>Document Type Definition</dd>
  <dt>XML</dt><dd>Extensible Markup Language</dd>
</dl>
```

HTML   HyperText Markup Language
DTD   Document Type Definition
XML   Extensible Markup Language

The Definition Term element is restricted to straight text and in-line elements, but text blocks, such as paragraphs, are allowed in the Definition Description element.

Font styles and phrases

A number of XHTML elements are used to format the content of text blocks.

Styles

The **Bold (B)** element specifies a bold typeface, and the **Italic (I)** element specifies an italic typeface. They may be nested to create combination styles:

```
<P>This paragraph contains <B>bold</B>,
<I>italic</I> and <B><I>bold/italic</I></B> text.</P>
```

This paragraph contains **bold**, *italic* and ***bold/italic*** text.

The **Teletype (Tt)** element specifies a monospaced font, such as Courier.

The **Big** and **Small** elements are complementary. They specify larger and smaller text respectively, but the actual size is determined by the browser.

Phrase styles

The **Abbreviation (Abbr)** element is used to identify an abbreviation in the text:

```
The term <abbr>Web</abbr> is used as an abbreviation
for 'World Wide Web'.
```

Similarly, the **Acronym** element holds a form of abbreviation that substitutes each word in a name with one letter:

```
... the <acronym >XML</acronym> language ...
```

The element **Strong** normally maps to a bold typeface and **Emphasis** (**Em**) to an italic typeface. The computer sample elements **Code** and **Var**, as well as the **Keyboard** (**Kbd**) element, normally map to a monospaced font. The **Sample** (**Samp**) element and **Citation** (**Cite**) element may both map to italic typefaces:

```
<p><em>Emphasized text</em>.
<strong>Strong text</strong>.
<code>Computer text</code>.
<kbd>Keyboard text</kbd>.
<var>Variable text</var>.
<samp>Sample text</samp>.
<cite>Citation text</cite>.</p>
```

Emphasized text. **Strong text**. `Computer text.`
`Keyboard text.` `Variable text.`
Sample text. Citation text.

The **Defining Instance** (**Dfn**) element encloses the first or most significant occurrence of a term used in the text. Potentially, this element may be used by search engines to determine keywords, and by stylesheets to highlight new terms as they are introduced:

```
... Although <dfn>XML</dfn> is related
to <dfn>SGML</dfn>, XML is also related
to <dfn>HTML</dfn> as HTML is an application
of SGML.
```

The **Subscript** (**Sub**) and **Superscript** (**Sup**) elements are complementary. The first encloses small text that appears below the baseline and the second encloses small text that appears above the baseline:

```
Water is just H<sub>2</sub>O, but is very powerful
when you consider that E = mc<sup>2</sup>.
```

Water is just H_2O, but is very powerful when you consider that $E = mc^2$.

Formatted text

It is sometimes important to be able to control the way in which the browser formats a block of text into individual lines.

Line breaks

The **Break Line** (**Br**) element forces following text to be placed on a new line. This is very useful for semi-formatted text, such as lines of poetry or computer code. It is an empty element:

```
<p>Break this line here <br />so this is line 2.</p>
```

The element can only hold the four core attributes (not the language or event attributes).

Pre-formatted text

The **Preformatted** (**Pre**) element composes its content in a monospaced font. All spaces and line-feed characters in the document are retained, making it possible to use these characters to create simple character-based diagrams or columns of text. If vertical alignment is important, the document author must use a monospaced font to ensure that the alignment is correct:

```
<pre>
Here is a face:    ---
                  /   \
                 [ o o ]
                  \ - /
                   ---
</pre>
```

The XML Space attribute is fixed in the DTD at the value 'preserve', to save document authors from having to specify this behaviour.

Apart from text, the content of this element is restricted to the Author, Break Line, Span, Bdo, Map, Teletype, Italic and Bold elements.

Images and image zones

Documents that consist entirely of text tend to be quite dull. Images add interest, and in some cases are truly 'worth a thousand words'.

Image references

The **Image** (**Img**) element identifies an image file, the content of which is to appear at the current location. This is an empty element. The **Source** (**Src**) attribute specifies the name and location of the image file using a URL reference (see Chapter 30):

```
...there is a GIF file <img src="myimage.gif" /> here.
```

This element takes additional attributes to specify the **Width** and **Height** of the image. By telling the browser the dimensions of the image, it can speed up presentation of the document because the rest of the page can be built before the image is downloaded:

```
<img ... width="5in" height="3in" />
```

Alternative text

Since some browsers are not able to display images, or can be configured for the visually impaired, an **Alternative** (**Alt**) attribute may be used to display alternative text. The second example below demonstrates its use:

```
...there is a GIF file
<img src="myimage.gif" alt="no picture" /> here.
```

```
                              --------
                       |              |
    ...there is a GIF file  --------   here.
```

```
    ...there is a GIF file [no picture] here.
```

Long description

The **Longdesc** attribute contains a URL link to a description (probably an XHTML page) of the image (and is usually longer than the content of an Alternative attribute). When the image has a server-sided image map, this description may explain what each of the regions are, and where they are in the image.

CGI image maps

It is possible to attach links to parts of an image. This is called an image map. For example, a map of the world could be linked to other XHTML documents that describe characteristics of each country. The source of the link is therefore defined as a specified area within the image.

In the well-supported concept of a 'server-sided' image map, the browser simply passes the coordinates of the mouse-click to the Web server, which calls a script that decides, depending on the coordinate values, which XHTML document to return to the browser. The Image element takes an additional attribute, **Ismap**, to indicate this requirement to the browser. This implied attribute has a single legal value of 'ismap':

```
<img src="myimage.gif" ismap="ismap" />
```

However, the Web server must also be told which script to activate when the mouse is clicked on this image. To do this, the Image element is enclosed in an Anchor element which uses a URL to locate the appropriate script:

```
<a href="/cgi-bin/imagemap/my.map">
  <img src="myimage.gif" ismap="ismap" />
</a>
```

This scheme relies upon the use of the HTTP protocol, a Web server and CGI scripts. It is not particularly suitable for simple intranet solutions or for publishing XHTML files on a CD-ROM.

Client-sided image maps

The concept of 'client-side' image maps overcomes the limitations of server-side image maps outlined above. The browser uses XHTML tags to identify image areas and associated URLs to other documents or to another part of the same document. This approach provides the benefits of less interaction with the server (making the process more efficient) and independence from the HTTP protocol (making it suitable for simple intranet use, when a Web server may not be needed), as well as giving prior warning of the effect of clicking on any part of the image (the target URL may be displayed as the pointer is moved over the image). The **Usemap** attribute is added to the Image element and holds the identifier of a **Map** element that defines areas within the image:

```
<img src="/images/myimage.gif" usemap="#mymap" />

<map name="mymap"> ..... </map>
```

The Map element has the usual core attributes, but the Id attribute is required instead of optional. It is not clear why this decision was made, because it is the Name attribute that holds the target value (for backward compatibility with HTML).

Within the Map element, each area is defined using an **Area** element. This element contains attributes to define the shape and coordinates of the area, and the URL associated with the area. The **Coordinates** (**Coords**) attribute defines the coordinates of the area and the **Href** attribute provides the URL. The **Alt** attribute contains a textual equivalent to the area, to be used by applications that cannot support this feature. The **Nohref** attribute indicates that this area is not active, and it has a single possible value of 'nohref'.

Consider an example of an image showing a new model of motor car. Each area of interest, such as the wheels or the engine, could be located and attached to an appropriate XHTML document:

```
<map name="mymap">
    <area coords="150 200 150 250"
          href="wheels/back.xhtml"
          alt="Back Wheels" />
    <area shape="circle"
          coords="350 200 50"
          href="wheels/front.xhtml"
          alt="Front Wheels" />
</map>
```

The default shape is a rectangle, with four coordinates representing in pixels the left edge, top edge, right edge and bottom edge of the area. The first example above defines an area for the back wheel – '50' pixels in, '150' pixels down for the left and top edges, and (as the diameter of the wheel is 100 pixels), '150' in and '250' down for the right and bottom edges. The optional **Shape** attribute may be used to make this area type explicit, 'shape="rect"'. Another shape option is 'circle', which requires three values; the horizontal and vertical coordinates for the centre of the circle, followed by the radius. The second example defines the area of the front wheel as a circle with a radius of '50' pixels, '350' pixels across and '200' down.

Using both mapping features

Backward compatibility can be provided for the benefit of browsers unable to use client-sided image maps. Both schemes for creating image maps can coexist by including both the Ismap attribute and the Usemap attribute in the same Img element. In the example below, a browser that does not support a client-side map scheme uses the Anchor to pass coordinates to 'myscript.cgi':

```
<a href="myscript.cgi">
   <img src="/images/myimage.gif" usemap="#mymap" ismap />
</a>

<map name="mymap">
  <!-- image mapping commands -->
  ...
</map>
```

Objects

The Image element is a historical relic from early versions of HTML. Today, images are only one of many forms of 'foreign' object that may be embedded in an XHTML document. Other options include sound and video clips, and program code (such as Java applets).

Object element

The **Object** element supersedes and extends the Image element. As its name implies, this element represents any 'foreign' object in an XHTML document, of which images are only one category. The **Data** attribute is a URL reference to the data to be loaded. The **Type** attribute is the MIME type of the data:

```
<object data="boat.gif" type="image/gif" ... />
```

```
<object data="bobbing_boat.mov"
        type="application/quicktime" ... />
```

Just as for images, an object can be given an area to work within using the **Height** and **Width** attributes. Also, the **Usemap** attribute may be used to make areas of the object act as hypertext links.

The **Standby** attribute holds text that is to be displayed until the object has been loaded.

Some additional attributes are intended for applications of the Object element that involve its use in loading software. When the object is a program, it may rely upon software libraries, possibly stored in archive files. A list of URL references to these archives can be supplied in the **Archive** attribute. Instead of the Data attribute, the **Classid** attribute may be used to identify the program to run. The **Codetype** attribute can be used in combination with this attribute to identify the data type, so that the browser can decide whether to download the object or not. Finally, it is possible to prevent immediate loading by including the **Declare** attribute, with its single possible value of 'declare'. A declared object is only loaded if it is referenced by another (loaded) object.

URLs provided in the Data and Classid attributes may be relative URLs, in which case the base location may need to be provided. This is done using the **Codebase** attribute.

The Object element can contain other elements. Browsers that do not understand the Object element should process the embedded elements (perhaps just an Image element). Browsers that do understand the Object element should ignore the embedded elements, and obey the Object element instead. When there is any doubt that a rendering engine could cope with a particular object type, it is also possible to put one object of a more generic type within another, more specific type. The first object that can be processed is used, and any embedded ones are ignored:

```
<object data="bobbing_boat.mov"
        type="application/quicktime" ... >
  <object data="boat.gif" type="image/gif" ... />
</object>
```

Parameters

The **Parameter** element, (**Param**), may be embedded within the Object element, and is used to pass parameters to a program launched by this object. There may be a number of parameters. Each empty element has two attributes, with the **Name** attribute supplying a parameter name, and the **Value** attribute supplying the value for this parameter:

```
<object data="file:///c:/programs/bobbingBoat.class" ...>
  <param name="sail_colour" value="red" />
  <param name="bobs_per_minute" value="15" />
</object>
```

It is further possible to specify what kind of value is being supplied. By default, the value is of type 'data', but using the **Valuetype** attribute, it can be set to 'ref' or 'object' instead. A 'ref' value is a URL reference. An 'object' value is a URL reference to another object in the XHTML document. The other object must have an Identifier attribute that matches the value of this parameter, and the entire remote object is passed to the current object.

Tables

The **Table** element encloses a two-dimensional grid that is composed of rows that are further divided into cells.

Frames and borders

The table is separated from surrounding objects with border lines, using the **Border** attribute. A number of pixels value may be specified for the thickness of the lines, such as '3' pixels, but a value of '0' indicates no border and no space for a border. The **Frame** attribute is used to constrain where border lines are drawn, and can take a value of 'void' (none), 'above', 'below', 'hsides' (horizontal sides), 'lhs' (left-hand side), 'rhs' (right-hand side), 'vsides' (vertical sides), 'box' (all sides) and 'border'.

The **Rules** attribute is used to draw lines between cells in the table, and can take a value of 'none', 'rows' (horizontal lines only), 'colls' (vertical lines only), 'groups' (vertical lines between identified groups of columns) and 'all'. If this attribute is absent, no rules are drawn to separate cells, except when the (older) Border attribute has a value.

Cell borders and padding

The space between cells can be adjusted. The **Cellspacing** attribute takes a numeric value that states how much space there is between cells (including their borders). If a value of zero is used, the border lines overlap each other:

cellspacing="1"   cellspacing="8"

The space between the cell contents and the borders of the cell can also be adjusted using the **Cellpadding** attribute:

There are no default settings for either of these attributes, so when they are absent the resulting layout is implied, and unpredictable.

Table width

Both the width and height of the table are often left under the control of the browser, which composes the table within the restrictions of the available window area. The **Width** attribute may be used to 'encourage' the browser to take into account the wishes of the document author.

This attribute takes a numeric value that dictates how many pixels wide the table should be, or what percentage of the available screen width it should occupy. A simple number is interpreted as a pixel value. A percentage symbol indicates a proportion of the screen dimensions:

```
<table width="800">...</table>
```

```
<table width="50%">...</table>
```

Table caption

The table may have a title, contained within a preliminary **Caption** element. This element is placed within the Table element but before the elements described later. The content is by default displayed above the main table grid:

```
<table>
   <caption>The Table Title</caption>
   ...
</table>
```

Note that the XHTML DTD seems to contain an error relating to captions. The original HTML model included an Align attribute, with the possible values 'top', 'bottom', 'left' and 'right', placing the caption above, below, or to either side of the table respectively. Yet in the XHTML DTD, despite that fact that an entity is defined for this purpose, the attribute is not declared. The caption can only appear in one position, presumably the top.

Simple table structure

The table structure is row-oriented, which means that the grid is built by first defining each row and then separating each cell within a row. Each row of data is enclosed in a **Table Row (Tr)** element and each cell is enclosed in either a **Table Header (Th)** element or a **Table Data (Td)** element, the only difference between them being one of emphasis. Th and Td elements may be mixed within the same row:

```
<tr>
  <th>Colour</th><th>Status</th><th>Level</th>
</tr>
<tr>
  <th>Red</th><td>Danger</td><td>1</td>
</tr>
<tr>
  <th>Green</th><tdD>Normal</td><td>3</td>
</tr>
```

Colour	Status	Level
Red	Danger	1
Green	Normal	3

Cells

Ultimately, every table is composed of a grid of cells. These cells have content, alignment and spanning characteristics. The Th and Td elements have exactly the same properties.

Note that when the term 'cell' is used here, this can be considered to stand in for either a Table Data or a Table Header element.

Cell content

As shown above, a cell may directly contain text. But it may also contain all of the in-line elements, and also any block-level element, including a complete embedded table. Although text and block-level elements can be mixed in the same cell, this is generally discouraged because it causes confusion over the meaning of whitespace around markup (see Chapter 8). The Break Line element is particularly useful for formatting text within the cell.

If a cell is empty, no border lines are drawn around it.

Cell alignment

The content of a cell may be aligned horizontally and vertically within the cell boundaries.

The **Align** attribute allows horizontal alignment to be set to 'left', 'right', 'center', 'justify' or 'char' (character align).

When 'char' is selected as the alignment, the **Character** attribute (**Char**) and **Character Offset** attribute (**Charoff**) supply additional information about which character to align on, and how far across the width of the cell from the left edge to place this character. The offset can be given as pixels, or as a percentage. For example, to align on a decimal point, and to position the point 50% of the way across (centred in the cell), the following values apply:

```
...<td align="char" char="." offset="50%">123.45</td>...
...<td align="char" char="." offset="50">9.987654</td>...
...<td align="char" char="." offset="50">.1</td>...
```

```
|    123.45     |
|      9.987654 |
|        .1     |
```

The **Vertical Align** (**Valign**) attribute allows vertical alignment to be set to 'top', 'middle', 'bottom' or 'baseline' (where all cells in the row are vertically aligned by last line, after the cell with the most lines is aligned to 'top').

There are no default alignments, though traditionally it has been 'left' in Td elements and 'center' in Th elements, and vertical alignment has been 'middle' for both types of cell.

Elements higher in the table structure can provide default settings for a whole column or row, but individual cells may override this setting. The Tr element has the Align and Vertical alignment attributes. When used, the settings apply to every cell in the row that does not have its own explicit definitions.

Cell spanning

By default, each cell occupies an area dissected by one column and one row, but a cell may be expanded across or down to overlap adjacent cell areas using the **Colspan** and **Rowspan** attributes. These attributes take numeric values, and have implied values of '1' (zero is not a legal option). Higher values than '1' stretch the cell over adjoining areas:

```
<tr>
  <td>Colour</td><td colspan="2">Status &amp; code</td>
</tr>
<tr>
  <td>Red</td><td>Danger</td><td>1</td>
</tr>
<tr>
  <td>Blue</td><td rowspan="2">No Priority</td><td>2</td>
</tr>
<tr>
  <td>Brown</td><!-- NO CELL --><td>3</td>
</tr>
```

Colour	Status & code	
Red	Danger	1
Blue	**No Priority**	2
Brown		3

Note that the first row in the example above has only two cell elements, because the second one ocupies the space where the third would appear. The final row also has only two cell elements, containing 'Brown' and '3', because the middle cell has been occupied by the cell above it.

Header and Footer rows

When presenting tables on paper, it is useful to be able to identify header rows, so that rendering software can repeat the headings of a large table at the top of each page. Similarly, footer rows can be repeated at the base of each page containing a reference to a footnote. Even when presenting to a scrollable window, this separation of headers and footers from the body of the table can be useful, as a large table body may be collapsed to just a few scrollable rows, sandwiched between fixed, permanently visible headers and footers. The elements **Table Head** (**Thead**), **Table Body** (**Tbody**) and **Table Footer** (**Tfoot**) enclose rows of each kind.

The Tbody element is optional. The table must either contain one or more of these elements, or one or more Table Row elements. Either way, they may be preceded by the Thead and TFoot elements.

The Thead and Tfoot elements are optional because not all tables have rows that fall into these categories. When present, the Thead element must occur first, as would be expected, but the Tfoot element must *also* precede the body. The reason for this unusual arrangement is that it allows rendering software to collect the content of a footer and then place it at the base of each page, without needing to process the table twice:

```
<table>
    <thead>...</thead>
    <tfoot>...</tfoot>
    <tbody>...</tbody>
</table>
```

In addition to the usual array of core, event and language attributes, these three elements also contain the **Align** and **Valign** attributes, so introducing another level of cell content alignment overriding. In a table containing mostly currency values, it may be suitable to state that all header cells are centred, that all body cells are aligned on a decimal point, and that all footer cells are left-aligned. Individual rows and cells can then override these values as appropriate.

Column settings

It is not uncommon to find tables where all the cells in a particular column are aligned in the same way. For example, a price table in a catalogue may have two columns, the first being a description of each product, with the text left-aligned, and the second being the price of that item, aligned on a decimal point. Using the table model described so far, each Td element would need to contain an Align attribute:

```
<tr>
    <td align="left">Red coat</td>
    <td align="char" char=".">12.4</td>
</tr>
<tr>
    <td align="left">Green coat</td>
    <td align="char" char=".">12.6</td>
</tr>
```

Clearly, when many rows are involved, this is very time-consuming to produce. It is therefore possible to define a style for all cells in a column, using the **Column (Col)** element.

In the example below, the first Column element specifies an alignment of 'left' for the first column, and the second Column element specifies an alignment on the decimal point for the second column, so removing the need to specify these alignments in individual entries:

```
<col align="left" />
<col align="char" char="." />
<tr>
  <td>Red coat</td>
  <td>12.4</td>
</tr>
<tr>
  <td>Green coat</td>
  <td>12.6</td>
</tr>
...
```

For horizontal alignments, the Column element overrides the Table Row element, though individual cell element styles are still the most significant:

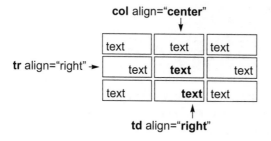

When several consecutive columns have the same settings, only one Column element is required, and the **Span** attribute is used to specify how many subsequent columns are to be grouped. The total number of columns in a table can be calculated by adding together the span values (when not present, a value of '1' is assumed). In the following example, the table has six columns (and it is assumed that if a Column element is used at all, then all table columns must be covered by these elements):

```
<col align="left" />
<col span="3" align="right" />
<col span="2" align="center" />
```

This element can also be used to define the width of a column (or columns), using the **Width** attribute, so that rendering software can start building the table presentation before reading the entire table. In the following example, the column widths are '30', '40', '40', '40', '50' and '50' pixels:

```
<col width="30" align="left" />
<col width="40" span="3" align="right" />
<col width="50" span="2" align="center" />
```

The width values may be given as a percentage of the full table width, using a '%' suffix. The values should add up to 100%. This approach has the great advantage of allowing the table to expand to fill the available horizontal width, but only if the Table element itself uses a width value that is also given as a percentage (of the width of the page or window), or has no width at all.

Finally, the width values may also be proportional, so that the table width can expand to the area available, and each column is assigned a 'fair' proportion of that width, based on the values in the Width attribute. A value followed by an asterisk, '*', denotes a proportional value. The effect is the same as for percentages, but slightly easier to calculate from existing fixed width values. To make the column widths defined above keep their relative sizes, but allow additional space to be exploited, it is only necessary to append the asterisk to the existing values, though the smaller values '3*', '4*', '4*', '4*', '5*' and '5*' would produce identical results. This approach is not yet universally supported, but one significant advantage over percentages is that the values do not have to total a pre-defined sum (100%); instead, the browser adds the values together then calculates each column width as a fraction of this total.

Column group settings

When a large number of consecutive Column elements share some attribute values, but not others, a more efficient technique may be employed using the **Column Group (Colgroup)** element. This element may enclose a number of Column elements, and has exactly the same attributes, which when used are deemed to apply to each embedded Column element that does not itself contain an explicit definition. In this example, both columns in the first group are given a width of '55' pixels:

```
<colgroup width="55">
   <col align="left" />
   <col span="3" align="right" />
</colgroup>
<colgroup width="50" align="center" />
```

Note that Column Group elements must not be mixed with Column elements. The only reason for the presence of the second Column Group element in the example above is because it would not be legal to use a Column element after a Column Group element.

The other major benefit of column groups is that they define an identifiable vertical component of a table, consisting of several columns and regardless of any degree of commonality in style between these columns. This defined object may be the target of a hypertext link, or the trigger for an event (see below). A Colgroup element does not even have to contain Col elements if their presence is not needed. In this case, it has its own **Span** attribute:

```
<colgroup span="3" width="35" />
<colgroup span="2" width="20" />
```

Forms

The 'form' concept gives the user the ability to send information back to the Web server. The document may contain a questionnaire, for example, which the user fills in and returns. A **Form** element encloses the entire form. It may contain all the normal elements described above (including the particularly useful table-building elements described above), plus the form-building elements described in this section. However, it must not contain an embedded Form element.

Sending a form

The Form element has a required attribute called **Action**, which identifies (using a URL) a script that can process the form when it is submitted, and an **Encoding Type** (**Enctype**) attribute that specifies the **MIME** type used to submit data to the server (the default value is 'application/x-www-form-urlencoded').

The Form element may contain a number of **Input** elements, of various kinds discussed below, but one of them must have an attribute **Type** value of 'submit' (the default value is 'text'), which the browser detects and takes as an instruction to send the content of the form to the Web server (another Input element may be used to define a button that resets the default settings of the form, using a Type attribute value of 'reset').

The example below sends the data entered into the form to the 'myscript.cgi' script running on the Web server when the 'Send' button is selected by the user of the browser:

```
<form method="POST" action="../mydir/myscript.cgi">
   <input type="submit" value="Send" />
   ...
</form>
```

Web server

Note that the Form element has an attribute called **Method**, which in the example has a value of 'post'. It may also take a value of 'get' (this is the default value). These values define the exact scheme by which the form sends information back to the server, a subject which is not covered further here.

Radio buttons

An Input **Type** value of 'radio' indicates that a radio button will appear in the form. The browser ensures that only the last radio button selected is highlighted at any one time within a group of buttons, and all Input elements sharing the same **Name** value are part of a single group. Each item specifies a **Value**. In the example below, two groups are defined, 'vehicle' and 'colour'. From the vehicle group the user may select the radio button labelled 'car', 'truck' or 'van', and from the colour group the user may select 'Red' or 'Blue'. The user may therefore select, for example, a blue car or a red van:

```
<input type="radio" name="vehicle" value="car" />
<input type="radio" name="vehicle" value="truck" />
<input type="radio" name="vehicle" value="van" />
<input type="radio" name="colour" value="Red" />
<input type="radio" name="colour" value="Blue" />
```

However, the user will not be able to see which buttons to select unless descriptive names also appear near the Input element, perhaps within Paragraph elements:

```
<p>
  <input type="radio" name="colour" value="red" />
  Red option.
</p>
<p>
  <input type="radio" name="colour" value="blue" />
  Blue option.
</p>
```

○ Red option
◉ Blue option

The browser is likely to pre-select the first item in each group when the form is displayed, because one option must always be selected, but it is the value selected when the 'submit' button is pressed that ultimately matters.

Check-boxes

The **Input** element can also be used to provide 'check-boxes,' which differ from radio buttons in that more than one can be selected at any one time. The **Type** attribute contains 'checkbox' and the **Name** attribute contains the name of the item that may be selected. An item can be pre-selected by including the **Checked** attribute, holding the single legal value of 'checked'.

In the example below, the user is presented with two options, 'leather' (seats) and 'CD' (player), and the CD item is already selected. The user can deselect CD player, select leather seats, select both or neither:

```
<p>
  <input type="checkbox" name="car" value="leather" />
  Leather
</p>
<p>
  <input type="checkbox" name="car" value="CD"
        checked="checked" />
  CD-player
</p>
```

☐ Leather
☒ CD-player

Text boxes

The **Input** element can be used to create text entry areas. The **Type** attribute either holds a value of 'text' or is absent (as this is its default value). The **Name** attribute holds the label for the text field. The **Size** attribute may be used to determine the length (in characters) of the text field, and if not present defaults to 20 characters. Also, the attribute **Maxlength** can be used to strictly limit the number of characters that can be entered, and may be smaller or larger than the text field size:

```
<input type="text" size="25" maxlength="15" />
```

Fifteen chars !

For multiple lines of text, the **Textarea** element is used instead. Each text area is identified using the **Name** attribute. The required **Rows** and **Columns** (**Cols**) attributes set the height and width of the visible text area in character-sized units. Scroll bars or other devices may allow extra characters or lines of text to be displayed within this area:

```
<textarea name="mybox" rows="3" cols="10">Here
is some content</textarea>
```

All line-feed characters in the data are retained, including one between the start-tag and the first word, if present (the example above would begin with a blank line if there were a line-feed before 'Here').

Other input types

Other Input element options available using the Type attribute include 'file' (attach a file to send with the form), 'hidden' (do not show to the user, used for passing state information between the server and browser) and 'image' (presents a graphic, though the **Src** attribute can also be used to locate an image file that will fill the background of the input field).

The 'reset' type identifies a button that tells the browser to ignore all changes made to the form since it was loaded.

The 'password' type identifies a text entry field in which the text entered is not visible, but often replaced by a stand-in character, such as '*'.

Selection menus

Selection menus may be created. The **Select** element encloses the menu. It uses the **Name** attribute to identify the menu. The number of rows visible is determined by the **Size** attribute.

By default, it is possible to select only one item from the list; each time a selection is made, the previous selection is lost. But the presence of the **Multiple** attribute (which can only take a single value of 'multiple') signifies that it is possible to select several options. Deselection then typically requires the user to reselect an already selected item.

Each option in the menu is defined using the **Option** element. The **Value** attribute may be used to replace the content of the element as the value returned to the server if that item is selected, and the **Selected** attribute may be used to pre-select one of the items, by including its only possible value of 'selected':

```
<select name="mymenu">
  <option>Car</option>
  <option selected="selected">Truck</option>
  <option>Van</option>
</select>
```

The later discussion on event triggers includes some form-specific features.

Field sets

Groups of form elements can be given a distinct identity, and perhaps have a line drawn around them, using the **Fieldset** element. This element may also contain a **Legend** element, to give the group a name, and to allow easy access to the group, because it contains the **Accesskey** attribute (this is explained below). Although the DTD does not contain this constraint (due to the possibility that text may occur directly inside the Fieldset element), there is a formal rule that only one Legend element can occur within the Fieldset element, and that it must precede all text or elements (it can only be preceded by whitespace characters).

Selection interface

Text that describes the purpose of an object on the form can be made 'active'. Using the **Label** element, the user can select the text instead of the actual button. For check-boxes and option buttons, selecting a label changes the value just as selecting the object itself does:

```
<label><input type="checkbox" ... />Leather</label>
```

If it is not convenient for the Label element to enclose the button or field it relates to, then it can use the **For** attribute instead, to refer to the Id attribute of the given object:

```
<label for="covertype">Leather</label>
...
<input type="checkbox" id="covertype" ... />
```

It is possible to use the tab key to select form objects in a pre-defined order using the **Tabindex** attribute. The form control with a Tabindex value of '1' is the first field selected. Alternatively, the **Accesskey** attribute allows a specific field to be selected instantly when the user depresses a specified key (in combination with the ALT key on a PC). It can be used with the Input, Select, Textarea, Button and Label elements (and also with image maps in the Area element):

```
<input type="checkbox" accesskey="L" .../> Leather
```

A number of items can be disabled in a form, to show that they are not applicable in the current circumstance. This may be done by 'greying out' the items, so that they are obviously not selectable. The Input, Select, Option Group, Option, Textarea and Button elements can all take the **Disabled** attribute, which if present must have the value 'disabled'. Similarly, the text items represented by the Textarea element and the Input element (when set to type 'text') may be enabled but not editable, becoming 'read-only' objects. The user can still select a range of text in the field, and copy this range elsewhere, but cannot change the content of the field itself. When present, the **Readonly** element has a single possible value of 'read-only'.

Descriptive markup

As stylistic elements were removed or deprecated from HTML, they were replaced by new descriptive elements. The following elements help stylesheet designers to develop more suitable formatting, and Web crawler search engines to perform more useful analysis of documents.

Spanning text

In place of numerous elements for styling text within a paragraph introduced earlier, XHTML promotes the use of stylesheet declarations to perform this kind of formatting. The **Span** element has the usual attributes, including the **Style** attribute, to achieve this:

```
Here is a <span style="font-weight:bold">bold</span> word,
and here is
an <span style="font-style:italic">italic</span> one.
```

Quotations

The **Quotation (Q)** element encloses in-line text that is a quote of another source. The tags may be replaced by language-dependent quotation delimiter characters when rendered:

```
... <q>To be or not to be</q>...
```

    ... "To be or not to be"...

The **Blockquote** element contains a block of text quoted from another source, and is typically indented by the browser.

The **Deletion (Del)** element identifies text that is to be considered redundant, and is only retained to bring attention to the fact that it once applied. Such text is typically presented with a line through it. Complementing this is the **Insertion (Ins)** element, which identifies new text. Typically, new text is highlighted with a change bar in the margin. By convention, these elements should be used consistently as block-level elements, or as in-line elements, but not both, as it may be difficult to apply a suitable style for both types:

```
... there are <del>fifteen</del><ins>nine</ins> days
left to Christmas ...
```

Both of these elements contain an optional **Datetime** attribute, indicating the time the document was changed.

Event trigger attributes

The 'On...' attributes that most elements can carry all specify an ECMAscript function that is to be activated when the user interacts with the element in some given way.

Standard events

The elements that can contain the core attributes can also contain the event attributes described here (with the exception of the Break Line (Br) element). In addition, these attributes can be used on the Map element.

The **Onclick** attribute activates the named function when the user clicks the mouse button over the element:

```
<p onclick="MyParaClickFunction()">Click here!</p>
```

Similarly, the **Ondblclick** attribute activates the named function when the user double-clicks the mouse button over the element and **Onkeypress** activates when a key is pressed (and released). Movement of the mouse pointer over the element is detected by the **Onmousemove, Onmouseover** and **Onmouseout** attributes. The **Onmousedown** and **Onmouseup** attributes detect the pressing and release of the mouse button while it is over an element. The **Onkeydown** and **Onkeyup** attributes work in the same way, but for key presses.

Additional event attributes can be used in the Body element, most of the form-building elements, and a few others.

Body events

The **Onload** and **Onunload** attributes may be added to the Body element. These attributes refer to scripts that are run when the document is displayed in a Web browser, and when it is either replaced or the browser is closed down.

Events in forms

All the usual event attributes can be used on the Form, Label, Input, Select, Option Group, Option, Text Area, Field Set and Button elements. But a number of additional event types are also available within forms.

The **Onfocus** and **Onblur** attributes trigger events that occur when the form component is given the primary focus of attention (by user selection), and when that focus is lost. They can appear on the Label, Input, Select, Text Area and Button elements.

The Form element can take the additional **Onsubmit** and **Onreset** attributes. They identify scripts to run when the user either submits the form or resets it to initial settings.

The Input (for text input fields) and Text Area elements have **Onselect** and **Onchange** attributes that are triggered when the user selects some text in the item. The second of these attributes can also be used on the Select element (to detect changes to the text).

Events in images

The **Onfocus** and **Onblur** attributes can be used on the Area element, as well as in forms.

Changes from HTML 4

Apart from the cosmetic changes that were necessary simply to make HTML 4 into an XML-compliant standard, the opportunity was taken to rationalize the language itself, just as HTML 4 rationalized earlier versions of HTML.

Removed frames

The focus on document rather than Web site construction means that the Frame, Frameset and NoFrames elements are not present in the strict XHTML DTD. They have been moved to another DTD.

Removed elements

A number of elements have been removed:

- Applet (use Object instead)
- Embed
- IsIndex
- Font (use Style and CSS)
- BaseFont (use Style and CSS)
- InIndex
- Listing
- Menu
- Plaintext
- Strike (strikethrough: use CSS style 'text-decoration:line-through')
- U (Underline: use CSS style 'text-decoration:underline').

Simplified lists

The Compact attribute has been removed from the Dir (Directory), Ol (Ordered List) and Ul (Unordered List) elements.

The Start and Type attributes have been removed from the Ol element.

The Type and Value attributes have been removed from the Li (List Item) element.

Added XML attributes

The XML Language attribute ('xml:lang') has been added to the core attributes, so is available on almost all elements.

The XML Space attribute ('xml:space') has been added to the Pre element (to ensure preservation of spaces and line-feeds), and to Script and Style elements (to preserve lines in scripts and formatting instructions).

Removed stylistic attributes

The Align attribute has been removed from the Caption, Div, H1, H2, H3, H4, H5, H6, Hr, Img, Input, Legend, Object, P and Table elements.

The Border attribute has been removed from the Object and Img (Image) elements.

The Hspace and Vspace attributes have been removed from the Img and Object elements.

The Target attribute has been removed from Area and Base elements.

The Width attribute has been removed from the Hr, Object, Pre, Td and Th elements, and the Height attribute has been removed from the Td and Th elements.

The BgColor attribute has been removed from the Body, Table and Tr elements.

24. Cascading stylesheets (CSS1)

- should use XSLT Instead

CSS, a stylesheet language in widespread use, is a popular choice for formatting XML. This chapter covers the well-supported CSS1 format (the next covers CSS2), and should be of particular interest to those wishing to use Web browsers to format XML or HTML documents. The language has different strengths to XSL/XSLT.

Background

The **CSS** standard was initially developed for use with HTML (by the W3C in 1996), specifically for implementation within Web browsers, and was born out of growing pressure for more author control over the presentation of Web pages. At the time of writing, only version 1 is fully supported by the most popular HTML Web browsers. This version can be obtained from http://www.w3.org/pub/WWW/ TR/REC-CSS1. An earlier chapter explores the XSL format, and demonstrates how powerful and flexible this language is. It is reasonable to ask why two stylesheet standards should exist, and why XSL users should even consider CSS. The answer is partly a simple issue of timing. At the time of writing, CSS exists and is supported by the popular Web browsers, whereas XSL is still just a draft standard. In addition, CSS may be used when XSL is considered too complex for the task, as it is easier to learn. Although CSS is relatively simple in comparison with many stylesheet languages, its concentration on screen formatting gives it some unique advantages in this area.

It should be noted that the latest drafts of XSL include formatting properties that are copied from CSS equivalents, and that even the names of these properties are the same. This means that once CSS is understood, it should be easier to learn XSL as well.

Format overview

The CSS format utilizes the ASCII text format, so style definitions can be easily created and edited in any text editor or word processor. However, unlike XSL, it does not use XML constructs.

Rules

A CSS stylesheet is composed of at least one style rule. A rule is simply a style specification for an element, pseudo-element or group of similar elements. A typical stylesheet will contain many such rules.

A rule begins with a selector, which must start a new line in the text file. In the simplest case, the selector is the name of an XML or HTML element. In the following example, the selector is 'title', so the style definition will apply to the content of the Title element, wherever it is used in a document. Curly brackets enclose the style definition, which may span any number of lines:

```
title { ... }
```

Note that when used with HTML, the name is not case-sensitive, so 'body', 'BODY' and 'Body' all identify the HTML Body element. In XML, however, element names are case-sensitive, so the stylesheet names must also be case-sensitive, and care must be taken to match exactly the name used in the DTD declaration of XML Schema definition.

In some cases, styles can be applied to just part of the text of an element, such as the first line or word, and in other cases user activity can affect the style. Keywords representing these conditions are separated from the element name using a colon:

```
title:first-line { ... }
```

Declarations

A style definition consists of at least one declaration. Each declaration defines a specific style, such as the name of a font, or size of an indent. A declaration is composed of a property, such as 'font-size', and a value for that property, such as '32pt'. The property is separated from its value by a colon:

```
font-size:32pt
```

For improved readability, spaces may also be included. Although it is possible to place spaces before the colon, perhaps the most readable combination is a colon followed by a space:

```
font-size: 32pt
```

Multiple declarations are separated by semicolons. In this case, legibility may be improved by including spaces both before and after the separator:

```
font-size: 32pt ; color: blue
```

The semicolon can also be thought of as a declaration terminator, as there is no harm in having a semicolon after the last declaration in the list. This can even be considered a good thing to do, as syntax errors are less likely to happen when further declarations are added to the list later.

Complete rule

To summarize these rules, a complete style definition that specifies 23pt blue text for a H1 element appears as follows:

```
h1   { font-size: 32pt ; color: blue }
```

The definition may also span multiple lines.

Comments

Comments can be added to a stylesheet, and take the same form as in the C and Java programming languages, beginning with the character sequence '/*', and ending with the sequence '*/':

```
H1   { ... }   /* HTML Header One Style */
```

Styling properties

CSS has many styling properties, including text properties (dealing with fonts and character styles), colours and backgrounds, margins, and whitespace around elements, and general object type classifications.

Colours

Wherever colours are allowed, the choice is from 'aqua', 'black', 'blue', 'fuchsia', 'gray', 'green', 'lime', 'maroon', 'navy', 'olive', 'purple', 'red', 'silver', 'teal', 'white' and 'yellow'. An RGB value can be given, with the keyword 'rgb(r, g, b)' ('r' represents red, 'g' represents green and 'b' represents blue), or with a hexadecimal number in the form '#rgb' or '#rrggbb'. The examples below are equivalent:

```
emph   { ... ; color: rgb(128, 0, 255)  }
emph   { ... ; color: #8000FF  }
```

Sizes

Wherever sizes are allowed, the choice is from absolute sizes given in points ('pt'), inches ('in'), centimetres ('cm'), millimetres ('mm') or picas ('pc'), and from relative sizes 'em' (height of the element's font), 'ex' (the height of a letter) and 'px' (pixels relative to the canvas). Values can have a '+' (the initial setting) or '-' prefix.

Often, sizes can be given as a percentage of an inherited size, so that '50%' means half the current size. Note that percentage values can be greater than 100, and a size value of '200%' indicates that the object should be twice the inherited size.

External references (URLs)

Sometimes, an external resource can be called in using a URL (see Chapter 30). The function 'url(...)' is used for this purpose. Relative URL references have the stylesheet document location as their context location. Quotes may enclose the actual URL. Significant characters need to be escaped, including '(', ')', ' ' ', ' " ' and ',', by placing a '\' character before them, such as '\('.

Font style properties

Characters are presented in a specified font, at a given size, and possibly rendered with style characteristics such as bold, italic and small caps.

Font family

The 'font-family' property specifies the font to display the text in, such as Helvetica. When the font name includes spaces, the name must be quoted, as in the following example:

```
para    { font-family: "Times New Roman" }
```

Because not all systems have the same fonts available, alternatives can be expressed, and are separated by commas. An application should pick the first one that matches an installed font, reading from left to right through the list. To cover situations where no font names match, there are some generic names available, and one of these should be added to the end of the list. They are 'serif' (a font like Times, or the font used for this paragraph, with lines on the end of each major stroke), 'sans-serif' (a font without serifs, such as Arial or Helvetica, and the titles and headings in this book), 'cursive' (Zapf-Chancery), 'fantasy' (Western) and 'monospace' (a font where all characters are the same width, such as Courier, the font used for the examples in this chapter):

```
title   {font-family: Arial, sans-serif }
```

Font style

The 'font-style' property affects the text in other ways, either slanting the letters, properly italicizing them, or using small caps in place of lower-case letters. The values 'normal', 'italic' and 'oblique' (slanted) are used:

```
title { ... ; font-style: italic }
```

Note that oblique is not quite the same as italic, and is often achieved by simply slanting the text electronically.

Font weight

The 'font-weight' property darkens or lightens the text using the values 'bold' (or '700'), 'normal' (or '400') (the default), '100', '200', '300', '500', '600' and '800', with 'bolder' and 'lighter' adjusting an inherited value up or down by 100:

```
title    { ... ; font-weight: bold }
```

Small caps

The text can also be displayed in small-caps style, using the 'font-variant' property, which takes a value of 'normal' (the default) or 'small-caps':

```
title { ... ; font-variant: small-caps }
```

The 'font-size' property determines the size to display the text, and is usually given in point sizes, though more vague measures such as 'xx-large', 'x-large', 'large', 'medium', 'small' , 'x-small' and 'xx-small' are also available. It is also possible to increase or decrease the size from an inherited value using 'smaller' and 'larger':

```
title    { ... ; font-size: 24pt   }

para     { ... ; font-size: medium  }

comment { ... ; font-size: smaller  }
```

The 'line-height' property specifies a gap between lines. A value of 'normal' means that no gap is added. A percentage of the inherited value can be given, and a number can be used as a calculation of the inherited height:

```
title    { ... ; line-height: 32pt   }

para     { ... ; line-height: normal  }

comment { ... ; line-height: 0.9   }
```

Combined font details

The 'font' property conveniently combines the properties described above into a single statement, with parameters that specify the font style, the variant, the weight, the size and line height (separated by a '/' character), and the font family. The Title element example below combines all the statements for this element shown above:

```
title    { font: italic small-caps bold
                    24pt/32pt Arial, sans-serif }
```

Colour and background properties

Colours, used carefully, greatly enhance the appearance of a document. CSS is able to specify a colour for the text itself, and for the area behind the text. For example, the content of a Warning element could be displayed in red text on a yellow background.

Colors

The 'color' property specifies the colour of the text:

```
warning    { ... ; color: red }
```

The 'background-color' property specifies the colour of the background, both behind the text and in the padding area (see below). Apart from the name of a colour, the value can be 'transparent', meaning that the existing background colour shows through, and this is the default setting:

```
warning    { ... ; background-color: yellow }

para    { ... ; background-color: transparent }
```

Background images

In addition to the colour, a background can also incorporate an image, referenced by URL. The 'background-image' property has a default value of 'none', but can take a URL parameter:

```
warning    { ... ; background-image: url(skull-Xbones.gif) }
```

A background image may be smaller than the area it needs to cover. It can therefore be repeated, both across and down, until the whole area is filled. The 'background-repeat' property takes the values 'repeat' (across and down), which is the default value, as well as 'repeat-x' (across only), 'repeat-y' (down only) and 'no-repeat':

```
warning    { ... ; background-repeat: repeat-x }
```

A browser may be able to scroll a background image, along with the text, as the user adjusts the display to read more. Alternatively, it may be able to keep the image in place as the text scrolls over it. Some browsers may be able to do both. The intended behaviour can be set using the 'background-attachment' property, which takes a value of 'scroll' (the default) or 'fixed':

```
warning    { ... ; background-attachment: fixed }
```

The top-left corner of a background image normally lies over the top-left corner of the first character in the text block, so does not cover the padding area (but see below for exceptions). Large, non-repeating images in particular may need to be moved to another location. The 'background-position' property allows the image to be moved to the 'top', 'center' or 'bottom', as well as to the 'left' or 'right' edge. Percentage values or simple length values can also be used, in which case the first parameter specifies the horizontal, followed by an optional vertical position:

```
warning    { ... ; background-position: center }
```

For the sake of brevity, all the background settings can be combined within the 'background' property:

```
warning    { ... ;
             background: yellow url(skull-xbones.gif)
                         repeat-x fixed center }
```

Text style properties

Using the following properties, indentation of first lines, the spacing between words and letters, automated transformation to upper-case or lower-case letters, underlines and overlines, and the horizontal and vertical alignment of lines and words, can all be achieved.

Word spacing

Additional space can be inserted between words using the 'word-spacing' property. It takes a length parameter, or 'normal' (the default):

```
important    { ... ; word-spacing: 3pt }
```

Letter spacing

Additional space can also be inserted between letters in a word, using the 'letter-spacing' property. It takes a length parameter, or 'normal' (the default):

```
important    { ... ; letter-spacing: 1pt }
```

Text decoration

Lines can be added to the text using the 'text-decoration' property, which takes the values 'none' (the default), 'underline', 'overline', 'line-through' (for displaying invalid or replaced text) and 'blink' (strictly for browser rendering):

```
important    { ... ; text-decoration: underline }
```

Vertical text alignment

The 'vertical-align' property aligns the text vertically, taking values of 'baseline' (the default), 'sub', 'super', 'top', 'text-top', 'middle' (useful for centering in-line images), 'bottom' or 'text-bottom', or a percentage value of the current line height:

```
subscript    { vertical-align: sub }
superscript  { vertical-align: 50% }
```

Forced letter-case

Whatever use of upper-case and lower-case letters actually occurs in an element, a standard may apply to which they must conform when presented. For example, title text may need to be presented in capitals, even when capitals have not been used in the title text. The 'text-transform' property transforms characters, when necessary, to the desired case. It takes a value of 'capitalize' (the first character of each word is upper-case, the remainder are lower-case), 'uppercase', 'lowercase' or 'none' (no transformations, and overriding inherited value) (the default):

```
title    { ... ; text-transform: uppercase }
```

Text can be aligned in different ways within the space reserved for it. It can be justified (like the text in this paragraph), left justified, right justified or centred, with the 'text-align' property taking the value 'left', 'right', 'center' or 'justify' (align on both sides):

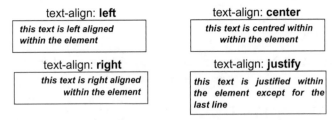

Text indentation

Often, the first line of each paragraph is indented. The 'text-indent' property takes a length or percentage value, with the percentage value representing a fraction of the parent element's width.

```
para    { ... ; text-indent: 3em }
```

Boxes

Text is formatted within a box, called the 'content box'. But text boxes rarely lie directly adjacent to each other. Margins separate these containers, and border lines may also be added, with padding between the text and the border lines, and between the lines and adjacent text blocks. There are properties for each of these areas, including variants that allow the top, right, bottom or left sides to be given individual styles. In the diagram below, a paragraph block is shown, enclosed between two other vertically stacked blocks:

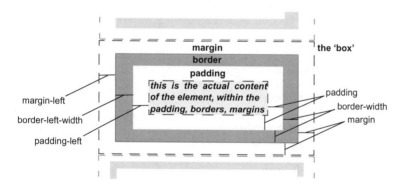

Note that background colours cover the padding area as well as the content area, and that background images should not cover this area.

Border lines

The border can be given a specific thickness, colour and style. The 'border-width', 'border-color' and 'border-style' ('none', 'dotted', 'dashed', 'solid', 'double', 'groove', 'ridge', 'inset' or 'outset') properties set these characteristics individually, but the 'border' property combines these features into a single statement. The two examples below are equivalent:

```
p  { ... ; border-width: 2pt ; border-color: red ;
           border-style: solid }
```

```
p  { ... ; border: 2pt solid red  }
```

When separate styles are required for different borders, the more specific 'border-left', 'border-right', 'border-top' and 'border-bottom' properties can be used instead:

```
p  { ... ; border-left:   2pt solid red ;
           border-right:  2pt solid red ;
           border-top:    4pt dotted black ;
           border-bottom: 4pt dotted black  }
```

Widths can also be set for individual borders, using the 'border-left-width', 'border-right-width', 'border-top-width' and 'border-bottom-width' properties:

```
p  { ... ; border-left-width:   2pt ;
           border-right-width:  2pt ;
           border-top-width:    4pt ;
           border-bottom-width: 4pt }
```

Padding (between text and borders)

The 'padding' property defines the size of the gap between the content and the border. If the padding is different on each side, the 'padding-left', 'padding-right', 'padding-top' and 'padding-bottom' properties are available, although individual top, right, bottom and left values can be defined in the 'padding' property by adding parameters. The examples below are equivalent:

```
p  { ... ; padding-top:    2pt ;
           padding-right:  3pt ;
           padding-bottom: 4pt ;
           padding-left:   5pt }

p  { ... ; padding: 2pt 3pt 4pt 5pt }
```

Margins (around borders or text)

The 'margin' property (and the more specific 'margin-left', 'margin-right', 'margin-top' and 'margin-bottom' properties) defines the size of the gap between this entire box and any adjacent boxes. Multiple values in the 'margin' property also identify separate top, right, bottom and left margins respectively. The following examples are equivalent:

```
p  { ... ; margin-top:    2pt ;
           margin-right:  3pt ;
           margin-bottom: 4pt ;
           margin-left:   5pt }

p  { ... ; margin: 2pt 3pt 4pt 5pt }
```

Fixed height and width

Some elements (especially images) may need to be resized (or scaled). The 'height' and 'width' properties can be used to reduce or enlarge the area reserved for the content of the element, and in the case of images actually reduce or increase the size of the image by scaling it.

Both properties can take a length value, or a value of 'auto' (the default). When 'auto' is used for just one of these properties, the scaling replicates the given scaling for the other property (for images, the ratio is maintained). If both properties use the 'auto' value, an image will appear at its original size. The 'width' property also allows a percentage value:

```
image    { ... ; width: 50% ; height: auto }
```

Floating boxes

The 'float' property is used to move boxes to the 'left' or 'right' of the display area, though the default value is 'none'. Other text may wrap around the element. This property is very useful for placing images amongst text.

The 'clear' property ensures that floating elements do not appear next to the current element; it clears the area to the 'left', 'right' or 'both' sides of the element, though the default value is 'none'.

When a floating element would otherwise have appeared to the left or right of this element, this element is moved down until it is clear of the floating element. For example, if there is a danger that there will be a floating image immediately preceding a title, it would not be appropriate for the image to occupy the same horizontal space as the title:

```
title    { ... ; clear: both }
```

Display properties

There are a number of additional properties that are used to distinguish between block and in-line elements, identify lists and list items, and elements in which multiple spaces must be preserved.

These properties are not essential for working in HTML, where the names of relevant elements in each category are hard-wired into HTML-aware Web browsers. But they are vital for working with XML. The 'display', 'white-space', 'list-style-type', 'list-style-image', 'list-style-position' and 'list-style' properties are therefore discussed later, when exploring important XML-specific features of CSS.

Simple element mapping

As previously described, defining a style rule for a given element requires specification of the element name (the selector), followed by a set of declarations:

```
head1    { font-size: 32pt ; color: blue }
```

More than one rule may be defined for each element. Providing that the declarations do not conflict, they simply accumulate as if they had been defined in a single rule. The example below is functionally identical to the less verbose version above:

```
head1    { font-size: 32pt }
head1    { color: blue }
```

When separate rules *do* conflict, the last rule in the stylesheet applies. In the following example, the Head1 element is displayed in green:

```
head1    { font-size: 32pt ; color: blue }
head1    { color: green }
```

Importance override

However, this behaviour can be reversed by adding an **important** clause to a declaration:

```
head1    { font-size: 32pt ; color: blue ! important}
head1    { color: green }
```

Of course, the original order of importance can be restored by also adding an important clause to the second declaration.

Shared rules

If a number of elements share the same styles, their style specifications can be combined into a single rule. The selector simply consists of all relevant element names, separated by commas:

```
head1, head2, head3    { color: blue }
```

Practical design consideration

Good stylesheet design practice combines the techniques described above to avoid unnecessary repetition. In the following example, the three main header elements should appear in blue, italic style, but have differing point sizes:

```
head1, head2, head3    { color: blue ; font-style: italic }
head1                  { font-size: 18pt }
head2, head3           { font-size: 14pt }
```

Contextual rules

There may be occasions where the style of an element should depend on where it appears within the document. For example, an XML DTD may define an element called Title, which is used to hold the title text of a book, its chapters, their embedded sections and all tables. Typically, the style of the title text should vary, depending on where it is applied. A book title would, for example, be larger than a section title. Reflecting this requirement in a stylesheet is known as contextual style mapping:

```
<book>
  <title>The Book Title</title>
  <chapter>
    <title>The First Chapter</title>
    <section>
      <title>The First Section</title>
      <table>
        <title>A Table</title>
        ...
      </table>
      ...
    </section>
    ...
  </chapter>
  ...
</book>
```

Broad context

The simplest kind of context rule defines a style for an element that applies only when that element is enclosed by another specified element. In the example below, a style is specified for a Title element when it appears within a Book element:

```
book title    { color: blue ; font-size: 36pt }
```

Specific context overrides

But the rule above applies to any descendant. The example above applies to any Title element within the book, even if it is the title of a chapter or table. CSS1 has no ability to specify a particular parent element, but can override a rule with a more specific rule.

In the example below, a Title element inside a Table element is associated with both rules, but the second rule is more specific, and has the final say (so the title text appears in 12pt):

```
book title     { color: blue ; font-size: 36pt }
table title    { font-size: 12pt }
```

Multiple rules

It is possible to combine simple selectors and contextual selectors within the same rule. In the example below, the declarations apply to both the Header element, wherever it might appear, and to the Title element, but only when it appears inside a Table element:

```
header, table title  { color: blue ; font-size: 36pt }
```

Inheritance

When a single element has a number of styles, depending on its context, one approach would be to define a rule for each context:

```
book title     { color: blue ; font-size: 36pt }
chapter title  { color: blue ; font-size: 18pt }
section title  { color: green ; font-size: 16pt }
table title    { color: blue ; font-size: 12pt }
```

However, when some or all of these contexts have properties in common, it is more efficient to first define a more generalized description of the element, in a simple, non-contextual rule. In the example above, it is obvious that most of the contexts require the title text to appear in blue, so this rule should be placed in the general Title description, and inherited by the others (unless overridden):

```
title          { color: blue }
book title     { font-size: 36pt }
chapter title  { font-size: 18pt }
section title  { color: green ; font-size: 16pt }
table title    { font-size: 12pt }
```

This approach avoids repetition, and so reduces the size of the stylesheet, improves legibility, highlights important rules and makes it easier to modify the stylesheet.

Precedence rules

When some rules are more specific than others, the simple precedence rule for resolving conflicts does not operate. The most specific rule takes precedence, even if it appears before the less specific rule in the stylesheet.

However, it is good design practice to define the general case first, as shown above, as this allows the reader to absorb the information in a more natural way. Taking the example above, when a title appears in a book, the first and second rules apply, and the title text appears in 36pt blue style.

But when there are conflicting rules, such as the font size property in the chapter title, the more specific rule overrides the less specific rule, so the title text appears in 18pt. In this case, the second rule is effectively ignored, because its single declaration is overridden by the third rule.

Care must be taken, however, because unforeseen and undesirable effects may result. It may not be immediately obvious from the example above that the title of a table will in fact appear in green, when it is embedded within a section. This is because the fourth rule also applies, which specifies the colour green, and is more specific than the first rule, and the final rule does *not* override this setting.

A good percentage of the time taken to design and debug a stylesheet revolves around locating and resolving such clashes.

First letter and line

Traditional formatting techniques include distinct styling of the first character, or the first line of text, particularly within the first paragraph of a chapter or book. But it is not possible to add markup to identify the content of a single text line, as the actual number of characters involved is determined only when the browser or pagination engine renders the text to screen or page.

The ':first-letter' keyword tells the application to style the first character in a given way, and the ':first-line' keyword similarly applies a given style to all the characters on the first line. These definitions can be combined, as shown below:

```
book title:first-letter { ... ; font-size: 14pt }
book title:first-line   { ... ; font-weight: bolder }
```

Larger first letter and bolder
first line than the rest of the
text.

Accessing and overriding styles

When using CSS with HTML, the standard can be applied in various ways. But XML is more restrictive. Where possibly conflicting styles are defined in different places, decisions need to be made regarding which styles to use.

Importing

To assist with the management of stylesheets, an importing mechanism is included. This allows one stylesheet to call in another. The '@import' keyword has a URL parameter that locates the other stylesheet document. These commands must appear at the top of the stylesheet, before any of the rules:

```
@import url(file:///library/tables.css)
```

One of the ways in which CSS exploits its 'cascading' nature is that, when conflicts arise, imported rules are considered less important than the rules defined in
the main stylesheet.

HTML

There are three ways that CSS styles can be applied to HTML documents. These
are the in-line method, the embedded method and the linked method.

The **linked stylesheet** approach places the stylesheet in a separate data file that is
simply referred to by each document. The remote stylesheet is referenced either by
a Link element, or by an 'import' command:

```
<!-- HTML -->
<head>
<link rel="STYLESHEET" href="red-colors.css"
                                    type="text/css">
</head>
```

In the **embedded stylesheet** approach, the stylesheet appears at the top of the
document, within the HTML Style element. The styles apply only to the document
containing them:

```
<!-- HTML -->
<head>
<style type="text/css">
p { color: green }
</style>
</head>
```

Finally, an **in-line style** is a rule that is applied directly to a specific instance of an
element. This approach uses the HTML Style attribute, and does not involve the
concept of a style 'sheet' at all:

```
<!-- HTML -->
<p style="color: blue">A blue paragraph.</p>
```

Although not part of the specification itself, the 'cascading' nature of CSS may
include distinguishing between the three levels of implementation described
above. A style specified in a linked stylesheet can be replaced by one defined in an
embedded stylesheet, which can in turn be overridden by an in-line style. The
popular browsers work in this way:

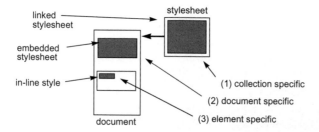

This principle is illustrated below, with the external stylesheet defining all elements to be red in colour, the embedded one redefining paragraphs to be green, and an in-line style on one of the paragraphs overriding this to make the paragraph blue:

```
<!-- HTML -->
<head>
<link rel="STYLESHEET" href="red-colors.css"
                                type="text/css">
<style type="text/css">
p { color: green }
</style>
</head>
<body>
<h1>A Red Header</h1>
<p style="color: blue">A blue paragraph.</p>
<p>A green paragraph.</p>
```

XML

As shown above, the mechanisms for attaching styles to an HTML document are to a large extent built in via extensions to the HTML specification. Implementors of XML systems need a different approach. There is no equivalent to the Style element in XML, and while in-line styles may be used, the attribute name 'style' would need to be added to every element in the DTD, or some other mechanism must be found for identifying an equivalent attribute.

It is clear that the linked stylesheet approach is the most suitable.

It is possible for an XML document to refer to the stylesheet that should be applied to it using a processing instruction. There is an agreed W3C standard for such instructions that works for both CSS and XSLT. The target name is 'xml-stylesheet', and parameters that look like XML attributes (called 'href' and 'type') are used to locate the stylesheet, using a URL, and to identify the type of stylesheet in use. In this case, the type is 'text/css' (see Chapter 22 for more details):

```
<?xml-stylesheet href="MyBook.css" type="text/css" ?>
```

XML specifics

Because HTML tags are hard-wired into HTML-sensitive Web browsers, some information does not need to be supplied by a stylesheet. For example, it is known that the Emphasis element is an in-line element, so no line breaks are to be generated around it. It is also known that the Ordered List element contains numbered list items, and that the Preformatted element dictates no formatting of the embedded text. An XML-sensitive formatter, however, requires explicit information to identify elements that perform these and other roles.

Block and in-line elements

When presenting information the formatting program must distinguish between two types of element content. Some elements contain text that forms just part of a larger block of text. Emphasized text, superscript numbers and hypertext links are typical examples. None of these items, when enclosed by an element, should create a break in the text. They are known as **in-line elements**. In other cases, an element contains text that must be separated from preceding and following information. A title, paragraph, list item or footnote would fall into this category. Such items are described as **block elements**.

```
<p>A block containing an <em>in-line</em> element.</p>
```

At first sight, it is tempting to equate in-line elements with mixed content DTD models, and block features with element content models. But there is no direct correlation.

For example, a Paragraph element will usually have mixed content (text and further elements), but an embedded Emphasis element may also have mixed content, yet the first is a block element, and the latter is an in-line element (it *is* possible to detect which elements are block elements from a DTD, though it can only be done by analysing all content models, starting with the smallest element in each hierarchy, to find the outermost element with mixed content).

The **display property** is used to identify block and in-line elements. The 'display' property can hold values of 'block', 'inline', 'list-item' and 'none' (CSS2 adds some more options). The default value, if the display property is not present, is 'block'. Therefore, the following two examples are equivalent:

```
title   { color: blue }
title   { color: blue ; display: block }
```

A 'block' display value indicates that line breaks will be generated above and below the element content. An 'inline' display value indicates that no line breaks will be generated. A display value of 'none' indicates that the content of the element should not be presented at all:

```
p       { display: block }
secret  { display: none }
em      { display: inline }


<p>This is a paragraph.</p>
<secret>THIS IS A SECRET!</secret>
<p>This is another block, with an
<em>in-line</em> embedded element.</p>
```

This is a paragraph.

This is another block, with an **in-line** embedded element.

Lists

It is possible for list item numbers to be generated automatically. The 'list-item' display value indicates that a list item marker is to appear against the content of this element:

```
item { display: list-item }

...
<item>This is an item.</item>
<item>This is another item.</item>
...
```

```
...
3. This is an item.
4. This is another item.
...
```

It may also be necessary to identify the element that encloses the entire list, if only to reset item counting, though an application may just assume that numbering starts from the first sibling in a list of items. Whether necessary or not, the parent of the items is a good place to specify the form the numbering will take.

The 'list-style-type' property specifies the marker type that will appear against each item. There are many options: 'disc', 'circle', 'square', 'decimal' (1. 2. 3. 4.), 'lower-roman' (i. ii. iii. iv.), 'upper-roman' (I. II. III.), 'lower-alpha' (a. b. c. d.), 'upper-alpha' (A. B. C. D.) and 'none' (blank). The default value is 'disc', which is a non-sequenced list (sometimes described as a 'bulleted' or 'random' list):

```
list { ... ; list-style-type: disc }
item { display: list-item }
```

- item one

- item two

- item three

List item position

The 'list-style-position' property specifies whether the marker appears within the left boundary of the text block ('inside'), or to the left of this block ('outside'). By default, the number is placed outside:

1. This is the first list item, with
   the item number appearing inside or outside.

2. This example shows the same effect.

When set to 'inside' the marker is 'brought in' to the text block:

```
list { ... ; list-style-position: inside }
```

1. This is the first list item, with
the item number appearing inside or outside.

2. This example shows the same effect.

Combined list properties

These disparate properties make list definitions quite cumbersome. Fortunately, all this information can be specified using the 'list-style' property, which takes a number of parameters: first the type, then an optional image URL and finally the position:

```
r-list    { list-style: lower-roman inside }

n-list    { list-style: decimal outside }
```

List item image

As an alternative to the list type marker, an image can be displayed before each list item. The image is identified by a URL in the 'list-style-image' property. Apart from its obvious use as a mechanism to include an infinite number of new item markers, this feature is particularly useful for generating appropriate icons against items of different types.

For example, the brochure for a hotel could list its features in this way. To achieve this effect, however, the image property must be included in the definition of the item element(s) themselves:

```
food   { list-style-image:
                      url(file:///images/knife-fork.tif) }
beds   { list-style-image:
                      url(file:///images/bed.tif) }
pool   { list-style-image:
                      url(file:///images/pool.tif) }
```

```
<features>
<beds>64 bedrooms</beds>
<pool>full sized swimming pool</pool>
<food>first class restaurant</food>
</features>
```

Whitespace

Under normal conditions, any surplus spaces and line-break codes are removed from a block of text. For example, if a text editor is used to create an HTML or XML document, it is normal practice to insert line-break codes into a paragraph at convenient points, so that the text will be legible:

```
<p>This paragraph is quite long so it has[CR]
been broken into separate lines in the text[CR]
editor used to create it. Yet these[CR]
line-breaks are artificial, and should[CR]
not be retained in formatted output.</p>[CR]
```

> This paragraph is quite long so it has been broken into separate lines on the text editor used to create it. Yet these line-breaks are artificial, and should not be retained in formatted output.

Most line-break codes are converted into spaces, as shown above, but there are exceptions that apply when the line breaks or original spaces appear between markup tags and text. In the example below, the leading space and carriage returns are removed:

```
<p> [CR]
This paragraph is quite short.[CR]
</p>
```

> This paragraph is quite short.

This behaviour is described as 'collapsing' the content of the element, effectively into a single text line (though it is re-split by the application at convenient column or window boundaries).

The 'white-space' property must take a value of 'normal' (collapsed), 'pre' (pre-formatted) or 'nowrap' (an HTML-specific feature used in conjunction with the Break element), and has a default value of 'normal'. All spaces and line-break codes can be preserved by setting the 'white-space' property to 'pre':

```
program    { white-space: pre }
```

```
<program>
10 REM This is a BASIC program[CR]
20 PRINT "Hello world"[CR]
30 GOTO 20[CR]
</program>
```

```
10 REM This is a BASIC program
20 PRINT "Hello world"
30 GOTO 20
```

See Chapter 8 for more details on this complex but important issue.

Batch composition to HTML

When using an XML-sensitive browser to display an XML document, it is only necessary to create a suitable CSS stylesheet, and reference it from the document. But when using an HTML-sensitive browser to display an XML document, a software 'filter' is used to transform the document into HTML format.

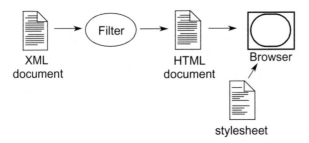

When using a filter program (or XSLT stylesheet), HTML in-line styles become a practical, and sometimes preferred, option. A filter program does not object to repeatedly generating the same style rule, it simply adds the Style attribute directly to each element:

```
<p style="font-size: 9pt ; color: blue">...</p>
<p style="font-size: 9pt ; color: blue">....</p>
<p style="font-size: 9pt ; color: blue">.....</p>
```

Although in-line styles were originally intended for 'tweaking' the appearance of specific objects on design-centred Web pages, the advantage of this approach is the total flexibility it provides. The filter software is able to take complex element and attribute value-based context rules into consideration when determining the style of each HTML element.

For example, the content of a Person element may need to be presented in different colours, according to some age grouping category, such as baby, toddler, child, teenager, adult and pensioner, for which appropriate age ranges are assigned, but working from an Age attribute that contains a simple value such as '36'. The software would supply the appropriate colour value using a look-up table of age ranges.

The disadvantages of this approach are the need for an intelligent filter program, and the larger size of the resulting HTML document.

HTML features

HTML contains elements and attributes that have been included specifically to facilitate styling by the CSS mechanism. Conversely, the CSS standard itself contains features aimed at its use with HTML documents. This section is aimed at readers who also work with HTML (either directly, or as an output format derived from XML source documents), and would like to apply CSS to HTML documents.

New attributes (Style and Class)

A new attribute, called Style, appears in the HTML 4.0 standard. This attribute contains a style rule that applies only to the specific instance of the element containing it. This in-line rule overrides all other rules:

```
<!-- HTML -->
h3    { color: blue }
...
<h3>Blue Header</h3>
...
<h3 style="color: green">Green Header</h3>
```

This feature is primarily aimed at design-led documents, where there are no predictable patterns to the layout of the text. As such, it is of little relevance to XML (though it was earlier shown how this feature can be used in unexpected ways).

An attribute called Class effectively provides a mechanism for extending the HTML DTD. For example, if the document author requires three different kinds of paragraph, the Class attribute can be used to define variants of the single Paragraph element:

```
<!-- HTML -->
<p class="first">The first paragraph.</p>
<p>A normal paragraph.</p>
<p class="note">NOTE: a note paragraph.</p>
```

The stylesheet can refer to the content of the Class attribute, creating different rules for each variant. The classification name is placed after the element name, separated by a full point. For the example above, three rules would be needed:

```
P            { color: blue ; font-size: 12pt }
P.first      { txt-indent: .5in }
P.note       { font-size: 9pt ; margin-left: 1in }
```

When a Class attribute does not appear in a specific paragraph instance, the first of these rules applies. When the Class attribute contains 'first', the second rule *also* applies. When the Class attribute contains 'note', the paragraph is indented, and the point size of the text is reduced.

It is not necessary to match the case of the text. 'FIRST' will match 'first' or 'First', though consistency is encouraged, if only for the sake of legibility.

Spanning and dividing blocks

Two additional elements have been defined to extend the capabilities of HTML. These are the **Span** and **Division** (**Div**) elements. Unlike other HTML elements, such as Emphasis, they have no implied meaning, and no default styles. Simply adding a Span element or Division element to an HTML document has no effect on embedded text, and in any case they are ignored by older browsers. These elements are only intended to be used to help build stylesheet rules (though Div was first introduced to isolate areas of the document that had different alignments, and has an Align attribute to affect embedded structures – but this usage should now be discontinued).

The Span element is an in-line element, which can be used to produce any *ad hoc* styles the author requires. Whenever the author requires an in-line element that does not exist in HTML, the Span element can be used. For example, if the name of a country is significant, and is to be presented in a unique style, the country name could be embedded within a Span element:

```
<!-- HTML -->
<p>I hear that <span>Belgium</span> is a nice
place to visit.</p>
```

If more than one additional element type is required, the Class attribute can be used. For example, if animal names are to be styled differently, the Class attribute can distinguish these domains:

```
SPAN.country { color: blue }
SPAN.animal  { color: green }
...
<!-- HTML -->
<P>I hear that <span class="country">Belgium</span>
is a nice place to visit. But there are no
<span class="animal">Giraffes</span> there.</p>
```

Link styling

Hypertext links can be styled in different ways, depending on whether or not the link has recently been traversed, and whether or not it is currently selected. The ':link' keyword identifies a hypertext link that has not been activated and is not currently selected. The ':visited' keyword identifies one that has been traversed (assuming that the browser has remembered this fact). The ':active' keyword identifies one that is currently being selected:

```
A:link       { color: green }
A:visited    { color: blue }
A:active     { color: red }
```

25. Cascading stylesheets 2 (CSS2)

CSS2 adds a number of features to the standard that increases its power generally, and improves its utility with XML specifically, yet retains backward compatibility with CSS1. It is necessary to read Chapter 24 before this one, as concepts in common are not repeated.

Improvements

This version includes more contextual rules and features to support output to paper. Of most importance to XML users, though, are its new display types, which allow arbitrarily named elements to be described as table-building constructs.

The language has more than doubled in size with this release, as it includes 77 new property types.

Improved selection options

Some obvious holes in the element selection capabilities of CSS have been filled in the new version. It is now possible to select an element that is the direct child of another specified element, that is immediately preceded by another specified element, or that is the first child of its parent. In addition, attribute values can be taken into consideration.

Wildcards

The '*' symbol is used as a 'wildcard', substituting for every element in the document, and also for any number of embedded element levels. However, unlike the XML use of this character in DTDs, it represents one or more descendants (not zero or more).

The rule below applies to all titles in the book, except for the book title itself (because there must be another element between the two elements):

```
book * title { ... }
```

Required parent element

The '>' symbol indicates that the target element must be a child of another specified element. In the following example, the style only applies to Paragraph elements that are directly embedded within Intro elements:

```
intro > para { ... }
```

Child and ancestor selection criteria may be combined. In the following example, the Intro element must also be a descendant of the Book element:

```
book intro > para { ... }
```

Required previous element

The '+' symbol is used to indicate that the target element must immediately follow another specified element. In the following example, the style only applies to a Paragraph element that immediately follows a Title element:

```
title + para { ... }
```

Again, this rule may be mixed with others. The following rule applies to paragraphs that immediately follow a title, but only when they are children of a Chapter element:

```
chapter > title + para { ... }
```

Required no previous element

The ':first-child' keyword is used to identify an element that has no prior siblings. For example, the first Paragraph element in a child sequence may be formatted differently to others (perhaps by not having the usual indent on the first line):

```
para:first-child { ... }
```

Unique element instance targeting

The '#' symbol, followed by an ID value, targets an instance of the given element when it has a matching unique identifier. Note that *no* mechanism is included for identifying the name of the attribute concerned when that information is unavailable due to the absence of a DTD. In the following example, the style only applies to the Paragraph element that has a Name value of 'para33':

```
para#para33 { ... }
```

Constraints using attributes

Attribute restrictions are enclosed in square brackets, '[' and ']', following the element name:

```
para[ ... ] { ... }
```

Multiple attributes may be considered, in which case the square brackets are repeated for each one:

```
para[ ... ][ ... ] { ... }
```

The mere presence of a particular attribute may be considered sufficient to select a category of elements. For example, every Paragraph element containing a Security attribute may be indented and displayed in a different colour, regardless of its value:

```
para[security] { ... }
```

Attribute value constraints

However, it is also possible to specify the value the attribute must contain for the match to be successful:

```
para[security="secret"] { ... }
```

A further refinement of this is the ability to match one word in an attribute that contains several space-separated values, by employing the '~' symbol before the equals sign. For example, a Keywords attribute may contain the value 'xml xsl css', but the rule may apply if the text 'css' is present within the value:

```
para[keywords~="css"] { ... }
```

A more constrained variant uses the vertical bar, '|', to match only the first part of an entry, leading up to a hyphen. This feature is mainly intended to be used with language codes, such as 'en-GB'. The following rule would match an English paragraph, no matter what the geographical location:

```
para[keywords|="en"] { ... }
```

When a rule should apply to any element containing a specified attribute, or particular attribute value, the element name is simply omitted. However, it is considered good practice to include the wildcard symbol, '*'. The following two examples are equivalent:

```
[security="secret"] { ... }
*[security="secret"] { ... }
```

Miscellaneous improvements

All properties now have an 'inherit' value option. When this value is used, the element inherits its setting for this property from the current setting, as specified in an enclosing element.

In some cases, the 'inherit' option is the default value, which means that the element inherits the characteristic from the parent element (unless an override value is explicitly set):

The 'vertical-align' property can now take a length value, such as '2pt'.

The 'text-align' property can now take a string value that represents the character or characters to centre the text on. This is of most use in tables, where columns of figures may need to be centred on a decimal point:

```
salary      { ... ; text-align: "." }
```

Some languages are written right to left. The 'direction' property takes a value of 'ltr' (left to right) or 'rtl' (right to left). This property specifies the base writing direction of blocks, the direction of table column layouts, the direction of horizontal overflow, and the position of the last line in a block with a 'text-align' property value of 'justify'. The 'unicode-bidi' property works in conjunction with the 'direction' property to control processing of in-line elements. Refer to the standard for details:

```
hebrew-text   { direction: rtl; unicode-bidi: embed }
```

Fonts and styles

Characters can be stretched or squeezed using the 'font-stretch' property. They can be 'ultra-condensed', 'extra-condensed', 'semi-condensed', 'condensed', 'normal' (the default), 'expanded', 'semi-expanded', 'extra-expanded' or 'ultra-expanded'. The values 'wider' and 'narrower' specify a move to the next setting:

```
warning-para { ... ; font-stretch: extra-expanded }
```

Shadows can appear around characters using the 'text-shadow' property. Each shadow effect is separated from others using a comma. Each effect involves up to four parameters, including the horizontal offset (which may be negative for backward shadows), the vertical offset (which may also be negative, for shadows above the text), then an optional blurring radius factor, and finally an optional colour:

```
shade-it { text-shadow: 2pt 2pt red }
```

```
shade-it-vivid { text-shadow: 2pt 2pt red,
                              -3px -3px 1px green }
```

Font substitution can be risky when a preferred font is not available and a small point size is specified. The reason is that some fonts are more legible than others at small point sizes, and this is usually due to something called the 'aspect ratio'. This is the height of small, lower-case letters, such as 'x', in relation to the line height. This difference is expressed as a value, such as '0.45'. Substitute fonts with a smaller aspect ratio than the preferred font should be presented at a larger point size to compensate. The 'font-size-adjust' property takes as a parameter the aspect ratio of the preferred font. The application must perform a calculation from the known aspect ratio of the substitution font in order to adjust its size accordingly:

```
para { font: bold italic large Palatino, serif ;
       font-size-adjust: 0.58 }
```

Boxes

The 'border-color' property can now take the value 'transparent'. It is then invisible, but still has its given width.

Independent border styles

The new properties 'border-left-color', 'border-right-color', 'border-top-color' and 'border-bottom-color' allow each side to be coloured differently (though 'border-color' with four parameters has the same effect). Similarly, the new properties 'border-left-style', 'border-right-style', 'border-top-style' and 'border-bottom-style' allow each side to be styled differently (though 'border-style' with four parameters has the same effect). The two examples below are equivalent:

```
para { border-color: red green yellow blue ;
       border-style: dotted dashed }
```

```
para { border-top-color:    red ;
       border-right-color:  green ;
       border-bottom-color: yellow ;
       border-left-color:   blue ;
       border-top-style:    dotted ;
       border-right-style:  dashed ;
       border-bottom-style: dotted ;
       border-left-style:   dashed}
```

Overflow text

When the content of an element is too much to fit in its containing box, some of the content will overflow. This will only happen when the box cannot expand to encompass the data, because it has been given a set width or height. The content is normally still 'visible', but, using the 'overflow' property, it is possible to make this content 'hidden', though still make it accessible by giving this property the value 'scroll' (a scroll bar is added to the field). The value 'auto' is also available, but will often be interpreted as being the same as 'scroll':

```
colours-list { ... ; width: 30mm ; height: 80mm ;
                     overflow: scroll }
```

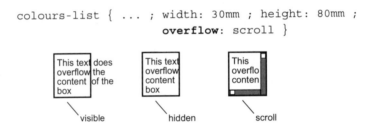

Clipped regions

In addition, the normally visible region within a box can be clipped, using the 'clip' property, which by default takes the value 'auto' (the clip region is the same size as the content box, so has no effect). In the future, it should be able to take parameters that represent a number of shapes, such as triangles and ovals, but for now it can only take a rectangular-shaped clipping region, 'rect(...)'. This function takes four parameters, each representing the distance from the top, right, bottom and left side of the content box:

```
clip-it { ... ; clip: rect(0px, 10px, 0px 10px) }
```

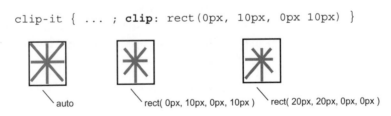

Invisible text

The content box is normally 'visible', but using the 'visibility' property it is possible to make the content 'hidden', while still taking the equivalent space in the flow, or even to 'collapse' the content entirely. The default value is 'inherit':

```
top-secret { ... ; visibility: collapse }
```

Lists

Additional options have been added to the 'list-style-type' property, including 'decimal-leading-zero', 'lower-greek', 'upper-greek', 'lower-latin' (the same as 'lower-alpha'), 'upper-latin' (the same as 'upper-alpha'), 'hebrew', 'armenian', 'georgian', 'cjk-ideographic', 'katakana', 'hiragana-iroha' and 'katakana-iroha'.

The leading zeros in the 'decimal-leading-zero' option refers to padding to the same length as the longest number in the list. If the largest number is '87', then values below 10 are padded to two digits, as in '06'. If the largest number is '264', then all values below 100 are padded to three digits, as in '006' and '098':

```
098  ninety-eighth item
099  ninety-ninth item
100  last item
```

Prefix and suffix generation

In XML documents, the ability to generate prefix and suffix text automatically is very important. For example, a Note element should not actually contain the prefix 'note:', or anything similar, but should only contain the note text itself:

```
<note>This is a note</note>
```

Prefix text

To indicate that this text is in fact a note when it is presented, a suitable prefix may be added. CSS is now able to do this using the 'before' pseudo-element, in conjunction with the new 'content' property:

```
note:before { content: "NOTE: " }
```

As the default value of the display property is 'inline', the prefix 'NOTE: ' is added to the text content of the Note element:

NOTE: This is a note

However, explicitly changing this value to 'block' puts the prefix above the text:

```
note:before { content: "NOTE: " ; display: block }
```

NOTE:
This is a note

All other style properties are available. For example, to make the heading bold, the font-weight property may be used:

```
note:before { content: "NOTE: " ; font-weight: bold }
```

NOTE: This is a note

Suffix text

For suffixes, there is an 'after' pseudo-element that works in exactly the same manner.

```
reference:before { content: "[" }

reference:after { content: "]" }
```

Quotes

To enclose the content of an element in quotes, it is advisable to use the 'open-quote' and 'close-quote' keywords:

```
quote:before { content: open-quote }

quote:after { content: close-quote }
```

What actually appears depends on a setting elsewhere, made using the 'quotes' property. For example, an English book may contain the following declaration, which states that left and right double-quote characters will be used, but then goes on to state, using additional parameters, that embedded quotes will be represented by single quote characters:

```
book[xml:lang="en"] { quotes: '"' '"' '"' '"' }
```

Attribute display

The 'attr(...)' function is replaced by the value of the named attribute. For example, to supply the name of the speaker for each speech in a play:

```
speech:before { content: attr(speaker) }
<speech speaker="Macbeth">...</speech>
```

Combinations

More complex options are made possible due to the fact that the 'content' property can take a number of parameters:

```
speech:before { content: "SPEAKER " attr(speaker) ":"}
```

SPEAKER Macbeth: ......

Complex item numbering

Finally, it is possible to generate sequential item numbering, in a more powerful way than could be achieved using the 'list-item' property. The 'counter-reset' property defines, and optionally also specifies, the starting value (default '0'). Then the 'counter-increment' property is used to increase the named value. Each increase can be more (or less) than the default of '1', by adding the increment (or decrement) value after the counter name. To display the counter, the 'counter()' function in the 'display' property is used (note that the value shown is one that is current after any reset or increment property is processed, regardless of the ordering of properties in the rule). The following example adds numbers to each item in a list:

```
list          { counter-reset: item 0 }
item          { display: block }
item:before { counter-increment: item ;
                content: counter(item) ". " }
```

1. first item

2. second item

Display options

The 'display' property has some additional options, including 'run-in', 'compact' and 'marker'.

Run in heading

The 'run-in' option is useful for creating specific styles for a range of text at the beginning of a block. An element given this style is assumed to be an in-line element that begins the block content of the next element. The style information only applies to the 'run-in' part of the resulting block. A single space character should appear between the content of the two elements. For example:

```
name { display: run-in ; font-weight: bold }
summary { display: block ; font-weight: medium }
```

```
<name>J Smith</name>
<summary>Software Developer, working in Java,
C++ and Perl.</summary>
```

> **J Smith** Software Developer, working in Java, C++
> and Perl.

Compact into margin

The 'compact' option is used to position text in the margin of the following block element. This feature is especially useful for creating glossaries and definition lists. The example above can be modified slightly as follows:

```
name { display: compact ; font-weight: bold }

summary { display: block ; font-weight: medium }
```

The content is treated as an in-line block if it is followed by a block element, and the content is short enough to fit in the margin. Otherwise, it is treated as a preceding block element, as shown below:

```
...
<name>M Pumpernickel</name>
<summary>Manager.</summary>
```

Markers

The 'marker' option is used within ':before' and ':after' pseudo-elements to separate prefix and suffix items from the main block, and can be used to create flexible list options. Also, the distance between the marker text and the main block can be controlled using the 'marker-offset' property. For example, it could dictate a gap of '3em':

```
note:before { display: marker ;
              marker-offset: 3em ; content: NOTE> }

note:after { display: marker ;
             marker-offset: 3em ; content: <<< }
```

```
<note>This is a long note that spans over lines.</note>
```

NOTE> This is a long note that spans over lines.   <<<

Size limits

There may be a need to constrain the width or height of an object to a specific mini-mum and/or maximum size. The 'min-width' and 'min-height' properties take a length or percentage value (with the latter defaulting to '0' and the former being application dependant). The 'max-width' and 'max-height' properties are similar, but both have a default value of 'none'.

```
sidebox    { min-width:  3cm ; max-width: 4cm ;
             min-height: 9cm ; max-height: none }
```

Object positioning

Boxes can be moved out of the normal flow, using the 'position' property.

A value of 'static' (the default) produces a box in the normal flow, but a value of 'relative' allows the box to be moved to a new location relative to its normal posit-ion, without affecting subsequent boxes, and a value of 'absolute' allows the box to be moved to a location relative to the position of the containing box (the box generated by the parent of the current element, such as a list box surrounding its item boxes, or the root element box that surrounds all others). A 'fixed' value is similar to 'absolute', but specifies a fixed location in respect to the page or browser view port. A fixed item does not move when the document is scrolled:

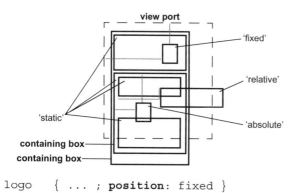

```
logo    { ... ; position: fixed }
```

Relatively placed boxes are positioned relative to the box itself. To move the box outside its own boundaries (as in the illustration above), negative values are used.

Positioned boxes can also be placed over or beneath other boxes, creating a stack. The root element automatically creates a default stack, and this element has the position '0' within this stack.

By default, all embedded elements share the same position value, so there is no stacking. But positioned elements given a higher stack number, using the 'z-index' property, lie above the the other elements, fully or partially masking them. When 'z-index' is given a value, instead of the default 'auto', the element is positioned in the stack, and also creates a new stacking context for embedded elements:

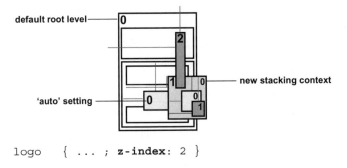

```
logo    { ... ; z-index: 2 }
```

Sizes

Boxes that are *not* positioned in a 'static' (normal flow) manner can be sized. The default value for the 'top', 'bottom', 'left' and 'right' properties is 'auto', meaning that the box is sized to fit the content, but a length or percentage value can be used to size the box relative to the containing block, or, in the case of relative positioning, to the originally calculated position of this box in the flow.

The 'left' property specifies the distance from the left edge of the containing block (or view port) to the left edge of the fixed or absolutely positioned box, and the 'right', 'top' and 'bottom' properties work in the same way for their respective sides. It may be more convenient, however, just to set the left and top edges in this manner, then use the 'width' and 'height' properties to size the box:

```
logo    { ... ; top:    20mm ; left: 150mm ;
                width:  40mm ; height:  40mm }
```

Tables

The table extensions in CSS2 should be of particular interest to XML users wishing to render the content of arbitrary XML elements in a tabular grid. Chapter 25 includes a brief discussion on the use of CSS to apply table styles to arbitrary XML elements, but the model is more powerful than the simple mapping to the table, the row and the cell elements shown there. As the properties described here have been developed to match the capabilities of the HTML 4.0 table model, readers unfamiliar with this model are advised to read the relevant descriptions in Chapter 25 before continuing.

Table grid

The display value 'table' corresponds to the HTML Table element. The display values 'table-row' and 'table-cell' correspond to the HTML elements Tr and Td (as well as Th).

These three display values are sufficient to map a simple XML structure onto a row-oriented table grid (column-oriented tables cannot be mapped, despite the first impression given by the inclusion of the display types 'table-column' and 'table-column-group', which actually serve a very different purpose):

```
<prices>
  <prod><code>XYZ-15</code><price>987</price></prod>
  <prod><code>XYZ-22</code><price>765</price></prod>
  <prod><code>ZZZ-01</code><price>119</price></prod>
</prices>
```

```
prices { display: table }

prod   { display: table-row }

code   { display: table-cell }

price  { display: table-cell }
```

XYZ-15	987
XYZ-22	765
ZZZ-01	119

Header and footer rows

In HTML 4.0, table row groups specified using the Thead, Tbody and Tfoot elements are allowed.

Header rows may repeat at the top of each page, and footer rows may repeat at the base of each page containing a reference to them. The equivalent display values are 'table-header-group', 'table-row-group' and 'table-footer-group':

```
<prices>
  <headers><head>Code</head><head>Price</head></headers>
  ...
</prices>
```

```
headers { display: table-header-group }

head    { display: table-cell }
...
```

Implied structure

In the previous example, there is no single row-separating element in the header section. The Head element defines a cell and the Headers element defines a table header group of rows. The missing intermediate level need not be explicitly stated, and is assumed to exist around all consecutive cell-level elements. Similarly, a group of row-level elements need not be explicitly encased in a table-level or row-group level element. In the previous example, the two Prod rows are deemed to be table body rows. It would even be possible to create a single-row table using nothing but cell-level elements:

```
<para>Normal text.</para>
<cell>danger</cell><cell>red</cell><cell>1</cell>
<para>More normal text.</para>
```

Width and height

The means by which the width and height of various parts of a table are determined includes automated calculations based on the content of the elements, or the use of attributes to make these measurements explicit. The 'table-layout' property takes a value 'auto' to specify that this task will be left to the rendering engine, or 'fixed' to ensure that fixed values are used. This property type may be used in the table-level element:

```
prices { display: table ; table-layout: auto}
```

Text alignment

Text can be aligned within a cell using the 'text-align' and 'vertical-align' properties (though only the 'top', 'bottom', 'middle' and 'baseline' values apply for vertical alignment):

```
<prices>
  <prod>
    <code>XYZ-15</code>
    <price>987</price></prod>
  <prod>
    <code>XYZ-22</code>
    <price>312</price></prod>
  </prod>
</prices>
```

```
code    { display: table-cell ; text-align: center }

price   { display: table-cell ; text-align: right }
```

XYZ-15	987
XYZ-22	312

Attribute control

Note that it is not possible to extract attribute values to dictate alignment, or to control cell spanning. The 'attr()' function mentioned earlier can only be used in the 'content' property, and only to present the content of an attribute. Perhaps the next version of CSS will address this problem. However, there is a crude technique available for providing some of this functionality:

```
code { display:table-cell ; text-align: center }

code[align="L"]     { ... ; text-align: left }

code[align="R"]     { ... ; text-align: right }
```

Column formatting

It is possible to assign XML elements to the roles played by the HTML Col and Colgroup elements, using the 'table-column' and 'table-column-group' display types:

```
left-block   { display:    table-column-group ;
                text-align: left }
```

Borders

There are property types to present borders around the table, or individual rows, columns and cells, including 'border' and 'border-collapse', but there are too many options and complications to cover here. See the specification.

Captions

A caption can be added to a table, using the 'table-caption' display type, and its location relative to the table can be specified using the 'caption-side' property ('top' (the default), 'bottom', 'left' or 'right'):

```
table title { display: table-caption ;
              caption-side: bottom }
```

Border lines

Using the 'border-collapse' property, borders around cells can be 'separate' (each cell has four border lines around it, not touching the borders around other cells) or can 'collapse' (adjacent cells share border lines on common edges, so they span the entire table). Collapsed borders are the default setting, but when separate borders are specified, the amount of space between the borders of each cell can be given using the 'border-spacing' property, which takes at least one length value, and up to four values representing the top, right, bottom and left edges respectively.

Also, in this model it is possible to omit borders around empty cells, using the 'empty-cells' property, and giving it the value 'hide' ('show' is the default):

```
table  { ... ; border-collapse: separate ;
              border-spacing: 2pt, 1pt, 2pt, 1pt }
```

Spoken headers

When the table is presented as speech, the content of a relevant table header is spoken before each cell, but by default is not repeated if the current cell shares the same header as the previous one. To repeat the header for every cell, the 'speak-header' property can be assigned the value 'always' (the default is 'once').

Printed output

CSS1 concentrates on the task of formatting text for presentation on-screen, within a Web browser. The different needs of printed output are not addressed, though it is possible simply to print out a document using the formatting already applied for screen presentation (the document is simply divided into page-sized chunks and printed in the same format).

CSS2 extensions give the stylesheet designer the ability to specify the size and orientation of the page output, the elements that should start a new page, decide how multi-line element content is broken over pages, define styles that only apply to screen or to page, and to define the active areas on the page to be printed on.

Separate print and screen formats

Before investigating these features in detail, the issue of separating instructions for print from instructions to display must be addressed. An **at-rule**, '@', with a keyword of 'media' and a parameter of 'screen' or 'print', is used to separate screen formatting rules from paper formatting rules.

In the example below, the Emphasis element is given differing definitions. For screen, bold style is an appropriate highlighting technique. For paper, italic style is feasible (and often preferred):

```
@media screen { em { font-weight: bold } }

@media print  { em { font-style: italic } }
```

More media options are available, including 'aural', 'braille', 'embossed', 'handheld', 'projection', 'tty' (teletype) and 'tv'. The term 'all' is used to encompass all these media types. Combinations are separated by commas:

```
@media screen, tv, handheld { ... }
```

Pages

The features of a page, such as its width and height, do not correspond to any element, so another at-rule, the 'page' rule, is used to contain the properties that may be used to specify page-oriented information:

```
@media print {
   @page  { ... }
   ...
}
```

The declarations allowed in the 'page' rule include those available to block elements ('margin', 'margin-top', 'margin-right', 'margin-bottom' and 'margin-left') plus 'size' and 'marks'.

First page

The first page of a document is often treated differently to the others, particularly when it takes the role of a cover sheet, having narrower margins or a smaller page depth. The 'first' pseudo-class identifies the first page of a document:

```
@page :first { ... }
```

Page size

The 'size' property defines the page area within a sheet of paper. The default setting, 'auto', denotes the same size and orientation as the sheet. However, it should be noted that printers cannot usually print to the edges of a sheet, so borders should be used to clear some space around the edges (see below).

The value 'landscape' specifies printing across the wider page dimension. A single explicit value provides both the width and height of the page box (defining a square). When two values are provided, the first value defines the width and the second defines the height. The target sheet must be at least this size for the page to be printed successfully:

```
@page { size: 8.5in 11in }
```

Left and right pages

It may also be necessary to consider the space that the binding takes from the reading area. It is common practice to make the inner margin wider than the outer margin, which in practice means defining different margin widths for left-hand and right-hand pages:

```
@page :left  { margin-left: 2cm ; margin-right: 4cm }
@page :right { margin-left: 4cm ; margin-right: 2cm }
```

Crop marks

Printed sheets may need to be trimmed to create a bound document, but the page box area defined above is not usually apparent on the sheet. The 'marks' property ensures that marks are added to reveal the print box area. Crop marks are used to show where the page should be trimmed. Cross marks are used to align pages.

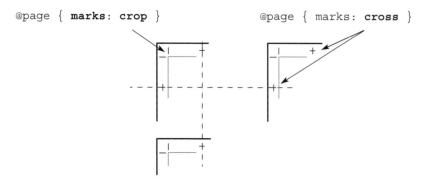

Page-break control

As on-screen browsing involves simply scrolling down through a single (possibly very long page), there is usually no indication as to how this material should be split when it is printed across multiple pages. The most obvious approach is simply to fill each page, regardless of the objects that appear before or after each page-break. If there are any chapter or section titles, for example, they can appear anywhere on the page, even though this does little to highlight their importance:

normal text flow

The 'page-break-before' property can be used to override this simple behaviour, and is represented by the value 'auto' (the default). Alternative values are 'always', 'avoid', 'left' or 'right'. This property may be used with any block element (except those in tables).

The default setting specifies that a page-break is not necessary, unless the element happens to fall naturally at the start of a new page.

A value of 'always' indicates a forced page-break before this element, even when this means generating a large amount of whitespace at the bottom of the current page.

The value 'avoid' is used to ensure that the element is never the first on a page (the content of the previous element may have to be dragged down to the top of the new page, leaving an even larger space on the previous page).

A value of 'left' or 'right' indicates that the element should be placed at the top of the next left-hand or right-hand page respectively. For example, if the text flow had reached the middle of a right-hand page when an element with a 'right' page-break setting was encountered, the rest of that page would be left blank, and the following left-hand page would also be left blank. This technique is typically found in books (like this one) where each chapter begins a new right-hand page:

```
chapter title    { page-break-before: right }
section title    { page-break-before: always }
```

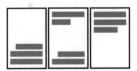

The 'page-break-after' property works in exactly the same manner, except that the page-break appears below the content of the element.

Page-breaks can be prevented from occurring within a text block, by moving the entire block down onto the following page. The 'page-break-inside' property can be set to 'avoid' (the default value is 'auto'). Note that this action may create whitespace at the bottom of the page that would have contained the first part of the block.

Widows and orphans

When a paragraph is broken over pages, the split could normally occur at any point within the paragraph, including just after the first line, or just before the last line. A single line at the bottom of a page is called an orphan. A single line left at the top of the page is called a widow. This is considered bad practice, and most type-setters avoid such splits by adjusting inter-line and inter-word spacing.

It is possible to specify a minimum number of lines that must appear at the bottom or top of a page using the 'widows' and 'orphans' properties. For example, setting both properties to a value of '2' in the Paragraph element would ensure the following kinds of paragraph break:

User interface

Cursor design

The design of the cursor may be changed as the user places it over a particular element. The 'cursor' property takes a value of 'auto' (the default), 'crosshair', 'default' (*not* the default), 'pointer', 'move', may be resized in a given compass direction ('e-resize', 'ne-resize', 'nw-resize', 'n-resize', 'se-resize', 'sw-resize', 's-resize' and 'w-resize'), 'text',' 'wait' or 'help', or may take a URL that identifies an image to show instead. Some of the more common representations are shown below:

Outline highlights

Lines around objects may be added to highlight a default or currently selected item, particularly within forms. Outlines are similar to borders, except that they do not occupy additional space, and are the same shape as the object (not necessarily rectangular).

An outline can have a style, with the same options as the border styles (default 'none'), a colour (with 'invert' added to the normal colour list, and made the default setting) and a width (default 'medium'). The 'outline-style', 'outline-color' and 'outline-width' properties apply to these characteristics. Pseudo-classes called ':focus' and ':active' are used to identify an element that has the current focus, or is currently active:

```
:active    { outline-style: dotted ;
             outline-color: red ;
             outline-width: 2pt }
```

These three properties can be combined within the 'outline' property, which specifies first the colour, then the style, and finally the width:

```
name:focus { outline: dashed }

:active    { outline: red dotted 2pt }
```

Aural styles

CSS2 includes a large number of properties to assist with the audible presentation of material. Speech presentation is important, not just to those who are visually disabled, but to anyone who is not able to switch their visual attention from some other task, such as driving.

Speech and spelling-out

The 'speak' property is used to render text audibly when given the value 'normal' (the default), or 'spell-out'. The 'spell-out' option is used to pronounce text such as CSS, by spelling out each letter, 'C', 'S', 'S'. A value of 'none' indicates no audible presentation of the content.

Volume

One of the most important properties of speech is volume. The 'volume' property can take a number of different types of value. This is simply a recommended or default value that the listener should be able to adjust.

A simple numeric value in the range 1–100 denotes a volume from barely audible to barely comfortable. A percentage value is used for volumes that are relative to inherited values:

```
para     { volume: 60 }

whisper { volume: 50% }

shout    { volume: 150% }
```

```
    <para>you should <shout>shout</shout> this and
    <whisper>whisper</whisper> this.</para>
```

The value 'silent' switches off sound (it should be recalled that a volume of '0' does not indicate silence, just very quiet speech), and there are several named volume values that represent common requirements, including 'x-soft' (the same as a volume of 0), 'soft' (the same as 25), 'medium' (50), 'loud' (75) and 'x-loud' (100).

Type of voice

Voices are distinguished by type. The most obvious categories are male, female and child, but it is also possible to specify more specific categories (though the standard does not contain such a list of options), or even name an individual.

Voice characteristics use an override system that is similar to the font specification, so that generic types can be chosen when specific types are not available on the local system. The 'voice-family' property is used:

```
john      { voice-family: male-cockney, male }

mary      { voice-family: female-irish, female }

ageto12   { voice-family: child }

churchill { voice-family: churchill, male }
```

Speech rate

Rate of speech can be defined with the 'speech-rate' property. As before, the listener should be able to override the initial setting.

This property takes a numeric value that represents words per minute, though some convenient named values are also available, including 'x-slow' (80 words per minute), 'slow' (120), 'medium' (180–200), 'fast' (300) and 'x-fast' (500). The values 'slower' and 'faster' adjust an inherited speech rate by 40 words per minute.

Pitch of voice

When generic voice types are used, it is possible to add some variety by specifying the 'pitch'. This property takes a value of 'x-low', 'low', 'medium', 'high' or 'x-high', or a numeric value giving the pitch in Hertz. The named values do not have a pre-defined Hertz equivalent, as it depends on the main voice characteristic chosen, such as 'male' or 'female' (the average pitch for a male voice is around 120Hz, but for a female voice it is around 210Hz):

```
churchill { voice-family: male ; pitch: 90Hz }
```

Some people speak with a steady pitch, and others vary the pitch, even in normal conversation. The 'pitch-range' property specifies the degree to which the pitch can change during the speech, from '0' (no change, a monotonous voice) to '100' (a wildly animated voice), with '50' representing a normal variance:

```
churchill { voice-family: male ; pitch:90Hz
                         pitch-range: 20 }
```

The voice can be further refined using 'stress' and 'richness' properties that affect the inflection and the prominence or brightness of the voice.

Pauses

Pauses between words are very important in speech. The ends of sentences, paragraphs and larger divisions of text are marked by pauses of different lengths.

The 'pause-before' property creates a pause before the content of the element is presented. A set duration can be given, such as '20ms' (20 milliseconds), or a time span that is relative to the speed of the speech can be specified instead, such as '50%' ('100%' represents the time it takes to speak one word, on average, at the current speech rate).

The 'pause-after' property works in the same way, but creates a gap after the content.

When specifying a pause both before and after, a more convenient 'pause' property is available that takes two parameters, with the first parameter providing the before value, and the second parameter providing the after value.

The 'pause' property can take a single parameter, to represent both locations. The following two examples are therefore equivalent:

```
item { pause: 30ms 20ms }
item { pause-before: 30ms ; pause-after: 20ms }
```

Punctuation and digits

In some cases, the pauses they produce may not be sufficient to identify punctuation, and it may be necessary to be ensure that punctuation is clearly identified. The 'speak-punctuation' property takes a value of 'code' to specify that punctuation is to be read out. For example, 'this, and that' would be read out as 'this comma ...(pause)... and that'. The value 'none' (the default) disables punctuation speech.

Similarly, while numerals are normally spoken as 'continuous' digits, so that '237' is pronounced 'two hundred and thirty seven', it is possible using the 'speak-numeral' property to dictate that the digits are to be read out separately. The value 'digits' ensures that this example is pronounced 'two three seven':

```
code { speak-numeral: digits }

<p>The alarm code is <code>1254</code>.</p>
```

Sound effects

Sound effects can be played before or after the spoken content. The 'cue-before' property specifies a sound to be played before the speech, and 'cue-after' plays a sound afterward. The 'cue' property is more convenient if surrounding sounds are required, as it takes two values, one for before and one after. Note that a single value to the 'cue' property specifies that the given sound should be played both before and after the speech.

Sounds can be inherited from parent elements, but existing sounds can be over-ridden using the value 'none' (to avoid playing a sound). A sound is identified by URL, using the 'url' function:

```
emergency { cue: url("BELL.WAV") }
```

The 'play-during' property allows a sound to be played throughout the speech. A value of 'auto' means that an existing sound, activated by an ancestor element, should continue to play throughout this fragment of the speech.

If there is a possibility (or even a certainty) that the sound will end before the speech ends, it is possible to repeat the sound using the 'repeat' parameter.

It is also possible to mix a new sound with one that is already playing, by adding the 'mix' parameter. These two parameters must follow the 'url' value, and when both are present they must appear in the order described above:

```
humm { play-during: url("HUMM1.WAV") repeat }

humm-harmony { play-during: url("HUMM2.WAV") mix repeat }
```

Spacial location

Advanced sound systems are able to provide stereo sound, and maybe also surround-sound effects. When there are several people speaking, it can be useful to give each one a separate spatial location.

Horizontal locations are specified using the 'azimuth' property, which accepts a value between '0deg' (zero degrees) and '360deg' (the same position). Values increase clockwise from the front-centre.

For convenience, some named values are available to correspond to different degree settings, including 'center' (zero degrees), 'center-right' (20 degrees), 'right' (40), 'far-right' (60), 'right-side' (90), 'left-side' (270), 'far-left' (300), 'left' (320) and 'center-left' (340).

The values 'leftwards' and 'rightwards' take an inherited value and move the sound left (by deducting 20 degrees) or right (by adding 20 degrees), though both appear to move sound in the wrong direction when it is behind the listener.

The parameter 'behind' can be added to a value, moving the sound to the back:

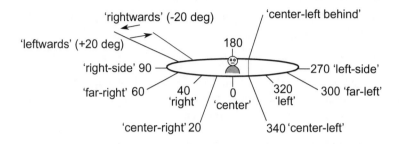

The following example places the judge at the centre-front, with prosecution and defence at each side:

```
judge          { azimuth:center }

prosecution { azimuth:left-side }

defence        { azimuth:right-side }
```

Sound sources may also be located at different vertical locations. For example, a judge should perhaps be elevated above the other speakers.

The 'elevation' property specifies a vertical location, from '0deg' (zero degrees) to '90deg' (overhead) or '-90deg' (beneath), with 'level', 'above' and 'below' also representing these extreme positions. The values 'higher' and 'lower' add and subtract 10 degrees respectively:

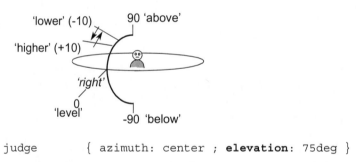

```
judge          { azimuth: center ; elevation: 75deg }
```

26. Managing XML documents

Many XML documents have a long or repeating life-cycle between creation and obsolescence. Apart from general issues of document management that apply to all types of electronic document, the XML language has features which may be utilized by software designed to simplify the creation and long-term management of documents. This chapter describes the options available, from the simplest use of operating system directory structures, public entities and catalogues to the most sophisticated document management systems.

Introduction

XML document and file management becomes an important issue when a large number of documents and components of documents are involved, when they have a long life-span, and when a number of authors are involved. It is important that XML documents are not misplaced, corrupted or stolen, and can be relocated without causing breaking links between related documents. A number of techniques are available for effective management of XML documents, at various levels of sophistication (and cost), including:

- storing documents as files in a directory-based operating system
- as above, but using public identifiers and catalogues to enable documents to be moved without breaking inter-document relationships
- as above, but utilizing formal public identifiers to make inter-document relationships more meaningful
- putting files under the control of a database system
- storing files in a document management system
- as above, but utilizing an XML-sensitive document component management system for increased flexibility.

Simple file storage

The simplest way to manage XML documents is to store them in a fixed location within the file system. In the example below, the main documents are stored in the 'docs' directory, common text entities are stored in the 'entity' directory and image entities are stored in the 'images' directory. Necessary configuration files, such as the DTD and character entity lists, are stored in the 'config' directory:

```
\work\xml\docs\X123456.xml
              X123457.xml
              X123458.xml
        \entity\disclaim.xml
              rights.xml
        \images\0001.tif
              0002.tif
              0003.tif
        \config\article.dtd
              isolat1.ent
              isogrk1.ent
```

Weaknesses

The operating system is designed to be a suitable storage manager for document files of any data format, including XML files, and standard features of the operating system may be utilized to prevent unauthorized access to some or all of the directories that are used to classify documents.

The URL-based linking scheme embodied in XML is also ready-made for file-to-file linking. A standard XML browser would allow users to follow links between documents.

All desktop applications expect to work directly with files, so do not need to be customized. And, best of all, this approach is essentially free.

Weaknesses

There are, however, a number of weaknesses with this approach.

It is difficult (and in some cases impossible) to control access to specific documents. Only entire directories are easy to control access to.

It is certainly impossible to control access to parts of a document. Documents tend to have short, and therefore cryptic file names (essential in older operating systems, and still desirable), so may not be easy to identify.

Two document authors may simultaneously access the same document without realizing and only changes made by the author who saves the work last are retained.

The status and history of a particular document are not stored, and there is no means to identify and notify an operator when the document is ready for a specific process.

It is also not easy to preserve old versions of a document as it is updated.

Another issue to be addressed with the file management technique is management of entities. A URL reference identifies a fixed location for each entity, and must be edited if the entity is moved to a new location, and relative URL references only partially resolve the problem.

Free-text searching

All of the approaches described here can now commonly include a **search engine**. These products analyse the text content of documents, and allow system users to quickly find relevant documents from words or phrases entered at a system prompt.

A search engine may have a number of techniques for locating documents that contain specified words or phrases. The most basic technique employs an **inverted word index**, which is a simple list of all the words used in a collection, sorted alphabetically, with links back to the documents containing these words.

XML is based on plain text formats, so is naturally easy to index using a search engine.

Increasingly, search engines are becoming XML-sensitive, and are able to identify text that occurs within specific elements. This is called '**zoning**'. For example, it is possible to locate all documents containing the word 'Wellington' within an element called Name, and by this means avoid all documents about footwear and military aircraft:

```
FIND "Wellington" IN Name AND "Waterloo" IN Title
```

Maintaining document links

The fundamental weakness of system identifiers is that they specify the exact, known location of a resource, so they fail to work if the resource is moved, or if the original resource is not accessible, but a copy elsewhere is to be used instead. While relative URL references (see Chapter 30) can be helpful when linked resources are moved together to a new location (and directory names involved in the bundle are not changed), they do nothing to avoid the other problems discussed here.

Avoiding this problem requires the use of **entity management** techniques, and a different kind of identifier.

An **entity manager** uses **public identifiers** to locate external entities. Entries in catalogue files simplify the management of entities (though they complicate transfer of data over the Internet). The various means by which the entity manager can provide access to an external entity can be illustrated using the example of an external DTD, referenced from the document type declaration. However, the following explanations apply equally to all external entity declarations.

A public identifier always assumes use of a catalogue file, but descriptive text replaces the file name in the document type declaration:

```
<!DOCTYPE mybook
          PUBLIC "-//MyCorp//DTD My Book//EN"   ""   >
```

The keyword 'PUBLIC' identifies this example as a public identifier. The catalogue file simply matches the delimited text to a specific data file on the local system:

```
PUBLIC "-//MyCorp//DTD My Book//EN" C:\XML\MYBOOK.DTD
```

Formal public identifiers

A formal definition for the format of public identifiers exists, and was originally defined for use with SGML. These identifiers include useful information about the resource, including the owner of the entity, the nature of its contents and even the human language used. A **formal public identifier** has a rigid structure composed of several parts: the **identifier type**, the **owner identifier**, the **public text class**, the **public text description** and the **public text language**. A public identifier should either conform strictly to the rules described below, or ignore this standard completely. Adopting the appearance but not the rigid rules of a formal public identifier would be confusing to people attempting to interpret it.

Registered and ISO entities

The **identifier type** describes the status of the identifier. For a public identifier to be guaranteed unique, it must be **registered**. The **ISO** standard **ISO 9070** covers the generating of a unique public identifier.

A **registered owner identifier** has the symbol '+' for the identifier type. An **unregistered owner identifier** has the symbol '-' (hyphen). An **ISO owner identifier** contains the text 'ISO 8879:1986'.

The identifier type is separated from the rest of the name by a double solidus, '//':

```
<!ENTITY ..... PUBLIC "+//....."> 
<!ENTITY ..... PUBLIC "-//....."> 
<!ENTITY ..... PUBLIC "ISO 8879:1986//..">
```

Note: There has been a change of character separating the ISO numbers from the dates. Originally a hyphen, it has changed to a colon. For example, 'ISO 8879-1986' has become 'ISO 8879:1986'.

Entity owner details

The **owner identifier** is the name of the person or organization that owns the entity content (or perhaps the owner of just the identifier itself). The owner identifier is not applicable in the case of ISO entities, as the identifier type has already established that the ISO is the owner.

Another double solidus separates the owner identifier from following details:

```
"+//MyCorp//....." 
"-//MyCorp//....." 
"ISO 8879:1986//....."
```

Entity contents

The **public text class** comprises a keyword that specifies the type of information contained by the entity. The classes of possible relevance to XML are listed here (there are several others used in SGML).

The 'DTD' class indicates that the entity contains a **Document Type Definition**, possibly including declarations for elements, entities and notations.

The 'ENTITIES' class indicates that the entity contains an **entity set**, containing declarations only for entities (commonly for character sets, such as the ISO sets).

The 'NOTATION' class indicates that the entity contains **character data** that documents the format of a notation. The 'TEXT' class indicates that the entity is a **text entity**:

```
"-//MyCorp//TEXT  ....."
```

Entity description

The **public text description** provides additional information about the content of
the external data:

```
"-//MyCorp//ENTITIES Superscript Chars  ....."
```

Human language used

The final component is the **language** identifier, which is a keyword from the list
provided in **ISO 639** (see Chapter 33). Again, it is separated from the public text
description by a double solidus '//'. The keyword for the English language, for
example, is 'EN' (note that letter-case is not really significant, but despite the conventions used in this and other examples, lower-case letters are now recommended):

```
"-//MyCorp//ENTITIES Superscript Chars//EN"
```

XML Catalog format

Although the use of catalogue files simplifies storage maintenance of XML documents, each XML-sensitive software application may use its own syntax for the
catalogue filing system, in which case the information must be repeated for each
application. In an attempt to avoid this unnecessary duplication, the **SGML Open**
group has produced a standard format for SGML documents, and more recently a
proposal has emerged for XML documents, called **XML Catalog**.

SGML Open

Two problems were identified by the SGML Open committee relating to the locating of entities on a system. First, when each application that accesses SGML entities uses its own catalogue format, entity location details must be duplicated.
Second, the recipient of an SGML document consisting of several files (not
merged using **SDIF**) needs a simple method to identify the base document and all
of its components. Both problems were solved by defining a common catalogue
format. The 'SGML Open Technical Resolution 9401:1995 (Amendment 1 to
TR9401)' paper on entity management defines such a format.

This simple format comprises a number of identifier mappings consisting of a keyword, followed by a public identifier or entity name and an equivalent system identifier.

In the example below, the file 'MYBOOK.XML' is identified as the base document (the starting point). The DTD is located in the system file 'BOOK.DTD', and the first chapter of the document is referred to by an entity called 'chap1', which is associated with a file named 'CHAPTER1.XML':

```
DOCUMENT   "MYBOOK.XML"
PUBLIC     "-//myCorp//DTD My DTD//EN"    BOOK.DTD
ENTITY     "chap1"                        CHAPTER1.XML
```

However, this standard is no longer in widespread use. The main criticism levelled at it was that its syntax did not conform to SGML (or indeed XML) conventions, so making it unnecessarily difficult to parse and validate, author and display catalogues.

Introducing XML Catalog

The scope and syntax of the proposed **XML Catalog** format (see http://www.ccil.org/~cowan/XML/XCatalog.html) is derived in part from the earlier attempt to define a standard for SGML documents described above. It is a private initiative, but is already widely accepted and incorporated into several parsers. The version of XML Catalog described here is the draft version 0.4 (though this version appears to be stable, and has been current for some years). Note that the name 'XCatalog' was formerly used for this standard, but the name was changed due to a conflict with the name of a commercial product.

Catalog syntax options

The XML Catalog standard defines two alternative syntaxes for catalogues. The first is fully backward-compatible with the SGML Open standard. The second is functionally equivalent, but uses an XML-based syntax. The second variant is often more interesting, because this makes it possible to create or edit a catalogue file using an XML editor, which can use the DTD shown below to guide the author.

Converting between formats is a task that can be automated. The following examples are directly equivalent:

```
BASE   "file:/xml/"
PUBLIC "-//ACME//DTD MyBook//EN" "DTDs/MyBook.DTD"


<XMLCatalog>
  <Base href="file:/xml/" />
  <Map PublicId="-//ACME//DTD MyBook//EN"
       HRef="DTDs/MyBook.DTD" />
</XMLCatalog>
```

Functionality

The XML Catalog standard allows public identifiers to be mapped to system identifiers (URLs), existing system identifiers to be mapped to other (locally relevant)
system identifiers, a base location to be defined from which relative URLs can be
given a context, a mechanism for incorporating one catalogue within another
(much like the external entity mechanism), and another for delegating some mappings to other catalogues.

Mapping public identifiers

The most fundamental reason for the existence of this standard is to provide a
product-independent mechanism for dealing with external entities that are referenced using a public identifier. The **Map** element provides a system identifier
equivalent that software can use to actually locate the entity.

In the following examples, an entity called '-//ACME//DTD MyBook//EN' is
given a location 'DTDs', and a filename of 'MyBook.DTD':

```
PUBLIC "-//ACME//DTD MyBook//EN" "DTDs/MyBook.DTD"
```

```
<Map PublicId="-//ACME//DTD MyBook//EN"
     HRef="DTDs/MyBook.DTD" />
```

Mapping system identifiers

The heavy emphasis on using system identifiers rather than public identifiers in
XML, due to its perceived primary use as a language of the Web, where catalogues
do not (yet) exist, means that public identifiers will often not be present in an entity
declaration. Only a system identifier will exist. However, the issue of mapping
identifiers to locally relevant URLs often remains. This standard therefore allows
a global system identifier to be mapped, or more accurately remapped to a local
identifier, using the **Remap** element (the older format uses the keyword
'SYSTEM').

In the following examples, the file 'MyBook.DTD' has no location context in the
system identifier, but is mapped locally to the 'DTDs' directory:

```
SYSTEM "MyBook.DTD" "DTDs/MyBook.DTD"
```

```
<Remap SystemId="MyBook.DTD"
       HRef="DTDs/MyBook.DTD" />
```

Base locations

The example above includes a relative URL reference as the system identifier. This is commonly done to make it easy to move collections of documents and entities to a new system location without needing to edit all the paths (or simply to avoid having to type the full path into the attribute). When a relative URL is included in a document, the path is considered to be relative to the source document, but in this case there is no source document. The location of the catalogue file itself is therefore used as the default base location:

```
HRef="DTDs/MyBook.DTD"
```

```
/XML/catalog.xml
     ...
     DTDs/MyBook.DTD
```

However, it is possible to override this default by including an instruction that names a specific base location, using the **Base** element:

```
<Base HRef="DTDs/" />

<Map PublicId="-//ACME//DTD MyBook//EN"
     HRef="MyBook.DTD" />
```

```
DTDs/MyBook.DTD
```

Extending and delegating

In large-scale systems, a single catalogue file may be too large to be either processed or maintained comfortably. It is therefore possible for a number of separate catalogue files to contain references to each other.

Common sets of mappings can be grouped together, and included in various 'main' catalogue files using the **Extend** element (the keyword 'CATALOG' is used in the older syntax). In the following example, a number of mappings for entities related to the ACME company are held in a catalogue file called 'ACME.CAT':

```
CATALOG "ACME.CAT"
```

```
<Extend HRef="ACME.CAT" />
```

A more sophisticated mechanism is provided for delegating related groups of entities, with similar public identifiers, to specialist catalogue files.

For example, a number of entities may all begin with the prefix '-//ACME'. The **Delegate** element is used to identify the prefix, as well as the catalogue file to delegate the mappings to:

```
DELEGATE "-//ACME" "ACME.CAT"
```

```
<Delegate PublicId="-//ACME" HRef="ACME.CAT" />
```

When an entity such as '-//ACME//DTD MyBook//EN' is encountered, the 'ACME.CAT' file is opened, and a matching public identifier is searched for in that file.

The DTD

The DTD for catalogue documents that comply with the XML variant of the draft is shown here:

```
<!ELEMENT Map        EMPTY>
<!ATTLIST Map        PublicId   CDATA   #REQUIRED
                     HRef       CDATA   #REQUIRED>

<!ELEMENT Remap      EMPTY>
<!ATTLIST Remap      SystemId   CDATA   #REQUIRED
                     HRef       CDATA   #REQUIRED>

<!ELEMENT Delegate EMPTY>
<!ATTLIST Delegate PublicId   CDATA   #REQUIRED
                     HRef       CDATA   #REQUIRED>

<!ELEMENT Extend     EMPTY>
<!ATTLIST Extend     HRef       CDATA   #REQUIRED>

<!ELEMENT Base       EMPTY>
<!ATTLIST Base       HRef       CDATA   #REQUIRED>
```

Note that the enclosing root element is not part of this DTD fragment, since it is envisaged that these mapping declarations may appear as part of larger configuration file structures. If it were included, it would probably have something like the following definition:

```
<!ELEMENT XMLCatalog  ( Base?,
                        (Map | Remap | Delegate)+,
                        Extend* ) >
```

The name '**XMLCatalog**' should certainly be used to ensure maximum portability of catalogue documents between systems.

Classification

One significant issue hardly addressed by the solutions described above is the need to find documents in a more rigorous and reliable manner than free-text searching can deliver. Often, documents need to be classified in a number of ways. For example, a document could be classified under the year it was created, by its theme and also by its authors.

Directory classification

At best, the use of sub-directory structures offers only a single way to classify documents (and manually crafting alias files in other directories would be tortuous).

Search zones

As already indicated, many free-text search engines are now able to restrict searches to specific elements. It should therefore be relatively simple to create zones for Year, Theme and Author elements:

```
<document>
  <year>2001</year>
  <theme>Image Formats</theme>
  <author>J.Smith</author>
  ...
</document>
```

As documents are added to the repository, the search engine takes particular note of the content of these elements. A search form can then be created that targets search queries at the content of these elements across all of the documents:

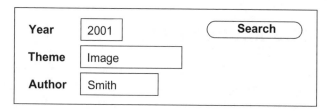

Database management

The jumble of technologies discussed so far are not easy to integrate, and some are not well supported. In addition, using a search engine to classifies documents is not satisfactory if the classifications are likely to change. For example, if all the documents classified under 'vector image formats' and 'raster image formats' needed to be re-classified under the single, new classification 'image formats', it might be necessary to edit all of the affected documents and then re-index them (though some advanced products allow new terms to be mapped to indexed terms). If the only reason for considering a search engine happens to be for classification purposes, then a **database** should be considered as an alternative.

A database can hold **meta-data** on each document, including **fields** to hold such items as the publishing date, author and any keywords or other details that would assist with identifying the document, as well as a pointer to the file that holds the document content:

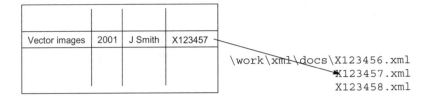

Databases can also take full charge of the documents, and by doing so secure them from unauthorized access and inadvertent deletion.

Basic document management

When documents have a 'life-cycle', ranging from creation to eventual publication, a number of issues arise. This includes protection of documents from unauthorized users, prevention of simultaneous updates to a single document, and preservation of old versions of a document in case of data corruption or incorrect updates. It is possible to develop an application around a database that adds appropriate features to support these requirements, but fortunately this has already been done, and packaged as **document management** systems by a number of software vendors. Standard features include:

- locking: the ability to prevent any of the actions below to be applied to a document

- check-out: the ability to assign a document to an author, while locking it to prevent other authors from accessing it (a 'check-in' operation places updates back into the system, and unlocks the document)
- versioning: the ability to preserve the original document after an updated version is checked-in.

Some document management systems also incorporate, or link into, an existing professional **workflow** tracking system, or offer basic workflow features directly. When such a document management system also includes other features aimed at 'factory' production of documents, it is termed an **editorial system**. Many publishers, for example, use an editorial system for the production of books, journals and magazines. Additional features may include tracking of operator time spent on each document.

Another class of product, termed **asset management** systems, offers similar features, but their main strength is in the storage of huge numbers of large data files, and emerged from the needs of some organizations to maintain a huge image library. They tend to be weaker than document management systems at editorial support, but stronger at extracting and bundling large numbers of assets for delivery to publishing systems or third parties (possibly to support content 'syndication' activity). These systems are rarely considered for XML document management alone, but can be adequate if such a system has already been purchased for other purposes.

Document component management

None of the approaches discussed so far exploit the (almost) unique characteristics of the XML document format. Apart from zoned-text searching, they treat XML documents as just another data format. Yet the structured nature of XML documents should allow individual sub-components to be isolated and individually exploited in various ways.

An author or editor wishing to amend one paragraph in a book should not need to check-out and open the entire book, or even one chapter of it. It should be possible to identify and access the required paragraph, check-out the paragraph and edit it in isolation, allowing other systems users to access neighbouring text blocks at the same time.

A document **component management** system (also termed a 'compound document management system') can 'pull apart' an XML document, storing each element separately. This allows documents to share standard blocks of text, and for documents to be assembled from standard components:

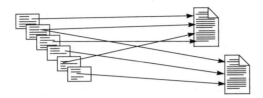

These systems emerged as early as the 1980s, initially to support SGML applications, and remain particularly prevalent in the engineering sector (especially for maintenance manuals, where multiple models, custom variants and constant improvements to equipment specifications need to be handled efficiently).

With this approach, the actual document is stored inside the database. As before, another major advantage of this is that the data is protected by the system to the same degree as the meta-data. It is included in incremental backups, and hidden from unauthorized users.

There is, however, some argument about what kind of database should be used at the heart of a component management system (discussed next).

Document disassembly techniques

There are at least two database technologies that have been exploited to disassemble XML documents in order to create a component management system. But, before discussing these techniques, it is beneficial to understand what document disassembly actually involves.

Disassembly principles

Consider the following document fragment:

```
<para>An example
<em>paragraph<xref idref="#para"/></em>
that demonstrates
<em>disassembly</em>
into hierarchical structures.</para>
```

Breaking this fragment down into its components reveals three levels of structure. The Paragraph element has a total of five children, including two elements and three pseudo-elements (text strings). The first Emphasis element has two children: first a pseudo-element, then an empty element. The second Emphasis element has one child, the pseudo-element string 'disassembly':

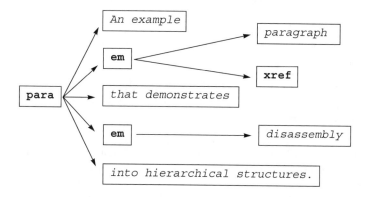

Relational database storage

A simple method of storing this information in a relational database table assigns a record with a unique identifier to each element and pseudo-element.

element	id	parent	childNum	string
para	100	???	?	
	101	100	1	An example
em	102	100	2	
	103	100	3	that demonstrates
em	104	100	4	
	105	100	5	into hierarchical structures

Other fields in the record contain a reference to its parent element, and a child number that records its position in relation to its siblings. The five rows shown above demonstrate how the five siblings of the Paragraph element are numbered ('1' to '5') and refer to their parent ('100').

The first Emphasis element contains two children:

	id	parent	childNum	string
	106	102	1	paragraph
xref	107	102	2	

The second Emphasis element contains one child pseudo-element:

	108	**104**	1	*disassembly*

Using this simple scheme, it would be possible to reconstruct the original paragraph using queries that refer to the identifiers. For example, to find the children of the Paragraph element, the following query would retrieve them:

```
SELECT element, id WHERE parent = ParaId
```

More efficient designs would utilize multiple tables, particularly to separate element hierarchies from textual content, and to store attribute values.

Relational databases have their limitations. Specifically, it is not a simple matter to represent information that does not fall into a simple tabular model. XML elements have many relationships, few of them tabular. Each element has a parent, and may have children, creating a hierarchical relationship. Each element may have siblings, and must know its position in the sequence. Although it is possible to define fields to hold sequential and hierarchical relationships between elements, as demonstrated in the example application above, such a model requires a considerable amount of software support to cope with amendments to the document.

Object database storage

An alternative **object database** technology has emerged, and most commercial component document management systems utilize object database systems.

Instead of tables built from rows containing fields, a much looser structure is built using uniquely identifiable units of information, or objects, containing 'attributes' that hold either simple data or pointers to other objects. Just as in XML, each attribute has a name and a value. In the example below, object 'A' contains two attributes, one called 'colour' that contains the value 'red', and another called 'ptr' that contains a list of pointers (to objects 'B' and 'C'):

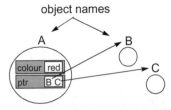

Object database technology has primarily been developed for permanent storage of data objects created by object-oriented software applications. But this technology is also suited to the storage of XML documents, as it can easily describe sequential and hierarchical relationships. An XML document can be decomposed into its constituent parts, as described previously, using attributes to hold the name of the element, and an array of pointers to identify child elements, in the order that they appear in the document.

However, the additional power of this approach comes at the cost of performance, and this technology is still considered by many to be inadequate for industrial strength applications. Despite this, the relational database vendors have replied to the threat with the **object-relational database**, which is essentially an object layer that sits on top of an existing relational database product, offering a compromise on both performance and object awareness.

XML or SQL

There is a clear case to be made for the use of XML as a storage format for information that can be conveniently treated as a structured document. Few would argue that XML is ideal for handling information comprised of sequentially and hierarchically arranged sub-components. There is a similar strong case to be made for the use of relational database technologies to create, store, query, updated and extract large volumes of highly structured information. Again, few people would argue that this information should be stored in XML documents instead (though XML remains a good candidate for exchange of information between systems). However, some material cannot be categorized quite so easily, and in this circumstance the decision is less easy to make.

This problem is particularly acute when attempting to manage a range of material that includes a mixture of semi-structured and highly structured content. The pressure to adopt a single technology can be intense; a single system saves on purchase costs, reduces the range of skills needed for maintenance, and provides a single, consistent interface to users of the system (without complex and expensive system integration). But when this approach is taken, significant compromises may need to be made to incorporate all of the information. The compromises may be just too great to make.

Entries

The term 'entry' is used in the following discussion to describe any meaningful collection of information units.

In XML terms, an entry is simply an XML document, though when the entries are particularly small, they may be grouped (enclosed by a 'wrapper' element) into a much larger document for storage or transfer convenience.

In relational database terms, the entry might be spread across a number of tables. There would typically be a central, or 'main' table, then other ancillary information that is shared with other entries (the concept of 'normalization' is discussed next).

It should always be possible for an entry to be stored in either fashion. Indeed, it is common practice for XML to be used as a reliable transfer medium for entries stored in databases (copying entries to other databases, or to client software applications).

Normalized data

A concept that is fundamental to relational databases is the idea of 'normalizing' data. The main principle of normalization is that there should be no unnecessary duplication of data that could lead to errors when information is updated. Instead, relationships between tables are used, making it possible to rebuild a database entry from data stored across these tables. In a one-to-many relationship, a single value (or set of values) can be used in many entries. If this value is updated, then all entries automatically receive the update.

A number of techniques for normalizing information in XML documents can be considered, including XML entities, and the XInclude and XLink standards. But none of these are particularly satisfactory, and all require sophisticated software support that, at the time of writing, hardly exists in mature and cost-efficient products.

XML databases

The case for XML can be strengthened somewhat simply by giving XML documents the same software support that relational data automatically gets. This seems only fair. Authoring, querying and manipulating XML data using an XML-capable database is a possibility, of course, but a note of caution is required. These databases are rarely what they seem.

The term 'XML database' is often applied to any system that is able to support the structures that XML describe. But, just because these systems are able to import XML data without loss of information, and then export data in XML document form as well, this does not mean that they are actually handling XML documents internally. When this is the case, it is almost meaningless to describe such a system as an 'XML solution'. These are proprietary solutions, and must be acknowledged as such. Some rely upon relational or object databases, but others are totally proprietary. Either way, the biggest concern here is the maturity of this technology, its future viability, and the ease with which trained support personnel can be found to support it.

Also note that when an XML database product happens to use an underlying relational database to break apart an XML document (as discussed in the previous section), this is not remotely the same thing as using a relational database to model the information directly. The relational model is describing the structure of *any* XML document, not the structure of the information a specific document happens to contain.

Decision Factors

The questions that can be raised include the following:

- how important is maturity of technology and availability of skills?
- do entries need to be normalized for reliable updating of duplicated data?
- do single updates sometimes span a number of entries?
- is versioning required?
- are parts of the entry restricted to certain users?
- are there sequential structural relationships?
- are there hierarchical structural relationships?

Technology maturity and available skills

A number of relational database tools have existed for some considerable time now, and are considered to be mature. Furthermore, the SQL standard for accessing databases has been widely accepted and supported by these products.

With mature and widespread technology comes a ready supply of professionals with relevant experience who can maintain and further develop a system. Again, the widespread use of a standard, in this case SQL, reduces the issue of transferring skills to new products. At the time of writing, no single standard has been adopted for use with XML documents, though XPath for queries shows some promise.

Normalization need

As already stated, relational databases are built around the concept of being able to normalize data.

For XML documents, using a search and replace tool that can update multiple files, it is possible in this crude way to emulate the required functionality. Nevertheless, this approach requires that all the files are accessible for updating, the task is arduous and therefore time-consuming, and the repetition is wasteful of disk space. On the plus side, however, it is not necessary to 'join' separated data objects in order to collate the information for review.

Multiple updates

Beyond the simple case of updating the value of a field that is (using a one-to-many relationship) shared by many entries, SQL updates may include statements that simultaneously update many entries, with the values of specific fields being tested to determine whether or not to update another field value. This is difficult to emulate using text-based search and replace tools.

Versioning

It is quite difficult to version entries in a relational database, though it is possible to export a 'snapshot' of old data (perhaps in XML format). Otherwise, it would be necessary to add version or date fields to each table involved in the entry.

In XML, versioning is quite easy to achieve at many different levels. First, attributes can be added to elements that give a version or date, and more elements can be easily added to hold changed content. Second, entire XML documents can be versioned simply by copying the file and using the new copy. Storing XML documents in a professional document management system makes document versioning even simpler and safer.

Security constraints

Relational databases permit certain tables, or even particular fields within a table, to be hidden from some users. Again, normalization helps here, as different users may be permitted to edit different tables, and may not even need to know about the existence of the other tables. The concept of a database 'view' (or 'virtual table') also helps.

XML documents are either totally available for editing, or totally hidden from view. Authors can change any part of an XML document. However, an XML document could be split into multiple smaller pieces, some more restricted than others.

Sequential relationships

In a relational database, entry components that have an unpredictable but significant relationship to each other must be maintained by adding a field that holds a sequential count value. Software is needed to maintain the list, allowing components to be reordered and new components to be inserted or appended.

XML documents maintain sequential relationships by default, due to the sequential nature of textual data files.

Hierarchical relationships

Relational databases divide data into records and fields. There is no concept of fields within fields.

XML is particularly suited to hierarchies that involve a mixture of text and elements. These 'in-line' elements have a sequential relationship with each other and with the text around and between them. Relational databases, however, have particular difficulty with this concept. Often, this constraint has been overcome by inserting XML tags into the text content of a field, but this is a particularly poor combination of techniques. The database is unaware of the significance of these tags, and does not validate them, take them into account when searching for text in the field, or hide them from users.

Summary

In general, the major strengths of SQL-based relational database solutions are that:

- this is a mature technology
- there is a wide skill base
- they are optimized for retrieving normalized information.

The equivalent strengths of an XML-based solution are:

- sequential relationships are easy to maintain
- hierarchical relationships are easy to maintain
- versioning is easy to incorporate
- document management tools can be used to add effective locking, tracking and versioning.

Document editing

A significant aspect of most document management needs is the requirement to be able to modify XML documents.

Document editing is essentially indistinguishable from document authoring, if only because editing often involves the creation of new or replacement material. Certainly, product vendors do not distinguish between these activities, and supply the same tools for both tasks.

There are three distinct approaches that can be taken to XML document editing, and editing tools exist in each of these categories (described below).

Structured editing tools

On first seeing a structured editing tool, many remark on its similarity to database record entry forms. The content of the element to be edited is displayed in a field, and edited in isolation. However, unlike database screens these editors must support the sequential and hierarchical structures inherent in an XML document, and typically include a navigation tree of some kind to allow users to select the element to be edited:

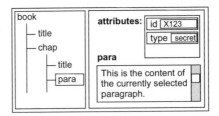

These tools are relatively simple to develop, and many are freely available; most support multiple computer platforms and operating systems.

Unfortunately, this is not a natural environment for most document authors. As well as being unfamiliar, it is inefficient when attempting to author significant amounts of new text. A more serious problem occurs when the smallest block-level elements, such as paragraphs, contain in-line structures such as emphasized text. It then becomes necessary to work on each part of the paragraph separately (to select a specific in-line element for editing, or one of the ranges of text between and around these elements).

The real niche for these tools is the editing, rather than authoring, of highly structured data (not loosely structured narrative text). These products are data editors rather than document editors.

Standard word processors

Since the tools described above do not provide an elegant narrative document authoring or editing environment, other products have emerged that adapt existing, general-purpose word-processing applications to the task of creating and editing XML documents. These XML 'extension' tools sit above the main application, in some cases intercepting keystrokes and formatting commands, so as to perform constant, interactive validation against the DTD.

The benefits of this approach are that authors get to use familiar, mature and capable products, and that these solutions tend to be cheaper than the XML document authoring packages described next (especially if the underlying word processor required is already in the user's possession).

Although styles can be applied to the text, these styles are ignored when the XML document is saved to disk. Yet formatting of the text remains very useful, as it helps document authors to verify that the correct elements have been chosen for components of the text. A formatted printout of the document is also a desirable practical format for proofreading, and even acceptable for simple publishing purposes.

However, the underlying word processor remains ignorant of the XML standard (and particularly of hierarchical document structures), and therefore needs constant and careful controlling and monitoring to make it work as an XML editor. Some consider this approach to be akin to trying to sail a yacht by attaching the tiller and winches to the wheels of a car placed within it, and steering the boat from within the car. It can be clumsy and inefficient, and it is also very difficult to prevent authors from ignoring the extension and breaking the document modelling rules by directly working with the word processor's own features. Finally, as the native data format is not XML, it is necessary to 'import XML' and 'save as XML' each time the product is used to edit an XML document, which is not very efficient, and makes integration with document management systems more difficult.

XML word processors

Some vendors promote the opinion that only purpose-built XML document authoring tools can offer an effective XML authoring environment. A small number of such products exist. These products were originally developed as SGML authoring tools many years ago, so are more mature than many people would initially think (despite the new name and low version number some are given).

They tend to be more expensive than previously described solutions, and (despite their heritage) less mature than general-purpose word processors. However, they are built to 'understand' XML, and this makes them very fast, efficient and relatively easy to use (certainly in comparison with the simpler editing tools described above).

While attempting to make the user interface as friendly and familiar to word processor users as possible, some of these products stop short of creating a fully-WYSIWYG (*What You See Is What You Get*) interface. While most will emulate the formatting and styling capabilities of standard word processors, in order to provide immediate feedback to authors, some also include visual representations of the start-tags and end-tags.

The following diagram was first seen in Chapter 2, and shows a typical interface of this type:

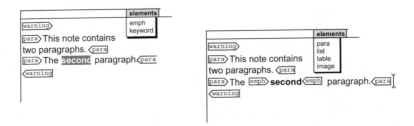

Typically, as shown above, the tags are replaced by icons that are easier on the eye, and impossible to corrupt through accidental editing of the content or delimiter characters. More significantly, however, the presence of these tags makes it possible to be precise about mapping the current editing position to a location in the documents structure. Their presence removes any ambiguity. Consider the following example; with the tags hidden from view it is not clear whether inserting a character at the cursor position will place the new character within the Emphasis element or not:

The **second** paragraph.

Similarly, it is not clear what should happen if the cursor is at the end of a bulleted list item paragraph when the user presses the 'enter' key. Depending on the DTD in use, at least three possibilities may arise:

- start a new bulleted item (the default result in many word processors)
- start a new paragraph within the same item (indented, but not given its own bullet)
- end the list and start a new, normal paragraph.

But with the tags present on-screen, the exact location of the cursor can be used to decide which of these options is relevant; within the paragraph, it splits the paragraph into two (within the same item); within the list item, but outside the paragraph, it splits the item into two items; within the list but outside the item, it ends the list and starts a normal paragraph.

Even if some tools do not provide the exact context-specific editing functionality described above, it is nevertheless important to be able to position the cursor precisely within the document structure. The current location determines, from information in the document model, which elements can be inserted at this position, and the editor needs to display the possible options.

A number of vendors have released products that attempt to make XML authoring and editing as natural as working with a traditional word processor. They do this by hiding the markup from view, to the point of almost pretending the product is a normal word processor. However, many people find this approach counter-intuitive, and feel a certain lack of control (much as a driver familiar with manual gear-changing becoming nervous when first faced with an automatic). Doubts return about matching cursor position to document model location, and it is argu-able that the effort of learning how to work efficiently with such a tool is at least as great as learning to live with a tags-showing view of the document.

27. Extended links (XLink)

This chapter covers the extensive linking capabilities provided by the XLink standard (released June 2001), which greatly improves upon the limited support for linking provided by the XML standard (as described in Chapter 7). XLink applications are required to be able to interpret XBase (see Chapter 11) and relative URL base instructions.

Background

The **XLink** standard is much more sophisticated than the linking scheme built in to the XML standard, and involves a number of concepts that need to be understood before the details of the syntax of this standard can be explored.

Resources, links and traversal

The purpose of a **link** is to allow **transversal** from one **resource** to another (from a '**starting-resource**' to an '**ending-resource**'). In the following example, it is possible to traverse from resource 'A' to resource 'B':

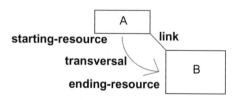

It is important to reinforce the distinction between linking and traversing. In the example above, it is only possible to traverse from 'A' to 'B' because these two resources have already been linked. The link itself is a supporting feature, not the actual process of traversing between resources. As a consequence of this distinction, if 'A' is linked to 'B', then it is equally true to say that 'B' is linked to 'A'. Traversal is therefore not necessarily uni-directional (single directional). For example, it may be made possible for traversal to occur in the opposite direction:

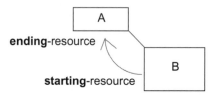

The terms **source** and **target** (introduced in Chapter 7) are also often used in place of starting-resource and ending-resource. The meanings are identical (and this more concise terminology tends to be used in preference throughout this chapter).

A resource is any object that can be made the target of a link, including an XML document, a document fragment, an image file or even a 'service', such as a database query that is resolved dynamically (the actual text may differ depending on the time it is requested, or on the values of various query parameters).

Arcs

Numerous resources may be linked to become **participating resources**. It is also possible to limit the user to specific starting-point resources and ending-point resources, by creating a number of explicit **arcs**, each one specifying a path from one resource to another.

In the following example of three participating resources, it is only possible to traverse from 'A' to 'B', and from 'B' to 'C':

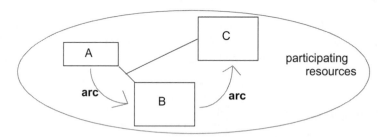

Hypertext links

Note that when a link is created for human consumption, rather than for software processing alone, it is often termed a **hypertext link**:. This is particularly the case when users are given a choice as to whether to traverse the link or not, and traversal is performed by such action as clicking on a reference to the target resource:

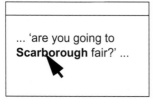

Single-direction hypertext links to target objects in the same document are a primitive form of linking supported by an XML DTD feature. But proposals for more advanced forms of linking appeared decades ago. Readers familiar with HTML and URLs will already be aware of a scheme that allows links to be made to other documents. Indeed, this scheme is incorporated into the XLink standard. But this standard goes well beyond the capabilities of HTML too.

SGML Note: Although the sophisticated HyTime standard has already been developed for use with SGML, it has not been widely implemented. If software support for the linking scheme described in this chapter is more forthcoming, there is little reason why such applications could not also be adapted to work with SGML documents.

Local and remote resources

XLink links and arcs are built using XML document markup, and make particular use of significant attribute names. Links can be created within narrative documents, and some participating resources may even be physically enclosed within the linking markup. These are known as **local resources**. Typically, however, most resources are **remote resources** that are not present within (or even near) the linking markup. Remote resources have to be found, using a **resource locator**:

A remote resource may occur in a different document. This is a major improvement on the XML linking scheme, but should be familiar to users of Web browsers, and HTML coding experts. In the following example there are three resources ('a', 'b' and 'c') that are spread across two documents:

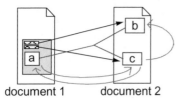

document 1   document 2

When an arc has a starting-point resource within the link markup, it is an **outbound** arc. The resource in 'document 1' above has an outbound arc to resource 'c' in 'document 2'. This resource in the second document, however, also happens to have an **inbound** arc, back to the same (the local) resource in 'document 1'. Finally, any arc between remote resources is a **third-party** arc. The two resources in 'document 2' are connected by a third-party arc.

The significance of inbound and third-party arcs is that they enable links to be made to resources within read-only documents, including documents owned by other parties, and for these resources to be starting-points of an arc (though the resources and links between them are only apparent to those who have access to the document containing the linking markup).

Link markup

All XLink features are provided using reserved attributes. The most significant of these specifies what kind of link to make. The Namespaces standard (see Chapter 10) is used to identify the elements and attributes that contribute to the creation of links. The namespace URL reserved for this purpose is 'http://www.w3.org/1999/xlink'. As in the standard itself, the prefix 'xlink' is used in the following examples, but, as usual, a document author may choose any legal prefix. Note that, for the sake of brevity, most of the following example document fragments do not involve a namespace declaration, but it should be assumed that one is present on an unseen root element.

Types

The **Type** attribute is used to identify what XLink role a particular element type in the document is to take. For example, an element called 'simpleLink' could be assigned to the role of a 'simple' XLink link:

```
See <simpleLink xlink:type="simple" ... >book
9</simpleLink> for details.
```

Note: It is not relevant to refer to specific element names in this chapter, yet it is necessary to discuss elements that adopt specific XLink roles. The convention in the draft standard, and in this chapter, is to refer to '*role*-type' elements, such as 'simple-type', with the understanding that the actual element name could be 'simple', 'link', 'A' or any other valid XML element name.

The Type attribute can take the value '**simple**' (as shown above) or '**extended**', and within extended links there can be '**locator**', '**arc**', '**resource**' or '**title**' constructs, which are also identified using this attribute.

A prefix, such as 'xlink:', is always required on this XLink attribute (and on all other XLink attributes). The Namespaces standard makes it clear that attributes without a prefix do *not* belong to the default namespace, and it is generally understood that such attributes belong to the namespace of the elements they are attached to. The XLink namespace does not include *any* element definitions, so an XLink attribute can never belong to the same namespace as the element it is attached to.

Resource identifiers

The XLink standard uses the URL scheme (see Chapter 30), the XPointer scheme (see Chapter 28), or a combination of the two, to locate the target resource. The URL is held in the **Href** attribute:

```
See <simpleLink xlink:type="simple"
                xlink:href="file://book9.xml">book
9</simpleLink> for details.
```

DTDs

When a DTD or XML Schema document is available to validate documents that will contain XLink constructs, it is highly desirable to update the model to take account of the XLink standard. Elements should be added to the model, if existing elements cannot be adapted to take XLink roles, and these new or existing elements can then be mapped to specific roles using fixed attributes. This simplifies document creation and maintenance by hiding unnecessary complications from the document authors.

While the names of the elements are not constrained in any way (beyond the usual constraints dictated by the XML standard itself), typically the DTD or XML Schema author would choose to name new elements after the XLink roles they are supporting. For example, an element called 'simpleLink' could be defined, and given an XLink Type attribute with a fixed value of 'simple':

```
<!ELEMENT simpleLink  (#PCDATA)>
<!ATTLIST simpleLink  xlink:type CDATA #FIXED "simple"
                      ... >
```

Document authors do not then need to know or care about the Type attribute, and can focus on the purpose of the element it is assigned to instead. In the following example, the document author simply adds a URL to the SimpleLink element:

```
See <simpleLink xlink:href="..." >book 9</simpleLink>
for details.
```

Simple links

This standard includes a similar feature to the primitive, one-directional linking scheme supplied by the XML standard, but makes it possible to traverse links between documents (as the HTML standard already permits). This is termed a **simple link**, and is identified using a **simple-type** element. As a simple link contains only one resource locator, this locator is stored in the **linking element** itself, using the **Href** attribute, as shown in previous examples:

```
<simpleLink ... xlink:href=" locator">local resource
name</simpleLink>
```

The content of the simple-type element would typically become 'active text' when the link is a hypertext link.

Internal links

The simplest form of link identifies an object in the same document. These 'semi-local' references must be preceded by a hash symbol, '#'. The target resource is identified as an element that contains an identical value (but without the hash symbol) in its **Id** attribute. A small part of the XPointer standard (see Chapter 28) is used here, and the example below is an abbreviation of the XPointer expression '#xpointer(id("X123"))':

```
<chapter id="X123">

...<simpleLink xlink:href="#X123">...</simpleLink>...
```

It is clear from the above description that this standard does not require the use of a DTD to identify attributes with values that can serve as unique target resource identifiers. However, such a DTD, with significant attributes assigned to the ID attribute type, could still be useful to ensure that target resources identified using attribute values *do* have unique identifiers.

External links

Using a URL, simple links can identify other documents on the local system:

```
<simpleLink xlink:href="file:///myDoc.xml">
  ...
</simpleLink>
```

The XML Base standard (see Chapter 11) is used to help resolve relative URLs.

Documents can also be accessed over the Web, using the HTTP protocol:

```
<simpleLink xlink:href="http://myHost.com/myDoc.xml">
  ...
</simpleLink>
```

Finally, an XPointer can be added to a URL to identify a sub-resource in another document.

```
<simpleLink xlink:href="file:///myDoc.xml#X123">
  ...
</simpleLink>
```

HTML emulation

The simple link feature is identical in nature to the use of the Anchor element in HTML, and it is also not a coincidence that the locator attribute name is 'Href'. In fact, it is possible to emulate HTML almost completely by naming the linking element 'A' (anchor), although a prefix is still needed on the Href attribute:

```
<!ELEMENT a      (#PCDATA)>
<!ATTLIST a      xlink:type    CDATA  #FIXED "simple"
                 xlink:href    CDATA  #REQUIRED >

    See <a xlink:href="book9.xml">book 9</a> for details.
```

Titles

It is useful for a resource to be labelled, so that the user can decide whether or not it would be profitable to follow the link to that resource. For example, if the name 'Scarborough' is highlighted in the title of the song 'Are you going to Scarborough fair?', it is not immediately obvious where the link leads to, and why. A label, containing the word 'location' (that perhaps appears when the cursor is placed over the name), makes it obvious that the resource says something about the location of this town. The **Title** attribute is used to hold this label (it is shown later how this title is even more useful when multiple links are involved):

```
<!ATTLIST simpleLink ...
                      xlink:title CDATA #IMPLIED>


... are you going to
<simpleLink xlink:href="#Sca" xlink:title="Location">
Scarborough
</simpleLink> fair?
```

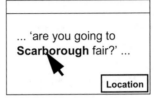

Roles

A 'role' can be assigned to a locator, and is used by the system to apply a different style to the linking element content, or to affect linking behaviour in some way. For example, if all links are classified as 'internal' (referring to objects in the same document) or 'external', then these links can be given different colours so that users will be aware of the distinction.

The **Role** attribute is used to create these categories. While a browser may simply use the attribute value to apply different styles to the linking text (both CSS and XSLT are able to apply different styles to an element, depending on the value of one of its attributes), a more specialized browser may perform role-specific actions as well.

The value of this attribute must be an absolute URL that is meant to point to a document that explains the purpose of the role. While this is a good idea in principle, the draft standard makes no comment on whether or not the existence of such a document is critical, or even on the format of the contents of this document if it does exist. The standard does not even suggest whether an XLink application should attempt to find and read the document, or make any deductions based on its contents. Perhaps the intent is for the application to simply show the document to a user upon request. But it could also be assumed that the document is optional, and that the URL is simply used to supply a unique identifier text string for the role (just as URLs are used in the Namespaces standard):

```
<!ATTLIST simpleLink ...
                   xlink:role CDATA #IMPLIED>

... are you going to
<simpleLink xlink:href="#Sca"
                   xlink:role="file:///describe">
Scarborough
</simpleLink> fair?
```

Perhaps in the next draft, or in the final release of the standard, there will be a number of typical roles defined, along with URLs that will be understood and interpreted intelligently by most XLink applications.

Linking behaviour

The means by which a link can be activated, and its behaviour once it has been activated, can be influenced by attributes in the linking element.

The **Actuate** and **Show** attributes suggest which action to take, though they may be ignored by an application. These attribute can be used on simple-type elements, and on arc-type elements (see below), to describe the behaviour desired when accessing the resources that they identify as targets. However, note that these attributes are ignored when a link is made to a 'linkbase' (see below).

Both of these attributes can hold values of 'other' and 'none'. The first of these values indicates that the behaviour is to be determined by analysing surrounding markup, and the latter simply indicates that the application must decide for itself what to do.

Actuate attribute

The **Actuate** attribute has a value of '**onLoad**' or '**onRequest**' (or 'other' or 'none'). A default value could be defined in a DTD or XML Schema model, but would typically be set to 'onRequest', indicating that the link is only traversed when explicitly selected by a user. When this attribute is set to 'onLoad', the link is activated automatically, as soon as the document is accessed.

Show attribute

The **Show** attribute specifies how the target resource is to be presented, and has a value of 'replace', 'embed' or 'new' (or 'other' or 'none'). These actions are interesting in their own right (and are described below), but are even more interesting when combined with one or other of the two actuate options described above.

Replace starting-resource

The Show attribute value '**replace**' dictates behaviour familiar to users of HTML browsers when following a hypertext link. The browser replaces the source text with the resource required (it 'jumps' to the new location). This method is ideal when the user is simply scrolling to a more interesting portion of the same document, or skipping to another, more interesting document (perhaps never to return).

In the following example, the user is scrolling down to a later fragment of the document:

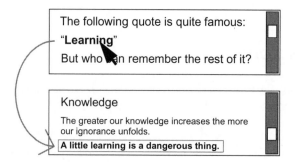

When used in conjunction with the 'onLoad' actuate option, transfer takes place automatically, which is useful when the document has been moved to another location, leaving behind only a redirection document:

```
<simpleLink xlink:show="replace"
            xlink:actuate="onLoad"
            xlink:href="..." >This page has
moved.</simpleLink>
```

Embed starting-resource

When the Show attribute has a value of '**embed**', the resource is brought in to the source text at the point from which it was referenced (this is formally termed a **transclusion**). When used in conjunction with the 'onLoad' option, reference merging will be transparent to the user.

In the following example, both the chapter title and number replace the reference text. In addition, the title and number of the chapter are inserted before the reference text is displayed. This means that these items can be altered at any time, with all references subsequently updated automatically. But the disadvantage is that the XML document is harder to understand and work with when using editing and viewing tools that are not link-aware:

```
As stated in Chapter
<simpleLink xlink:href="#MSnum"
            xlink:show="embed"
            xlink:activate="onLoad" />
(<simpleLink xlink:href="#MStitle"
             xlink:show="embed"
             xlink:activate="onLoad" />), ...


    <chapter>
      <num id="MSnum">7</num>
      <title id="MStitle">Market Research</title>
      ...
    </chapter>
```

As stated in Chapter 7 (Market Research), . . .

An earlier draft of the XLink standard included a mechanism for specifying that when a fragment of another document is being selected, the whole document is not to be retrieved and displayed. The 'l' symbol was used in place of the '#' symbol, as an alternative fragment identifier with this meaning. This concept has been abandoned, and it is not obvious what has replaced it. Perhaps it could just be assumed that when embedding a fragment, it would not make sense to actually embed the whole document (and then scroll to the fragment).

At first sight this feature is reminiscent of the fragment embedding facility provided by the XInclude standard (see Chapter 12) but it actually differs in a fundamental respect. XInclude is used to create a new XML document that permanently incorporates XML data copied from elsewhere. The feature described here simply presents other material (including non-XML data), making no permanent changes to any of the XML documents involved.

This is also reminiscent of an XML entity reference being replaced by the entity content. However, the link approach has the advantage that there are no declarations to create, and that the resource can also be accessed elsewhere using more conventional linking techniques.

New ending-resource window

If the Show attribute has a value of '**new**', the browser should open a new window (or utilize an equivalent mechanism) to display the resource, still leaving the original text on-screen. Again, this technique is commonly seen in HTML-based Web browsers. The advantage of this approach is that the source resource is not lost; it is not necessary to for the user to follow another link to get back to this resource. The disadvantage is that the user may be required to explicitly close the window in order to avoid clutter, or perhaps even to reveal the original window. In the following example, the user is shown a new (overlapping) window that contains the target text:

```
...  "<simpleLink xlink:href="file:///Learn.xml"
                  xlink:show="new"
                  xlink:actuate="onRequest">
Learning</simpleLink>"  ...
```

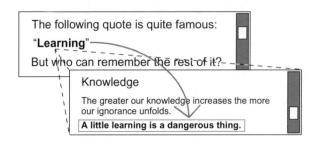

Simple link limitations

The simple links described above are a very minor part of the XLink specification, and have only been included for backward compatibility with earlier SGML and HTML schemes, and to simplify as far as possible the markup needed to support the most basic, but also most widely used, form of hypertext link. The simple link scheme is very limited. A simple link cannot:

- start from a read-only document
- be bi-directional
- have multiple target ending-point resources
- be stored with other links in a single place for ease of maintenance.

The linking element is embedded in the text, so cannot be added to a read-only document (perhaps a document that is owned by another party).

A simple link is one-directional. Although a browser may be able to return from the target resource, using a 'back' button, this is not the same as being able to start from the other end of the link. To do that, it would be necessary to include a second simple link at the other end. While possible (when the remote document is not read-only), this requires some effort, and link maintenance becomes much more difficult.

It is sometimes desirable to have multi-directional links. For example, a number of on-line works may contain some material on a famous person, such as Napoleon. A book on warfare may include a chapter on his campaigns, a book on famous French people may include a chapter on his life, and a book on psychiatry may include a case study of someone who thought they actually were Napoleon. It could be useful for all of these resources to be linked to each other (without needing to create three simple links in each of the three resource locations).

When linking markup is scattered throughout one or more XML documents, link maintenance becomes very difficult. Even listing the links takes some effort.

The XLink standard addresses these issues by including a much more sophisticated mechanism for creating links (and the rest of this chapter discusses this mechanism).

Extended links

Using an **extended link**, a number of resources can be cross-related. An extended link contains **locator** elements, each one pointing to a different resource. However, the extended link may still be an in-line element, containing one of the resources:

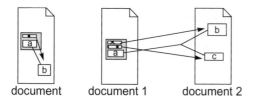

document   document 1   document 2

The ends of the link have equal status, even if one resource is a single word reference and the other is an entire book. It is also irrelevant which end of the link actually contains the linking markup.

Extended type

Extended links refer to a number of resources by including embedded resource locators. Each locator is stored in a **locator-type** element, and all related locator elements are grouped within an **extended-type** element. If the link markup occurs at the point of one of the resources to be included, then a **resource-type** element is used to isolate and identify this (local) resource. The **Type** attribute is again used to identify the elements that take these roles.

A DTD author must ensure that the extended-type element can contain the locator-type element and the resource-type element, as well as any DTD-specific elements appropriate at this point:

```
<!ELEMENT para            (#PCDATA | extendedLink | emph)* >

<!ELEMENT extendedLink    (#PCDATA | localResource |
                           remoteResource | emph)* >
<!ATTLIST extendedLink    xlink:type="extended" ... >

<!ELEMENT localResource   (#PCDATA) >
<!ATTLIST localResource   xlink:type="resource" ... >

<!ELEMENT remoteResource (#PCDATA) >
<!ATTLIST remoteResource xlink:type="locator" ... >
```

```
<para>Here are
  <extendedLink>some <emph>extended</emph>
    <localResource>links:</localResource>
    <remoteResource xlink:href="...">
      Locator a
    </remoteResource>,
    <remoteResource xlink:href="...">
      Locator b
    </remoteResource>.
  </extendedLink>
</para>
```

Here are some *extended* links: **Locator a**, **Locator b**.

A browser should recognize that the embedded LocalResource and RemoteResource elements form a related group, and deduce that it would be useful to dynamically create arcs between them all (in this case, between the fragment shown above;, the fragment identified as 'Locator a' and the fragment identified as 'Locator b'.

Note: An assumption is being made here that when resource-type elements are not empty, their content text can act as jump-off points for hypertext links (just as it can in simple-type and resource-type elements).

Empty links

The example link above creates three resources (one local, two remote). But it is possible for a link to contain a single, local resource, or even to contain no resources at all. This might be done simply to utilize XLink identification attributes that give the resource a role, title or label, or to create a placeholder for later updating.

Multiple titles

It can be very useful to attach a title to each participating resource when these resources are not mentioned individually in the document text. It is also possible to give each resource multiple titles.

Titles as selection text

In the example above, each linked resource is referred to in the text, and these references are treated as labels by enclosing them in LocalResource and RemoteResource elements. Typically, users would follow a specific link simply by selecting the appropriate reference text. But this approach cannot work when one or more of the targeted resources is not mentioned in the text at all. The **Title** attribute can be used to overcome this problem:

```
<para>... and the quote 'not tonight Josephine' is
attributed to
<extendedLink>
  <localResource>Napoleon</localResource>
  <remoteResource xlink:title="Campaigns"
                  xlink:href="..." />
  <remoteResource xlink:title="Life Story"
                  xlink:href="..." />
  <remoteResource xlink:title="Famous Generals"
                  xlink:href="..." />
  <remoteResource xlink:title="French Law"
                  xlink:href="..." />
  <remoteResource xlink:title="Delusions"
                  xlink:href="..." />
</extendedLink>.</para>
```

These descriptions may be presented in a selection window:

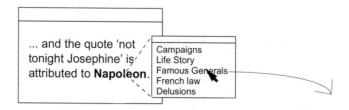

The same Title attribute can be used on simple links, and on arcs (explained below).

Title elements

It is also possible to designate entire elements as **title-type** elements, and to use these elements within the other elements that take the roles of extended link, locator and arc structures. Indeed, any one of these objects can contain multiple title

elements, with each one perhaps containing the same text, but in a different language (using the xml:lang attribute to identify the language concerned). While it
is possible for each of these constructs to contain both a Title attribute and one or
more Title elements, the draft standard does not suggest any particular significance
to such combinations.

```
<remoteResource ...>
  <resourceTitle xlink:type="title" xml:lang="...">
    ...
  </resourceTitle>
  <resourceTitle xlink:type="title" xml:lang="...">
    ...
  </resourceTitle>
</remoteResource>
```

More titles and roles

The two attributes that describe resource (Title and Role) can also be used to
describe both an entire link and a local resource.

Whole link information

The **Role** and **Title** attributes may be used on the extended-type element, and are
used here to describe the entire link, rather than any particular resource that partici-
pates in the link:

```
<!ATTLIST extendedLink ...
                       xlink:role   CDATA  #IMPLIED
                       xlink:title  CDATA  #IMPLIED>
```

It could be imagined that a browser would show the title, for example, as soon as
the link appears on-screen, and only show the title of a particular resource when
the cursor hovers over the reference to that resource.

Local resource information

A local resource can also have a Role and a Title attribute, so that information
about this resource can be gathered and presented elsewhere, and in particular at
the location of the other participating resources:

```
<!ATTLIST localResource ...
                        xlink:role   CDATA  #IMPLIED
                        xlink:title  CDATA  #IMPLIED>
```

```
<song>
  <songTitle>Are you going to
    <extendedLink>
      <localResource xlink:title="song"
                     xlink:role="reference">
        Scarborough
      </localResource>
      <remoteResource xlink:title="location" ... />
      <remoteResource xlink:title="history" ... />
    </extendedLink>
  fair?</songTitle>
  ...
</song>
```

The title is presented to users browsing other documents who may wish to link to the local resource, in the following case depending on whether or not the user wishes to learn the lyrics to a song about Scarborough:

Arcs

An extended link can group a set of related resources, and allow links to be made from each resource to all other resources in the group. Yet this degree of freedom is not always desirable. Some resources may not be suitable starting points, and others may be equally unsuitable as target resources from some of the starting points. The 'arc' concept provides a means for specific traversal options to be specified between resources in the group.

Arc-type elements

An **arc-type** element, identified by the **Type** attribute value 'arc', has **From** and **To** attributes to identify the starting point (or points) and ending point (or points) of a possible traversal between participating resources. But these two attributes must refer to the starting point and ending point unambiguously, by reference to a 'label' value.

The **Label** attribute may be used in locator-type and resource-type elements (it is not appropriate to the simple-type link, because there is already a single, implied arc from the linking markup to the targeted resource):

```
<localResource xlink:label="X" ... >...</localResource>

<remoteResource xlink:label="Y" ... />
<remoteResource xlink:label="Z" ... />

<arcLink xlink:type="arc" xlink:href="..."
                    xlink:from="X" xlink:to="Z"/>
<arcLink xlink:type="arc" xlink:href="..."
                    xlink:from="Z" xlink:to="Y" />
```

Note that as soon as at least one explicit arc is specified, the assumption that all resources connect directly to all other resources should be abandoned. In the example above, a user cannot navigate to 'X' from either 'Z' or 'Y', because there are explicit arcs present, but none of them specify these paths.

Duplicate labels

Interestingly, label values do not have to be unique within a group. For example, consider two resources that both have the label 'Z'. Any arc that targets this label will automatically target both resources. Also, any arc that starts from this label has two starting points:

```
...
<remoteResource xlink:label="Z" ... />
<remoteResource xlink:label="Z" ... />

<arcLink xlink:from="X" xlink:to="Z" />
<arcLink xlink:from="Z" xlink:to="Y" />
```

Missing From and To attributes

The To and From attributes are optional, but their absence has interesting implications.

If the **From** attribute is omitted, it is implied that all of the resources are starting points (even resources that have no explicit Label value still have an implied value). Even the ending point resource gains its own starting point:

```
...
<arcLink xlink:to="Z" />
```

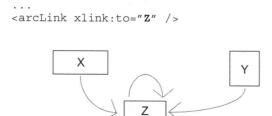

Similarly, if the **To** attribute is omitted, then every resource is targeted (including the starting-point resource):

```
...
<arcLink xlink:from="Z" />
```

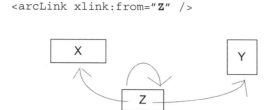

Arc link behaviour

An arc-type element may contain **Show** and **Actuate** attributes. In this case, these attributes suggest the behaviour for accessing the target resource when that particular arc is followed. Apart from the simple-type element, this is the only place that these attributes can be used. Note that this means it is not possible to specify such behaviours when arcs are not defined in a complex link: an XLink-sensitive application must then make its own decisions on how to present resources.

Arc roles

The **Arcrole** attribute defines the role of an arc, rather than the role of the target resource (or the source resource). The target resource may have a different meaning in respect to each starting point. For example, a resource describing the life of Napoleon may be the target of several arcs, including one from a resource describing his wife, and one from a resource describing the history of France. In the first case, the arc is targeting the 'husband' of the source resource. In the second case, the arc is targeting the 'emperor' of the source resource (at one point in its history). The arc roles are known as 'has' relationships (though the examples here might be better described as 'had' relationships). Josephine *has* a husband called Napoleon; France *has* an emperor called Napoleon.

This attribute may also be used in the simple-type element, to define the role of the implied arc from the link markup to the targeted resource.

Out-of-line links

It is often neater to separate an extended link from all of the resources it identifies. An **out-of-line** link is simply a link that has no local resource. While an out-of-line link may physically appear in-line, in the sense that it can be placed in the flow of text, this has no significance, and only makes the linking mechanism more difficult to find and maintain. A more obvious place to put out-of-line links is at the top of the document:

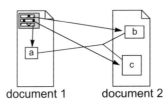

document   document 1   document 2

It is important to note that some documents may not contain any information on the resources they hold, as in 'document 2' in the example above, because their linked resources are identified in another document. The possible absence of linking markup in a participating document has interesting benefits. As already noted, a document that cannot be edited, perhaps because it resides on a remote system and is not owned by the link creator, can nevertheless be remotely provided with links, both to other parts of the same document, and to other documents.

However, there is also a disadvantage to this approach. A processor given 'document 2' would be unaware of the existence of the first document, and therefore of any of the links defined there. A mechanism called a **link database** (or '**linkbase**') may be used to overcome this problem. In this scenario, all or most links reside in a separate 'linking file' (a 'database of links').

When a large number of internal or third-party arcs are needed, general management of the link markup is greatly assisted if all of this markup is placed in a single, separate data file, placed in a well-known location accessible to all potential users of the links defined within this file:

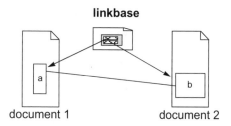

linkbase

document 1   document 2

But there needs to be some mechanism for finding and selecting a linkbase file, as soon as a user decides to open one of the documents that contains some of the starting point resources. Although the draft standard does not constrain XLink-compatible applications in this respect, it does include a single technique that will often be appropriate. Each document that contains participating resources (in particular, starting-point resources) could include a link that targets the linkbase.

```
<simpleLink xlink:href="file://myLinkBase.xml" ... />
```

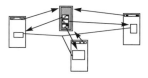

But the XLink application needs to be aware of the special purpose of this link, and not attempt to display the linkbase document to the user. The reserved **Arcrole** attribute value 'http://www.w3.org/1999/xlink/properties/linkbase' can be used to ensure that the link is interpreted correctly:

```
<simpleLink xlink:href="file://myLinkBase.xml"
    arcrole =
    "http://www.w3.org/1999/xlink/properties/linkbase" />
```

A linkbase file could also include further arcs to other linkbase files to achieve effective management of huge numbers of links that form natural sub-groupings, though an XLink-sensitive application may wish to set a limit to how many such arcs it will follow. The application must also watch for and avoid cyclical arcs between link bases, and ignore duplicate links.

Note that linking using this technique cannot start from a read-only document, as it would not contain the link to the link group file, unless the browser is also given the link group file previously.

28. Advanced links (XPointer)

It is possible to improve on the simple fragment identifiers that can be used with HTML documents. The XPointer standard provides the ability to reference many items, elements without identifiers, and points and ranges of text. This chapter is not essential reading for those who only need to be able to link to single elements that have unique identifiers.

XPointer is largely built on XPath expressions, so an understanding of this standard is essential (see Chapter 13).

Concepts

The **XPointer** standard provides a way to create hypertext links that does not depend on the target object being an XML element, or on a target element having a unique identifier. Although primarily aimed at support for hypertext linking for user navigation through documents, it may also be used in other application areas.

Absent identifiers

There may be times when it is necessary to provide a link to an object that has no unique identifier. Those responsible for preparing the text may not be able to identify the elements that will later be the target of hypertext links, and the cost of adding unique values to all elements (just in case) may not be justifiable.

Ranges and text

Consider a very large paragraph that contains a single short phrase of interest. A link to the element containing the entire paragraph is hardly helpful in this circumstance. The ability to link directly to the embedded range of text is preferable.

XPath and beyond

The navigation techniques provided by the **XPath** standard (described in Chapter 13) are exploited by the XPointer standard. This is a very flexible technique, as a selection of examples demonstrates. Using XPointer expressions, it is possible to target:

- the third chapter
- the second child element of the third chapter
- the second paragraph in the section with an identifier of 'Sec12'
- the fifth paragraph of the fourth chapter
- all chapter titles
- the last-but-one item in the first list of the third chapter
- the second list with a Type attribute value of 'indented'
- the first paragraph with a Level attribute value of 'top-secret', in the first section with a Level attribute value of 'secret'
- the second occurrence of the phrase 'A little learning is a dangerous thing' in the fifth chapter
- the word 'dangerous' within the string 'A little learning is a dangerous thing'.

Most of these examples should not be surprising to those already familiar with XPath. However, a few of the later examples could not be supported by XPath alone.

XPointer

At its heart, the XPointer standard describes how to use XPath expressions as URL reference fragment identifiers.

XPointer identifier

A simple XPointer is identified using the **xpointer**() scheme as the URL reference fragment identifier:

```
http://.../xml/doc9.xml#xpointer(...)
```

This function contains an XPath expression, enhanced with the XPointer object types and functions explained below.

Initial context

The initial context location for an XPointer expression is usually the root node of a selected document. When the XPointer expression is used as a fragment identifier on the end of a URL, this URL is deemed to select the document in question. Although other uses of XPointer expressions can be envisaged, the standard does not attempt to dictate how these other applications should determine which document to apply the expression to.

Pointing to identifiers

The most obvious way to point to an element is to reference its unique identifier. This technique is well known to developers of HTML Web sites. Although alternative pointing techniques are described later, this approach remains the most efficient and robust, and should always be used in preference when the target is an element, when this element has a unique identifier, and when the identifier is known to the person creating the link.

Identifier function

XPointer can point to an element with a unique identifier using the XPath Id function:

```
http://.../xml/doc9.xml#xpointer(id("sect2.1"))
```

It does not matter what the names of the elements and attributes are, though both must be defined in a DTD:

```
<section identifier="sect2.1">...</section>
```

Bare names

The standard includes a minimization technique that attempts to retain backward compatibility with the HTML mechanism for linking to objects within Web pages. When the expression is simply the value of an element identifier attribute, this is termed a '**bare name**'. The example below is fully equivalent to the more verbose example above:

```
http://.../xml/doc9.xml#sect2.1
```

However, this can be a little misleading to those familiar with HTML fragment linking. This mechanism only works for XML documents, not HTML documents. The document must be both well-formed (most HTML documents are not), and must reference a DTD. The target object can be any XML element that has an attribute defined in a DTD to be an identifier attribute.

XHTML anchor targets

In the XHTML standard the Name attribute in the Anchor element is not classified as an identifier attribute in the DTD (see Chapter 23). However, this element has an Id attribute that serves this purpose:

```
<a id="sec2.1" name="SomethingElse">...</a>
```

To target an XHTML Anchor element that uses the traditional Name attribute for its unique identifier, the following XPath expression would be used:

```
xpointer(//a[@name='sect2.1'])
```

```
<a name="sect2.1">...</a>
```

Fallbacks

It is possible to add extra XPointer expressions to act as fallbacks in the event that previous ones fail. The first expression that succeeds is used, and the remainder are ignored:

```
xpointer(...)xpointer(...)xpointer(...)
```

This technique can be used to cater for the possibility that an XML document will not reference a DTD. The following example contains three expressions. The first will be applied if the document references a DTD that includes attributes declared to be of type ID. The second will be applied only if this is not the case, but makes the assumption that the name of the attribute is 'id'. Finally, it may be known that some elements have an attribute called 'name', and it may not be known which of these two attributes contains the requested identifier value. Therefore, the third expression is tried if the second one fails:

```
xpointer(id("sect2.1"))xpointer(//*[@id="sect2.1"])
xpointer(//*[@name="sect2.1"])
```

Location context

Typically, not every element in an XML document has an explicit unique identifier attached to it. However, all elements in an XML document *do* have a unique structural location. For example, only one element instance can be the third sibling of the second child of the root element. If the exact position of a target element is known, then it can be referenced unambiguously using this 'address'.

The XPointer standard offers a very simple scheme for identifying an element by its location in the document tree. It counts elements at each level. This is called a '**tumbler**' mechanism, or '**stepwise addressing**' scheme, but officially it is now known as a '**child sequence**':

```
http://.../xml/doc9.xml#xpointer(/1/3/2)
```

```
1
        <book>
          <title>Book Title</title>
3       <chapter>...</chapter>
        <!-- third child of this book -->
        <chapter>
          <title>Chapter Title</title>
2       <!-- second child of this chapter -->
          <section id="sec2.1">...</section>
```

Note that comments are ignored, as are other markup constructs such as processing instructions.

The following example is an abbreviated version of the same expression:

```
http://.../xml/doc9.xml#/1/3/2
```

If this feature were not present it would be possible to achieve the same effect using standard XPath expressions. But the following example, which uses '*' to represent any element, and a predicate filter to indicate the required occurrence, is both less intuitive and more verbose:

```
http://.../xml/doc9.xml#xpointer(/*[1]/*[3]/*[2])
```

First step options

It should be noted that the first step in the absolute paths shown above will generally have the value '1' when pointing to an object in the document, because only one element is allowed at the root of the document. However, higher values may be used to reference the content of parsed external entities, which for this purpose are considered to be appended to the end of the main document (though the order in which they are appended seems to be uncertain).

The first step can also be the identifier of a specific element. In the following example, the second child of the element with an identifier of 'thisOne' is selected:

```
http://.../xml/doc9.xml#xpointer(thisOne/2)
```

```
<book>
  ...
  <section ident="thisOne">
    <para>first paragraph.</para>
    <para>Selected paragraph.</para>
  </section>
  ...
</book>
```

Escaping characters

There are some potentially complex character-escaping requirements that need to be fully appreciated in order to avoid errors when creating XPointer expressions, particularly because XPointer expressions need an escaping mechanism of their own, in addition to the XML language and URL syntax escaping schemes.

XPointer bracket escaping

XPointer expressions include functions that use brackets, such as 'string-range()' (described later). To prevent confusion, if a bracket forms part of the text it must be escaped. In the XPointer standard, the '^' character is used as an escape character; so '^(' represents '(' and '^)' represents ')'. In addition, due to the special significance of this character, its appearance in data must also be escaped, giving '^^':

```
xpointer(string-range(/book/title, "the ^^ and
                       the ^( characters are significant"))
```

```
<section>
  <title>It should be noted that the ^ and
  the ( characters are significant in XPointer</title>
  ...
</section>
```

XML attribute value escaping

When an XPointer expression is embedded within an XML attribute, any chevrons, quotation marks (when conflicts cannot be avoided) and ampersand characters must be escaped as normal. In addition, any characters not covered by the character set in use by the document must be escaped:

```
<target href="xpointer(string-range(/book/title,
          &quot;the ^^ and the ^( characters
          are significant&quot;))">...</target>
```

URL escape characters

In addition to any XPointer and XML escape characters, it may be necessary to ensure that the text string is conformant with the URL standard (see Chapter 30). For example, all spaces must be escaped as '%20', and circumflex characters, '^' with '%5E'. Often, the need for a URL escape sequence means that the XML escape sequence is not necessary. For example, '"' is not necessary because '%22', the URL equivalent, is valid XML:

```
<target href="xpointer(string-range(/book/title,
   %22the%20%5E%5E%20and%20the%20%5E(%20
          characters%20are%20significant%22))">
   ...
</target>
```

Multiple targets

A single XPath expression may (as explained in Chapter 13) apply to multiple elements. Indeed, the simpler the expression the more likely it is that it pertains to two or more element instances. Depending on how it is applied, the expression 'title' may apply to all elements of this type that are children of the current element, or to all Title elements in the document. Similarly, the expression '/book/chapter/title' applies to every chapter title.

At first sight, this concept may not appear relevant to the XPointer standard. Yet the idea of multiple targets has already been discussed (in the previous chapter), and it is actually a very powerful feature. While the behaviour of browsers that may allow this is not described by the standard, it could be imagined that a browser would immediately scroll to the first occurrence, and provide 'previous' and 'next' buttons to allow instant access to other occurrences (or simply highlight each subsequent occurrence):

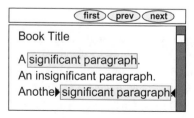

When this effect is not desired, the child sequence method described above may be used to ensure that a single element is targeted. Otherwise, it is necessary to be very careful when creating expressions that need to target a single element. For example, '/book/chapter[2]/title' will target a single Title element, providing that the document model specifies that the Title element is not repeatable within the Chapter element.

Extension functions

There are a number of functions that the XPointer standard defines for use in expressions. These are:

```
location-set start-point(location-set)
location-set end-point(location-set)
location-set range(location-set)
location-set range-to(location-set)
location-set range-inside(location-set)
location-set string-range(location-set, string, number?,
                          number?)

location-set here()
location-set origin()

xmlns(prefix=namespaceURL)
```

The first five deal with points and ranges, allowing groups of elements or characters to be treated as a single target object. The next two deal with alternative, relative context locations for the start of the path. The final function is used to manage namespace mappings in expressions, and deals with multiple mappings to the same prefix, as well as unknown prefix usage in the document. They are all described in more detail in following sections.

Points and ranges

XPointer expressions do not have to target an entire, single element instance. Instead, they can target a point in the document structure between elements, or a range of elements. These concepts are analogous to editing tool user interfaces, which have a current cursor position, or a range of selected material (and these concepts should also be familiar to those readers of Chapter 21 (DOM Level 2)).

Points

A **point** is a single location in the document. This location is identified as being within a specific container node, and between specific sibling nodes within that container. Its position within the sibling nodes is a simple index value that starts at zero. The following example shows the points within a container Book element that has a title and a single chapter. There are only three points in this example:

When an element contains text, this text is represented by a single text node:

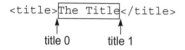

Note that text nodes containing nothing but whitespace may be used in a document simply to format element tags. Such nodes have no effect on the meaning of the document, but they certainly have an impact on the number of location points in the container. A larger number of points are present when the first example above is re-formatted in this way:

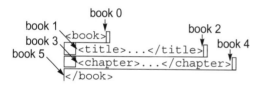

When the container is a text node, a comment or a processing instruction, the points are between the characters in that node:

```
The Title
```
text 0 text 4 text 9

The point index number relates to a location immediately after the character at that position in the string. Point 15 can therefore be seen to be a 'cursor' situated between character 15 and character 16.

Ranges

A **range** is a series of document components, such as elements, other markup and text characters, that lie between two specific points. For example, a range could be a block of text consisting of three consecutive paragraphs:

The only exception to this rule occurs when two points occupy the same location; in this scenario, there are no document components between the two points, so it does not make sense to talk about there being a **range** of material between them. However, the term '**collapsed range**' is used to describe this situation.

The first point in a range is termed the '**start-point**'. The other point is termed the '**end-point**':

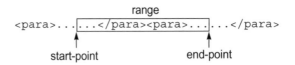

Naturally, both points must be in the same document. However, ranges do not respect of XML rules for well-formed document structrures. For example, the start-point may occur in the middle of one element, and the end-point may occur in the middle of the next sibling element:

Similarly, ranges do not have to share the same container element. However, ranges that start within a comment or processing instruction must end within the same instruction.

Locations

Ultimately, an XPointer expression is used to identify a **location** in the document. A location can be an XPath object, such as an element instance or a text node, but it can also be a point or a range.

Many of the functions described below take a **location-set** as a parameter. This is simply a set of locations throughout the document, maintained in document order, though the set may actually be just a single element, point or range. These functions also return a location-set that may again be just a single element, other node type, or a point or range.

Range-to function

The **range-to()** function specifies the location of the end-point, and makes the assumption that the preceding part of the expression locates the start-point. For example, to create a range that begins at the third paragraph in a given chapter, and ends at the end of the fifth paragraph, the following expression can be used:

```
xpointer(//chapter[3]/para[3]/range-to(follow-
ing::para[2]))
```

Note the value '2' in the last part of the expression above. This is the second paragraph after the currently selected paragraph, making it the fifth paragraph in the chapter:

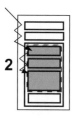

The unique feature of this function is that it alone can appear as a step in a location path. The other functions described below (as well as those defined in the XPath standard) cannot. The XPath specification has been deliberately broken (or 'modified') within the XPointer standard to allow this single case.

Note that if the context expression that precedes this function identifies multiple locations in the document, then multiple ranges are created. The parameter expression is re-evaluated at each of these locations. In the following example, a range is created at the start of every chapter. Each range covers the title and everything up to the end of the first paragraph in that chapter:

```
xpointer(//chapter[3]/title/range-to(following::para[1]))
```

Point functions

It is possible to target a point instead of a node. The **start-point()** function returns a point, but the exact position of this point depends on the nature of the material selected by a parameter to this function.

If the embedded expression targets the root node of the document, or an element, a comment, a processing instruction or a text node, then the point returned is the first point within this node. In the example below, the point returned is immediately within the start-tag of the Chapter element:

```
xpointer(start-point(/book/chapter[1]))
```

```
<book>
  <chapter>|...</chapter>
```

The **end-point()** function is similar, but simply identifies the last point in the container element or other node type, instead of the first. In the following example, the point between the last character of the title and its end-tag is targeted:

```
xpointer(end-point(/book/title))
```

```
<book>
  <title>The Book Title|</title>
```

When the embedded expression targets a range, the start-point or end-point of this range is returned, depending on which of these functions is used.

When the nodes returned by the embedded expression are already points, then there is no difference between using start-point() and end-point().

Range function

The **range()** function returns ranges around each object targeted by its parameter expression. The following example creates range targets around every third paragraph in each chapter:

```
xpointer(range(/book/chapter/para[3]))
```

Range-within function

The **range-inside()** function is similar to the range() function described above, but selects the contents of each node, instead of the whole node. The nodes selected by its parameter are treated as container nodes for the ranges to be created. When the nodes are elements, the start-points and end-points are placed immediately within the elements tags. The following example creates range targets within every third paragraph in each chapter:

```
xpointer(range-inside(/book/chapter/para[3]))
```

It should be noted that if these ranges are presented visually in a browser, the distinction between range() and range-inside() may be too subtle to distinguish.

Relative links

In all previous examples, the origin of the XPath expression is the root of the document. XPointer adds two kinds of 'relative context' to allow an external or internal starting point to be specified instead.

Local context

Relative linking is possible using the **here**() function at the beginning of the expression. There are two possible interpretations of what 'here' actually means, though they are similar.

In the first scenario, the XPointer expression is the text content of an element. In this case, 'here' refers to the enclosing element node. In the following example, it refers to the Link element, so the expression can target the previous Paragraph element using the previous-sibling() axis:

```
<para>The link below targets this paragraph.</para>
<link>xpointer(here()/previous-sibling::para[1])</link>
```

In the second scenario, the pointer is anything other than text content of an element, and 'here' refers to the enclosing node. Typically, this will be an attribute node. It is almost always necessary to back out of the attribute node to (at least) the parent element, before starting to navigate around the document:

```
<para>The link below targets this paragraph.</para>
<link to="xpointer(here()/ancestor::link/
          previous-sibling::para[1])"/>
```

Origin context

A mechanism is provided for relative links that are defined out-of-line, using the **origin**() function. It is a feature that only seems to make sense when an extended XLink link contains references to two resources, with the second one defining a location relative to the first, as in the following example, which links two adjacent paragraphs:

```
<extendedLink>
  <locateResource
          xlink:href="#xpointer(id("chap1")/para[5])" />
  <locateResource
          xlink:href="#xpointer(origin()/
                      following-sibling::para[1])" />
</extendedLink>
```

However, if this is the intention, it serves only as a form of shorthand, as it would always be possible to include the full path to the second resource.

Targeting text strings

One of the most significant features of the XPointer language is its ability to target a specific character, word, phrase or sentence of interest, without having to rely upon the presence of an identifying element. For example, the name 'Scarborough' may be of interest in the following text, but the enclosing Paragraph element also contains other text:

```
<Para>Are you going to Scarborough fair?</Para>
```

However, the name 'Scarborough' *does* have an exact location in the document relative to other occurrences and surrounding element structures. But it is not necessary to know and specify the position of the string (in the way that it *is* necessary to know the identifier or exact location of an element). Instead, an XPointer-based system is able to find the string for itself.

String-range function

Designating a string of text as a link resource is accomplished using the **string-range()** function:

```
xpointer(string-range(...))
```

The first parameter is the node set to search through, and the second is the text string to be found. In the following example, the second chapter of the book is searched for paragraphs that contain the string 'find me':

```
xpointer(string-range(//chapter[2]/para, "find me"))
```

```
<book>
  <chapter>...</chapter>
  <chapter>
    <para>You will find me here.</para>
    <para>You will also find me here.</para>
  </chapter>
</book>
```

Ignored markup

Element tags and other markup tags are all ignored when matching strings. The example above would work equally well in the following circumstance:

```
<para>You will find <emph>me</emph> here.</para>
```

```
<para>You will also <emph>find</emph> me here.</para>
```

As already stated, this means that the selection can span parent structures too:

```
string-range(//, "here to here")
```

```
<para>Select the text from <emph>here</emph></para>
<para> to <emph>here</emph>. But not this.</para>
```

Select the text from *here*
to here. But not this.

Occurrence identifier

A specific instance of the string can be isolated using normal XPath predicate filters. The following example selects the second occurrence of the string 'find me' within the second chapter of the book:

```
string-range(/book/chapter[2], "find me")[2]
```

As stated above, any embedded markup is ignored, so it does not matter if the second occurrence of 'find me' is actually inside an embedded element. In the following example, the second occurrence of the string is found in every chapter:

```
string-range(/book/chapter, "find me")[2]
```

```
<chapter>...find me find me...</chapter>
<chapter>...find me <emph>find me</emph>...</chapter>
```

Finally, in this example the second occurrence of the string in every text node, comment and processing instruction is targeted:

```
string-range(/, "find me")[2]
```

Partial string selection

Sometimes, the string to be found is not quite the same as the string to be highlighted, but also contains an essential context for this string. For example, it may be desirable to point to the name 'Scarborough', but only when it occurs within the string 'going to Scarborough fair'.

Two further parameters can be added to the **string-range()** function to select just part of the given string. The first parameter is a starting position number, which must not be zero. The value '1' indicates a position just prior to the first character in the string (this being the default value). The value '10' indicates a position just before the tenth character (character ten is to be included in the selection):

```
string-range(//para, "going to Scarborough fair", 10)
```

```
<para>Are you going to Scarborough fair?</para>
         1         10
```

The next parameter value is the number of characters to select from this starting position. By default, all characters up to the end of the string are selected, as indicated above. A value of '0' indicates no characters, and a point rather than a range is specified. In the following example, only the name 'Scarborough' is selected:

```
string-range(//para, "going to Scarborough fair", 10, 11)
```

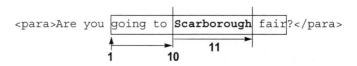

Finally, it is even possible to select additional characters:

```
string-range(//para, "find me", 1, 12)
```

```
<para>You can find me here</para>
                   1        12
```

Non-normalized whitespace

Multiple whitespace characters are *not* normalized to a single space when matching strings. A search for 'find me' would not find the string 'find   me'.

Namespace issues

When XML documents include elements from multiple namespaces (see Chapter 10), it is possible that the document will contain element instances with the same name, but from different namespaces. Consider the following example (a modified version of an example first introduced in Chapter 10). There are two Score elements in this document fragment:

```
<competitionEntry xmlns:M="...">
  <competition>Piano</competition>
  <competitor>J Smith</competitor>
  <score>57</score>
  <M:played>
    <M:composer>George Gershwin</M:composer>
    <M:composition>Rhapsody in Blue</M:composition>
    <M:score>Ferde Grofé</M:score>
  </M:played>
</competitionEntry>
```

This example causes no issues for XPointer expressions, as the two XPointer examples below make clear. The first selects all the competitor scores; the second selects the people responsible for scoring a composition:

```
xpointer(//score)

xpointer(//M:score)
```

But when the same prefix is used for both elements, using namespace overriding, the following expression will apply to both of these element types:

```
xpointer(//M:score)
```

```
<M:competitionEntry xmlns:M="competitorNamespace">
  <M:competition>Piano</M:competition>
  <M:competitor>J Smith</M:competitor>
  <M:score>57</M:score>
  <M:played xmlns:M="musicNamespace">
    <M:composer>George Gershwin</M:composer>
    <M:composition>Rhapsody in Blue</M:composition>
    <M:score>Ferde Grofé</M:score>
  </M:played>
</M:competitionEntry>
```

The solution to this problem is to specify in advance the namespace that the prefix will map to. This is done using the **xmlns()** function:

```
xmlns(prefix=namespaceURL)xpointer(... prefix:name ...)
```

Because a single XPointer expression may refer to elements from various namespaces, there may be multiple namespace functions preceding the xpointer function (or functions):

```
xmlns(X=...)xmlns(Y=...)xmlns(M=...)xpointer(...)
```

The example below makes it clear that the name of the person who scored the composition is wanted (not the score of the competitor):

```
xmlns(M=musicNamespace)xpointer(//M:score)
```

Another advantage of this feature is that it is not necessary for the prefix used in the XPointer expression to match the prefix used in the document. This is very important if the prefix used in the document is not known, or if the same expression is used on numerous documents that use various different prefixes:

```
xmlns(X=musicNamespace)xpointer(//X:score)
```

```
<M:score>Ferde Grofé</M:score>
```

29. Character sets

XML markup and document text can only be recognized when the characters they are comprised of conform to recognized standard encoding schemes. This chapter describes character encoding schemes in general, and the most important standards used today (including ASCII, ISO 8859, Unicode and ISO 10646). An understanding of the intentions and limitations of these formats is fundamental to the appreciation of the purpose and scope of XML.

Characters

XML data is composed of a simple sequence of **characters**, including the text of the document and the markup that describes and structures this text. In order to store any text on a computer, it is necessary to specify what characters are available, and how to store them electronically.

Character sets

The term **character set** is used to describe a collection of characters that are related in some way. A character set is not a physical thing. It is only a concept, defined by a specification or standard. A typical character set will include letters, numbers and commonly used symbols:

```
abcdefghijklmnopqrstuvwxyzABCDEFGHIJKLMNOPQRSTUVWXYZ
0123456789!"#$%&'()*+,-./:;<=>?@[\]^_`{|}~
```

Encodings

Computers do not directly understand characters (or character sets). They are basically calculating machines (or 'number crunchers') that can store and manipulate numbers. In order to store text in a computer, a unique numeric value is therefore used to represent each character in a given character set, usually including letters, digits and punctuation marks. This is termed an **encoding** scheme.

For example, the value 51 may be used to represent the digit '3', the value 33 may be used to represent the exclamation mark, '!', and the value 84 may be used to represent the letter 'T'. When a user presses the letter 'T' key on their keyboard, a signal is sent to the computer, which uses a look-up table to determine the value to be stored on disk or in memory:

The actual shape of the character will vary depending on which **font** is used to display or print that character. A font table provides a suitable shape for each character in the character set (and in the simplest cases, each shape has a numerical position that matches the character value):

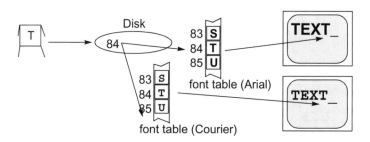

Confusing sets and encodings

It is important to recognize that an encoding is not conceptually the same as a character set, but that a single standard may define both simultaneously. For example, there is no distinction between the two with ASCII (see below), which is both a character set that includes 'A' and '1' in its set, and an encoding that specifies that 'A' has a value of 65 and '1' has a value of 49. But in other languages, such as Japanese, the same character set may be made available in several different encodings.

Incompatibility

When information is transferred between two computers that use incompatible encoding schemes, the numeric values are preserved but the number-to-character mappings differ, and the text becomes unintelligible when presented to a user of the second system.

Assuming the incompatible representation schemes shown below (where every character on System B has a value one lower than on System A), the word 'TEXT' would be corrupted to 'UFYU' on transfer to System B. Clearly, there is a need for standards to prevent such problems:

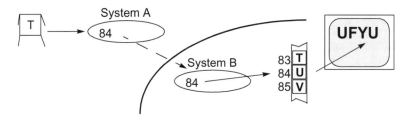

ASCII

Moves to avoid the problem of incompatible encodings resulted in the defining of **ASCII** (the *American Standard Code for Information Interchange*), which assigns an agreed value to commonly used characters (it is pronounced 'ask-key'). For example, two systems that use the ASCII standard will both assume that the value 84 represents the letter 'T', so they can exchange simple text data without risk of corruption.

Although ASCII is the predominant basic standard character set, there are a few alternatives. This includes **EBCDIC**, which is used on IBM mainframe systems and assigns the value 129 to the letter 'A' (instead of the ASCII value 65). Others include character sets for some foreign languages, such as Japanese.

Scope

ASCII defines values for 128 characters (a **7-bit** representation). Each byte of computer memory holds a single ASCII character. Although there are eight bits in a byte, the final bit is used as a check-bit to detect errors in data transmission:

```
1 0 1 0 1 0 0  = 84 = 'T'
```

This number of characters is sufficient for handling English text (and in fact only 94 of these values are used for visible characters). ASCII copes with all the characters and symbols that appear on English typewriters and computer keyboards, and also includes a few invisible control characters required to crudely format the text for viewing or printing, and for other purposes.

The full range of visible ASCII characters are listed below by order of ascending value. Unsurprisingly, this list of characters is the same as the one above, though the ordering appears to be less logical:

```
!"#$%&'()*+,-./
0123456789
:;<=>?@
ABCDEFGHIJKLMNOPQRSTUVWXYZ
[\]^_`
abcdefghijklmnopqrstuvwx
yz{|}~
```

ISO 646

The ASCII format was standardized by the **ISO** (the ***International Organization for Standardization***) under the designation **ISO/IEC 646**. The only modification made was to replace the country-specific currency symbol, such as '$', with the international currency symbol, '¤'.

Limitations

Unfortunately, ASCII and ISO 646 do not have the scope to represent the wide range of characters needed for many foreign languages. For example, there are no spare values to represent the accented characters 'Üàó', or the Greek letters 'αεφγ'. In addition, there are no available values for scientific symbols such as '!∀≤∃'.

PI codes

One approach to extending the range of characters that can be represented using the standard ASCII character set is to use several ASCII characters to represent one non-ASCII character (called 'PI codes' in traditional typesetting systems). This technique (under a different name) is in common use in SGML and HTML documents, and may be applied to XML equally well.

An entity may be defined for each 'extended' character, and given a suitable name such as 'eacute' for the 'é' character. Whenever the character is required in the text, the entity reference 'é' is inserted. Alternatively, the value of a character can be inserted, such as 'é', without needing an entity definition, but relying on an agreed definition of what character the value maps to. But these approaches are unwieldy, and should be made redundant when all computer systems have adopted the extended character set schemes described below.

Text files

A data file that contains only characters conforming to the ASCII standard is called a **text file** (though this term also applies to platform-specific alternatives such as EBCDIC).

A text file is often used as a simple data format for transfer of information between systems and application software. Many word processors, for instance, have an option such as 'Save as Text' or 'Export ASCII'.

Data exchange formats that rest upon the ASCII format include **CSV**, **RTF** and **PostScript**, amongst many others. Significantly, this also includes XML. Text editor applications are designed to work with text files, allowing them to be created, viewed, edited and printed. A simple text editor is therefore a suitable tool for editing XML documents (provided that interactive validation is not required).

Extended ASCII

With the greater reliability of modern computer systems and networks, a check-bit is no longer needed, so an **8-bit** character set is no longer unsafe. Using the extra bit actually doubles the number of values available, giving an extra 128 character values.

There was originally no agreement between system vendors on which extra characters to include, and which values to assign to those characters that they happen to have in common. For example, the Apple Macintosh OS uses the value 142 to represent the character 'é', whereas the same character is given a value of 130 in one configuration of an MS-DOS system. Therefore, a Macintosh text file should not be copied to an MS-DOS system without passing it through a filter that moves the extra characters to their correct positions in the latter's character set. The problem that ASCII was originally intended to resolve thus returned.

ISO 8859

The problem of incompatible 8-bit encodings was addressed by **ISO 8859**, which defines (amongst others) a standard Latin alphabet character set (**ISO 8859/1**) consisting of 255 characters, currently used by Web browsers, Microsoft Windows and Sun OS UNIX (a chart of this character set is shown in Chapter 33).

These sets were designed in the 1980s by **ECMA**. Backward compatibility with ISO 646 is maintained, so if the high bit of every byte in a 8859 document is zero, it automatically counts as a 646 document as well. Conversely, every 646 document is automatically also an 8859/1 document as well:

```
0 1 0 1 0 1 0 0  = 84 = 'T'
1 1 0 1 0 1 0 0  = 212 = 'Ô'
```

The '/1' part of the name identifies just one variant of 8859 (the standard Latin alphabet). There are other variants that include different accented characters, to cover the requirements of various languages:

ISO 8859/x	Languages covered
1	ISO Latin-1. ASCII characters plus Danish, Dutch, English, Faroese, Finnish, German, Icelandic, Irish, Italian, Norwegian, Portuguese, Spanish and Swedish characters.
2	ISO Latin-2. ASCII characters plus Croatian, Czech, Hungarian, Polish, Romanian, Slovak and Slovenian characters.
3	ISO Latin-3. ASCII characters plus Esperanto, Maltese, Turkish (though 8859/5 is now preferred for this language) and Galician characters.
4	ISO Latin-4. ASCII characters plus Latvian, Lithuanian, Greenlandic and Lappish.
5	ASCII characters plus Cyrillic characters to cover Byelorussian, Bulgarian, Macedonian, Russian, Serbian and Ukrainian.
6	ASCII characters plus Arabic.
7	ASCII characters plus modern Greek.
8	ASCII characters plus Hebrew.
9	ISO Latin-5. As Latin-1 except six Turkish characters replace six Icelandic letters.
10	ISO Latin-6. ASCII characters plus Lappish, Nordic and Inuit.

Despite the existence of the more powerful standards described later, work still continues on yet more variants of 8859.

Japanese

Probably the most significant non-Roman alphabet in use today on the Web is Japanese. There have been several attempts to define encodings for this language, including ISO 2022-JP (which includes ASCII as a subset, so XML tags can still look the same), JP-EUC and JIS X 0201-1997.

On UNIX platforms, JP-EUC has been dominant, but under Microsoft Windows Shift_JIS is more popular.

Limitations

Even 8-bit character sets are very limited in scope, as they can only directly handle 256 characters. The obvious solution is to use notations that use more than one byte to hold each character.

Unicode and ISO/IEC 10646

As there are far more than 256 symbols in use in the world, even ISO 8859 cannot represent them all. One obvious solution is to use more than one byte to encode each character, and two standards have emerged that use this technique. These are the Unicode and ISO/IEC 10646 standards (see hwww.unicode.org).

Unicode

The **Unicode** standard, now at version 3.0 (September 1999), was the first of these initiatives. It uses two bytes for each character, immediately raising the scope to 65,536 characters (though it actually contains just under 50,000 at the time of writing). Online charts of the characters covered can be found at www.unicode.org/charts. The number of characters of different types are listed below:

- Alphabetics and Symbols: 10236
- CJK Ideographs: 27786
- Hangul Syllables: 11172
- Private Use: 6400
- Surrogates: 2048.

Note that font support gets a little more complicated when dealing with such a large set. The fonts have names rather than numbers, and Unicode characters are mapped to these names using a configuration file. No font covers all Unicode characters, and the mapping file may include multiple character mappings to the same font shape, as in the following example, where two Unicode characters are both mapped to the Latin Small Letter S with Cedilla font shape (glyph). The characters are references below using **hexadecimal** notation (base 16):

```
015F;scedilla;LATIN SMALL LETTER S WITH CEDILLA
F6C2;scedilla;LATIN SMALL LETTER S WITH CEDILLA
```

ISO 10646

As even the scale of Unicode is insufficient for some needs, such as representing the vast range of Chinese characters, the ISO devised the capacious **ISO 10646** scheme, which employs up to four bytes to handle over two billion characters. In response, Unicode 2.0 contained some additional variable-size representation schemes to access some of these additional characters, and Unicode 3.0 is aligned with the latest version of ISO 10646 (ISO/IEC 10646-1 second edition). XML has adopted ISO 10646 as its character encoding format, as this is seen as the ultimate encoding scheme. It is expected that all operating systems and applications will eventually move to this universal standard. ISO 10646 consists of a number of encoding schemes, some aimed at efficient software processing, and others at efficient data exchange. Each scheme is discussed in detail below.

UCS

The simplest schemes utilize a fixed number of bytes to store each character, and are known as **UCS** (**Universal Character Set**) schemes. **UCS-4** is a four-byte scheme, and **UCS-2** is a two-byte scheme:

```
                    00000000 01010100  = 84 = 'T' (UCS-2)
   00000000 00000000 00000000 01010100  = 84 = 'T' (UCS-4)
```

Values below 128 represent the same characters as the equivalent values in ISO 646 (and therefore also ASCII, with only the currency symbol exception). In addition, values between 128 and 256 are the same as ISO 8859/1, so the character 'é' has the value 233 in both.

As identification of a character by its 16-bit value is hardly intuitive, names have been assigned to groups of values on different scales. For example, a character can be identified as being in group 13, plane 253, row 4, cell 129:

```
 -0000000    00000000    00000000    00000000
```

```
  group (128)  plane (256)  row (256)    cell (256)
```

Note that UCS-2 therefore represents all the characters in plane 0, and UCS-4 all the characters in group 0.

BMP

As shown above, there are 32,768 planes of 65,536 characters each. The first plane (plane 0) is known as the **BMP** (the **Basic Multilingual Plane**).

All XML names must be comprised of characters from the BMP (from UCS-2).

At the time of writing, only the BMP has been assigned characters; the vast land-scape beyond this set is reserved for future use, which will certainly include the huge Chinese character set.

Note that the standard two-byte Unicode format is now directly equivalent to the BMP set. A valid Unicode character is automatically the same character in the UCS-2 representation, and with two zero-value bytes added is also a valid UCS-4 character. However, discrepancies have temporarily occurred in the past, when-ever one standard has been updated before the other.

UTF

The UCS schemes are certainly simple and efficient. Memory is now relatively cheap, so using two, or even four bytes for each character is not usually of concern, and processing data when all characters occupy the same number of bytes is inher-ently very easy and efficient. For example, the location in memory of the 39th character is simple to determine (multiply 39 by four, then deduct three).

Yet this technique is not suitable in all cases. It can appear wasteful when storing data, and dramatically hinders the flow of information over networks.

In many scenarios, the great majority of characters in a file will be the standard alpha-numerics found on the keyboard, in which case only 25 per cent of the bytes stored or transmitted contain useful information (the first three bytes of each char-acter contain zero values).

To reduce the size of such files, a scheme that allows common characters to be rep-resented by a smaller number of bytes would be ideal. Less common characters could still be represented by large values, stored in four, or even more bytes. Schemes that work in this way are termed **UTF** (*UCS Transformation Format*) schemes.

Using UTF, when an ASCII character is encoded, only one byte is needed to rep-resent it, but more exotic characters are encoded using several bytes. In the worst case scenario, where exotic characters comprise the majority of characters in the file, the UTF format produces a slightly larger file than its UCS equivalent, but in the best case it is just one-quarter of the size.

UTF-8

UTF-8 uses a single byte to represent 7-bit ASCII characters, and between two and six bytes to represent extended characters. For example, to represent the character with a binary value of '011 11000000 11110000 00111100', it actually employs five bytes.

The first byte first states that it is the first of five ('11111'), then represents the first three digits ('011'). Subsequent bytes start with '10' to indicate that they are part of a larger value, then store six bits of the value each:

```
00000000 00000000 00000000 01010100  = 84 = 'T' (UCS-4)
                            01010100  = 84 = 'T' (UTF-8)
```

```
00000011 11000000 11110000 00111100                    (UCS-4)

11111011 10110000 10001111 10000000 10111100  (UTF-8)
```

= 5 bytes   continuation bytes

Although the second example above demonstrates that UTF-8 representation of a character can actually take more bytes than UCS-4, in the vast majority of cases it will take considerably fewer, and most frequently just one byte per character.

All XML processors must be able to process UTF-8 format data. Indeed, XML processors are expected to default to this encoding if the XML document contains no information on the notation it uses.

UTF-16

As the limitations of Unicode became apparent (compared with ISO 10646), a technique to access more than just the BMP set of characters from ISO 10646 was developed, first called UCS-2E ('E' for extended), but now known as **UTF-16** (*UCS Transformation Format for Planes of Group 00*). This scheme provides access to a further 16 planes. This is achieved in a similar manner to the UTF scheme described above. Some values are reserved to 'switch in' other planes.

All XML processors must be able to process UTF-16 format data.

Unicode compatibility

Many operating systems and programming languages have now adopted Unicode as their standard character encoding format. As explained above, Unicode is based on UCS-2, and includes the same 65,536 encoding values.

By implication, Unicode is therefore the same as the low-order bytes of UCS-4. However, it also contains some tricks for accessing the full UCS-4 set.

Unicode = UCS-2 = BMP

Character sets summary

A large number of character sets and encodings have been discussed here. But the main point to recall is that most of these standards overlap each other:

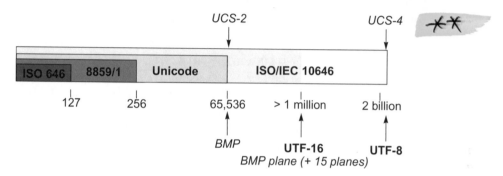

It should be noted, however, that ISO 8859/1 does not fit comfortably into this picture. It is not possible to 'pretend' that an ISO 8859/1 format file is in fact one of these other standards (even Unicode, because it uses just one byte for each character). It is unfortunate that the encoding scheme that is the most popular in the early days of XML is *not* a default XML format.

use this move to save space

It should be recalled that *all* XML processors must accept UTF-8 and UTF-16 formats as standard.

Character set declarations

An XML processor is informed of the character set used in an XML document via the encoding parameter of the XML declaration. Valid names are listed at www.isi.edu/in-notes/iana/assignments/character-sets:

```
<?xml ... encoding="ISO-8859-1" ... ?>
<?xml ... encoding="UTF-8" ... ?>
<?xml ... encoding="Shift_JIS" ... ?>
<?xml ... encoding="ISO-2022-JP" ... ?>
```

Defaults

The encoding parameter is not required. An XML document is assumed to be encoded in UTF-8 if the first four bytes of the file have the values '3C 3F 78 6D' (in **hexadecimal** notation), which represent the characters '<?xm'. If these characters are not present, then UTF-8 is still assumed.

If UTF-16 is in use, the characters expected at the start of an XML document could be represented by the values '00 3C 00 3F 00 78 00 6D', as might be expected, or equally by the byte-reversed values '3C 00 3F 00 78 00 6D 00'. In order to resolve this **lo-byte/hi-byte** ordering problem, which is caused by microprocessor design constraints, the first two bytes of any UTF-16 file *must* be reserved for use as a byte order mark. The byte order mark should be 'FF FF' for the first ordering shown above, and 'FF FE' for the latter.

Explicit declarations

A declaration is required for formats other than UTF-8 and UTF-16. A document that conforms to ISO 646 can 'pretend' to be a UTF-8 file, as it is a valid subset, but an ISO 8859 document must be explicitly identified:

```
<?xml ... encoding="ISO-8859-1" ... ?>
```

Note that a variant of this tag, the **Encoding Processing Instruction**, should appear at the top of each external entity, where it is used to identify entities with a different character encoding to the main file:

```
<?xml encoding="EUC-JP" ?>
```

MIME types

If an XML document is delivered over the Internet, the encoding scheme in use may be determined from the MIME header. When the MIME type is 'text/xml', the character encoding is provided in the 'charset' parameter of the MIME header.

XHTML declarations

In XHTML, the Meta element is used to specify character sets:

```
<meta http-equiv="content-type" content="text/xhtml;
      charset=EUC-JP" />
```

Entities for characters

Until the more advanced character set schemes described above become widely used in operating systems and transfer media, many users of XML may prefer to continue to work with 7-bit ASCII, and rely upon entities to describe additional characters. Many XML DTDs, for example, contain references to ISO entity sets:

```
<!ENTITY % ISOlat1 PUBLIC "ISO 8879:1986//
         ENTITIES Added Latin 1//EN"
         SYSTEM "../ISOlat.ent">
<!ENTITY % ISOgrk1 PUBLIC "ISO 8879:1986//
         ENTITIES Greek Letters//EN"
         SYSTEM "../ISOgrk.ent">

%ISOlat1; %ISOgrk1;
```

However, it is perhaps too easy just to add entity declarations that refer to the ISO sets. An ISO set may be added because it contains a few (or even just one) required character definitions. But, once added, a document author can use all of the characters defined in the set. Difficulties then arise if a character is used that is not supported by an available font in the printer or browser used to publish the material. Although more work is required, it is better to create an application-specific entity set that contains exactly the characters required. It is still advisable to use the official ISO-defined names for these characters, as these names are widely recognized and understood.

XML language

The **xml:lang** attribute is loosely related to the issue of character sets, in that they both contribute to supporting an application's ability to present information in different languages. The xml:lang attribute it not vital, but is useful because it tells the application which language the encoded text is in, and this may affect the way the application displays and breaks lines.

Even the country code that this attribute is able to hold can have an effect on presentation. Some applications include use dictionaries of hyphenation rules to ensure that words which break over lines are broken at reasonable points. Each country may have its own hyphenation dictionary.

30. URLs

A standard scheme for locating documents on local and remote computer systems, and particularly over the Internet, is essential to the practical use of XML. URLs are used in numerous places in the XML standard and in other, related standards such as Xlink and XInclude. But they are often misunderstood and used incorrectly, thus causing software errors and preventing a successful link to the remote resource.

URLs and URIs

The need to locate documents on the Internet in a standard way led to the development of the **URL** (*Uniform Resource Locator*) scheme. This scheme can also be used to identify resources on a local intranet, network or local computer. URLs are used in Web browsers, to find the home page of a Web site, then to navigate around the site. In XML, URLs are used to locate entities and now, as in HTML, to create hypertext links between documents (see Chapter 27). They also play a role in XInclude (Chapter 12), and in the Namespaces standard (Chapter 10). Strictly speaking, the URL scheme is just part of a wider scheme, known as the **URI** (*Uniform Resource Identifier*) standard. There have been several attempts to define URIs, such as **RFC 2396** (1989), which can be found at www.ietf.org/rfc/rfc2396.txt. As the precise meaning of 'URI' and 'URL' has changed, the W3C has released a note that clarifies this (www.w3.org/TR/2001/NOTE-uri-clarification-20010921). The URL part of the URI standard is used to access files at a given physical location, generally using a file specification that includes at least a file name, but may also include a path to the file, as well as the method to be used to access it.

Although the term 'resource' is used in the standard, often this means a data file, or data that can be generated as the result of a search query. XML documents,

DTDs, stylesheets, images and other required resources are usually stored as files.

URL construction

A URL is a simple text string. This string can appear in any form. It can be printed on paper, and still be termed a URL. But a URL is most useful in electronic form. It can then be interpreted by software that needs to access the resource it identifies.

Syntax

The characters allowed in a URL string are restricted to digits, upper-case and lower-case letters, and a few symbols (though some additional symbols are allowed in specific parts of a URL):

```
0123456789
abcdefghijklmnopqrstuvwxyzABCDEFGHIJKLMNOPQRSTUVWXYZ
-_.!~*'()
```

All other characters are represented by an escape code comprising a percent symbol, '%', followed by a hexadecimal two-digit ASCII (see Chapter 29) character value ('%00' to '%FF'). For example, '%20' represents a space, and the percent symbol itself must be represented by the code '%25':

My Document.xml

```
My%20Document.xml
```

Components

A URL is divided into a number of components, each with a different task to perform. The following diagram shows how the components of a typical URL combine to target a file on a remote computer system (but note that the last part, the '#' identifier, is not officially part of the URL):

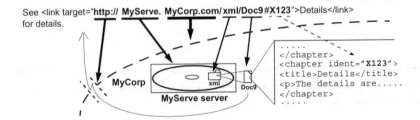

The following sections describe each of these components in detail.

Protocols

URLs are used in a number of circumstances, to retrieve data using many techniques for many purposes. For example, they are used for e-mail, for file transfer and for USENET news. The first part of the URL therefore gives an indication of the scheme it belongs to. The scheme, or **protocol**, is separated from the rest of the URL using a colon:

```
protocol:scheme-specific-part
```

The protocols for the uses given above are 'mailto:', 'ftp:' (File Transport Protocol) and 'news:':

```
mailto:scheme-specific-part

ftp:scheme-specific-part

news:scheme-specific-part
```

The syntax of the remainder of the URL depends on the requirements and characteristics of the scheme involved. Here, the discussion concentrates on the **file URL** scheme and **HTTP URL** scheme, as the former is used to locate files elsewhere on the local computer system or network, and the latter is the usual method for retrieving information from anywhere on the Internet. They are both regularly used in XML to access entities (particularly DTDs), XML Schemas and stylesheets.

File and HTTP URLs

The protocols for the two schemes discussed in detail in this chapter are 'file:' and 'http:':

```
file:...

http:...
```

These two schemes have much in common, and share a very similar syntax.

In both cases, the protocol is followed by two forward-slash characters, '//', indicating that these schemes follow a convention for URLs called the 'Common Internet Scheme Syntax':

```
file://...

http://...
```

A file URL takes the form:

```
file://host/path
```

An HTTP URL takes the form:

```
http://host:port/path?search-part
```

As can be seen, the file scheme is a simpler version of the HTTP scheme. It does not include the port and search-part components. As these two parts are also optional in the HTTP scheme, it is quite common for file and HTTP URLs to look identical apart from the protocol name at the start.

Note that the third slash in both schemes is part of the path, and not present merely to separate the host name from the path. This may seem a trivial point, but has significance when discussing relative paths later.

File hosts

Typically, file URLs refer to files on the local computer system or network, where the disk containing the file is directly 'visible' to the computer. In this case, the host part of the URL can be empty, or the string '**localhost**'. The two fragments below are therefore equivalent:

```
file:///path
```

```
file://localhost/path
```

It is also possible to refer to remote hosts using this scheme, but the file protocol is not a true Internet protocol, so its use in this form is limited:

```
file://mac.myRemoteHost.co.uk/path
```

HTTP hosts

The HTTP scheme requires a connection to a remote system, using a client/server protocol. Yet a number of server-based applications may be listening simultaneously for requests over the Internet, and to avoid confusion each one therefore listens on a different **port** number.

By default, an application that can deal with requests using the HTTP protocol listens on port '80'. When this is the case, the port number is not required to be present in the URL:

```
http://myHost/...
```

To connect to an application not listening for connections on the default port, it is necessary to supply the port number in the URL. It follows the host name, and is preceded by a colon:

```
http://myHost:1234/...
```

Queries

A required resource may not be an existing, static file, residing on a disk. It may instead be data that need to be generated from details provided in the URL. The classic example is a URL that requests information that resides in a database. A question mark character, '?', precedes the query. In the following example, a script called 'get' is run, and is passed parameters that indicate that it should return the address of the person with the name 'John':

```
<!ENTITY JohnAddress
    SYSTEM "http://.../.../get.cgi?find=Addr&name=John">
```

It makes sense that this concept applies to HTTP URLs but not file URLs. When HTTP is in use, there must be a server elsewhere that receives the request, activates the program and passes the parameters to it, then receives output from this program and passes it on to the client. When using the file protocol, no such assumption can be made.

Within queries, additional characters are allowed, but ';', '/', '?', ':'. '@', '&', '=', '+', ',' and '$' are still reserved. They must be escaped if appearing in the query itself. Typically, the '&' symbol is used to separate each part of a multi-part query, and '=' is used to separate the field name from the value it is required to hold.

File paths

Selecting a file takes more than just locating the system that contains it and naming the file required. Most modern computer systems divide file storage into areas called **directories**, which can also contain sub-directories, so creating a directory hierarchy. Many files may have the same name, and be distinguished only by their location in this hierarchy. It is therefore necessary to find the directory containing the file. This is done by stepping down through the hierarchical layers to home in on the file.

Folders

Users of modern GUI (*Graphical User Interface*) systems will be familiar with the 'folders' that can be opened to reveal files and more folders. These nested folders are just visual representations of the directory structure.

In the following example, there is an XML document in the 'xml' folder, and an image file in the 'images' sub-folder:

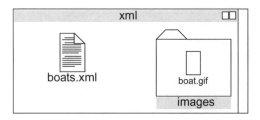

Root directory

The URL can ignore the issue of directories entirely if the file it refers to is in the 'root' directory. This directory is the one at the top of the hierarchy (just as the same term is used for the document element in XML). It may, however, be the root of the entire system, or just the root of a smaller part of the system that is enclosed within a secure 'sandbox' area that is visible to a Web server. If a Web server were to operate within a 'working' directory, then the following URL would refer to the file 'start.xml' within this directory:

```
file:///start.xml
```

Steps

The URL must otherwise 'tunnel down' through the directory levels to locate the file required. Fortunately, a syntax for this task had already been developed for other purposes. In earlier times, computers were limited to more primitive interfaces that required commands to be typed at the keyboard (they are still useful today). A simple and efficient notation was required to include directory hierarchies in commands that locate files, or establish a new working directory.

The journey to the file required is termed a **file path**. This path is built from a number of **steps**. Each step selects a particular directory along the journey, and is separated from the other steps using a reserved symbol. The URL standard specifies the '/' symbol for this purpose, though this has been an area of some confusion, as different symbols are used on different operating systems:

```
step1/step2/step3/filename
```

URLs were first most widely used on UNIX computers, and it is therefore not surprising that UNIX command-line conventions were adopted for URLs. These conventions include the use of the forward-slash character, '/', as the separator of steps. For example, the file 'boat.gif' in the diagram above can be identified as being in directory 'images', which is within directory 'xml', using the following URL fragment:

```
/xml/images/boat.gif
```

It should be noted again that complete paths begin with a '/' symbol. The absence of a directory name (or other step option) preceding this symbol indicates that the path begins at the root. This is important for the later discussion on relative paths.

Within paths, additional characters are allowed, including ';', '@', '&', '=', '+', '$' and ','. Other symbols (not included in the global set) must still be escaped if appearing in the path.

Computer platform complications

UNIX

On a UNIX computer system, no matter how many disk drives are attached to it, the computer 'sees' only a single file system, with a single root directory. As new disks are added to an existing system, the root of the file system on that drive is simply 'attached' to a branch on the main hierarchy. There are therefore no complications as far as URLs are concerned. But the other popular platforms discussed below do not map all drives to a single hierarchy in this way. The disk drives are considered separate, and the relevant drive needs to be specified in the URL.

UNIX file systems have case-insensitive directory and file names. This means that two files with the same name can be stored in the same directory. For example, 'index.htm' and 'Index.HTM' are considered to be two different files. A directory or file may not be found if the case is wrong (though most Web servers correct such errors automatically).

Windows

When the whole system is visible on Windows (and MS-DOS) systems the drive letter is required, followed by a colon. If the required file is on drive 'C', then the URL must include 'C:' as the first step in the hierarchy:

```
file:///C:/.../.../...
```

Macintosh

When the whole system is visible on Macintosh systems the drive name must appear as the first step. The added complication here is that Macintosh disk drive names can be quite long, and may include spaces, as in the following example. When a space is present, it must (as usual) be represented by the escape code '%20':

```
file:///Macintosh%20HD/.../.../...
```

URL references

XML documents often contain references to URLs. A **URL reference** (properly, a URI reference) is a complete, extended or partial reference to a URL. It may include information that has been appended to the end of the URL to indicate processing that is to take place after the resource has been retrieved, or it may be incomplete simply to avoid unnecessary repetition of the host name, port number or file path, or to allow interlinked documents to be moved as a group to another system location, without the need to edit all the references.

When the URL reference is incomplete, the program that interprets the reference must fill in the blanks. A **relative URL** reference is resolved into a complete URL by the application processing the reference, using existing knowledge it has of the current context.

Absolute references

An **absolute URL** reference is simply a URL, as described above. The only extra concern is how the URL can be isolated from and identified within the document containing it. When the URL is an attribute value, the quotes act as unambiguous delimiters. When the URL appears as just part of a longer string of text, it must be delimited in a similar fashion. Normally, this is again done with quotes, or with chevrons. But these delimiters alone may also be for other purposes, so it is also preferred that URLs be unambiguously identified using the prefix 'url:':

```
Requests For Comments (RFC) and Internet
Draft documents are available
from <url:ftp://ftp.internic.net> and
numerous mirror sites.
```

Relative references

A referenced document may also contain further references to other documents. For example, an HTML Web page often contains references to images (to be included in the page when it is displayed). These related resources are usually stored on the same system. The location of the system and the protocol used to retrieve the other resources will be the same as before, and it should not be necessary to repeat them. A reference that begins with a single forward-slash character is a relative URL reference to the same domain, using the same protocol, but containing an absolute path from the root of that domain. For example:

```
<!ENTITY boat SYSTEM "/xml/images/boat.gif">
```

```
/xml/boats.xml
    /images/boat.gif
```

Relative paths

When a URL reference does not begin with a forward-slash character, it contains a **relative path**. The full path is calculated from combining the relative path with a pre-defined fixed 'home' location (but not the system root). Relative paths in URLs make maintenance of related files much easier. A collection of documents and directories can be moved to another system, without needing to edit any of the URL references. This will always work, providing that the documents retain their locations relative to each other.

By default, the home location from which relative paths are calculated is the directory holding the document that contains these references. When the resource is in the same directory as the source, it should only be necessary to give its name in the URL reference:

```
<!ENTITY boat SYSTEM "boat.gif">
```

/xml/boats.xml
　　　/boat.gif

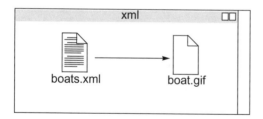

When the resource is in a sub-directory, the URL reference begins with the name of the directory:

```
<!ENTITY boat SYSTEM "images/boat.gif">
```

/xml/boats.xml
　　　/**images**/boat.gif

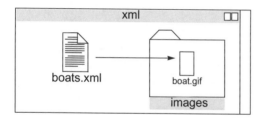

When the resource is elsewhere on the system, it is necessary to 'back out' of the current directory. This is done using the '..' symbols. A relative link to a file in a directory which shares the same parent directory as the source document appears as follows:

```
<!ENTITY boat SYSTEM "../images/boat.gif">
```

```
/xml/docs/boats.xml
    /images/boat.gif
```

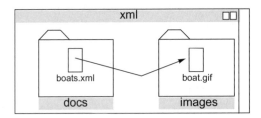

To back out more than one level, additional steps of the same kind are added. But care must be taken to avoid stepping back beyond the root directory. In the following example, the file 'home.xml' is in a directory three levels out from the current document:

```
/../../../home.xml
```

Earlier it was implied that the initial forward slash acts as a separator between the host details and the file path. Then it was revealed to be an important part of the file path itself, and only appears when it is an absolute path. This apparent dual role raises the theoretical problem of how to deal with the scenario of an absolute URL that contains a relative path, as the required separator slash would not be present. However, this scenario cannot arise because an absolute URL must, by definition, include an absolute file path.

Relative to what?

As already indicated, the home location for calculating relative paths is often the location of the document containing the references, but does not have to be. It can be convenient to make another directory the base from which relative URL paths are calculated.

In HTML, this is achieved using the Base element (see Chapter 23). Its Href attribute must hold a complete, absolute URL, which identifies the new home location. In the following example, the base location is set to the Images directory:

```
<BASE HREF="http://work/xml/images">
```

A later reference to an image will resolve to this directory, regardless of the location of the document containing this element:

```
<IMG SRC="boat.gif">
```

The XML standard has no equivalent feature, but the adjunct XML Base standard (see Chapter 11) now replicates, and improves slightly upon, this HTML feature.

These features of HTML and XML take advantage of the principles by which the base is determined, as established in the URI standard:

- If a mechanism for explicitly defining a base is present within the document, as explained above, it takes precedence.
- If the document containing the reference has a specific location (is not generated dynamically), then this location is deemed to be the base for all relative references.
- If the document has no explicit location, the original URL used to access the document is used to set the context.

Fake paths

Some Web servers are able to intercept URLs, and look up replacement paths. This allows the physical location of the files to change, without breaking existing URL references (though see the URN standard below). It should not therefore be assumed that the file path in the URL is the real file path on the system, especially when using the HTTP protocol.

Fragments

Often, only part of the file identified by the URL is required. It is therefore possible to supply further information, which is appended to the URL but is not formally part of it (but *is* part of the specification provided by RFC 2396). This is known as a **fragment identifier**. In HTML, the fragment identifier, '#', usually refers to the value of the Name attribute in an Anchor element:

```
...<A HREF="../myfiles/detail.xml#part3">
See details, part 3</A>...
...
<H2><A NAME="part3">Part Three</A></H2>
...
```

A Web browser first separates the fragment from the true URL, retrieves the file using the URL, then uses the fragment name to scroll to the desired part of the document.

When a URL reference consists of nothing but a fragment identifier, the reference is assumed to be made to the current document, and the document is not re-accessed.

The same kind of link can be made in an XML document when using the XPointer standard (see Chapter 28).

Common errors

Inconsistent and variable software tolerance to corrupted URL references has caused some confusion about this standard. URLs that work in one package tend to be broken when processed by other software. The most significant issues are incorrect path step separators, missing URL components and missing slashes.

Wrong path step separators

While UNIX systems use '/' to separate path steps, some systems use different characters. Under MS-DOS and Windows, '\' is used. On Macintosh systems, ':' is used. While Web browsers may accept URLs that contain these characters, it is important to recognize that they are not true URLs:

```
file:///C:\xml\entities.xml
```

Missing components

It has now become common practice for only part of a URL to be quoted in written form; particularly in advertising. This is possible only because Web browsers have sufficient intelligence to complete the URL automatically.

Consider the URL 'http://www.acmeCorp.com/index.htm'. A Web browser could be given the incomplete URL 'www.acmeCorp.com' and deduce the rest. First, it would anticipate that the most likely access method will be 'http:'. Second, it would by default look for a page called 'index.htm' or 'index.html'.

Going still further, some software would find the site and page from nothing more than the name 'acmeCorp', as 'www' is a common prefix and '.com' is a common suffix.

The most important point here is that software other than the popular Web browsers do not make the same assumptions, so it is always safest to use the full URL in XML documents.

Missing separators

There was some early confusion regarding the exact syntax of the file protocol. Because it is not a true Internet protocol, some people had assumed that it should not include the '//' separator:

```
file:/absolute-path
```

This point has since been clarified, and three forward slashes are required:

```
file:///absolute-path
```

URNs

URLs are just one form of reference, and are part of a wider standard called **URI** (***Universal Resource Identifier***). Apart from the URL standard, the other standard that URIs embrace is called the **URN** (***Uniform Resource Name***) standard.

Background

The URN concept is described in a specification called **RFC 2141**. While URLs describe *where* a resource is (using domain names, and file paths or specific queries), URNs describe *what* the resource is instead.

A URN has the advantage of being independent of the location of the resource, so it remains applicable even when the resource is moved, but has the consequent disadvantage that a look-up mechanism is required to resolve the URN into a URL whenever the resource is requested. This mechanism must be available at all times, and must be constantly maintained.

The difference between URLs and URNs is therefore analogous to the theoretical difference between a PUBLIC and SYSTEM identifier in XML entities (see Chapter 4). It is also analogous to domain names, which are descriptive and independent of Internet addresses.

Syntax

All URNs are divided into three components. URNs are composed of a 'urn' prefix (not case-sensitive), a 'namespace' identifier, and a namespace-specific unique resource identifier. Colons are used to separate each part:

```
URN:namespace:resource-identifier
```

One example of a namespace would be book references, which are governed by ISBN (*International Standard Book Number*) codes. The resource identifier of a book conforming to this standard consists of 10 digits giving the country (or other area), publisher and title of the book, plus a check digit (with hyphens or spaces between each part):

```
URN:ISBN:0-201-67487-4
```

The namespace identifier must consist of between one and 31 characters, consisting only of Roman letters and digits.

The resource identifier can be of any length, and may include the symbols '(', ')', '+', '-', ':', '=', '@', ';', '$', '_', '!', '*' and ' '. A particular namespace may permit other characters, but these characters must be escaped in the URN in the same manner as reserved characters are escaped in URLs (using the '%' escape code mechanism).

A URN is deemed to be complete when a character not in the allowed set is encountered, such as a space, right-chevron or quote:

```
<URN:ISBN:0-201-67487-4>
```

31. Past and future context

This chapter describes the influences that shaped the XML standard, and the earlier standards and technologies that prompted the development of XML, before going on to look at the future of these standards.

Overview

XML builds on the principles and conventions of two existing languages, **HTML** and **SGML**, to create a simple yet powerful mechanism for information storage, processing and delivery. These standards were in turn influenced by earlier markup languages, and by the Internet, and have in turn influenced newer standards for delivery of various kinds of information to many media outlets:

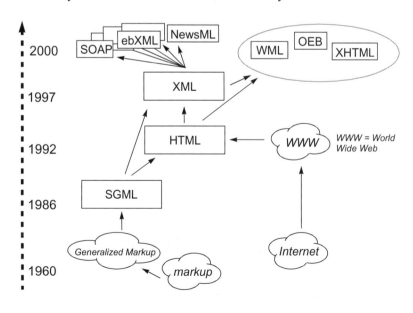

Markup

Tags

In traditional **typesetting** systems, **markup** instructions are used to facilitate more flexible formatting by **composition** software. The software accepts and outputs normal characters according to the current style setting, but detects markup characters and interprets them as instructions. Such an instruction, or **tag**, may for example dictate a switch to another **font**, or signify a line break, but will not itself appear in the presented text:

```
Are you going to *ITA Scarborough *ROM fair?
```

Are you going to *Scarborough* fair?

Typesetting languages

Most traditional **typesetting languages** comprise an allowed list of tags, each one with a pre-defined purpose. Of particular interest, in comparing this approach with XML, is that these systems tend to focus on the appearance of the information, and the language comprises a set of instructions for specifying the appearance and location of the text on the page.

Modern word processors and DTP systems hide markup codes from the author by employing a **WYSIWYG** (*What You See Is What You Get*) interface. The markup still exists, in one form or another, though it may take the form of a less intelligible (to humans), more efficient machine-readable scheme. It is an interesting exercise (if not enlightening) to open a word-processor document file using a simple text editor. At best, some words or sentences may be recognizable amongst the unintelligible mess.

Macros

Some typesetting languages allow a commonly used sequence of formatting instructions to be grouped and stored, for reference by a single tag whenever they are needed. The **macro** concept involves the use of named groups of instructions, called **macro definitions**, and references (**macro calls**) to these groups:

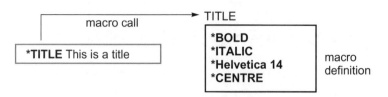

This technique introduces the concept of **generic** coding, because the macro name is likely to reflect its intended use, not the style of the following text. A macro called '*TITLE' has an obvious meaning: it is only necessary to identify a title in the document, and apply this macro to it, not to remember and apply a series of style tags. The document author need not be concerned with either specifying or understanding the formatting codes held in the macro definition. In addition, the author need not be concerned with the final appearance of the title. Most modern word processors and DTP packages have '**stylesheet**' definition facilities, which can be considered an equivalent concept.

SGML

The generalized markup concept emerged in the early 1960s, but did not become well established until the introduction of **SGML** (see Chapter 32), which was ratified by the **ISO** in 1986.

SGML has remained essentially unchanged in its first ten years of use. It is certainly a measure of how robust SGML was from the beginning that a decade passed before even minor revisions were considered necessary. Indeed, the specification for SGML was perhaps too advanced, with several of its features to this day under-utilized.

Yet it is the very power of SGML that has been its major handicap. Development of software to support even a typical subset of the language is a huge programming task. SGML-aware applications have therefore tended to be slow in arriving, incomplete or error-prone, yet at the same time expensive in comparison with proprietary solutions.

By the mid-1990s, a large number of experts in the field considered that the time was right to specify a simplified version of SGML that would make the generalized markup approach attractive to a wider audience.

HTML

The Internet has become an established medium for information retrieval and exchange. This medium was a natural platform for a hypertext service, linking documents around the world into a **World Wide Web** of information. But a tagging language was needed to provide the linking mechanism, and to apply some basic text formatting to the document containing these links.

The **HTML** language was developed to meet this need. Although the syntax of SGML was largely adopted by HTML, its principles were not. Only in later incarnations was HTML made fully compatible, and could then be described as an application of SGML (and defined by a suitable DTD). Although a standards committee is responsible for the development of HTML, vendors of the most popular Web browsers have also added incompatible tags for commercial advantage, causing considerable confusion. Yet HTML provides no mechanism for allowing document authors to extend the language by adding their own tags.

XML

The pressure to simplify SGML coincided neatly with the pressure to enhance HTML, and the **W3C** saw the need for a new language to fill the gap. In 1996 the process began with the definition of ten design goals that the new language should satisfy. These goals would be used to ensure that the final specification addressed the concerns that first prompted the drive for a new language. The ten goals they defined are listed below, together with some personal and rather subjective assessments of their realization or otherwise in the final specification.

Goal 1 – easy to use

XML shall be straightforwardly usable over the Internet. XML has purposely adopted HTML conventions to make the progression to XML as simple as possible, and XML may be used without a DTD.

Goal 2 – widespread application

XML shall support a wide variety of applications. XML provides a convenient mechanism for describing a very wide variety of information, from highly structured database fields to semi-structured publishing material, and from push technology and client-sided processing to document management and multiple media publishing. Within three years of its release, XML has become a pervasive, fundamental technology.

Goal 3 – SGML compatibility

XML shall be compatible with SGML. XML is defined as a subset of SGML, so can be processed using SGML tools, occasionally at the expense of clarity in the XML specification. (Whenever it is perceived that some detail of the XML language is superfluous, redundant or irrelevant, it is almost invariably included to provide backward compatibility with the more complex SGML format.)

Goal 4 – easy to support

It shall be easy to write programs which process XML documents. The major differences between XML and SGML are the removal of minimization and other options, and stricter rules on the format of remaining markup. For example, in XML the literal string '`<![CDATA[`' is significant, whereas in SGML the same instruction may be formatted in various ways, such as '`<![   CDATA    [`' or '`${CharData{`'. An XML processor is therefore much easier to develop than a similar SGML tool, because there are fewer options and variants to consider in the data syntax. However, this advantage is beginning to be eroded by the pressure to also support other standards, such as XML Schemas, Namespaces, XInclude and Xlink.

Goal 5 – limited optional features

The number of optional features in XML is to be kept to the absolute minimum, ideally zero. In one sense, almost all the features of XML are optional, so it is difficult to assess the success of this goal. However, in the sense that there are rarely two or more ways to achieve one effect, XML has met this aim. This goal is really just part of Goal 4.

Goal 6 – clear and human readable

XML documents should be human legible and reasonably clear. As XML is based on SGML, a human-readable markup language resting on the ASCII text format, and also has no minimization features (see Goal 10), it is a given that XML is legible and clear (but see Goal 3 for exceptions).

Goal 7 – quick development of XML standard

The XML design should be prepared quickly. This goal is difficult to assess. Development began in the summer of 1996 and the final specification was released in February 1998. It is left to the reader to decide whether this goal was met.

Goal 8 – formal and concise design

The design of XML shall be formal and concise. XML is specified by a set of rules that conform to a formal grammar (see Chapter 34, which illustrates the design of XML in chart form).

Goal 9 – easy to create documents

XML documents shall be easy to create. Software can create an XML document using simple text line output commands, and humans can create XML documents using any tool that can export ASCII text.

Goal 10 – minimization unimportant

Terseness in XML markup is of minimum importance. The SGML language includes many optional features that allow a document author to omit keying tags or parts of tags, when context alone allows software to infer the presence of this markup. Even in HTML, it is possible to omit end-tags, such as the '</p>' tag, without introducing ambiguity. XML has no such minimization features. All tags must be present and complete, which helps with Goal 4, and reflects the fact that modern XML-sensitive word processors make issues of keying individual markup characters irrelevant.

The future

The most influential software vendors have backed XML, and have released numerous products to support it. XML is also at the heart of a number of industry initiatives (available from www.oasis-open.org/cover/xml.html#applications). If there was ever any serious doubt, the future of XML is certainly now secure. But there remains the question about its continued relationship with SGML and HTML, and whether there is room for all three languages.

HTML and XHTML

HTML should survive. It has some unique features that XML does not aim to replicate, and is particularly suited to form-based interaction with the user. Also, there are times when customized tags are unnecessary, and even counter-productive. Such examples as displaying information extracted from a database, and creating marketing-oriented Web sites, illustrate the point. In the first case, a DTD has no useful role to play, and, in the second case, the constraints of structured markup would stifle creativity in design. Finally, Web browsers are simply more efficient when dealing with formatting markup they natively understand, particularly when a stylesheet is not needed.

HTML should remain a popular standard, and one that will gradually improve. The recent move to 'XML-ise' HTML, called **XHTML** (see Chapter 23), demonstrates its continued importance.

SGML

XML is more likely to replace SGML in the medium term. While there are a number of additional features in SGML that still have their uses in serious document management and publishing applications, this advantage is gradually being eroded by the new standards supporting XML (such as Xlink, Xpointer, XML

Base and XInclude). Software vendors with a history of developing SGML products are, for the moment, continuing to support it. But new vendors are ignoring
SGML, and only supporting XML.

A good test of the popularity of any technology is the number of books that focus
on it. It has been several years since any new books on SGML have appeared, and
the existing books are often hard to find. But there are many books dedicated to
XML, to XSLT and now to XML Schemas.

32. SGML

SGML is the older brother of XML. There are several books dedicated to describing SGML in detail (see *The Concise SGML Companion* (Addison-Wesley – ISBN 0-201-41999-8)). This chapter should be of particular interest to readers who need to convert existing SGML documents and DTDs into XML format (possibly including DTD to XML Schema conversions), and those who wish to use SGML tools to process XML documents. Otherwise, this material is of historical interest only, and explains some of the quirks of the XML standard.

History and usage

SGML (the ***Standard Generalized Markup Language***) has, at the time of writing, been in existence for over 15 years. The developers of the XML language used their experience of SGML to determine the shape and scope of the new language, and there are therefore many similarities. However, SGML is also a larger (some would say more unwieldy) language.

Due to the complexity of SGML, and the consequential expense of implementing a system based around this format, relatively few organizations have adopted it for document storage, publishing and interchange. Initially, it was almost totally confined to use in government organizations and large publishers. As supporting tools became more affordable, and more mature, SGML branched out into new domains and became a popular solution for some demanding publishing needs.

SGML Declaration

One major difference to XML is that all SGML documents begin with an **SGML Declaration**, which can be seen as a kind of configuration file. Instructions in this section provide values for the characteristics and limitations described below.

The SGML declaration logically precedes the DTD. It may be present in the same physical data file as the DTD and document instance, but more typically it applies to many documents, and even to many document types, so is located in a separate data file.

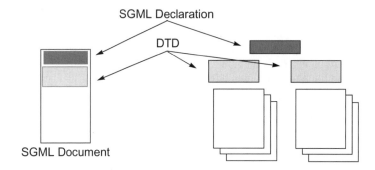

There are default settings for all the features affected by the SGML Declaration. When the default settings are satisfactory, there is no need for an actual SGML Declaration to be present.

The **SGML Declaration** segment of an SGML document prepares the parser for the remaining data by specifying character sets in use (usually based on ASCII or ISO 646), setting system variable space limits and selecting optional parts of the SGML standard.

These considerations are not relevant to XML, which can take advantage of recent technological developments and has a different target audience. However, it is necessary to know about the SGML declaration if SGML tools are to be used with XML documents, because the default SGML settings need to be modified to make the tools accept documents conforming to the XML syntax.

The start of an SGML declaration is defined by the characters '<!SGML', followed by the version of the standard. It is completed by the close chevron, '>':

```
<!-- SGML -->
<!SGML ISO 8879:1986 ..........>
```

Abstract syntax

The SGML standard defines the rules that apply to an SGML document, but does not specify exactly how to apply them. Implied rules are defined by an **abstract syntax** and include, for example, a rule stating that a special character will be used to begin an element start-tag, but without specifying which character this is.

Concrete syntax

A mechanism is provided for defining a **concrete syntax** from the abstract syntax. The concrete syntax specifies the actual keywords and special characters that separate markup from data. For example, it includes a physical value for the character to be used to begin an element start-tag, such as '<'.

Reference concrete syntax

There is a default concrete syntax, which is known as the **reference concrete syntax**. As the values and settings of the reference concrete syntax are 'hard-wired' into the parser, they need not be physically included in the declarations. The defaults include specifying the use of the '<' character to begin a start-tag, and '>' to end one. For example, a start-tag for an element called Name would by default be expected to appear as '<name>'.

Variant concrete syntax

It was foreseen that some implementors would work in environments where the default markup delimiters would be inconvenient, perhaps because the characters used as delimiters are already in common use in the document text. Any change to any part of the concrete syntax must be declared, and creates a **variant concrete syntax**.

For example, the element start-tag open delimiter, by default a '<' character, could easily be changed to '!', so that '<' characters can be used in the data:

```
!code> <a<b<c !/code>
```

Reference quantity set

There is also a **reference quantity set** that puts limits on the number or size of various objects, and works in a similar manner. For example, it states that an element name consists of at most eight characters. These limits can be changed, and were generally relaxed as SGML began to be used on increasingly powerful computer platforms.

CALS standard

Every SGML application could have its own unique SGML declaration (including a variant concrete syntax and/or a variant quantity set), but due to the desirability of maintaining standards only one variant is in common use. Devised by the US Department of Defense, it is sometimes referred to as the **CALS declaration**. The **CALS** (*Continuous Acquisition and Life Cycle Support*) variant differs from the reference quantity set mainly in respect of the legal scope of some constraints.

For example, the reference quantity set restricts tag names to a maximum length of eight characters, but the CALS variant permits up to 32 characters. The default declaration would enforce a brief element name to identify a 'procedure summary', such as '`<procsum>`', whereas the CALS variant would allow the code to be '`<procedure-summary>`' (if so desired).

Adapting for XML compliance

SGML declarations are only relevant to XML when using SGML tools to maintain XML documents. Generally, it is possible to modify an existing declaration, and if the size or number of certain objects is present, they should be reset to '9999999'. It is also necessary to change the definitions for empty elements and processing instructions. This allows document instances to be formatted as required by XML:

```
<!-- SGML -->
CAPACITY
      SGMLREF
      ELEMCAP 999999


DELIM   GENERAL   SGMLREF
        NET   "/>"
        PIC   "?>"


<!-- SGML -->
<p>This is an <empty/> element</p>
<?PROCESS instruction ?>
```

DTD features

The SGML standard incorporates the concept of a **DTD** (a *Document Type Definition*).

The SGML DTD scheme is similar to, but more complex than the XML DTD mechanism, as it contains additional features. In some cases, these features can be emulated using other techniques.

An SGML DTD and its associated documents can be converted into equivalent XML files, should there be any reason to replace SGML tools with XML tools, or to process, deliver or publish SGML data using XML tools. But it may not always be possible to achieve this without human intervention.

Any content

A content model can simply include the keyword ANY, which indicates that any combination of text and the other elements defined in the DTD can be used in the content.

```
<!-- SGML -->
<!ELEMENT anything - - ANY>
```

This was never widely used, due to the lack of control it permits. However, this feature has been resurrected in the XML Schema standard (the 'any' element, or default 'anyType' data type).

'and' groups

Beyond the sequential and optional model group types that XML DTDs permit, SGML also has an option that requires all elements in a group to be present, but allows them to occur in any order. The 'and' connector, '&', is used to signify this rule. For example, an entry in a catalogue may require the presence of Description, Price and Code elements, without dictating what order they must appear in:

```
<!-- SGML -->
<!ELEMENT entry - - (desc & pr & cd)>
```

The three examples below all conform to this rule:

```
<!-- SGML -->
<entry><desc>...</desc><pr>...</pr><cd>...</cd></entry>

<!-- SGML -->
<entry><cd>...</cd><desc>...</desc><pr>...</pr></entry>

<!-- SGML -->
<entry><cd>...</cd><pr>...</pr><desc>...</desc></entry>
```

This concept has returned in the XML Schema standard (see Chapter 15) using the 'all' element, though in a simpler form (the 'all' group must be the only group in the model, and no element in the group may repeat).

Inclusions

It is possible to specify the inclusion of a given element in the content models of all elements below a certain point in the DTD hierarchy. For example, instead of explicitly stating that the Indexterm and Emphasis elements are allowed in the content model of each mixed content element, such as the Paragraph, Item, Title and Note elements, they could be defined as 'global' elements at the root of the document. After the model group, a list of included elements appears, separated by one of the token separator characters, 'I', '&' or ',' (though it is irrelevant which is chosen) and bounded by brackets that are preceded by a plus symbol, '+'. In this

example, a paragraph before the first chapter cannot contain index terms or emphasis, but any paragraph within a chapter can.

```
<!-- SGML -->
<!ELEMENT book       - - (para*, chapter+)>
<!ELEMENT chapter    - - (para|list|note)*
                                  +(indexterm|emph)>
<!ELEMENT para       - - (#PCDATA)>
<!ELEMENT list       - - (item+)>
<!ELEMENT note       - - (#PCDATA)>

<!ELEMENT indexterm  - - (#PCDATA)>
<!ELEMENT emph       - - (#PCDATA)>


<!-- SGML -->
<para>This is an <emph>important</emph> paragraph.</para>
```

Note that the Chapter element can also directly contain the included elements, so
revealing this technique to be a rather blunt instrument, often causing possibly
unintended side effects.

Exclusions

It is also possible to specifically exclude an element from the content of all sub-
elements, whether they are explicitly (but optionally) defined as part of the model
group of some of these sub-elements, or are just included (using the mechanism
just described) at a higher level in the document hierarchy. The approach is the
same, except that a minus symbol, '-', is used in place of the plus symbol. For
example, it may be considered unwise to allow an Indexterm element to contain
another Indexterm element, and for an Emphasis element to contain another
Emphasis element:

```
<!-- SGML -->
<!ELEMENT indexterm (#PCDATA) -(indexterm)>
<!ELEMENT emph      (#PCDATA) -(emph)>
```

Ignoring markup

When it is inconvenient for significant characters in a particular element to be
interpreted as markup, the element content can be defined to consist of normal
character data, '**CDATA**', or normal character data that may also contain entity
references, '**RCDATA**' (*Replaceable Character Data*):

```
<!-- SGML -->
<!ELEMENT statement CDATA>
...
<statement>The characters '&<>' are used in
the Standard Generalized Markup Language</statement>


<!-- SGML -->
<!ELEMENT statement RCDATA>
...
<statement>The characters '&amp;<>' are used in
the &SGML;</statement>
```

When this requirement applies only to a range of text, instead of the whole content of an element, marked sections may be used to enclose and identify the text range. XML has adopted the CDATA marked section, but not the **RCDATA** variant:

```
<!-- SGML -->
<statement>The characters <![RCDATA[ '&amp;<>' ]]>
are used in the &SGML;</statement>
```

Similarly, the content of an entity (both internal and external) may be defined as CDATA or as **SDATA** (*System Data*). SDATA is the same thing as CDATA, except that it indicates system-dependent content, which would need to be edited if transmitted to another system.

Markup minimization techniques

At the time SGML was defined, memory and disk space were vastly more expensive than today. The limited memory available to computers in the early 1980s was a concern. A document could be too large, or too complex for the parser to deal with. The size of documents was therefore a major concern, and keeping markup to a minimum was seen as essential. There was also no expectation that WYSIWYG editing tools would be made available to authors. XML document authors were expected to type every character in every tag. So techniques designed to minimize the task of keying markup constructs was of prime importance. For these two reasons, the SGML specification includes a number of **markup minimization** techniques. Markup tags may be shortened or omitted without disrupting the document structure; but only where the context permits, where the DTD rules allow, and when some optional SGML features are enabled on the local system.

HTML Note: Some of these minimization techniques found their way into HTML. In particular, some end-tags may be omitted, and some attribute names are not required (or indeed expected) as in '`<ul compact>`'.

Normalized SGML

Minimization in SGML was always an optional feature. When SGML documents are created without using any of the minimization techniques described below, they are considered to be fully **normalized**. With only a few very minor exceptions, fully normalized SGML looks identical to XML. The following fragment is a fully normalized structure identifying a company employee:

```
<!-- SGML -->
<employee>
    <name>J. Smith</name>
    <number>9876</number>
    <title>XML Developer</title>
</employee>
```

For the sake of following examples, it will be assumed that all the elements shown above are required by the DTD, in the strict order given.

Omitted elements

Though it may seem a confusing contradiction, an element that is officially required to be present may in fact be *omitted* from the document, simply because its presence can be implied.

The DTD may contain switches within element declarations that specify whether or not the start-tag or the end-tag may be omitted from the document (providing that their presence can be implied by context). When this feature is enabled (by the SGML declaration) two single character tokens appear immediately after the element name. Each token must be either '-' (required) or 'o' (omit), and the first applies to the start-tag, the second to the end-tag. In the following example, the Paragraph element end-tag may be omitted:

```
<!-- SGML -->
<!ELEMENT para - o (.....)>


<!-- SGML -->
<chapter>
<para>This is a paragraph.
<para>This is another paragraph.
</chapter>
```

Omit start-tag

In some cases, the start-tag may be omitted. This is an option where it is obvious by context that the element must have started. In this case, the presence of the Employee start-tag is enough to signify the start of its first required child element, Name, and the presence of the Name end-tag similarly signifies the start of its next sibling element, Number:

```
<!-- SGML -->
<employee>
    J. Smith</name>
    9876</number>
    XML Developer</title>
</employee>
```

Omit end-tag

In some cases, as shown below, the end-tag may be omitted. This is an option where it is obvious by context that the element has ended. In this case, the Number start-tag is enough to signify the end of the Name element, and the Employee end-tag similarly signifies the end of the embedded Title element:

```
<!-- SGML -->
<employee>
    <name>J. Smith
    <number>9876
    <title>XML Developer
</employee>
```

Empty end-tag

Alternatively, the end-tags may be present, but may omit the element names. These are known as **empty end-tag** elements:

```
<!-- SGML -->
<employee>
    <name>J. Smith</>
    <number>9876</>
    <title>XML Developer</>
</employee>
```

Null end-tag

Another technique abbreviates both the start-tag and end-tag. The end-tag is a **null end-tag**, '/', and the start-tag is a **net-enabling start-tag** (net = null end-tag), which ends with the same character, '/':

```
<!-- SGML -->
<employee>
    <name/J. Smith/
    <number/9876/
    <title/XML Developer/
</employee>
```

This feature can be convenient when the element content is restricted to text and is likely to be brief:

```
Water is H<sub/2/O
```

Water is H_2O

Empty start-tag

The start-tag may be empty if it is the same as the previous start-tag. This is known as an **empty start-tag**:

```
<!-- SGML -->
<title>XML Developer</title><>Java Developer</title>
```

Here, the '<>' tag has an implied meaning of '<title>', as this is the previous element in the data stream.

Short references

Markup can be implied from the contextual use of normal text characters using **short reference** mappings. This can be considered the ultimate minimization technique, as it may involve the insertion of *no* extra characters. For example, the use of the quotation mark character to surround quoted text could be interpreted as markup, in which case the following fragments would be considered equivalent:

```
<!-- SGML -->
<p>Alice in Wonderland thought "What is the
use of a book without pictures or convers-
ations?".</p>
```

```
<!-- SGML -->
<p>Alice in Wonderland thought <quote>What
is the use of a book without pictures or
conversations?</quote>.</p>
```

The mapping of strings or individual characters to element tags can be made context-sensitive. Taking the example above, a quotation mark found within a Paragraph element is mapped to the start-tag '<quote>', whereas a quotation mark found within a (now opened) Quote element is mapped to the end-tag '</quote>'.

This technique is especially suitable for tabular material, where the line-end codes are mapped to Row elements and tab or comma characters are mapped to Entry elements:

```
<!-- SGML -->
Red [TAB] 1 [TAB] Danger [CR][LF]
Yellow [TAB] 2 [TAB] Alert [CR][LF]
Green [TAB] 3 [TAB] Normal [CR][LF]
```

Attribute minimization

When an attribute value is restricted to a single word or number the quotes are not necessary. This is because the next space or chevron unambiguously ends the value (though this feature may be disabled in some systems):

```
<!-- SGML -->
<list offset=yes indent=15>
```

An attribute value may be further restricted to one word from a group of words, termed a **name group** (as in XML). In the following example, the Offset attribute value is restricted to a value of either 'yes' or 'no'. Any other value would be illegal (though this is not obvious from the example – the limitation is defined in and controlled by the DTD). In this situation, the attribute name and the **value indicator** ('=') may also be absent:

```
<!-- SGML -->
<list yes>
```

Attribute inheritance

An attribute value may be inherited from the value of the previous occurrence of that attribute. This is a useful technique when its value is likely to switch only occasionally. The declaration includes the **#CURRENT** keyword to indicate this behaviour. In the following example, the second and third paragraphs are 'English', whereas the fifth is 'French':

```
<!-- SGML -->
<!-- English paragraphs -->
<para lang="English"> ... English ... </para>
<para> ... English ... </para>
<para> ... English ... </para>

<!-- French paragraphs -->
<para lang="French"> ... Francais ... </para>
<para> ... Francais ... </para>
```

Converting to XML

The wide range of software supporting XML will prompt some to consider converting SGML documents to XML format. Unfortunately, this is not as simple a task as converting the other way. This is due to the fact that SGML has a far wider range of capabilities.

The SGML Declaration

XML uses the same characters for markup delimiters as specified by the default SGML declarations. For example, the characters '</' indicate the start of an end-tag in XML, just as they do in the SGML reference concrete syntax. If the SGML declaration in use redefines any delimiters, both the SGML declaration must be changed to the default case, and all affected DTDs and document instances must be processed accordingly:

```
<!-- SGML -->
GENERAL
        SGMLREF
        STAGO  "**"          (start-tag open)
        ETAGO  "@@"          (end-tag open)
        TAGC   "!!"          (tag close)

**p!!This is a simple paragraph@@p!!
```

The example declaration and document fragment shown above must be changed as follows:

```
<!-- SGML -->
GENERAL
        SGMLREF
        STAGO  "<"           (start-tag open)
        ETAGO  "</"          (end-tag open)
        TAGC   ">"           (tag close)

<!-- SGML -->
<p>This is a simple paragraph</p>
```

In fact, the instructions can be removed entirely when their values are all the same as the reference concrete syntax. There are a number of SGML books on the market which provide a full list of the keywords used to modify capacity limits and markup delimiters, along with their default, reference concrete syntax values.

Converting the DTD

Element and attribute names are not usually case-sensitive in SGML. It is possible for the DTD to contain a definition of an element using lower-case letters, yet for a conforming document instance to contain upper-case letters. Care must be taken to ensure that all names defined in the DTD are consistent with each other, and with element names in the document, unlike the following example (see Chapter 6 for suggested convention for XML names):

```
<!-- SGML -->
<!ELEMENT Chapter .....>
<!ELEMENT para .....>

<Chapter>
<PARA>This is a paragraph</Para>
...
</CHAPTER>
```

As element minimization techniques are not part of the XML standard, the minimization tokens must, if present, be removed from SGML element declarations. Alternatively, they can be replaced by a parameter entity reference. This will be accepted by an XML processor, though the entities concerned must contain no text when processed as XML. This approach is useful if the DTD is still to be applied to SGML documents as well as XML documents:

```
<!-- XML -->
<!ENTITY % YesYes ''>    <!-- for SGML make 'o o' -->
<!ENTITY % NoNo ''>      <!-- for SGML make '- -' -->
<!ENTITY % NoYes ''>     <!-- for SGML make '- o' -->
<!ENTITY % YesNo ''>     <!-- for SGML make 'o -' -->

<!ELEMENT para %NoYes; (#PCDATA)>
```

SGML allows comments to be embedded in declarations of various types, including element declarations. An embedded comment must be moved out of the declaration, and, if it is still required, must be placed within dedicated comment declarations:

```
<!-- SGML -->
<!ELEMENT IMG EMPTY -- Image Reference -->


<!-- XML -->
<!-- Image Reference -->
<!ELEMENT IMG EMPTY>
```

SGML allows PCDATA to be mixed with elements (in a mixed content model), with the tokens appearing in any order. XML insists on the PCDATA token appearing first:

```
<!-- XML -->
<!ELEMENT para %NoYes (#PCDATA | sub | super)*>
```

Although strongly discouraged, connectors other than the choice connector may be used in a mixed content model, and the content may not have to be repeatable. But XML insists on the choice connector and repeatability in mixed content models, so as to avoid ambiguities:

```
<!-- SGML -->
<!ELEMENT title - - (prefix, #PCDATA)>


<!-- XML -->
<!ELEMENT title %NoNo; (#PCDATA | prefix)*>
```

When several elements share the same content model, a single element declaration may be used to define them all. The element names are grouped. It is necessary to create individual element declarations for the XML DTD:

```
<!-- SGML -->
<!ELEMENT (para|note|item) - - (#PCDATA|emph)*>


<!-- XML -->
<!ELEMENT para    %NoNo;    (#PCDATA|emph)*>
<!ELEMENT note    %NoNo;    (#PCDATA|emph)*>
<!ELEMENT item    %NoNo;    (#PCDATA|emph)*>
```

SGML allows a content model to include tokens that represent elements which must appear, but in any order, using the 'and' connector, '&'. In practice, it is rarely used, but where it *is* used it can often be changed to a sequence connector without many complaints from document authors. However, doing this may invalidate old documents which include these elements in a different order to that chosen in the new DTD. Alternative approaches to this problem include re-sequencing invalid combinations (see *Converting the Document instance* below) or explicitly allowing all combinations. The latter approach involves less work, but can result in complex chains of rules, particularly because it is necessary to avoid ambiguity in DTD models. The XML equivalent shown below is actually illegal, because it is ambiguous:

```
<!-- SGML -->
<!ELEMENT entry - - (desc & pr & cd)>


<!-- XML (illegal) -->
<!ELEMENT entry    ( (desc, pr, cd) | (desc, cd, pr) |
                     (pr, desc, cd) | (pr, cd, desc) |
                     (cd, desc, pr) | (cd, pr, desc) )>
```

On encountering the element Desc, for example, the parser would not know which of the first two model groups apply. The solution is to modify the example as follows:

```
<!-- XML -->
<!ELEMENT entry    (
                   (desc, ((pr, cd)  | (cd, pr))  )  |
                   (pr,   ((desc, cd) | (cd, desc)) )  |
                   (cd,   ((desc, pr) | (pr, desc)) )
                   )>
```

But note that XML Schemas have the All element to replicate this functionality.

A number of SGML attribute types are not available in XML. The table below shows all SGML attribute types, and gives recommended substitutions for those types not supported by XML:

SGML	XML	XML Schema
CDATA	CDATA	string
ENTITY	ENTITY	ENTITY
ENTITIES	ENTITIES	ENTITIES
ID	ID	ID
IDREF	IDREF	IDREF
IDREFS	IDREFS	IDREFS
NAME	**NMTOKEN**	*pattern*
NAMES	**NMTOKENS**	*list of* NMTOKEN
NMTOKEN	NMTOKEN	NMTOKEN
NMTOKENS	NMTOKENS	NMTOKENS

NUMBER	NMTOKEN	integer
NUMBERS	NMTOKENS	*list of* integer *(space instead of '+' separator)*
NUTOKEN	NMTOKEN	*pattern*
NUTOKENS	NMTOKENS	*list of* NUTOKEN *(space instead of '+' separator)*
NOTATION	NOTATION	NOTATION

In all cases, the more specific token types are simply reassigned to name tokens, which in their XML incarnation are less rigidly defined (for example, they may start with a digit).

In SGML, marked section keywords may be surrounded by spaces, and the TEMP keyword is available. In XML, marked section keywords must not have spaces around them, and 'TEMP' is not allowed, so 'TEMP' should be converted to 'INCLUDE' (or 'IGNORE' if not currently wanted) (the same is true for keywords specified via an entity reference).

Inclusions and exclusions

Where an inclusion has been used purely as a convenience, to avoid specifying the element in many content models, conversion is a simple matter of entering the element name in these content models.

For example, a DTD that includes an Indexterm element at the root element must be modified to specify the Indexterm element explicitly in each element where it may be used. The DTD becomes more verbose, but this is unavoidable.

There is, in fact, one virtue to doing this, as more control is provided over the placement of the included element. For example, an Indexterm element could contain a Chapter element (assuming it has a content of ANY):

```
<!-- SGML -->
<!ELEMENT book      - - (chapter)* +(indexterm) >
<!ELEMENT chapter - - (title, para+) >
<!ELEMENT title   - - (#PCDATA)*>
<!ELEMENT para    - - (#PCDATA|emph)*>


<!-- XML -->
<!ELEMENT book    (chapter)*>
<!ELEMENT chapter (title, para+) >
<!ELEMENT title   (#PCDATA|indexterm)*>
<!ELEMENT para    (#PCDATA|emph|indexterm)*>
```

Where an inclusion is used to enable certain structures within parts of a document, it is necessary to invent new elements. For example, where an Indexterm may be used in paragraphs contained in chapters, but not paragraphs contained within pre-liminary matter, the solution is to replace the single Paragraph element with two elements, one containing the Indexterm element:

```
<!-- SGML -->
<!ELEMENT book     - - (para*, chapter+)>
<!ELEMENT chapter - - (para|list|note)* +(indexterm|emph)>
<!ELEMENT para     - - (#PCDATA)>


<!-- XML -->
<!ELEMENT book        (intro_para*, chapter+)>
<!ELEMENT chapter     (para|list|note)* >
<!ELEMENT intro-para (#PCDATA)*>
<!ELEMENT para        (#PCDATA|indexterm)>
```

Where an exclusion has been used for the same purpose, an identical approach should be used, but where an exclusion has been used to avoid recursion, either the rule must be removed (and replaced with written instructions), or more drastic remodelling introduced. For example, a Table element may include an exclusion on embedded tables, because each cell of the table may contain any block-level element, including the Table element, yet some software applications may not be able to handle embedded tables:

```
<!-- SGML -->
<!ENTITY % block "para|list|table">
...
<!ELEMENT table - - (row)*    -(table)>
<!ELEMENT row    - - (cell)*>
<!ELEMENT cell   - - (%block)*>


<!-- XML -->
<!ENTITY % block "para|list|table">
...
<!ELEMENT table  (row)*>
<!ELEMENT row    (cell)*>
<!ELEMENT cell   (para|list)*>
```

Converting the document instance

The default SGML Declaration states that element and attribute names are not case-sensitive. Although it can be changed, most SGML documents conform to this setting. When the DTD and document authors work with case-insensitive material it is typically the case that inconsistent use will be made of upper- and lower-case letters in names. These inconsistencies must be removed during the conversion to XML. Entities are usually case-sensitive in SGML, so no further thought needs to be given to these.

SGML documents containing minimized and/or omitted tags must be **normalized**. All start-tags and all end-tags must be present and complete to be valid XML element tags. Thankfully, most modern SGML-sensitive applications produce fully normalized data. In other cases, there are a number of SGML tools that can perform the normalization process quickly and efficiently.

SGML allows external entities to be identified by only a public identifier. Resolution to an actual file name is assumed to be the task of an entity manager:

```
<!-- SGML -->
<!DOCTYPE mybook PUBLIC "-//MyCorp//DTD My Book//EN">
```

XML does not allow for public identifiers without accompanying system identifiers. A public identifier in a document type declaration must be converted to a system identifier, which unambiguously locates a named file on the system:

```
<!-- SGML or XML -->
<!DOCTYPE mybook SYSTEM "file:///DTDS/MYBOOK.DTD">
```

Primarily, conversion of the document instance requires the reformatting of empty elements:

```
<!-- SGML -->
This is an <empty> element.
```

```
<!-- XML -->
This is an <empty/> element.
```

All processing instructions must start with a keyword, and end in '?>', but it is unlikely that existing processing instructions will be relevant in a new XML-based environment. It is more likely that old processing instructions would simply be removed by eliminating all text beginning '<?' and ending '>'.

Marked section content defined as RCDATA must be converted to CDATA, and any embedded entities must be replaced by their content:

```
<!-- SGML -->
<statement>The characters <![RCDATA[ '&amp;<>' ]]>
are used in the &SGML;</statement>
```

```
<!-- XML -->
<statement>The characters <![CDATA[ '&<>' ]]>
are used in the &SGML;</statement>
```

In addition, markup characters in elements defined to be of type CDATA or RCDATA must be replaced by entity references (as well as changing the DTD to #PCDATA).

```
<!-- SGML -->
<!ELEMENT statement CDATA>
...
<statement>The characters '&<>' are used in
the Standard Generalized Markup Language</statement>


<!-- XML -->
<!ELEMENT statement (#PCDATA)>
...
<statement>The characters '&amp;&lt;&gt;' are used in
the Standard Generalized Markup Language</statement>
```

33. Charts and tables

The charts and tables included in this chapter:

- SAX methods (page 684)

- DOM methods (page 691)

- XSLT elements and attributes (page 691)

- CSS properties (page 693)

- This book DTD (page 699)

- ISO 8859/1 character set (page 702)

- ISO 639 language codes (page 708)

- ISO 3166 country codes (page 710)

- HTML 2/3/4 elements and attributes (page 713).

SAX 1.0 methods

The following table shows all the methods in the SAX API, in alphabetical order, the interfaces or classes they are defined in, the parameters they take and their return values:

Method	Interface/Class	Parameters	Return value
characters	DocumentHandler	char ch[], int start, int length	void
endDocument	DocumentHandler		void
endElement	DocumentHandler		void
error	ErrorHandler	SAXParseException err	void
fatalError	ErrorHandler	SAXParseException err	void
getByteStream	InputSource	InputStream byteStream	InputStream
getCharacterStream	InputSource	Reader charStream	Reader
getColumnNumber	Locator		int
getEncoding	InputSource		String
getLength	AttributeList		int
getLineNumber	Locator		int
getName	AttributeList	int i	String
getPublicId	Locator, InputSource		String
getSystemId	Locator, InputSource		String
getType	AttributeList	int i *or* String name	String
getValue	AttributeList	int i *or* String name	String
ignorableWhitespace	DocumentHandler	char ch[], int start, int length	void
InputSource	InputSource	*NONE or* String SysId *or* InputStream byteStream *or* Reader charStream	
notationDecl	DTDHandler	String name, String pubId, String sysId	void
parse	Parser	InputSource src, *or* String url	void
processingInstruction	DocumentHandler	String target, String data	void

resolveEntity	Entityresolver	String pubId, String sysId	InputSource
getByteStream	InputSource	InputStream byteStream	InputStream
setByteStream	InputSource	InputStream byteStream	void
setCharacterStream	InputSource	Reader charStream	void
setDocumentHandler	Parser	DocumentHandler dh	void
setDocumentLocator	DocumentHandler	Locator myLoc	void
setDTDHandler	Parser	DTDHandler dtdh	void
setEncoding	InputSource	String encoding	void
setEntityResolver	Parser	EntityResolver er	void
setErrorHandler	Parser	ErrorHandler eh	void
setLocale	Parser	Locale loc	void
setPublicId	InputSource	String pubId	void
setSystemId	InputSource	String sysId	void
startDocument	DocumentHandler		void
startElement	DocumentHandler		void
unparsedEntityDecl	DTDHandler	String name, String pubId, String sysId, String notaName	void
warning	ErrorHandler	SAXParseException err	void

SAX 2.0 methods

The following table shows all the additional methods in the SAX 2.0 API, in alphabetical order, the interfaces or classes they are defined in, the parameters they take and their return values (SAX 2.0 includes all SAX 1.0 methods listed above, but deprecates some of them (those belonging to the Parser, DocumentHandler and AttributeList interfaces)):

Method	Interface/Class	Parameters	Return value
characters	ContentHandler	char[] ch, int start, int length	void
endDocument	ContentHandler		void
endElement	ContentHandler	String namepaceURI, String localName, String qName	void
endPrefixMapping	ContentHandler	String prefix	void
getContentHandler	XMLReader		ContentHandler
getDTDHandler	XMLReader		DTDHandler
getEntityResolver	XMLReader		EntityResolver
getErrorHandler	XMLReader		ErrorHandler
getFeature	XMLReader	String name	boolean
getProperty	XMLReader	String name	object
getIndex	Attributes	String qname	int
getIndex	Attributes	String uri, String local-Name	int
getLength	Attributes		int
getLocalName	Attributes	int index	String
getParent	XMLFilter		XMLReader
getQName	Attributes	int index	String
getType	Attributes	int index	String
getType	Attributes	String qname	String
getType	Attributes	String uri, String local-Name	String
getURI	Attributes	int index	String
getValue	Attributes	int index	String
getValue	Attributes	String qName	String

getValue	Attributes	String uri, String local-Name	String
ignorableWhitespace	ContentHandler	char[] ch, int start, int length	void
parse	XMLReader	InputSource input *OR* String systemId	void
getProperty	XMLReader	String name	object
processingInstruction	ContentHandler	String target, String data	void
setContentHandler	XMLReader	ContentHandler handler	void
setDocumentLocator	ContentHandler	Locator locator	void
setDTDHandler	XMLReader	DTDHandler handler	void
setEntityResolver	XMLReader	EntityResolver resolver	void
setErrorHandler	XMLReader	ErrorHandler handler	void
setFeature	XMLReader	String name, boolean value	void
setParent	XMLFilter	XMLReader parent	void
setProperty	XMLReader	String name, Object value	void
skippedEntity	ContentHandler	String name	void
startDocument	ContentHandler		void
startElement	ContentHandler	String namespaceURI, String localName, String qName, Attribute atts	void
startPrefixMapping	ContentHandler	String prefix, String uri	void

DOM methods

The following table shows all the methods in the DOM API in alphabetical order, the interfaces they are defined in, the parameters they take and their return values:

Method	Interfaces	Parameters	Returns
appendChild	Node	Node newChild	Node
appendData	CharacterData	String arg	void
cloneNode	Node	boolean deep	Node
createAttribute	Document	String name	Attr
createCDATASection	Document	String data	CDATASection
createComment	Document	String text	Comment
createDocumentFrag-ment	Document		DocumentFragment
createElement	Document	String tagname	Element
createEntityReference	Document	String name	EntityReference
createProcessing-Instruction	Document	String target, String data	ProcessingInstruct-ion
createTextNode	Document		Text
deleteData	CharacterData	int offset, int count	void
getAttribute	Element	String name	String
getAttributeNode	Element	String name	Attr
getAttributes	Node		NamedNodeMap
getChildNodes	Node		NodeList
getData	CharacterData		String
getDoctype	Document		DocumentType
getDocumentElement	Document		Element
getElementsByTagName	Document, Element		NodeList
getEntities	DocumentType		NamedNodeMap
getFirstChild	Node		Node
getImplementation	Document		DOMImplementa-tion
getLastChild	Node		Node

getLength	CharacterData, NodeList, Named NodeMap		int
getName	DocumentType, Attr		String
getNamedItem	NamedNodeMap	String nodeName	Node
getNextSibling	Node		Node
getNodeName	Node		String
getNodeType	Node		short
getNodeValue	Node		String
getNotationName	Entity		String
getNotations	DocumentType		NamedNodeMap
getOwnerDocument	Node		Document
getParentNode	Node		Node
getPreviousSibling	Node		Node
getPublicId	Entity, Notation		String
getSpecified	Attr		boolean
getSystemId	Entity, Notation		String
getTagName	Element		String
getValue	Attr		String
hasChildNodes	Node	String value	boolean
insertBefore	Node	Node newChild, Node oldChild	Node
insertData	CharacterData	int offset, String arg	void
item	NodeList, Named NodeMap	int index	Node
normalize	Element		void
removeAttribute	Element	String name	void
removeAttributeNode	Element	Attr oldAttr	void
removeChild	Node	Node oldChild	Node
removeNamedItem	NamedNodeMap	String nodeName	Node
replaceChild	Node	Node newChild, Node oldChild	Node
replaceData	CharacterData	int offset, int count, String arg	void

setAttribute	Element	String name, String value	void
setAttributeNode	Element	Attr newAttr	void
setData	CharacterData	String data	void
setNamedItem	NamedNodeMap	Node theNode	Node
setNodeValue	Node	String value	void
setValue	Attr	String value	void
splitText	Text	int offset	Text
substringData	CharacterData	int offset, int count	String

XSLT elements and attributes

The elements and attributes defined in the XSLT DTD are shown in the table below, sorted into alphabetical order. This DTD includes the attribute 'xmlns:xsl' to declare the namespace of XSLT elements. It may be necessary to add at least one more attribute, to declare the namespace for the output document, such as 'xmlns:fo' or 'xmlns:html'. Also, a stylesheet document author may elect to ignore this attribute, and use another prefix, or simply use the default namespace:

Element	Attributes
apply-imports	*(none)*
apply-templates	select, mode
attribute	name, namespace, xml:space, use-attribute-sets
attribute-set	name, use-attribute-sets
call-template	name
choose	xml:space
comment	xml:space
copy	xml:space, use-attribute-sets
copy-of	select
decimal-format	name, decimal-separator, grouping-separator, infinity, minus-sign, NaN, percent, per-mille, zero-digit, digit, pattern-separator
element	name, namespace, xml:space, use-attribute-sets
fallback	xml:space
for-each	select, xml:space
if	test, xml:space
import	href
include	href
key	name, match, use
message	terminate, xml:space
namespace-alias	stylesheet-prefix, result-prefix
number	level, count, from, format, lang, letter-value, grouping-separator, grouping-size, value
otherwise	xml:space
output	method, version, encoding, omit-xml-declaration, standalone, doctype-public, doctype-system, cdata-section-elements, indent, media-type

param	name, select
preserve-space	elements
processing-instruction	name, xml:space
sort	select, lang, data-type, order, case-order
strip-space	elements
stylesheet	id, xmlns:xsl*, xml:space, extension-element-pre-fixes
template	match, name, priority, mode, xml:space
text	disable-output-escaping
transform	(*see* stylesheet)
value-of	select, disable-output-escaping
variable	name, select
when	test, xml:space
with-param	name, select

CSS properties

The following table lists all the CSS properties (53 from CSS1 and an additional 77 from CSS2) and the values that they can take, grouped by appropriate function. Common parameter value types are described below.

Length – inches (in), centimetres (cm), millimetres (mm), points (pt), picas (pc), ems (em), x-height (ex), pixels (px). A '+' or '-' prefix is allowed.

Percent – '+' or '-', followed by number, then '%', e.g. 200% = twice size.

Color – black, navy, blue, aqua, purple, maroon, green, red, gray, fuchsia, teal, lime, yellow, white, olive, silver, #rgb (hexadecimal), #rrggbb (hexadecimal), rgb(r,g,b) (each value decimal, or percent).

Number – digits, optionally prefix with '+' or '-', may include decimal point.

Integer – digits, optionally prefix with '+' or '-', not including decimal point.

Time – Number plus 'ms' (milliseconds) or 's' (seconds).

String – Quotes characters, single or double, no embedded quotes of same type, use '\"' or '\'' instead. Newline is '\A' and just '\' to split text over lines in style-sheet.

Note that, beyond the values shown below, CSS2 also adds the Inherit value to all properties.

Property	Ver	Example values	Values
Font properties			
font	1	italic small-caps bold 18pt/22pt Helvetica, sans-serif	combination of next six properties – font-style, font-variant, font-weight, font-size, line-height and font-family, with '/' between size and line height
	2	caption	... caption, icon, menu, message, small-caption, status-bar
font-style	1	italic	normal (the default), italic, oblique
font-variant	1	normal	normal (the default), small-caps
font-weight	1	bold	normal (the default), bold, bolder, lighter, 100, 200, 300, 400, 500, 600, 700, 800, 900
font-size	1	18pt larger	*Length*, xx-large, x-large, large, medium (the default), small, x-small, xx-small, smaller, larger

font-family	1	Helvetica, sans-serif 'Times New Roman'	comma separated alternative font names, first has preference, can be generic name (serif, sans-serif, cursive, fantasy, monospace), (quote name with spaces, "Times New Roman" (use single quotes in Style attributes))
font-size-adjust	2	0.58	*Number*, none (the default)
font-stretch	2	narrower	normal (the default), wider, narrower, ultra-condensed, extra-condensed, condensed, semi-condensed, semi-expanded, expanded, extra-expanded, ultra-expanded
Color and background			
color	1	blue #FF0	*Color*
background	1	red url(boat.gif) no-repeat scroll 10% 10%	combination (background-color, background-image, background-repeat, background-attachment, background-position)
background-color	1	green	*Color*, transparent (the default)
background-image	1	url(boat.gif)	URL, none (the default)
background-repeat	1	repeat-x	repeat (default), repeat-x, repeat-y, no-repeat
background-attachment	1	fixed	scroll (default), fixed
background-position	1	top 10mm 15mm	top, center, bottom, left, right, *Percent*, (*Length* – x, y)
Text properties			
text-decoration	1	underline	none (the default), underline, over-line, line-through, blink
vertical-align	1	sub	baseline (the default), sub, super, top, text-top, middle, bottom, text-bottom, *Percent*
	2	2pt	... *Length*
text-align	1	center	left, right, center, justify
	2	"."	... *String*
text-indent	1	1cm	*Length* (default '0') (first line of text block, minus value gives hanging indent), *Percent*
letter-spacing	1	2pt	normal (the default), *Length*
word-spacing	1	normal	normal (the default), *Length*
text-transform	1	uppercase	capitalize, uppercase, lowercase, none (the default)
line-height	1	22pt	none, (default), *Number*, *Length*, *Percent*
text-shadow	2	3px 3px red 2pt 4pt, -2pt -4pt 1pt blue	normal (default), *Length* (across) *Length* (down) *Length*? (blur angle) *Color*? (plus more optional shadows separate by commas)
Box properties			

margin	1	.3cm	*Length*, *Percent*, auto – repeated ('x' = all margins, 'x x' = vertical and horizontal and 'x x x x' = top/right/bottom/left)
margin-left	1	.3cm	*Length* (default 0), *Percent*, auto
margin-right	1	.3in	*Length* (default 0), *Percent*, auto
margin-top	1	9pt	*Length* (default 0), *Percent*, auto
margin-bottom	1	10%	*Length* (default 0), *Percent*, auto
padding	1	1pt	*Length* (default 0), percent*** – repeated ('x' = all edges, 'x x' = vertical and horizontal and 'x x x x' = top/right/bottom/left)
padding-left	1	1pt	*Length* (default 0), *Percent*
padding-right	1	auto	*Length* (default 0), *Percent*
padding-top	1	1em	*Length* (default 0), *Percent*
padding-bottom	1	5pt	*Length* (default 0), *Percent*
border	1	1in	*Length* – repeated ('x' = all borders, 'x x' = vertical and horizontal and 'x x x x' = top/right/bottom/left) or URL (or from V2, also set width, color and style – see below)
border-left	1	.3cm	*Length* or URL (or from V2, also set width, color and style – see below)
border-right	1	.3in	*Length* or URL (or from V2, also set width, color and style – see below)
border-top	1	9pt	*Length* or URL (or from V2, also set width, color and style – see below)
border-bottom	1	10%	*Length* or URL (or from V2, also set width, color and style – see below)
border-width	1	thick, thin 2pt 4pt 2pt 4pt	thin, medium, thick, *Length* – repeated ('x' = all borders, 'x x' = vertical and horizontal and 'x x x x' = top/right/bottom/left)
border-left-width	1	thick	thin, medium (default), thick, *Length*
border-right-width	1	thin	thin, medium (default), thick, *Length*
border-top-width	1	medium	thin, medium (default), thick, *Length*
border-bottom-width	1	3pt	thin, medium (default), thick, *Length*
border-color	1	blue green	*Color* - repeated ('x' = all borders, 'x x' = vertical and horizontal and 'x x x x' = top/right/bottom/left)
	2	transparent	... , transparent
border-left-color	2	red	*Color*
border-right-color	2	black	*Color*
border-top-color	2	white	*Color*
border-bottom-color	2	red	*Color*
border-style	1	solid ridge solid ridge	none, hidden, dotted, dashed, solid, double, groove, ridge, inset, outset – repeated ('x' = all borders, 'x x' = vertical and horizontal and 'x x x x' = top/right/bottom/left)
border-left-style	2	dotted	none, hidden, dotted, dashed, solid, double, groove, ridge, inset, outset

border-right-style	2	ridge	none, hidden, dotted, dashed, solid, double, groove, ridge, inset, outset
border-top-style	2	dashed	none, hidden, dotted, dashed, solid, double, groove, ridge, inset, outset
border-bottom-style	2	dotted	none, hidden, dotted, dashed, solid, double, groove, ridge, inset, outset
width	1	50px	*Length*, *Percent*, auto (default)
min-width	2	50px	*Length*, *Percent*
max-width	2	50px	*Length*, *Percent*, none (default)
height	1	auto	*Length*, auto (default)
	2	15%	*... Percent*
min-height	2	50px	*Length*, *Percent*
max-height	2	50px	*Length*, *Percent*, none (default)
float	1	left	left, right, none (the default)
clear	1	left	left, right, both, none (the default)
overflow	2	hidden	visible (the default), hidden, scroll, auto
clip	2	auto	*Shape*, auto (the default)
visiblity	2	visible	visible, hidden, collapse (default is 'inherit')
z-index	2	12	auto (the default), *Integer*
Generated content			
content	2	open-quote "My prefix" close-quote	*String*, URI, *Counter*, attr(...), open-quote, close-quote, no-open-quote, no-close-quote (and any combination)
quotes	2	none "«" "»" "<" ">"	none, *String String* (repeating)
counter-reset	2	section -1 imagenum 99	none (the default) or *Identifier Integer?* (repeating)
counter-increment	2	section 10 item 1	none (the default) or *Identifier Integer?* (repeating)
list-style	1	decimal outside	combination of list-style-type, list-style-image, list-style-position
list-style-type	1	circle	disc, circle (the default), square, decimal, lower-roman, upper-roman, lower-alpha, upper-alpha, none
	2	circle	... decimal-leading-zero, lower-greek, upper-greek, lower-latin, upper-latin, hebrew, armenian, georgian, cjk-ideographic, hiragana, katakana, hiragana-iroha, katakana-iroha
list-style-position	1	inside	inside, outside (the default)
list-style-image	1	url(boat.gif)	URL, none (the default)
Paged media			
size	2	8cm 12cm	auto (the default), protrait, land-scape, *Length* (one or twice)
marks	2	crop cross	none (the default), crop cross
page-break-before	2	left	auto (the default), always, avoid, left, right

page-break-after	2	always	auto (the default), always, avoid, left, right
page-break-inside	2	avoid	auto (the default), avoid
page	2	auto	auto (the default), *Identifier*
orphans	2	3	*Integer* (default '2')
widows	2	3	*Integer* (default '2')
Tables			
caption-side	2	left	top (the default), bottom, left, right
table-layout	2	fixed	auto (the default), fixed
border-collapse	2	separate	collapse (the default), separate
border-spacing	2	3pt 3pt 5pt	*Length* (default '0') *Length*?
empty-cells	2	hide	show (the default), hide
speak-header	2	always	once (the default) always
User interface			
cursor	2	crosshair, default url(eggtimer.gif), wait	auto (the default), crosshair, default, pointer, move, e-resize, ne-resize, nw-resize, n-resize, se-resize, sw-resize, s-resize, w-resize, text, wait, help, or URL() (repeating?)
outline	2	red dashed 2pt	combination of outline-color, out-line-style, outline-width
outline-width	2	2pt	thin, medium (the default), thick, *Length* – repeated ('x' = all borders, 'x x' = vertical and horizontal and 'x x x x' = top/right/bottom/left)
outline-style	2	dashed	none (the default) , hidden, dotted, dashed, solid, double, groove, ridge, inset, outset – repeated ('x' = all borders, 'x x' = vertical and horizontal and 'x x x x' = top/right/bottom/left)
outline-color	2	red	invert (the default), *Color*
Aural styles			
volume	2	medium	*Number, Percent*, silent, x-soft, soft, medium (the default), loud, x-loud
speak	2	spell-out	normal (the default), non, spell-out
pause	2	12ms 9ms	combination of pause-before and pause-after
pause-before	2	12ms	*Time, Percent*
pause-after	2	9ms	*Time, Percent*
cue	2	url(squeek.gif) url(go.gif) url(stop.gif)	combination of cue-before and cue-after
cue-after	2	url(squeek.gif)	url(...), none (the default)
cue-before	2	url(squeek.gif)	url(...), none (the default)
play-during	2	url(squeek.gif) repeat auto	auto (the default), none, url(...) mix? repeat?

azimuth	2	far-right behind 240deg	*nnn* deg, leftwards, rightwards or left-side, far-side, left, center-left, center (the default), center-right, right, far-right, right-side followed by behind
elevation	2	far-right behind 240deg	*nnn* deg, below, level (the default), above, lower, higher
speech-rate	2	faster 120 *(words per minute)*	*nnn*, x-slow, slow, medium (the default), fast, x-fast, faster, slower
voice-family	2	churchill female	male, female, child, (specific voice such as 'comedian')
pitch	2	low 200Hz	x-low, low, medium (the default), high, x-high, *nn* Hz
pitch-range	2	44	0–100 (default 50)
stress	2	53	0–100 (default 50)
richness	2	70	0–100 (default 50)
speak-punctuation	2	code	code, none (the default)
speak-numerals	2	digits	digits, continuous (the default)
Classifications			
display	1	inline	none, block (**default**), inline, list-item
	2	block compact table-row	none, block, inline (**default**), list-item ...*PLUS*... run-in, compact, marker, table, inline-table, table-row-group, table-header-group, table-footer-group, table-row, table-column-group, table-column, table-cell, table-caption
marker-offset	2	section 10 item 1	*Length*, auto (the default)
position	2	relative	static (the default), relative, absolute, fixed
top	2	2pt	*Length*, *Percent*, auto
bottom	2	2pt	*Length*, *Percent*, auto
left	2	2pt	*Length*, *Percent*, auto
right	2	2pt	*Length*, *Percent*, auto
direction	2	rtl	ltr (the default), rtl (right-to-left)
unicode-bidi	2	embed	normal (the default), embed, bidi-override
white-space	1	pre	normal (the default), pre (pre-formatted), nowrap (single line)

This book DTD

The following is an example DTD (based on the SGML DTD that was used to produce this book), included to illustrate the concepts described in Chapters 5 and 10:

```
<!-- XML BOOK DTD
          DTD for The XML Companion
          AUTHOR: N.Bradley (neil@bradley.co.uk)
          VERSION: 1.4 (9/3/2001) -->


<!-- ENTITY DECLARATIONS -->

<!-- specify names and locations of external entities -->
<!ENTITY % CALStable SYSTEM "TABLE.DTD">
<!ENTITY % ISOnum
      PUBLIC "ISO 8879:1986//ENTITIES Numeric and Special
               Graphic//EN" SYSTEM "ISOnum.ent">
<!ENTITY % ISOlat1
      PUBLIC "ISO 8879:1986//ENTITIES Added Latin 1//EN"
      SYSTEM "ISOlat1.ent">
<!ENTITY % ISOgrk1
      PUBLIC "ISO 8879:1986//ENTITIES Greek Letters//EN"
      SYSTEM "ISOgrk.ent">
<!ENTITY % ISOpub
      PUBLIC "ISO 8879:1986//ENTITIES Publishing//EN"
      SYSTEM "ISOpub.ent">

<!-- merge-in the external entities -->

%CALStable;
%ISOnum;
%ISOlat1;
%ISOgrk1;
%ISOpub;

<!-- define internal entities -->
<!ENTITY % Blocks      "(para | markupPara | graphic |
                        list | table | roadMap)*" >

<!ENTITY % SuperSub    "sup | sub" >
<!ENTITY % Hilite      "markup | emphStrong | emphWeak" >


<!-- MAIN STRUCTURE -->

<!-- Book document element -->
<!ELEMENT book          (front, body, back)>
<!ATTLIST book          id      ID      #REQUIRED>

<!-- Title -->
<!ELEMENT title         (#PCDATA | %SuperSub;)*>


<!-- FRONT SECTION -->

<!-- front matter -->
```

```
<!ELEMENT front          (title, edition, author, publisher)>

<!-- edition of book -->
<!ELEMENT edition        (#PCDATA)>

<!-- author of book -->
<!ELEMENT author         (first, second, eMail?)>
<!ELEMENT first          (#PCDATA)>
<!ELEMENT second         (#PCDATA)>
<!ELEMENT eMail          (#PCDATA)>

<!-- publisher of book -->
<!ELEMENT publisher      (pubName, address)
<!ELEMENT pubName        (#PCDATA)>
<!ELEMENT address        (#PCDATA)>


<!-- BODY SECTION -->

<!ELEMENT body           (part+ | chapter+)>

<!-- part (in body) -->
<!ELEMENT part           (title, chapter+)>

<!-- chapter (in body or part) -->
<!ELEMENT chapter        (title, %Blocks;, section*)>
<!ATTLIST chapter        id    ID    #REQUIRED>

<!-- section (in chapter) -->
<!ELEMENT section        (title, %Blocks;, subSection*)>
<!ATTLIST section        id    ID    #REQUIRED>

<!-- subsection (in section) -->
<!ELEMENT subSection     (title, %Blocks;)
<!ATTLIST subSection     id    ID    #REQUIRED>

<!-- roadmap charts have different pagination and
     font size rules -->
<!ELEMENT roadMap        (para | markupPara)*>


<!-- BACK SECTION -->

<!-- back matter -->
<!ELEMENT back           (glossary)>

<!-- glossary (special form of chapter) -->
<!ELEMENT glossary       (para*, section*)>


<!-- BLOCK STRUCTURES -->

<!-- paragraph -->
<!ELEMENT para           (#PCDATA | %Hilite; | %SuperSub; |
                          xRef)*>

<!-- graphic image - placeholder -->
<!ELEMENT graphic        EMPTY>
<!ATTLIST graphic        id    ID       #IMPLIED
```

```
                              ident   ENTITY    #REQUIRED>

<!-- list -->
<!ELEMENT list           (item+)>

<!-- list item -->
<!ELEMENT item           (#PCDATA | %Hilite; |
                          %SuperSub; | xRef)*>
<!ATTLIST item           type     (number|random)   "random"

<!-- text block dislayed in mono-space -->
<!ELEMENT markupPara     (markupLine*)>
<!ATTLIST markupPara     splitable (loose | together)
                                              "loose">

<!-- markup line - one line of text in markup fragment-->
<!ELEMENT markupLine     (#PCDATA | %Hilite; | %SuperSub; |
                          presented)*>


<!-- IN-LINE STRUCTURES -->

<!-- example of rendered output -->
<!ELEMENT presented (#PCDATA | %Hilite; | %SuperSub;)*)>

<!-- XML example fragments in text -->
<!ELEMENT markup         (#PCDATA | %SuperSub; |
                          emphStrong | emphWeak)*>

<!-- emphasized text - shown in bold -->
<!ELEMENT emphStrong     (#PCDATA | markup | emphWeak |
                          %SuperSub; | xRef)*>

<!-- stressed (names) - shown in italic -->
<!ELEMENT emphWeak       (#PCDATA | markup |
                          emphStrong | %SuperSub; | xRef)*>

<!-- superscript -->
<!ELEMENT sup            (#PCDATA)>

<!-- subscript -->
<!ELEMENT sub            (#PCDATA)>

<!-- cross-references to other text in the book -->
<!ELEMENT xRef           (#PCDATA)>
<!ATTLIST xRef           source  IDREF   #REQUIRED>

<!-- END END END -->
```

ISO 8859/1 character set

The character set describing European letters, numbers and symbols. This character set is used by HTML, and forms the basis of Microsoft Windows fonts (although reserved places are filled with extra characters in the Windows version) and UNIX fonts (for example, Open Windows). The first 128 characters are derived from the **ISO/IEC 646** version of **ASCII**. The remaining 128 characters cover European accented characters, and further common symbols. The official ISO name for each character is placed in brackets, for example 'Solidus (slash)'.

The ISO character entity sets, **ISOnum** (numeric and special graphic), **ISOlat1** (latin accents) and **ISOdia** (diacritic marks), provide an alternative means of specifying most of the characters in this set. Each entity reference is identified as belonging to one of these sets as follows:

- N = ISOnum
- L = ISOlat1
- D = ISOdia

For example, '< N' indicates that entity reference '<' belongs to the ISOnum set. Those not covered by any ISO entity set are shown as character entities, '&#...;'. When an entry appears in italic, the character is easily available from the keyboard, and has no significance in any XML context (so the entity reference is not generally needed), or it is unused within an XML context (mainly redundant control codes).

All the entities in the following table may be used in HTML documents presented using Internet *Explorer 3.0* and *Navigator 3.0* onwards, except for ', | (use the normal vertical bar '|') and ½ (use the alternative form: ½).

Decimal and Hex		Character entities	Description
000 00		*&#00;*	*NUL – no effect*
001 01		*&#01;*	*SOH – Start of Heading*
002 02		*&#02;*	*STX – Start of Text*
003 03		*&#03;*	*ETX – End of Text*
004 04		*&#04;*	*EOT – End of Transmission*
005 05		*&#05;*	*ENQ – Enquiry*
006 06		*&#06;*	*ACK – Acknowledge*
007 07		*&#07;*	*BEL – Bell*
008 08		*&#08;*	*BS – Backspace*
009 09		*	*	HT – Horizontal Tab, **HTML** Tab
010 0A		*
*	LF – Line Feed, **HTML** new-line (with or without '013'), **record start (RS)**
011 0B		*&#11;*	*VT – Vertical Tabulation*

012 0C		&#12;	FF – Form Feed
013 0D		&#13;	CR – Carriage return, **HTML** new-line (with or without '010'), **record end** (**RE**)
014 0E		*&#14;*	*SO – Shift Out*
015 0F		*&#15;*	*SI – Shift In*
016 10		*&#16;*	*DLE – Data Link Escape*
017 11		*&#17;*	*DC1 – Device Control (1)*
018 12		*&#18;*	*DC2 – Device Control (2)*
019 13		*&#19;*	*DC3 – Device Control (3)*
020 14		*&#20;*	*DC4 – Device Control (4)*
021 15		*&#21;*	*NAK – No Acknowledge*
022 16		*&#22;*	*SYN – Synchronize*
023 17		*&#23;*	*ETB – End of Transmission Block*
024 18		*&#24;*	*CAN – Cancel*
025 19		*&#25;*	*EM – End of Medium*
026 1A		*&#26;*	*SUB – Substitute Character*
027 1B		*&#27;*	*ESC – Escape*
028 1C		*&#28;*	*FS – File Separator*
029 1D		*&#29;*	*GS – Group Separator*
030 1E		*&#30;*	*RS – Record Separator*
031 1F		*&#31;*	*US – Unit Separator*
032 20		&#32;	Space (space)
033 21	!	*!* N	Exclamation (exclam)
034 22	"	" N	Quotation (quotedbl), literal (use " in attributes with literal delimiters)
035 23	#	*#* N	Number sign (numbersign), **reserved name indicator** ('#PCDATA')
036 24	$	*$* N	Dollar sign (dollar)
037 25	%	*%* N	Percent sign (percent), parameter entity reference open delimiter ('%ent;')
038 26	&	& N	Ampersand (ampersand), entity reference open delimiter ('&ent;'), character reference open delimiter ('&#26;')
039 27	'	*'* N	Apostrophe sign, literal alternative delimiter (use ' in attributes with literal alternative delimiters)
040 28	(	(N	Left parenthesis (parenleft), group open delimiter ('(a, b)')
041 29	)	) N	Right parenthesis (parenright), group close delimiter ('(a, b)')
042 2A	*	*** N	Asterisk (asterisk), optional and repeatable symbol ('a, b*')
043 2B	+	*+* N	Plus sign (plus), required and repeatable symbol ('a, b+')
044 2C	,	*,* N	Comma (comma), **sequence connector** ('a, b, c')
045 2D	-	*‐* N	Hyphen (hyphen), comment delimiter ('-- my comment --')
046 2E	.	*.* N	Full point (period)
047 2F	/	/ N	Solidus (slash), end-tag open delimiter ('</tag>')

048 30	0	&#48;	Zero (zero)
049 31	1	&#49;	One (one)
050 32	2	&#50;	Two (two)
051 33	3	&#51;	Three (three)
052 34	4	&#52;	Four (four)
053 35	5	&#53;	Five (five)
054 36	6	&#54;	Six (six)
055 37	7	&#55;	Seven (seven)
056 38	8	&#56;	Eight (eight)
057 39	9	&#57;	Nine (nine)
058 3A	:	: N	Colon (colon)
059 3B	;	; N	Semicolon (semicolon), **reference close** ('&ent;')
060 3C	<	< N	Less than (less), start tag open delimiter, end-tag open delimiter ('</'),
061 3D	=	= N	Equals (equal), **value indicator** ('attrib=" value" ')
062 3E	>	> N	Greater than (greater), **markup declaration close** ('<!.......>'), **processing instruction close** ('<?proc>'), **tag-close** ('<tag>')
063 3F	?	? N	Question mark (question), **optional occurrence indicator** ('a | b'), **processing instruction open** ('<?')
064 40	@	@ N	Commercial at (at)
065 41	A	&#65;	A
066 42	B	&#66;	B
067 43	C	&#67;	C
068 44	D	&#68;	D
069 45	E	&#69;	E
070 46	F	&#70;	F
071 47	G	&#71;	G
072 48	H	&#72;	H
073 49	I	&#73;	I
074 4A	J	&#74;	J
075 4B	K	&#75;	K
076 4C	L	&#76;	L
077 4D	M	&#77;	M
078 4E	N	&#78;	N
079 4F	O	&#79;	O
080 50	P	&#80;	P
081 51	Q	&#81;	Q
082 52	R	&#82;	R
083 53	S	&#83;	S
084 54	T	&#84;	T
085 55	U	&#85;	U
086 56	V	&#86;	V
087 57	W	&#87;	W
088 58	X	&#88;	X
089 59	Y	&#89;	Y
090 5A	Z	&#90;	Z

091 5B	[	[N	Left square bracket (bracketleft), **declaration subset open** ('<!DOCTYPE ... [...]>'), **data tag group open**
092 5C	\	\ N	Reverse solidus (backslash)
093 5D	]	] N	Right square bracket (bracketright), **declaration subset close** ('<!DOCTYPE ... [...]>'), **data tag group close, marked section close** (']]')
094 5E	^	*ˆ* D	Caret (asciicircum)
095 5F	_	*―* N	Underscore (underscore)
096 60	`	` D	Grave accent
097 61	a	*a*	a
098 62	b	*b*	b
099 63	c	*c*	c
100 64	d	*d*	d
101 65	e	*e*	e
102 66	f	*f*	f
103 67	g	*g*	g
104 68	h	*h*	h
105 69	i	*i*	i
106 6A	j	*j*	j
107 6B	k	*k*	k
108 6C	l	*l*	l
109 6D	m	*m*	m
110 6E	n	*n*	n
111 6F	o	*o*	o
112 70	p	*p*	p
113 71	q	*q*	q
114 72	r	*r*	r
115 73	s	*s*	s
116 74	t	*t*	t
117 75	u	*u*	u
118 76	v	*v*	v
119 77	w	*w*	w
120 78	x	*x*	x
121 79	y	*y*	y
122 7A	z	*z*	z
123 7B	{	*{* N	Left curly brace (braceleft)
124 7C			| N	Vertical bar (bar), **or connector**
125 7D	}	} N	Right curly brace (braceright)
126 7E	~	*˜* D	Tilde (asciitilde)
127 7F		*&#127;*	Delete (del), Checkerboard effect
128 80			WINDOWS CHARS, delete (del)
....			...
....			...
....			...
159 9F			WINDOWS CHARS
160 A0		N	NBS – Non-break space
161 A1	¡	¡ N	Inverted exclamation (exclamdown)
162 A2	¢	¢ N	Cent sign (cent)
163 A3	£	£ N	Pound sterling (pound)
164 A4	¤	¤ N	General currency symbol (currency)

165 A5	¥	¥ N	Yen sign (yen)
166 A6	¦	¦ N	Broken vertical bar (pipe)
167 A7	§	§ N	Section sign (section)
168 A8	¨	¨ D	Umlaut (dieresis)
169 A9	©	© N	Copyright (copyrightserif)
170 AA	ª	ª N	Feminine ordinal (ordfeminine)
171 AB	«	« N	Left angle quote (guillemotleft)
172 AC	¬	¬ N	Not sign (logicalnot)
173 AD	-	&#173;	Soft hyphen (hyphen)
174 AE	®	® N	Registered trademark (registerserif)
175 AF	¯	¯ D	Macron accent (macron)
176 B0	°	° N	Degree sign (ring)
177 B1	±	± N	Plus or minus (plusminus)
178 B2	²	² N	Superscript two (Reserved)
179 B3	³	³ N	Superscript three (Reserved)
180 B4	´	´ D	Acute accent (acute)
181 B5	µ	µ N	Micro sign (Reserved)
182 B6	¶	¶ N	Paragraph sign (paragraph)
183 B7	·	· N	Middle dot (periodcentered)
184 B8	¸	¸ D	Cedilla (cedilla)
185 B9	¹	¹ N	Superscript one (Reserved)
186 BA	º	º N	Masculine ordinale (ordmasculine)
187 BB	»	» N	Right angle quote (guillemotright)
188 BC	¼	¼ N	Fraction one-fourth (Reserved)
189 BD	½	½ N ½ N	Fraction one-half (Reserved)
190 BE	¾	¾ N	Fraction three-fourths (Reserved)
191 BF	¿	¿ N	Inverted question mark (questiondown)
192 C0	À	À L	Capital A grave (Agrave)
193 C1	Á	Á L	Capital A acute (Aacute)
194 C2	Â	Â L	Capital A circumflex (Acircumflex)
195 C3	Ã	Ã L	Capital A tilde (Atilde)
196 C4	Ä	Ä L	Capital A umlaut (Adieresis)
197 C5	Å	Å L	Capital A ring (Aring)
198 C6	Æ	Æ L	Capital AE dipthong (AE)
199 C7	Ç	Ç L	Capital C cedilla (Ccedilla)
200 C8	È	È L	Capital E grave (Egrave)
201 C9	É	É L	Capital E acute (Eacute)
202 CA	Ê	Ê L	Capital E circumflex (Ecircumflex)
203 CB	Ë	Ë L	Capital E umlaut (Edieresis)
204 CC	Ì	Ì L	Capital I grave (Igrave)
205 CD	Í	Í L	Capital I acute (Iacute)
206 CE	Î	Î L	Capital I circumflex (Icircumflex)
207 CF	Ï	Ï L	Capital I umlaut (Idieresis)
208 D0	Ð	Ð L	Capital Eth Icelandic (Reserved)
209 D1	Ñ	Ñ L	Capital N tilde (Ntilde)
210 D2	Ò	Ò L	Capital O grave (Ograve)
211 D3	Ó	Ó L	Capital O acute (Oacute)
212 D4	Ô	Ô L	Capital O circumflex (Ocircumflex)
213 D5	Õ	Õ L	Capital O tilde (Otilde)
214 D6	Ö	Ö L	Capital O umlaut (Odieresis)
215 D7	×	× N	Multiply sign (Reserved)
216 D8	Ø	Ø L	Capital O slash (Oslash)

217	D9	Ù	Ù L	Capital U grave (Ugrave)
218	DA	Ú	Ú L	Capital U acute (Uacute)
219	DB	Û	Û L	Capital U circumflex (circumflex)
220	DC	Ü	Ü L	Capital U umlaut (Udieresis)
221	DD	Ý	Ý L	Capital Y acute (Reserved)
222	DE	Þ	Þ L	Capital THORN Icelandic (Reserved)
223	DF	ß	ß L	Small sharp s, sz ligature (germandbls)
224	E0	à	à L	Small a grave (agrave)
225	E1	á	á L	Small a acute (aacute)
226	E2	â	â L	Small a circumflex (acircumflex)
227	E3	ã	ã L	Small a tilde (atilde)
228	E4	ä	ä L	Small a umlaut (adieresis)
229	E5	å	å L	Small a ring (aring)
230	E6	æ	æ L	Small ae dipthong, ligature (ae)
231	E7	ç	ç L	Small c cedilla (ccedilla)
232	E8	è	è L	Small e grave (egrave)
233	E9	é	é L	Small e acute (eacute)
234	EA	ê	ê L	Small e circumflex (ecircumflex)
235	EB	ë	ë L	Small e umlaut (edieresis)
236	EC	ì	ì L	Small i grave (igrave)
237	ED	í	í L	Small i acute (iacute)
238	EE	î	î L	Small i circumflex (icircumflex)
239	EF	ï	ï L	Small i umlaut (idieresis)
240	F0	ð	ð L	Small eth Icelandic (Reserved)
241	F1	ñ	ñ L	Small n tilde (ntilde)
242	F2	ò	ò L	Small o grave (ograve)
243	F3	ó	ó L	Small o acute (oacute)
244	F4	ô	ô L	Small o circumflex (ocircumflex)
245	F5	õ	õ L	Small o tilde (otilde)
246	F6	ö	ö L	Small o umlaut (odieresis)
247	F7	÷	÷ N	Division sign (Reserved)
248	F8	ø	ø N	Small o slash (oslash)
249	F9	ù	ù N	Small u grave (ugrave)
250	FA	ú	ú N	Small u acute (uacute)
251	FB	û	û N	Small u circumflex (ucircumflex)
252	FC	ü	ü N	Small u umlaut (udieresis)
253	FD	ý	ý N	Small y acute (Reserved)
254	FE	þ	þ N	Small thorn Icelandic (Reserved)
255	FF	ÿ	ÿ N	Small y umlaut (ydieresis)

ISO 639 language codes

ISO 639 language codes are used in **xml:lang** attributes and **public identifiers**. The following table shows some of the most common. The full list can be found in **RFC 1766** (see ftp://ds.internic.net/rfc/rfc1766.txt):

Code	Language	Code	Language
aa	Afar	mk	Macedonian
ab	Abkhazian	ml	Malayalam
af	Afrikaans	mn	Mongolian
am	Amharic	mo	Moldavian
ar	Arabic	mr	Marathi
as	Assamese	ms	Malay
ay	Aymara	mt	Maltese
az	Azerbaijani	my	Burmese
ba	Bashkir	na	Nauru
be	Byelorussian	ne	Nepali
bg	Bulgarian	nl	Dutch
bh	Bihari	no	Norwegian
bi	Bislama	oc	Occitan
bn	Bengali	om	Oromo
bo	Tibetan	or	Oriya
br	Breton	pa	Punjabi
ca	Catalan	pl	Polish
co	Corsican	ps	Pashto
cs	Czech	pt	Portuguese
cy	Welsh	qu	Quechua
ch	Chinese	rm	Rhaeto-Romance
da	Danish	rn	Kirundi
de	German	ro	Romanian
dz	Bhutani	ru	Russian
el	Greek	rw	Kinyarwanda
en	English	sa	Sanskrit
eo	Esperanto	sd	Sindhi
es	Spanish	sg	Sangro
et	Estonian	sh	Serbo-Croatioan
eu	Basque	si	Singalese
fa	Persian	sk	Slovak
fi	Finnish	sl	Slovenian
fj	Fiji	sm	Samoan
fo	Faeroese	sn	Shona
fr	French	so	Somali
fy	Frisian	sq	Albanian
ga	Irish	sr	Serbian
gd	Gaelic	ss	Siswati
gl	Galician	st	Sesotho
gn	Guarani	su	Sudanese
gr	Greek	sv	Swedish
ha	Hausa	sw	Swaheli
he	Hebrew	ta	Tamil
hi	Hindi	te	Tegulu

hr	Croatian	tg	Tajik
hu	Hungarian	th	Thai
hy	Armenian	ti	Tigrinya
ia	Interlingua	tk	Turkman
id	Indonesian	tl	Tagalog
ie	Interlingue	tn	Setswana
ik	Inupiak	to	Tonga
in	Indonesian	tr	Turkish
is	Icelandic	ts	Tsonga
it	Italian	tt	Tatar
iu	Inuktitut	tw	Twi
ja	Japanese	ug	Uigur
jw	Javanese	uk	Ukrainian
ka	Georgian	ur	Urdu
kk	Kazakh	uz	Uzbek
kl	Greenlandic	vi	Vietnamese
km	Cambodian	vo	Volapuk
kn	Kannada	wo	Wolof
ko	Korean	xh	Xhosa
ks	Kashmiri	yi	Yiddish
ku	Kurdish	yo	Yoruba
ky	Kirghiz	za	Zuang
la	Latin	zh	Chinese
ln	Lingala	zu	Zulu
lo	Laothian		
lt	Lithuanian		
lv	Latvian		
mg	Malagasy		
mi	Maori		

ISO 3166 country codes

ISO 3166 country codes are used in e-mail addresses, such as '... .co.uk' and in the **xml:lang** attribute to identify variations on the same languages (such as 'en-UK' and 'en-US'):

Code	Country	Code	Country
AD	Andorra	LA	Laos
AE	United Arab Emirates	LB	Lebanon
AF	Afghanistan	LC	Saint Lucia
AG	Antigua and Barbuda	LI	Liechtenstein
AI	Anguilla	LK	Sri Lanka
AL	Albania	LR	Liberia
AM	Armenia	LS	Lesotho
AN	Netherland Antilles	LT	Lithuania
AO	Angola	LU	Luxembourg
AQ	Antarctica	LV	Latvia
AR	Argentina	LY	Libya
AS	American Samoa	MA	Morocco
AT	Austria	MC	Monaco
AU	Australia	MD	Moldova
AW	Aruba	MG	Madagascar
AZ	Azerbaijan	MH	Marshall Islands
BA	Bosnia-Herzegovina	MK	Macedonia
BB	Barbados	ML	Mali
BD	Bangladesh	MM	Myanmar
BE	Belgium	MN	Mongolia
BF	Buerkina Faso	MO	Macau
BG	Bulgaria	MP	Northern Mariana Islands
BH	Bahrain	MQ	Martinique
BI	Burundi	Mr	Mauritania
BJ	Benin	MS	Montserrat
BM	Bermuda	MT	Malta
BN	Brunei Darussalam	MU	Mauritius
BO	Bolivia	MV	Maldives
BR	Brazil	MW	Malawi
BS	Bahamas	MX	Mexico
BT	Bhutan	MY	Malaysia
BV	Bouvet Island	MZ	Mozambique
BW	Botswana	NA	Namibia
BY	Belarus	NC	New Caledonia
BZ	Belize	NE	Niger
CA	Canada	NF	Norfolk Island
CC	Cocos Islands	NG	Nigeria
CF	Central African Republic	NI	Nicaragua
CG	Congo	NL	Netherlands
CH	Switzerland	NO	Norway
CI	Ivory Coast	NP	Nepal
CK	Cook Islands	NR	Nauru
CL	Chile	NU	Niue
CM	Cameroon	NZ	New Zealand

CN	China	OM	Oman
CO	Colombia	PA	Panama
CR	Costa Rica	PE	Peru
CU	Cuba	PF	Polynesia
CV	Cape Verde	PG	Papua New Guinea
CX	Christmas Island	PH	Philippines
CY	Cyprus	PK	Pakistan
CZ	Czech Republic	PL	Poland
DE	Germany	PM	St Pierre and Miquelon
DJ	Djibouti	PN	Pitcairn
DK	Denmark	PR	Puerto Rico
DM	Dominica	PT	Portugal
DO	Dominican Republic	PW	Palau
DZ	Algeria	PY	Paraguay
EC	Ecuador	QA	Qatar
EE	Estonia	RE	Reunion
EG	Egypt	RO	Romania
EH	Western Sahara	RU	Russian Federation
ER	Eritrea	RW	Rwanda
ES	Spain	SA	Saudi Arabia
ET	Ethiopia	SB	Solomon Islands
FI	Finland	SC	Seychelles
FJ	Fiji	SD	Sudan
FK	Falkland Islands	SE	Sweden
FM	Micronesia	SG	Singapore
FO	Faeroe Islands	SH	St Helena
FR	France	SI	Slovenia
FX	France	SJ	Svalbard and Jan Mayen Islands
GA	Gabon	SK	Slovakia
GB	Great Britain (UK)	SL	Sierra Leone
GD	Grenada	SN	Senegal
GE	Georgia	SO	Somalia
GF	Guyana	SR	Surinam
GH	Ghana	ST	St Tome and Principe
GI	Gibraltar	SV	El Salvadore
GL	Greenland	SY	Syria
GM	Gambia	SZ	Swaziland
GN	Guinea	TC	Turks and Caicos Islands
GP	Guadeloupe	TD	Chad
GQ	Equatorial Guinea	TF	French Southern Territory
GR	Greece	TG	Togo
GS	South Georgia and South Sandwich Islands	TH	Thailand
GT	Guatemala	TJ	Tadjikistan
GU	Guam	TK	Tokelau
GW	Guinea Bissau	TM	Turkmenistan
GY	Guyana	TN	Tunisia
HK	Hong Kong	TO	Tonga
HM	Heard and McDonald Islands	TP	East Timor
HN	Honduras	TR	Turkey
HR	Croatia	TT	Trinidad and Tobago
HT	Haiti	TV	Tuvalu

HU	Hungary	TW	Taiwan
IE	Ireland	TZ	Tanzania
IN	India	UA	Ukraine
IQ	Iraq	UG	Uganda
IR	Iran	UK	United Kingdom
IS	Iceland	US	United States
IT	Italy	UY	Uraguay
JM	Jamica	UZ	Uzbekistan
JO	Jordan	VA	Vatican City State
JP	Japan	VC	St Vincent and Grenadines
KE	Kenya	VE	Venezuela
KG	Kyrgyz Republic	VG	Virgin Islands
KH	Cambodia	VN	Vietnam
KI	Kiribati	VU	Vanuatu
KM	Comoros	WF	Wallis and Futuna Islands
KN	St Kitts Nevis Anguilla	WS	Samoa
KP	Korea (North)	YE	Yemen
KR	Korea (South)	YT	Mayotte
KW	Kuwait	YU	Yugoslavia
KY	Cayman Islands	ZA	South Africa
KZ	Kazachstan	ZM	Zambia
		ZR	Zaire
		ZW	Zimbabwe

HTML and XHTML elements and attributes

The following table shows the elements and attributes defined in each significant version of HTML. Items marked with an asterisk, '*', are not supported by the latest version of at least one of the most popular Web browsers, so should be used with caution.

There are a very large number of attributes first defined in HTML 4.0. Many of them are defined using entities. To keep this table to a reasonable size, these groups are described here, and given the names 'Core', 'Events' and 'Lang' for reference under appropriate elements.

Core attributes: Id, Title, Class, Style.

Language attributes: Lang (and xml:lang in XHTML), Dir.

Event attributes: Onclick, Ondblclick, Onmousedown, Onmouseup, Onmouseover, Onmouseout, Onkeypress, Onkeydown, Onkeyup (and Onmousemove in XHTML).

However, note that when an attribute in one of these groups applies to earlier versions of HTML, it is also included explicitly.

Similarly, HTML 2.0 contains a number of SDA attributes to aid conversion of HTML elements into the ICADD DTD format. These attributes are not covered here.

Elements and Attributes	HTML 2.0	HTML 3. 2	HTML 4.0	XHTML 1.0 (strict)
A	YES	YES	YES	YES
Core & Events & Lang			YES	YES
accesskey *			YES	YES
coords *			YES	YES
charset *			YES	YES
href	YES	YES	YES	YES
hreflang *			YES	YES
methods	YES	obsolete		
name	YES	YES	YES	YES
onblur *			YES	YES
onfocus *			YES	YES
rel	YES	YES	YES	YES
rev	YES	YES	YES	YES
shape *			YES	
tabindex *			YES	
target			YES	
type *			YES	YES
title	YES	YES	YES	YES

urn	YES	obsolete		
ABBR			**YES**	**YES**
Core & Events & Lang			YES	YES
ACRONYM			**YES**	**YES**
Core & Events & Lang			YES	YES
ADDRESS	**YES**	**YES**	**YES**	**YES**
Core			YES	YES
Events & Lang				YES
APPLET		**YES**	deprecated (use Object)	
align		YES		
alt		YES		
archive				
code		YES		
codebase		YES		
height		YES		
hspace		YES		
name		YES		
object *				
title				
vspace		YES		
width		YES		
AREA		**YES**	**YES**	**YES**
Core & Events & Lang				YES
accesskey *			YES	YES
alt		YES	YES	YES
coords		YES	YES	YES
href		YES	YES	YES
nohref		YES	YES	YES
onblur *			YES	YES
onfocus *			YES	YES
shape		YES	YES	YES
tabindex *			YES	YES
target			YES	
B	**YES**	**YES**	**YES**	**YES**
Core & Events & Lang			YES	YES
BASE	**YES**	**YES**	**YES**	**YES**
href	YES	YES	YES	YES
target			YES	
BASEFONT		**YES**	deprecated	
color *				
face *				
id *				
name *				
size		YES		
BDO			**YES**	**YES**
Core			YES	YES
Events				YES
dir *			YES	YES
lang *			YES	YES
xml:lang				YES
BIG *		**YES**	**YES**	**YES**
Core & Events & Lang			YES	YES
BLOCKQUOTE	**YES**	**YES**	**YES**	**YES**

Core & Events & Lang			YES	YES
cite *			YES	YES
BODY	**YES**	**YES**	**YES**	**YES**
Core & Events & Lang			YES	YES
alink		YES	deprecated	
background		YES	deprecated	
bgcolor		YES	deprecated	
link		YES	deprecated	
onload *			YES	YES
onunload *			YES	YES
text		YES	deprecated	
vlink		YES	deprecated	
BR	**YES**	**YES**	**YES**	**YES**
Core			YES	YES
clear		YES	deprecated	
BUTTON			**YES**	**YES**
Core & Events & Lang			YES	YES
accesskey *			YES	YES
clear		YES		
disabled *			YES	YES
name *			YES	YES
onblur *			YES	YES
onfocus *			YES	YES
tabindex *			YES	YES
type *			YES	YES
value *			YES	YES
CAPTION		**YES**	**YES**	**YES**
Core & Events & Lang			YES	YES
align		YES	deprecated	
CENTER		**YES**	**deprecated**	
Core & Events & Lang				
CITE	**YES**	**YES**	**YES**	**YES**
Core & Events & Lang			YES	YES
CODE	**YES**	**YES**	**YES**	**YES**
Core & Events & Lang			YES	YES
COL *			**YES**	**YES**
Core & Events & Lang				
align				
char *				
charoff *				
span				
valign *				
width				
COLGROUP *			**YES**	**YES**
Core & Events & Lang				
align *				
char *				
charoff *				
span *				
valign *				
width *				
DD	**YES**	**YES**	**YES**	**YES**
Core & Events & Lang			YES	YES

DEL			**YES**	**YES**
Core & Events & Lang				
cite *				
datetime *				
DFN *		**YES**	**YES**	**YES**
Core & Events & Lang			YES	YES
DIR	**YES**	**YES**	**deprecated** (use UL)	
Core & Events & Lang			YES	
compact *	YES	YES	YES	
DIV		**YES**	**YES**	**YES**
Core & Events & Lang			YES	YES
align		YES	YES	
DL	**YES**	**YES**	**YES**	**YES**
Core & Events & Lang			YES	YES
compact	YES	YES	YES	
DT	**YES**	**YES**	**YES**	**YES**
Core & Events & Lang			YES	YES
EM	**YES**	**YES**	**YES**	**YES**
Core & Events & Lang			YES	YES
EMBED			**YES**	
Core & Events & Lang				
FIELDSET			**YES**	**YES**
Core & Events & Lang				YES
language *				
title *				YES
FONT		**YES**	**deprecated**	
Core & Lang				
color		YES		
size		YES		
FORM	**YES**	**YES**	**YES**	**YES**
Core & Events & Lang			YES	YES
action	YES	YES	YES	YES
accept				YES
accept-charset *			YES	YES
enctype *	YES	YES	YES	YES
method	YES	YES	YES	YES
onreset			YES	YES
onsubmit			YES	YES
target			YES	
FRAME			**YES**	
Core				
frameborder				
langdesc *				
marginheight				
marginwidth				
name				
noresize				
scrolling				
src				

FRAMESET			YES	
Core				
cols				
onload *				
onunload *				
rows				
H1	YES	YES	YES	YES
Core & Events & Lang			YES	YES
align		YES	deprecated	
H2	YES	YES	YES	YES
Core & Events & Lang			YES	YES
align		YES	deprecated	
H3	YES	YES	YES	YES
Core & Events & Lang			YES	YES
align		YES	deprecated	
H4	YES	YES	YES	YES
Core & Events & Lang			YES	YES
align		YES	deprecated	
H5	YES	YES	YES	YES
Core & Events & Lang			YES	YES
align		YES	deprecated	
H6	YES	YES	YES	YES
Core & Events & Lang			YES	YES
align		YES	deprecated	
HEAD	YES	YES	YES	YES
Lang			YES	YES
profile *			YES	YES
HR	YES	YES	YES	YES
Core & Events			YES	YES
Lang				YES
align		YES	deprecated	
noshade		YES	deprecated	
size		YES	deprecated	
width		YES	deprecated	
HTML	YES	YES	YES	YES
Lang			YES	YES
version *			deprecated	
xmlns				YES
I	YES	YES	YES	YES
Core & Events & Lang			YES	YES
IFRAME			YES	
Core				
align *				
frameborder *				
langdesc *				
marginwidth *				
marginheight *				
marginwidth *				
name *				
scrolling *				
src *				
width *				
IMG	YES	YES	YES	YES

Core & Events & Lang			YES	YES
align	YES	YES	deprecated	
alt	YES	YES	YES	YES
border		YES	deprecated	
height		YES	YES	YES
hspace		YES	YES	
ismap	YES	YES	YES	YES
longdesc *			YES	YES
src	YES	YES	YES	YES
usemap		YES	YES	YES
vspace	YES	YES	YES	
width	YES	YES	YES	YES
INPUT	**YES**	**YES**	**YES**	**YES**
Core & Events & Lang				YES
accept *				YES
accesskey *				YES
align	YES	YES		
alt *				YES
checked *	YES	YES		YES
disabled *				YES
langdesc *				
maxlength *	YES	YES		YES
name *	YES	YES		YES
onblur *				YES
onchange *				YES
onfocus *				YES
onselect *				YES
readonly *				YES
size	YES	YES		YES
src	YES	YES		YES
tabindex *				YES
type	YES	YES		YES
usemap *				YES
value	YES	YES		YES
INS			**YES**	**YES**
Core & Events & Lang				
cite *				
datetime *				
ISINDEX	**YES**	**YES**	**deprecated**	
Core & Lang			(use INPUT)	
prompt		YES		
KBD	**YES**	**YES**	**YES**	**YES**
Core & Events & Lang			YES	YES
LABEL			**YES**	**YES**
Core & Events & Lang				YES
accesskey *				YES
for *				YES
lang *				
language *				
onblur *				YES
onfocus *				YES
title *				YES
LEGEND *			**YES**	**YES**

Core & Events & Lang			YES	YES
accesskey *			YES	YES
align *			deprecated	
LI	**YES**	**YES**	**YES**	**YES**
Core & Events & Lang			YES	YES
type		YES	YES	
value		YES	deprecated	
LINK	**YES**	**YES**	**YES**	**YES**
Core & Events & Lang				
charset *				
href	YES	YES		
hreflang *				
media *				
rel	YES	YES		
rev	YES	YES		
title	YES	YES		
LISTING	**deprecated**	**deprecated**	**obsolete** (use PRE)	
MAP		**YES**	**YES**	**YES**
Core & Events & Lang			YES	YES
name		YES	YES	YES
MENU	**YES**	**YES**	**deprecated** (use UL)	
Core & Events & Lang				
compact	YES	YES		
META	**YES**	**YES**	**YES**	**YES**
Lang				
content	YES	YES		
http-equiv	YES	YES		
name	YES	YES		
scheme *				
NEXTID	**YES**	**obsolete**		
N	YES	obsolete		
NOSCRIPT			**YES**	**YES**
Core & Events & Lang			YES	YES
NOFRAMES			**YES**	
Core & Events & Lang			YES	
OBJECT *			**YES**	**YES**
Core & Events & Lang			YES	YES
align *			YES	
archive *			YES	YES
border *			deprecated	
classid *			YES	YES
codebase *			YES	YES
codetype *			YES	YES
declare *			YES	YES
height *			YES	YES
hspace *			YES	
name *			YES	YES
standby *			YES	YES
tabindex *			YES	YES
type *			YES	YES
usemap *			YES	YES
vspace *			YES	

width *			YES	YES
width *				YES
OL	**YES**	**YES**	**YES**	**YES**
Core & Events & Lang			YES	YES
compact	YES	YES	deprecated	
start		YES	deprecated	
type		YES	deprecated	
OPTGROUP			**YES**	**YES**
Core & Events & Lang				
disabled *				
label *				
OPTION	**YES**	**YES**	**YES**	**YES**
Core & Events & Lang			YES	
selected	YES	YES	YES	
value	YES	YES	YES	
disabled				
label				
P	**YES**	**YES**	**YES**	**YES**
Core & Events & Lang			YES	YES
align		YES	deprecated	
disabled *			YES	
label *			YES	
PARAM		**YES**	**YES**	**YES**
id *				
name		YES		
type *				
value		YES		
valuetype *				
PLAINTEXT	**YES**	**deprecated**	**obsolete** (use PRE)	
PRE	**YES**	**YES**	**YES**	**YES**
Core & Events & Lang			YES	YES
width	YES	YES	deprecated	
xml:space				YES
Q			**YES**	**YES**
Core & Events & Lang			YES	YES
cite *			YES	YES
SAMP	**YES**	**YES**	**YES**	**YES**
Core & Events & Lang			YES	YES
SCRIPT		**YES**	**YES**	**YES**
charset *			YES	YES
defer *			YES	YES
language			deprecated	
src *			YES	YES
type *			YES	YES
xml:space *				YES

SELECT	YES	YES	YES	YES
Core & Events & Lang				
disabled *				
multiple	YES	YES		
name	YES	YES		
onchange *				
onblur *				
onfocus *				
size	YES	YES		
tabindex *				
SMALL *		YES	YES	YES
Core & Events & Lang			YES	YES
SPAN			YES	YES
Core & Events & Lang				YES
align				
STRIKE		YES	deprecated	
Core & Events & Lang			YES	
STRONG	YES	YES	YES	YES
Core & Events & Lang			YES	YES
STYLE		**YES**	YES	YES
Lang			YES	
media *			YES	
title *			YES	
type *			YES	
xml:space *				
SUB *		YES	YES	YES
Core & Events & Lang			YES	YES
SUP *		YES	YES	YES
Core & Events & Lang			YES	YES
TABLE		YES	YES	YES
Core & Events & Lang			YES	YES
align		YES	deprecated	
bgcolor *			deprecated	
border		YES	YES	YES
cellpadding		YES	YES	YES
cellspacing		YES	YES	YES
frame *			YES	YES
rules *			YES	YES
summary *			YES	YES
width		YES	YES	YES
TBODY *			YES	YES
Core & Events & Lang			YES	
align *			YES	
valign *			YES	
char *				
charoff *				
TD		YES	YES	YES
Core & Events & Lang			YES	YES
abbr *			YES	YES
align		YES	YES	YES
axis *			YES	YES
colspan		YES	YES	YES
headers *			YES	YES

height		YES	deprecated	
nowrap		YES	deprecated	
rowspan		YES	YES	YES
scope *			YES	YES
valign		YES	YES	YES
width		YES	deprecated	
char				YES
charoff				YES
TEXTAREA	**YES**	**YES**	**YES**	**YES**
Core & Events & Lang				
accesskey *				
cols	YES	YES		
disabled *				
name	YES	YES		
onblur *				
onchange *				
onfocus *				
onselect *				
readonly *				
rows	YES	YES		
tabindex *				
TFOOT *			**YES**	**YES**
Core & Events & Lang			YES	
align *			YES	
valign *			YES	
char				
charoff				
TH		**YES**	**YES**	**YES**
Core & Events & Lang			YES	YES
abbr *			YES	YES
align		YES	YES	YES
axis *			YES	YES
colspan		YES	YES	YES
headers *			YES	YES
height		YES	deprecated	
nowrap		YES	deprecated	
rowspan		YES	YES	YES
valign		YES	YES	YES
width		YES	YES	
char				YES
charoff				YES
THEAD *			**YES**	**YES**
Core & Events & Lang				
align *				
valign *				
char				
charoff				
TITLE	**YES**	**YES**	**YES**	**YES**
Lang			YES	YES
TR		**YES**	**YES**	**YES**
Core & Events & Lang			YES	YES
align		YES	YES	YES

bgcolor *			YES	
valign		YES	YES	YES
char				YES
charoff				YES
TT	**YES**	**YES**	**YES**	**YES**
Core & Events & Lang			YES	YES
U		**YES**	**deprecated**	
Core & Events & Lang			YES	
UL	**YES**	**YES**	**YES**	**YES**
Core & Events & Lang			YES	YES
compact	YES	YES	deprecated	
type		YES	deprecated	
VAR	**YES**	**YES**	**YES**	**YES**
Core & Events & Lang			YES	YES
XMP	**deprecated**	**deprecated**	**obsolete** (use PRE)	

34. XML road map

This chapter is intended to be used as an aid to 'steering' through the XML standard, and the enclosed charts are referenced from terms appearing in the Glossary. The maps have been updated from earlier editions to take account of minor modifications to the XML standard made in the second edition of XML, and includes notes to indicate where changes have been made.

Map formats

The 'road map' appearing in this chapter is derived from the rules that comprise the XML 1.0 standard, released in February 1998, and modifications made in the second edition of 6 October 2000. Each rule defines a **symbol**, using an **expression**:

```
symbol ::= expression
```

The expression is composed of at least one **token**. A token may be literal text, such as '<!', or the name of another rule, which may be considered a 'sub-rule' (so building a hierarchy of rules):

```
symbol ::= expression
           /     \
          /     symbol ::= expression
         /
     symbol ::= expression
               /    \
              /    symbol ::= expression
             /
         symbol ::= expression
```

Each rule is numbered (from 1 to 93 in the Syntax specification, and 1 to 21 in the Linking specification), and is represented in this chapter by an appropriately numbered chart. The charts appear in numeric order, just as the rules do in the standard. However, alphabetically ordered listings are included in tables that precede the charts, and the rules are also described in alphabetical order in the Glossary.

Each chart has a two-digit number, enclosed by curly brackets. For example, rule 8 is represented by the chart numbered '{08}'. The symbol name appears next to the number, and the associated expression is drawn beneath the symbol name, using a simple diagrammatic structure. In the example below, symbol one, 'aRule', includes two tokens. In this case, both components of the expression happen to be references to other expressions:

```
{17} aRule

----- anotherRule
      |
      lastRule
```

The connecting lines can only be followed across to the right or down, starting from the top-left corner of the chart. In the example above symbol one, 'anotherRule', leads down to symbol two, 'lastRule'.

The next example shows how optional structures are represented. In this example, the expression describes a structure that consists of either 'aRule' or 'alternate Rule' (followed by 'lastRule'):

```
----- aRule
  |
  --- alternateRule
      |
      lastRule
```

Occurrence rules for each token are shown using the official convention, '?' for optional, '+' for repeatable and '*' for optional and repeatable.

```
----- aRule ?
  |
  --- alternateRule *
        |
      lastRule +
```

Most charts are followed by one or more examples of their use, which appear in italic style. For example:

```
----- "</"
       |
      Name
       |
      S ?
       |
      ">"
```

</mytag>

Most examples only show typical usage, and should not be assumed to cover all possibilities. In some cases, however, several examples are employed to show various options. In this case, the examples are numbered:

```
1. </mytag>
2. </mytag    >
```

A space character is represented by the '^' symbol when it is not otherwise obviously present.

```
1. name
2. ^^name^^^
```

Most expressions contain symbols that refer to other rules. The reader can locate a 'sub-rule' by referring to the number appearing in curly brackets after the symbol name:

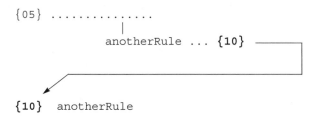

When studying a rule, it is sometimes useful to know how and where that rule is used in other charts. This can be described as 'backward' linking, and allows the reader to analyse a rule, then trace its contextual location in the standard. Every symbol in an expression is numbered, as in '{05.8}' in the example above. This is done to facilitate precise location of the reference in the other chart. Most rules form sub-units of a larger rule. The location of the reference to this rule appears next to the symbol name:

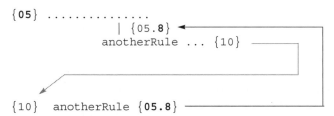

A rule may be referenced from more than one other location, in which case there will be multiple references to it, such as '{05.8} {19.12}'. When a rule is referenced several times from a single expression, an abbreviated format is used, giving '{05.8 .11}' in place of '{05.8} {05.11}'.

When specific characters are referred to, they are identified by a four-digit hexadecimal number that specifies their location in the Unicode/UCS-4 ISO 10646 character set. Note that the first 256 characters in this set are identical to ISO 646, so the ASCII/ISO 646 value for the TAB character, which is given as hexadecimal value '#x09', would be represented as '#x0009'.

Content lists

The structure of an XML document is described by hierarchies of charts. Apart from the obvious hierarchy describing the logical structure of a complete XML document, **document**[01], there are other 'top-level' charts that describe a data file that contains an external DTD, **extSubset**[30], or fragment thereof, **extPE**[79], an external text entity, **extParsedEnt**[78], and the value of an attribute when it is a set of names, **Names**[06], name tokens, **Nmtokens**[08], or a language code, **languageID**[33].

The table below lists the charts in the order that they are defined in the standard, and as they are presented in this chapter:

01 document	31 extSubsetDecl	61 conditionalSect
02 Char	32 SDDecl	62 includeSect
03 S	**33 LanguageID**	63 ignoreSect
04 NameChar	34 Langcode	64 ignoreSectContents
05 Name	35 ISO639Code	65 Ignore
06 Names	36 IanaCode	66 CharRef
07 Nmtoken	37 UserCode	67 Reference
08 Nmtokens	38 Subcode	68 EntityRef
09 EntityValue	39 element	69 PEReference
10 AttValue	40 STag	70 EntityDecl
11 SystemLiteral	41 Attribute	71 GEDecl
12 PubidLiteral	42 ETag	72 PEDecl
13 PubidChar	43 content	73 EntityDef
14 CharData	44 EmptyElemTag	74 PEDef
15 Comment	45 elementdecl	75 ExternalID
16 PI	46 contentspec	76 NDataDecl
17 PITarget	47 children	77 TextDecl
18 CDSect	48 cp	**78 extParsedEnt**
19 CDStart	49 choice	**79 extPE**
20 CData	50 seq	80 EncodingDecl
21 CDEnd	51 Mixed	81 EncName
22 Prolog	52 AttlistDecl	82 NotationDecl
23 XMLDecl	53 AttDef	83 PublicID
24 VersionInfo	54 AttType	84 Letter
25 Eq	55 StringType	85 BaseChar
26 VersionNum	56 TokenizedType	86 Ideographic
27 Misc	57 EnumeratedType	87 CombiningChar
28 doctypedecl	58 NotationType	88 Digit
29 markupdecl	59 Enumeration	89 Extender
30 extSubset	60 DefaultDecl	

The table below lists the charts in alphabetical order:

53 AttDef	09 EntityValue	58 NotationType
52 AttlistDecl	57 EnumeratedType	
41 Attribute	59 Enumeration	72 PEDecl
54 AttType	25 Eq	74 PEDef
10 AttValue	42 ETag	69 PEReference
	89 Extender	16 PI
85 BaseChar	75 ExternalID	17 PITarget
	78 extParsedEnt	22 Prolog
20 CData	**79 extPE**	13 PubidChar
21 CDEnd	**30 extSubset**	12 PubidLiteral
18 CDSect	31 extSubsetDecl	83 PublicID
19 CDStart		
02 Char	71 GEDecl	67 Reference
14 CharData		
66 CharRef	36 IanaCode	03 S
47 children	86 Ideographic	32 SDDecl
49 choice	65 Ignore	50 seq
87 CombiningChar	63 ignoreSect	40 STag
15 Comment	64 ignoreSectContents	55 StringType
61 conditionalSect	62 includeSect	38 Subcode
43 content	35 ISO639Code	11 SystemLiteral
46 contentspec		
48 cp	34 Langcode	77 TextDecl
	33 LanguageID	56 TokenizedType
60 DefaultDecl	84 Letter	
88 Digit		37 UserCode
28 doctypedecl	29 markupdecl	
01 document	27 Misc	24 VersionInfo
	51 Mixed	26 VersionNum
39 element		
45 elementdecl	05 Name	23 XMLDecl
44 EmptyElemTag	04 NameChar	
81 EncName	**06 Names**	
80 EncodingDecl	76 NDataDecl	
70 EntityDecl	07 Nmtoken	
73 EntityDef	**08 Nmtokens**	
68 EntityRef	82 NotationDecl	

Maps

{01} document *(no enclosing structures – describes logical document structure)*:

```
          {01.1}
----- Prolog ... {22}
       | {01.2}
       element ... {39}
       | {01.3}
       Misc * ... {27}

<?XML version="1.0"?>
<!-- start document type -->
<!DOCTYPE mybook SYSTEM "mybook.dtd">
<!-- start actual document -->
<mybook> ... </mybook>
<!-- end document -->
<?END my end of file processing instruction ?>
```

{02} Char (Character) {15.1} {16.3} {20.1} {65.1} {S37.1} *(also a general description of the characters allowed in a document)*:

```
----- #x0009 (tab)
   |
   --- #x000a (line-feed)
   |
   --- #x000d (carriage return)
   |
   --- #x0020 > #xD7FF
   |
   --- #xE000 > #xFFFD
   |
   --- #x10000 > #x10FFFF
```

{03} S (Space) {16.2} {23.4} {24.1} {25.1 .2} {27.3} {28.1 .3 .5 .8 .9} {31.4} {32.1} {40.2 .4} {42.2} {44.2 .4} {45.1 .3 .5} {49.1 .3 .4 .6} {50.1 .3 .4 .6} {51.1 .2 .3 .4 .5 .7} {52.1 .3 .5} {53.1 .3 .5} {58.1 .2 .4 .5 .7} {60.1} {62.1 .2} {63.1 .2} {71.1 .3 .5} {72.1 .2 .4 .6} {75.1 .3 .5} {76.1 .2} {77.3} {80.1} {82.1 .3 .6} {83.1}:

```
-----
   |
(repeatable)
   |
   --- #x0020 (space)
   |
   --- #x000a (line-feed)
   |
   --- #x000d (carriage return)
   |
   --- #x0009 (tab)
```

{04} NameChar (Name Character) {05.2 .3 .4} {07.1}:

```
          {04.1}
----- Letter ... {84}
|     {04.2}
--- Digit ... {88}
|     (04.3}
--- CombiningChar ... {87}
|     (04.4}
--- Extender ... {89}
|
--- '.'
|
--- '-'
|
--- '_'
|
--- ':'
```

{05} Name {06.1 .3} {17.1} {28.2} {40.1} {41.1} {42.1} {44.1} {45.2} {48.1} {51.6} {52.2} {53.2} {58.3 .6} {59.1 .3 .4 .6} {68.1} {69.1} {71.2} {72.3} {76.3} {82.2}:

```
          {05.1}
----- Letter ... {84}
|     |  {05.2}
|     Namechar * ... {04}
|
--- " "
|     |  (05.3}
|     NameChar * ... {04}
|
--- ":"
      |  (05.4}
      NameChar * ... {04}
```

1. *My•Name*
2. *_MyName*
3. *:SPECIAL*

{06} Names *(not part of any other rule – however,* **TokenizedType**[56] *refers to 'IDREFS' content, which is of type Names)*:

```
          {06.1}
----- Name ... {05}
      |
   (optional)
   (repeatable)
      |
   (space character)
      |  {06.3}
      Name ... {05}
```

Note: This was removed in the second edition of XML to allow only space characters between names, instead of any whitespace character.

1. *MyName*
2. *My_Name Another_Name*

{07} Nmtoken (Name Token) {08.1 .3} {59.2 .5}:

```
          {07.1}
----- NameChar + ... {04}
```

66_Token

{08} Nmtokens (Name Tokens) *(not part of any other rule – however, **Token-izedType**[56] refers to 'NMTOKENS' content)*:

```
              {08.1}
----- Nmtoken ... {07}
        |
   (optional)
   (repeatable)
        |
      (Space character)
        |   {08.3}
      Nmtoken ... {07}
```

Note: This was removed in the second edition of XML to allow only space characters between tokens, instead of any whitespace character.

```
1. 66_Token
2. 66_Token Another_Token
```

{09} EntityValue {73.1} {74.1}:

```
----- " " "
   |     |
   |    ----
   |      |
   |   (optional)
   |   (repeatable)
   |         |
   |        ---(text except for '%', '&' and '"')
   |        |      {09.1}
   |        --- PEReference ... {69}
   |        |      {09.2}
   |        --- Reference ... {67}
   |        |
   |       ----
   |         |
   |        " " "
 " ' "
   |
   ----
      |
  (optional)
  (repeatable)
        |
       ---(text except for '%', '&' and ' ' )
       |      {09.3}
       --- PEReference ... {69}
       |      {09.4}
       --- Reference ... {67}
       |
      ----
        |
       " ' "
```

```
1. "An entity value"
2. 'an entity value with %paramRef; and &reference; in it'
```

{10} AttValue (Attribute Value) {41.3} {60.2}:

```
----- " " "
  |     |
  |    ----
  |       |
  |   (optional)
  |   (repeatable)
  |       |
  |      ---(text except for '<', '&' and '"')
  |       |       {10.1}
  |       --- Reference ... {67}
  |       |
  |      ----
  |         |
  |        " " "
 " ' "
  |
   ----
     |
  (optional)
  (repeatable)
     |
    ---(text except for '<', '&' and '"')
     |       {10.2}
    --- Reference ... {67}
     |
    ----
       |
      " ' "
```

```
1.  "An attribute value"
2.  'the % is not significant'
```

{11} SystemLiteral {75.2 .6}:

```
----- " " "
  |     |
  | (chars except for " " ")
  |     |
  |   " " "
 " ' "
  |
(chars except for " ' ")
  |
 " ' "
```

```
1.  "C:\DTDS\MyDoc.DTD"
2.  'C:\DTDS\MyDoc.DTD'
```

{12} PubidLiteral (Public Identifier Literal) {75.4} {83.2}:

```
----- " " "
  |     |   {12.1}
  |   PubidChar * ... {13}
  |     |
  |   " " "
 " ' "
  |   {12.2}
 PubidChar * (except for " ' ") ... {13}
  |
 " ' "
```

```
1.  "The Big DTD"
2.  'Another DTD Version 1.4'
3.  '-//MyCorp/ENTITIES My Entities/EN'
```

{13} PubidChar (Public Identifier Character) {12.1 .2}:

```
----- #x000a (line-feed)
  |
  --- #x000d (carriage return)
  |
  --- #x0020 (space)
  |
  --- "a - z" "A - Z" "0 - 9"
  |
  --- " -'()+,./:=?;!*#@$_% "
```

{14} CharData (Character Data) {43.1 .3 .5 .7 .9 .11}:

```
----- (not '<', '&' or ']]>')
```

This is character data

{15} Comment {27.1} {29.6} {43.10}:

```
----- "<!--"
     | {15.1}
     Char * (except "--") ... {02}
     |
     "-->"
```

<!--A Comment, characters < & % are all ignored-->

{16} PI (Processing Instruction) {27.1} {29.5} {43.8}:

```
----- "<?"
     | {16.1}
     PITarget ? ... {17}
     | {16.2}
     S ... {03}
     | {16.3}
     Char * (not including "?>") ... {02}
     |
     "?>"
```

<?MyInstruct AVOID ? BEFORE > IN PI ?>

{17} PITarget (Processing Instruction Target) {16.1}:

```
         {17.1}
----- Name (not including "xml" or "XML") ... {05}
```

MyInstruct

{18} CDSect (Character Data Section) {43.6}:

```
         {18.1}
----- CDStart ... {19}
     | {18.2}
     CData ... {20}
     | {18.3}
     CDEnd ... {21}
```

<![CDATA[This is <normal> text]]>

{19} CDStart (Character Data Start) {18.1}:

```
----- "<![CDATA["
```

<![CDATA[

{20} CData (Character Data) {18.2}:

```
          {20.1}
----- Char * (excluding "]]>") ... {02}
```

This is <normal> text

{21} CDEnd (Character Data End) {18.3}:

```
----- "]]>"
```

]]>

{22} Prolog {01.1}:

```
          {22.1}
----- XMLDecl ? ... {23}
      | {22.2}
      Misc * ... {27}
      |
  (optional)
      | {22.3}
      doctypedecl ? ... {28}
      | {22.4}
      Misc * ... {27}
```

```
<?XML version="1.0"?>
<!-- start document type -->
<!DOCTYPE mybook SYSTEM "mybook.dtd">
^^^<!-- start actual document -->^^<?SHOW Show this message?>^
```

{23} XMLDecl (XML Declaration) {22.1}:

```
----- "<?xml"
        | {23.1}
        VersionInfo ... {24}
        | {23.2}
        EncodingDecl ? ... {80}
        | {23.3}
        SDDecl ? ... {32}
        | {23.4}
        S (Space) ? ... {03}
        |
        "?>"
```

```
1. <?XML version="1.0"?>
2. <?XML version='1.0' encoding="UTF-8" ?>
3. <?XML version='1.0' encoding="UTF-8" standalone="yes" ?>
```

{24} VersionInfo {23.1}:

```
          {24.1}
----- S (Space) ... {03}
      |
      "version"
      | {24.2}
      Eq (Equals) ... {25}
      |
      ----- " " "
      |       | {24.3}
      |       VersionNum ... {26}
      |       |
      |       " " "
      |
      " ' "
      | {24.4}
      VersionNum ... {26}
      |
      " ' "
```

Note: This was changed in the second edition of XML to make it clearer.

```
1. VERSION="1.0"
2. version = '1.0'
```

{25} Eq (Equals) {24.2} {32.2} {41.2} {80.2}:

```
          {25.1}
----- S (Space) ? ... {03}
      |
     "="
      |  {25.2}
     S (Space) ? ... {03}
```

{26} VersionNum {24.3 .4}:

```
-----
      |
 (repeatable)
      |
      --- "a - z" "A - Z" "0 - 9"
      |
      --- " - "
```

```
1. 1.0
2. 1.1
3. version X99
```

{27} Misc (Miscellaneous) {01.3} {22.2 .4}:

```
          {27.1}
----- Comment ... {15}
    |    {27.2}
    --- PI (Processing Instruction) ... {16}
    |    {27.3}
    --- S (Space) ... {03}
```

```
1. <!-- end document -->
2. <?MY-PROC my processing instruction ?>
3. ^^^
```

{28} doctypedecl (document type declaration) {22.3}:

```
----- "<!DOCTYPE"
     |   {28.1}
     S (Space) ... {03}
     |   {28.2}
     Name ... {05}
     |
     |-----
     |     |   {28.3}
     |     S (Space) ... {03}
     |     |   {28.4}
     |     ExternalID ... {75}
     |     |
     |-----|
     |     |   {28.5}
     |     S ? (Space) ... {03}
     |     |
     |     |-----
     |     |     |
     |     |     " ["
     |     |     |
     |     |     (repeatable)
     |     |     |         {28.6}
     |     |     --- markupdecl ... {29}
     |     |     |         {28.7}
     |     |     --- PEreference ... {69}
     |     |     |         {28.8}
     |     |     --- S (Space) ... {03}
     |     |     |
     |     |     -----
     |     |     |
     |     |     "]"
     |     |     |   {28.9}
     |     |     S ? (Space) ... {03}
     |     |     |
     |     ----------------
     |                    |
                          ">"
```

```
1. <!DOCTYPE mybook>
2. <!DOCTYPE mybook SYSTEM "mybook.dtd">
3. <!DOCTYPE mybook SYSTEM "mybook.dtd" [ ... ] >
4. <!DOCTYPE mybook [ ... ] >
5. <!DOCTYPE mybook PUBLIC "MyPublicId" "mybook.dtd" [ ... ]>
6. <!DOCTYPE mybook PUBLIC "-//MyCorp//DTD My Book//EN" "mybook.dtd">
```

{29} markupdecl (Markup Declaration) {28.6} {31.1}:

```
-----
     |
     (optional)
     (repeatable)
          |    {29.1}
          --- elementdecl ... {45}
          |    {29.2}
          --- AttlistDecl ... {52}
          |    {29.3}
          --- EntityDecl ... {70}
          |    {29.4}
          --- NotationDecl ... {82}
          |    {29.5}
          --- PI ... {16}
          |    {29.6}
          --- Comment ... {15}
```

```
<?SHOW formatted?>
<!NOTATION ......>
^^^<!-- DTD fragment -->
%OtherDecs;
<!ENTITY ...>
<!ELEMENT ...>   <!ATTLIST ...>
```

{30} extSubset (External Subset) *(no enclosing structures – the DTD file)* :

```
            {30.1}
--- TextDecl ? ... {77}
      |  {30.2}
    extSubsetDecl ... {31}

<!xml version="1.0" encoding="ISO-8859-1">
<!NOTATION ......>
<!ELEMENT ...>
%elementSet;
<!ATTLIST ...>
<![IGNORE[
   <!ELEMENT ...>
]]>
```

{31} extSubsetDecl (External Subset Declaration) {30.2} {62.3} {79.2}:

```
------
       |
    (optional)
    (repeatable)
       |     {31.1}
       --- MarkupDecl   ... {29}
       |     {31.2}
       --- conditionalSect ... {61}
       |     {31.3}
       --- PEReference ... {69}
       |     {31.4}
       --- S (Space) ... {03}

<!NOTATION ......>
<!ELEMENT ...>
%elementSet;
<!ATTLIST ...>
<![IGNORE[
   <!ELEMENT ...>
]]>
```

{32} SDDecl (Standalone Document Declaration) {23.3}:

```
            {32.1}
----- S (Space) ... {03}
         |
      "standalone"
         | {32.2}
      Eq (Equals) ... {25}
         |
         |--------------------
         |                    |
       " " "                " ' "
         |                    |
       --- "yes" -----      --- "yes" -----
         |           |        |            |
       --- "no" ------|      --- "no" -------|
                  |                      |
                " " "                  " ' "

1. standalone="no"
2. ^^^standalone = 'yes'
```

{33} LanguageID (Language Identifier) *(no enclosing structures – the value of the 'xml:lang' attribute, as described in RFC 1766)*:

```
            {33.1}
----- Langcode ... {34}
         |
      (optional)
      (repeatable)
         |
       "-"
       |  {33.2}
      Subcode ... {38}
```

Note: This was removed in the second edition of XML. The standards IETF RFC 1766 and ISO 639 are referenced instead.

```
1. en
2. en-GB
3. i-Yiddish
4. x-MyCode
```

{34} Langcode (Language Code) {33.1}:

```
            {34.1}
------ ISO639Code ... {35}
      |     {34.2}
      --- IanaCode ... {36}
      |     {34.3}
      --- UserCode ... {37}
```

Note: This was removed in the second edition of XML. The standards IETF RFC 1766 and ISO 639 are referenced instead.

```
1. en
2. i-Yiddish
3. x-Cardassian
```

{35} ISO639Code {34.1}:

```
-----  "a - z" "A - Z"
         |
       "a - z" "A - Z"
```

Note: This was removed in the second edition of XML. The standards IETF RFC 1766 and ISO 639 are referenced instead.

```
1. en
2. fr
```

{36} IanaCode {34.2}:

Note: This was removed in the second edition of XML. The standards IETF RFC 1766 and ISO 639 are referenced instead.

```
1. i-Yiddish
2. I-Yiddish
```

{37} UserCode {34.3}:

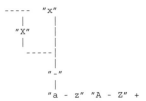

```
-----   "x"
  |      |
 "X"     |
  |      |
  -----  |
         |
        "-"
         |
       "a - z" "A - Z" +
```

Note: This was removed in the second edition of XML. The standards IETF RFC 1766 and ISO 639 are referenced instead.

```
1. x-Cardassian
2. X-Cardassian
```

{38} Subcode {33.2}:

```
-----  "a - z" "A - Z" +
```

Note: This was removed in the second edition of XML. The standards IETF RFC 1766 and ISO 639 are referenced instead.

GB

{39} element {01.2} {43.2}:

```
              {39.1}
-----  EmptyElemTag ... {44}
  |         {39.2}
  --- STag ... {40}
      | {39.3}
      content ... {43}
      | {39.4}
      ETag ... {42}
```

```
1. <image name="image13"/>
2. <para>Some content</para>
3. <para></para>
4. <para/>
```

{40} STag (Start Tag) {39.2}:

```
-----  "<"
     |   {40.1}
     Name ... {05}
     |
     -----
     |     |
     |  (repeatable)
     |     | {40.2}
     |   S (Space) ... {03}
     |     | {40.3}
     |   Attribute ... {41}
     |     |
     -------
           | {40.4}
         S (Space) ? ... {03}
           |
          ">"
```

```
1. <emph>
2. <emph type="2">
3. <emph type = "2" style = "bold" >
```

{41} Attribute {40.3} {44.3}:

```
          {41.1}
----- Name ... {05}
      | {41.2}
      Eq (Equals) ... {25}
      | {41.3}
      AttValue ... {10}
```

```
1. type="2"
1. border = '5mm 10mm 2" 3"'
```

{42} ETag (End Tag) {39.4}:

```
----- "</"
        | {42.1}
        Name ... {05}
        | {42.2}
        S ? (Space) ... {03}
        |
        ">"
```

```
1. </emph>
2. </emph >
```

{43} content {39.3} {78.2}:

```
-----
      |     {43.1}
      --- CharData ? ... {14}
      |
   (optional)
   (repeatable)
      |    {43.2}
      --- element ... {39}
      |     |     {43.3}
      |     --- CharData ? ... {14}
      |    {43.4}
      --- Reference ... {67}
      |     |    {43.5}
      |     --- CharData ? ... {14}
      |    {43.6}
      --- CDSect ... {18}
      |     |    {43.7}
      |     --- CharData ? ... {14}
      |    {43.8}
      --- PI ... {16}
      |     |     {43.9}
      |     --- CharData ? ... {14}
      |    {43.10}
      --- Comment ... {15}
      |     |     {43.11}
      |     --- CharData ? ... {14}
```

Note: This was edited in the second edition of XML. The position of character data is made clearer now.

```
<!-- Some Content -->
<?ACME-WP  new_page ?>
<para>
An entity reference, such as &ref;, is not recognised in
when <![CDATA[appearing in here]]>.
</para>
```

{44} EmptyElemTag {39.1}:

```
----- "<"
      |   {44.1}
    Name ... {05}
      |
      -----
      |    |
      |  (repeatable)
      |    |   {44.2}
      |  S (Space) ... {03}
      |    |   {44.3}
      |  Attribute ... {41}
      |    |
      -------
           |   {44.4}
         S (Space) ? ... {03}
           |
         "/>"
```

```
1.  <revisionStart/>
2.  <image name="image13" />
```

{45} elementdecl (element declaration) {29.1}:

```
----- "<!ELEMENT"
      |   {45.1}
    S (Space) ... {03}
      |   {45.2}
    Name ... {05}
      |   {45.3}
    S (Space) ... {03}
      |   {45.4}
    contentspec ... {46}
      |   {45.5}
    S ? (Space) ... {03}
      |
    ">"]
```

Note: An entity reference that contains nothing may appear after the name (because it is then just part of the space). It is included to allow the entity to contain SGML tag omission indicators, '- O', in an SGML variant of the same DTD.

```
1.  <!ELEMENT image EMPTY>
2.  <!ELEMENT para (#PCDATA | sub | super)* >
3.  <!ELEMENT %para; (#PCDATA | sub | super)* >
4.  <!ELEMENT para %paraContent;>
```

{46} contentspec (content specification) {45.4}:

```
-------- "EMPTY"
        |
     --- "ANY"
     |      {46.1}
     --- Mixed ... {51}
     |      {46.2}
     --- children ... {47}
```

```
1.  EMPTY
2.  ANY
3.  (#PCDATA | sub | super)*
4.  (title, para*)
```

{47} children {46.2}:

```
          {47.1}
----- choice ... {49}
   |      |
   |       --47------------------
   |      {47.2}
   |-- seq (sequence) ... {50}   |
   |       |                     |
   |        ---------------------|
                                 |
                            --- "?"
                            |
                            --- "*"
                            |
                            --- "+"
                            |
                            *
```

1. *(name, address, telphone)*
2. *(para | list)**

{48} cp (content particle) {49.2 .5} {50.2 .5}:

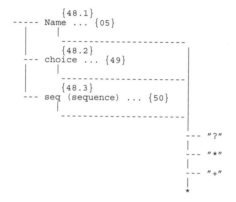

```
          {48.1}
----- Name ... {05}
   |      |
   |       ---------------------
   |      {48.2}
   |--- choice ... {49}
   |      |                     |
   |       ---------------------|
   |      {48.3}
   |--- seq (sequence) ... {50}
   |      |                     |
   |       ---------------------|
                                |
                            --- "?"
                            |
                            --- "*"
                            |
                            --- "+"
                            |
                            *
```

1. *address*
2. *address+*
1. *(..., ..., ...)*
2. *(... | ...)**

{49} choice {47.1} {48.2}:

```
----- " ("
      | {49.1}
      S ?(Space) ... {03}
      | {49.2}
      cp ... {48}
      |
      -------
      |      |
      | (repeatable)
      |      | {49.3}
      |      S ? (Space) ... {03}
      |      |
      |      " | "
      |      | {49.4}
      |      S ? (Space) ... {03}
      |      | {49.5}
      |      cp ... {48}
      |      |
      ---------
                | {49.6}
                S ? (Space) ... {03}
                |
                " ) "
```

Note: This was improved in the second edition of XML.

```
1.  (para|list)
2.  ( para | Nlist | Alist )
3.  ( para | %listTypes; )
4.  ( company | (firstname, secondname) )
```

{50} seq (sequence) {47.2} {48.3}:

```
----- " ("
      | {50.1}
      S ?(Space) ... {03}
      | {50.2}
      cp ... {48}
      |
      -------
      |      |
      | (repeatable)
      |      | {50.3}
      |      S ? (Space) ... {03}
      |      |
      |      " , "
    . |      | {50.4}
      |      S ? (Space) ... {03}
      |      | {50.5}
      |      cp ... {48}
      |      |
      ---------
                | {50.6}
                S ? (Space) ... {03}
                |
                " ) "
```

Note: This model was improved in the second edition of XML.

```
1.  (para)
2.  ( %paraType; )
3.  ( name, address, tel )
4.  (name, %addrType;, tel)
5.  (title, (para | note)* )
```

{51} Mixed (mixed content) {46.1}:

```
------ " ("
   |    | {51.1}
   |    S ? (Space) ... {03}
   |    |
   |    "#PCDATA"
   |    | {51.2}
   |    S ? (Space) ... {03}
   |    |
   |    ")"
   |
  "("
   | {51.3}
  S ? (Space) ... {03}
   |
  "#PCDATA"
   |
   |-----
   |    |
   |  (repeatable)
   |    | {51.4}
   |    S ? (Space) ... {03}  .
   |    |
   |    "|"
   |    | {51.5}
   |    S ? (Space) ... {03}
   |    | {51.6}
   |    Name ? ... {05}
   |    |
   -----------
              | {51.7}
              S ? (Space) ... {03}
              |
              ")*"
```

1. `(#PCDATA)`
2. `( #PCDATA )`
3. `( %someMixedContent; )*`
4. `(#PCDATA|emph)*`
5. `(#PCDATA | emph | code | name)*`
6. `(#PCDATA | emph | %other; | name)*`

{52} AttlistDecl (Attribute list Declaration) {29.2}:

```
----- "<!ATTLIST"
      | {52.1}
      S (Space) ... {03}
      | {52.2}
      Name ... {05}
      | {52.3}
      S ? (Space) ... {03}
      | {52.4}
      AttDef * ... {53}
      | {52.5}
      S ? (Space) ... {03}
      |
      ">"
```

1. `<!ATTLIST report date    NMTOKEN        #REQUIRED`
   `                author CDATA          #IMPLIED`
   `                status (draft|final) "draft"  >`
2. `<!ATTLIST %para  type   CDATA          "normal"`
   `                %otherAttrib;                  >`

{53} AttDef (Attribute Definition) {52.4}:

```
          {53.1}
----- S (Space) ... {03}
      | {53.2}
      Name ... {05}
      | {53.3}
      S (Space) ... {03}
      | {53.4}
      AttType ... {54}
      | {53.5}
      S (Space) ... {03}
      | {53.6}
      DefaultDecl ... {60}
```

1. *date NMTOKEN #REQUIRED*
2. *author CDATA #IMPLIED*
3. *status (draft|final) "draft" >*
4. *%colourAttName; %colourGroup; %colourDefault; >*

{54} AttType (Attribute Type) {53.4}:

```
          {54.1}
----- StringType ... {55}
   |      {54.2}
   --- TokenizedType ... {56}
   |      {54.3}
   --- EnumeratedType ... {57}
```

1. *CDATA*
2. *NMTOKEN*
3. *(draft|final)*
4. *NOTATION (Tex|TROFF)*

{55} StringType {54.1}:

```
----- "CDATA"
```

{56} TokenizedType {54.2}:

```
----- "ID"
   |
   --- "IDREF"
   |
   --- "IDREFS"
   |
   --- "ENTITY"
   |
   --- "ENTITIES"
   |
   --- "NMTOKEN"
   |
   --- "NMTOKENS"
```

NMTOKEN

{57} EnumeratedType {54.3}:

```
          {57.1}
----- NotationType ... {58}
   |      {57.2}
   --- Enumeration ... {59}
```

1. *NOTATION (Tex|TROFF)*
2. *(draft|final)*

{58} NotationType {57.1}:

```
----- "NOTATION"
        | {58.1}
       S (Space) ... {03}
        |
       " ("
        | {58.2}
       S ? (Space) ... {03}
        | {58.3}
       Name   ... {05}
        |
        -----
        |    |
        |  (repeatable)
        |    | {58.4}
        |   S ? (Space) ... {03}
        |    |
        |   "|"
        |    | {58.5}
        |   S ? (Space) ... {03}
        |    | {58.6}
        |   Name   ... {05}
        |    |
        -------
             | {58.7}
            S ? (Space) ... {03}
             |
            ")"
```

1. *NOTATION (Tex|TROFF)*
2. *NOTATION (Tex | TROFF)*
3. *%NOTA; (%imageFormats; | PostScript | %mathFormats;)*

{59} Enumeration {57.2}:

```
----- " ("
        | {59.1}
       S ? (Space) ... {03}
        | {59.2}
       Nmtoken ... {07}
        |
        -----
        |    |
        |  (repeatable)
        |    | {59.3}
        |   S ? (Space) ... {03}
        |    |
        |   "|"
        |    | {59.4}
        |   S ? (Space) ... {03}
        |    | {59.5}
        |   Nmtoken ... {07}
        |    |
        -------
             | {59.6}
            S ? (Space) ... {03}
             |
            ")"
```

1. *(Activate)*
2. *(yes|no)*
3. *(red | amber | green)*
4. *(%colours;)*

{60} DefaultDecl {53.6}:

```
------ "#REQUIRED"
   |
   --- "#IMPLIED"
   |
   --------- "#FIXED"
      |         |  {60.1}
      |         S (Space) ... {03}
      |         |
      --------|
                |  {60.2}
                AttValue ... {10}
```

1. *#REQUIRED*
2. *#IMPLIED*
3. *"giraffe"*
4. *%defaultAnimal;*
5. *#FIXED "giraffe"*

{61} conditionalSect {31.2}:

```
              {61.1}
------ includeSect ... {62}
  |    {61.2}
  --- ignoreSect ... {63}
```

1. *<![INCLUDE[...]]>*
2. *<![IGNORE [...]]>*

{62} includeSect (included Section) {61.1}:

```
----- "<!["
  |  {62.1}
  S ? (Space) ... {03}
  |
  "INCLUDE"
  |  {62.2}
  S ? (Space) ... {03}
  |
  "["
  |  {62.3}
  extSubsetDecl ... {31}
  |
  "]]>"
```

1. *<![INCLUDE[...%decl1;...%decl2;...]]>*
2. *<![%Switch;[...]]> <!-- when entity value is "INCLUDE" -->*

{63} ignoreSect (ignored Section) {61.2}:

```
----- "<!["
  |  {63.1}
  S ? (Space) ... {03}
  |
  "IGNORE"
  |  {63.2}
  S ? (Space) ... {03}
  |
  "["
  |  {63.3}
  ignoreSectContents * ... {64}
  |
  "]]>"
```

1. *<![IGNORE[...%decl1;...%decl2;...]]>*
2. *<![%Switch; [...]]> <!-- when entity value is "IGNORE" -->*

{64} ignoreSectContents (ignored Section Contents) {63.3} {64.2 (recursive)}:

```
            {64.1}
----- ignore ... {65}
       |
  (repeatable)
       |
     "<![ "
       | {64.2}
       ignoreSectContents ... {64}  (RECURSIVE)
       |
     "]]>"
       | {64.3}
       ignore ... {65}
```

Note: This rule calls itself, allowing nesting of ignored sections.

```
1. "ignore contents of this string"
2. ...<!-- a comment-->...
3. ...<?CODE new-page?>...
4. ...<![IGNORE[ ... <![IGNORE[...]]> ... ]]>...
```

{65} Ignore {64.1 .3}:

```
            {65.1}
----- Char * (but not '<![' or ']]>') ... {02}
```

This text must not contain consecutive "< ! [" or "]] >".

{66} CharRef (Character Reference) {67.2}:

```
----- "&#"
  |    |
  |   "0"-"9" +
  |    |
  |   ";"
  |
  --- "&#x"
       |
      "0"-"9" "a"-"f" "A"-"F" +
       |
      ";"
```

```
1. &#123;
2. &#xE2;
3. &#x7FFF;
```

{67} Reference {09.2 .4} {10.1 .2} {43.4}:

```
            {67.1}
----- EntityRef ... {68}
  |         {67.2}
  --- CharRef ... {66}
```

```
1. &myent;
2. &#123;
3. &#x7FFF;
```

{68} EntityRef (Entity Reference) {67.1}:

```
----- "&"
       | {68.1}
      Name ... {05}
       |
      ";"
```

```
&myref;
```

{69} PEReference (Parameter Entity Reference) {09.1 .3} {28.7} {31.3}:

```
----- "%"
      |   {69.1}
      Name ... {05}
      |
      ";"
```

```
%myref;
```

{70} EntityDecl {29.3}:

```
            {70.1}
----- GEDecl ... {71}
  |       {70.2}
  --- PEDecl ... {72}
```

```
1. <!ENTITY myent      "a general entity" >
2. <!ENTITY myent      %someGeneralContent>
3. <!ENTITY %EntName; "a general entity">
4. <!ENTITY % myent      "a parameter entity" >
5. <!ENTITY % %otherEnt; "a parameter entity">
6. <!ENTITY % %otherEnt; %someParameterContent; >
```

{71} GEDecl (General Entity Declaration) {70.1}:

```
----- "<!ENTITY"
      |  {71.1}
      S (Space) ... {03}
      |  {71.2}
      Name ... {05}
      |  {71.3}
      S (Space) ... {03}
      |  {71.4}
      EntityDef ... {73}
      |  {71.5}
      S (Space) ? ... {03}
      |
      ">"
```

```
1. <!ENTITY myent      "a general entity" >
2. <!ENTITY myent      %someGeneralContent;>
3. <!ENTITY %EntName; "a general entity" >
```

{72} PEDecl (Parameter Entity Declaration) {70.2}:

```
----- "<!ENTITY"
      |  {72.1}
      S (Space) ... {03}
      |
      "%"
      |  {72.2}
      S (Space) ... {03}
      |  {72.3}
      Name ... {05}
      |  {72.4}
      S (Space) ... {03}
      |  {72.5}
      PEDef ... {74}
      |  {72.6}
      S (Space) ? ... {03}
      |
      ">"
```

```
1. <!ENTITY % myent      "a parameter entity" >
2. <!ENTITY % %otherEnt; "a parameter entity">
3. <!ENTITY % %otherEnt; %someParameterContent; >
```

{73} EntityDef (Entity Definition) {71.4}:

```
            {73.1}
----- EntityValue... {09}
  |       {73.2}
  --- ExternalID ... {75}
        |  {73.3}
        NDataDecl ? ... {76}
```

1. *"this is my entity"*
2. *PUBLIC "-//MyCorp/TEXT My entity/EN" "/ents/myent.ent"*
3. *SYSTEM "file:///ents/myent.ent" NDATA cgm*

{74} PEDef (Parameter Entity Definition) {72.5}:

```
            {74.1}
----- EntityValue... {09}
  |       {74.2}
  --- ExternalID ... {75}
```

1. *"this is my entity"*
2. *PUBLIC "-//MyCorp/TEXT My entity/EN" "/ents/myent.ent"*
3. *SYSTEM "file:///ents/myent.ent"*

{75} ExternalID {28.4} {73.2} {74.2} {82.4}:

```
----- "SYSTEM"
  |   |  {75.1}
  |   S (Space) ... {03}
  |   |  {75.2}
  |   SystemLiteral ... {11}
  |
  --- "PUBLIC"
       |  {75.3}
       S (Space) ... {03}
       |  {75.4}
       PubidLiteral ... {12}
       |  {75.5}
       S (Space) ... {03}
       |  {75.6}
       SystemLiteral ... {11}
```

1. *SYSTEM "/ents/myent.ent"*
2. *PUBLIC "-//MyCorp/TEXT My entity/EN" "/ents/myent.ent"*

{76} NDataDecl (Notational Data Declaration) {73.3}:

```
            {76.1}
----- S (Space) ... {03}
       |
       "NDATA"
       |  {76.2}
       S (Space) ... {03}
       |  {76.3}
       Name ... {05}
```

^^^NDATA TeX

{77} TextDecl (Text Declaration) {30.1} {78.1} {79.1}:

```
----- "<?xml"
       |  {77.1}
       VersionInfo ? ... {24}
       |  {77.2}
       EncodingDecl ... {80}
       |  {77.3}
       S ? (Space) ... {03}
       |
       "?>"
```

Note: Describes optional information appearing at the top of each external XML format entity file.

```
1. <?XML encoding = "UTF-8"?>
2. <?XML VERSION="1.0" encoding = "UTF-8"?>
```

{78} extParsedEnt (external Parsed Entity) *(no enclosing structures – well-formed entity containing a document fragment)*:

```
         {78.1}
----- TextDecl ? ... {77}
     | {78.2}
       content ... {43}
```

```
<?XML encoding = "UTF-8"?>
<chapter>...</chapter>
```

{79} extPE (external Parameter Entity) *(no enclosing structures – the external DTD or fragment of the DTD)*:

```
         {79.1}
----- TextDecl ? ... {77}
     | {79.2}
       extSubsetDecl ... {31}
```

```
<?XML version="1.0" encoding = "UTF-8"?>
<!ELEMENT book ...>
<!ATTLIST book ...>
<!ELEMENT chapter ...>
```

{80} EncodingDecl (Encoding Declaration) {23.2} {77.2}:

```
         {80.1}
----- S (Space) ... {03}
     |
     "encoding"
     | {80.2}
     Eq (Equals) ... {25}
     |
     |--- " " "
     |       | {80.3}
     |         EncName ... {81}
     |       |
     |       " " "
     |       |
     ------|
             |
           " ' "
           | {80.4}
             EncName ... {81}
           |
           " ' "
```

```
1. encoding="UTF-8"
2. ^^^encoding = 'UTF-8'
```

{81} EncName {80.3 .4}:

```
----- "A"-"Z" "a"-"z"
     |
   (optional)
   (repeatable)
     |
       --- "A"-"Z" "a"-"z" "0"-"9"
     |
       --- "-"
     |
       --- "_"
     |
       --- "."
```

```
UTF-8
```

{82} NotationDecl (Notation Declaration) {29.4}:

```
----- "<!NOTATION"
     | {82.1}
     S (Space) ... {03}
     | {82.2}
     Name ... {05}
     | {82.3}
     S (Space) ... {03}
     | {82.4}
     |----- ExternalID ... {75}
     |              |
     | {82.5}       -------------
     PublicID ... {83}          |
     |                          |
     --------------------------
                               | {82.6}
                           S ? (Space) ... {03}
                               |
                             ">"
```

1. `<!NOTATION  mynota  SYSTEM  "/nota/mynota.not"  >`
2. `<!NOTATION mynota PUBLIC "MY NOTATION" "/nota/mynota.not">`
3. `<!NOTATION mynota SYSTEM "">`
4. `<!NOTATION %aNotatName; SYSTEM "/nota/mynota.not">`
5. `<!NOTATION mynota &aNotatID;>`
6. `<!NOTATION %aNotatName; %aNotatID>`

{83} PublicID (Public Identifier) {82.5}:

```
----- "PUBLIC"
     | {83.1}
     S (Space) ... {03}
     | {83.2}
     PubidLiteral ... {12}
```

Note: Describes optional information appearing at the top of each external XML format entity file.

1. `<?XML encoding = "UTF-8"?>`
2. `<?XML VERSION="1.0" encoding = "UTF-8"?>`

{84} Letter {04.1} {05.1}:

```
          {84.1}
----- BaseChar ... {85}
     |    {84.2}
     --- Ideographic ... {86}
```

Note: This rule is too large to illustrate in chart form – refer to the standard.

1. `e`
2. `e´`

{85} BaseChar (Base Character) {84.1}:

```
----- (a large range of letters from many languages)
```

Note: This rule is too large to illustrate in chart form – refer to the standard.

{86} Ideographic {84.2}:

```
----- (various unicode character ranges)
```

Note: This rule is too large to illustrate in chart form – refer to the standard.

{87} CombiningChar (Combining Character) {04.3}:

```
----- (various unicode character accents, such as "´")
```

Note: This rule is too large to illustrate in chart form – refer to the standard.

{88} Digit {04.2}:

```
----- "0"-"9"
  |
  --- (various Unicode non-Arabic digits)
```

Note: This rule is too large to illustrate in chart form – refer to the standard.

{89} Extender {04.4}:

```
----- "•" (middle dot)
  |
  --- (various Unicode characters)
```

Note: This rule is too large to illustrate in chart form – refer to the standard.

35. XPath road map

This chapter is intended to be used as an aid to 'steering' through the XPath standard.

The 'road map' appearing in this chapter is derived from the rules that comprise the XPath standard, released in November 1999. The maps follow the same structure as those in the previous chapter, describing the XML standard, and the first section of that chapter should be read before studying the charts in this chapter.

Content lists

The structure of an XPath expression is described by hierarchies of charts. These charts are highly recursive, and it can be difficult to establish which are 'top-level' charts. Nevertheless, significant entry-points include **LocationPath**[1], **Predicate**[8], **Expr**[14], **ExprToken**[28] and **ExprWhitespace**[39]. The table below lists the charts in the order that they are defined in the standard, and as they are presented in this chapter:

01 LocationPath	**14 Expr**	27 UnaryExpr
02 AbsoluteLocationPath	15 PrimaryExpr	**28 ExprToken**
03 RelativeLocationPath	16 FunctionCall	29 Literal
04 Step	17 Argument	30 Number
05 AxisSpecifier	18 UnionExpr	31 Digits
06 AxisName	19 PathExpr	32 Operator
07 NodeTest	20 FilterExpr	33 OperatorName
08 Predicate	21 OrExpr	34 MultiplyOperator
09 PredicateExpr	22 AndExpr	35 FunctionName
10 AbbreviatedAbsoluteLocation	23 EqualityExpr	36 VariableReference
11 AbbreviatedRelativeLocationPath	24 RelationalExpr	37 NameTest
12 AbbreviatedStep	25 AdditiveExpr	38 NodeType
13 AbbreviatedAxisSpecifier	26 MultiplicativeExpr	**39 ExprWhitespace**

The table below lists the charts in alphabetical order:

13 AbbreviatedAxisSpecifier	**28 ExprToken**	32 Operator
10 AbbreviatedAbsoluteLocation	**39 ExprWhitespace**	33 OperatorName
11 AbbreviatedRelativeLocationPath	20 FilterExpr	21 OrExpr
12 AbbreviatedStep	16 FunctionCall	19 PathExpr
02 AbsoluteLocationPath	35 FunctionName	**08 Predicate**
25 AdditiveExpr	29 Literal	09 PredicateExpr
22 AndExpr	**01 LocationPath**	15 PrimaryExpr
17 Argument	26 MultiplicativeExpr	24 RelationalExpr
06 AxisName	34 MultiplyOperator	03 RelativeLocationPath
05 AxisSpecifier	37 NameTest	04 Step
31 Digits	07 NodeTest	27 UnaryExpr
23 EqualityExpr	38 NodeType	18 UnionExpr
14 Expr	30 Number	36 VariableReference

Expression structure overview

It can be difficult to follow some of the labyrinthine ways in which XPath rules include each other. Yet there is a major chain of rules for expressions (**Expr**$^{\{14\}}$), as shown below. The order in which the following roles are linked (exclusively) to each other also indicates the order in which they are processed (so that, for example, '=' is evaluated after '<'):

```
{14} Expr              ... and ... or ... (adds nothing)
      |
   {21} OrExpr         ... and ... or ...
         |
    {22} AndExpr    $a=$b and $y < $z ...
          |
     {23} EqualityExpr        $y < $z = $a < $b + $f * -2
           |
      {24} RelationalExpr          $a < $b + $f * -2
            |
       {25} AdditiveExpr                $b + $f * -2
             |
        {26} MultiplicativeExpr              $f * -2
              |
         {27} UnaryExpr                          -2
               |
          {18} UnionExpr    warning/chapter[9]/para    2
                |
           {19} PathExpr            chapter[9]/para     2
                 |
            {20} FilterExpr          chapter[9]         2
                  |
             {15} PrimaryExpr        chapter            2
```

Expression tokens

Tokens within an expression (**ExprToken**$^{\{28\}}$) take the following form. Whitespace can appear before and after each of these tokens:

```
----- '('                                    position ( )
  |
  --- ')'                                     position ( )
  |
  --- '['                         para [ @id='x1' ] /
  |
  --- ']'                         para [ @id='x1' ] /
  |
  --- '.'                                    . /emph
  |
  --- '..'                        .          .. / .. /title
  |
  --- '@'                                    / @ id
  |
  --- ','               translate( . ,  'abc' ,  'ABC')
  |
  --- '::'                                   child ::
  |      {28.1}
  --- NameTest ... {37}        acmeNS:*    acmeNS:widget
  |      {28.2}
  --- NodeType ... {38}        processing-instruction
  |      {28.3}
  --- Operator ... {32}                and   +   //
  |      {28.4}
  --- FunctionName ... {35}                  position
  |      {28.5}
  --- AxisName ... {6}              child   ancestor
  |      {28.6}
  --- Literal ... {29}              'another string'
  |      {28.7}
  --- Number ... {30}                        .55
  |      {28.8}
  --- VariableReference ... {36}        $myVariable
```

Among other surprises, this chart shows that it is possible to have spaces between axis names and the '::' suffix, such as 'child ::', and between function names and parameters, such as 'position ()'.

Maps

{01} LocationPath {19.1}:

```
         {01.1}
----- RelativeLocationPath ... {03}
  |      {01.2}
  --- AbsoluteLocationPath ... {02}
```

```
ancestor::acmeNS:*
para
@id
(none - assume child) text()
processing-instruction(Acme)
chapter/section[3]//para/text()
.
../section/title
./section//para
```

```
/
/book
/book/@id
/book/chapter/section[3]//para/text()
/book//para[99]/..
//para
```

{02} AbsoluteLocationPath {01.2}

```
----- '/'
  |      |    {02.1}
  |    RelativeLocationPath? ... {03}
  |      {02.2}
  --- AbbreviatedAbsoluteLocationPath ... {10}
```

```
/
```

```
/book
/book/@id
/book/chapter/section[3]//para/text()
/book//para[99]/..
```

```
//para
```

{03} RelativeLocationPath {01.1} {02.1} {03.2} {10.1} {11.1} {19.4 .6}

```
         {03.1}
----- Step ...  {04}
  |       {03.2}
  --- RelativeLocationPath ... {03}   (immediate recursive)
  |    |
  |    '/'
  |    |  {03.3}
  |    Step ... {04}
  |       {03.4}
  --- AbbreviatedRelativeLocationPath ... {11}
```

```
ancestor::acmeNS:*
para
@id
(none - assume child) text()
processing-instruction(Acme)
chapter/section[3]//para/text()
.
../section/title
./section//para
```

{04} Step {03.1 .3} {11.2}

```
              {04.1}
----- AxisSpecifier... {05}
  |     |  {04.2}
  |   NodeTest ... {07}
  |     |  {04.3}
  |   Predicate * ... {08}
  |       {04.4}
   --- AbbreviatedStep ... {12}
```

ancestor::acmeNS:*
child::acmeNS:widget[...]
para
@*
@id
(none - assume child)*text()*
(none - assume child)*node()[...][...]*
processing-instruction(Acme)

.

..

Note: "range-to()[5]" (XPointer defined step type (use in XPointer only)).

{05} AxisSpecifier {04.1}

```
              {05.1}
----- AxisName ... {06}
  |       |
  |      '::'
  |      {05.2}
   --- AbbreviatedAxisSpecifier ... {13}
```

ancestor::
child::
@
(none) (following word is an element name)

{06} AxisName {05.1} {28.5}

```
----- 'ancestor'
  |
  --- 'ancestor-or-self'
  |
  --- 'attribute'
  |
  --- 'child'
  |
  --- 'descendant'
  |
  --- 'descendant-or-self'
  |
  --- 'following'
  |
  --- 'following-sibling'
  |
  --- 'namespace'
  |
  --- 'parent'
  |
  --- 'preceding'
  |
  --- 'preceding-sibling'
  |
  --- 'self'
```

self
preceding

{07} NodeTest {04.2}

```
               {07.1}
    ----- NameTest ...  {37}
    |          {07.2}
    --- NodeType ...  {38}
    |        |
    |       '('
    |        |
    |       ')'
    |
    --- 'processing-instruction'
             |
            '('
            |   {07.3}
         Literal ...  {29}
             |
            ')'

    *
    acmeNS:*
    acmeNS:widget
    text()
    node()
    processing-instruction("Acme")
```

{08} Predicate {04.3} {20.3}

```
    ----- '['
          |   {08.1}
        PredicateExpr ...  {09}
          |
         ']'

    [...]
```

{09} PredicateExpr {08.1}

```
          {09.1}
    ----- Expr ...  {14}

    [...]
```

{10} AbbreviatedAbsoluteLocationPath {02.2}

```
    ----- '//'
          |   {10.1}
        RelativeLocationPath ...  {03}

    //
    //para
```

{11} AbbreviatedRelativeLocationPath {03.4}

```
           {11.1}
    ----- RelativeLocationPath ...  {03}  (recursive)
          |
         '//'
          |   {11.2}
        Step ...  {04}

    chapter//para
```

{12} AbbreviatedStep {04.4}

```
    ----- '.'
      |
    --- '..'
```

```
 .
 . .
```

{13} AbbreviatedAxisSpecifier {05.2}

```
----- '@' ?

@
(none)  (assume child::)
```

{14} Expr {09.1} {15.2} {17.1}

```
        {14.1}
----- OrExpr ... {21}

-153
5 * 6 = 6 * 5 and $myVariable != $anotherVariable or 3=$myvariable
5 > $myVariable != 6 > $anotherVariable
/book/chapter/title | para/emph
```

{15} PrimaryExpr {20.1}

```
              {15.1}
----- VariableReference ... {36}
  |
  --- '('
  |    |   {15.2}
  |    Expr ... {14}
  |    |
  |   ')'
  |        {15.3}
  --- Literal ... {29}
  |        {15.4}
  --- Number ... {30}
  |        {15.5}
  --- FunctionCall ... {16}

$myVariable
(...)
"a string"
153
range() (XPointer function)
acmeFunc()
```

{16} FunctionCall {15.5}

```
            {16.1}
----- FunctionName ... {35}
         |
        '('
         |
        --------
               | {16.2}
            Argument ... {17}
              |
              ---------
                     |
                 (repeatable)
                     |
                    ','
                     | {16.3}
                 Argument ... {17}
                     |
                  ---------
         |
        -------
         |
        ')'

range() (XPointer function)
acmeFunc()
```

{17} Argument {16.2 .3}

```
         {17.1}
----- Expr ... {14}
```

{18} UnionExpr {18.2} {27.1}

```
            {18.1}
----- PathExpr ... {19}
  |        {18.2}
  --- UnionExpr ... {18} (immediate recursive)
      |
    ' | '
      |    {18.3}
      PathExpr ... {19}
```

/book/chapter/title | para/emph

$myVariable | $anotherVariable
(...) | (...)
"a string" | 'another string'
153 | 456
acmeFunc() | acmeFunc2()[12]

current()/@id | current/@name

{19} PathExpr {18.1 .3}

```
            {19.1}
----- LocationPath ... {01}
  |        {19.2}
  --- FilterExpr ... {20}
  |        {19.3}
  --- FilterExpr ... {20}
  |        |
  |      ' / '
  |        |   {19.4}
  |      RelativeLocationPath ... {03}
  |        {19.5}
  --- FilterExpr ... {20}
           |
         ' // '
           |   {19.6}
        RelativeLocationPath ... {03}
```

/book/chapter/title
para/emph

$myVariable
(...)
"a string"
153
range() (XPointer function)
acmeFunc()
range()[15] (XPointer function)
acmeFunc()[15]

current()/@id

origin()//following-sibling::para[1]

{20} FilterExpr {19.2 .3 .5} {20.2}

```
            {20.1}
----- PrimaryExpr ... {15}
  |        {20.2}
  --- FilterExpr ... {20} (immediate recursive)
           |   {20.3}
        Predicate ... {08}
```

```
range()[15]  (XPointer function)
acmeFunc()[15]

$myVariable
(...)
"a string"
153
range()  (XPointer function)
acmeFunc()
```

{21} OrExpr {14.1} {21.2}

```
           {21.1}
----- AndExpr ... {22}
  |        {21.2}
  --- OrExpr ... {21}  (immediate recursive)
          |
         'or'
          | {21.3}
       AndExpr ... {22}

-153
5 * 6 = 6 * 5 and $myVariable != $anotherVariable or 3=$myvariable
5 > $myVariable != 6 > $anotherVariable
/book/chapter/title | para/emph
```

{22} AndExpr {21.1 .3} {22.2}

```
           {22.1}
----- EqualityExpr ... {23}
  |        {22.2}
  --- AndExpr ... {22}  (immediate recursive)
          |
         'and'
          | {22.3}
       EqualityExpr ... {23}

-153
5 * 6 = 6 * 5 and $myVariable != $anotherVariable
5 > $myVariable != 6 > $anotherVariable
/book/chapter/title | para/emph
```

{23} EqualityExpr {22.1 .3} {23.2 .4}

```
            {23.1}
----- RelationalExpr ... {24}
  |          {23.2}
  --- EqualityExpr ... {23}  (immediate recursive)
  |      |
  |     '='
  |      | {23.3}
  |   RelationalExpr ... {24}
  |          {23.4}
  --- EqualityExpr ... {23}  (immediate recursive)
          |
         '!='
          | {23.5}
       RelationalExpr ... {24}

-153
5 * 6 = 6 * 5
5 > $myVariable != 6 > $anotherVariable
5 * 6 = 6 * 5 = 2 * 15 != 2 + 2 != 3 + 3
/book/chapter/title | para/emph
```

{24} RelationalExpr {23.1 .3 .5} {24.2 .4 .6 .8}

```
                {24.1}
----- AdditiveExpr ... {25}
    |        {24.2}
    --- RelationalExpr ... {24} (immediate recursive)
    |        |
    |       '<'
    |        |  {24.3}
    |    AdditiveExpr ... {25}
    |        {24.4}
    --- RelationalExpr ... {24} (immediate recursive)
    |        |
    |       '>'
    |        |  {24.5}
    |    AdditiveExpr ... {25}
    |        {24.6}
    --- RelationalExpr ... {24} (immediate recursive)
    |        |
    |       '<='
    |        |  {24.7}
    |    AdditiveExpr ... {25}
    |        {24.8}
    --- RelationalExpr ... {24} (immediate recursive)
             |
            '>='
             |  {24.9}
         AdditiveExpr ... {25}

- $anotherVariable
-153
5 * 6 + 7 * 8 < $myVariable
5 div 6 + 7 mod 8 > $myVariable
5 mod $myVariable + 9 <= 123
5 * 6 * 7 + 2 * 3 >= 987 + $myVariable
/book/chapter/title | para/emph
```

{25} AdditiveExpr {24.1 .3 .5 .7 .9} {25.2 .4}

```
                {25.1}
----- MultiplicativeExpr ... {26}
    |         {25.2}
    --- AdditiveExpr ... {25} (immediate recursive)
    |        |
    |       '+'
    |        |  {25.3}
    |    MultiplicativeExpr ... {26}
    |        {25.4}
    --- AdditiveExpr ... {25} (immediate recursive)
             |
            '-'
             |  {25.5}
         MultiplicativeExpr ... {26}

- $anotherVariable
-153
5 * 6 + 7 * 8
5 div 6 + 7 mod 8
5 mod $myVariable + 9
5 * 6 * 7 + 2 * 3
5 * 6 div 7 + 7 mod 8
/book/chapter/title | para/emph
```

{26} MultiplicativeExpr {25.1 .3 .5} {26.2 .5 .7}

```
              {26.1}
   ----- UnaryExpr ... {27}
      |      {26.2}
      --- MultiplicativeExpr ... {26}  (immediate recursive)
      |      | {26.3}
      |   MultiplyOperator ... {34}
      |      | {26.4}
      |   UnaryExpr ... {27}
      |        {26.5}
      --- MultiplicativeExpr ... {26}  (immediate recursive)
      |         |
      |       'div'
      |        | {26.6}
      |   UnaryExpr ... {27}
      |        {26.7}
      --- MultiplicativeExpr ... {26}  (immediate recursive)
               |
             'mod'
              | {26.8}
          UnaryExpr ... {27}
```

```
- $anotherVariable
-153
5 * 6
5 div 6
5 mod $myVariable
5 * 6 * 7
5 * 6 div 7
/book/chapter/title | para/emph
```

{27} UnaryExpr {26.1 .4 .6 .8} {27.2}

```
            {27.1}
   ----- UnionExpr ... {18}
     |
     --- '-'
         | {27.2}
        UnaryExpr ... {27}  (immediate recursive)
```

```
/book/chapter/title | para/emph
```

```
$myVariable
- $anotherVariable
-153
```

{28} ExprToken

```
----- '('
|
--- ')'
|
--- '['
|
--- ']'
|
--- '.'
|
--- '..'
|
--- '@'
|
--- ','
|
--- '::'
|       {28.1}
--- NameTest ... {37}
|       {28.2}
--- NodeType ... {38}
|       {28.3}
--- Operator ... {32}
|       {28.4}
--- FunctionName ... {35}
|       {28.5}
--- AxisName ... {6}
|       {28.6}
--- Literal ... {29}
|       {28.7}
--- Number ... {30}
|       {28.8}
--- VariableReference ... {36}
```

range (XPointer adds various function names, such as 'range' and 'start-point')
acmeFunc

{29} Literal {07.3} {15.3} {28.6}

```
----- '"'
|       |
|     characters (no double quotes)
|       |
|      '"'
|
--- "'"
        |
      characters (no single quotes)
        |
       "'"
```

"a string"
'a string'

{30} Number {15.4} {28.7}

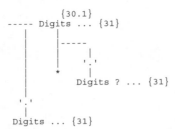

```
              {30.1}
----- Digits ... {31}
|       |
|       |-----
|       |    |
|       |   '.'
|       *    |
|           Digits ? ... {31}
|
'.'
|
Digits ... {31}
```

```
3
3.
3.3
.3
```

{31} Digits {30.1 .2 .3}

```
----- (one or more digits)

3
33
```

{32} Operator {28.3}

```
               {32.1}
----- OperatorName ... {33}
  |        {32.2}
  --- MultiplyOperator ... {34}
  |
  --- '/'
  |
  --- '//'
  |
  --- '|'
  |
  --- '+'
  |
  --- '-'
  |
  --- '='
  |
  --- '!='
  |
  --- '<'
  |
  --- '<='
  |
  --- '>'
  |
  --- '>='

and
or

*

!=
//
```

{33} OperatorName {32.1}

```
----- 'and'
  |
  --- 'or'
  |
  --- 'mod'
  |
  --- 'div'

and
or
```

{34} MultiplyOperator {26.3} {32.2}

```
----- '*'

*
```

{35} FunctionName {16.1} {28.4}

```
         {35.1}
----- QName - NodeType   (Namespaces standard qualified name
                         (but must not be a node type name))

range (XPointer adds various function names,
       such as 'range' and 'start-point')
acmeFunc
```

{36} VariableReference {15.1} {28.8}

```
----- '$'
      |  {36.1}
      QName ...  (Namespaces standard - qualified name (possible prefix))

$myVariable
```

{37} NameTest {07.1} {28.1}

```
----- '*'
   |
   --- NCName ...  (Namespaces standard - an XML name but no ':' in it)
   |     |
   |    ':'
   |     |
   |    '*'
   |
   --- QName ...  (Namespaces standard)

*
acmeNS:*
acmeNS:widget
```

{38} NodeType {07.2} {28.2}

```
----- 'comment'
   |
   --- 'text'
   |
   --- 'processing-instruction'
   |
   --- 'node'

text
node
```

{39} ExprWhitespace

```
----- S ...  (XML standard (space, tab, LF, CR))
```

Glossary

This glossary contains a list of terms related to XML and to the additional topics covered in this book. It includes:

- XML and Xlink concepts, delimiter characters, keywords and production charts
- SGML concepts
- other related ISO and *de facto* standards
- database and publishing-related terminology, including popular image formats.

All bold terms in the body of the book have an entry in the glossary, except for:

- element names belonging to a specific standard document model
- attribute names belonging to elements defined in a specific standard model
- method, class and interface names in SAX and DOM.

All text before the dash, '—', is used to sort the entries.

When a term has more than one definition, each definition is preceded by a number in square brackets, starting at '*[1]*'.

Acronyms are pronounced by spelling out the letters ('XML' is pronounced 'ex-em-el') except when the entry contains '[pronounced ...]'. For example, the JPEG entry contains '[pronounced 'jay-peg']'. To make the pronunciation as clear as possible, the term is sometimes expanded to a commonly known word that contains the sound. For example, the entry for SAX contains '[pronounced 'sax'ophone]'.

A reference to another entry is highlighted in bold typeface. In some cases, a term is not referenced from the main text at all, only from other entries in the glossary. Note that in this case the term does not appear in the index, because the index does not cover this glossary. On the other hand, the index references all bold words in the rest of the book, including terms that do not appear in the glossary, as discussed above.

Symbols and digits

" — Literal delimiter, 'attrib="value"' (alternative to " ' ").

— [1] Reserved name indicator delimiter, prefixing **REQUIRED**, **IMPLIED**, **FIXED** and **PCDATA**, as in '#REQUIRED'. [2] Character separating a URL for an Internet-based document from a subdocument location, http:www.myserver.com/mydoc#chapter2. [3] Also part of character reference delimiter.

% — Parameter entity reference open delimiter, '%entity;'.

& — Entity reference open delimiter, '&entity;'.

&# — Character reference open delimiter, '{'.

' — Literal alternative delimiter, 'attrib='value'' (alternative to ' " ').

(— Group open delimiter, '((a & b) | c)'.

) — Group close delimiter, '((a & b) | c)'.

* — [1] Optional and repeatable indicator, '(a*,b,c+)'. [2] In expressions, used as a wildcard to represent any element name.

+ — Required and repeatable indicator, '(a*,b,c+)'.

, — Sequence connector, '(a,b,c)'.

-- — Comment delimiter (both open comment and close comment), '-- comment --'.

. — In **XPath** expressions, used to represent the current node.

.. — In **XPath** expressions, used to represent the parent node.

/ — In **XPath** expressions, used as a location path step separator.

/> — Empty element close indicator, 'The house<image id="x123" />'.

; — Reference close delimiter, '&entity;'.

: — In **Namespaces**, used to separate the namespace prefix from the element name, as in 'html:h3'.

:: — In **XPath** expressions, used to separate a location direction keyword, such as 'parent' or 'child', from the name of the element, as in 'parent::chapter'.

< — Start-tag open delimiter, '<element>'.

<! — Markup declaration open delimiter, '<!ELEMENT ..>'.

</ — End-tag open delimiter, '</element>'.

<? — Processing instruction open, '<?BREAK page?>'..

= — [1] Value indicator, 'attrib="value"'. [2] In expressions, used to compare two expressions, returning true or false.

> — [1] Markup declaration close delimiter, '<!ELEMENT ..>'. [2] Tag close delimiter, '</element>'. [3] Used in expressions to indicate larger-than comparison, returning true or false.

? — Optional occurrence indicator, '(a?, b, c?)'.

?> — Processing instruction close delimiter, '<?BREAK page?>'.

@ — [1] Used in Internet mail addresses to separate the user ID from the domain name, as in 'neil@bradley.co.uk'. [2] Used in **CSS** to identify an **at-rule**. [3] Used in expressions to indicate an attribute (the name follows).

[— Declaration subset open delimiter, '<!DOCTYPE [...]>'.

] — Declaration subset close delimiter. '<!DOCTYPE [...]>'.

]] — Optional section close delimiter. '`<![INCLUDE[...]]>`'.

I — Optional connector. '`(a|b|c)`'.

16-bit — Character set that uses 16 binary digits, which allows 65,536 values for representing characters. **Unicode** is a 16-bit character set.

32-bit — Character set that uses 32 binary digits, which allows 4,294,967,296 values for representing characters. **ISO/IEC 10646** is a 32-bit character set. See **7-bit** and **8-bit**.

7-bit — Character set or image format that uses 7 binary digits (**bits**) for each character or pixel. The smallest memory unit most computer systems deal with is a **byte**, which is **8 bits**. But data formats that use 7 bits employ the final bit for validating data transmitted between systems (making all values even or odd by setting the last bit on or off accordingly, then checking that no even (or odd) values are received at the other end). The bit combinations '0000000' to '1111111' are used to represent the decimal values '0' to '127'. **ASCII** and **ISO/IEC 646:1991** are 7-bit character sets. More reliable systems have made 7-bit data formats unnecessary. See **8-bit**.

8-bit — Character set or image format that uses 8 binary digits (**bits**) for each character or pixel. The binary values '00000000' to '11111111' are used to represent decimal values '0' to '255'. **ISO/IEC 8859/1** is an 8-bit character set.

A

AAP *(American Association of Publishers)* — Organization of publishers that have defined various standard **DTDs** for **SGML**, which have been used as the basis for the latest **ISO** DTDs. See **ISO 12083**.

absolute link — A **hypertext link** that identifies a resource by its full address. See **relative link**.

absolute path — An **XPath** navigation method that locates an object by its unique identifier, rather than by its contextual location. See **relative path**.

abstract syntax — An **SGML** concept not applicable to XML that allows SGML markup syntax to be configurable, so that a **start-tag** could, for example, be described by '[para]' instead of '<para>'.

accent — A diacritical mark that modifies a base letter. For example, 'é'. The **ISOlat1** set of **entities** defines references for common European accented characters. For example, '`&eacute;`'.

access server — A computer that provides access to remote users, providing transparent access to remote networks. Sometimes called a **remote access server**.

address resolution protocol — See **ARP**.

Adobe Acrobat — A program that displays page images on-screen, or outputs them to paper, using the **PDF** data format. A suitable electronic publishing method when the screen presentation must exactly match page formatting.

agent — A program that operates on a user's behalf, performing its task in the background and delivering results at the end of its task. A **Web** agent may roam over the **Internet** for information of interest to the user.

American Standard Code for Information Interchange — See **ASCII**.

amp — The name of a reserved entity that represents the ampersand character, '&', used to avoid confusing a data character with an entity reference delimiter.

ancestor — A concept derived from the family tree describing an **element** that encloses the subject element, either directly as a **parent**, or indirectly as part of a larger **hierarchy** of elements. For example, a Book element would be the ancestor of a Paragraph, and also of the Chapter containing the Paragraph. See **child** and **sibling**.

ancestor:: — An **XPath** expression that selects an ancestor of the current node, with the given name. See **descendant::**.

anchor — A **tag** embedded in the text that serves as the **source** or **destination** of a **hypertext link**. The link is 'anchored' because it stays with the relevant text if it is moved due to insertions or deletions earlier in the document. Sometimes used to describe an element that serves as both the **target** and **source** ends of a link.

and — Used in an expression in **XPath** to test two sub-expressions, returning true only if both sub-expressions are true. See **or**.

ANY — A keyword used to indicate that an **element** may contain all other elements defined in the **DTD** (including itself). Rarely used in practice, due to the lack of constraint on structure it encourages.

API *(Application Program Interface)* — A specification for the interface of a software package by which other programs can utilize that package. An **XML processor** must have an API through which applications can receive XML data. See **SAX** and **DOM**.

apos — The name of a reserved entity that represents the apostrophe character, ' ' ', used to avoid confusing a data character with an attribute value delimiter.

applet — A self-contained program that runs in a specific environment, usually a **Web browser**. See **applet (Java)**.

applet (Java) — A semi-compiled **Java** program accessed by a **Web browser** for activation on the local system. Source code has an extent of '.java'. Semi-compiled code, or 'bytecode', has an extent of '.class'. Machine-specific compilers are available from http://java.sun.com/download.html.

arc — A connection between two **nodes**, creating a relationship.

architectural form — The use of XML constructs to add a further layer of meaning. A syntax that rests upon XML, just as XML rests upon **Unicode**. Only specialist software applications make use of the additional information. Typically, a processing instruction format, element name, or attribute name and value provides the extra information. See **ICADD** and **XLink** for example applications.

ARP *(address resolution protocol)* — A **TCP/IP** protocol for locating the physical address of a node on the network.

ASCII *(American Standard Code for Information Interchange)* — [pronounced 'ass-key'] The most popular scheme for representing common characters (Latin alphabet, Arabic digits and typewriter symbols) in computer memory. Defined by ANSI *(American National Standards Institute)*. A unique **7-bit** value is assigned to each character, including '65' for the letter 'A' and '49' for the digit '1' (the value of a character should not be confused with a digit character, such as '1'). The values 0 to 31 are non-printing control characters; 32 to 127 represent letters, numbers and symbols. The only relevant alternative is **EBCDIC**, used on IBM mainframe systems. See **ISO/IEC 646:1991**, **ISO/IEC 8859/1** and **Unicode**.

at-rule — A **CSS** rule that is used to create definitions for objects that do not map to elements, such as page layout characteristics. So called because it is identified by a 'commercial at' symbol', '@'.

AttDef[53] *(Attribute Definition)* — The part of an **attribute list declaration** (**AttlistDecl**[52]) that describes one attribute for the **element**, including its name and any restrictions on the value it can take.

ATTLIST keyword — The keyword that identifies an **attribute declaration**, used to declare and define the content of one or more attributes.

AttlistDecl[52] *(Attribute list Declaration)* — The markup used to define attributes and assign them to a specific element. Although there may be more than one attribute list declaration for an element, for compatibility with SGML only one should be used.

attribute — An **element** parameter that modifies or refines the meaning of the element, and consists of a name and a value. The attribute is named to distinguish it from other attributes and values in the same element.

Attribute — See **Attribute**[41].

attribute:: — An **XPath** expression that selects a given attribute of the current node.

Attribute[41] — The name and value of a single attribute instance, embedded in the **start-tag** (**STag**[40]), or **EmptyElemTag**[44].

Attribute definition — A single **attribute** definition, including its name, its requirement status and possibly its default and allowed values. See **AttDef**[53].

attribute list declaration — See **AttlistDecl**[52].

attribute name — The name of a defined **attribute**.

attribute type — An attribute is assigned to a category, such as 'CDATA' (character data) or 'ID' (unique identifier). See **AttType**[54].

attribute value — The value of a specific **attribute** instance. See **AttValue**[10].

AttType[54] *(Attribute Type)* — A category of attribute, applied to a specific attribute. Whenever that attribute is used, its value is simply restricted in some way ('**NMTOKEN**', '**NMTOKENS**' and **enumerated** values) or may also be deemed to have some special significance ('**ID**', '**IDREF**', '**IDREFS**', '**ENTITY**', '**ENTITIES**' and '**NOTATION**').

AttValue[10] *(Attribute Value)* — The value of an attribute as its appears in the element start-tag.

AVI *(Audio Video Interleave)* — Full motion video format developed by Microsoft.

axis — In **XPath**, a direction through the document structure. Ascendents, descendants, parent, children, preceding siblings, following siblings, preceding elements (to the start of the document) following elements (to the end of the document), and attribute lists are all examples. Used in expressions with a keyword and a node filter, separated by double colons, '::', as in 'parent::chapter'.

B

bandwidth — The capacity of a communications channel (the amount of data transferrable in a given unit of time), specified by megabits per second (Mbps). Standard Ethernet has a bandwidth of 10Mbps.

Base Character — See **BaseChar**[85].

base64 — A data encoding scheme that transforms a **binary data** object into plain **ASCII**, so that it can be safely transferred over networks designed to handle only text. There are suggestions around for a special mechanism in XML to be defined to include embedded base64 data, usually representing image data.

BaseChar[85] *(Base Character)* — Part of a compound character, being combined with an accent or other **Ideographic**[86].

Basic Multilingual Plane — See **BMP**.

batch composition — Document format preparation done automatically, usually on many documents in series. A suitable approach only when the source data is self-describing, such as XML documents. See **database publishing**.

batch validation — The comparison of one or more document instances against its (or their) DTD as a single process. The result is a report of errors encountered (if any). See **interactive validation**.

baud rate — The rate at which discrete signal events are transmitted on a communications channel. See **bps**.

binary date — Data that does not conform to a textual encoding scheme. Most **image format**s, particularly **raster image** formats, use binary data files, where each byte represents a combination of pixels. In a binary format, no pre-determined meaning can be given to any particular value, as any value is possible in an image. There can be no 'end-of-file' or 'end-of-line' code.

binary entity — An **entity** with content that is either not XML format, or is XML but is not to be parsed as part of the document. It must be an **external entity**. Typically used for image data (see http://www.cis.ohio-state.edu/text/faq/usenet/graphics/fileformats-faq/part3/faq.html).   See   **parsed entity**.

bit — A 'binary digit'. The smallest unit of information on a computer, taking a value of '0' or '1' (or 'on' or 'off'). Collections of bits make larger units, with values that can be calculated using binary arithmetic ('00' = 0, '01' = 1, '10' = 2, '11' = 3). For example, 8 bits combine to form a **byte**, and a **7-bit** character set uses 7 bits to store unique character values, allowing only 128 possibilities.

Bits Per Second — See **BPS**.

block element — An **element** that contains a block of text, such as a title, paragraph or table cell. When foramtted, the content of a block element is separated from previous and following elements by at least a line break. See **in-line element**.

BMP *(Basic Multilingual Plane)* — The first 65,536 characters of **ISO/IEC 10646**, and equivalent to **Unicode** (though the two standards have diverged slightly as one is updated before the other).

BNF *(Backus-Naur Form)* — See **EBNF**.

bold — A heavy variation of a normal typeface. Cross-referenced terms in this glossary appear in bold typeface.

boolean() — A function in an expression used in **XPath** that returns the boolean value of the enclosed expression. See not().

BPS *(Bits Per Second)* — A measurement of the rate of transfer of data. A 100bps transfer rate means 12 **ASCII** characters are transmitted by one system and received by the other each second.

Browser — An application designed to read and display tagged text, allowing **hypertext links** to be followed. See **HTML Browser**.

BTW — Abbreviation for 'By The Way' used in online conversation. Others include **IMHO** (In My Humble Opinion), **FWIW** (For What It's Worth), **FYI** (For Your Information) and **OTOH** (On The Other Hand).

byte — A unit of memory composed of 8 **bit**s (short for 'by eight'). Using binary arithmetic, a byte can store values between '00000000' and '11111111' (or '0' to '255' in decimal). Currently, most **character set**s use one byte to represent one character, giving 256 combinations for an **8-bit** character set. When one bit is ignored, or used for parity checking, this leaves only 128 character values available in a **7-bit** set, such as **ASCII**. Proposed character sets use two or four bytes for each character, vastly expanding the range of available characters. Some image formats use byte values to represent pixels.

C

CALS *(Continuous Acquisition and Lifecycle Support)* — [pronounced 'kalz'] Set of standards (before 1994 standing for *Computer-aided Acquisition and Logistics Support*), including **DTD**s, **CCITT Group IV**, **CGM** and **IGES**, and an electronic delivery standard for transfer of documentation between defence contractors and the US Department of Defense. Notable for **CALS table**s and the **CALS declaration**. Contact http://www.acq.osd.mil/cals/.

CALS declaration — An **SGML Declaration** defined for use with **CALS** DTD. Notable primarily for extending the number of characters allowed in element and attribute names from 8 to 32.

CALS table — An **SGML** table model defined in the **DTD**s developed in the **CALS** initiative, now used in many other applications due to widespread software support, including **WYSIWYG** editing. Defined in 'MIL SPEC 28001-B Appendix A-50', and refined by the **SGML Open** committee in 1995 (largely superceded by newer, related HTML table model).

canonical — An idea or object reduced to its simplest possible representation. This concept applies to string comparisons when each string may contain the same information, but originally coded using different options.

CAPS *(Computer Aided Publishing System)* — [pronounced 'caps'] Combined database and pagination system, possibly used for on-demand printing, and feasibly involving the use of XML.

carriage return — See **CR**.

Cascading Style Sheets — See **CSS**.

case folding — The act of converting **lower-case** characters to **upper-case** equivalents to assist with string comparisons where differences of case are not relevant. After case folding, the string 'This Text' will match the string 'THIS TEXT', or 'this text'.

catalog — A file containing mappings between a **public identifier** and its **system identifier** counterparts. For example, 'MyEnt' may be mapped to '/ENTS/MYENT.XML' and '-//MyCorp//DTD My DTD//EN' may be mapped to '/ENTS/MYDTD.DTD'. Used by an **entity manager**. See **SGML Open** for a standard catalog format.

catalogue — UK spelling of **catalog**.

CCITT Group IV — Compression scheme for bi-level (on/off pixels, not suited for representing gray scales or colours) bit-mapped (**raster**) image data, optimized for images containing lines of text. Adopted as an **ODA** format (along with CCITT Group III). Adopted as one of the **CALS** standards. May be stored in a **TIFF** file 'wrapper'.

CDATA *(Character Data)* keyword — The keyword that identifies data consisting of normal text characters; no markup recognition is attempted within this data on encountering significant markup delimiter characters.

CData[20] *(Character Data)* — Data consisting of normal text characters; no markup recognition is attempted on encountering significant markup delimiter characters. Part of a Character Data Section (**CDSect**[18]).

CDEnd[21] *(Character Data End)* — The terminating markup delimiters of a Character Data Section (**CDSect**[18]). The characters ']]>' end the special treatment of characters.

CDF *(Channel Definition Format)* — A standard for the use of XML markup to identify a Web site with push capability, including which pages are channel pages, the icon to display, a title and a description of the channel.

CDSect[18] *(Character Data Section)* — A section of the document consisting of normal text characters; no markup recognition is attempted on encountering significant markup delimiter characters. It is bounded by the **CDStart**[19] delimiter, '<![CDATA[', and the **CDEnd**[21] delimiter, ']]>'.

CDStart[19] *(Character Data Start)* — The starting markup delimiters of a Character Data Section (**CDSect**[18]). The characters '`<![CDATA[`' begin special treatment of characters.

ceiling() — Used in an expression in **XPath** to convert a real number into an integer by rounding up to the nearest whole number. See **round()** and **floor()**.

CERT *(Computer Emergency Response Team)* — Organization formed to increase awareness of Internet security issues. Contact cert@cert.org.

CGI *(Common Gateway Interface)* — A standard method for software to dynamically create customized **XHTML** pages, facilitating a two-way exchange of information between the **Web server** and the user of a **Web browser**. A CGI script can be written in any language (though the most popular is Perl), and can therefore access various sources of information, such as an SQL database. One use of a CGI script is to process **form**s that are filled in by the user (using the **Action** attribute), and another is to create and return customized HTML pages based on information gathered from such a form. Contact comp.infosystems.www.authoring.cgi' news group and http://hoohoo.ncsa.uiuc.edu/cgi/interface.html.

CGM *(Computer Graphics Metafile)* — An **ISO** standard (ISO 8632) representing two-dimensional object-based **vector** images. Adopted as part of the **CALS** standard (MIL-D-28003). Contact http://www.agocg.ac.uk:8080/agocg/CGM.html.

Channel Definition Format — See **CDF**.

Char[02] *(Character)* — The character set of XML, from the **ISO 10646** set. Also see **Unicode**.

character — A letter, digit or symbol represented within a computer by a numeric code. Generally grouped into **character set**s.

Character — See **Char**[02].

Character Data — Data that does not contain markup, so markup delimiter characters may be safely used without risk of confusion. See **CData**[20].

Character Data End — The markup construct that identifies the end of a **Character Data Section**. See **CDEnd**[21].

Character Data Section — Part of an XML document that may contain markup delimiter characters which are not to be interpreted as markup. See **CDSect**[18].

Character Data Start — The markup construct that identifies the start of a **Character Data Section**. See **CDStart**[19].

character number — A value that represents a character. For an **8-bit** character set, the number will be in the range 0–255. As the letter 'A' has a value of 65 (decimal) in **ASCII**, its character number would be '65'. **Hexadecimal** notation is often used, especially in **Character Reference**s.

Character Reference — A markup construct that represents a single character (usually a character that is normally interpreted as a markup delimiter or is not possible to generate directly from the keyboard). For example, '`&#1234;`' represents the **Unicode** character with the **hexadecimal** value 1234. See **CharRef**[66].

character set — An ordered set of **character** definitions. A value is assigned to each character shape (or '**glyph**'). The number of characters held in a set is determined by the number of **bits** assigned to each character. Currently, most character sets are **8-bit** sets, holding 256 characters. See **ASCII**, **EBCDIC**, **ISO/IEC 646:1991** and **ISO/IEC 10646**.

CharData[14] *(Character Data)* — The textual content of an XML document, as distinct from the various **markup** constructs.

CharRef[66] *(Character Reference)* — A special form of **entity reference** that has a replacement value of a single **character**. Requires a preceding '#' symbol. For example, '`&#1234;`'. A **hexadecimal** value can be used by inserting the letter 'x' before the digits. For example, '`&#x1F8D;`'.

Chemical Markup Language — See **CML**.

child — A concept derived from family trees that describes an **element** that is enclosed by another element (as part of a **hierarchy** of elements). One element is the child of another, and an element may have several children. For example, a Chapter element may be the child of a Book element, and itself may contain several Section children. See **parent** and **sibling**.

child:: — An **XPath** expression that selects a node by name that is a child of the current node. Abbreviates to nothing, so 'child::para' is the same as 'para'.

Children[47] — The legal content of an element, including text and/or **child** elements.

Choice — See **Choice**[49].

Choice[49] — The content of an element, when defined in the **DTD** to be a choice of one or more elements. The 'I' symbol is used to separate the names of available elements. The alternative model is **Seq**[50] (sequence).

choice connector — The 'I' symbol used to separate the names of available elements, to be used in any order.

client — An application that requests services from a **server** application, usually over a network. For example, a **Web browser** acts as a client to each **Web server** it connects to. See **peer-to-peer**.

CML *(Chemical Markup Language)* — A private initiative to determine an XML markup scheme for chemical formulae. See www.venus.co.uk/omf/cml/doc/index.html.

collapsed space — The replacement of a consecutive **whitespace** characters with a single space character, such as ' [TAB] [CR][CR] [LF][TAB] ' with ' '.

Combining Character — See **CombiningChar**[87].

CombiningChar[87] *(Combining Character)* — Various characters built from two **Unicode** character shapes. This technique avoids having to define thousands of extra characters, and forms part of the **NameChar**[04] rule for defining names of markup constructs.

Comment — See **Comment**[15].

Comment[15] — A **markup** declaration that holds explanatory text not considered part of the document content. Similar to comments in program source code. Comments have no effect on processing and do not appear in published documents. A comment may be inserted by a **DTD** author or by a document author. It is delimited by '<!--' and '-->'.

comment() — A function of a navigation expression used in **XPath** that identifies any **comment** object in the document tree. See **node()**.

Common Gateway Interface — See **CGI**.

compile — The automated conversion of information from a human-readable form into a more efficient, machine-readable format. For example, keywords are converted into numeric tokens, which can be read faster by machine, but are unintelligible to people. A computer program that is compiled (such as C) operates faster than one that is merely **interpreted** (using an **interpreter**) (such as Perl). An XML DTD and even XML documents may be compiled for use with a specific software application in order to improve performance (though often at the expense of usability with other software).

compiler — A software application or module of a larger program that **compiles** information.

component management — The storage of document parts in a document management system that is able to re-create the document or parts of the document at will and allows parts to be shared by many documents.

compose — The process of converting **tagged** data into formatted output, including hyphenation and justification of the text.

composition — See **compose**.

compound document — A document containing more than just text, for example images and sound.

concat() — In an **XPath** expression, used to concatenate strings into a single string.

concrete syntax — In **SGML**, the instructions that define the system environment and choose optional features of the language in the **SGML Declaration**.

conditional Section — See **conditionalSect**[61].

conditionalSect[61] *(Conditional Section)* — A segment of the document that is marked for explicit inclusion (**includeSect**[62]) or exclusion (**ignoreSect**[63]), using a **markup declaration** that includes the 'INCLUDE' or 'IGNORE' keywords respectively. Only allowed in the **external subset** of a **DTD**.

connector — A symbol that connects tokens and describes the relationship between them. The optional connector, '|', indicates a choice of tokens; 'a | b' provides a choice between A and B. The sequence connector, ',', indicates a sequence; 'a , b' specifies that A precedes B.

container element — An element that contains text and/or other elements, enclosed in a **start-tag** and **end-tag** pair. See **empty element**.

contains() — Used in an expression in **XPath** to test for the presence of one string within another. See **starts-with()** and **normalize()**.

content — See **content**[43].

content[43] — The content of an **element**, delimited by a **start-tag** and **end-tag**. An **empty element** has no content.

content specification — See **contentspec**[46].

contentspec[46] — The definition of the content of an **element**, including **child** elements, **mixed text**, or **empty** element.

content particle — See **cp**[48].

content token — Part of a **model group**, defining the use of text, or an **element** or **group** of elements.

control character — A non-visible character that is used by the system to perform special tasks, such as end a line or page of text.

count() — Used in an expression in **XPath** to return the number of matches found by the embedded expression.

cp[48] *(content particle)* — One token in a list of elements in an element declaration, including an occurrence indicator for the named element, which can be '?' (optional), '*' (optional and repeatable) or '+' (must occur and is repeatable).

CR *(Carriage Return)* — A control character used to terminate lines, alone or in combination with **LF** *(Line-Feed)*, by many operating systems. In **SGML**, the RE *(Record End)* is assigned to this character by the **reference concrete syntax**.

CRLF — See **CR**.

crop marks — Marks on a sheet of paper that identify the edge of the page it contains, so that it can be cut (or 'cropped') for binding into a book. See **cross marks**.

cross marks — Marks on a sheet of paper that allow pages to be aligned for folding and binding into a book. See **crop marks**.

CSS *(Cascading Style Sheets)* — A **W3C** standard for applying styles to elements. A 'stylesheet' is a set of instructions (at least one **CSS rule**) held remotely from the elements they refer to. It is 'cascading' because an **in-line** definition overrides a definition at the top of a document, which in turn overrides a definition in a separate stylesheet. Supported by the most popular **Web browser**s. An extended version, known as 'CSS2', is also complete (see www.w3.org/TR/REC-CSS2/), and work has commenced on CSS3. See **XSL**.

CSS declaration — A **CSS** instruction that defines styles for an element, possibly in a specific context, using at least one **CSS rule**.

CSS rule — A **CSS** instruction that defines a style to an element, all or part of a **CSS declaration**.

CSS selector — Each **CSS rule** must start with a 'selector' which identifies an element, or an element in context, that 'trips' this rule.

CSV *(Comma Separated Values)* — A **text file** that uses commas to separate values and line-end characters to separate rows. Typically used as an interchange format between spreadsheet applications and simple **flat-file databases**.

current attribute — An **SGML** attribute requirement option of 'CURRENT', indicating that the attribute value, if not stated, is the same as a previously declared value. For example, if the Section element for section one had a Status value of 'secret', and the Section element for section two had no value, its Status attribute would inherit the value of 'secret'.

D

data content — The element can only contain data, not **child** elements. Not described by a formal rule, but an informal name for any content model that includes the #PCDATA keyword.

data entity — Non-parsable, non-XML data. See **parser** and **XML Entity**. Alternative term for **binary entity**.

data stream — Term used to describe the processing of a data file, character by character, with the first character in the file heading the stream of input to the application. Some data formats are designed to assist processing in a single direction, including XML, which is why the **prolog** must precede the **document instance** (at no point should a **parser** need to 'rewind' to an earlier point in the file).

database — A collection of information, organized to be easily accessible. The term is often used in a stricter sense, to describe a **table**, containing **record**s, or several tables that are interlinked via unique record identifiers. See **flat-file database**, **relational database** and **object database**.

DataBase Management System — See **DBMS**.

database publishing — Publishing directly from a database. Suitable for highly structured information. For example, a bus timetable. The term may be used in a wider sense, to describe publishing of highly organized, self-describing information, such as a collection of XML documents, when it would include **batch composition** as a necessary component of the system.

DBMS *(DataBase Management System)* — The software that provides access to a **database**, controlling concurrent access to the data, and interpreting commands framed in a **query language**.

DDML *(Data Definition Management Language)* — See **schema**.

declaration — A **tag** that is used to help specify the document structure.

declaration subset — A mechanism by which some **declaration**s can contain other declarations, by enclosing them in square brackets, '[' and ']'. For example, the declarations that form all or part of the **DTD** are enclosed in the **doctypedecl**[28].

Default Declaration — See **DefaultDecl**[60].

DefaultDecl[60] — The final part of an attribute definition (**Attdef**[53]), which declares whether the attribute is required, optional, fixed, or has a default value should none be provided by the document author.

default entity — An **SGML** concept (not applicable to XML). An entity that provides a replacement value for all references to non-existent entities. Possibly used to prevent error messages, or replace references to unknown entities with a message, such as 'SOMETHING MISSING HERE'. There can be only one default entity in an SGML **DTD**.

default namespace — A **namespace** that does not have to be made explicit in each element or attribute, by adding a prefix.

default value — The value of an **attribute** when no value is entered by the document author during insertion of the **element** containing that attribute. Alternatively, the value can be pre-defined (FIXED), be REQUIRED or optional (IMPLIED), or take the same value as the previous occurrence of the attribute (CURRENT).

delimiter role — A character or series of characters that identify **markup** embedded within the text have a delimiter role. The '<' character has a delimiter role, sometimes in conjunction with other characters, such as '<!' and '<?'.

descendant — An element that is enclosed either directly or indirectly by another element. All elements are descendants of some other element, except for the **document element** (the 'root' element).

descendant:: — An **XPath** expression that selects a descendant of the current node, with the given name. See **ancestor::**.

descendant-or-self:: — An **XPath** expression that selects all nodes that conform to the given name and are children, or other descendants of the current node. 'self:node()/descendant-or-self::node()' is the same as './/'

descriptive markup — A **markup** scheme that describes the significance of each part of a document, without referring to how the document should appear when published, which is the task of **procedural markup**. Both XML and **SGML** facilitate descriptive markup, but do not enforce it. A descriptive document can easily be translated into procedural markup, but the opposite is not true.

designed document — A document that consists of individually designed pages, and little or no pre-defined structure to the contents. **XML** often has little or no role in such documents. See **structured document** and **templated document**.

DeskTop Publishing — See **DTP**.

digit — A numeric character ('0'–'9'). See **digit**[88].

digit[88] — The characters '0'–'9'. Optionally appearing as part of a name (**Name**[05]), or name token (**Nmtoken**[07]).

Directed Linked Graph — See **DLG**.

DIS *(Draft International Standard)* — An **ISO** standard in progress to becoming an **IS** *(Industry Standard)*.

display property — A CSS property type that is rarely used in HTML stylesheets but is vital for XML as it defines what kind of object the XML element is. For example, a Paragraph element and a Title would be assigned as 'block' types, whereas Emphasis and Subscript elements would be 'in-line'.

DLG *(Directed Linked Graph)* — A system of representing relationships using **arc**s and **node**s. Inherent in the **XML-Data** and **RDF** schemes.

DNS *(Domain Name Server)* — A server that stores the relationships between **domain name**s and **IP address**es (e.g. 'bradley.co.uk' is the domain name for IP address '194.73.182.107').

DocBook DTD — See **OASIS**.

doctypedecl[28] *(document type declaration)* — A markup declaration that appears at the top of an XML **document**, specifying the document element, enclosing the **internal subset** of a **DTD** and pointing to the **external subset**.

document — In this context, an entire XML formatted document, but not including the external DTD subset or other entity. See **document**[01].

document[01] — The top-level rule describing the format of an XML document, including the **internal subset** of a **DTD**.

document element — The outermost **element** in the document **hierarchy**. The ultimate **ancestor** of all elements in the document. The 'root' element.

document entity — The **entity** that is not called in from any other entity, contained in the file that is selected by the user or given to the **parser**. It contains the **document type declaration** and *may* contain the bulk of the **document instance** data.

document instance — The 'real' document, following system and document defining rules. Defines the content of the document, including **markup** and text.

document management — The task of storing and controlling documents. A document management system provides receipt, creation, referencing, retrieval, distribution, output and disposal features. A **database** forms the core of the system, so allowing documents to be located quickly and easily. See **editorial system**.

Document Object Model — See **DOM**.

document structure — The allowed combination of elements in a given document type, including hierarchical and sequential constraints.

Document Style Semantics and Specification Language — See **DSSSL**.

Document Style Semantics and Specification Language – Online — See **DSSSL-O**.

document type declaration — See **doctypedecl**[28].

Document Type Definition — See **DTD**.

DOM *(Document Object Model)* — [pronounced 'dom'estic] A software interface to the document structure, with methods that allow a program to manipulate the elements in a document or read their contents. See www.w3.org/markup/dom/drafts/requirements.html. For event-driven processing see **SAX**.

domain name — The natural language equivalent of an **IP address**. For example, 'bradley.co.uk' is the domain name for IP address '194.193.96.10'. The **IANA** *(Internet Assigned Numbers Authority)* is responsible for coordinating and managing the assignment of domain names, which must be unique (there cannot be two 'bradley.co.uk' names). The database that matches domain names to IP numbers is maintained by Network Solutions Inc. (NSI). Part of the name denotes the type of organization ('.org' = organization, '.com' = commercial, '.co' = commercial, '.edu' = education, '.gov' = governmental). The final part of the name denotes the country (see **ISO 3166**) (omitted for the United States). See www.networksolutions.com or www.nominet.org.uk for UK names.

Domain Name Server — See **DNS**.

Dots Per Inch — See **DPI**.

dotted decimal — The notation used for domain names, which are composed of four numbers, each having 256 possible values. The representation '194.193.96.10' shows these numbers in decimal form (0–255), with dots between them.

down-convert — Term used to describe the process of converting data from an information-rich format, such as XML, to a less rich, or display-oriented format, such as **RTF**. Generally categorized as a **low energy** conversion process. See **up-convert**.

DP *(Draft Proposal)* — See **ISO**.

DPI *(Dots Per Inch)* — A measure of the **resolution** of text or image data as presented on screen or page. Better quality results from a 'higher' resolution. A 600 DPI laser page proof is easier to read than a 72 DPI screen presentation.

DSSSL *(Document Style Semantics and Specification Language)* — [pronounced 'dis-sell'] An **ISO** standard (ISO/IEC 10179:1995) language (based on the Scheme programming language) used to specify transformation and format information relating to **SGML** structured documents, replacing the more limited **FOSI** approach. More recently, used as the basis for the XML Style specification. Released in April 1996. Contact http://occam.sjf.novell.com:8080/dsssl/dsssl96. For a brief tutorial see http://itrc.uwaterloo.co:80/~papresco/dsssl/tutorial.html. See **DSSSL-O**. Due to reliance on programming language concepts, considered too complex for many users, an issue addressed by the development of **XSL** and **XSLT**.

DSSSL Lite— Previous name for **DSSSL-O**.

DSSSL Online— See **DSSSL-O**.

DSSSL-O *(Document Style Semantics and Specification Language – Online)* — Previously called 'DSSSL Lite', this is a subset of the full **DSSSL** standard aimed at adding remote formatting instructions to **SGML** documents. The online version is used to **compose** SGML documents on-screen. This approach potentially offers a more powerful alternative to the current use of **XHTML** on the **Web**, as no prior conversion is needed to a generic **DTD**, and the information provider controls the appearance of the information when it is rendered on the user's system. Contact http://occam.sjf.novell.com:8080/docs/dsssl-o/do951212.htm or http://sunsite.unc.edu/pub/sun-info/standards/dsssl/dssslo.htm.

DTD *(Document Type Definition)* — The instructions that codify rules for a particular type of document. Used by a **parser** to check that a **tag**ged document conforms to the pre-defined document structure rules.

DTP *(DeskTop Publishing)* — An application designed to **compose** and **paginate** documents, and operate on desktop computers, usually employing a **WYSIWYG** interface.

DTR *(Draft Technical Report)* — See **ISO**.

Dynamic HTML — A marketing term used to describe the capabilities of the latest **Web browser**s, but resting on the new capabilities of **HTML 4.0**, in particular the now universal **Id** attribute and the various 'on...' event attributes, as well as **Cascading Style Sheets**.

dynamic information — Information that is constantly updated, usually from a database. A feature of online publishing is the continual update of the information. See **static information**.

E

EBCDIC *(Extended Binary Coded Decimal Interchange Code)* — [pronounced 'ebserdick'] An equivalent to **ASCII** used on IBM mainframe systems. Similar characters are represented, but are assigned different values (in fact there are several variants of EBCDIC). A text file copied from an EBCDIC-based computer to an ASCII-based computer should be translated, or the result will be unintelligible.

EBNF *(Extended Backus-Naur Form)* — A notation for expressing the rules of a language in a formal, precise and terse manner. The **XML** specification uses EBNF to define the syntax of XML documents and **DTD**s. EBNF is very difficult to understand (the charts in this book representing the XML specification are included for this reason).

ECMA *(European Computer Manufacturers Association)* — [pronounced 'eck-ma'] Organization responsible for **ECMAScript** and for the **ISO 8859** character sets. Contact www.ecma.ch.

ECMAScript — [pronounced 'eck-ma-script'] A scripting language employed in **Web browsers**, defining a standard version of the popular 'JavaScript' language, produced by **ECMA**. Formally named ECMA-262.

EDI *(Electronic Data Interchange)* — [pronounced 'ed-dee'] The exchange by electronic means of structured business information, such as inventories and accounts. An abstract concept that requires concrete specifications, such as **EDIFACT**. See www.geocities.com/WallStreet/Floor/ 5815/ for an XML initiative.

EDIFACT — [pronounced 'ed-dee-fact'] An implementation of **EDI** aimed at administration, commerce and transport, and involving a standard character set, and agreed field separators ('+' is a segment tag and data separator, ' ' ' is a segment terminator, ':' is a component data element separator and '?' is a release character) and identifier codes ('5848' stands for 'amount'). Sections of an EDIFACT message may be mandatory or optional, and may be repeatable (simply changing the specification to XML syntax would bring the advantages of cost-effective, off-the-shelf parsers, format translators and output engines, but the parser cannot check field lengths and restricted field contents, until the **XML Schema** standard is widely supported).

editorial system — A **document management** system that includes **workflow** features and is aimed at supporting document production departments.

Electronic Data Interchange — See **EDI**.

element — See **element**[39].

ELEMENT keyword — The keyword that identifies an **element declaration**, used to declare and define the content of an element.

element[39] — An identifiable object in a text document. When the object contains text and/or other elements it is a **container element**, otherwise it is an **empty element** (**EmptyElemTag**[44]). The legal content of an element may be pre-defined in a **DTD** using an **elementdecl**[45]. The attributes allowed may also be pre-defined using an **AttlistDecl**[52].

element declaration — See **elementdecl**[45].

element content — *[1]* An element that may contain **child** elements, but not text (see **mixed content**). All line-feed characters in element content are ignored (not treated as spaces). *[2]* The text and/or child elements contained within an element. An **empty element** has no content.

element instance — One instance of an element appearing in a document. For example, a book that contains nine chapters will have nine Chapter element instances. This term is often used to avoid confusion with an **element declaration**.

elementdecl[45] *(element declaration)* — A markup declaration that contains the specification of an element, including the element name and its allowed content, which may include the names of other elements, so building the **document hierarchy**. It may be associated (by name) with an attribute declaration (**AttlistDecl**[52]), which specifies attributes allowed in this element.

Element Structure Information Set — See **ESIS**.

embed — To place one **element** inside another element. When an element can directly or indirectly contain instances of its own type, such elements are termed **nested** elements.

emphasis — Text that is highlighted to bring attention to its importance, often using bold or italic styling.

Empty Element — See **EmptyElemTag**[44].

empty end-tag — An **SGML** markup minimization feature, where '`</>`' signifies the end of the element last opened in the text stream. Not applicable to XML.

empty start-tag — An **SGML** markup minimization feature, where '`<>`' signifies reoccurrence of the previous element in the text stream. Not applicable to XML.

EmptyElemTag[44] *(Empty Element Tag)* — An empty element is simply an element with no content. The **end-tag** may be omitted, but if present must immediately follow the start-tag. An element represented by a single tag, there being no element content. If the end-tag is omitted, the **start-tag** takes a different form from usual, indicating its empty status to a parser (which should not then look for the end-tag). The end of tag **delimiter** is '`/>`' in place of '`>`'. For example, '`<x></x>`' or '`<x/>`'.

EncName[81] — A parameter of the **Encoding declaration** that specifies the character set in use in the document.

encoding — A parameter of the **XML Declaration**, stating the character encoding in use in the document.

Encoding Declaration — See **EncodingDecl**[80].

EncodingDecl[80] *(Encoding declaration)* — A parameter of the **XMLDecl**[23] and **TextDecl**[77] codes, specifying the character set in use.

Encoding Name — See **EncName**[81].

end-tag — Markup that ends a **container element**, and optionally ends an **empty element**, providing it immediately follows the **start-tag**. See **ETag**[42].

entity — A named object that can be referred to. In **SGML**, a data fragment usually stored in a separate file or delimited by quotes, referred to by an **EntityDecl**[70].

entity declaration — The **markup declaration** that defines an **entity** name and associated content (either directly or by reference). See **EntityDecl**[70].

Entity Definition — See **EntityDef**[73].

entity end — See **EE**.

ENTITY keyword — The keyword that identifies an **entity declaration**, used to declare and define the content of an **entity**.

entity manager — Software designed to locate and access data held in an **entity**. An essential component of a **parser**. May use a **catalog** file to match **public identifier**s to **system identifier**s.

entity reference — Special character sequence identifying an external object (an **entity**) to be inserted at the current point in the data. In the document a **general entity** is used. In the DTD a **parameter entity** is used.

entity set — A group of **entity** declarations within the **document type declaration**. May be held in an **external entity**, where they are typically used to represent extended characters, such as the **ISOlat1** set. See **ENTITY**.

entity text — The content of an **entity**, either enclosed in quotes within the declaration, or referenced from the declaration.

entity type — The type of an **entity**, identifying its content as a sub-document, character data, system specific data or non-SGML data with associated notation name.

entity value — See **EntityValue**[09].

EntityDecl[70] *(Entity Declaration)* — The declaration of an entity name, and the content of the entity, which may be held in the declaration itself, or may be stored elsewhere (in which case the declaration contains a pointer to it).

EntityDef[73] *(Entity Definition)* — The value of a **general entity**, or a reference to the value if it is stored remotely. For parameter entities see **PEDef**[74].

EntityRef[68] *(Entity Reference)* — A reference to a **general entity**. For example, '`&myentity;`'. Declared using a **GEDecl**[71]. For parameter entity references see **PEReference**[69].

EntityValue[09] — A literal value for the entity that appears within the entity declaration.

enumerate — Create a list of possible values, which, for ease of computer processing, are assigned unique numeric values. See **Enumeration**[59].

enumerated type — See **EnumeratedType**[57].

EnumeratedType[57] *(Enumerated Type)* — An Attribute Type (**AttType**[54]) that constrains its value to one of a list of options, being either a list of notation types or of other tokens. For example, '`(draft|final)`' or '`NOTATION (TEX|TIFF)`'.

enumeration — See **Enumeration**[59].

Enumeration[59] — An Attribute Type (**AttType**[54]) that constrains its value to one of a list of tokens. For example, '`(red|amber|green)`'.

EPS *(Encapsulated PostScript)* — A **PostScript** fragment that is not part of a specific page, so may be included in any number of pages, and is considered a separate object that can be stored and transmitted. A file format.

Eq[25] *(Equals)* — The equals symbol, '=', optionally surrounded by spaces, as used to separate attribute names from their values.

equals — See **Eq**[25].

escape code — A character sequence in a **data stream** that generates a special character, or performs some other function.

ESIS *(Element Structure Information Set)* — [pronounced 'ee-sys'] The **ISO** standard (**ISO/IEC 13673:1995**) that describes the content and structure of a document. Used for conformance testing.

ETag[42] *(End Tag)* — A **tag** that indicates the end of the named **element**. For example, '`</book>`'. See **STag**[40].

event-driven — Software that reacts to markup as it is encountered while reading the **data stream**. Such software is unable to 'look ahead' for context, copy or move material to earlier points in the stream. See **tree-manipulation**.

expression — *[1]* A rule that defines part of the **XML** or **XLink** language. The expression comprises at least one **token** and is given a name (the **symbol**). *[2]* A means of locating elements by their context in a document, used to create a **pattern** for matching **XSLT** templates to source document elements, possibly including a **location path** to the element, and to target objects for reuse or extraction (in **XQL**) or linking (in **XPointer**). All three use an expression language defined by the **XPath** standard.

extended — See **extended link**.

extended link — A **hypertext link** concept in **XLink** that allows a number of **resources** to be linked together, so each target points to multiple sources, and all links are two-directional. See **simple link**.

Extended Pointer — A hypertext link that refers to an object by its contextual location.

Extender[89] — Used in **NameChar**[04] only to include special characters.

extender — See **Extender**[89].

Extensible Markup Language — See **XML**.

Extensible Stylesheet Language — See **XSL** (and also **XSLT**).

external entity — An **entity** stored outside the main XML document, usually in a separate file, and located by a **public identifier** or **system identifier**. A **binary entity** *must* be an external entity.

External Identifier — See **ExternalID**[75].

external link — A **hypertext link** to another document, or to part of another document, which is not supported by the **ID** and **IDREF** linking scheme, but is supported by the **HyTime** and **XLink** standards and by **Web browser**s working with **HTML** documents. See **internal link**.

external Parameter Entity — See **extPE**[79].

external Parsed Entity — See **extParsedEnt**[78].

external subset — See **extSubset**[30]

external text entity — An **entity** held in a separate file (an **external entity**) that contains XML data to be parsed and merged into the document.

ExternalID — See **ExternalID**[75].

ExternalID[75] *(External Identifier)* — A **system identifier** and possibly also a **public identifier** that identifies an **external entity**.

extParsedEnt[78] *(External Parsed Entity)* — An **external entity** that contains a fragment of the XML document, so will be parsed as part of the document structure.

extPE[79] *(External Parameter Entity)* — An **external entity** that contains a fragment of the **DTD**.

expression — In **XPath**, a text string that represents a query regarding objects in an XML document. This includes **patterns** (`'position() = 3'`) and **location paths** (`'book/chapter/title'`).

extranet — An **intranet** that has been opened up to selected clients, partners or suppliers, but is still closed to the wider **Internet** community.

extSubset[30] — Part of the **DTD** that is held in a separate file so that it can easily be applied to many documents. Consisting of **extSubsetDecl**[31] declarations. See **internal subset**.

extSubsetDecl[31] — DTD building declarations that are embedded in a remote file or inside an **included section**.

F

false() — An **XPath** expression function that returns the value 'false' in a boolean test.

family — A group of related **fonts**. Perhaps a **roman** typeface, *italic* typeface and **bold** typeface, all based on the same character shape designs.

FAQ *(Frequently Asked Questions)* — Abbreviation for a document, usually made available on the **Intnernet**, that includes answers to the most common questions asked of a particular technology or protocol.

field — A single unit of information in a **record**. Every record in a **table** has the same fields, which can be thought of as the columns of the table. Each column has a name, such as 'name', 'employee number' and 'department', but each record may have a different field value, such as 'J. Smith', '6435' and 'Accounts'. In some ways similar to an **attribute** in XML, and information transferred between an XML document and a database is typically copied from attributes to fields, or vice versa. See **key-field**.

firewall — Software or hardware that protects an internal network from unauthorized external access. A firewall may be needed to separate private **intranet** pages from public **Internet** pages.

FIXED keyword — An attribute type that contains a pre-defined value which cannot be altered by the document author. Used mainly in **architectural form**s.

fixed-pitch — See **monospaced**.

fixed attribute — See **FIXED**.

flat-file — A simple type of **database**, which contains a single **table**. The problem with flat-file databases is that they may contain duplicate information in some of the columns. The **relational database** or **object database** approach avoids this problem. Information is typically transferred between flat-file database systems using the **CSV** format.

flat-file database — See **flat-file**.

floating image — An **XHTML** concept that allows images to be placed in the left or right margin of the document. They are 'floating' because text within the document is not broken by the presence of the images.

floor() — Used in an expression in **XPath** to convert a real number into an integer by rounding down to the nearest whole number. See **round()** and **ceiling()**.

following:: — An **XPath** expression that selects a node that follows the current node in document order. Similar to **following-sibling::**, except that the search goes forward to the end of the document, at all levels in the following structures. See **preceding::**.

following-sibling:: — An **XPath** expression that selects a sibling of the current node, that follows the node in document order. See **preceding-sibling::**.

font — A set of **characters**, including at least the standard alphabet, conforming to a consistent design, traditionally of a fixed size and style, and tailored for a particular output device (though this is no longer typical). Also called 'fount'. Several related fonts may form a **family**.

Formatting Objects DTD — A **DTD** defined as part of the **XSL** standard that is used to describe documents that contain XSL formatting instructions as well as the raw text data. Also called the **FO DTD**. This DTD defines such elements as 'block' to hold text blocks and 'inline-sequence' to hold in-line text.

formal public identifier — An organized and strictly formatted version of a **public identifier**. Each required part of the name is separated from other parts by two solidus characters '//'.

Formatting Output Specification Instance — See **FOSI**.

FOSI *(Formatting Output Specification Instance)* — [pronounced 'fozi'] A **CALS** defined (MIL-STD-28001 Appendix B) vendor-independent format for specifying publishing formats and styles for each tagged object in an **SGML** document. Currently supported by several applications that are designed to work with technical manuals. A precursor to the **DSSSL** and **XSLT/XSL** standards that is rapidly losing favour. A FOSI is in fact an SGML document that conforms to the FOSI 'out-spec' **DTD**. The elements and attributes defined in this DTD are used to describe the formats and styles to be applied to elements defined in the user's own DTD. Contact http://www.neuro.sfc.keio.ac.jp/~ayako/CALS/CALS2/MIL-M-28001.app-b10-. In the example below, the 'e-i-c' element (element-in-context) specifies settings for an element called 'Sub', when it appears within an element called 'Para'. The Charlist element (characteristics list) specifies that the 'Sub' element inherits all style information from the current settings, but then the Font element overrides the point size and baseline positioning to create the effect of subscript text:

```
<e-i-c gi="sub" context="para">
 <charlist inherit="1">
 <font size="6pt" offset="-1pt">
</e-i-c>
```

fragment identifier — The '#' symbol following a URL that indicates the presence of information that identifies a specific fragment of the document.

frame — An **XHTML** feature already supported by the popular **Web browsers**. A single window is split into frames, each frame holding a different document which can be scrolled independently. Particularly useful for holding a table of contents or banner.

FTP *(File Transfer Protocol)* — A standard method for computers to access files on other, remote computers. Used to locate and access documents on servers that supports FTP anywhere on the **Web**. Specified in a **URL** using 'ftp://.....'. See alternative **HTTP** connection method.

FWIW — Abbreviation for 'For What It's Worth' used in online conversation. Others include **BTW** (By The Way), **IMHO** (In My Humble Opinion), **FYI** (For Your Information) and **OTOH** (On The Other Hand).

FYI *(For Your Information)* — *[1]* A document explaining an Internet protocol defined by one or more **RFC**s. To reach the index file, contact ftp://ds.internic.net/rfc/fyi-index.txt. *[2]* Abbreviation used in online conversation. Others include **BTW** (By The Way), **IMHO** (In My Humble Opinion), **FWIW** (For What It's Worth) and **OTOH** (On The Other Hand).

G

G4MIL-R-28002 — The **CALS** standard for a bit-mapped image format and compression scheme (actually **CCITT group IV**).

GCA *(Graphic Communications Association)* — A non-profit association formed in 1986 to apply computer technology to printing and publishing. A promoter of XML and other standards through training and development committees and the organization of conferences, including 'SGML/XML 200*x* Europe' and 'SGML/XML 200*x* (USA)' (at which **SGML Open** holds its committee meetings). Contact http://gca.sgml.com.

GEDecl[71] *(General Entity Declaration)* — A declaration for a **general entity**, which can be referred to in document text using an **EntityRef**[68]. For parameter entities see **PEDecl**[72].

general entity — An **entity** that may be referenced from the general text, as opposed to a **parameter entity**, which can only be used within **markup**. A reference to a general entity is preceded by an ampersand character ('&myent;'). See **general entity reference**.

General Entity Declaration — See **GEDecl**[71].

general entity name — The name of the **general entity**.

generalized — See **generic**.

generalized markup — Document markup that uses **generic coding** techniques, and also defines the document structure to aid automated processing. A generalized markup language is sometimes also called a DMA (Declarative Markup Language). See **SGML** and, of course, XML.

generic — Not designed for a specific purpose. A generic **tag** would describe an important word as an emphasized word instead of an italic word, so allowing a different choice of style to be applied depending on the needs of particular media (for example, italic for paper output, red for screen output). See **generic coding**.

generic coding — Document markup that does not specify format and style explicitly, but refers to general names, such as 'title'. The name identifies a **macro** or stylesheet name which contains the explicit format or style information. This is a significant step toward **generalized markup**.

geometric graphics — See **vector**.

GIF *(Graphic Interchange Format)* — [pronounced 'gif't] The *de facto* **raster** 8-bit image format used with **HTML** on the **Web**. Although the data is compressed (using **LZW**), no information is ever lost. Originally GIF 87, transparent backgrounds were added with **GIF 89**. Up to 256 colours are available, and are chosen from the image content, so a picture of a sunset could contain 256 shades of red. Used in preference to **JPEG** on the Web for graphical logos, button images and rules, but not for natural colour images (particularly photographs). See **X-Bitmap**, **X-Pixelmap** and **PNG**.

GIF 87 — See **GIF**.

GIF 89 — Latest version of **GIF** that adds transparent backgrounds. Also provides multiple pass decompression, slowly improving image quality while allowing the download to be cancelled at any time.

glyph — A graphic symbol, as it appears on paper or screen. Every **character** is realized as a glyph from a specified **font**.

GML *(Generalized Markup Language)* — Precursor to **SGML**, developed in 1969 by IBM. A pioneer of the **generic markup** approach.

granularity — The degree to which an element is divided into **child** elements. A complex **hierarchy** denotes a 'fine' granularity. Simple structures with few levels indicate a 'coarse' granularity. For example, a Name element may simply contain a person's name in full, or may contain child elements that separate the first name from the second name. It should be noted that the cost of **up-converting** legacy data to XML format is affected by the degree of granularity chosen. A fine granularity is likely to involve more manual intervention. A difficult and costly process of this kind may be termed a **high energy** process. The reward for this effort, however, is **low energy**, totally automated **down-conversion** to various output formats. The choice of granularity is therefore dictated by balancing the extra cost of a finer granularity, against the likely future benefits of having a richer database. For example, creation of a list of names, sorted by second name, is much simpler to achieve using a finer granularity, as the required information is unambiguously identified for software extraction

Graph Representation Of property ValuEs — See **grove**.

Graphic Communications Association — See **GCA**.

group — A collection of names, typically **element** names, possibly organized in a strict fashion using the connector symbols, '&', '|' and ',', and possibly quantified using the symbols '*', '+' and '?'. A group is bounded by brackets, '(' and ')'.

grove *(Graph Representation Of property ValuEs)* — An abstract description of a means to represent SGML constructs, which may be given concrete form in terms of a **grove plan**.

grove plan — A strategy for deciding what types of information are to be held in a grove for a specific purpose. For example, one plan may omit **comment** and **processing instruction** tags if they are not needed for the processing that will be performed on the grove.

gt — The name of a reserved entity that represents the greater-than character, '>', used to avoid confusing a data character with a tag delimiter. See also **lt**.

H

head — Start-point of a **hypertext link**. Equivalent to the **source** of a link. Points to the **tail**.

here() - In an **XPointer** expression, indicates the current node.

hexadecimal — The base 16 notation for representing numeric values. In this notation there are 16 value symbols in place of the normal 10. The first 10 are the same, '0' to '9', and the letters 'A' to 'F' represent the additional six values. A = 10, B = 11, C = 12, D = 13, E = 14 and F = 15. Hexadecimal is popular in computing because base 16 is a multiple of two, so is a simple multiple of binary, or base 2. Four bits can represent values between zero ('0000' in binary) and 15 ('1111' in binary), which can be represented by a single hexadecimal digit. Two digits are required to represent the value of a single byte, with 'FF' standing for 255, or '11111111' (binary).

hi-byte — When a single value requires more than one byte to store it, because it may be larger than 255, a sequence of bytes are assigned. Depending on the microprocessor used, a two-byte value may be stored in an unexpected order, **lo-byte** followed hi-byte. To determine the full value stored, the value in the hi-byte is multiplied by 256, then the value in the lo-byte is added to the result.

hierarchy — A concept derived from family trees that describes **element** relationships. The elements Book/Chapter/Section/Paragraph would form a hierarchy, with each layer viewed as one branch of a **tree**, from which smaller branches diverge to create the next level.

high energy — A complex task involving human intervention, which is therefore costly. A term typically used to describe the process of **up-convert**ing data to XML format. See **low energy**.

home page — The initial 'welcome' **Web page** that contains links to other pages on an **Internet** site. Usually named 'index.html' (which is assumed by the **Web browser** if no file name appears in the **URL**).

host — A computer that is connected to the **Internet**. A host may be a server or a client in any particular transaction.

hot spot — An area of a graphical image that acts as a link to associated information when selected.

HTML *(HyperText Markup Language)* — A non-application-specific **DTD** developed for delivery and presentation of documents over the **Web**, to be **compose**d using an **HTML browser**. Contact alt.html and comp.infosystems.www.html newsgroups. See **HTML Level One**, **HTML Level Two** and **HTML Level Three**.

HTML 1.0 — See **HTML Level One**.

HTML 2.0 — See **HTML Level Two**.

HTML 3.0 — A proposed version of HTML that was never accepted due to its complexity. This version was abandoned, but some of its ideas were later incorporated into **HTML 3.2**.

HTML 3.2 — See **HTML Level Three**.

HTML 4.0 — See **HTML Level Four**.

HTML browser — A **browser** application that understands and **compose**s from HTML markup.

HTML Level Four — Latest version of **HTML** (4.0), released by the **W3C** on 18 December 1997. It can be downloaded from www.w3.org/TR/REC-html40. An **SGML** application, including a **DTD**. Includes support for **frame**s, more complex tables, and attributes to support processing via a **DOM**.

HTML Level One — First and universally supported version of **HTML**. Loosely related to **SGML** (a **DTD** was later retro-fitted). No support for **form**s, tables or **frame**s. Superseded by **HTML Level Two**.

HTML Level Three — Most widely adopted version of **HTML**. Released June 1996. It can be downloaded from www.w3.org/pub/WWW/TR/REC-HTML32.dtd. An **SGML** application, including a **DTD**. Includes support for tables and **frame**s. Now superseded by **HTML Level Four**.

HTML Level Two — Second and well-supported version of **HTML**. Closely related to **SGML**, including a **DTD**. Includes support for **form**s. Superseded by **HTML Level Three**.

HTML-aware — An application that is able to produce or understand **HTML** markup, such as a Web browser or authoring package.

HTML+ — See **HTML**.

HTTP *(HyperText Transfer Protocol)* — The commonest means of communication between a **Web server** and **Web browser**, using a **URL**. Used by **Anchor** elements in **HTML** to locate and access documents on servers that support HTTP anywhere on the Web, 'http://www. ...'. Contact ftp://info.cern.ch/pub/www/doc/http-spec.txt.Z. See **HTTP 1.1** and **HTTPS**. Also see **FTP**.

HTTPS *(HTTP Security)* — A variation of HTTP that provides security for online transactions, using the SSL scheme. Also called **S-HTTP**.

HTTP 1.0 — See **HTTP**.

HTTP 1.1 — A new version of HTTP that allows multiple transactions without having to reconnect to the server each time, so saving time.

hyperlink — See **hypertext link**.

hypermedia — The same concept as **hypertext**, with the addition of allowing a mix of information types, including audio and visual media. See **HyTime** and **multimedia**.

Hypermedia/Time-based Document Representation Language — See **HyTime**.

hypertext — Text that does not follow a single narrative flow. A **hypertext link** allows the reader to follow an alternative path through a document. In electronic versions of traditional documents, this may mean simply activating references to other parts of the text. Sometimes, the 'text' part of the name is taken to mean any part of a document, including images, and the term is then used interchangeably with **hypermedia**.

hypertext link — A link between a **source** reference and a **target** object. Sometimes called a 'hyperlink'. Such links enable the creation of **hypertext** documents. See **ID** and **IDREF**, **XLink** and **Hytime**. See **absolute link** and **relative link**.

HyperText Markup Language — See **HTML**.

HyperText Transfer Protocol — See **HTTP**.

HyTime *(Hypermedia/Time-based Document Representation Language)* — Standard mechanism for use of **SGML** to represent time-based data such as music, animation or film. Released in 1992, and defined as **ISO/IEC 10744**. See **HyTime application**. Several techniques allow **hypertext** linking between SGML documents and between SGML and other format documents, including methods that identify target objects by their location in the file. Contact http://www.sgmlopen.org/sgml/docs/library/archform.html and http://www.techno.com/TechnoTeacher/HyTime.html.

HyTime application — A **HyTime**-compliant **DTD**, including **HyTime elements** that conform to a **HyTime architectural form**.

HyTime architectural form — An **architectural form** defined in the **HyTime** standard. Specific attribute names and value are recognized by a HyTime-aware application.

HyTime element — An **SGML** defined **element** that includes **attributes** and attribute values recognizable to a **HyTime** application. An attribute called 'HyTime' takes a value that identifies the **HyTime architectural form** – for example '`hytime NAME #FIXED 'clink'`'.

I

IANA *(Internet Assigned Number Authority)* — Authority responsible for assigning default **port numbers** to common applications on the **Internet**. Also responsible for character set identifiers, and the current list can be accessed from ftp://ftp.isi.edu/in-notes/iana/assignments/languages (the procedure for proposing a new variant is described in **RFC 1766**. See **IanaCode**[36]).

IanaCode[36] — A language identifier defined by the **IANA** (the *Internet Assigned Number Authority*), used for variants not covered by **ISO 639**. Part of the **Langcode**[34] rule, which is used in the **xml:lang** attribute.

ICADD *(International Committee for Accessible Document Design)* — A committee formed in 1992 to promote access to documents by print-impaired readers. An ICADD-compliant **DTD** uses **fixed attribute**s to map complex structures to a simpler pre-defined document structure. The DTD effectively carries information on how to convert a **document instance** to another document conforming to the ICADD DTD. Once converted, existing software can represent the contained information in various forms suitable for those who are print-impaired, including Grade 2 Braille, large print and voice synthesis. Included in **ISO 12083** (the SGML DTD for general book and periodical publishing). See **SDA**. See www.sil.org/sgml/ICADDiso.html.

ICR *(Intelligent Character Recognition)* — An improved form of **OCR**, which does not use pre-defined templates to locate characters on an image. The ICR software understands the general shape of each character, and analyses lines and curves to deduce the character, so is not restricted to specific **font**s.

id() — A function in an expression used in **XPath** that selects the node with the given unique identifier. It can only be used at the start of an **absolute path**. See **key()**.

ID keyword — The keyword that defines an **attribute** to be the **target** of an **internal link**. The 'identifier' keyword. See **IDREF**.

identifier type — The type of **public identifier**, '-//', (unregistered), '+//' (registered) or 'ISO ...//' (ISO defined).

Ideographic — See **Ideographic[86]**.

Ideographic[86] — A category of character in **ISO/IEC 10646**.

IDREF keyword — The keyword that identifies an attribute as one that references another element. The value of this attribute must match the value of another attribute of type **ID** in another element.

IDREFS keyword — The keyword that identifies an attribute as one that contains several values of type **IDREF**.

IEC *(International Electrotechnical Commission)* — Organization working on standards, sometimes in partnership with the **ISO**. The next version of **SGML** will be labelled 'ISO/IEC 8879'. Contact www.hike.te.chiba-u.ac.jp/ikeda/IEC/.

IETF *(Internet Engineering Task Force)* — The international community (comprising network designers, operators, researchers and vendors) concerned with the smooth operation and future of the **Internet** architecture. An IETF working group defined **HTML**, but this group dissolved in 1995 after defining version 2.0 (the role was taken over by the **W3C**). Contact www.ietf.org/.

IGES *(Initial Graphics Exchange Specification)* — A three-dimensional **vector** CAD drawing data format. Used as part of the **CALS** standard (MIL-D-28000).

ignorable whitespace — Spaces and line-end codes that occur directly within elements that are defined in a DTD to contain only other elements (not #PCDATA). This whitespace is deemed not to be part of the content of the actual document, but only appears to format the tags.

Ignore[65] — A sub-rule of **ignoreSectContents[64]** that helps distinguish characters in an ignored section from embedded ignored section contents.

IGNORE keyword — The keyword that identifies a segment of the document (the **ignoreSect[63]**) which is not to be processed. Replacing this keyword with 'INCLUDE' enables processing.

ignore Section — See **ignoreSect[63]**.

ignore Section Contents — See **ignoreSectContents[64]**.

ignoreSect[63] *(ignore Section)* — A section of the document marked for non-inclusion. Enclosed declarations are to be ignored by parsers building the document model. See **includeSect[62]**.

ignoreSectContents[64] *(ignore Section Contents)* — The content of an excluded portion of the document (an **ignoreSect**[63]), which is not processed, but may include further, embedded ignored sections. All the content is ignored, even if an embedded include section is present.

image format — A data format that is used to store graphic data, as opposed to text data. Two main categories are **raster** and **vector** types. On the **Internet**, **GIF** and **JPEG** are commonly used, but **PNG** should also be popular. **CGM** (vector) is used for technical drawings and publishers tend to use **TIFF** (raster). Compression techniques such as **LZW**, **JPEG** and **CCITT Group IV** are used to reduce the file size (a monochrome A4 sized image at 300 dpi would be over one megabyte if uncompressed, but Group IV would typically reduce it to about 30 kilobytes, assuming it comprised mainly of lines of text (this format is used by FAX machines)). Unlike **text format**s, even uncompressed image formats are rarely readable due to the need to keep the file size down. See www.cis.ohio-state.edu/text/faq/usenet/graphics/fileformats-faq/part3/faq.html.

image map — An **Internet** concept. Areas within an image, such as a circle or rectangle, can be identified and made active. When the mouse is clicked on an image associated with a map, the coordinates of the cursor are transmitted to the **Web server**, which uses the map coordinates to determine whether an active area has been selected, and an appropriate script is activated. This is termed a 'server-sided' image map. Some **Web browser**s can link areas directly to **URL**s specified in the **XHTML** page. This, more direct method, is called 'client-sided'. Typically, an image map is used to provide an attractive menu screen that accesses other **page**s. See the **Ismap** attribute.

IMHO — Abbreviation for 'In My Humble Opinion' used in online conversation. Others include **BTW** (By The Way), **FWIW** (For What It's Worth), **FYI** (For Your Information) and **OTOH** (On The Other Hand).

IMPLIED keyword — The keyword that identifies an attribute which does not have to be explicitly given a value by a user. There may be a default value assigned in the DTD. If not, the application must decide on a default action (if any) to take. See **REQUIRED**.

implied attribute — See **IMPLIED**.

in-line — *[1]* An object that is embedded in a sequence of other objects, such as a Paragraph element that follows and precedes similar text structures. See **out-of-line**. *[2]* Element content that does not force a **line break** in the flow of text. See **in-line element**. *[3]* An element that identifies a **hypertext link** which is embedded with (or surrounds) the referencing text, so moves with that text when earlier text is added or deleted. See **in-line link**.

in-line element — An element that does not imply a line break in the flow of text. Typical examples are Emphasis, Name, Superscript and Xref elements. See **block element**.

in-line link — A **hypertext link** that is specified by an element embedded in (or around) the text that forms the **source** of the link. The benefit of this approach is that the source part of the link is maintained if preceding text is edited, because the linking element is 'anchored' to the reference text. See **out-of-line** link.

in-line style — A style definition that is applied to a particular instance of an element in one document, giving document authors the ability to 'design' a page, but a wasteful technique when every instance should be styled the same. See **stylesheet**.

inbound — An **XLink** link with a destination that is the resource embedded within the link markup. The opposite of an **outbound** link.

INCLUDE keyword — The keyword that identifies an included section (**includeSect**[62]). The content must be included in **XML processor** output (in other words, it has no effect but may be easily changed to **IGNORE** and back as required).

include section — See **includeSect**[62].

includeSect[62] *(include Section)* — A section of the document explicitly marked for inclusion in **XML processor** output. It has no effect on the document in itself, but it may be changed to an **ignore Section** at any time by changing the keyword from '**INCLUDE**' to '**IGNORE**'.

inferior — See **subscript**.

infobahn — An alternative term used for the 'information superhighway' (the **Internet**).

information superhighway — An alternative term used for the 'infobahn' (the **Internet**).

insignificant whitespace — Spaces, tabs, and **line break** codes which are not considered to be part of the document text, but are only used to make markup easier to read, so should not appear when the document is presented. See **significant whitespace**.

instance — A specific document that conforms to a class of documents, possibly identified using a **DTD** or an **XML Schema** model (an **XML application**).

interactive validation — Comparison of an XML DTD with a document instance that should conform to it, while that document is being created or edited. A technique used by XML-aware text editors to prevent document structure rules from being broken. See **batch validation**.

internal entity — An **entity** that exists within the main XML document, and is named and stored within an **entity declaration**. The content is delimited by quote characters. See **external entity**.

internal link — A **hypertext link** that has a **source** point and a **target** point in the same document. See **external link**.

internal reference — See **internal link**.

internal subset — Part of a **DTD** that is stored at the top of a document instance, allowing a document author to add document-specific characteristics. See **external subset**.

internal text entity — A **text entity** that includes the replacement text inside the **entity declaration**. See **external text entity**.

International Committee on Accessible Document Design — See **ICADD**.

International Electrotechnical Commission — See **IEC**.

International Organization for Standardization — See **ISO**.

International Standards Organization — See **ISO** (which, despite appearances, is not actually an abbreviation of this name, and in any case is properly called the 'International Organization for Standardization').

Internet — Scheme for connecting computer systems using the **TCP/IP** network protocols, originating in US defence, gaining popularity within universities, then business, and latterly as a general platform for the **Web** and electronic mail. Overseen by the **IETF**. For details on standards see www.ietf.cnri.reston.va.us/1id-abstracts.

Internet Assigned Number Authority — See **IANA**.

Internet Engineering Task Force — See **IETF** .

Internet protocol — The Internet supports a number of communication protocols, including **HTTP** (the *HyperText Transfer Protocol*) and **FTP** (the *File Transfer Protocol*), file (local file access), gopher, mailto, news, telnet, rlogin, tn3270 and wais (*Wide Area Information Servers*).

Internet server — An application that accepts requests from other systems connected to the Internet, returning the data requested. A form of Internet server that accepts **HTTP** requests for **HTML** documents is termed a **Web server**.

InterNIC — The organization responsible for assigning unique **IP addresses** (or blocks of numbers) to individuals, organizations and companies, or to intermediaries (the access providers). Contact User Assistant Services on 1-703-742-4777.

interpret — The step-by-step process of a software application that reads a data file containing instructions that are mainly designed to be human legible. This is known to be a slow process, and must be repeated each time the file is read. To improve speed, such information is often processed by a **compiler** (though the resulting compiled file may not be readable by other software not familiar with the compacted format).

interpreter — A module of a larger program that needs to read data designed to be also human-readable. See **interpret**.

intranet — A local 'closed' version of the **Internet**, for access by a local community (typically by company employees) using tools developed for the Internet, including **Web browser**s. See **extranet**.

inverted word index — The index created by a **search engine** of the words found in the document.

IP *(Internet Protocol)* — The method by which computers connected to the **Internet** communicate with each other. See **TCP** and **IP address**.

IP address — Unique **Internet** host identifier number, for example '145.123.252.231'. For ease of use they are associated with easier to remember **domain name**s, such as 'bradley.co.uk', on a **DNS**.

IP number — See **IP address**.

IPng — See **IPv6**.

IPv6 — The 'next generation' of **IP address**, which allows for many more unique machine identifiers, data security, support for mobile computing and many other initiatives. Developed by the **IETF**.

IRV *(International Reference Version)* — Standard version of **ISO/IEC 646:1991**, using the currency symbol, '¤', in place of the dollar character, '$', found in **ASCII**.

IS *(International Standard)* — A standard released by the **ISO**.

ISO *(International Organization for Standardization)* — [pronounced 'eye-so'] The organization responsible for release of the **SGML** standard under the designation 'ISO 8879' and various other standards. Most of the related standards discussed in this book are released by the working group **WG8**. An 'IS' is an International Standard. A DTR is a 'Draft Technical Report'. Located at 'ISO Central Secretariat/1, rue de Varembe/CH-1211 Geneva 20/Switzerland'. The name 'ISO' is not an abbreviation, but is intended to describe equality, just as it is used in a name such as '*iso*sceles' (a triangle with two *equal* sides).

ISO 10179 — See **DSSSL**.

ISO 10180 — See **SPDL**.

ISO 10744 — See **HyTime**.

ISO 12083 — Ratified versions of the **AAP DTDs**. Devised for general publishing needs.

ISO 2022 — A standard for extending the range of a character set by the use of the **ESC** 'escape sequence' codes, which switch in and switch out alternative blocks of characters.

ISO 3166 — A list of two-letter country codes, such as 'UK' (United Kingdom), as used in e-mail addresses such as 'neil@bradley.co.uk' and in **xml:lang** attributes to specify a dialect, such as 'en.UK' and 'en.US'.

ISO 639 — Definition of codes specifying the language of an **entity**. For example, 'EN' identifies the English language. Used in the **xml:lang** attribute. See **IANA**.

ISO 646 — See **ISO/IEC 646:1991**.

ISO 8632 — See **CGM**.

ISO 8859 — A group of character sets now controlled by the **ISO**, but originally defined by **ECMA**. See **ISO/IEC 8859/1** for one common character set in this group.

ISO 8859/1 — See **ISO/IEC 8859/1**.

ISO 8879 — See **SGML**.

ISO 8879:1986 — See **SGML**. '1986' is the year of issue.

ISO 9069 — See **SDIF**.

ISO 9070 — Official scheme for determining an **owner identifier** in a **formal entity declaration**.

ISO owner identifier — An **external entity** that has been defined by the **ISO**, and has owner details consisting of the ISO publication number. For example 'ISO 8879:1986'. The first part of a **formal public identifier** referring to an ISO-owned entity.

ISO text description — The formal text description of an **ISO**-defined **entity** within a **formal public identifier**. For example, the text description for one of the character entity sets is 'Added Latin 1'.

ISO/IEC 10179 — See **DSSSL**.

ISO/IEC 10180 — See **SPDL**.

ISO/IEC 10646 — An **ISO**-defined **32-bit** coded **character** set for information interchange. See **ASCII** and **ISO/IEC 646:1991**. It defines a unique computer value for 4,294,967,296 characters. The lower seven bits correspond to the **ASCII** (US) **7-bit** character set, the lower eight bits correspond to **ISO/IEC 8859/1** (Latin-1), and the lower 16 bits correspond to the **Unicode** character set.

ISO/IEC 10744:1991 — See **HyTime**.

ISO/IEC 13673:1995 — See **RAST**.

ISO/IEC 646:1991 — The **ISO** defined **7-bit** coded **character set** for information interchange. Almost identical to **ASCII**, from which it is derived. See the first 128 entries of the **ISO/IEC 8859/1** character set. Also see **ISO/IEC 10646**.

ISO/IEC 8859/1 — A **character set** based on **ASCII**, but adding symbols and European accented characters (see **ISOlat1**) by employing an **8-bit** character set. Used in **HTML**, Microsoft Windows and some UNIX systems. See also **ISO/IEC 646:1991**, of which it is a superset, and both **Unicode** and **ISO/IEC 10646**, of which it is a subset.

ISO/IEC 8859/2 — A **character set** based on **ASCII**, but adding characters for Croatian, Czech, Hungarian, Polish, Romanian, Slovak and Slovenian languages.

ISO/IEC 8859/3 — A **character set** based on **ASCII**, but adding characters for Esperanto, Maltese, Turkish (though 8859/5 is now preferred for this language) and Galician languages.

ISO/IEC 8859/4 — A **character set** based on **ASCII**, but adding characters for Latvian, Lithuanian, Greenlandic and Lappish languages.

ISO/IEC 8859/5 — A **character set** based on **ASCII**, but adding characters for Cyrillic characters to cover Byelorussian, Bulgarian, Macedonian, Russian, Serbian and Ukrainian languages.

ISO/IEC 8859/6 — A **character set** based on **ASCII**, but adding characters for the Arabic language.

ISO/IEC 8859/7 — A **character set** based on **ASCII**, but adding characters for modern Greek.

ISO/IEC 8859/8 — A **character set** based on **ASCII**, but adding characters for Hebrew.

ISO/IEC 8859/9 — A **character set** based on **ASCII**, similar to 8859/1, but replacing Icelandic characters with Turkish characters.

ISO/IEC 8859/10 — An **character set** based on **ASCII**, but adding Lappish, Nordic and Inuit characters.

ISO/IEC 8879 — Official designation of the update to the **SGML** standard.

ISO/IEC TR 9573 — Technical report complementing **ISO 8879**, which includes techniques for encoding general text, tables, mathematical formula and Japanese text. The mathematical structures are widely supported by software, but tables are commonly coded using the **CALS table model**.

ISO639Code[35] — A language identifier that conforms to the **ISO** standard **ISO 639**.

ISOdia *(ISO Diacritics)* — A **character set**, grouped under **formal public identifier** 'ISO 8879:1986//ENTITIES Diacritical Marks//EN', consisting of marks that are added to letters such as '¨' (German umlaut) and '´' (French acute).

ISOgrk1 *(ISO Greek Letters)* — A **character set**, grouped under **formal public identifier** 'ISO 8879:1986//ENTITIES Greek Letters//EN', consisting of Greek letters such as '&Agr;' (Alpha Greek).

ISOlat1 *(ISO Added Latin 1)* — A **character set**, grouped under **formal public identifier** 'ISO 8879:1986//ENTITIES Added Latin 1//EN', consisting mostly of European accented letters such as 'é'.

ISOnum *(ISO Numeric and Special Characters)* — A **character set**, grouped under **formal public identifier** 'ISO 8879:1986//ENTITIES Numeric and Special Graphic//EN', consisting mostly of fractions such as '⅜', mathematical symbols such as '÷' and currency symbols such as '¥'.

ISOpub *(ISO Publishing)* — A **character set**, grouped under **formal public identifier** 'ISO 8879:1986//ENTITIES Publishing//EN', consisting of characters used in publishing, such as ' ' (em space) and 'ﬁ' (fi ligature (the 'f' and the 'i' character are merged into a single symbol)).

ISOtech *(ISO General Technical)* — A **character set**, grouped under **formal public identifier** 'ISO 8879:1986//ENTITIES General Technical//EN', consisting mostly of mathematical symbols such as '∞' (infinity).

italic — Characters that are slanted and cursive (script-like), as in '*italic*'. See **roman**.

J

Java — A multi-platform object-oriented programming language developed by Sun. Originally developed in 1992, it was intended to be embedded in consumer devices. In 1995 it was enhanced, and aimed at **Internet** applications. Semi-compiled Java code modules, or **applet**s, are accessed by a **Web browser**, interpreted or compiled (just-in-time compilation), then executed on the local machine. Platform independence includes machine and operating system neutral interfaces, including a graphical user interface. Contact http://Java.sun.com and comp.lang.java newsgroup.

Java API XML — See **JAX**.

JPEG — [pronounced 'jay-peg'] Popular 24-bit **raster** image format devised by the Joint Photographic Experts Group. An efficient compression scheme, but at the cost of accuracy as it does not faithfully reproduce the original image, and is therefore described as a 'lossy' format. May be stored within a **TIFF** file 'wrapper'. Used on the **Web** and **Internet** in general, in preference to **GIF** for natural colour images, particularly photographs, but not for button images, rules or logos. See **PNG**.

K

key() — A function in an expression used in **XSLT** that selects the node with the given unique key identifier. The first parameter names a key set, as defined using the **Key** element.

key-field — A **field** with the special property that it must contain a different (unique) value in every **record** in the **table**. It is especially useful in a **relation** database, because it allows information stored across a number of tables to be unambiguously linked.

keyword — A word appearing in **markup** that identifies the purpose of the tag, or some part of it. For example, 'IGNORE' is a keyword that identifies a portion of the document to be ignored.

L

Langcode[34] — A human language identifying code, possibly user defined, but preferably an **ISO** or **IANA** defined code.

language — *[1]* Defined **markup** scheme. See **meta-language**. *[2]* Part of a **public identifier** that indicates the human language used in the data contained in the **entity**. English text contains the identifier 'EN'.

Language Code — See **Langcode**[34].

Language Identifier — See **LanguageID**[33].

LanguageID[33] — A human language identifying code, possibly user defined, but preferably an **ISO** or **IANA** defined code, and possibly including a subcode that identifies a regional dialect.

last() — A function in an expression used in **XPath** that returns the location of the last node in its list of siblings, as returned by the expression. Usually used for comparions, such as '[not(position() = last())]'. See **position()**.

L^{A}T$_E$X — [pronounced 'lay-teck'] Popular **macro**-based extension to the **T$_E$X** typesetting language, facilitating **descriptive markup**.

leaf — A node that has no sub-nodes. In **DTD** markup, an **empty element** or element that contains only text. In document markup, an element that contains no child elements or text (pseudo element).

Letter — See **Letter**[84].

Letter[84] — A subset of the **Unicode** character set containing characters that are deemed to be described as 'letters'.

LF *(Line-Feed)* — Special character used to end a line in **ASCII** and **ISO/IEC 646:1991**. Theoretically, the action of moving down one line, with the carriage return (**CR**) used to move back to the left edge of the page, though operating systems vary in their usage of one or both of these characters to start a new line.

line break — A break in a line of text due to the presence of the right edge of the page or border of the screen, or because a line break control character (or combination) is present. See **CR** and **LF**.

line-feed — See **LF**.

link — A connection between two or more resources, allowing users to 'follow' a link from one resource to another. See **hypertext**.

link database — See **linkbase**.

linkbase — An **XLink** document that contains sets of third-party links between other documents.

linked stylesheet — The term used to describe a **stylesheet** conforming to the **CSS** standard which is held separately from the document or documents to which it applies.

linking element — An **element** that contains an **attribute** that identifies another **resource** (of possible interest to the reader).

lo-byte — When a value is too large (greater than 255) to be stored in a single byte, two bytes must be used. This gives 256 multiplied by 256 possible values (65,536), and is known as a **16-bit** value. But one byte must be identified as the one that increments by one each time the other reaches 255. This is the **hi-byte**. The other byte is the lo-byte.

local-part() — Used in an **XPath** expression to extract the local name part of an element name that includes a **Namespace** prefix, as in 'h3' from 'html:h3'. See **namespace()**.

local resource — A resource that is embedded within link markup, so does not need to be referenced.

location path — A form of **XPath** expression that is used to unambiguously identify one or more objects within an **XML** document.

locator — In **XLink**, something that points to a resource. A 'locator' is actually an attribute value in a **linking element**.

low energy — A process that is fully or highly automated, relatively effortless to perform (once the necessary software filters are written), and therefore cost efficient. Often used to describe conversions from XML format to other formats (known as a **down-convert**ing process). See **high energy**.

lower-case — Small letters. The lower-case equivalent of the **upper-case** letter 'A' is 'a'. The name is derived from the fact that these **character**s were found in the lower part of the printer's type case.

lt — The name of a reserved entity that represents the less-than character, '<', used to avoid confusing a data character with a tag delimiter. See also **gt**.

LZW — An compression scheme for **image format** data, owned by CompuServe and used in **GIF**.

M

macro — A group of typesetting instructions that may be activated by reference to a name. One instruction replaces many, and may take a meaningful name. A feature of **generic coding** schemes. For example, a **macro call** named 'Title' will activate a **macro definition** of the same name (it may contain instructions to centre the following text, and compose it in 18pt Helvetica typeface). An equivalent feature, termed 'style-sheets', is found in some modern word processors and DTP systems.

macro call — A named reference to a **macro definition**. See **macro**.

macro definition — A collection of one or more **markup** tags given a name for use by a **macro call** in the **data stream**. See **macro**.

many-to-many — A term used to describe relationships between items in separate domains. Most frequently found describing records in separate tables of a **relational database**, where a many-to-many relationship, such as 'an author (possibly) writes many documents and a document is (possibly) written by many authors' would be normalized into a more manageable form by adding an intermediate table, with **one-to-many** relationships to the original two tables. Also see **one-to-one**.

markup — A **tag** added to electronic data to specify style (**descriptive markup**) or add structure (**procedural markup** or **generalized** markup) to the data. In XML, a document component is identified by an **element**[39].

markup declaration — A special tag in XML that is *not* used to mark up a document, but is used for many other purposes, such as to build the document structure rules (the **DTD**), identify and locate each **entity** or define alternative document segments. Delimited by '<!' and '>' characters. See **markupdecl**[29].

Markup Declaration[29] — See **markupdecl**[29].

markup delimiter — A character or characters that signify the start or end of **markup** embedded in the text. In XML, some markup delimiters are '<', '</', '>', '/>', '<?', '?>', '<!', '&', '%' and ';'. If these characters are required as data, they are represented by an **entity reference** such as '<' (less than, '<'). In **SGML**, they may be changed in a **variant concrete syntax**.

markup language — A computer language that involves the use of pre-defined tags inserted into text. The tags either describe the meaning of the text (**XML**) or specify how to format the text for presentation (see **RTF**, **XHTML** and **TROFF**).

markup minimization — A feature of **SGML** (and to some extent **HTML**) whereby some parts of a tag (or even the whole tag) can be safely omitted as its presence can be implied. XML does not have any minimization features.

markupdecl[29] — The various markup declaration tags that define **entities** and construct a **DTD**.

MathML — A standard from the **W3C** for encoding of mathematical formulae using XML markup, described using an XML **DTD**. As with earlier schemes, such as part of the **ISO 12083** standard, some of the tags describe the formatting of a formula, but to this model is added another which describes the content of the formula logically, making it possible to compare formula when searching data. MathML is designed to be compatible with both ISO 12083 and T_EX, to the extent that data can be automatically converted into MathML. Work began in 1994, and version 2 is now complete. See www.w3.org/TR/MathML2/.

MCF *(Meta-Content Framework)* — A proposal for an XML-based standard to describe information about information (meta-data). See **XML-Data** and **RDF**.

meta-data — Data about data, existing only to identify or describe some 'genuine' information. In a book, the table of contents and index are types of meta-data. In a relational database, the primary key may only exist to link records in different tables. Online databases often have a 'keywords' field for finding appropriate records.

meta-language — A language for defining another **language**. XML is an example, using a **DTD** to define a bespoke **markup** language.

MIME *(Multi-purpose Independent Mail Extensions)* — [pronounced 'mime'] A standard for identifying the formats in a mixed media mail or **HTTP** message, including pictures and text. **HTML** is a MIME format, as specified by the header line 'Content-Type: text/html'. **JPEG** is another, identified by 'content-Type: image/jpeg'. MIME is used by the **Web** to send information on the file content type. Contact 'comp.mail.mime' newsgroup. See **RFC 1590**.

minimization — In **SGML** and **HTML**, one or more techniques for omitting markup that can be implied from context. Not applicable to XML.

Miscellaneous — See **Misc**[27].

Misc[27] *(Miscellaneous)* — Non-hierarchically sensitive markup that may occur after the **document element**, and around the document type declaration (**doctypedecl**[28]). Any mixture of spaces (S[03]), **Comment**[15] and processing instructions (**PI**[16]).

Mixed — See **Mixed**[51].

Mixed[51] — The definition of the content of an **element**, when both sub-elements and document text are allowed, in any combination. The keyword '**#PCDATA**' identifies the allowed presence of text, and must appear first in the content model ('(#PCDATA | emph | quote)').

mixed content — A combination of text and elements. For example, a paragraph may contain text and Emphasis and Quote elements. See **Mixed**[51].

mod — Used in an expression in **XPath** to get the remainder after dividing one number by another.

mode — In **XSLT**, different style rules may apply to the content of an element, depending on the context in which that content is presented. For example, the content of a Title element typically appears differently for its presentation at the top of a new chapter, compared to its appearance in a table of contents.

model group — A sequence or option group in an element declaration, possibly enclosing other model groups. Brackets enclose the group.

monospaced — A font that contains characters that are all the same width, which can be useful for illustrating typewriter or old computer output, or for lining up vertically aligned textual structures. Also termed 'fixed pitch'.

Multi-purpose Independent Mail Extensions — See **MIME**.

multimedia — The same as **hypermedia**, except that differing information types may be synchronized – for example, music accompanying a video clip, described by a scrolling caption. See **HyTime**.

multiple namespace — A document that contains elements from two or more **namespaces**.

N

Name — See **Name**[05].

Name[05] — A group of characters that can be considered the name of an element, attribute etc. By definition, starting with a letter, '-' or ':', and thereafter consisting of optional further letters, digits, '.', '-', '_', ':' and other **Unicode** characters.

Name Character — See **NameChar**[04].

name group — A set of tokens that define an attribute's possible values.

name resolution — The replacement of a **domain name** by its associated **IP number**, as the first step to finding a resource on the **Internet**.

name server — A computer attached to the **Internet** that converts **domain name**s into **IP address**es.

name token — See **Nmtoken**[07].

name token group — A **DTD** feature that defines a list of options for a given attribute value.

name tokens — See **Nmtokens**[08].

name() — An **XPath** function that returns the name of the **node** identified by an enclosed expression.

NameChar[04] *(Name Character)* — A subset of the Unicode character set that defines characters allowed in a **Nmtoken**[07] and, except for the first character, allowed in a **Name**[05], consisting of letters, digits and miscellaneous characters ('.', '-', '_' and ':').

Names — See **Names**[06].

Names[06] — One or more names (**Name**[05]) words separated by **whitespace**. A top-level rule, but referred to as value constraints in attribute values.

namespace — An 'environment' within which element names and attribute names are guaranteed to be unique. A DTD defines a single namespace. The namespace 'problem' emerges when documents include elements from different DTDs or schema. See http://www.w3.org/TR/1999/REC-xml-names-19990114/.

namespace() — Used in an **XPath** expression to extract the global part of an element name that includes a **Namespace** prefix, as in 'html' from 'html:h3'. See **local-part()**.

Namespace attribute — An optional **XSLT** attribute to the **Element** and **Attribute** elements, used to declare the **Namespace** prefix (the rest of the element name is provided by the **Name** attribute).

NDataDecl[76] *(Notational Data Declaration)* — The information that an external entity conforms to a **notation** type other than XML, such as 'NDATA TeX'.

NDATA keyword — The **reserved name** for the keyword that indicates the content of an **external entity** is composed of non-XML data (for example, an image format). The 'non-XML data' keyword. A name follows the keyword, identifying the format to match declarations to references. Such entities must be referenced using an attribute value, not an entity reference.

nested element — An **element** that may contain itself, directly, or indirectly via another element, thus allowing potentially endless recursion.

net-enabling start-tag — Single character delimiter option for brief elements in **SGML**. Set to solidus, '/', in the **reference concrete syntax**. For example, 'Water is H<sub>2/O' is shorthand for 'Water is ₂O'.

Network Information Center — See **NIC**.

new — An **XLink** value in the **Show** attribute, indicating that the resource pointed to should be displayed in a new window, leaving the source text on-screen.

NIC *(Network Information Center)* — A system that holds information on **Internet** standards, including **RFC** documents and FYI (For Your Information) documents, made available using **FTP**.

NMTOKEN — A keyword that restricts the value of an attribute to a single word. See **Nmtoken**[07].

Nmtoken[07] *(Name token)* — An attribute type that consists of a single word. Similar to a **Name**[05], except that there is no special restriction on the first character value.

NMTOKENS — A keyword that restricts the value of an attribute to one or more **NMTOKEN**s. See **Nmtokens**[08].

Nmtokens[08] *(Name tokens)* — More than one name token, separated by spaces, such as 'green red white blue'.

node — An object in a **grove**, consisting of at least one **property**. An element definition in a DTD can be represented by a node, with properties for its attribute definitions and its content model. An element instance in a document can also be represented by a node, with properties for its attribute values and its actual content. See **leaf** and **node()**.

node() — A function of a navigation expression used in **XPath** that identifies any object in the document tree, including elements, attributes, comments, processing instructions and text. See **text()**, **processing-instruction()** and **comment()**.

non-validating — An **XML processor** that does *not* compare usage of elements and attributes against the rules defined in a **DTD**. However, correct use of syntax and requirement for the document to be **well-formed** is checked. See **validating parser**.

normalization — When **minimization** has been used in a document, normalization is the process of inserting the missing markup. For example, in **SGML** and **HTML** it is possible to omit end-tags. A document is normalized if these tags are inserted. A significant part of converting SGML documents into valid XML documents involves normalizing it.

normalize() — Used in an expression in **XPath** to remove leading and trailing spaces, and reduce multiple spaces to a single space.

normalized space — To separate terms in various contexts it is sufficient to insert a single space character between them, yet **DTD** and document authors may use other **whitespace** characters, or multiple spaces. To facilitate parsing and text comparison, an **XML processor** detects a sequence of whitespace characters and reduces it to a single space.

not() — A function in an expression used in **XPath** that returns the opposite boolean value to the result of the embedded expression. This example returns true if the current node is not the last in the list: '[not(position() = last())]'.

notation — Representation of natural phenomena by signs. Speech is represented by a written notation (involving letters, punctuation and left-to-right or right-to-left ordering), and also by a Braille notation. In computing this term is used interchangeably with 'data format', such as **ASCII**, **CGM** and **SGML**.

NOTATION — The keyword that asserts the value of an attribute will be a valid **notation** name, as defined in a **Notation Declaration**.

notation declaration — A **declaration** that assigns a unique name to a non-XML format, and may identify a document describing the format, and/or a program capable of processing the format. See **NotationDecl**[82].

notation type — An attribute type, indicating that the attribute contains the name of a notation for a data format other than XML. See **NotationType**[58].

Notational Data Declaration — See **NDataDecl**[76].

NotationDecl[82] *(Notation Declaration)* — A declaration that names a notation and identifies the location of a program that can process the data.

NotationType[58] — Part of an attribute definition (**AttDef**[53]) that is used to identify the notation used for the data in the element, when it is not XML format.

NSGMLS — The 'New SGML Structured' parser that replaces **SGMLS**. A freely available command-line-based SGML parser, but with the correct **SGML declaration** may also be used to validate XML documents. Contact jjc@jclark.com.

null end-tag — An SGML **end-tag** that consists of a single special character, which is used again at the end of the **start-tag**. For example, 'H<sub/2/0' is the same as 'H₂0'.

number() — Used in an expression in **XPath** to convert the result of an embedded expression into a number. See **string()** and **boolean()**.

numeric character reference — A **character reference** containing a numeric value representing a character. Identified by leading '&#', consisting of the decimal value of a character, and concluding with a semi-colon, ';'. For example, 'A' represents 'A' in **ASCII**.

O

o — The reserved name for the **SGML** keyword that indicates that a **start-tag** or **end-tag** may be omitted from the document. The 'omit' keyword. May be changed to another name in a **variant concrete syntax**.

OASIS — The new name for **SGML Open**.

object — An identifiable unit of information, possibly containing both discrete data units and also functions that operate on that data.

object-relational database — A database technology that combines relational and object oriented storage and retrieval technologies. Usually, a relational database system with added object-oriented features.

object database — A database technology that can represent complex data structures easily, unlike the **relational database** approach, which organizes data into simple tables. The **ODMG** *(Object Database Management Group)* devised the ODMG object database standard, which includes OQL (the *Object Query Language*). Suitable for permanent storage of objects created using object-oriented programming languages, such as **Java**. Also utilized by SGML-aware and XML-aware **document management** systems for storage of document components. Contact www.odmg.org.

OCR *(Optical Character Recognition)* — The automated recognition of character shapes on an image of a page containing text, from which **ASCII** text is output to allow manipulation or searching of this text. More explicitly the earliest technology for achieving this, which relied on pre-defined template matching to specific shapes on the image. The weakness of this approach is that unknown **fonts** are not recognized. See **ICR**.

ODA *(Open Document Architecture)* — Until 1990 known as 'Office Document Architecture'. A standard (ISO 8613) for defining document components for interchange between differing word processors and desktop publishing systems. An attempt to classify the features of such systems. It combines a structure view of the document (in similar fashion to **SGML**), with a layout view that specifies where on the page, and possibly on *which* page, an object appears. Contact http://sil.org/sgml/odanov10.html. In 1986 this format was discontinued as an ISO standard.

Office Document Architecture — Old name for 'Open Document Architecture'. See **ODA**.

omitted tag minimization — Determines whether the SGML **start-tag** or **end-tag** of a declared **element** may be absent in the document. See **o**.

one-to-many — A term used to describe relationships between items in different domains. For example, 'an author (possibly) writes many documents'. An ideal form of relationship in a **relational database**, but see also **one-to-one** and **many-to-many**.

one-to-one — A term used to describe relationships between items in different domains. For example, 'a document has one title'. See **one-to-many** and **many-to-many**.

Open Document Architecture — See **ODA**.

Open Trading Protocol — See **OTP**.

optional feature — A feature of the **SGML** language that is optional, switched on or off within the **SGML declaration** using **reserved name**s ('SHORTREF', 'CONCUR', 'DATATAG', 'OMIT-TAG', 'RANK', 'SHORTTAG', 'SUBDOC', 'FORMAL', 'IMPLICIT' and 'EXPLICIT'). Not applicable to XML.

or — Used in an expression in **XPath** to test two sub-expressions, returning true if either sub-expression is true. See **and**.

OTOH — Abbreviation for 'On The Other Hand' used in online conversation. Others include **BTW** (By The Way), **IMHO** (In My Humble Opinion), **FYI** (For Your Information) and **FWIW** (For What It's Worth).

OTP *(Open Trading Protocol)* — A proposed, independent standard for an interoperable message protocol for payments, invoices and receipts. Contact www.otp.org.

out-of-line — An object that is not part of a sequence of objects, such as paragraphs on a page. Used to describe a type of **hypertext** link where the element that describes the link is not embedded in the text, and also used to describe document objects, such as images, which do not need to appear at the point in the text where they are referenced. See **in-line**.

out-of-line link — A type of **hypertext** link where the element that describes the link is not embedded in the text. The benefit of this is that links can be added to read-only documents, and are more easily maintained if grouped together.

outbound — An **XLink** link with its source located at the resource enclosed in the linking markup. The opposite of an inbound link.

owner identifier — The part of a **formal public identifier** that identifies the owner of the specified **external entity**.

P

page — Common term for an **HTML** or **XHTML** document. See **Web page**.

Page Description Language — See **PDL**.

paginate — The process of placing **compose**d text and other parts of a document, such as images, onto at least one page, or as an intermediate step into a **PDL** *(Page Description Language)* such as **Post-Script**.

parameter — Feature of a **tag** that can contain modifying variables. A parameter value may have a meaning associated with its location in the tag (for example, name followed by size, '*FONT times

`18:`') or indicated by a parameter name (for example, 'name' and 'size', '`<font size="18" name="times">`'). An **attribute** is an XML element parameter, and each attribute has a name and value (so the order of parameter appearance is not significant).

parameter entity — An **entity** that may be referred to only within **markup**. Used mostly to aid construction of a **DTD**, but may also be used by document authors in the **internal subset** to override or select DTD options. A parameter entity may share the same name as a **general entity** without confusion, as it is distinguished by the '%' character in both the declaration and reference.

Parameter Entity Declaration — See **PEDecl**[72].

Parameter Entity Definition — See **PEDef**[74].

parameter entity reference — An **entity reference** that can be entered only within **markup**, so is mostly the province of the **DTD** author rather than the document author. See **general entity reference**.

Parameter Entity Reference — See **PEReference**[69].

parent — A concept derived from family trees that describes an **element** that encloses another element as part of a **hierarchy** of elements. For example, a Book element may be the parent of several Chapter elements. See **child** and **sibling**.

parent:: — An **XPath** expression that selects the parent of the current node, if it conforms to the given name, which may be '**node()**' to avoid exclusion in all cases. Abbreviates to '..', so '`parent::node()`' is the same as '..'.

parse — Decoding and understanding, using the rules of a grammar. In XML, the process of checking the legal use of **markup**, as performed by the **validating parser** module of an **XML processor**.

parsed entity — An entity whose content is valid XML data, forming part of the document structure, so is required to be parsed by any validating **parser**. See **binary entity**.

parser — Software designed to **parse** the content of a document for syntactical and possibly also logical errors, forming part of an **XML processor** software module. May aid and control the authoring or editing process. A term that is casually used to describe the entire XML processor. See **validating parser**.

parsing — The use of a **parser** to process and validate a document.

participating resources — Two or more resources that are related to each other using a **link**, thus allowing **transversal** between them.

pattern — An **expression** that is used to match a given node in the document tree against a pre-defined template. The pattern '`chapter/title`' matches any title that is the direct child of a Chapter element.

PCDATA — The **keyword** that represents normal character data. The 'parsable character data' keyword. Preceded by the hash-symbol, '#', to avoid confusion with an identical **element** name, when used within a **model group** (for example, '`(#PCDATA | PCDATA)*`'). See **Mixed**[51].

PDF *(Portable Document Format)* — The **PDL** used by **Adobe Acrobat**, derived from **PostScript** for on-screen page display. Contact comp.text.pdf newsgroup.

PDL *(Page Description Language)* — Data format for describing the content of a page of information. Includes commands for positioning each line of text on the page, drawing lines and painting graphics. **PostScript** is a popular PDL.

PEDecl[72] *(Parameter Entity Declaration)* — A declaration that defines a **parameter entity**, referred to in the **DTD** using a **PEReference**[69]. For general entities see **GEDecl**[71].

PEDef[74] *(Parameter Entity Definition)* — The part of a **PEDecl**[72] that holds the actual entity value or the identifier of an external value.

peer-to-peer — Two computers connected on a network where neither system has the set role of **server** or **client**, and at least some applications running on both systems can assume either of these roles.

PEReference[69] *(Parameter Entity Reference)* — A reference to a **parameter entity**, which must occur within markup, so as not to be confused with document entity references. For general entities see **EntityRef**[68].

PI[16] *(Processing Instruction)* — A special instruction that is to be interpreted by the receiving application, only to be used for information that cannot be expressed by the XML language.

PICT — [pronounced 'pict'ure] A Macintosh-based **vector** (but also **raster**) **image format**. See **WMF** for PC variant and **CGM** for widely used standard.

PITarget[17] *(Processing Instruction Target)* — The part of a **PI**[16] that identifies the application which the instruction is aimed at. The target name 'xml' is a special case.

placeholder — An **element** with no content, and with no **attributes**. Its presence alone is sufficient to indicate its purpose, and its importance at the specific point in the data where it appears.

PNG *(Portable Network Graphics)* — An **Internet**-based **image format** devised in 1995 over the Internet by a number of independent developers. Likely to be a successor to **GIF** due to its vendor independence and increased capabilities. Strengths include consistent appearance on different computer platforms and a faster interlacing technique.

port — A communication channel through which an Internet application sends or receives data. See **port number**.

port number — To distinguish one application from another when a computer receives data or requests from other systems, each application is assigned a number. The client must know the port number of the server application in order to communicate with it. A port number must be in the range '0' to '65535' (a 16-bit number). Some applications are so common that they are assigned 'well known' port numbers by the **IANA**, including 7 for the echo utility, 25 for smtp (simple mail transport protocol), 70 for gopher and 80 for **HTTP**. Other registered port numbers fall into the range 1024 through 49151. A port number may appear in a **URL** when a server application is 'listening' on a different port to the default. A secondary HTTP server may be assigned to port '8080' (although this number is registered, a browser looks on '80' unless told otherwise), such as http://occam.sjf.novell.com:**8080**/dsssl/dsssl96. Remaining values are left unassigned for user-specific applications.

Portable Document Format — See **PDF**.

Portable Network Graphics — See **PNG**.

position() — A function in an expression used in **XPath** that returns the location of the current node in its list of siblings, as returned by the expression. See **last()**.

PostScript — The widely used **PDL** developed by Adobe. See **PDF**.

preceding:: — An **XPath** expression that selects a node that precedes the current node in document order. Similar to **preceding-sibling::**, except that the search goes back to the beginning of the document, at all levels in the document structure. See **following::**.

preceding-sibling:: — An **XPath** expression that selects a sibling of the current node, that precedes the node in document order. See **following-sibling::**.

predicate filter — In an **XPath** expression, used to 'filter out' undesirable nodes of a given type.

preserve — Retain all whitespace characters; do not normalize down to a single space character.

preserved space — A sequence of **whitespace** characters that are not normalized to a single space for presentation, parsing or comparison.

procedural markup — A **markup** scheme that describes how a document should look, possibly including **font** descriptions, and character styles such as **roman** and **italic**. See **RTF** and **descriptive markup**.

processing instruction — Application-specific text (to be processed by an application). To be used only when absolutely necessary.

Processing Instruction — See **PI**[16].

processing-instruction() — A function of a navigation expression used in **XPath** that identifies any **processing instruction** object in the document tree. See **node()**.

Processing Instruction Target — See **PITarget**[17].

Prolog — See **Prolog**[22].

Prolog[22] — The first part of a **document**[01], specifying the version of XML in use, the document character set and requirements for DTD processing, and possibly either containing or referring to a **DTD**.

property — One piece of information in an **object**. For example, an object that describes a person may have a property for the age of that person and another to describe their height. See **property type**.

property type — The 'template' for a **property** within an object. Each instance of that property may have a different value. For example, three objects that each describe a person may all have an 'age' property, but each age property may hold a different value.

pseudo-element — A unit in the document hierarchy that is not a markup construct. Specifically, a string of text appearing before, after or between **in-line** elements, so that it can be considered a sibling to these elements when the document is viewed as a **tree**. The term has relevance to the advanced hypertext linking schemes in **XLink**, the **DOM** and **grove**s in general. For example, '`<p>this is a pseudo-element <em>but not this</em>.</p>`'.

PubidChar[13] *(Public identifier Character)* — One character in the quoted text of a **public identifier**, which identifies an object by a non-location-specific name. The text must not contain the same quote character used to enclose it.

PubidLiteral[12] *(Public identifier Literal)* — The literal text that identifies an object by a neutral name, including quotes to define the boundaries of the text, which may contain spaces.

PUBLIC — A keyword that precedes and identifies a name for an entity, rather than a location pointer to that entity (see **SYSTEM**).

public identifier — An **external entity** identifier that is not system specific (in terms of identifying either format or **entity** location). This identifier is expected to be compared with an entry in a **catalog** file, which provides the location and name of the system file. The public identifier may be a **formal public identifier**, in which case it has a rigid format that describes the owner, registered status and language of the entity.

Public Identifier — See **PublicID**[83].

Public identifier Character — See **PubidChar**[13].

Public identifier Literal — See **PubidLiteral**[12].

public text class — The part of a **formal public identifier** that describes the content of an **external entity**. Various class options include 'DTD' and 'ENTITIES'. In the latter case, the entity may only contain more entities.

public text description — The part of a **formal public identifier** that describes the information contained in the **external entity**. Enlarges on information provided by the **public text class**.

public text display version — The part of a **formal public identifier** that distinguishes between versions of public text stored in an entity.

public text language — The part of a **formal public identifier** that identifies the language used in the **external entity**. A two-character **ISO 639** defined code, such as 'EN' for English.

PublicID[83] *(Public Identifier)* — Strictly as used, a public identifier for a notation declaration. Perhaps this rule should also form part of **ExternalID**[75], which includes an identical fragment for identifiers in various other constructs.

publishing database — A **database** that exists purely to provide a platform from which information can be published. Often a half-way house for information derived from a number of different databases that are used for other purposes.

pull-data — One way to access XML data, using a **parser** that waits for instruction to retrieve the next portion of the file, as opposed to the event-drive (**SAX**) method, where the application must deal with everything that is thrown at it from the parser.

push technology — A term used to describe selected information that is delivered to a **Web browser** based on prior user selection of categories of interesting material. In reality, with current technology the browser still 'pulls' the **Web page** from the server.

Q

qualified name — An element or attribute name that includes a **namespace** prefix, to ensure that it is unique when mixed among markup from other namespaces.

quantity indicator — The number of times an **element** may appear at a given point in the document structure is governed by a special symbol, '?' (optional), '+' (repeatable) or '*' (optional and repeatable). When no symbol is present, the element is required and may not repeat. For example, '(title,para+)' indicates a required Title element, followed by at least one Paragraph element.

query — A question asked of a **DBMS** to retrieve specific information. The **SQL** query 'SELECT NAME FROM EMPLOYEES WHERE DEPARTMENT = 'Accounts'' returns the names of all employees (held in the 'name' **field** of the 'employees' **table**) in the accounts department.

query language — A computer language designed for the purpose of requesting information from a database. A request formed in such a language is termed a **query**.

quot — The name of a reserved entity that represents the double quote character, ' " ', used to avoid confusing a data character with an atribute value delimiter. See also **apos**.

R

raster — Method of representing images electronically using computer memory to create a grid, with one or more bits representing a pixel (one bit allows black and white pictures, four bits allow 16 colours, or shades of grey, and 16 bits allow over 65,000 colours). The resolution (pixels per inch) is determined at the time of creation, and the resulting picture is not usually amenable to scaling or rendering at a different resolution. Compression schemes include **JPEG** and **CCITT Group IV**. The alternative representation scheme, designed to overcome some of the limitations of the raster technique, is the **vector** scheme.

Raster Image Processor — See **RIP**.

RCDATA — An **SGML** concept that identifies text which may contain entity references, but no other markup is expected, so other **markup delimiter**s, such as '<', are safely considered to be data characters. Not applicable to XML.

RDF *(Resource Description Framework)* — A W3C working draft for a foundation for processing metadata on the Web. Applications cited in the specification include providing better search engine capabilities and cataloguing the content of a Web site. See www.w3.org/RDF.

RE *(Record End)* — An **SGML** concept that surrounds each 'record' of data with **RS** *(Record Start)* and RE characters.

record — One row of a **table** in a **database**. A table containing details on employees would have one record for each employee. The record is split into a number of **field**s (which are the columns of the table).

record end — See **RE**.

record start — See **RS**.

recursive — Something that may contain itself. From programming circles, the term is used to describe a function that is able to call itself in order to break down a problem into smaller chunks. In XML, an element that may directly or indirectly contain another instance of itself (an **embedded** element).

Reference — See **Reference**[67].

Reference[67] — A reference to a **general entity**, such as '`&myEnt;`' or the value of a character, such as '`&#123;`'.

reference concrete syntax — A number of default concrete settings in **SGML** that define quantity limits and the SGML language syntax. For example, the length of a tag has the implied maximum value of '960' and a start tag open delimiter is '<' by default. Values may be overridden within the **SGML declaration**.

reference capacity set — A number of default concrete settings in **SGML** that define the maximum number of various object types allowed. For example, the maximum number of elements that may appear in a document. Not applicable to XML, where no limits are defined.

registered — A **public identifier** for an **external entity** that is registered to ensure that it is unique, so that it can be referred to without ambiguity. See **registered owner identifier**.

registered owner identifier — A **public identifier** registered with the **ISO**, and therefore guaranteed unique. The public identifier begins with '+//', followed by the name of the owner. When an entity is owned by the ISO it has a different format, consisting of the publication number. See **ISO owner identifier**.

relational database — A **database** technology that allows a number of **tables** to be interlinked by **keyfield**s. This approach allows all duplication to be removed, by creating new tables where necessary, thus helping to ensure better consistency of the content than a **flat-file** database can provide. See **object database**.

relative link — A **hypertext link** that identifies the location of a resource in relation to some other resource, typically the location of the source document or element. See **absolute link**.

relative location — A hypertext link target that is not identified by a unique code, but by its location relative to other elements. For example, a link could be made to the fifth paragraph in the third chapter in a document. **XLink** has this capability. The weakness of this approach is that insertions and deletions to the text before the target make the link invalid. See **relative path**.

relative path — A navigation method in **XPath** that locates an object by its contextual location, rather than by a unique identifier. See **absolute path**.

RELAX — Now discontinued competitor to **XML Schema**, merged with **TREX** in the later **RELAX NG** specification. Also see **Schematron**.

RELAX NG — The latest attempt to produce a competitor to **XML Schema**, combining the now abandoned **RELAX** and **TREX** efforts. See www.oasis-open.org/committees/relax-ng.

remote resource —A resource that is not embedded within link **markup**, so needs to be referenced and bounded.

replaceable character data — Text that may contain an **entity reference**, but not element tags. Any references will be replaced by the entity content. See **RCDATA**.

replacement text — The text defined in an **entity** that replaces all references to that entity.

required attribute — An **attribute** that must have a value entered by the document author as the **element** is created. In the **element declaration** this is indicated with the '**REQUIRED**' keyword. Typically, an XML-aware word processor automatically presents a dialogue box for entry of a required attribute value when such an element is inserted into the document. See **implied attribute**.

REQUIRED keyword — A keyword that identifies an **attribute** that must be given a value each time the element containing it is used.

reserved attribute — An **attribute** name that cannot be defined for ad hoc use by DTD authors, because it has special significance in all XML applications. All reserved attributes begin with 'xml'. For example 'xml:lang' is always used to identify the language of the content of an element.

reserved name — In **SGML**, the default name for a keyword, used to help create a **concrete syntax** from the **abstract syntax**. For example, the reserved name for the keyword that allows characters to be assigned to the role of indicating the beginning of a **start-tag** is 'STAGO', and a definition of 'STAGO !' assigns '!' to this role (replacing the default value of '<'). Not applicable to XML.

reserved name indicator — The symbol that precedes a keyword when it is used where element names or other special tokens are also allowed, to avoid confusing one with the other. The '#' symbol is used. For example, if the **DTD** author creates an element called PCDATA, it must not be confused with the PCDATA keyword: '(#PCDATA | PCDATA)*'.

resolution — The size of pixels (on screen) or dots (on paper). The smaller the dots, the 'higher' the resolution, and the better the quality of the text or image. Quantified in 'dots-per-inch', or **DPI**.

resource — An object that is the target of a **hypertext link**.

Resource Description Framework — See **RDF**.

resource locator — The means by which a remote resource is identified, using a **URL**, an **XPointer** expression, or both.

resource title — The title of a **resource**, used to provide a user with information prior to selecting a link to that resource.

RFC *(Request For Comments)* — An Internet-related standard proposal. There are usually a number of RFCs for each Internet protocol. Every RFC has a number, and most are accessible over the Internet. RFCs are maintained by the **IETF**. To reach the index file, contact ftp://ds.internic.net/rfc/rfc-index.txt. See **FYI**.

RFC 1590 — An **RFC** that describes the codes which may be used to identify a data type for multimedia-capable e-mail and **HTTP** browsers. The formal description of **MIME**.

RFC 1766 — An **RFC** that describes the codes which may be used to identify a human language.

Rich Text Format — See **RTF**.

RIP *(Raster Image Processor)* — [pronounced 'rip'tide] A program or computer chip that converts **vector** format data into **raster** output at a specified **resolution**. A **PostScript** RIP converts PostScript data into a page 'image', ready for output to screen or paper.

role — A feature of **XLink** that uses an attribute (default name **Role**) to create categories of link which may affect the style of the linking text or the behaviour of a specialist browser.

roman — A character style. The characters are printed upright, as these words are. See **italic**.

root element — Another term for **document element**. The element that encloses the entire document (the only element that has no **parent**).

round() — Used in an expression in **XPath** to convert a real number into an integer by rounding down or rounding up to the nearest whole number. See **ceiling()** and **floor()**.

router — A intermediate computer that passes **Internet** data between other systems.

RS *(Record Start)* — An **SGML** concept that surrounds each 'record' of data with **RE** *(Record End)* and RS characters.

RTF *(Rich Text Format)* — A proprietary format developed by Microsoft that describes the format and style of a text-based document using **tags**. Particularly suited to exchange of documents between computer platforms. For the specification, contact ftp://ftp.primate.wisc.edu/pub/RTF.

S

S-HTTP *(Secure HTTP)* — A variant of **HTTP** that offers security for commercial transactions using authentication (the client is who they say they are) and encryption (the data cannot be read by other parties). Also called 'HTTPS'.

S[03] *(Space)* — A character with no visible appearance, used to separate words and markup parameters, and to break the document into convenient lines of text. Apart from the space character itself, ' ', this includes the horizontal tab character and the two characters commonly used to start a new text line (**CR** and **LF**).

SAX *(Simple API for XML)* — [pronounced 'sacks'] An open, standard method for interfacing with **event-driven** XML processors. For tree-driven processing see **DOM**. Advantage over DOM approach includes far less memory consumption, and ability to abort processing before reaching the end of the document.

schema — The definition of a document structure, including value constraints and relationships between objects. Similar to a **DTD**, but potentially more powerful. Several schema standards compete, but XML Schema is the most widely supported. Plural is 'schemas' or 'schemata'. See **DDML**.

Schematron — An approach to validating XML documents that, unlike **XML Schema**, **TREX** and **RELAX NG**, uses **XPath** expressions to test various propositions that the document should conform to.

SDA *(SGML Document Access)* — A specification for an **architectural form**, specifically using **fixed attributes** to support the **ICADD** initiative. Attribute names are significant; they specify how the following fixed value should be used in the SDA **DTD**. This DTD defines the following elements: Anchor (mark spot on page); Au (author); B (bold); Book (document element); Box (sidebar info); Fig (figure title); Fn (footnote); H1–H6 (headers); Ipp (ink print page); It (italic); Lang (language); Lhead (list heading); List; Litem (list item); Note; Other (emphasis); Para (paragraph); Pp (print page number); Term (or keyword); Ti (book title) and Xref (cross-reference). Allowable attribute names are Sdaform, Sdarule, Sdabdy, Sdapref and Sdasuff. See **ISO 12083** (Annex A.8) for more details. An example, mapping the Title element of a user-defined DTD to the ICADD element H1:

```
<!ATTLIST title SDAFORM   CDATA  #FIXED "h1"

<!ATTLIST chap SDARULE   CDATA #FIXED  "title h2"
<!ATTLIST sect SDARULE   CDATA #FIXED  "title h3"
```

SDATA — A keyword used in **SGML** to identify element and attribute content that is system dependent, so will need editing when the document is transferred to another system.

SDDecl[32] *(Standalone Document Declaration)* — The part of the **XMLDecl**[23] that states whether or not an external DTD needs to be read in order to accurately interpret the content of the document. A value of 'no' indicates the **DTD** is required, perhaps because it contains fixed attribute values, default attribute values of defines entities that are used in the document. A value of 'yes' indicates that the document can stand alone.

SDIF *(SGML Document Interchange Format)* — [pronounced 's-dif'ference] An **SGML**-related **ISO** standard (ISO 9069) for combining related **entity** objects into a single file object, generally for transfer to another system. Not widely used.

search engine — A software application that analyses the content of data files (documents), and created as index of all of the words it finds, so making it possible to quickly establish if the document does (or does not) contain a specific word or phrase.

self:: — An **XPath** expression that selects the current node, if it conforms the given name, which may be '**node**()' to avoid exclusion in all cases. Abbreviates to '.', so 'self::node()' is the same as '.'.

self-describing — The main feature of a **generalized markup** language is that the names of elements make the information they contain self-describing. For example, text enclosed in an element called Quote is obviously a quote. The benefit is that software can process the data meaningfully, and document style decisions can be made later, using a **stylesheet**.

separator — One or more characters used within a defined context to separate objects, such as one markup **parameter** from another.

seq[50] *(sequence)* — The definition of the content of an **element** when the content must be a strict series of other (child) elements and/or groups ('(title,author,(chap|sect),index)').

Sequence — See **seq**[50].

sequence connector — The character that takes the role of specifying a choice of token, 'l'. For example, '(#PCDATA | emph | subscript | superscript)'.

serialization — The process of converting multidimensional object relationships and **one-to-many** relationships into a simple data stream, to facilitate transfer of information between systems. XML is a suitable carrier for serialized data.

server — An application that provides services to a **client** application, usually over a network. For example, a **Web server** provides HTML pages to **Web server**s. See **peer-to-peer**.

SGML *(Standard Generalized Markup Language)* — The ISO 8879 standard developed in 1986 to assist electronic delivery and publication of text-based documents. Classified under 'Information processing – Text and office systems'. Developed and maintained by the ISO/IEC JTC1 SC18/WG8 committee. A language is defined for creation of document structure rules in a **DTD**. Contact comp.text.sgml newsgroup. See **SGML Users' Group** and **SGML Open**.

SGML Declaration — The first part of an **SGML** document, providing defaults such as the **concrete syntax** and the **reference capacity set**.

SGML Document Access — See **SDA**.

SGML Open — A non-profit international consortium of suppliers supporting and promoting **SGML** and **XML** (now renamed **OASIS**). Responsible for setting or rationalizing standards that rest upon SGML. As examples, a standard **catalog** format has been agreed (but see **XML Catalog**), and the **CALS table** model refined and harmonized. Contact www.sgmlopen.org/. See **GCA** and **SGML Users' Group**. For **HTML** equivalents see **IETF** and **W3C**.

SGML Users' Group — A non-profit organization formed in 1984 to promote the use of **SGML** and the sharing of information. It has many regional and national chapters. Contact http://sil.org/sgml/sgmlug.html. See **GCA** and **SGML Open**.

SGMLS — A popular and freely available **parser** developed for use with **SGML**, but with the correct **SGML declaration**, may also be used to validate XML documents. See **NSGMLS**.

short reference — An **SGML** feature that allows data characters to stand in for markup. This is an ultimate **minimization** feature. For example, the quote character can be recognized as both a Quote element start-tag and end-tag (depending on the context). In a table, the tab character could be equivalent to a Cell element and the line-end character to a Row element. This feature is not applicable to XML.

sibling — A concept derived from the family tree that describes an **element** that is adjacent to other elements within a **hierarchy** of elements (much like brothers and sisters). It is at the same level, following and/or preceding other elements. For example, a Chapter element is likely to be a sibling to other Chapter elements. See also **parent** and **child**.

significant whitespace — Spaces, tabs, and **line break** codes which are considered to be part of the document text, so should be preserved and appear when the document is presented. See **insignificant whitespace**.

Simple API for XML — See **SAX**.

simple link — An **XLink** link that is in-line and one-directional.

SMDL *(Standard Music Description Language)* — Standard use of **SGML** to describe real-time music samples, related to (and precursor of) the **HyTime** concept. Contact www.techno.com/SMDL.html.

SMIL *(Synchronized Multimedia Integration Language)* — An application of XML designed to provide a platform for multimedia presentations over the Web, composed from disparate multimedia objects. For example, a SMIL file may refer to a number of image files and to an oral narrative (audio file), specifying what order to display the images and when to start the audio track.

socket — A single **Internet** server program may be communicating simultaneously with several client applications. Each message received includes a socket number (assigned by the server when the connection is first initiated) that allows the data to be processed by the correct thread.

soft line-break — A break in the flow of text produced by the presentation software due to reaching a page, column or screen edge. Typically, 'hard' line-end codes are replaced by spaces before this happens.

source — A resource from which a **link** can be made to another resource. See **target**.

Space — See $S^{\{03\}}$.

SPDL *(Standard Page Description Language)* — An **ISO** standard (ISO/IEC 10180) that defines a language for representing text and graphics on a page. Released in December 1995. Equivalent and similar to the *de facto* **PostScript** language, except that PostScript commands are embedded within **SGML** elements (in the 'clear-encoding', non-compressed form).

```
<picture>
 <tkseqn>
    200 200 moveto
    100 200 rlineto
 </tkseqn>
</picture>
```

SQL *(Structured Query Language)* — [pronounced 'S.Q.L.' or 'sequel'] A very popular, vendor-neutral **query language** for extracting information from a **relational database**. For example, the SQL query 'SELECT name, telephone FROM employees WHERE name = "John"' returns the telephone number of a person from an employee database table.

SSADM *(Structured Systems Analysis and Design Method)* — A scheme developed by the UK government in 1982 for development of information systems by government departments, but now more widely used.

STag[40] — First part of an **element**, coupled with the end-tag (**ETag**[42]) to hold the content of the element, when not empty. Also the container of **attribute** values.

standalone — The name of a parameter in an **XML declaration** that is used to specify when a separate **DTD** file is (or is not) required to correctly interpret the content of the document. This means that the DTD does not define any default attribute values, or any entities that are referred to in the document. See **SDDecl**[32].

Standalone Document Declaration — See **SDDecl**[32].

Standard Generalized Markup Language — See **SGML**.

Standard Page Description Language — See **SPDL**.

Standard Vector Graphics — See **SVG**.

Start Tag — See **STag**[40].

start-tag — The first part of a **container element**, '<...>'. The *only* part of an **empty element** defined using the alternative syntax, '<.../>'. See **end-tag**.

starting-resource — The resource from which a **link** is made to the **ending-resource**. Both of these resources are **participating resources**.

starts-with() — Used in an expression in **XPath** to test for the presence of one string within another, but only if the contained string is at the start of the larger string. See **contains()** and **normalize()**.

static information — Information that is not easily updated, typically because it takes the form of a published document or book. See **vector information**.

string() — Used in an expression in **XPath** to convert the result of an embedded expression into a string value. See **boolean()** and **number()**.

string-length() — In an **XPath** expression, used to return the length in characters of the string identified by the parameter. 'string-length("abc")' returns three.

StringType[55] — An attribute type, indicating normal characters may be used in the attribute, including spaces, using the '**CDATA**' keyword in the **DTD**.

structured document — A document that belongs to a class of documents with a common, pre-defined structure, such as one reference book in a series. Ideal for representation in **XML** format, and formal definition using a **DTD** or **schema**, and also ideal for automated presentation using a stylesheet. See designed document and templated document.

Structured Query Language — See **SQL**.

style — The appearance of text when it is printed or presented on-screen, including the font used and the point size.

stylesheet — A set of style rules held together, perhaps in a separate data file, to be applied to all element instances which match, in name and context, one or more of these rules. See **in-line style**.

subcode[38] — Additional information about a language in the **LanguageID**[33], such as the country, 'en-GB' (Great Britain).

subelement — An **element** that is directly contained within another element. Formal name for the **child** of another element.

subscript — Text positioned below the baseline, as in 'H_2O'. Also known as 'inferior' text. See **superscript**.

substring() — Used in an expression in **XPath** to extract part of a string, from a given character, for a specific number of characters. See **substring-before()** and **substring-after()**.

substring-after() — Used in an expression in **XPath** to extract the last part of a string, from a given character in that string. See **substring-before()** and **substring()**.

substring-before() — Used in an expression in **XPath** to extract the first part of a string, up to a given character in that string. See **substring-after()** and **substring()**.

superior — See **superscript**.

superscript — Text positioned above the base line, as in 'E = MC^2'. Also known as 'superior' text. See **subscript**.

SVG *[Standard Vector Graphics]* — An XML application for describing vector graphics, using XML syntax to draw lines, curves, and to position text.

symbol — A rule that defines part of the XML or **XLink** language. The symbol is a name given to an **expression**, which is composed of at least one **token**.

Synchronized Multimedia Integration Language — See **SMIL**.

syntax — All languages, including English, have defined rules of grammar. The XML syntax defines how **tags** and **markup declarations** are stored and identified.

SYSTEM — A keyword that precedes and identifies a **URL** reference to an external resource, such as an external entity. See **PUBLIC**.

System Data — An **SGML** concept that describes data which is system dependent, and must be modified when transmitted to an incompatible system. Not applicable to XML. See **SDATA**.

system identifier — System-specific **external entity** identifier. Typically a file name and location. For example, '../ENTS/MYBOOK.DTD'.

System Literal — See **SystemLiteral**[11].

SystemLiteral[11] *(System Literal)* — A quoted string containing a file name, and possibly a file path, used to locate entities and notational data handlers.

T

tab — An invisible character, similar to a space character, but signifying a possibly wider gap that may be used in consecutive lines to create columns of information.

table — A collection of data arranged into rows and columns, from which a **flat-file** or **relational** database package can locate required information.

tag — A code embedded in the text, signifying the structure, format or style of the data. A tag is recognized from surrounding text by the use of **delimiter** characters. A common delimiter character for an XML tag is the chevron, '<'.

tag close — The character(s) indicating the end of a tag.

tail — The end-point of a **hypertext link**. Equivalent to the **target** of a link. A reference is traversed from the **head** to the tail. For example, a chapter Title element may be the tail of many references.

target — The object of a **hypertext link**. It must be identified by a unique name or code, which can be used within a **source** object to form the link. See **Target attribute** and **ID**.

TCP *(Transmission Control Protocol)* — See **TCP/IP**.

TCP/IP *(Transmission Control Protocol/Internet Protocol)* — Data transport protocol for the **Internet**. Used by **HTTP** and **FTP** file transfer protocols. Contact 'comp.protocols.tcp-ip/newsgroup'.

TEI *(Text Encoding Initiative)* — A group of representatives from learned societies in the humanities and social sciences, defining common **DTDs** for the coding and interchange of relevant documents. Contact http://mes01.di.uminho.pt/Manuals/HTML/html-howto/tei.html or www.uic.edu:80/orgs/tei/.

template — In **XSLT**, a template is used to describe how a specific element in the source document is to be transformed in an output document. This may involve formatting the content of the element by replacing source elements with elements from the **FO DTD**, defined in the **XSL** specification.

templated document — A document that consists of highly-granular, pre-defined components, often originating from database records. **XML** may play an intermediary role, between authoring/storage and presentation, or as a simple transfer format. See **structured document** and **designed document**.

T$_E$X — [pronounced 'teck'] Popular typesetting language. Particularly strong on mathematical formulae. It is sometimes found embedded in **SGML** documents due to the absence of a widely accepted SGML-based tagging convention for formulae (but see **MathML** for XML). Contact www.fi.muni.cz/TeXhelp/TeX-homepage.html and comp.text.tex newsgroup. See **L^{A}T$_E$X**.

text() — A function of a navigation expression used in **XPath** that identifies any text object in the document tree. See **node()**.

text — A series of **character**s.

Text Declaration[77] — See **TextDecl**[77].

Text Encoding Initiative — See **TEI**.

text entity — In a **public identifier**, an **entity** that contains simple text.

text file — A data file containing textual characters, possibly conforming to the **ASCII** standard, or to **Unicode**. Each character is represented by a unique value. There is no provision for styling the text, and little provision for formatting the text. A **markup** language assigns significance to sequences of ASCII characters, forming **tag**s. A text editor works directly with ASCII data, and most word processors can export and import text files.

text format — A data format that contains text characters, usually to represent textual information. Simple text formats comprise of nothing more than **character set**s like **ASCII**, **Unicode** and **EBCDIC**. More complex data structures are described by assigning significance to some characters, such as the comma in **CSV**. Using **markup**, even more complex structures are described in **XHTML**, **XML**, **SGML** and **TeX**. See **image format**.

Text identifier — The major part of a **formal public identifier**, describing the type, description and language of an **entity**.

Text Run OFF — See **TROFF**.

TextDecl[77] *(Encoding Processing Instruction)* — A processing instruction that appears at the top of a **DTD** file, a fragment thereof, or an external **parsed entity**, when its content conforms to a different character set or version of XML to the main document.

TIFF *(Tagged Image File Format)* — [pronounced 'tiff'] An **image format** devised by Microsoft and Aldus, now maintained by Adobe. The actual image data is held in one of several **raster** formats, depending on the compression requirements. Options include **CCITT Group IV** and **JPEG** compression, or no compression at all. The current version is 6.0. Contact http://www.adobe.com/Support/TechNotes.html.

token — *[1]* A unit of information in a **group**. Either a single object, such as the name of an **element**, or an entire embedded group which also contains tokens. *[2]* A building block of the rules that comprise the definition of the XML and XLink standards. A number of tokens build an **expression**, which is named with a **symbol** (which may be used as a token in another expression).

Tokenized Type — See **TokenizedType**[56].

TokenizedType[56] *(Tokenized Type)* — An **attribute type** declared in the **DTD**. A single word, or **token**, or a list of tokens.

transclusion — A **hypertext** concept that involves replacing the **source** reference with the **target** resource. The link is not so much followed, as brought to the reference. An ideal mechanism for ensuring that a reference to a title is always accurate, even when the target title is edited, or for calling in an image without needing to use an **entity declaration**.

translate() — Used in an expression in **XPath** to replace specific characters with other characters.

transversal — The act of moving from a **source** resource to a **target** resource by way of a **link** between these resources.

Transmission Control Protocol — See **TCP/IP**.

transversal — A term used for following a **hypertext link** to a references **resource**.

tree — A hierarchical structure which resembles a tree in that the structure can be viewed as branches. **SGML** elements form hierarchies, and are sometimes described using the family tree concept, including the use of names such as **ancestor**, **parent**, **child** and **sibling**.

tree-manipulation — Editing a tree, such as changing the order or location of an element, inserting or deleting an element, or duplicating an element.

tree walking — The process of stepping from one document **node** to another, processing the document in the same order as treating the content as a linear **data stream**. A common technique when processing using the **DOM**.

TREX — Now discontinued competitor to **XML Schema**; merged with **RELAX** to create **RELAX NG**. Also see **Schematron**..

TROFF *[Text Run OFF]* — A markup language used on UNIX systems for document formatting (see also **TEX**).

true() — An **XPath** expression function that returns the value 'false' in a boolean test. See **false()** and **boolean()**.

typesetting — The process of converting tagged data, possibly in XML format, into completed pages. A combination of the **compose** and **paginate** operations.

typesetting language — A computer language that comprises a list of codes to be embedded in a **text file**, specifying a style or location for text that follows the code.

U

UCS *(Universal Multiple-Octet Coded Character Set)* — The core **ISO10646** multi-byte data format. Transformation formats reduce the size by using single bytes for common characters. These formats are called **UTF**, with 'U' standing for UCS.

UCS Transformation Format — See **UTF**.

UCS Transformation Format 16 Bit Form — See **UTF-16**.

UCS-2 — An **ISO/IEC 10646** and **Unicode** character encoding scheme that uses two bytes to store each character. See **UCS-4**. May be converted to a **UTF** format for transfer.

UCS-4 — An **ISO/IEC 10646** and **Unicode** character encoding scheme that uses four bytes to store each character. See **UCS-2**. May be converted to a **UTF** format for transfer.

unavailable text indicator — An entity that is not available to the general public, perhaps only for use within an organization. Part of a **formal public identifier**, following the **public text class** and consisting of the trailing characters '-//'. For example, '+//MyCorp//DTD MyDTD -// . . . . . . '.

Unicode — A **16-bit** character set devised by the Unicode Consortium (a group of largely American hardware and software suppliers). Several coding schemes are allowed, but in the canonical scheme every bit combination represents a distinct character. Using this scheme, Unicode can be viewed as a superset of **ASCII** (US) with '0000' to '00FF' (hexadecimal) being equivalent to ASCII '00' to 'FF'. Unicode has been adopted as a subset of **ISO/IEC 10646**, with '00000000' to '0000FFFF' being equivalent to the Unicode characters '0000' to 'FFFF'. Contact http://www.stonehand.com/unicode.html.

Universal Character Set — See **UCS**.

Universal Multiple-Octet Coded Character Set — See **UCS**.

Universal Resource Identifier — See **URI**.

Uniform Resource Locator — See **URL**.

unparsed entity — An entity that is given a notation, so is not deemed by the XML processor to be XML data that can be parsed (even if it does happen to be XML, or simple text data). It must be an external entity.

unregistered owner identifier — A **public identifier** that has not been officially registered, so cannot be guaranteed to be unique. See **registered owner identifier**.

up-convert — Conversion of typeset data to XML format. Usually a semi-manual, **high energy** task. The expense of up-converting to XML is often cited as the main reason for not adopting XML, though in some cases this cost is more than offset by the reduced cost of **down-convert**ing to various output formats.

upper-case — Capital letters, such as 'THIS'. The upper-case equivalent of the **lower-case** letter 'a' is 'A'. The name is derived from the fact that these **character**s were found in the upper part of the printer's type case.

URI *(Uniform Resource Identifier)* — The **Internet** addressing scheme. Includes the **URL** and **URI** standards. Contact www.w3.org/pub/WWW/Addressing/Addressing.html.

URL *(Uniform Resource Locator)* — Subset of the **URI** protocol for schemes that require direct reference to a location, then to a file or by specifying a search requirement. See **URN**.

URN *(Uniform Resource Name)* — Subset of the **URI** protocol for schemes that do not require direct reference to a filename and location. See **URL**.

UserCode[37] — A user-defined language code used in the **xml:lang** attribute. Must begin with 'x-' or 'X-'. See **IanaCode**[36] and **ISO639Code**[35].

UTF *(UCS Transformation Format)* — A mechanism for compressing **UCS-2** and **UCS-4** encoded data for transfer between systems. The two-byte or four-byte UCS character representation schemes are often wasteful when relatively common characters are in use. A text file can easily be compressed by as much as 75 per cent. Two variants, UTF-8 (8-bit) and UTF-16 (16-bit), offer different levels of character range support.

UTF-16 — See **UTF**.

UTF-8 — See **UTF**.

V

V.32bis — A modulation protocol for modems that transmit or receive data at a maximum of 14,400 bits per second (bps).

V.34 — A modulation protocol for modems that transmit or receive data at a maximum of 28,800 bits per second (bps). More recently allowing up to 33,600 bps.

V.42 — A modulation protocol for modems that allows errors to be corrected by retransmitting packets of data.

V.42bis — A modulation protocol for modems that includes data compression to achieve greater throughput.

validate — The process of comparing a **document instance** against its **DTD**. See **validating parser**.

validating parser — A **parser** that compares the usage of **element**s and **attribute**s in a document against the rules of a **DTD** or schema. For example, if the DTD states that a Chapter element can only contain a Title element followed by Section elements, then an error will result should a document contain a Paragraph element directly within a Chapter element.

value indicator — In **SGML**, the equals sign that separates an attribute name from its value may be redefined to another character, but is always called a 'value indicator'. In some SGML **minimization** techniques, the character may be omitted.

variant concrete syntax — An **SGML** concept whereby the default characters used as **markup delimiter**s are changed to suit the requirements of a particular computer platform or document type. A concept that does not apply in XML.

vector — Method of representing images electronically using resolution and scale independent drawing commands, producing lines, points, arcs, filled areas and text. For example, 'DRAWTO 60 35; MOVETO 75 90; CIRCLE 50; ...'. Also known as 'geometric graphics'. Some formats use text-based commands as in the example, others use more compact machine-readable schemes. **CGM** allows for both representations. The alternative representation is called a **raster** format (though a vector-based image must be converted into a raster-based image when rendered using an appropriate resolution). See also **IGES**, **PICT** and **WMF**.

Version Information — See **VersionInfo**[24].

Version Number — See **VersionNum**[26].

VersionInfo[24] *(Version Information)* — A statement of the version of XML in use by the document. Part of the XML declaration (**XMLDecl**[23]). At the time of writing, the only version of XML that exists is '1.0'.

VersionNum[26] *(Version Number)* — The actual value of the version of XML in use, such as '1.0'.

Virtual Reality Modelling Language — See **VRML**.

VRML *(Virtual Reality Modelling Language)* — A language that describes three-dimensional objects. Used on the **Internet** to create 'virtual worlds'. Developed by Silicon Graphics, who also shaped VRML 2.0 (1996), which adds behaviours, sensors, sound and animation (from its 'Moving Worlds' specification). Contact http://vrml.sgi.com/moving-worlds.

W

W3C *(World Wide Web Consortium)* — An industry consortium founded in 1994 that comprises over 120 organizations. Involved in the establishment of standards for the **Web**, including **XML** and **DTD**s for versions of **HTML**. In agreement with major vendors, responsible for the latest versions of HTML, starting with **HTML 3.2** in June 1996 and **HTML 4.0** on 18 December 1997. This organization has a close relationship with the **IETF** (see **SGML Open** for equivalent **SGML** monitoring organization). Also responsible for **XHTML**. Contact http://www.w3.org/.

Web — Common abbreviation for the World Wide Web. An **Internet** service that uses the **HTTP** protocol and **HTML** format data files to provide an attractive document delivery service over standard telephone lines. Information is passed between a **Web server** and a **Web browser**. Various graphic formats are also supported, including **GIF** and **JPEG**. Created by researchers at CERN in Switzerland (www.w3.org). Not owned by any company, the Web is overseen by the **W3C** (and the Internet is overseen by the **IETF**).

Web browser — A computer application that receives **Web page**s from a **Web server** via the **Internet**, and **render**s them on-screen. See **Web**.

Web page — A data file containing **HTML** or XML tagged text ready to be displayed by a **Web browser**. Although called a 'page', the file may be much longer than a physical page, and a closer analogy would be a scroll. However, Web page designers are encouraged to split long documents into smaller units, so as to keep network traffic to a minimum, and the name 'page' is a reminder of this philosophy.

Web server — A computer attached to the **Internet** that stores **Web page**s and delivers them to a **Web browser**. See **Web**.

well-formed — An XML or SGML document that contains properly embedded tags, with all objects explicitly bounded by start-tags and end-tags. An **SGML** document *may* be well-formed, but an XML document *must* be well-formed in order to be valid. In addition, the document must be complete (an **entity** defined outside the document must not be referenced).

WG8 *(ISO/IEC JTC1 SC18/WG8)* — The **ISO** working group responsible for a number of standards, starting with **SGML** in 1986, but recently including **HyTime** (1992), **SPDL** (1995) and **DSSSL** (1996). Contact www.ornl.gov/sgml/wg8/wg8home.htm.

whitespace — A character used to separate words in text, and parameters in markup, including the space character, ' ', the horizontal tab character and the end-of-line codes **CR** and **LF**. See **ignorable whitespace**.

Windows MetaFile — See **WMF**.

WMF *(Windows MetaFile)* — A Microsoft Windows-based **vector** image format. See **PICT** and **CGM**.

workflow — The movement of documents through a number of separate preparation stages, such as 'create', 'proof', 'edit, 'approve' and 'publish'. A necessary component of an **editorial system**, which may automatically deliver documents to operators assigned given tasks as they become ready. A workflow system may also automatically re-route documents as necessary, alert users to scheduling problems and provide statistics on throughput.

World Wide Web — See **Web**.

World Wide Web Consortium — See **W3C** .

WWW *(World Wide Web)* — See **Web**.

WYSIWYG *(What You See Is What You Get)* — [pronounced 'wizz-e-wig'] Acronym describing one approach to viewing data on-screen, where an attempt is made to replicate published output (What You See *on the screen* Is What You Get *on the page*). Text markup is hidden, and the text is composed using representative fonts and styles.

X

X-Bitmap — Simple 1-**bit** per pixel **raster** image format used on UNIX systems and also used by the **Web**. Pixels are set to black or transparent. Typical file extent is '.xbm'. Actually C language source code (an array) to be read by a compiler rather than a graphic viewer. See **JPEG**, **GIF** and **X-Pixelmap**.

X-Pixelmap — Simple 8-**bit**s per pixel **raster** image format used on UNIX systems (and X-Windows icons) and used by the **Web**. Pixels are set to one of 256 colours. Actually C language source code (an array) to be read by a compiler rather than a graphic viewer. Less memory efficient than **GIF**. Typical file extent is '.xpm'. See **JPEG** and **X-Bitmap**.

XBM — See **X-Bitmap**.

XHTML — An XML compliant version of **HTML 4.0**. A **markup language** focussed on formatting rather than describing the contents of a document.

XInclude — A standard for placing references in one XML document that are used to 'call-in' parts of other XML documents; a simple alternative to using external entities for this purpose.

XLink *(XML Linking Language)* — An adjunct standard to XML that defines a specification for hypertext linking. See www.w3.org/TR/WD-xml-link. See **XPointer**.

XML — A **generalized markup language** based on **SGML**, with some influence from **HTML**, aimed primarily at the **Web**. Subscribe to xml-dev@ic.ac.uk.

XML Application — One usage of **XML**, probably defined by a **DTD** or **XML Schema** model, creating a class of document instances that conform to that application.

XML Base — A proposed standard for setting the base location from which relative **URLs** are calculated. See **xml:base**.

XML Catalog — A private initiative, well supported, for defining a standard format for entity management catalogues. Based on **SGML Open** format, but simplified and with an optional XML-based syntax.

XML Declaration — See **XMLDecl**[25].

XML Include — See **XInclude**.

XML processor — A software module that allows XML documents to be read by an application. It includes an **entity manager**, and optionally a **parser**. The XML document is made available to the application as a **data stream**, or as a **grove**. Commonly, the term 'parser' is used to describe what is formally an XML processor. See **SAX** and **DOM**.

XML Schema — An **XML** standard that replicates and improves upon the inherant **DTD** modelling capability, using an XML-based syntax. See **RELAX NG** and **Schematron**.

xml:base — The attributes used in the **XML Base** standard to specify the base location from which all relative **URLs** will be calculated. It uses a URL to set this location.

xml:lang — A reserved XML attribute name, used to identify a value that represents the human language used for the content of the current element. Its value is a code, defined in **LanguageID**[33]. See **IANA** and **ISO 639**.

xml:space — A reserved XML attribute name, used to identify elements that contain **white space** which must be preserved.

XML-aware — A software application that recognizes the XML data format and understands XML concepts, such as document structure, entities, and possibly also the hypertext linking or stylesheet supplementary standards, so is able to perform meaningful operations on that data. An XML-aware editor, for example, would use the **DTD** to control and guide the authoring process. Other terms used include 'XML-capable' and 'XML-sensitive'. An XML-aware application must include at least an **XML processor**.

XML-capable — See **XML-aware**.

XML-sensitive — See **XML-aware**.

xml-stylesheet — The target name for a processing instruction that is used to link a stylesheet to the XML document to format that document.

XML Stylesheet Language — See **XSL**.

XMLDecl[25] *(XML Declaration)* — The first part of an XML document, specifying the version of XML in use (**VersionInfo**[24]), the character set in use (**EncodingDecl**[80]) and the requirements, or otherwise, of DTD processing to correctly interpret the content of the document (**SDDecl**[32]).

xmlns — The reserved attribute name that indicates a **namespace declaration**.

XPath — A standard for an **expression** language that can be used for searching an XML document (see **XQL**), creating links into documents (see **XPointer**) and applying specific formats to each element type within contextual constraints (see **XSLT**). Contact www.w3.org/TR/xpath.

XPM — See **X-Pixelmap**.

XPointer — A proposed standard that complements **XLink** to allow links to objects that do not have a unique identifier, but do have a significant contextual location in the document.

XQL *(XML Query Language)* — A proposal for a query language to extract information from XML documents.

XSL *(XML Stylesheet Language)* — A proposal for a **stylesheet** language for XML, including **CSS** equivalent features. See www.w3.org/TR/WD-xsl or www.mulberrytech.com/xsl/xsl-list. An **XSLT** stylesheet may be used to create an XML document that contains elements and attributes as a concrete format for XSL features, confroming to the **FO** DTD.

XSL Transformations — See **XSLT**.

XSLT *(XSL Transformations)* — A transformation language that has the primary use of creating **XSL** documents from arbitrary XML documents, but can also be used to translate one XML document into another XML document of a different structure, including **XHTML**. Contact www.w3.org/TR/WD-xslt.

XSLT processor — A software application that is able to read and understand an **XSLT** stylesheet, and use it to transform an XML document into another format (XML or otherwise).

Z

zoning — The ability of a **search engine** to divide a document into zones, such as those defined by XML **elements**, and allow documents to be found that contain specific words and phrases only within selected zones.

Index

NOTES: This index identifies terms introduced in the main text (where they are displayed in bold). The glossary is not indexed, so a term in the glossary that is *only* referenced from other terms in the glossary will not appear in this index. All entries are shown in the present tense, singular form (except where the term is a syntactic token name or keyword, or is always used in another form). For example the 'hierarchy' entry also identifies usage of the word 'hierarchical.' Entries in capitals, such as 'ENTITY,' are XML keywords. Entries with an initial capital letter, such as 'Table,' are DTD-specific element or attribute names, and as they may be used in more than one DTD they are identified using bracketed qualifiers; for example, there is an entry for 'Title (XLink)' and another entry for 'Title (HTML)' (but note that these names are case-sensitive, and usually differ from this convention).

Also by the same author...

The XSL Companion
Neil Bradley

A concise, comprehensive and accessible guide to the scope, strengths and limitations of XSL (eXstensible Stylesheet Language) family of stylesheet standards for XML. This book explains the practical ways in which XSL can be utilized for formatting and manipulating information held in the immensely popular data format.

The huge expansion in usage of XML created the need for a powerful standard for formatting and transforming XML documents – the XSL standard, which developed into the family of three specific standards examined in detail in this book. XSL enables the further expansion of XML technology into new domains of content management, audience-targeted presentation and distributed document processing.

If you are a current or potential XML user looking for just one reference to get you up to speed on styling or manipulating your XML documents with clarity, comprehensive coverage and precision, then this book will be your essential and constant companion.

This book covers in detail the family of three separate stylesheets that make up XSL:

- Xpath locates specific information within XML documents
- XSLT transforms XML documents into other data formats
- XSL embeds formatting information in XML documents

Together these form a powerful array of tools that allow you to control and optimize the formatting of your XML documents, and thus deliver content and information in a dynamic and flexible way.

Visit us on the world wide web at:
www.it-minds.com or www.aw.com/cseng/